THE CULTURE OF WAR

THE
CULTURE
OF WAR

MARTIN van CREVELD

PRESIDIO
PRESS

BALLANTINE BOOKS

NEW YORK

Published in the United States by Presidio Press, an imprint of
The Random House Publishing Group, a division of Random House, Inc., New York.

PRESIDIO PRESS and colophon are trademarks of Random House, Inc.

Grateful acknowledgment is made to the following for permission
to reprint previously published material:

Barbara Levy Literary Agency on behalf of the Estate of George Sassoon:
"To the Warmongers" by Siegfried Sassoon. Reprinted by permission of Barbara Levy
Literary Agency on behalf of the Estate of George Sassoon.

The Free Press, a division of Simon & Schuster Adult Publishing Group:
Title page from *The Goose Step Is Verboten: The New German Army* by Eric Waldman,
copyright © 1964 by The Free Press and copyright © renewed 1992 by Eric Waldman.
All rights reserved. Reprinted by permission.

Viking Penguin, a division of Penguin Group (USA) Inc. and Barbara Levy Literary Agency
on behalf of the Estate of George Sassoon: "In Barracks" from *The Collected Poems of
Siegfried Sassoon* by Siegfried Sassoon, copyright © 1918, 1920 by E. P. Dutton,
copyright © 1936, 1946, 1947, 1948 by Siegfried Sassoon. Rights in Canada and the
United Kingdom are controlled by Barbara Levy Literary Agency. Reprinted by
permission of Viking Penguin, a division of Penguin Group (USA) Inc. and
Barbara Levy Literary Agency on behalf of the Estate of George Sassoon.

LIBRARY OF CONGRESS CATALOGING-IN-PUBLICATION DATA
Van Creveld, Martin
The culture of war / Martin van Creveld.
p.   cm.
Includes bibliographical references and index.
ISBN 978-0-345-50540-8 (hbk. : alk. paper)
1. Sociology, Military.   2. War.   3. Military art and science—History.   I. Title.
U21.5.C74 2008
306.2'7—dc22   2008025740

Printed in the United States of America on acid-free paper

www.presidiopress.com

2 4 6 8 9 7 5 3 1

FIRST EDITION

Book design by Mary A. Wirth

To you, bold venturers, adventurers, and whoever has embarked
With cunning sails upon dreadful seas—

To you, who are intoxicated with riddles, who delight in twilight, and whose souls
Are drawn by flutes to every dizzying abyss;

For you do not want, with cowardly hand, to grope for a rope
And where you can guess, there you disdain to decipher.

—FRIEDRICH NIETZSCHE, *Also Sprach Zarathustra*

CONTENTS

V. Contrasts   333

INTRODUCTION

I n theory, war is simply a means to an end, a rational, if very brutal, activity intended to serve the interests of one group of people by killing, wounding, or otherwise incapacitating those who oppose that group.[1] In reality, nothing could be further from the truth. Even economists now agree that human beings, warriors and soldiers included, are not just machines out for gain. Facts beyond number prove that war exercises a powerful fascination in its own right—one that has its greatest impact on participants but is by no means limited to them. Fighting itself can be a source of joy, perhaps even the greatest joy of all. Out of this fascination grew an entire culture that surrounds it and in which, in fact, it is immersed. Like any other culture, the one associated with war consists largely of "useless" play, decoration, and affectations of every sort; on occasion, affectations, decoration, and play are even carried to counterproductive lengths.[2] So it has always been, and so, presumably, it will always be.

A full discussion of the culture of war would require not a single volume but an entire library. The culture in question ranges from the often far from utilitarian shapes and decoration of armor (or, before there was armor, war paint) to today's "camouflage" uniforms and "tiger suits"; from war games played by the ancient Egyptians with the aid of tokens on specially made boards all the way to the enormous variety of present-day war games, exercises, and maneuvers; and from Yahweh's commandments in the book of Deuteronomy,[3] which laid down some elementary rules for the treatment of various kinds of enemies confronted in certain kinds of war, to the numbered paragraphs of today's international law. It includes the values and traditions of warriors as manifested in their deportment, customs, literature, parades, reviews, and other assorted ceremonies, as well as the endlessly varied ways in which wars have been declared, brought to a formal end, and commemorated.

In many societies, especially tribal ones as described by Tacitus and feudal ones such as Homeric Greece, medieval Europe, Mamluk Egypt, and samurai Japan, the culture of war enjoyed extremely high status. For example, Chrétien de Troyes in *Perceval* says it was "the highest that God has created and commanded"; a sixteenth-century French knight, Brantôme, called *chevallerie* "the religion of honor" and claimed that it ought to be given priority over all other forms of culture.[4] By contrast, in today's self-styled "advanced" countries, for the culture of war to be held in such high esteem is rare. Soldiers, war gamers, collectors of militaria, and even military historians know the score. At best, their culture is seen as a quaint leftover from a previous, presumably less rational, less utilitarian, and less humane, past. At worst, it is denied, put aside, ignored, ridiculed, or denounced as childish "warmongering." As countless jokes about the (supposed) quality of military intelligence, military law, military music, and even military cooking imply, too often it is despised as loud, vulgar, and crude.

Some people go so far as to claim that war and culture are absolute opposites. Like Lord Byron, all they see is "the windpipe-slicing, brain-splattering art"; as a result, each time a flag is raised or a bugle calls, they look away or stop their ears. Others, while prepared to admit that a culture of war does exist, look at it as an expression of that worst of all bad things, "militarism." Academics, many of whom are politically on the left, are especially likely to consider things in this light. This may explain why, in spite of the undoubted popular appeal of works with titles such as *Medieval Arms and Armor, Uniforms of the Wehrmacht,* and *Military Aircraft of the World,* a scholarly, comprehensive study of the subject has yet to be written. Perhaps it also explains why one volume whose declared subject is "the symbols of war" in the ancient world is completely dominated by discussions of weapons, armor, and tactics.[5]

Even if the charges were true, it does not follow that the culture in question does not deserve close attention. War has always played a critically important role in human affairs. No empire, civilization, people, or religion has ever risen to greatness without, as one British officer once put it to me, excelling at "the smacking business." Very often, the most successful ideas, religions, peoples, civilizations, and empires are simply those that acquired the most cannon and, having done so, used them to crush the rest. Conversely, few if any great ideas, religions, peoples, civilizations, or empires have fallen without trying to reverse their fortune by force of arms first. Much as bleeding hearts may dislike the fact, war and its culture form an integral element of human history and human life and are likely to do so for all future to come. As part of human life, they need to be understood. To be understood, they deserve to be studied no less carefully, and no less sympathetically, than any other parts.

As this volume will try to show, very often the charges are not true. Even today, when most developed countries no longer have conscription and professional forces have made a comeback, no sharp line divides most people from soldiers.[6] True, soldiers are not a homogeneous lot. Some may even be insensitive, callous, and vulgar. Yet there is absolutely no reason to think that such men are more numerous in the military than anywhere else; conversely, it could be argued that one reason why so many "civilized" people can engage in refined feelings is because there are soldiers who do their dirty work for them. Thus only prejudice can explain why the culture they create, and in which they are immersed, is so often considered inferior to that of other groups, be they priests, merchants, professionals, workers, whites, blacks, women, or people who have recovered from cancer.

In truth, war paint, armor, uniforms, and weapons are quite as interesting, have quite as long a history, and are as intricately linked to every aspect of economic, social, and cultural development as civilian dress is. Not only are military ceremonies as sophisticated and as full of symbolism as civilian ones are, but they have often served as models for the latter. It is true that the law of war has often been ignored, violated, or used as a veneer to justify people's cold-blooded interests; however, the same applies to any other laws designed to regulate any other field. Starting with Homer and ending with Lincoln's Gettysburg Address, war, with its incomparable triumphs and unfathomable sorrows, has always inspired some of the greatest literature of all. From the Winged Victory of Samothrace to the black, V-shaped Vietnam Veterans Memorial in Washington, D.C., the same is true of the monuments erected in its honor.

Many of those who look down their noses on the culture of war may be dismissed as mere snobs, or else as people who, fortunately for them, have no idea what war is all about. Some of those who deliberately ignore it don't know a thing about it either, but, unfortunately for the rest of us, they are much more dangerous. I am referring to the self-styled "neo-realists," gremlin-like creatures who really think that war is the continuation of politics (or, as often as not, bureaucratic battles over budgets) and nothing else. Never having served, they are oblivious to the fact that war calls for the highest sacrifice of all, and that those who wage it are made of flesh and blood. Ensconced in their offices, they deal with mere abstractions. Closing their eyes to anything but "utility" and "interest," they see the culture in question as irrelevant to the "real" business at hand and treat it accordingly. Among them are some who, holding senior office in Washington, D.C., and other capitals, are in a position to drag their fellow citizens into war should they be so inclined.

Now, it is true that, as with any kind of culture, much of what surrounds war is based on unreason and does not fit into a utilitarian framework of any kind. However, this fact does not reduce its importance one whit. One reason for this is because, stripped of its "useless" culture, war will degenerate into a mere orgy of violence, a thing sustained by no organization, no purpose, and no sense. It goes without saying that history has witnessed many such orgies. On occasion, some of the best armies in history have been guilty of them. Throwing discipline to the wind, losing control, and lashing about them in a blind fury. However, such orgies do not war make. In general, those who failed to distinguish between the two have been no match for well-organized, well-regulated armies with all their cumbersome cultural accoutrements.

This brings us to the real reason why the culture of war matters: namely, the critical role it plays in overcoming men's natural inclination to avoid, or flee from, danger while at the same time preparing them to make the supreme sacrifice if and when required. Troops of every kind may be prepared to kill, rob, and destroy in order to serve this or that purpose. They may also possess every attribute needed for realizing those goals: resources, numbers, organization, equipment, whatever. However, unless they are also prepared to defy nature and risk their lives, they will be useless and worse.

Admittedly, Patton's quip that the purpose of war is to make the other guy die for *his* country contains a large measure of truth; nevertheless, it is only a half-truth. This in turn means that pundits who, whether out of ignorance or snobbery, refuse to take the culture of war seriously are committing an error so momentous as to cast doubt on anything else they may say, or write, or do about it. A story told about the German chief of staff Alfred von Schlieffen (1893–1905) sums it up very nicely. "Yes," he once told a carping critic, "it all comes down to this foolish question, how to win."

The outline of the volume is as follows. Part I deals with the culture of war as it manifests itself in ordinary times. This includes the decoration of military dress and equipment, the inculcation and transmission of martial values at military educational institutions of every sort, and the huge number of exercises and games whose objective is to prepare for war and simulate it. Part II deals with the culture as it may be observed during hostilities, including the transition into war and battle, the joy of fighting, the rules of war, and the transition from war back to peace. Part III briefly describes the culture that is created in the wake of war, such as monuments, literature, movies, museums, and so on. Part IV focuses on civilization since 1945—the so-called post-modern, post-military, post-heroic civilization. Here my aim is to show that a world without war is not in the cards. On the contrary, every one of the elements discussed in the book's previous parts remains alive and well. Though often treated with contempt and sometimes suppressed, they are present just under the surface, waiting to emerge.

Those are the historical parts of this volume. But what can we expect to happen in case the culture of war is absent? To answer that question is the purpose of the fifth and last part. Here the focus is on some of the things that have always been considered to stand, and in many ways do stand, in direct opposition to the culture in question, to wit: the wild horde, the soulless machine, men without chests, and feminism.

The objective of the exercise is a double one. First, I want to put any number of assorted "ists"—such as relativists, deconstructionists, destructivists, post-modernists, the more maudlin kind of pacifists, and feminists firmly in their place. *Pace* all these people, not only does such a thing as a culture of war exist, but much of it is magnificent and well worth studying. Furthermore, in many ways it has remained essentially the same at all times and in places. In one sense, my objective is just the opposite from that of John Keegan in *A History of Warfare* (1993). He tried to show how when culture changes, the conduct of war must follow. I, on the contrary, want to show how some very basic things stay the same in spite of all changes in weapons, tactics, and so on.

Flipping the coin to its other side, I want to confront the "neo-realists." Focusing almost exclusively on information, capabilities, weapon systems, and what the editor of one well-known periodical in the

field calls "strict strategy," all they do is prove their own inability to understand what motivates war as well as their unfitness to run it. By contrast, my aim is to bring back into the study of war all the vital things they,
and of course their amanuensis Clausewitz, have left out of it. Thus I am
taking on opponents on both sides of the political-cultural spectrum, the
more sentimental kind of left and the "hard-headed" right. But then I
have always enjoyed a good fight.

I

PREPARING FOR WAR

In theory, war is simply a means to an end, a rational, if very brutal, activity intended to serve the interests of one group of people by killing, wounding, or otherwise incapacitating those who oppose that group. In reality, nothing could be further from the truth. Whether war is profitable has often been doubted. However, its ability to fascinate men and, in a different way, women is beyond question. For every day that World War I lasted, several books were written about it and continue to be written about it; had anybody been made to see all the films ever made about World War II, no doubt he or she would have spent years doing so. More than any other factor, it is this fascination that accounts for the fabulous sums and enormous creative talent often spent in decorating men, equipment, and weapons. Other parts of the culture of war comprise the preparation of soldiers for battle as well as devising and playing war games of every kind, even to the point where, seen from a purely military point of view, the investment made was sometimes counterproductive.

.   .   .

1

From War Paint to Tiger Suits

L ogically, men should enter war decked out in the most economical, most utilitarian way possible—for is not war the most wasteful of human activities? In reality, very often they do just the opposite, covering themselves with elaborate decorations that might take hours, even days, to apply. As far back into prehistory as we can look, war paint has always been part of the culture of tribal societies.[1] Originally such paint may have been intended purely for going on campaign, thus helping create a sharp distinction between war and peace. As with so many other elements of what we have called the culture of war, though, very often it ended up being used for ceremonial purposes on other occasions as well, so much so that it is often very hard to say whether war has penetrated culture or culture war.

Usually the paint was made from locally available materials, especially vegetable ones mixed with small amounts of minerals ground or pounded into a powder. Occasionally, though, it was obtained by trade. Among the Indians of North America vermillion paint was highly desired; in 1756–63 it became one of the commodities in which both the French and the British paid their Indian allies. Usually it was applied with the aid of the fingers, though here and there specialized instruments were used. The objectives included magic—certain devices were considered capable of providing protection—inspiring fear, and to some extent identification.

Whereas normally each warrior decorated himself as he pleased, each tribe also had its own pattern to serve for identification. The Sioux used red, the Crow white. The fearsome reputation of the Catawba of the Carolinas may have had something to do with the asymmetrical way they painted their faces. One eye was surrounded by a white circle, the other by a black one; the rest was blackened as well. Often different colors indicated different moods. For example, among the Cherokee red stood for victory. Blue stood for defeat or trouble, black for death, and white for quiet, peace, and happiness. Very often entire mythologies were woven to explain why a people had chosen to put on this or that color for this or that purpose. Too often, all the tales did was to cover the fact that the choice was, in reality, perfectly arbitrary.

Originally the Indians of North America traveled and fought on foot. No sooner had horses been introduced, however, than the same colors started to be applied to them as well. Horses were painted symmetrically on both sides of their bodies, each side telling the same story. The symbols used included circles around one or both eyes of the horse, perhaps intended to make them look more threatening, as well as long zigzag lines that symbolized lightning, apparently with the intention of adding power and speed to terrify the enemy. The various symbols were not isolated but understood to build upon each other. They formed, or were meant to form, a whole that appeared harmonious to their creators even if it looked outlandish to outsiders.

What was true of the Indians of North America was equally true of other tribal societies scattered all over the world—even though, before the advent of the white man, very few of them can have so much as heard of each other's existence. Neither Zulu warriors in South Africa nor Sioux ones in South Dakota went into battle as their gods had created them. The same applies to the headhunters of New Guinea and fighters throughout Polynesia, as well as the braves of countless societies in what is now known as Latin America. Instead they did so with their bodies covered with decorative patterns and/or special hairdos, as in the case of the Meru of Kenya. Very often the paint was not laid on but permanently applied by means of tattoos painfully created during initiation rites; tattoos, indeed, were among the distinctive marks of the warriors. For example, Briton warriors around the time of Christ covered much of their bodies with animal designs. This gave them a bluish color and, as Julius Caesar commented, made them "frightful to look upon in battle."[2] Roman soldiers did not take long to adopt the practice. Over the next centuries they spread it throughout the empire until the first Christian emperor, Constantine I, banned it because he felt it went against "God's handiwork."

Nor is the use of paint to modify the appearance of men and animals at war limited to "barbaric" peoples most often met in ethnological museums. Thus eighteenth-century British regiments used to color their horses so as to make them look alike. Originally developed for parades, the practice was sometimes continued on campaign even though it was harmful to the animals' health, which was why it was finally prohibited in 1811.[3] Later in the century French officers whose moustaches happened to be blond were under standing orders to blacken them by applying shoe polish. In today's armies war paint is still in use—so much so that it is often employed as a synonym for preparation for battle. At least two books, Cynthia Enloe's *Does Khaki Become You?* and Andrew Bacevich's *The New American Militarism,* carry pictures of young soldiers, female and male respectively, their faces painted in a greenish black pattern, on the dust covers. A third, Bill Goshen's autobiographical novel about his experience fighting in Vietnam, uses the words "war paint" as its title.[4]

To tribal people, one reason for applying war paint was to exercise magic power either for protecting oneself or for harming the enemy. Other, more practical reasons may be to provide camouflage—especially during night operations, ambushes, and surprise raids—or to terrify the enemy. In the modern world the situation is even more complicated. On the one hand, with most people priding themselves on their rationality and freedom from superstition, the magical-power explanation (supposedly) no longer applies. On the other, since most soldiers, instead of clashing hand to hand with edged weapons, operate at such long ranges that they hardly see the faces of enemy troops, the second and third reasons do not apply either. Among the few exceptions—soldiers who still fight at close quarters—are commandoes. Not by accident did Goshen belong to, and write about, a Ranger unit.

This explains why, the practical uses of war paint aside, modern armies have turned it into the trademark of elite warriors. It is sometimes adopted by other soldiers who feel envious of them and want to imitate them so as to earn the kudos that are usually reserved for these elite warriors. To this should be added other reasons, among them the hope to draw courage by engaging in a ceremonial act as well as the need to mark the transition from an existence in which one's life is generally safe into another where it is in constant jeopardy. So intricate is the mixture of motives that accounts for the use of war paint—psychological, social, practical, and magical—that separating them is probably impossible. The same, we shall soon have occasion to see, is true of almost every other element in the culture of war.

In countless societies, war paint, whether applied to the skin or permanently tattooed, was complemented by other forms of decoration. Plumes made of feathers or the tails of animals, rings of every kind and shape, pieces of bone or wood or metal that pierced the nose or the ears, the horns and claws and teeth of various animals that were used to decorate headgear or put on a string and carried as necklaces—all these and many others were pressed into service. As with tattoos, the objectives varied greatly. One was probably to make warriors look larger and more ferocious than they were. Another was to ensure that the qualities of the animals whose body parts were thus taken into battle would transfer themselves to the warriors who wore or carried them. Another still was to bring protective magic into play so as to render the wearer invulnerable. In North and South America, Micronesia, Polynesia, New Guinea, New Zealand, and much of Southeast Asia "battle dress" might also include dried, shrunken, or pickled body parts of enemies who had been killed in previous encounters and now served to demonstrate the wearer's prowess.

Modern soldiers on campaign seldom carry real valuables other than sentimental items such as pictures of wives, children, girlfriends, and the like. The members of older societies often behaved quite differently. Going to war, they took their belongings along, wore them, and displayed them as prominently as they could. In part, this was because they had no choice; after all, there were no banks, often not even permanent dwellings, where they could leave their belongings knowing that they would still be there when they came back. In part, perhaps, wearing their finery was one way they inspired themselves with courage. As late as the aftermath of the Battle of the Nile in 1798, Napoleon's soldiers were found fishing in the river so as to catch their opponents' bodies and relieve them of the gold and silver coins they carried.[5]

From very early on, the warriors of many societies no longer fought more or less naked. Instead they covered themselves with some kind of dress that also provided protection; in other words, they wore armor and headgear. Others supplemented this by carrying defensive devices such as shields. In this study we are primarily interested in those aspects of dress and armor that are *not* functional, at least not in the sense that they are strictly bound up with the need to protect their wearers.

Historically, not all warriors wore protective clothing or armor or carried shields. In the case of some, such as the Roman *velites,* or "fast"
troops, this was because they preferred to rely on agility for protection.
More often, perhaps, it was because people could not afford the latter
two in particular; depending on the time and place, prices might vary
from the equivalent of a few days' work to a small fortune. The fact that
protective gear was costly also helped turn it into a status symbol, encouraging competition among the men. Right from the beginning, those
who did carry shields and/or wore armor or protective clothing usually
covered them with extremely elaborate, and frequently very costly, decoration.

As in the case of war paint, tattoos, and various objects carried on the
body, some of the decoration was meant to impress and to terrify. In
many societies, fighters used to put on battle dress made of the skins of
wild animals such as tigers, leopards, and pumas. Often the dress came
complete with the animal's head, glass eyes and teeth specifically included; the most famous case in point is the ancient Greek demigod
Heracles, who always wore a lion skin in battle. Also from Greece came
the warrior goddess Pallas ("robust") Athena. Her shield, the aegis, was
made of goatskin. To it was fixed the severed head of Medusa, who had
serpents growing from her head instead of hair. Myth had it that anyone
who so much as looked at the head was instantly turned into stone. To
Sigmund Freud, the myth arose because, to the unconscious mind, it
symbolized castration and a return to the mother's genital from which
men had come.[6]

The *Iliad* presents us with several elaborate descriptions of armor.
Old Nestor carries a shield made entirely of massive gold (probably the
poet meant that it was covered with a very thin layer of the material,
or else it would have been quite useless). Preparing for battle, King
Agamemnon starts by putting on "beautiful greaves with silver ankle
clasps." Next, he dons a corselet with "ten bands of enamel, twelve of
gold and twenty of tin. Enameled snakes arched towards the neck of the
piece, here on either side, like the rainbow which Zeus fixes firmly in the
clouds as a sign for mortal men." His "man-protecting, skillfully wrought"
shield had "ten circles of bronze; the twenty studs were of white tin
around its rim. On its middle was a boss of dark enamel enclosed by the
mouth of a ferocious Gorgon, and on each side of her were Fear and
Panic. . . . The strap for hanging the shield was of silver on which a dark
blue serpent of three heads twined on one trunk." The elaborate outfit

was completed by "a double-ridged helmet with four white crests of horsehair, which nodded terribly above it."[7]

Achilles's shield was even more famous. It was ornamented with a complete panorama of human life worked in gold, silver, tin, and lapis lazuli; among other things it showed the sky, the earth and the river thought to surround it, cities, people voting in the assembly, scenes from agricultural life, and much more.[8]

Clearly, Heracles, Nestor, and Agamemnon all put a high value on decoration. The first two were presumably prepared to pay what it cost, whereas the third had his equipment made for him by the divine smith Hephaistos. Their motives, as far as they can be made out, were different. Of the three shields, the one belonging to Achilles was the most elaborate and the most beautiful—art for art's sake, to use a modern phrase no ancient Greek would have understood. The one carried by Agamemnon was designed to terrify, and the one owned by Nestor showed how rich and powerful its owner was. All three motives existed during the Trojan War, more than three millennia ago, and all three are very much in evidence today.

Still remaining in ancient Greece, we have countless vases painted with scenes of warriors fighting and phalanxes advancing against each other. In these paintings we can clearly see how highly decorated greaves and armor were; Socrates at one point criticized the practice, arguing that close-fitting armor was preferable to the kind inlaid with silver and gold.[9] It was standard practice for citizen-soldiers to buy their own arms and armor from the craftsmen who made them. This may be one reason why, as far as we can judge, hardly two of them are identical. Some greaves and cuirasses were worked until they became real works of art, carrying reliefs of mythological figures, animals, birds, and symbols of every sort and description. More often, though, their decoration consisted merely of geometrical devices etched into the metal.

The shields carried by Greek warriors fell into three kinds, gilded, brazed, and white; discussing the advantages of ones made out of bronze over wooden ones, Xenophon simply says that they could be brought to a high polish.[10] Some shields carried geometrical devices. Others were painted with a variety of threatening animals, such as lions, bulls, boars, rams, snakes, scorpions, fighting cocks, and various birds of prey; another favorite emblem was a human eye. The Spartans used to paint the letter *lambda* (the initial of the Spartan state's name, Lacedaemon) on the shields they carried. However, this use of shields for identification seems to have been exceptional. Probably it is linked to the fact that, out of several hundred city-states, Sparta alone had a system whereby arms were centrally purchased and distributed to the troops; perhaps this system itself was meant to prevent soldiers from going their own way and indulging their taste for splendor. Less is known about the way the soldiers of Alexander and his successors decorated their shields. Still, our sources do tell us that some elite units carried expensive ones made of or covered with silver, and were accordingly called *argyraspides*.[11]

The helmets worn by Greek and Macedonian soldiers were, if anything, even more shaped by aesthetic considerations. The *Iliad* is full of references to waving crests, the most famous one being that decorating the helmet won by Hector, which terrifies his infant son Astyanax.[12] Helmets varied-according to the region where they were made. Depending on the identity of their owners, the particular corps of the warrior, or the class of the wearer they tended to become more elaborate over time, culminating in those worn by the royal guards of Alexander and his successors. Their elaborate visors, ear and neck flaps, and ostentatious plumes reflected both the need for visibility in mounted attack and the privileged status of the warrior. If wearing them risked attracting the attention of enemy pikemen, apparently it was felt that this was a risk worth taking.

In ancient times, as today, some of the more elaborate, more expensive pieces may have been part of the culture of war rather than of war itself. They were intended for reviews, parades, ceremonial occasions, presentation by important personages to each other and to their underlings, or simply the display cabinet. Some were plainly too delicate to serve for anything else.[13] That, however, was by no means always the case, for two important reasons. First, commanders and troops who only carry the most common, cheapest equipment on campaign are thereby making a statement about themselves: that they lack pride in themselves and that they do not trust in the outcome. In other words, they are at a psychological disadvantage before the fighting even gets under way. Second, as we shall see in greater detail later in this study, during most of military history battles themselves were the greatest parades of all.

In any case we have plenty of literary evidence that expensive, highly decorated equipment often *was* carried in battle and *was* used for fighting. Of Xenophon we know that he always wore his finest armor. So did other commanders; indeed, in the *Anabasis* he himself says so.[14] Describing the Samnite army in 309 B.C., Livy says that half of their fifty thousand men were dressed in white with crests and plumes on their helmets. The sight made enough of an impression for the Roman commander, Lucius Papirius Cursor, to tell his troops that "crests do not cause wounds, and the Roman javelin goes through painted and gilded shields."[15] Caesar, counting on his soldiers' avarice to make them fight better, encouraged them to use weapons inlaid with gold and silver. Conversely, at Pharsalus in 48 B.C. he worried lest the Pompeians' splendid equipment would have an adverse psychological effect on them.[16]

At Mont Graupius in A.D. 84, the British chieftain Calgacus told his men, "Be not frightened by [the Roman troops'] idle display, by the glitter of gold and of silver, which can neither protect nor wound."[17] The fourth-century A.D. writer Ammianus Marcelinus says that the Romans used their "magnificent" equipment in order to intimidate and overawe their Germanic enemies, sometimes with success. Vegetius adds that centurions' armor and helmets were ornamented with silver so that they might be more easily distinguished by their respective soldiers.[18] In fact, so overwhelming is the evidence that at least some expensive equipment was used in battle and not simply on parade that one can only wonder why some people refuse to believe it.

Both in classical Greece and in Republican Rome, soldiers were normally citizens of middle-class origin who purchased their own equipment and kept it at home, bringing it with them as they were called up for military service. Of imperial Rome we know, and of the Hellenistic monarchies we may guess, that their professional armies drew most of their rank and file from the lower classes; yet even in these periods it was the legion and the phalanx, not the individual, who counted.[19] As many surviving representations show, these facts were far from dictating absolute uniformity in dress and armor.[20] Still, they must have limited the extent to which soldiers competed with each other or were allowed to do so by the regulations; to armies whose strength consisted precisely of the fact that they fought in formation, such competition would have been damaging. The situation in proto-feudal and feudal societies as they developed—for example, during the European Middle Ages as well as in samurai Japan—was quite different. In them, the middle classes were absent almost by definition. By definition, too, they were dominated by warrior aristocrats who spurned regulation while treasuring their personal honor and independence above anything else.

In the field of aesthetics, as well as any other, such attitudes are likely to lead to strong competition between individuals. Hence it is no surprise that European armor of the period came in an amazing variety of shapes and forms. Excavations of Anglo-Saxon graves in Britain, pre-Viking ones in Scandinavia, and pre-Carolingian ones in Germany present an interesting picture. Whereas those that contain the remains of women are full of jewelry, those of men abound with highly ornate arms; evidently it was thought there was some kind of equivalence between the two. Of particular interest in the present context are so-called *Spangenhelme,* high, conical helmets found throughout Germany and spreading into northern Italy as well. Many are gilt and decorated with figures of animals and flowers. Some carry the mark of sword blows, proving that they were used in battle and not merely for display. Shields, made of wood, were also often highly decorated, coming as they did with metallic appliqués of silver or brass representing birds of prey, lions, and other animals.[21]

Though the suits of chain mail worn during the early Middle Ages were hard to decorate, pictorial representations such as the Bayeux Tapestry leave no doubt that warriors on both sides entered battle while carrying multicolored, highly ornamental shields. The next two centuries witnessed any number of developments, yet the most elaborate, as well as most expensive, forms of decoration had to wait until after plate began to replace mail late in the thirteenth century. From then until the middle of the sixteenth century the manufacture of armor became a highly developed, highly specialized craft whose centers were in such cities as Nuremberg, Augsburg, and Milan.

The basic material of which armor was made was iron, which was forged and hammered until it turned into what was, by our standards, low-quality steel. Very often it was inlaid, emblazoned to create various patterns, burnished, and brought to a high degree of polish. Those who could afford to do so had their sets decorated with gold and silver. They were encrusted with precious stones and etched with all kinds of emblems such as mottos, scrolls, coronets, crowns, biblical and mythological figures, and whatnot; some of the etchings were based on the work of famous artists such as Daniel Hopfer, Hans Holbein (both father and son), and Albrecht Dürer. An entire vocabulary, much of it incomprehensible to anybody but experts, developed to describe the various types: jacks, corselets, cuirasses, brigandines with and without ribs.

The "Chain-Mail Reinforced Period" having ended early in the four-teenth century, we go through the "Cyclas Period" (1325–35). Next come the "Studded and Splinted Period," the "Camail and Jupon Period," and the "Lancastarian or Surcoatless Period."[22] Since few pieces of armor dating to these periods survived, this particular periodization is based mostly on the brass reliefs found in English churches; other experts have produced their own systems. The Lancastarian Period in turn was followed by the "Tabard Period," also known as the "Gothic" one, from which many sets still survive. As the name indicates, armor took on elaborate Gothic forms. Even this was not the end, however, since later still it began to be fluted or ridged or gadrooned.

Now the pieces that covered the feet sported spikes in front—some were longer than the feet themselves and must have made it impossible for their wearers to walk; now they were broad and flat.[23] Now the pieces covering the shoulders and elbows were relatively simple; now they suddenly sprouted protrusions resembling nothing as much as cauliflower leaves. Gauntlets, too, varied enormously. Some were articulated to cover each finger. Others were shaped like mittens, whereas others still anticipated today's punk culture by carrying pointed spikes in front. Only a few of the endless variations can be explained on utilitarian grounds. Probably the great majority reflected changes in fashion in general; many manufacturers of armor sought to reproduce, in metal, the kind of decorative devices that high-class people wore on their clothes.[24]

Those styles apart, armor made in Italy, which had a characteristic "burly" look, differed from its more delicately fashioned German counterpart. Some modern researchers identify many substyles with names such as the Schott-Sonnenberg style, the Frederick the Victorious style, the Sanseverino style, and others. Depending on the place and period, we find high waistlines and low ones, high necklines and low ones (covered, in the case of armor, with chain mail), puffs, and slashes. Some suits, made toward the middle of the sixteenth century, carry that ultimate symbol of masculinity, a hefty codpiece. Others, manufactured only twenty years later, have the parts below the waist shaped like skirts; one might almost think they were meant to be worn by ballerinas.

As had been the case during many earlier periods, helmets in particular provided opportunities for display. Some helmets were boxlike, others rounded, others conical. Some were open in front, others had fixed visors, still others hinged visors that could be closed. Some had flaps to protect the ears and the rear of the neck, but others did not. Some had rims, but others did not. Some were provided with beaks to present a sharp corner to the enemy in front. Presumably to make them look threatening, some fifteenth- and sixteenth-century helmets even sported molded teeth, eyebrows, and/or moustaches.[25] Others still sought to achieve the same effect by being shaped in the form of various animals—lions, wolves, and birds of prey were special favorites—or else by being provided with spikes, combs, crests, and various kitelike devices so as to make their wearers seem taller than they were. Probably no item knights wore or carried, however humble, could escape the decorative urge of those who created it or ordered it. Witness spurs, often made of, and inlaid with, a variety of precious materials, and often lovingly fashioned into real, if minor, works of art.[26]

War horses, too, were covered with—one is tempted to say smothered by—decoration. Already ancient sources speak of bit bosses, other parts of harnesses, and even horse sandals being made of precious metals or else enameled. To horse trappings, the Middle Ages added stirrups and saddles. Some of the latter, while made of wood and leather, were so heavily covered with carvings as to make them resemble ivory; others were studded with precious stones.[27] Whereas the horses shown in the Bayeux tapestry appear as their creator made them, toward the end of the thirteenth century some of them began to have their heads protected by specially made iron masks with spikes protruding from them. Later still their breasts and sides were lined with armor, their tails carefully dressed or cropped, and their entire bodies covered by colored, embroidered coats, known as trappers, that almost hid their forms.[28] The closer to the middle of the sixteenth century we come, the more elaborate the decoration.

To the great Dutch historian Johan Huizinga (1872–1945), the trend toward more and more elaborate ornamentation presented a sign of decline. Political, economic, and technological factors were causing the ground on which chivalry has stood for so long to slip away under it; vaguely aware of this fact, people were trying to obtain one last lease on life by means of fantastic embellishment.[29] Others have disputed this, attempting to explain the development of arms and armor during this period on purely utilitarian grounds and coming close to denying that they involved any form of "culture" at all.[30] Personally, I do not find either of these arguments convincing. In his other great book, *Homo Ludens*, Huizinga himself argues that utility and decoration, practical considerations and playacting, have gone hand in hand not just during the late Middle Ages but at all times and places (except, sadly, those in which he himself has the misfortune to live).[31] There is no reason to think this is less true of war than of any other human field of endeavor; if anything, to the contrary.

Once again, this raises the question as to just when, and what for, the suits in question were made, purchased, and worn. Some, no doubt, could only be owned by real grandees and were intended solely for use on parade or in tournaments. On the other hand, some grandees are known to have ordered suits of armor specifically in order to prepare for wars in which they expected to serve; as, for example, Archduke Leopold V of the Tyrol did in 1618.[32] Some suits, now in various museums, are known to have been taken as spoils. Others belonged to *condottieri* or captains of Landsknechte, men who spent their entire lives fighting one engagement after the other. Some are even marked with the words "for the field." Turning the evidence around and looking not at the weapons but at the occasions on which they were used, for some battles we have explicit evidence. At Nicopolis, in 1396, magnificence, driven by competition among the Christian knights, was carried to the point where the army looked more like a pleasure party than a force preparing for war. The same was true at Granson in 1476.[33]

Moreover, until the middle of the sixteenth century, sometimes even later, princes, dukes, kings, and even emperors took an active part in the battles they commanded. Quite often they fought in person. Among English kings alone, Harald, William the Conqueror, Henry I, Henry II, Richard the Lionhearted, Edward I, Edward III, the Black Prince, and Henry V all did so as a matter of course. So, on the Continent, did Jean VI of France (taken prisoner at Agincourt in 1415), Charles the Bold of Burgundy (killed at Nancy in 1477), and Francis I of France (taken prisoner at Pavia in 1525). Commanding against the Turks at Bizerta in 1535, Emperor Charles V had several horses killed under him. King Sebastião I of Portugal was killed fighting the Moroccans at Alcazarquivir in 1578; fifty-four years later, King Gustavus Adolphus of Sweden lost his life while fighting the imperialists at Lützen. For reasons discussed earlier, such august persons could hardly afford *not* to wear their suits when leading their troops on campaign. Doing so, they forced their subordinates to imitate them.

Though social conditions and methods of warfare differed very greatly, developments in other parts of the world paralleled European ones. Proceeding in ascending order of cost, some Indian shields were made of bamboo shoots glued together. Some were fashioned out of rhinoceros hide, others of damascened steel, and others still of gold-plated steel—the last being reserved for the highest class of warriors. Yet however cheap or expensive they might be, almost all were heavily decorated with geometrical and floral patterns. Many sported various animals, especially lions and elephants. Others carried various letters that stood for magic formulae.[34] Even the armor worn by war elephants was decorated. Much the same applies to Arab armor, Persian armor, Chinese armor, Ottoman armor (made of oxhide and intended to be carried on horseback), and almost any other armor one can think of.

In the entire world, probably no warriors were more addicted to decorating their armor, often fashioning it in truly outlandish forms, than the samurai. In medieval Japan, as in the feudal West, most arms were not centrally distributed but commissioned by individual warriors from individual craftsmen. Even when this was not the case, samurai were supposed to wear their own personal crests as well as those of their lords.[35] As a result, in the whole of Japanese art one can hardly find two warriors whose dress and equipment were exactly the same. Any number of means was used to intimidate and, if possible, win the fight before it had even started. They included shining materials, especially polished metal and lacquer; emblems in the form of demons and ferocious animals; black helmets, some looking like the one worn by Darth Vader and others equipped with antlers (known as *kuwagata*) or else protruding fighting teeth; faces covered with war paint in red, black, and yellow; and much more.

Some of the equipment in question was so elaborate as to be clearly counterproductive, militarily speaking. A good example were the two-foot-high gold-lacquered conical helmets worn by the troops of Date Masamune (1566–1636) as they marched through Kyoto on their way to Korea in 1592.[36] As in the West, the real purpose—if that is the term—of such monstrosities might be to disguise an ongoing process of decline. As in the West, that is just one out of several possible explanations, and not necessarily the most persuasive one. Perhaps even more than in the West, warriors were willing to go to almost any length to present a suitable appearance. We even hear of one man, Kimurai Shinegari, who perfumed his head in order that it would make a more attractive trophy if it was taken—as, in the event, actually happened.

In both the West and Japan, the second half of the sixteenth century represented a turning point. In Japan this was because, after the Tokugawa victory of 1603, there were no more wars for two and a half centuries. In the West, it was because armor, in addition to being less and less effective against bullets, had become so elaborate and so expensive that only a handful of great lords could afford it. From about 1550 on,

Armor as decoration; a Western caricature of a samurai warrior admiring his grim self in the mirror
DVORA LEWY

armor began to shrink. First the pieces that used to cover the lower parts of the legs were done away with. Those providing protection to the rest of the legs and the arms followed, until finally only the breastplate remained, and then only for a certain type of heavy cavalry known as cuirassiers. From around 1650 on, its place began to be taken by uniforms. The origin of uniforms must be sought in the liveries issued by lords to their retainers, the objective being to save money (and, by overcharging those retainers, make it) as well as to provide identification. Very soon, though, aesthetic considerations were added until they became, in effect, playthings.

In today's armies, the purpose of many uniforms is to render their wearers as invisible as possible. With some exceptions, such as light troops and *Jaeger,* that was not at all the case for the ones that started to emerge in the seventeenth century and dominated the eighteenth and the first half of the nineteenth. This was a period when soldiers, relying on musket fire and often still carrying pikes, fought standing up in full view of the enemy, whose troops, also standing erect, were hardly ever more than a hundred meters away. It is true that after the War of the Spanish Succession pikes were finally discarded. The replacement of muskets by flintlocks did not, however, appreciably increase range so that battles were still fought by living walls of flesh that moved steadily toward each other. Only around 1860 did things finally change. The introduction of rifled small arms and cannon forced soldiers to lie down and take shelter; the replacement of muzzle-loaders by breech-loaders permitted them to do so. Until then, not unexpectedly, the development of uniforms followed a trajectory similar to that taken by plate armor during the period from 1300 to 1550. Some commanders, notably the Marshal de Saxe, raised their voices against the trend toward more and more elaborate, more and more expensive, and (sometimes) more and more useless uniforms.[37] Normally, however, they did so in vain.

Adding to the extravagance, uniforms during the period in question were often designed by amateurs who took to it as a hobby. One of those who did so was Queen Anne of England; she surrounded herself by a troupe of uniformed female archers whom she called "Amazons." Another was the "soldier king," Frederick William I of Prussia. He seems to have been the first monarch in history to wear a uniform; one story has it that, lying on his deathbed and hearing the chaplain sing "Naked shall I, too, appear before Thy stern countenance," he roused himself and shouted that he would be dressed in his uniform.[38] Others were Peter II of Russia, who (his wife, Catherine the Great, claimed) loved his boots so much that he did not take them off even in bed; Frederick William III of Prussia, who owned a huge collection; and George IV of England, who carried things to the point where he became the object of derision in the press.

Some of Napoleon's marshals also amused themselves by designing uniforms for themselves and their men. Joachim Murat, the dashing cavalry commander who later became the King of Naples, was a particularly vain man; so fanciful were some of the uniforms he made for himself that the emperor at one point compared him to a famous clown of the time. Far from being limited to crowned heads, the interest in uniforms spread down the social pyramid. Many colonels tampered with their units' uniforms out of misplaced vanity or sheer boredom, even to the point of spending their own money to make sure that coat buttons would be made of a certain material and carry a certain pattern. In the early decades of the nineteenth century children were able to buy for a few pennies sets of cardboard soldiers with interchangeable paper uniforms.

Many, though not all, of the devices discussed so far achieve their aesthetic effect by virtue of their individuality, as each warrior made or commissioned his own equipment and decorated it as he saw fit. This is not true of uniforms, which, as the term implies, do so by using standard patterns endlessly and relentlessly repeated—in other words, by appealing to what is probably man's innate sense of order.[39] Every late-seventeenth- and eighteenth-century army had its martinets. The original Martinet had Jean as his first name and acted as Louis XIV's inspector general. He was killed in 1672, but not before leaving his name to other officers and NCOs. Armed with the cat-o'-nine-tails—which, in French, is also named after him—their task was to enforce uniformity to the last gaiter button. This did not prevent uniforms from coming in a bewildering array of patterns, cuts, and colors, with accessories of every kind. The overriding objective was always to emphasize the men's trim, increase their stature, broaden their shoulders, exaggerate their strength, and conceal physical shortcomings (such as scrawny necks, narrow chests, protruding stomachs, and spindly legs)—in short, to make them look impressive to their selves, to their enemies, and to spectators of both sexes. Though codpieces had long fallen out of fashion, some uniforms used other means to focus attention on their wearers' masculinity, for example, by having V-shaped stripes or rows of buttons running down from the shoulders toward the groin.

Some of the heights of sartorial splendor were achieved by the British army in the early nineteenth century, which may therefore serve as our example for what could be and was done in this field.[40] Uniforms worn by different branches of the service varied greatly. Coat colors consisted primarily of the traditional scarlet for infantry and engineers, scarlet or dark blue for cavalry, dark blue for the artillery, and dark green for rifle units. However, when it came to collars, lapels, and cuffs, each regiment had its own coat colors, the favorites being yellow and green. On top of this, officers' coats were trimmed with gold or silver bullion lace, whereas other ranks had white worsted lace. Coats carried anywhere between twenty and forty shiny metal buttons. Each button was embossed with some sign and surrounded by its own button lace. Officers added to the effect by wearing bullion epaulets in silver or gold, whereas those worn by other ranks were made of worsted wool.

Headgear, too, received a good deal of attention. The cavalry in particular tended to adopt tall and imposing hats, their height further increased by the addition of plumes in red and white or green and white. Even in a period when tactics were as described earlier, such headgear was a study in military counterproductivity. As one board of inquiry reported, shakos were heavy—their "sickening weight" strained the neck and required broad and uncomfortable chin bands. Some types of hats provided little protection against the weather. Others directed rainwater "in an incessant stream" down the back of their wearers, whereas others still absorbed water, collected dust, or had an unfortunate attraction for insects both on campaign and while in storage. One amusing, though probably apocryphal, story describes how in 1829 the Duke of Wellington was blown off his horse during a review because of the huge hat he was wearing.

Among the colors soldiers sported, white, owing to its quality of showing every speck of dirt, occupied a special place. French, British, and Austrian units (the last of which were sometimes known as "white-coats") all wore uniforms that were at least partly white, and which had to be cleaned by applying pipe clay. Pipe clay, until it dried, restricted soldiers' movements since they had to avoid brushing against anything. Repeated applications of the material made uniforms inflexible and unpleasant to wear as well as reducing their life span. On the march it would come off in clouds of dust; one British officer noted that pipe clay, which he called "white dirt," was "more injurious to the sight and health of men than anything that can be conceived."[41]

Tight uniforms could restrict men's movements, especially those of cavalrymen trying to mount their horses, and the famous Wellington boots were extremely uncomfortable on the march. Yet the most counterproductive piece of dress of all was the neckstock, a device so quaint that it does not even appear in most modern dictionaries. Neckstocks were used in all armies, the U.S. one included. They consisted of a collar made of stiff leather, some four inches in height, which could be laced shut so as to keep the wearer's head erect in the correct martial position. In spite of many complaints about the discomfort and even injuries it caused, in peacetime it was supposed to be worn at all times; any attempts to shorten it or make it softer by scraping the leather were severely punished. Only in 1845 did the Duke of Wellington finally agree to introduce a more pliant variety, but even so some colonels resisted the change.

All this brings us to the really decisive question: namely, whether such counterproductive practices were found solely during peacetime parades or whether they were retained in wartime, too. The answer is that they were used during wartime, if not by everybody, then by some units, and if not all of the time, then much of the time. As if to put our doubts to rest, some contemporary illustrations showing Prussian troops in their blue coats and white trousers are explicitly entitled "*campagne uniform.*"[42] The dangers that colorful uniforms posed while on campaign were, of course, well understood.[43] Still British regiments operating in Europe were expected to wear full dress as a matter of course and, as far as we know, did so whenever possible; at Waterloo, officers famously entered battle dressed in the very same gala uniforms they had worn to a

Uniform as torture; the neckstock
in caricature   *PUNCH*, 1854

ball held at Brussels the previous evening.

In the absence of regulations that could bind the entire army, British colonels, taking their regiments on colonial service in different parts of the world, adopted different practices as it suited them. Some made concessions to the climate, which was often harsh, doing away with the more obnoxious items of dress and substituting more utilitarian ones. Others took the opposite course: hoping to impress the natives, they insisted that the troops continue to wear their red coats and white gloves even on campaign. The fact that in the colonies such items had value as booty and therefore made it even more likely that wounded soldiers left on the battlefield would be butchered was ignored. Apparently no place was considered so remote as to make it unnecessary for uniforms to have pipe clay applied to them. As Lord Elphinstone was besieging Kabul in 1841, three soldiers went looking for supplies in the nearby hills and were killed for their pains. Both during the Crimean War (1854–56) and the Second Burmese War (1855) some soldiers even insisted on wearing their neckstocks.[44]

Looking under the surface, we can easily detect a paradox at work. War is a matter of life and death. In it, every means is fair and practically every method permitted, to say nothing of the shortages and deprivations it entails, along with some of the most intense suffering men can endure. Logically speaking, therefore, war is the last place where we might expect nonfunctional practices to make their appearance or to be retained from peacetime life. In theory all this ought to have led to the abandonment of everything superfluous; yet there is a sense in which a piece of equipment or dress *has* to be superfluous if it is to produce any sort of psychological effect. It is like giving a woman a kitchen utensil for her birthday. The utensil may be highly practical, even nice to look at. Still, if the aim is to make her give one a kiss, one had better come up with a present that is *not* useful, such as flowers or, better still, diamonds.

To push this analogy a little further, perhaps the correct way to understand the age-old military tendency toward magnificence—not just in peacetime but often enough on the battlefield as well—is by referring to the so-called handicap theory.[45] Originally the theory was developed in the 1970s to explain the behavior of certain birds, such as peacocks with their enormous, clearly dysfunctional tails; later it was applied to other species, such as deer with their enormous antlers. The argument runs as follows. Males, in our case uniformed males, must demonstrate their strength and vitality so as to attract mates and deter rivals. To do so they must engage in types of display that are *not* essential for survival. This applies to war just as much as it does to love.

As already noted, changes in technology and tactics caused uniforms to become somewhat less elaborate from the middle of the nineteenth century on. During the Indian Mutiny of 1857–58 some British units started dyeing their white uniforms khaki, a much more practical color. The torture devices known as neckstocks disappeared, although men and especially officers were still expected to carry themselves as if they wore them—even today, cadets at Sandhurst Royal Academy must spend the first six weeks marching about as if they were robots. Other armies were also forced to give up their traditional bright colors, which had become too conspicuous and too dangerous to wear. They were replaced with others whose names, such as field gray, olive green, earth brown, and horizon blue, sufficiently indicated their purpose. Headgear, too, became less elaborate, though this process did not take place without some curious devices, such as the famous Prussian *Pickelhaube* (a spiked helmet), coming and going. As the huge epaulets characteristic of the first half of the nineteenth century were done away with, the amount of gold and silver braid worn by officers diminished and continued to do so in the wake of World War I. Still, there never was any question of military attire becoming purely utilitarian—as utilitarian, say, as business attire (which has now remained almost unchanged for about a century), or workers' clothes or track suits.

Civilians, buying as many new clothes as they want at times when they want to do so, easily adapt themselves to the dictates of fashion; as new clothes are added to the rack, old ones are phased out. By contrast, changing the dress worn by the members of an organization numbering tens of thousands, hundreds of thousands, or even millions of men represents a major logistic undertaking and is very expensive, causing such changes to be rare and far between. The outcome is that many a uniform is hopelessly out of date. For example, shoulder straps running diagonally across the chest originated in the bandoliers of seventeenth-century musketeers, but they continued to be worn into World War II and even after it. British, German, Soviet, and some American officers continued to wear riding breeches, riding boots, and spurs in World War II, long after their regiments had converted from horses to tanks and even after they no longer knew how to ride. The cord that runs around the shoulders of officers and NCOs and disappears into their left breast pockets originally had a whistle tied to it. These and any number of other dress items started as practical implements of war. All remained part of officers' outfit long after their original function had been lost and forgotten—the very fact that they were old turned them into objects for veneration.

Yet another reason why uniforms have retained, and presumably will always retain, more than their share of ornamental elements is the need to attract recruits. From the time when an ancient Egyptian poet complained that male children entering the pharaoh's service were destined to "have their bones scattered"[46] in the desert, military life has always had its dark side; as often as not it was brutish, nasty, and short. One function of gaudy uniforms—and, before there were uniforms, armor and war paint—was to compensate for this unpleasant fact or disguise it, creating an impression of glamour and attracting many a young man who might not otherwise have enlisted.

Very often, the tactic worked. In eighteenth-century Scotland, according to one observer,

> young men smitten with military ambition . . . talk vauntingly of [the Second Dragoons, the Scots Grays], their gray horses, their long white tails, the scarlet coats, the long swords, the high bearskin caps and the plumes of white feathers encircling them in front, the blue overalls with the broad yellow stripes on the outside, the boots and spurs, the carbines slung at the saddle side, the holster pipes and the pistols . . . Of these they talk proudly, and depict in their inward vision the figures of themselves thus accoutered and mounted.[47]

In Wilhelmine Germany, to be allowed to wear a uniform was the one great wish of every man; one story had it that officers' daughters, jealous of their menfolk, desired to have special military insignia made for them.[48] Yet there is no need to go back that far. In Israel in the 1950s, American-style combat boots, issued to paratroopers but not to other soldiers, were known as "heroes' shoes," and it was the dream of every youngster to wear a pair of them. In his memoirs, Colin Powell, former chairman of the U.S. Joint Chiefs of Staff, wrote:

> During the first semester at CCNY [City College of New York], something had caught my eye—young guys on campus in uniform . . . There came a day when I stood in line in the drill hall to be issued olive-drab pants and jacket, brown shirt, brown tie, brown shoes, a belt with a brass buckle, and an overseas cap. As soon as I got home, I put the uniform on and looked in the mirror. I liked what I saw.[49]

To help recruitment, armies organized, and continue to organize, parades, reviews, open days, and similar occasions in which splendidly attired soldiers form one of the chief attractions.

Modern uniforms must meet many different requirements, some contradictory. They must impose uniformity, but not to the point where individual and unit pride are offended. They must differ from civilian wear, but not to such an extent as to give rise to contempt or ridicule. They must change with the times, but not to the point where tradition is thrown to the wind. They must be comfortable, but they must be attractive, too. Perhaps most important of all, they must protect the body and emphasize its contours, but without giving rise to charges of foppishness and/or effeminacy. Present-day French cavalry uniforms, designed to be worn on ceremonial occasions such as the Bastille Day parade, do all this partly by dispensing with any pockets. In the view of at least one expert who worked with them, they enable the men to achieve a kind of elegance and panache hardly equaled even by the very best professional models.[50]

Very often these demands cannot be met by a single uniform—hence the need for different ones to be worn by different units on different occasions. In theory the simplest, roughest, least ornamental uniforms should be worn for combat, whereas the most elaborate ones should be reserved for peacetime balls. In practice, since anything that has to do with combat confers prestige, things are much more complicated. Visiting the Marine Corps University at Quantico, Virginia, in late 1990, I was surprised to see many of the faculty walking about in camouflage dress—these, of course, were the days just before the first Gulf War, when anybody who had been left behind in the continental United States was ipso facto suffering from an inferiority complex. Visiting the U.S. Air Force Academy in late 1999, I learned that cadets with the highest grades were rewarded by being allowed to wear pilots' suits on campus (for women in particular, this was highly impractical attire). Conversely, to display their courage, U.S. enlisted men in Vietnam sometimes defied the regulations, wearing shiny buckles as well as jewelry. On occasion, the same objective can be achieved by a carefully studied carelessness, as happened, for example, when U.S. bomber crews in World War II discarded the grommets they were supposed to wear on their berets.

Modern uniforms are, in one sense, all of a kind. Still, they do display clear national variations whose origins are by no means easy to explain.[51] Russian tsarist uniforms, and after them Soviet ones, tended to be on the baggy side. They also had large shoulder boards, a tradition still maintained in post-1991 Russia. Perhaps this was done to prove that Russians were, in fact, bears; another peculiarity was the attempt to cover the chests of their wearers not just with ribbons but with whole medals. The French retained the kepi, a nineteenth-century piece of headgear, long after other armies had adopted caps. Some of the most successful uniforms, combining a martial look with a businesslike appearance, were and still are being worn by British officers.

Pre-1945 German uniforms followed a different tradition. Here soldiers enjoyed exceptionally high status. Uniforms were very different from civilian dress and anything but casual. They were tight, snappy, and gaudy, with numerous multicolored ribbons attached; during the Nazi period, the same applied to the Waffen SS. In the judgment of one former Wehrmacht soldier who wore it for years on end, "no other uniform [was] so deliberately designed as the German to turn a man into a soldier, absolute and united with his fellows, and not just a civilian in special clothes."[52] Modern American reenactors, whose expertise is such that they will readily tell you whether this or that piece of equipment was or was not worn in 1943, agree.[53]

By contrast, U.S. uniforms bore, and still bear, a strong resemblance to civilian dress. Perhaps this reflects the wish to avoid anything smacking of "militarism"; as the Jewish linguist and Holocaust survivor Victor Klemperer noted, in comparison with their German enemies, American ones hardly looked like soldiers at all.[54] At least one American, the novelist Kurt Vonnegut, who had spent time as a prisoner of war, made a similar point. "The American Army however," he wrote, "sends its enlisted men out to fight and die in a modified business suit quite evidently made for another man, a sterilized but unpressed gift from a nose-holding charity which passes out clothing to drunks in the slums." Italian soldiers, officers in particular, tended toward dandyism and liked plumes, causing both allies and enemies to treat them as clowns. Visiting Rome in 1938, Nazi propaganda minister Joseph Goebbels poked fun at the uniforms Mussolini and other Fascists wore. Later, wags claimed that the blame for Italy losing the war fell not just on the troops and officers but on their fashion designers, too.

One modern country that, in spite of its reputation for martial excellence, has never invested much in the uniforms its troops wear is Israel. There are several reasons for this, all of them interesting since they shed light on the interaction between the military and the society it serves or is supposed to serve. First, the Israeli army originated in the pre-state paramilitary organization known as Palmach. Partly because it was illegal, partly because its members glorified agriculture as the highest occupation known to man, not only did Palmach do without spit and polish, but it despised them as signs of "bourgeois decadence." Second, a society that was initially extremely poor had better things to spend its money on than shiny buttons, leather straps, and peaked caps. Third, the climate discourages wearing neckties. Fourth, as any visitor knows, Israelis are among the least disciplined people in the world; the sloppy appearance of most civilians is carried over into the army as well. On top of this, during most of its history there was no doubt in anybody's mind that the army was absolutely vital to the country's survival. Under such conditions service personnel did not need gaudy uniforms to enhance their status. To the contrary, such uniforms indicated that, instead of serving in a combat unit, one spent one's days pushing paper from one side of a desk to another, as the saying went.

Not just the armed forces of different countries but different services and arms belonging to the same forces very often have their carefully cultivated sartorial traditions. A very good example is provided by the United States. For reasons that are by no means clear twentieth-century U.S. Army uniforms, colored first drab olive and then dark green, have always been the least attractive of all. The navy, the air force (which, wishing to distance itself from the army in which it had originated, copied the navy), and especially the marines all came up with much better ones; this may be one reason why, after the unpopular second war against Iraq dragged on and on, the marines found it easier than the rest to attract recruits. Such differences, which may also be observed in other countries, are hard to explain and indeed attempts to do so often lead to absurdities. Though outsiders may tend to trivialize them, to soldiers they are often very important indeed. For example, the U.S. Army in 2001 had the bright idea of putting all its personnel in black berets. This made the Rangers, who until then had been the only ones to wear that color, rise in revolt—and win their case.

At all times and places, a mere look at soldiers' attire ought to disprove the "realist" idea that, to the vast majority of them, war is merely a rational activity waged by robot-like creatures in cold blood to achieve this objective or that. The available raw materials and the technical capabilities of the societies from which they came; the class to which soldiers belonged and the position they occupied in social life; belief systems and religion; the tension between individualism and the need for unit cohesion; their own desire for distinction and commanders' demand for uniformity; the hope to overawe the enemy and the need, at other times, to render oneself as invisible as possible; pride, fear, and traditions of every kind, many of them unaccountable and some so irrational as to be counterproductive; the overall balance of forces—all these and many more interacted in a bewildering number of ways.

At all times and places, what people wore on campaign necessarily reflected the way society at large dressed (or did not dress). At all times and places, the fact that those who put them on were preparing to look death in the face tended to make uniforms, armor, and war paint more gaudy and more elaborate than anything people wore while going about their "ordinary" occupations. This tendency toward elaboration is one reason why, on countless occasions, "military" and "ceremonial" almost amounted to one and the same thing. Which, of course, is just another aspect of the culture of war.

2

From Boomerangs to Bastions

Chinese culture, one of the greatest and most ancient on earth, is often seen as fundamentally anti-military and peace-loving. Whether or not that is quite true we shall consider at greater length in Part IV of this volume; here, all that needs to be said is that already in the Bronze Age (ca. 2100–500 B.C.) Chinese craftsmen invested enormous efforts in the weapons they produced, decorating and beautifying them as much as the available techniques permitted.[1] Many ax blades, which today may be seen in various museums around the world, have devices, such as animals, dragons, and various geometrical patterns, etched into the metal; in at least two cases, five-legged swastikas are shown. Other ax blades were fenestrated, that is, provided with holes that may either have been intended as decoration—it is hard to see any practical advantages they may have offered—or else served to attach other ornaments such as feathers or trailers. Dagger blades, too, were decorated with a large number of different symbols and inscriptions as well as human faces etched into them. Their hilts were often made in the form of animals or covered with patterns; some of the decoration, such as a shaft mounting in the form of a tiger, is of very high quality indeed. Nor were such weapons restricted to China alone. A lively trade in Chinese weapons existed, with the result that they spread to Korea, Japan, Siberia, Russia, and as far away as the Ukraine. In all these countries, even the oldest known weapons were decorated.

Owing to the great antiquity of the objects in question, the meaning of the various symbols is often obscure; we can only guess that they had something to do with magic. The same is even more true of Bronze Age weapons produced in the Middle East (Asia Minor, Mesopotamia, Syria, Palestine, and Egypt).[2] Little or no contact seems to have existed between China and the civilizations of the Middle East during this period, yet in the latter, too, we find ax blades elaborately ornamented by means of etchings, reliefs, or fenestration. Here too, daggers often have elaborately shaped hilts inlaid with precious materials, whereas their blades come inscribed with all kinds of formulae. The blades of many daggers and spearheads are ribbed; once again, it is hard to see any reason for this except the desire for decoration. Aesthetic considerations, such as the wish to attain a high degree of polish, may also explain why the blades of some daggers and axes contain a higher proportion of lead than would have been the case if quality had been the only thing that mattered.

Whereas the population of China has long been relatively homogeneous, ethnically speaking the Middle East of the second millennium B.C. was an extremely diverse place. Here Hittites, Assyrians, Mittani, Amorites, Canaanites, Egyptians, and countless other peoples lived and interacted, which itself must have resulted in flux. The fact that the more elaborate the objects, the more often they were traded in and the larger the area over which they spread supports this interpretation. There may, however, have been other factors that pushed development along. Undoubtedly, the most highly decorated, most elaborate, most expensive weapons conferred prestige on those who owned and used them. People further down on the social ladder probably sought to emulate their betters by purchasing cheaper versions of the same weapons and decorating them in similar styles—a process familiar to modern fashion. The outcome must have been constant pressure toward change. Whether or not this is the correct explanation, of one thing we can be fairly certain: many of the forms had nothing to do with changes in the weapons' function. Such being the case, the demands of fashion are as good an explanation as there is.

What is true of Bronze Age China and the Middle East is equally true of other civilizations. The Australian Aborigines may not have had many kinds of weapons, but those they did have, such as boomerangs and throwing spears, were brightly painted with all kinds of complex patterns. The war clubs, bows, arrows, and tomahawks of North American Indian tribes, the metal knives and spears of African peoples, and ancient Greek, Roman, Celtic, and Germanic knives and swords were all manufactured in any number of shapes. Crude as it was in other respects, even the simplest medieval weapon of all, the war club, was often heavily decorated; even the simplest European halberds, intended for use by ordinary soldiers, almost always had their blades shaped into a variety of decorative forms or else fenestrated in the form of a small cross. Japanese arrowheads alone came in several hundreds of different styles; many were very beautiful. While some served different purposes, such as bird shooting, game hunting, armor piercing, and the like, it would be useless to pretend that all, or even most, did. There and elsewhere weapons were provided with decorative ribs, ornamented with beads, provided with colored feathers, tasseled. They were also inlaid with precious materials of every sort, etched, inscribed, and brought to such a high degree of polish that they could, and sometimes did, serve as mirrors.

On occasion things were carried to the point where even those who made the weapons and owned them no longer knew what their real function was. A striking example of such confusion is the fact that the Hebrew word for weapon, *zayin,* means "ornament" in Arabic, to which it is closely related. Another is an argument recorded in the Talmud. Rabbi A claimed that weapons constituted tools, hence they could not be carried on the Sabbath. Not so, said Rabbi B; people wore them as decoration and therefore they could be. In the end it was the latter interpretation that carried the day.

"Without tools, man is nothing; with tools, he is everything" (Thomas Carlyle). What applies to tools in general applies even more strongly to weapons in particular; without them, man, coming face-to-face with many other animals, would have been more or less helpless. Once war, meaning organized violence directed by one group of men against another, gets under way, weapons become even more vital. After all, it is on their quality, on their ability to crush or stab or slash or shoot or penetrate (or to prevent the enemy from causing damage by doing all this), that the existence of kings, countries, peoples, and men (as well as their most precious belongings, women and children) depends. They act as symbols and proof of the fact that their owners are still alive. Is it so surprising, therefore, that, in addition to being as well made as the available technical means permit, they are very often adorned, decorated, provided with every kind of embellishment, loved, treasured, cherished, worshipped almost? That there has grown around them an entire culture,

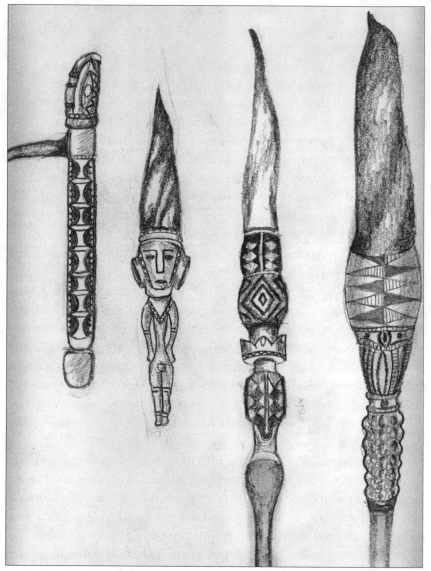

Decorated weapons from the Admiralty Islands   DVORA LEWY

one that was and is not a whit less sophisticated, less magnificent, and ultimately, less rational than any other?

From the beginning of history, proof that such attitudes did in fact
surround weapons is superabundant. Some of the best evidence is provided by graves; in countless civilizations around the world, so much did
people, especially but by no means exclusively high-class people, value

their weapons that they insisted on taking them when they died. Here
and there weapons became the subject of what can only be called love-
songs. A Punjabi poem, perhaps three thousand years old, will serve as
our example:

> With Bow let us win, Kine, with Bow in battle, with
> Bow be victory in our hot encounters,
> The Bow brings grief and sorrow to the foeman; armed
> With Bow may we subdue all regions.
> Close to his ear, as fain to speak, she presses, holding
> Her well-loved friend in her embraces;
> Strained on the Bow, she whispers like a woman—this
> Bow-string that preserves us in the Combat.[3]

Modern soldiers, too, are often told to look after their rifles as if they
were their wives.

By way of an example of a weapon that acted as the centerpiece of an
entire culture, consider the Malay kris.[4] To the uninitiated, the kris is simply a short, narrow steel dagger with a distinctive twisted blade. Modern
ones are mass manufactured in factories; they can be purchased, for a
few dollars, in any bazaar from Bangkok to Jakarta and beyond. Savants,
however, will know that traditionally there were no fewer than seven
basic kinds of kris. To these were added countless subtypes, all of which
could be distinguished from one another by the length and form of the
blade, the hilt, and the scabbard. Hilts in particular came in an endless variety of forms, ranging from simple geometrical shapes to fantastic birds,
animals, and demons. As to blades, suffice it to say that there were six
different ways for the buyer to measure them. Each of these was accompanied by its own special incantations, designed to make sure that the
weapon should bring its owner good rather than bad fortune.

Confirming the ideas of the ancient rabbis, the kris acted as decoration—"in the olden days," we are told, no Malay regarded himself as properly dressed if he did not carry one. Rulers issued regulations as to how
many might be worn and how they might be worn; the manner of doing so
in peacetime differed from the one used in war. In some modern countries, officers attending a wedding of one of their comrades will draw
their swords and form two lines with the swords crossed above so that
the bride and bridegroom may pass under them. The role of the kris in
Malay weddings was even greater, and indeed so closely identified were

the daggers and their owners that, in one type of ceremony, a kris might stand proxy for the groom. According to the most authoritative study of the subject, the kris represented "the essence of Malayness, being a symbol not only of Malay sovereignty but also of Malay masculinity." Among other things, they formed part of the court dress of sultans and may be seen in the emblem of today's Singapore armed forces.

Much, if not all, of this is replicated by other weapons in different cultures. Eleventh- and twelfth-century German poems tell us of marriage ceremonies in which the bride received her ring from the point of the groom's sword.[5] Similarly in eighteenth-century Scotland, dirks stood for manhood and, being endowed with personalities, as it were, stood as "witnesses" to their owners' veracity when swearing an oath. Here and in other European countries, officers and other aristocrats continued to wear swords long after most other edged weapons had fallen into disuse; twentieth-century Fascist and Nazi organizations such as the Blackshirts, the SS, and the Hitler Jugend (Hitler Youth) also issued their members with inscribed, highly decorative daggers. In Tokugawa Japan, swords stood at the heart of an entire aristocratic culture, and only noblemen were allowed to wear them. It is there, too, that we encounter an interesting paradox. By the time swords took over from bows as the samurai's principal weapon, wars had come to an end. As a result, almost their *only* remaining use was as status symbols. So much so, in fact, that knights had to be reminded to wear them at all times.[6]

The last example is the *shebariya*, or curved knife. To this day it remains an indispensable part of any Bedouin's dress, such that he would feel quite naked going out without it. In part, this fact reflects the practical demands of a widely scattered society that, until quite recently, did not have police forces of any kind, so each man had to defend himself if the occasion called. However, it is also linked to the role that the sword plays in Islam—which, of course, itself started as a Bedouin religion. Along with the crescent moon, the sword is one of Islam's principal symbols. It stands both for the weapons that made its early conquests possible and for the truth of its message. Consequently the Arabic word for it, *sayif*, is part of many a person's name. The list goes back at least as far as the seventh-century Sayif ibn Umar, who was one of the early commentators on the Koran. It reaches all the way to Sayif al-Islam Khadafi, son of the Libyan dictator Muammar, and the notorious Philippine terrorist Abu Sayif.

Things also worked the other way around. To gain respect, swords and other weapons had to be more than sharpened pieces of metal. As in the ancient Middle East, this led to a constant pressure to find new forms even if there were no utilitarian reasons for doing so. In Europe, between 980 and 1550, according to one expert, pommels alone fell into six different styles, subdivided into nineteen types.[7] Many swords achieved their exalted status by carrying all kinds of inscriptions on their blades. The meaning of some has been lost, but seems to have consisted of magic or cabbalistic formulae intended to protect their users or inflict harm on those users' enemies. +HDXOXCHMDRCHXORVI+ is the inscription on one sword fished out of the river Thames. Another, found in Norfolk and now at the British Museum, has ANTANANTANANTAN.

Some swords were inscribed with the names of their makers or owners. Others carry prayers, or benedictions, or dedications, such as "*In nomine domini,*" "*Sosmencrsos,*" and "*Si si non non,*" the last meaning, apparently, that the owner keeps his word.[8] At least one sword, dating to around 1500 and currently in the Hof-Jagd und Ruestung Kammer, Vienna, has a Latin inscription that translates, in part, as "If you ask: I am for war, not the chase." Many of these very expensive and, to their owners, very precious swords also had artistically shaped hand guards and pommels inlaid with precious stones—and again, those stones may have been valued not just for their appearance but for the magic qualities they were believed to possess. Pommels could also be shaped to provide cavities in which to place holy relics. The most famous sword of all, Durendal, owed its reputation partly to the fact that it had a whole array of them: a tooth of Saint Peter, blood of Saint Basil, hair of Saint Denis, and cloth from Mary's gown.

Durendal was not the only sword to have a proper name. King Arthur's sword was called Excalibur. Odin had Balmung, Siegfried Gram, Charlemagne Joyeuse. We can see similar practices in Japan and India. Both, as it happens, attributed the invention of the sword to the gods. In the former the original one was a gift from the sun goddess, Amaterasu, to her grandson; in the latter, it made its debut in a meteor-shaped lotus brought into the world when the god Brahma made a sacrifice.[9] Muhammad had four swords, called Dhu'l Fakar (the Trenchant), Al Battar (the Beater), Medham (the Keen), and Halef (the Deadly). Following him, Mogul rulers also named their swords. Thus we meet Dusman-Kush (Killer of Enemies), Alam-Sitam (World Conqueror), Fateh-Lashkar (Army Vanquisher), Kamar-Jeb (Waist Adorner), and Yare-Vafader (Faithful Friend).[10] Some swords were seen almost as living beings. As far back as the Bronze Age, some had pommels suggestive of human faces; Roland before his death bade a loving farewell to his faithful Durendal.[11]

Perhaps seeking to enhance their own prestige as well as the prices they could command, swordsmiths did what they could to surround them with mystery, linking them with the rites of sex, birth, and death. Japanese ones of the Heian period turned the process of forging blades into ritual occasions, decorating their workshops with rope and paper cutouts, washing, putting on special robes, and even refraining from sex, alcohol, and certain kinds of food.[12] Here as in other countries, the most precious swords became the subject of what can only be called genealogies. Lists were kept recording the names of those who had made them, those who had owned them, and those who had been killed by them. One sword, discovered by Galahad during his adventures, was supposed to go back all the way to King David himself. As history, such tales should not be taken too seriously. Yet they certainly conveyed attitudes, and provided the stories were believed, they were not without psychological value in battle.

Nor were swords the only instruments of war to carry proper names. The custom of naming warships goes back at least as far as the ancient Greeks. Originally it may have been a functional means of distinguishing one from another. In time, however, symbolism and probably affection got involved as well, or perhaps things worked the other way around. A series of fourth-century B.C. inscriptions, now at the Epigraphical Museum, Athens, provides us with the names of about three hundred Athenian triremes.[13] As in English, Latin, and many other languages, Greek ships were female, grammatically speaking. Some were named after gods or else mythological heroes and heroines. Others carried the names of places, districts, abstract qualities, or animals. The most famous Greek ship was the *Argos,* called after the district of that name and used by Jason and the Argonauts to cross the Black Sea on their way to find the Golden Fleece in Colchis. Other examples are *Amphitrite* (wife of the sea god, Poseidon), *Thetis* (a sea goddess who was Achilles's mother), *Eleusis* (the place where the mysteries were held), *Eleutheria* (self-determination), and *Dolphis* (dolphin).

The tradition of naming warships—and, of course, other conveyances—has been carried on straight to the present day and could easily form a subject for specialized study.[14] Nelson at Trafalgar had the *Victory.* The Italians at Lissa in 1866 had the *Re d'Italia,* which was sunk by the Austrians. The Germans in World War II had the *Bismarck.*

Originally it was supposed to be called *Deutschland;* later, though, it was renamed because the loss of a ship carrying that name might constitute too great a blow to morale. Some modern warships are still named after Greek gods, as when Britain commissioned a whole series of aircraft carriers called *Hermes.* Others carry the names of places (the former USS *Arizona,* sunk at Pearl Harbor), victorious battles (the former USS *Saratoga*), commanders (USS *Eisenhower, Nimitz, MacArthur*), abstract qualities considered especially precious or designed to terrorize the enemy (USS *Enterprise,* the former HMS *Dreadnought, Devastation*). Others are named after animals (the former HMS *Lion*), birds, or else climatic phenomena, such as *Tempest.*

The custom of naming rams, catapults, ballistae, and other engines of war also goes back to Greek times, if not before. Adopted by the Romans, it was revived when medieval warriors started using these machines sometime around A.D. 1000. No sooner did the first cannon make their appearance than they, too, were given names, such as the Demolisher, the Terrible, the Fury, the Madwoman, and others. In China, one famous cannon of the mid-1400s was known as the Invincible Generalissimo. Germany in World War I produced the Big Bertha, a huge 42 cm gun named after the stout wife of industrialist Gustav Krupp von Bohlen und Halbach and intended to demolish the Belgian frontier forts. No sooner did tanks make their appearance than they, too, started being given names. Ajax, Chablis, Dracula, Delilah, and Charlie Chaplin were particular favorites; surveying a field full of shot-up British tanks late in World War I, the famous German writer Ernst Jünger noted that not one was without a name, whether ironic, menacing, or lucky.[15] Half admiring, half terrified, Allied soldiers in Italy during World War II nicknamed the huge German railway gun used against them "Anzio Annie." Briefly, soldiers have always endowed weapons with personalities, and the larger and more powerful any weapon the more likely they were to do so. Perhaps the most famous named machine of all was the *Enola Gay.* Called after the pilot's mother, it is likely to be recalled with a shudder for all time to come.

Some of the names were intended to remind soldiers of past triumphs or else of the things for which they were supposed to put their lives at risk. Others were meant to impress the enemy, others still of an affectionate nature. In 1940, the three ancient biplanes that were all the British Empire could spare to defend Malta were named *Faith, Hope,* and *Charity.* During the Pacific War, one American crew named their B-29 *Boomerang.* The idea was that a boomerang always returns to the place it came from; a real boomerang, with marks corresponding to the number of missions flown, was carried along.[16] Ammunition, too, was often inscribed with names. Either the names were those of its owners, or those of the enemies for whom it was intended; in the latter case, wishful thinking, or perhaps some kind of sympathetic magic, may have been involved. At least one Macedonian arrowhead has been found with the name of King Philip II, father of Alexander, on it.[17] Roman slingstones, which were cast of lead, often carried the names of those who owned and fired them. Modern bombs, rockets, and missiles that are dropped on, or launched at, the enemy are more likely to carry the name of their intended victims. During the 1991 Gulf War, a huge "bunker-busting" bomb, rush-developed by the Americans for use against their enemy, was known as "the Saddamizer."[18] As was at least one U.S. Marine Corps tank.[19]

To return to decoration, when cannon made their appearance it was not long before they came to bear all sorts of symbols as well as other decorative devices, scrolls, and mottos—the best-known one being perhaps Louis XIV's *Ultima ratio regis.*" Guns and pistols, too, had their metal parts, locks and barrels in particular, inlaid or etched. The same was true of stocks. Though almost always made of wood, they were painted, carved, damascened, and inlaid with precious materials, such as gold, silver, and ivory; one early-seventeenth-century European pistol has a stock formed like a woman having sex with a creature half man, half goat.[20] Once again, the question arises whether such pieces were intended for real-life war or for other purposes, such as display, presentation, or the hunt. Once again, the answer seems to be that most of them were used for all of these. Conversely, any weapon, however beautiful, that is incapable of being fired in anger is a mere toy, more suitable for the nursery than for anything else. In some societies it would not be considered fit even for that.

Most decoration was probably harmless, affecting weapons' prices but not their performance in war. Some, however, was not only counterproductive but deliberately intended to be so. A very good example comes from World War I. In that war, as in all subsequent ones, victory in air combat depended very largely on the ability to spot one's enemy first. This led to the application of camouflage paint intended to make aircraft as invisible as possible both from above and from below. Thus their lower side might be colored gray or blue and their upper one covered with green and brown patterns so designed as to merge with the landscape below. Still, we meet aircraft flown by individual aces painted all sorts of bright colors. Tactically speaking, giving an aircraft a coat of bright blue, green, yellow, or red—the last being the color favored by the famous Manfred von Richthofen—was a foolish thing to do. From the point of view of morale, the effect was just the opposite. The colors were visible for miles around. They told the world that the pilots who flew these aircraft were a bunch of real bastards, ready to take on any opponent and fight him to the death.

Some modern air forces keep the names of their pilots secret, the aim being to conceal the identity of the 10 percent or so who are aces. This was not the case in World War I. At that time, to the contrary, French and Italian aces often had their aircraft embellished with individual designs such as coffins, lions' heads, and the like, thus mounting a challenge that probably cost some of them their lives. On both sides of the front, late in the war, some aircraft started having their front ends painted to resemble a shark's snout, complete with open jaws, rows of pointed teeth, and heavily shaded, threatening, eyes. Such eyes, incidentally, already figured on Greek and Roman warships; as the idea of an "evil eye" shows, at various times and places they may have had magic meanings associated with them.[21] In World War II some German fighter aircraft had a black spiral painted on yellow propeller shafts. This particular pattern may have been meant to hypnotize enemies for a split second, thus providing what could be an important advantage in combat. Other explanations have been advanced, but many seem contrived. Everything considered, probably the most important motive behind the decoration was men's pride in, and love for, the weapons they operated. Given that their lives depended on those weapons' performances, this is not surprising.

Most famous of all was the "nose art" painted on American combat aircraft, thousands upon thousands of them. Some paintings, such as bombs and other symbols corresponding to the number of missions flown and enemy aircraft shot out of the sky, were supposed to record past achievement and perhaps to taunt the enemy. Others reflected the men's wish to maintain their individuality amid the uniformity the Army Air Corps imposed on them, as well as their fantasy life. Given the context in which they were created, it is scant wonder that some were clearly sadistic, showing skulls, demons, devils, pirates, or dragons, as well as Hitler, Mussolini, or Tojo being beaten over the head with a stick. Even less surprisingly, given how young most aircrews were, others were unabashedly sexual. Many of these paintings drew their inspiration from contemporary magazine artists of the time. Very often they presented young women in various states of undress, and very often those women were shown seated on, or else in close proximity to, guns and various types of projectiles.

Some researchers have argued that the farther away from higher headquarters a unit, the more provocative the decoration, but such claims are hard to substantiate. Some of the art was very imaginative, combining the most disparate elements into a more or less coherent, often quite funny whole. Contrary to popular belief, much of it was not the work of amateurs. Instead it was competently done by professional artists who commanded good money for their services—another proof of how important it was to those who commissioned it. All the more pity that in our politically correct world such displays are usually prohibited. Prohibited, that is, until war breaks out, as happened, for example, in 1991. As life suddenly becomes serious and the smell of danger fills the air, soldiers are metamorphosed from expensive do-nothings into very valuable commodities. The niceties of peacetime are blown away like cobwebs, and men are again allowed to become what, just under their skins, they have never ceased to be.

So far, I have focused on the fact that many of the most heavily decorated weapons *were* intended for use in battle and *were* so used. However, this argument can also be turned around. Today, the very fact that a tool, machine, or even work of art is associated with war is usually sufficient to brand it as second-rate, artistically speaking; to admire it carries the risk of being called a "militarist." That was by no means the case at many previous times and places, when, to the contrary, they were often seen as objets d'art in their own right. Tribal societies in particular never knew our distinction between "crafts" on one hand and "art" on the other. Among them, even the most mundane objects intended for day-to-day use, such as furniture (the little they had), agricultural implements, containers of every sort, and musical instruments, were heavily decorated almost as a matter of course; if so, why not weapons? To adduce another example, some of the most elaborate European armor of the sixteenth and seventeenth centuries was certainly made for display either during tournaments (see chapter 4) or in the treasure rooms of the very rich. Yet nobody took it into his or her head that the suits in question were somehow less accomplished works of art simply because they were associated with war; if anything, to the contrary.

Today, too, some weapons are manufactured out of or inlaid with more or less precious materials. They are brought to a high state of polish, provided with all kinds of inscriptions, put into nice-looking cases, and used for either display or presentation. Even some weapons not so intended continue to be valued for their beauty. An excellent example comes from the Israel Air Force (IAF). Back in the 1960s the IAF was a true elite service characterized by tremendous pride, esprit de corps, and a tradition of victory. At that time Israel was a small, poor country where aircraft, combat aircraft in particular, were few in number and precious in proportion. This explains how IAF personnel came to claim that an effective fighter plane had to be good-looking, too. Odes were written to the deadly, streamlined beauty of the French Mirage IIIc that served as the IAF's first-line fighter. Nor did the Mirages stand alone; especially after the spectacular victory in the Six Days' War of June 1967, almost anything military was considered beautiful by definition. It remained so until 1973, when another, less successful war brought people back to earth and ended the cult in spite of the efforts of some people, such as Prime Minister Menachem Begin, to revive it.

As with everything else, ideas of what weapons are, or are not, considered beautiful vary. An excellent example is the contrast between Soviet and American warships as it developed during the last decades of the Cold War and, to the extent that the former are not lying at the bottom of the sea or rusting away in port, still persists. Soviet ships were festooned by array upon array of weapons (guns and missiles), antennae, and radar dishes mounted on decks and on masts; with them, they glowered at the world. Not so American ones, which tended to have lean, clean lines. The weapons U.S. ships carried, as well as the electronic gear needed for communication, surveillance, weapons guidance, and so on, were for the most part hidden from view. The result was a smooth superstructure that might have been designed by Walter Gropius or Ludwig Mies van der Rohe. The interesting thing is that many Soviet warships were actually more modern than their U.S. equivalents, having been built under Admiral Sergei Gorchakov from 1976 on; therefore, timing alone cannot explain such differences.

By way of another example, legend has it that late-nineteenth-century British navy personnel used to see guns as brutes that, when fired, caused the paint of warships to crack. With their U.S. successors the situation is exactly the opposite: judging from the way ships are configured, they must be deeply ashamed of their weapons. Similar differences may also be seen on other weapon systems, tanks in particular. A visit to the U.S. Army Ordnance Museum at Aberdeen, Maryland, will show that, compared with the World War II German and Soviet tanks on display, British, French, Italian, Japanese, and even American ones look like toys; perhaps this has something to do with the fact that the first two nations engaged in the largest, most ferocious land war that has ever been fought or is likely to be fought. As each generation of designers steps into their predecessors' footsteps, such differences tend to perpetuate themselves. Many of them have little, if anything, to do with military effectiveness.

A century after Freud established, in *The Interpretation of Dreams*, the way in which objects can act as sexual symbols, the similarity between many weapons and weapon systems and the male phallus has become a cliché.[22] No great psychoanalytical insight is required to see that one reason why edged weapons have so often been cherished by men and treated as representative of manhood is because they tear and enter another person's body; indeed, in Latin the word *gladius* (sword) could also be used as a slang term for penis. The analogy with firearms, which fire projectiles, as well as bullets, torpedoes, and missiles, which are fired or launched, is perhaps even closer. Many projectiles accentuate the similarity by having their tips brightly painted, red in particular being a favored color. In the case of bullets, incidentally, each color also has a meaning; red, for example, is usually used for tracer. At least one British missile, designed for air-to-air combat and now no longer in service, was officially designated "Red Top."

Often those who design the weapons are not naive but perfectly well aware of what they are doing.[23] Some weapons are "sexed up," which is slang for making them more attractive in the eyes of prospective buyers and users; a lick of paint, the right pattern applied at the right place, will do wonders. Others, such as combat aircraft and missiles of every sort, are provided with so-called penetration aids ("penaids" for short) to help them get through enemy defenses and reach their targets. Turning the argument around, all this may help explain why certain weapons that do not resemble phalli, such as mines, poison gas, and napalm, are disliked as strongly as they are. Instead of being elongated and sharp, they are boxlike, or round, or formless. Nor do they offer their users the supreme satisfaction of firing and penetrating somebody else's body. The same facts may also explain why women's attitudes toward weapons seem to be much more ambiguous than those of men. Though there are exceptions, a woman who collects weapons or replicas of them is a strange creature indeed.

If much modern military equipment is sleek and elegant, some pieces are anything but that. Consider the American Humvee. Originally developed to replace the nimble World War II jeep, it is a squat, angular, box-like vehicle that looks like nothing so much as a frowning garbage can turned on its side and provided with wheels. This very ugliness also constitutes its redeeming feature—some would say its only redeeming feature, since its usefulness in combat has been hotly debated.[24] Advertised as a "diesel-powered off-road beast," it disdains any pretense of aerodynamic form and thus of fuel efficiency (which, in the Pentagon, is considered "sissy"). Instead it offers the image of brute power; ready to run off the road anything else that moves. It is this quality that has turned the vehicle into a favorite among well-heeled civilians such as muscleman Arnold Schwarzenegger, former basketball star Dennis Rodman, and others. Not only are they happy to pay for it, but they have demanded and obtained special editions provided with various comforts the original did not have.

Another such weapon, whose role in war is growing all the time, is the attack helicopter. Such helicopters are among the most ungainly machines ever built. They are angular rather than streamlined, covered by oddly shaped plates which look as if they have never been properly joined, provided with stub noses and wings, and decorated, if that is the word, with bulges of different sizes in unexpected places. Attachments such as rotary guns, missiles, electronic warfare pods, and antennae, make the machines look even uglier. The entire contraption is crowned by a rapidly rotating piece of exceptionally complicated gearing. Combined with their characteristic *chop-chop* noise, the overall impression is that of brute power, pushed through regardless of any other consideration. Many observers have compared attack helicopters to huge winged insects, ready to sting, and indeed some recent models reinforce this image by carrying enormous optical eyes intended for infrared vision at night.[25] The typical tactic they use is to take cover behind a hill. Suddenly roaring into view, they are among the most feared weapons of all.

Finally, consider the history of fortification. Far from being merely utilitarian structures, many fortresses and castles are highly decorated (as, incidentally, are other military structures that cannot be examined here).[26] Quite a few represent masterpieces of architectural art. In fact, considering how proud people have always been of other kinds of building, how could it be otherwise? The Lion Gate at Mycenae, dating to the end of the second millennium B.C., is world-famous. The gates of ancient

Babylon, now at the Pergamon Museum in Berlin, were painted an intense blue, glazed, and decorated with various mythological animals, creating a stunning effect that never fails to impress visitors to the present day. The crenellated walls of Nineveh, carefully restored some 2,600 years after the city's fall, served aesthetic purposes as well as purely practical ones, as did those of the Alcazar in Toledo, Spain.[27]

Japanese castles, too, had symbolic as well as military value.[28] Curiously enough, the Japanese never developed crenellation, proving, one supposes, that even this most universal feature of pre-modern military architecture owed as much to cultural traditions as to utilitarian military considerations. Instead they use symmetry and evenly spaced roof beams to achieve their effect. The best examples appear as if they were ready to spread their wings and soar to heaven. Clearly great effort, love even, was invested in making sure they would be as beautiful as human hands could make them. A good example is Azuchi Castle, not far from Kyoto in Omi Province. Completed in 1576, a period of intense civil war, it not only utilized the best natural defensive features available but had its walls gaudily painted with dragons. The paradox is that, of the castles that still exist, almost every one was built after the peace of 1603, showing once again how much they have fascinated the minds of men.[29]

Civilians, too, like to share the feeling of brute martial power: a General Motors Hummer.   MARIANNE CANBY

Likewise, many medieval towns were inordinately proud of their for-tifications and did what they could to make them pleasing to the eye as well as effective. Islamic rulers followed similar traditions.[30] They embel-lished the walls with which they surrounded their cities with bands of col-ored stone or brick, various inscriptions, and animals in relief, one famous case in point being the panthers placed over Jerusalem's so-called Lions' Gate. Among the best examples of all are the fortifications of the Italian Renaissance. With their sloping walls, towers, crenellation, machicolation (largely rendered out of date by the advent of gunpowder, but still used for aesthetic purposes), and firing loops all carefully combined, they cre-ated a whole, which if not always effective was certainly as harmonious as any architectural style can be.[31] And no wonder: many designers were well-known artists. For example, the man who redesigned the fortifica-tions of Siena (and, in 1553, helped defend them) was Maestro Giorgio di Giovanni. Having been trained by Dominico Beccafumi, in peacetime he made his living as a fresco painter.[32] More celebrated artists, such as Leonardo, Michelangelo, and, north of the Alps, Albert Dürer, also tried their hand in this field.

Since space forbids even a cursory survey of this huge subject, I shall focus on one group of fortifications to give the reader a better idea of what was involved.[33] At least from the 1140s on, some English castles were clearly built with aesthetic considerations very much in mind.[34] This fact is particularly evident in those erected by Edward I in Wales, and even more so in the great fortress of Caernarfon. The very location se-lected for the castle provides a hint of imperial power, given that it stands right on top of what used to be Roman Segontium. The most important decorative effects include geometrical variety in the plan; banded, col-ored masonry in the walls, said to have been copied from similar ones in-corporated into the Theodosian wall of Byzantium; numerous turrets, far in excess of those required for observation; polygonal towers with six, eight, and even ten sides; and battlements carved with figures, including eagles on the west tower. As so often, the most elaborate feature of all is the King's Gate, from which visitors would get their first impression of the whole. The design is based on no fewer than three octagons so arranged as to form a triangle. It has no fewer than five sets of doors and six portcullises. On top of all this comes an elaborate sculpted niche. Inside is the seated figure of a king inspired, some authors say, by the imperial precedent of Frederick II's triumphal gate at Capua.

Putting their defensive value to one side, some of these features may have been meant to intimidate and to impress the Welsh tribesmen in whose country they were built. Others, such as loops and machicolation, must have been valued for their aesthetic effects, among other things. This is especially true of crenellation. Consisting of equally sized teeth positioned at equal distances from each other, crenellation probably appeals to man's sense of order, already mentioned in connection with uniforms. This may explain why not just great lords but ordinary people were prepared to purchase the license required to mount it on buildings; it served as a symbol of power as well as the latter's substance. Other features, such as water defenses, may have been intended not merely to present attackers with another obstacle but also to forge a link with the fashionable contemporary world of Arthurian romance.[35] Some of Edward I's castles, notably Acton Burnell in Shropshire, carry symbolism and decoration to the point where they become counterproductive, militarily speaking. I can do no better than to quote the modern historian to whose expertise I am indebted for this subject. "The overall impression made by Caernarfon and its companions," he says, "is of an elite group of men-of-war, long-standing comrades in arms of the king, indulging in an orgy of military expression on an almost unlimited budget; a medieval forerunner of the recent American 'star wars' program."[36]

Thus neither swords, nor cannon, nor ships, nor aircraft, nor fortresses, nor even humble pieces of ammunition, such as lead pellets intended to be hurled from a sling, have ever been simply "instruments" of war made for, and useful in, fighting alone. They have, of course, always been that, but they have been many other things besides. Some were highly prized, even cherished, objets d'art. They were produced and embellished at very great expense over and above the practical requirements of battle, though this did not prevent them from being used in combat. Some were associated with religion, whereas others were bearers of magic powers, whether defensive or offensive. Some were treated almost as if they had independent personalities. Others served their owners as emblems of manhood, whereas still others (even sometimes enemy ones) were regarded with a certain kind of affection. Arms and equipment acted as carriers of ideas and traditions, transmitted by means of the mottos inscribed on them and the names they were given; they inspired awe by virtue of their size, shape, and all kinds of special effects; and, whether because of their shape or because of the decoration they carried, they stood out as some of the most powerful sex symbols of all.

Above all, the fact that men depended on them for their lives and that they were capable of taking lives caused the implements and buildings of war to be surrounded by an aura. On one hand, they were often treated with a respect seldom shared by other implements. On the other, they served as insignia of power, even, sometimes, objects of worship. Thus, some Nazi leaders tried to develop a form of "German" Christianity in which the place of the cross would be taken by the sword.[37] Above the altar in the chapel of the U.S. Air Force Academy, built just before jet engines took over, there is a large cross, in the form of a propeller.

All these ideas, beliefs, and attitudes interacted with each other and reinforced each other. While the military technology at the disposal of a given society may be primitive, men's minds never are; as a result, even Stone Age societies, such as those of New Guinea, surrounded war with a culture that was anything but primitive.[38] The more any modern book or treatise focuses on "strategy," the less it has to say about all of this, and indeed, from reading most of them one would hardly guess that any of it existed. Yet without all of this, the behavior of men in war and battle can never be understood, let alone directed in such a way as to maximize our own fighting power while minimizing that of the enemy.

3

Educating Warriors

The goals and methods of educating young men on their way to becoming warriors are broadly similar at all times and places. Probably this indicates the existence of some very deep-rooted military requirements and psychological needs that no amount of mollycoddling, whether carried out in the name of democracy or feminism, can erase. In the words of one early-twentieth-century commander of cadets:

> Gentlemen, you have taken on the highest profession on earth. The goal you have set yourselves is the highest there is. We are here to show you how to reach that goal. Here you will learn the meaning of life and death . . . Everything you have experienced, seen and understood you must forget. Everything you now experience, see and understand will become your goal. From this point on you have no free will. You must learn to obey so you'll be able to command later on.[1]

While these methods and these goals may be readily seen in the armed forces of the most advanced modern countries, until not so long ago they could also be observed among some of the simplest tribal societies such as the Meru of Kenya.[2] In this chapter we shall focus mainly on the way attitudes, values, and traditions are inculcated and transmitted from one generation to the next; that, too, is part of the culture of war.

In present-day modern societies, most young people are brought up by their families at home. Often they only go their own way into the world at the age of eighteen or nineteen, if then. This was not true in a great many previous societies. In them, boys (not girls, who were usually allowed to remain at home until they were married) were taken away from their fathers and, above all, their mothers so that the process of making men (read warriors, or less often priests) out of them could get under way. In many societies, especially so-called segmentary ones constructed around age groups, a boy would leave home when he had reached the age of seven or so. Not by accident, the same was true in Sparta. Of all Greek city-states, Sparta was one of the most conservative, which meant that it retained the greatest number of characteristics of the tribal society in which it had originated.

The slave merchants who bought future mamluks for the Arab sultans and janissaries for the Ottomans took boys past their seventh birthday, though some appear to have been as old as fourteen. In the European Middle Ages, the normal age when the younger sons of the aristocracy were sent away to join the household of some great nobleman was around nine.[3] Other societies started training boys for war when they were eleven to twelve, as in the pre–World War I German cadet schools and traditional Japan. Youngsters who enroll in military high schools that are common in the United States as well as some other modern countries do so at ages fourteen or fifteen.

In any military education, the first indispensable step is to physically isolate the youngsters from "ordinary" society, its customs, its temptations, and the myriad ties by which its members are held together. In many tribal societies this is achieved by subjecting the boys to a whole series of stringent taboos. For example, they may be ordered never again to touch certain kinds of food. They may be forbidden to enter their parents' huts (except, perhaps, by passing through a door specially designated for the purpose) and prevented from talking to their female relatives in particular; if they are to turn into men, their womanish qualities must be driven out first. Many modern forces, such as the U.S. Marines, aim at achieving similar results by prohibiting any contact with the outside world during the first few weeks of basic training, not even a letter or a telephone call.

Special insignia will be provided, or paint or tattoos applied, in order to set the trainees apart and mark them off from the rest of society. Alternatively, they will be provided with clothing as different from ordinary garments as possible. By way of further distinguishing the fresh recruits both from their own senior comrades and ordinary society, they are likely to have their hair cut in some bizarre fashion or else shaved off altogether. In some societies isolation opens with a relatively short period that consists essentially of sitting around and waiting; deliberately or not, the same practice is followed by a great many modern induction systems.[4] By the time that period is over the trainees will be bored almost stiff. They will be frustrated and eager at the same time; briefly, they will be roaring to go.

Another method used is humiliation. Every military education system ever designed starts by humiliating its trainees, not just by way of serving punishment but also as part of a well-considered plan. The objective is to cut their ties with the rest of society, do away as far as possible with any regional and class differences that distinguish them from one another, strip them of their security and sense of self-worth, and provide

Educating warriors; a cadet at St. Cyr, circa 1880
FROM *NOS GRANDES ÉCOLES MILITAIRES ET CIVILES*

tangible proof that they are now entirely dependent on their superiors, making them receptive to discipline as well as the instruction to come. The methods used can be pretty barbaric. Invariably there are physical examinations. In the German Wehrmacht, these used to be carried out on men standing to attention, naked, with their comrades looking on, but many other armies of the time were not much better.

Then there are verbal forms of abuse. Some involve yelling, some ridicule, whereas others are merely coarse. The ability of drillmasters to invent such abuse, often incorporating highly charged sexual terminology, is legendary; in places where doing so is still permitted, they will call their charges "girls." Some drillmasters will add to the humiliation by moving their faces as close as possible to those of their trainees while simultaneously yelling at the tops of their lungs. Another favorite trick is to make recruits repeat formulae that are meaningless, ridiculous, or self-derogatory. Not only are they tormented, but they must inflict some of the torment on themselves.

Next, there is physical abuse. Trainees may be made to assume postures that are hard to maintain, such as squatting, supporting themselves on their arms, or hanging from horizontal bars; at the Citadel, a private military academy in South Carolina, there used to be an additional refinement in the form of bayonets stuck into the ground and pointing upward under the cadets hanging from such bars. They may be forced to stand motionless for long periods of time, made to do guard duty as if they were robots, go through strenuous exercises, or sustain beatings. Other methods may be more subtle. A particularly common one, used to teach trainees to operate under pressure, is to assign them certain tasks but insufficient time in which to perform them, such as making beds, changing uniforms, cleaning and arranging all kinds of gear, and the like.[5] All this must be done while paying meticulous attention to the smallest detail: blankets crisply folded, shoes polished to mirror-like perfection and precisely aligned. Having, inevitably, failed to perform the required tasks in the time allowed, the trainees are made to perform them again and again.

To reinforce the effects, sleep deprivation—in the U.S. Navy, recruits can expect no more than five to seven hours a night—hunger, thirst, loud noises, and flashing lights deliberately designed to unnerve and confuse may all be used. Thus individuality is eliminated as much as possible, and uniformity enforced, the objective being to make everybody respond with machine-like reliability and predictability. On one hand, showing signs of fear or failing to measure up is discouraged and punished (or used to be,

until political correctness and the kinder, gentler military took over). On
the other, those who try to stand out by boasting, or doing more than is
demanded of them, or telling their fellow trainees what to do, are considered an even greater nuisance; if there is one kind of person who cannot
be tolerated in training it is the smart alek. Either way, any instructor
worth his salt will quickly detect the problem and single out those who
show signs of it for special treatment.

To be taken into one of the elite Nazi schools, youngsters had to
demonstrate their courage by swimming a distance of ten meters under
the ice—not something that is entirely without risk, and certainly a somewhat terrifying experience for a twelve-year-old.[6] Wehrmacht infantry
trainers, who were often big, powerful men, had recruits lie supine on the
ground and then proceeded to walk right over them, a method also favored in some other armies.[7] Perhaps the worst abuse of all was inflicted
on Waffen SS recruits; they had to stand to attention while a hand
grenade was placed on their helmets and exploded. Recruits may find
themselves rolling in mud, as in the U.S. Marine Corps, or perhaps even
in less pleasant substances. In Israel, the phrase "crawling among this-
tles" has become synonymous with basic training as undergone by the
better infantry units; both there and in other countries people talk of recruits being "polished" as if they were pieces of metal or wood. How
much continuity there is in all this is shown by the fact that Spartan boys
had to go barefoot.[8] They were limited to wearing one shirt year-round
and slept on beds of rushes that they themselves had to gather, without
using knives, from the banks of the river Eurotas. Among the Meru, one
test aspiring warriors had to undergo was to sit on a bed made of a sort of
nettle and maintain their position for a long time without moving. The list
goes on and on.

Such methods appear to have something magical about them. What
happens to them during training, recruits are told, will change them forever. The childish, the weak, and the feminine must die to make way for
the manly and the strong; soldiers, in other words, are now prepared to
kill and be killed if necessary.[9] The same methods are also used as tests,
enabling instructors to weed out the weakest recruits and grade the rest
in preparation for more advanced training and assignments.

Even these, however, are not the only goals. Even as it humiliates
trainees, a well-considered, well-carried-out program will also instill in
them pride and self-confidence—in fact, this may be as important as any

skills it imparts. The tests must be devised in such a way as to make them hard to pass but not so hard as to cause too many trainees to fail. Looking back on the obstacles they have overcome, graduates will experience a sense of satisfaction and increased self-respect.[10] "Tests" of the kind often advocated by modern educators, tests in which what counts is not results achieved but honest effort made and which everybody is allowed to pass, cannot carry out this function. In this sense the success of most depends on the failure of some.

For example, we know that some Spartan boys failed to make it through the education course, or *agoge,* though just how many of them is impossible to say.[11] Possibly the Spartans went too far; thus helping explain for the decline in their numbers after about 400 B.C.[12] In the pre-1919 German cadet schools, considered so good at training future officers that the Allies in the Treaty of Versailles paid them the backhanded compliment of ordering them closed, the normal failure rate hovered between 4 and 13 percent. This did not deter the Germans; during the days of the Weimar Republic, only one-third of the officers entering the Kriegsakademie (which the Allies had also closed, but which continued to operate undercover) were finally taken into the Reichswehr's General Staff.[13] By contrast, the failure rate at West Point is about 20 percent over four years. When a misunderstanding once created the impression that I had failed 25 percent of my Marine Corps Staff College students at Quantico, Virginia, the scream of anguish could be heard all the way to the Pentagon thirty miles away. Such a result, I was told, was impossible; so good were the methods used in selecting students that everybody always passed.

On the other hand, the methods just mentioned cannot be used forever, for to do so would lead to demoralization. Although they always remain available should the need arise, once the initial objectives of isolation, humiliation, and providing the trainees with a better understanding of what is expected of them are achieved, their place will be taken by a more settled routine. Partly for practical reasons—very often, time is money—and partly in order to prevent boredom or worse, the program is organized in such a way as to make sure that the trainees have as little time for themselves as possible. Supervision is close, abating only when the trainees are asleep. During the first few weeks, trainees may have to ask permission to relieve themselves, let alone eat, speak, or go to sleep. Partly to keep the pressure up, partly because the large number of people often involved demands it, every minute is planned. Different activities follow one another seamlessly, and woe to those who fail to meet the schedule.

Hours may be punctuated by a simulated emergency, so designed as to create even more stress, or else by an occasional ceremony held to commemorate either a historical event or one in the life of the training organization itself. However, on the whole they tend to be long and regular. By permitting trainees to focus, such routines are supposed to facilitate the learning process. The following will give an idea of what the timetable of a German cadet school looked like around 1915:[14]

0600	Wake, wash, dress
0620	Breakfast
0635	Work time, sick call, prepare for classes
0655	Clothing inspection, gymnastics, free exercises
0705	Begin matins
0710–0720	Matins
0720–1220	Five class periods, 50 minutes each (second breakfast from 1010 to 1030)
1225	Sick call
1230–1255	Appel
1300–1330	Lunch
1330–1430	Recess or resting time
1430	Prepare for work time
1440–1755	Work time
1610–1630	Vespers, lining up
1730–1925	Exercises and sports
1940–2000	Supper
2000–2100	Free time
2115	Lights out

During this period, punishments will increasingly be replaced by rewards. Depending on the time and place, these may consist of freedom from certain fatigues such as kitchen patrol; the right to wear or carry certain kinds of dress, insignia, and weapons; a special place in the dining hall or while on parade; and the like. Outstanding trainees may have their achievements publicized; at West Point, the so-called merit system dates to the days of Superintendent Sylvanus Thayer in the 1820s.[15] Man, however, is a pliable animal. Very often, merely inviting trainees who have performed well to meet with a person of standing and receive a few words of praise will do the trick. They may also obtain special privileges such as passes, improved rations, the right to smoke (in the days before smoking was frowned upon), premiums, and so on. All these may be awarded either on a case-by-case basis for good behavior or else permanently, reflecting progress made and trust imparted. Some organizations have also set up special courses or classes. Their purpose is to take in the crème de la crème on the understanding that being selected for one of these will help a man in his future career.

The ultimate accolade is always to be given a position of authority and responsibility. Greek youngsters were often put into the charge of other youngsters somewhat younger than themselves. In Sparta they were known as *mastigophoroi* (whip carriers), a term that sufficiently explains their position. In Republican Rome, which surprisingly enough does not seem to have had a formal system for training fresh recruits or *tirones*, they consisted of selected *hastati*, the next oldest soldiers.[16] Modern organizations, including not only military academies but paramilitary movements such as the Fascist Balilla and the Hitler Jugend, have devised their own systems.

Quite often senior trainees are given the semblance of power but not its reality. The goal is to prevent excess; sometimes, however, the system backfires, as those rendered impotent in this way avenge themselves by hazing their charges. However it is done, the system of rewards, like that of punishments, must be handled very carefully if it is to achieve its purpose. Perhaps the most important thing is to avoid anything that smacks of favoritism. The reason is that if the system appears unfair, it may cause the rest of the trainees to join forces against the preferred ones, thus defeating its own purpose. Instead of building ties between individuals, it will prevent such ties from being forged; instead of causing trainees to embrace the culture of war, it will lead to cynicism.

The objective of the training programs is a dual one. On one hand, it is to break down the ties that bind young men to society at large, to isolate them and turn them into atoms. On the other, it is to build up new ties, such as are made up of discipline and comradeship. So strong should the ties be that when the time comes, the troops will go on obeying their superiors' orders. At all cost, they must stay with one another and continue to function in an organized way, even amid the chaos of battle, and even when looking death in the face. In any military worthy of the name, the entire structure is erected to support this single overriding need. The term usually used to describe the tie is *brothers,* as, for example, in the Israel Defense Force (including both the elite Golani Infantry Brigade and the navy), the Philippine Army, and, most famously, Shakespeare's *Henry V.*[17]

From ancient Sparta to West Point, the methods used to establish these ties have always been the same. One is to visit punishment for infractions of the rules not just on the individuals who committed them but on the entire group. This practice, too, is not without risk. If carried to extremes, it may lead to resistance and mutiny. Perhaps more commonly, it may cause the majority of trainees to turn on the minority even to the point where members of the latter suffer severe abuse or are killed, which explains why Nazi concentration camp guards (who, of course, did not mind if some inmates died) used it to prevent escape. Correctly and consistently handled, it will create a situation where trainees help each other and, by so doing, develop a strong esprit de corps.

Another way of achieving the same effect is to divide trainees into teams. Many tribal societies have developed a particularly ingenious way of doing this. Having reached the appropriate age and about to start their training, youngsters are sent to a specially selected sacred spot. There they are supposed to remain, without food or drink, until, at long last, they dream up the totemic animal of the clan to which, from this point on, they will belong. Spartan youths were also divided into tribes (which did not correspond to those comprising the citizenry) and subteams, though just how it was decided which boy would be assigned to what team can no longer be ascertained.[18] Modern training institutions invariably divide their charges into units modeled on those of the armed forces to which they belong, such as companies, platoons, squads, and so on. Sometimes this is done on the basis of all kinds of abstruse psychological considerations whose objective, in theory at any rate, is to achieve some kind of balance. In other cases the decision appears to be purely arbitrary.

Whatever the method used, each team will be given its own emblem, flag, or standard. Each team will also be assigned its own elder, commander, or spokesman, who is in charge of it and represents it in its dealings with higher authority. For example, in Sparta they were known as *bouagoi* and *eirenes;* they were selected, Plutarch tells us, for their keen intelligence as well as their prowess in fighting.[19] From the point of view of those in charge, one benefit of the system consists of the fact that authority over each team can be delegated, making it unnecessary for them to busy themselves with every detail. There are, however, other advantages. If only because each team shares the same room, tent, or mess, it is to some extent autonomous. Given enough time, this will cause it to differ from others in small but quite significant ways.

The team spirit that invariably results from such a system can be further reinforced by the deliberate use of marching cadences, songs, and slogans that have to be shouted in unison; in bases where recruits go through their paces, everything tends to be done *molto con brio*. Perhaps the most important method of all is to set up interteam competition with awards for the winners. In Sparta, boys are known to have competed both in singing and in playing what appears to have been some rough-and-tumble ball game inside a field marked with lime. From the little we know, it seems that the objective was "to catch hold of the moving ball and throw it back until one side pushes the other over the back line."[20] Is it necessary to point out that many modern military training institutes use similar methods?

Among the subjects taught, history is likely to take a major part, and the more advanced the education the more true this is.[21] In tribal societies, history consists of the legends and traditions of the tribe, stored in the memory of elders and orally transmitted to youngsters. In the European Middle Ages it was cultivated by means of the *chansons de geste*. The objective was to praise ancestors and present models for emulation. Hence, very often they did not draw a very sharp line between fact and fiction; when it comes to education rather than training, the fiction can serve just as well as fact, if not better. Later still, military history came to consist of tales and analyses of past wars, battles, and heroic deeds. Some of those involved in the education process saw history mainly as a source of examples from which trainees could draw inspiration. Others, starting with Polybios and proceeding to Machiavelli and beyond, saw it more as a practical tool from which practical lessons could and should be derived.[22] The rise of "scientific" history in the first half of the nineteenth century tended to strengthen the second of these approaches at the expense of the first. Whether, everything considered, that was a good idea is another question.

Though punishments and rewards do play a large role in education, they are not enough. In regard to attitudes perhaps even more than skills, the principal method of learning is imitation, but no imitation will take place when role models are absent. Traditionally this has meant that warriors had to be reared by other warriors, if possible those who had already seen action and distinguished themselves. In Sparta and other Greek city-states, this included erotic associations between youngsters and elders.[23] In many tribal, ancient, and feudal societies finding the necessary personnel presented no problem. For Greeks during the classical period, war was such a normal state of affairs that peace treaties were always concluded to last a set number of years only. For three quarters of a millennium Roman Republican armies took the field year in, year out, so the gates to the Temple of Janus almost never closed. European knights in the Middle Ages and Japanese samurai until 1603 were almost always fighting either on their lords' behalf or on their own. Thus there were plenty of men around who had experienced war and even distinguished themselves. This is often not the case in modern societies, some of which have not seen a real war for decades on end.

Sometimes, too, the opposite happened. As an armed force prepared for war and waged it, the best personnel took up or were assigned command positions. Consequently, training organizations had to make do with what was left—men unfit for command, men who were recovering from their wounds or permanently invalided, overage men. Things were made worse by the fact that serving in such an assignment, instead of being a mark of distinction, sometimes spelled the end of a man's career. At the U.S. Marine Corps Staff College, those selected for a faculty assignment referred to themselves as "children of a lesser god." The situation in other U.S. military colleges is hardly any better; in some, so small is the difference between instructors and students that they can hardly be told apart. Thus the future was being sacrificed for the present. Recognizing the danger, the pre-1945 German army took great care to ensure that the careers of instructors of every rank should not suffer because of their assignments.[24] The result was that men of the caliber of Erich Ludendorff, Heinz Guderian, Erich von Manstein, and many other famous commanders spent time teaching at the Berlin Kriegsakademie, educating themselves in the process. Unless this is done, the quality of training will be mediocre at best.

Almost as important as the quality of the training personnel are the physical surroundings involved. Among tribal societies that do not have large, permanent buildings, warriors are often educated in some field or clearing in the forest, located at some distance from the rest and so situated as to provide shelter from prying eyes. Some societies go much further, making future warriors leave society altogether and providing communal houses instead. There they are expected to remain for years, completely under their instructors' control. Spartan males entered some sort of barracks at the age of seven, staying until they married at the age of thirty or so; even then they had to wait until their first child had been born before they were finally able to set up their own households. The Zulu system, instituted by King Shaka kaSenzangakhona (ca. 1787–1828), kept the men in barracks for an even longer period.[25]

Training may be decentralized, meaning that no strict line is drawn between the places where it is carried out and those where the rest of the troops live. Or else it is centralized, implying a compound separated from its neighbors by a wall, distance, or both. The Roman army provides examples of both kinds. In Republican times there do not seem to have been specialized training bases, which, given that the armies of the period were disbanded each time a campaign ended, is not surprising. As the switch to a professional force was completed, though, things changed. Excavations in places as far apart as Britain and Iraq have laid bare several legionary camps dating to the imperial period which give every indication of having served to train recruits.[26] One medieval document, referring to a son of Harun al-Rashid named Abu Ishaq al-Mutasim (794–842), who ended up as sultan of Samarra, almost waxes poetic as it describes how things were done. "He built a wall stretching over a long distance which he called *Ha'ir Halayr*. Thus the Turks [the Mamluks are meant] were placed far away from the markets and from the congestion . . . and there were no other people, such as merchants or others, with whom they could mix . . . [and the sultan did not] allow any other strangers . . . to be their neighbors . . . He built within the streets of the Turks mosques and public baths, and established a small market in each."[27]

In our own day West Point, located up the Hudson Valley miles from anywhere, is based on the same idea. Originally there were a hotel and an inn located nearby, but pressure from the academy, whose heads did not take kindly to the sight of cadets stuffing themselves, forced them to close. Some other famous training facilities were initially almost as remote, only to be overtaken by urban development later on. Another very important reason for separating the compound from the rest of the world is because, as Plato explains, training for war, if it is not to degenerate into a childish game, should involve modest risk to life and limb.[28] To enable the hardship and terror of war to be reproduced as far as possible, it is essential to have a place that allows safety regulations to be instituted and enforced while keeping other people away.

Historically speaking, most of the installations where warriors were educated have tended to be on the austere side—even though some of the poorer trainees might find the conditions better than the ones to which they were accustomed at home. In part, it is a question of parsimony, since erecting buildings and maintaining them costs money. In part, austerity is imposed in a deliberate attempt to support a training program designed to produce hardiness by avoiding luxury. Needless to say, what constitutes "luxury" will vary from one case to the next; during my time at Quantico an Israeli student in the course, a lieutenant colonel and former battalion commander, told me that the quarters of a U.S. Marine Corps private were superior to those he himself had occupied at home. Trainees may be housed either in tents or in temporary structures, although experience shows that the latter often have an astonishing tendency to become permanent. Even when such is not the case, unsuitable base layouts, old and ill-maintained buildings, inadequate heating and/or cooling facilities, insufficient sanitary facilities, overcrowding, and lack of privacy are often the order of the day. This is the list of complaints surrounding one major American facility; imagine the rest.[29]

Still, there often is another side to the story. While conditions may be austere, even harsh, to make them so harsh as to give the trainees the feeling that the society to which they belong is out to get them or puts no value on them would be counterproductive. Volunteers, in particular, must be well treated if enrollment is not to decline. The more an army relies on them, and the more advanced the training, the more comfortable the facilities tend to be. Conversely, conscripts at the beginning of their career always get the short end of the stick. Above all, it must be remembered that the objective is not merely to impart skills but to inculcate and transmit values. Hence, it is probably best if the installation has been in use for long enough to acquire a certain aura.

In tribal societies the aura results from the place being inhabited by the part of the tribe that is dead, meaning the ancestral spirits, said to observe the living, bless those who behave themselves, and inflict magical punishment on those who do not. Alas, the armed forces of more advanced societies do not have such a wonderful instrument at their disposal. Hence they try to achieve a somewhat similar effect by naming the buildings and other facilities after past warriors, preferably those who were victorious, but sometimes those who set an example by sacrificing themselves for the cause. In Rome a similar purpose was served by the legionary standards. Introduced by Marius around 100 B.C. as part of the shift from a conscript force to a professional one that relied on volunteers, at first they were made of silver, later gilded. They acted as the physical expression of a unit's corporate spirit and were kept in a special shrine, carefully maintained, reverently treated, and brought out on suitable ceremonial occasions.[30] During imperial times the standards were supplemented by busts and statues of the reigning emperor, and perhaps his closet relatives—just as the dining room at the British Army Staff College, Camberley, used to have an oil portrait of Princess Anne.

In modern training institutions, especially those designed for future officers, inscriptions at the entrances to buildings will commemorate when they were built and by whom. There will be works of art, such as paintings and reliefs and statues, in which past wars and the men who fought and commanded in them are celebrated. Display cases are likely to contain old standards and flags—preferably ones whose tatters show they were taken from the enemy—uniforms, decorations, weapons, and similar memorabilia. The picture is completed by monuments to or lists of fallen comrades, who thus play a role not dissimilar to that of the spirits of old. Models of ambiences of this kind are provided by the military academies of developed countries such as Sandhurst, West Point, and Saint Cyr. Here each room resembles those of a well-arranged museum, and every corner reeks of past glories calling for, indeed commanding, emulation. But Dartmouth College, Kingston Academy (Canada), Annapolis Academy, and the newer U.S. Air Force Academy at Colorado Springs are not so bad, either.

The next chapter will go into a little more detail concerning some of the more technical aspects of training. Here, all it is necessary to say is that to be effective, training should be gradual. It should progress from the simple to the complex, each stage building on its predecessor and providing a building block for the one to follow. The really essential point to note is that if things are to be done properly, each step can and should also be used for a purpose other than simply strengthening the body and imparting skills (important as doing so is). Instead, the objective should be to reinforce the qualities warriors have always needed and will always need, such as obedience, courage, stamina, self-reliance, teamwork, honor, truthfulness (according to Zoroastrian wisdom, youngsters should be taught "to shoot the bow and speak the truth"), and the like; briefly, what people until 1945 or so were not ashamed to call "character."

All this is much more easily said than done. In case the attempts to do it are taken too far, they are likely to meet with resistance in the form of cynicism or indifference and thus become counterproductive. For this reason, the best training program is probably the one that instills these qualities without talking about them too often, as, for example, when West Point's Sylvanus Thayer accepted cadets' explanations of reported delinquencies without question as part of the honor system.[31] When they *are* talked about, though, this should be done in a suitably impressive manner.

Among the Meru, as among many other pre-modern societies, the education of future warriors included a stage when their ties with the rest of society were cut. Next, they were let loose to show what they could do. Among the ancient Germans and the North American Plains Indians they would go out in an attempt to find enemies and gather coups. In ancient Crete and Sparta they had to live by their wits, perhaps stealing or gathering or hunting for food. In the latter, they also acted as a kind of internal police, spying on the helots and killing those who looked as if they might become dangerous.[32] Alternatively, they might patrol outlying areas, looking for trouble. This was the case in Athens where, for as long as they remained *ephebes*, they could neither take up any kind of civic responsibility, sue, nor be sued.[33] Possibly the system of knight-errantry, under which young men teamed up with a few comrades and went looking for "adventure," should be understood in similar terms.[34] In traditional Japan, too, spending time as a *ronin* (literally, "one who is tossed on the waves") or masterless warrior was supposed to be a stage in the career of any samurai.

From the point of view of those who have put it into place and operate it, the system has an additional advantage. It permits older trainees to be put in charge of younger ones under something resembling operational conditions, thus providing another vehicle for educating the former, allowing them to gain experience, testing them, and selecting them. Here and there modern armies have tried to imitate the system, with mixed results. For example, the Wehrmacht during World War II moved some of its training bases into the occupied countries so that trainees could double as police forces when the occasion demanded. As time went on and resistance put up by the local people increased, however, all too often recruits were called upon to deal with emergencies. This caused the process of military acculturation to be disrupted rather than assisted. At the same time, the troops engaged in "anti-bandit" operations, as the Germans called them, were likely to be less proficient than they were supposed to be.[35]

In modern societies, courses usually last between nine weeks— which is probably the shortest period that must be spent in basic training if it is to do any good—and four years, which is the time needed to go through a military academy or full ROTC program. In previous, socially less differentiated societies, courses could last far longer, getting under way not when youngsters reached their eighteenth or nineteenth year but much earlier. Ten-year programs, during which youngsters were prepared not merely for their future as warriors but for every other aspect of manliness as well, were quite common. Here and there, some lasted even longer than that.

Old or modern, the more extended a program the more likely it was to fall into several distinct stages. Each constituted a full cycle, and each had a recognizable beginning and end. In Sparta there appear to have been four of these, although the exact ages at which youngsters passed from one to another are not known; other city-states had two or three.[36] In theory at any rate, to be knighted one had to first pass from page to squire, though the decentralized nature of feudal society meant that many lords interpreted the hierarchy in different ways if, indeed, they worried about it at all. Once again, a system whereby a program was divided into several different stages made it easier to put advanced trainees in charge of younger ones. It also opened the possibility of demoting trainees, whether permanently because they had failed to make it or temporarily as a punishment for some specific offense.

However long the program, inevitably the time will come when it must end. First the recruits may be put through one final test of endurance, hardiness, and skill. In some societies this is when they are circumcised, an extremely painful procedure that must be withstood without flinching; in others they are severely beaten. In others still they may be tattooed, or else have parts of their bodies pierced with the decorative objects that will signify their new status. For example, during the later Middle Ages dubbing ceremonies were often held on the battlefield, either just before combat to inspire courage or else just after it as a reward for proven courage and loyalty.[37]

Modern troops, too, have to prove their mettle either officially or unofficially, by means of hazing. Israeli infantry units have something known as the "beret march." In it, as the name implies, soldiers must earn the right to wear a red or violet beret. It involves a sixty-six-mile nonstop trek on foot, at the end of which participants are so exhausted they can barely stand; at the other end of the scale, fresh crewmembers are "welcomed" aboard navy ships by being doused with sewage water or else subjected to a mock gang rape.[38] Parachutists may have to jump out of an aircraft for the nth time, perhaps (to increase the danger or the impression of it) with a parachute that, instead of opening automatically, must have its cord pulled. Some U.S. Marines had to stand to attention as pins marking their new status as members of the corps were pounded into their chests. This ceremony, known as "blood winging," was condoned until media revelations created a public outcry and brought it to an end.[39]

After the tests have been passed, the men will probably spend days or even weeks preparing for the moment when they will "come out" on a specially selected, specially prepared ground. Decked out in all their finery, they are handed their weapons. Next they are made to swear a solemn oath. In Athens, where the ceremonies took place in front of the assembled people (*ekklesia*), it went as follows:

> I will not shame the sacred arms [I have been given] nor will I desert the man at my side wherever I am positioned in line. I shall defend what is sacred and holy and I will not pass on to my descendants a diminished homeland but rather one greater and stronger as far as I am able and with the assistance of all. I will offer my ready obedience at any time to those who are exercising their authority prudently, and to the established laws and to those laws which will be judiciously in force in the future.[40]

In many societies this is followed by some religious ceremony. In Sparta, the first act young adults performed after completing the *agoge* was to sacrifice to Heracles, god of endurance in the face of adversity;[41] in modern armed forces this is the time to call in the chaplain, rabbi, or mullah. Dignitaries will give speeches and present awards to graduates who have distinguished themselves. A sacred text, such as Nietzsche's *Thus Spake Zarathustra* (in the Wehrmacht) or the Bible (in the Israeli Army), may be distributed. There will take place a war dance, review, parade, war game, or some other demonstration of prowess, with friends and relatives (if at all possible including female ones as well) watching and applauding. A good meal or a round of drinks, intended not just to fill bellies but to reconcile the former trainees with those who have tormented them for so long, concludes the official part of the festivities. Finally, the recruits may be given a period of liberty to go on celebrating.

One very good way to understand the culture of any society, organization, or institution is to examine its education system, the instrument par excellence by which that culture is made explicit, inculcated, and transmitted. In the case of warriors and soldiers, this is represented by the age-group systems of tribal societies, the *agoge* of Sparta and other Greek city-states, the military apprenticeship systems of feudal Europe and Japan, and of course the various training systems, military schools, cadet schools, and military academies that modern armed forces started developing from the second half of the seventeenth century on. All of these create, formalize, inculcate, and transmit values. To do so, very often they resort to ceremony, ritual, play, and make-believe of every kind. All of them are an integral part of human culture, not a whit inferior to or less deserving of study than their opposite numbers in civilian life, be they those of the Church, the professions, or whatever.

The political, economic, social, cultural, and technological context in which education for war is carried out may lead to enormous variety in detail. Yet many of the underlying objectives are the same at all times and places. Since the qualities required of the warrior hardly change, this is not surprising. Did not Alexander's soldiers need courage, loyalty, and hardiness just as much as modern soldiers do? Then as now, was it not necessary to weed out those who did not have those qualities while identifying and promoting those who did? What *is* surprising is how many modern works about military training are so obsessed with imparting and acquiring "skills" that they do not even mention the culture of war; reading them, one might think the objective is to produce not warriors but a cross between machines and bean counters.[42]

The methods just outlined may not be to everybody's liking. Still, the fact that they have remained essentially the same for millennia on end speaks for itself. Should any system or organization fail to make correct use of them in educating warriors, then almost certainly it will betray both its own purpose and those who are entrusted to its care.

4

Games of War

As everybody knows, the Battle of Waterloo was won on the playing fields of Eton. True, the Duke of Wellington almost certainly never said anything of the kind.[1] Yet a myth as persistent as this one seems to indicate a large measure of hidden truth; if he did not actually utter the words, then he should have. That play constitutes part and parcel of human culture that few, if any, people will deny. Some have gone much further still, describing it as the most important cultural activity of all on which all others are, in one way or another, built.[2] Here the question that interests us is how play and games relate to war, and what this relationship tells us about the role of war in culture.

When we play, what we do is engage in a game. A game might be defined as any activity that is carried on for its own sake, rather than for some other purpose. Games result when people break free from the world in which they live, so to speak. They create an artificial universe, one in which the normal relationships of daily activity—that is, "because of" and "in order to"—are suspended. At the place the game is played, for as long as it is played, the overriding motive is the desire for enjoyment that is shared by players and onlookers alike. Thus almost any activity, no matter how trivial or how serious, can be turned into a game. In fact, hardly any activity exists that is not occasionally turned into one, from playing with a miniature railway to closing a multimillion-dollar deal. I'll never forget how I asked my grandfather (who was a self-made multimillionaire) why he went on and on making more money, and he answered that it was a game. It is less the nature of an activity than the way we relate to it that makes it so.

But what, in the present context, is meant by joy? Much the best answer to this question is provided by Friedrich Nietzsche: joy is what results when we take on a challenge.[3] To enjoy, one must pit oneself against resistance, wrestle with it, and, as one does so, be sufficiently successful as to feel one's own power growing. This does not necessarily mean that to enjoy playing a game we must never lose, but it does mean that the resistance should be neither so strong nor so weak as to render the outcome a foregone conclusion. This is something those who are in charge of organizing competitive sports such as football, baseball, or soccer know very well. While a team that loses all the time will become demoralized, nothing is as boring as a victory endlessly repeated. Things must therefore be arranged in such a way as to give all teams a fairly reasonable chance, with new blood infused from time to time. Provided these conditions are met, the precise nature of the resistance is almost immaterial.

To define the kind of resistance in question, the methods by which it may be countered, and the equipment that may be used is the function of the rules. In some games the rules dictate that the game involve danger (even if, as is very often the case, it is make-believe danger). Good examples are parachuting, bungee jumping, and riding a roller coaster; they may be classified as games of courage. In others it is a question of luck or fortune, as in gambling and Russian roulette; to a greater extent even than in parachuting and bungee jumping, what is really being tested is pure nerve. Many games require players to accomplish a task that takes skill (for example, putting together a puzzle or target shooting) or endurance and strength (running, swimming). In others the resistance may consist of animals (as in hunting and fishing) or of other people, acting either alone (as in singles tennis) or in groups (baseball).

Recent decades have added games that are played on a screen and in which the resistance comes from a computer. The games in question require skills that are either physical (such as good coordination and quick reflexes), intellectual, or both. Those who design the games and program the computers know exactly what they are doing; as time goes on, the challenge becomes harder and harder. Nor is there any reason why any given game should be limited to just one kind of resistance; many games exist in which players are required to cope with, and overcome, several different kinds.

Games in which the resistance consists of people, which are our main interest, fall into two kinds. Games whose rules allow each side to try to win, but prevent him from directly interfering with the other's attempts to do the same, as in a foot race, are called *contests*. By contrast, games such as chess and football in which both sides are allowed both to strive after their own goals and to interfere with each other are known as games of *strategy;* indeed, strategy itself might be defined as a "system of expedients" (Helmut von Moltke) designed to do precisely those two things.[4] Regardless of where they are played and what their rules are, games of strategy require players to consider not just their own intentions and capabilities but those of the opponent as well; as a result, they tend to be more complex than any others. The larger the number of participants on each side, the more varied the equipment they use, and the more complex the environment in which the game is played, the more true this is.

Finally, many games of strategy, such as chess, do not allow physical contact with or the use of force against the opponent, whereas others, such as boxing and football, do (within certain limits). Among the latter, quite a number permit the use of at least some violence, and they are therefore known as combat sports. A few combat sports even permit, not to say demand, deadly violence, either deliberately inflicted, as in the Roman gladiatorial games, or taken in stride so that the fun may go on, as in early medieval tournaments and modern boxing. Here it should be emphasized that violence, including deadly violence, is not always the opposite of culture. For example, the Maya of Yucatán had a ball game in which prisoners of war, forced to play in such a way that they always lost, ended up by being decapitated.[5] Though the outcome was inevitably deadly, still the game was very much part of the culture in question. On it centered a whole complex of religious beliefs; unless it was played, the gods would be angered and disaster would result.

Next, how does war fit into this picture? The simple answer is that war is a collective, exceptionally complicated, extremely violent form of combat sport. Like any other combat sport, it involves two (rarely, more) sides. The existence of two sides means that the combatants must make use of strategy, along with all the intellectual complexity the latter involves. Like any other combat sport, it is a test of skill, strength, endurance, and courage as well as strategy. As in other combat sports, the resistance is the strongest imaginable—the most intelligent, most dominant, and, we like to think, the most powerful creatures ever to walk this earth. More than any other combat sport, it permits, even demands, the full mobilization of all the participants' intellectual, moral, and physical qualities; this is because in war there are few if any rules that would prevent whatever qualities the combatants have from being used to the full extent. Taken together, all these factors explain why war is so often capable of generating joy, even ecstasy. Very often it involves, even demands, disengagement from the ordinary world; in short it is the ultimate game, which makes all the rest pale.

To see how closely related play and war are, it is enough to look at linguistics. In the Bible, we find that when Abner, servant of Saul, challenged the followers of David, then king of Judea, to a duel of twelve against twelve he used the words "Let the lads rise and play in front of us"; only when all twenty-four had been killed did the proceedings come to an end.[6] In ancient Greece, the term *agon* could stand for both athletic competition and war; at the Olympic stadium in Delphi, the statue personifying it stood right next to that of Ares, the god of war. In Rome, the deadly gladiatorial combats were known as *ludi,* "games." In Dutch, the word *oorlog* (war) seems to derive from *oor* (original, primeval) and *log* (leap, dance, game). The British at the height of their empire talked of "the great game." The term seems to have been coined by the greatest imperialist writer, Rudyard Kipling, in order to describe the endless round of petty hostilities, intrigues, counterintrigues, ambush, and raid that was going on in Central Asia; a little later, it also came to be applied to war as such. Though expressions such as "the play of cannon" may be outdated (as, to a large extent, are cannon themselves), we continue to speak of "swordplay."

Just as war in many ways is but an extreme form of sport, so sport in turn is completely permeated by the language of war. The very term *exercise* is derived from the Latin *exercitus,* meaning "army." Mountain climbers regularly call their expeditions "campaigns." Launching one, they try to overcome the "resistance" of mountains, which, they like to pretend, put up a "fight" so as to avoid being "conquered."[7] In many other sports, each time two individuals or teams prepare to play a game they start by gathering "intelligence" about their opponents. They collect statistics, watch videos, send out observers, and may even resort to espionage in order to sniff out "game plans." Having identified their opponents' strengths and weaknesses and how they fit into their own, they sit down to work out a "strategy" and, perhaps, "tactics" as well.

Once the game has started, one side defends, the other attacks. One side retreats, the other advances. One tries to hold, stop, and block, the other maneuvers, breaks through, and ends by "shooting" at the goal. One triumphs, the other loses. (So attractive is this military terminology that it is used even in golf, which is basically a game of skill, not strategy, and where the rules do not allow any of the players to do anything to obstruct the others.) Players who have been hurt and leave the field or are carried from it are sometimes called "casualties"; in some sports, they *are* casualties. Every sports commentator knows these terms and exploits them as much as he can. Frequently the more sanguinary the language he uses, the greater his success.

As the ultimate game, war demands from players all the physical, moral, and intellectual qualities required by lesser games and then some. Conversely, the fact that many other games also necessitate some of the qualities demanded in war has turned the former into a method par excellence for training and educating those about to fight in the latter. Even some of the oldest, most elementary steps in training warriors, such as teaching them to run, leap, climb, cross obstacles, and so on, can be and very often have been turned into games. The same applies to assembling and disassembling weapons, target shooting, and the like. Many former recruits remember the time spent in these activities as great fun; they like to sit around recalling them. At all times and places, most trainees have been men and normally young ones to boot. Hence, usually all that was needed to make them enjoy an activity was to add a challenge in the form of competition and prizes for the winner—in short, turn it into a game.

Contests in archery or in throwing the javelin have been used to train warriors ever since ancient Egypt and until very recently they could still be found among some people such as the Yanomamo of the upper Amazon forest. At the Athenian Panatheneia, a sort of minor Olympic games, one contest known as *euandria* (literally "good manliness") apparently involved running in full armor and possibly a tug-of-war as well; festivals held by other Greek cities may have had similar events.[8] Other exercises still were designed to teach men first to ride and then to use their weapons on horseback. The Mamluks, for example, had a whole series of them: the lance game, the mace game, the gourd game. In part, these exercises were simply a means to an end. In part, however, they were understood as games, as is shown by the fact that, around the *furusiyya* (the art of horsemanship, from *furus*, "horseman"), there gradually developed an entire culture.[9] Mastery of the relevant skills and attitudes made up the difference between Mamluks and other mortals. As a result, quite often *furusiyya* was carried to the point where it interfered with, rather than assisted, the military performance it was supposed to serve. If play could be put to serious use as training, very often serious training was turned into something close to play.

Exercises similar to those of the Mamluks, be they target shooting or throwing hand grenades, are still being used by every modern armed force around the world. As if to prove how closely related war and play are, some have even been turned into real sports, such as target shooting (either with the bow or with the rifle) and the triathlon, which are practiced at countless contests from the Olympic games down. Perhaps the most important difference between such contests and military exercises is that in the former the rules are much tighter. Very precise regulations lay down the kind of weapon that may be used, the ways in which they may be used, and the like. Besides minimizing danger, this serves to level the field, puts all the contestants on a strictly equal footing, and allows them to be graded much more precisely than military life requires.

However useful such games or exercises may be when it comes to developing the warrior's skills, they suffer from the fact that they are one-sided, whereas war is two-sided by definition. Using real weapons in two-sided training would be extremely dangerous, leading to more casualties than even Plato was ready to tolerate. As each side tries to win by landing the strongest blows of which he is capable, restraint may be thrown to the wind and escalation is almost inevitable. Things might get out of hand altogether—not an improbable eventuality, as the history of medieval tournaments and some modern football games show. Perhaps the oldest solution to the dilemma is to replace humans by animals. Did not Plato say that war is simply a different kind of hunt?[10] It is true that animals have their limits. No animals, not even chimpanzees, possess joints that enable them to throw objects well. If only for this reason, none of them has developed weapons. Even more important, none has the intelligence and communication skills needed to set up a military organization in our sense of that term: appoint a commander, follow orders, institute a division of labor, and offer collective resistance to the humans who hunt them. What many animals do have are advantages of size, protection, power, ferocity, agility, and/or speed. Unfortunately for them, this turns them into opponents worth tackling.

Not just people but animals, too, hunt. Some, such as lions, wolves, hyenas, and chimpanzees, do so in groups; if a sophisticated organization is lacking, cooperation is not. Some anthropologists argue that man owes his intelligence to hunting for meat and, even more so, the "political" interaction that is necessary in order to distribute the spoils.[11] Originally, hunting must have developed as a method for self-defense in the face of large animals—which, given the primitive weapons in use, could only be done in groups—as well as obtaining food. Still, however far back into history we look, it has always been practiced for fun, too;[12] some believe it was the oldest form of sport, from which all the rest developed.[13] Judging by descriptions of chimpanzee hunts, perhaps one might conclude that they, too, enjoy the activity. Certainly they show excitement by hooting, screaming, drumming, and waving branches.[14]

Though there are exceptions, usually the larger and the more dangerous the animals, the more people enjoyed hunting them and the greater the prestige to be derived from doing so.[15] This may explain why, in Greek vase paintings, small animals such as hares are sometimes depicted so as to appear huge in relation to the hunters.[16] However far back into history we look, too, very often hunting did not consist just of pursuing and killing "game." Instead, it also involved all sorts of rituals. Some of the rituals were no doubt intended to make it easier to catch the quarry. Others invoked the souls of soon-to-die or dead animals, appeased them, and commemorated them; English fox hunters have been known to observe a minute of silence for the dead.[17] Cynics might point out, with reason, that all this was done merely for the hunters' own benefit and that none of it was of any use to the poor animals involved. That is true enough, but it does not change the fact that the ceremonies in question constituted culture.

In this chapter, our main interest is to look at hunting as functional training for war. Certainly the ancient Greeks, the Romans, medieval knights, American Indians both north and south, and countless other societies practiced hunting for that reason among others. Xenophon recommended it highly, saying that male children should take it up as the first step on the way to becoming men and that it provided "excellent training for war";[18] so, almost two millennia after him, did Machiavelli.[19] Both of these men were famous military writers. Equally important, both had successfully commanded troops in action and neither can be said to be more romantically inclined than the average person. Nineteenth-century English upper-class culture also glorified hunting, whether in the form of riding to hounds, pig sticking, tiger shooting, or anything else. It was credited with the development of almost every martial virtue, and adduced as one of the main causes behind Britain's prowess in warfare.[20]

Depending on the society in question, the identity of the hunters, the technology in use, and the nature of the "game," hunting took a very large number of forms. It ranged from the time when a handful of cavemen armed with wooden spears brought down a lion or a bison to the time when old, semi-incapacitated dignitaries were given a high-powered rifle with sniper sights and installed on a raised platform so they could safely butcher the hapless deer being driven toward them. In between these extremes, often it involved the certainty of physical effort and a very real possibility of danger. Homer's Odysseus cannot have been the only man who bore on his leg a scar acquired while hunting, nor the emperor Hadrian the only one to grow a beard so as to conceal one inflicted on his face.

In the millennia before the automobile was invented most commanders depended on their equestrian skills to move and fight, and in this, too, hunting provided useful practice. In addition it taught, or could teach, skills such as rough living in the open, reading the terrain—a quality specifically mentioned by Machiavelli—stealthy movement, understanding the prey's mind, rapid decision making, and teamwork; in fact, few if any major military tactics exist that do not have their counterparts, some would say their origins, in hunting. Finally, hunting taught men how to draw blood and kill, even when the quarry consisted of smaller animals that could not strike back. Especially in modern society, where few people hunt for a living or work on the farm, butchering for meat takes place in special factories, and the death penalty is no longer carried out in public, this capacity is not something most people are necessarily equipped with.[21] As an American commander such as George Patton and an Israeli one such as Yitzhak Sadeh understood very well, it must be deliberately inculcated.[22]

While all of this explains why hunting has so often been associated with war, it is also true that the two are not the same.[23] The qualities of humans differ from those of animals, especially, of course, when it comes to intelligence. To make up for this, it was necessary to introduce games that, though they did pit men against each other, only allowed them to use certain carefully regulated and circumscribed forms of violence. The oldest games that may clearly be identified as such go back to Sumer around 3000 B.C.[24] However, there is scarcely any tribal society that does not have them; therefore, there is good reason to think that they must be much older still. Even more significant to the topic at hand, paintings from ancient Egypt show wrestling scenes side by side with various kinds of military activities. This suggests that already at that time wrestling was considered part of a soldier's training.

By the time of the Egyptian New Kingdom soldiers certainly engaged in wrestling, whether as part of their normal training or on other occasions. Reliefs found at Thebes show contests held in front of the deified pharaoh Tuthmosis III, who perhaps not accidentally was one of the greatest conquerors of all. In one of them the victor is made to say: "Alas for you, O miserable soldier, who boasted with his mouth! I'll make you say, O the folly of taking the hand of a soldier of his majesty!" In other carvings from Medinet Habu, a wrestler, again in the presence of the pharaoh, exclaims, "Stand up to me! I'll make you see the hand of a [real] warrior!"[25]

Whether the Greeks took over combat sports from Egypt, as they did so many other things, or developed them on their own need not be considered here. Certainly in the epics, war and games are never far apart. The games held in honor of the dead Patroclos included a boxing competition as well as the famous duel between Diomedes and Ajax; so much did the latter resemble real war that Achilles had to call it off lest the latter lose his life.[26] Later writers often compared battlefields to a wrestling ground,[27] and one commander was said to "wear down" his opponent just as some good athletes do.[28] Wrestling apart, the Greeks practiced boxing and *pankration* (literally, "smash by all available means"). In it, holding, punching, and kicking were all permitted; apparently the only techniques not allowed were eye gouging and biting. All three seem to have formed a normal part of the education of young Greek males. Other competitions included running, leaping, swimming, throwing the discus or the javelin, chariot racing, and the like. The compound in which they and the rest were practiced, the *palaestra,* served as a cultural center in any one of hundreds of city-states scattered all over the Mediterranean.

For the Greeks, the way to enjoy two-sided contests while avoiding casualties was to engage in various forms of unarmed combat. Not so the Romans who introduced gladiatorial games. Tradition has it that they were taken over from the Etruscans; another people who held them were the Thracians. In Rome itself, the first ones were held in 264 B.C. when the sons of Junius Brutus Pera, a former consul, organized a show to honor their dead father.[29] Combining this fact with other evidence, some modern scholars have argued that in both Rome and Greece, armed combat was the earliest combat sport of all. According to this theory, combat sports first appeared as part of the religious ceremonial surrounding funerals and only later did they become secularized. As the process took hold, weapons were discarded (except, of course, for those used by the gladiators). This made the games less lethal, although then as today they never became entirely safe.[30] Their origins, so the argument runs, were not military but ritual.

However that may be, as time passed the games changed their character.[31] They were turned into almost pure entertainment—in fact, the greatest entertainment Rome had to offer and the kind for which the largest building of all, the Colosseum, was ultimately built. Political candidates, consuls, and emperors lent their names to them and, seeking to curry favor with the people, spent fortunes to organize them. Tertulian, a good observer, says that men surrendered their souls to gladiators, and women their bodies as well as their souls.[32] Some gladiatorial combats took place between individuals whereas others involved groups or teams. From the first century A.D. on there was a growing tendency to select some famous past battle and reenact it in the arena.

According to Augustine in his *Confessions,* so exciting were the games that people were caught up by them even against their will;[33] centuries before him, Cicero had said something similar.[34] Some of the appeal must have resulted from displays of unusual bravery and skill. Much of it, however, resulted from the spectacle of dying men. According to Suetonius, the emperor Claudius, who by Roman standards was not particularly bloodthirsty, even made a special point of looking into their faces at the moment they expired.[35] What made all this carnage possible was, of course, the fact that players, *luderi,* were slaves or condemned criminals, so their lives were forfeited anyhow. Only later were they joined by volunteers including, in imperial times, an emperor or two. Which shows, one supposes, how much glory there was to be won in them.

Already in ancient times, the exact link between all these different kinds of games and preparation for real-life warfare was moot. To add interest, Roman gladiators were divided into many different kinds of fighters. Some carried all sorts of weapons, including tridents and nets, which were not normally part of soldiers' equipment. They fought in pairs rather than in organized formations. For these reasons, gladiators had little to offer soldiers. Normally their careers were entirely separate. The former spent their lives in and around the arena; the latter, in camp or on campaign. The same was even more true of Greek sports, combat sports included. In the *Iliad* the boxer Epheus (who later built the Trojan horse) admitted he was no great warrior.[36] Xenophon says the same of Boiscos, the boxing champion of the day.[37]

The Spartan war poet Tyrtaeus, who probably lived during the seventh century B.C., was also unimpressed with athletic achievement. "No man," he sang, "is any good in warfare unless he dares look at bloody slaughter."[38] The list is completed by Euripides. In one of his plays, now lost but for a few lines, a character who can no longer be identified had some very harsh things to say about athletes: "What outstanding wrestler, what swift-footed man, or discus hurler, or expert at punching in the jaw has done his ancestral homeland a service by winning a crown? Do they fight with enemies holding discuses in their hands or by kicking through shields with their feet expel their country's enemies? No one standing next to steel indulges in this stupidity."[39]

Wrestling apart, Plato, too, had strong misgivings about the relevance of athletics as preparation for war; the former, he says, were insufficiently like the latter.[40] Epaminondas, Alexander, and Philopoemen echoed his words.[41] All three were famous commanders. In one way or another, all three considered wrestling, boxing, and *pankration* (to which, Plutarch says, Alexander took a special dislike) and other forms of athletics to be too unlike war to serve a useful purpose and sought to replace them by more realistic exercises involving formations and/or weapons. Epaminondas, who in his youth had himself been a wrestler of repute, even told his troops that the place to prepare for war was the camp and not the *palaestra*—a statement that, at the time and in the cultural context it was made, almost amounted to heresy.

There was, however, another side to the question. Perhaps we may disregard authors such as Lucian, Philostratos, and Plutarch.[42] All three wrote in the second century A.D., and all three were trying to defend Greek culture against Roman accusations of frivolity. Hence their praise of athletics in the service of war and "Greek freedom" may have done no more than to reflect nostalgia.[43] Yet the role games could play in physical conditioning was, of course, recognized centuries before the Roman conquest.[44] For every athlete who did not excel in war it was possible to name another one who did, such as Eurybates of Argons (victor at Nemea in the pentathlon), Promachos of Pellene (an Olympic victor in *pankration*), Timasitheos of Delphi (took two crowns at Olympia and three at Delphi in *pankration*), and others. From Aristophanes, we learn that at least some of his contemporaries considered the old style of physical education responsible for the victory at Marathon.[45]

Furthermore, Spartan training certainly played a vital part in creating the famous Spartan military excellence. It included annual contests in honor of Artemis Ortiya (the huntress). Typical of Sparta, an object without any intrinsic value—a piece of cheese—was placed on the goddess's altar. One team of youngsters was appointed to try to steal the cheese, another to defend it. Not just wrestling but gouging, biting, and punching were all allowed; taken as a whole, so strenuous and so violent was the *agoge* that Aristotle thought it produced beasts, not men.[46] Finally, neither Epaminondas nor Alexander nor Philopoemen denied that some kinds of exercises and games were essential for military training. Rather, and as Plato's reference to the need to accept casualties also shows, what they really wanted to do was to replace games they regarded as insufficiently martial by others that would be more so.

As to the Roman gladiators, any reluctance to mix them up with war may have had more to do with social considerations than with military ones. After all, most gladiators were captive foreigners (which partly accounts for the different ways in which they were armed and trained) and slaves. When given the opportunity, as under Spartacus, they proved their ability to fight very effectively not merely in the arena but in real-life war as well. Of them, Florus says that the men fought to the death, as befitted gladiators; adding that Spartacus himself died bravely "as became a general."[47] On more than one occasion in Roman military history, gladiators and their trainers, or *lanistae,* were called upon to help train regular soldiers as well.[48] Significantly, one of those responsible for initiating the practice was Marius, himself a scion of the lower classes and famous for his disdain of upper-class pretensions. All this shows that, for all the obvious differences between the two, the *ludi* on one hand and *bellum* (war) on the other were not as far apart as some Roman snobs liked to think.

War games dating to later periods, such as the medieval tournaments, were held for similar reasons and gave rise to similar problems. Set in the ninth century A.D., the Arthurian legends present their heroes as champions at the "tourney." This, however, is an anachronism; historically speaking, the earliest known tournaments seem to have been held in the years just before 1100.[49] By definition, they were two-sided affairs. They were also very rough, barely different from real skirmishes. First, a day and a place were announced. Next, those present were divided into two teams, if possible following existing divisions, such as town A against town B, southerners against northerners, and the like. A signal was given, and the two sides, mounted and armed as if for war, went at each other with virtually no holds barred until night came and separated them, as would normally happen in real war.

In the absence of an arena there was nothing to prevent combat from spreading over hill and dale, trampling over fields and gardens, damaging crops, and sometimes spilling over into settled areas. Not just participants but spectators often became casualties. As with many modern soccer matches, they were by no means always innocent; one late-fourteenth-century English ordinance prohibited "they who shall come to see the Tournament" from bringing along sword, dagger, staff, mace, or stone.[50] Among the few things that mitigated the ferocity of the proceedings was the fact that for most participants the goal was not to kill or injure their opponents but to take them prisoners so as to extract ransom—as, to some extent, was true of real-life war as well.

Once tournaments had been invented, the authorities never quite knew what to do with them.[51] However wild tournaments might be, they acted as safety valves for the excess energy of members of the "chivalrous" classes. As such, they were preferable to real-life war among knights, in the same way that many people prefer to see soccer hooligans beat each other up inside the stadium than outside it. Given how little they differed from war, they must also have constituted great training for the latter; in fact, given how decentralized and lacking in formal military institutions the feudal system was, they constituted training par excellence.[52] As time went on many tournaments began to be held at regular times. They were announced months in advance, and attracted participants near and far. While this fact meant that some people were able to display their prowess and make a handsome profit as well, it also enabled rulers to use the tournaments in order to test prospective followers and take them on.[53]

Things were even more complicated than that, however. Whether because they liked doing so or because their positions as knights hardly left them a choice, many rulers, even very powerful ones such as England's three Edwards and the same country's Richard III, took an active role in tournaments; the last-named even had some lances painted red especially for the purpose. Others, such as Henry II of England, placed a ban on them, whereas some, such as Henry II's son Richard II, sought to regulate them, either in order to limit casualties or so that they themselves could profit by requiring that a license be taken out for holding them and participating in them. All these various factors must have acted and interacted, producing a true mélange.

Above all, tournaments, which spread quickly from northern France all over Europe and even into the lands conquered by the Crusaders across the sea, were enormously popular not only among the nobility, where they originated, but also in an urban context, as in Italy.[54] Obviously, one reason for this was because of the spectacle they provided. Then as now, people liked to watch carnage, especially when mixed with pageantry; late-fifteenth- and sixteenth-century prints show windows, roofs, and even trees crowded with onlookers.

Toward the end of the twelfth century, by which time the introduction of specially designated arenas had made tournaments a little less dangerous to attend, the women of the chivalrous classes also started attending them.[55] Some came in the hope of catching a husband, others with less moral encounters in mind. They watched the proceedings, stimulated their favorites by giving them tokens to wear or carry, awarded prizes, and organized the games themselves when in a position to do so. In 1331, the stands that carried Queen Philippa, wife of England's Edward III, collapsed. She and her ladies fell on top of the knights, who were sitting farther down.[56] Here and there mock tournaments were held as the ladies took shelter in a "castle of love" and were besieged by opposing parties of gentlemen, with everybody using cakes as weapons.

But even that does not come to the core of the matter. Tournaments were not just a kind of violent game that involved fighting and, on occasion, bloodshed. They were that, but they were also—more and more so, as time went on—festive occasions in which the members of the chivalrous classes gathered. It was at tournaments, often organized to celebrate some ruler's birthday, wedding, or anniversary, that they displayed themselves, practiced their unique customs, went through their unique rites, celebrated their triumphs, and bemoaned their defeats. Tournaments, in short, stood at the very heart of an entire aristocratic culture roughly known as chivalry, one akin in many ways to the role feast days used to play and still play in religion. No wonder the Church, seeing them as competition, consistently opposed them and tried to ban them. To no avail; in 1471, a tournament was even held right in Saint Peter's Square.

Over time the appeal of tournaments as cultural events seems to have grown, whereas their value in providing serious training for war declined. Paradoxically, one reason for this may have been because they had become too dangerous; as the list of nobles who had died fighting in them indicates, those of the thirteenth century had been ferocious affairs indeed. From about 1300 on, this led to greatly increased regulation. Elaborate measures were taken to ensure that the champions should be well matched in military as well as social terms (it would not, of course, do for a great noble to fight a commoner, however valiant the latter might be). A partition, known as the lists, was added to separate the combatants and their horses so they could no longer physically crash into each other. Specially made *armes de plaisance* made their appearance, and rules were sometimes added to decide what armor might be worn, how many blows might be delivered by each kind of weapon, and so on. To choose the winner an elaborate point system, like the one used in present-day boxing, was added.[57]

Adding to the play element, from about 1400 on participants also began to take on roles. They presented themselves in elaborate disguises and amid elaborate boasts. They defended passes and bridges, slew dragons, rescued tearful maidens who were being held captive, and the like, causing tournaments to become scripted. As in Rome, in other words, mere fighting was no longer considered enough. Instead, it was dressed up in elaborate tales so as to endow it with a pseudo-historical, pseudo-moral meaning. Still, even in this period, *combat à outrance* often remained an option for participants to choose from—in fact, of the many kinds of competition into which tournaments had now divided, at least some were always sufficiently like war to serve as serious training for it. In 1559, the accidental death of King Henry II of France provided dramatic proof of how dangerous such competitions could still be.

In all of this, one interesting question is the role of firearms. Firearms, of course, were never admitted in tournaments. Many knights regarded them as the ultimate in unchivalrous weapons, inflicting ferocious punishments on those who used them in war.[58] Until about 1520, those who could afford to do so tried to counter firearms by commissioning and wearing ever stronger, heavier, and more elaborate armor. This in turn called for larger horses, longer and heavier lances, and so on in a self-reinforcing cycle that ended by turning knights into human tanks. Whereas originally many *milites* (knights) could afford the necessary equipment, by the beginning of the sixteenth century only a few grandees could; meanwhile, on the battlefield, soldiers' reaction to firearms was to discard armor as useless. Thus tournaments, now known as jousts, and real warfare went their separate ways. Under such circumstances it is scant wonder that by the first decades of the seventeenth century jousts had all but disappeared.

Firearms did not end men's interest in rough team games and combat sports, both of which continue to be practiced and to attract hundreds of millions of spectators to the present day. What they did do was to make the use of real-life weapons in two-sided war games much too dangerous; from this point on, the best one could do was to use blank cartridges, which make noise but do not cause injuries. This very fact may have encouraged the spread of yet another kind of simulated warfare, board games. Certainly not all board games are modeled on war, and quite a number of them, such as Chutes and Ladders, do not involve strategy in the abovementioned sense. Even those that are so modeled differ from combat sports and group sports in that they exclude danger, bloodshed, violence, and physical effort, as well as the kind of fighting spirit and determination that are needed to cope with them.

Board games, though, also have advantages. One is cost; neither requiring elaborate equipment nor taking up much space, usually they are cheap to organize and run. More important, they are able to capture the intellectual side of war as a two-sided contest. Games that do this, or attempt to do this, go back all the way to ancient Egypt. They fall into a vast number of different types, of which the best known by far is chess. Chess originated in India around A.D. 600. From there it spread to Persia, which provided some of the terminology used, and the Middle East, and reached Europe around A.D. 1000. According to legend, it was a deliberate attempt to model war for the purpose of instruction and entertainment. It did so by putting a king, a queen, chariots, horsemen, elephants, and foot soldiers on a board and having them slog it out.[59]

Partly in order to increase the value of chess for training, planning, and simulation and partly as pure entertainment, at least as early as the second half of the seventeenth century various attempts were made to modify it so as to make it more like war.[60] In some games the number of pieces on each side was increased, as was the number of squares on the board. For example, the young Louis XIV is said to have owned a set of toy soldiers, comprising five thousand pieces, made entirely of silver. Presumably it could be played with on the palace floor; later he had it melted down to help pay for his many real-life wars. Lesser mortals had to make do with the tin soldiers that industry started to produce in the eighteenth century. Others, such as the staff officer and military writer Bourcet, used blocks of wood or cardboard counters with various marks on them.

Next, game rules were modified so as to make the pieces' moves and actions more like those of real troops and units; this might or might not include logistic factors. One way to do this was to have a board made up not

just of black and white squares but of squares of green, red, and other colors as well, making it possible to represent various kinds of terrain on
which different kinds of units could be made to move and operate in different kinds of ways. Another was to substitute maps for boards, using a
pair of dividers in order to measure distances. Some games substituted in-
complete information for complete. Some used pieces whose characteristics could be read only by their owners but not by the other side, as is the
case with card games (which, however, do not resemble war) and in a relatively little-known game called Stratego.[61] Others introduced a screen to
separate the players and appointed an umpire whose task was to decide
which information should be passed to the other side and which should
not. Others still made use of dice, either simple ones or ones with as many
as eighteen sides, which introduced the missing element of chance.

The best-known game of this kind was devised by two Barons von
Reisswitz, father and son, during the 1820s. After much effort, they succeeded in having it presented to the then Prussian chief of the general
staff, General Friedrich von Mueffling, who is said to have exclaimed,
"This is not a game, this is training for war!"[62] Next, he ordered sets to
be made and distributed to all units; they, and the boxes in which they
were contained, may still be seen at German military museums. During
the middle years of the nineteenth century *Kriegspiele,* derived from the
one developed by the Reisswitzes, started serving the Prussian army as
training and planning tools.

Once that army had won its great victories against Austria and
France in 1866–71, war games spread to the armies of other nations as
well. Some games were tactical and were played with miniature soldiers
around sandboxes, the advantage being that terrain could be plastically
modeled and not just represented on a two-dimensional map. Others
were operational or strategic and took place in offices where officers sat
behind desks. Using the same large-scale maps as they would in war, they
wrote or, from the beginning of the twentieth century on, telephoned orders for imaginary units to be moved about against each other. Especially
in the U.S. Navy, which in the 1890s equipped an entire hall at the War
College to simulate all kinds of possible wars,[63] and in the German armed
forces, which always gamed major operations before mounting them,[64]
the role of war games was critical.

As so often in everything connected with war, it would be hard to say
where serious activity ended and sheer amusement got under way. For
example, in Germany around 1900 *Kriegspiele,* in the form of tactical

problems that had to be solved on paper and were published in newspapers much as crossword puzzles are, formed a fairly popular pastime. Nor were Germans the only ones to amuse themselves in this way. One of H. G. Wells's less well-known endeavors was a book called *Little Wars: A Game for Boys from Twelve Years to One Hundred and Fifty and for That More Intelligent Sort of Girl Who Likes Games and Books.*[65] In it, he recommended playing with soldiers on the floor of a large room as a relaxing but challenging form of intellectual exercise; whereas most other game-designers used dice and statistical tables to calculate casualties, Wells wanted to incorporate spring-operated miniature pellet-firing cannon. He was a popular author, and the entire book is written very much tongue in cheek. By contrast, Wells's near contemporary Frederick Jane was as serious a defense intellectual as they come, as is also proved by the fact that he started the series of publications still known after him. He, too, devised a war game, but one that had nothing frivolous about it and was intended for the use of naval officers in training.[66]

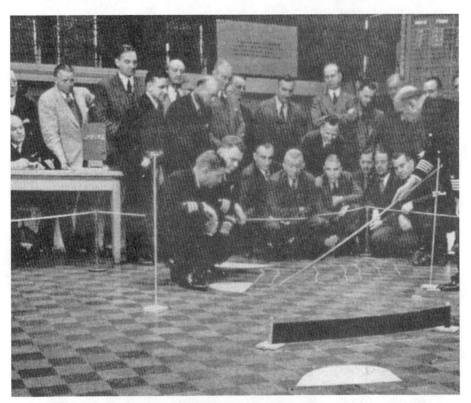

Preparing for war; war gaming for professionals   NAVAL WAR COLLEGE

Making the line between serious training and playacting even harder to draw, war was and remains far too complex an activity to be modeled as a whole. Instead of a single model there are countless different ones. Some games seek to model past wars, whether for serious study (although historians, a notoriously conservative lot, hardly ever use them) or for mere amusement.[67] Some, especially those that are played by military training and planning organizations around the world, deal with what *could* take place on the basis of existing technology, whereas others are entirely imaginary and involve elves, gremlins, dragons, and similar creatures. Some are strategic or even grand-strategic, meaning that they try to incorporate the politics of which war is (or is supposed to be) merely the instrument. Others focus on the operational level or on tactics. Some games have countless, extremely detailed rules that take intense study to master. Others, known as free games, seek to simplify things by assuming knowledge of what is and is not possible and introducing an umpire. Doing so may save much time, but only at the cost of adding an element that is often arbitrary and, since real life does not have umpires, always completely unrealistic.

Many games are played on a one-against-one basis, but some permit several players to match their wits against each other or else the formation, on each side, of teams with a commander and a clear division of labor. Most are realistic in that they leave ample room for the operation of chance (which, however, also means that the role of skill is downgraded), but some do not. Just as a map that shows every aspect of a certain piece of land would be equivalent to it, so a game incorporating every aspect of war would be hard to distinguish from war itself. Even if such a game could be developed, it would be so complex as to be unplayable—as things are, the real wonder about some of the larger strategic ones on the market is that some people *do* bother to learn the hundreds of rules involved in playing them. The outcome is that even the most sophisticated, most realistic games, developed at huge cost and intended for the most serious purposes, contain a large element of make-believe. To that extent, they are mere play.

No game however complex or simple, no sport however rough, no form of unarmed combat between protagonists, not even hunting, is capable of fully capturing every aspect of war, let alone doing so while remaining sufficiently safe and sufficiently simple as to be playable as well. As the strictures of Euripides, Plato, and the rest show, the limitations of such sports and such games qua preparation for war have always been understood perfectly well. Though some commanders have been good chess players, clearly playing chess is not in itself sufficient preparation for war; as for other exercises discussed in this chapter, suffice it to say that in 1995 not a single Russian polled believed that he or she could contribute anything to the country's defense by keeping fit.[68] As thousands of years of history show, finding reasons why games and sports do not constitute adequate preparation for war is easy. As thousands of years of history also show, devising an alternative to take their place is a different matter. As a result, they continue to be used in countless training institutions all over the world. Dwight D. Eisenhower may have been the most famous cadet to injure his knee while playing football at a military academy. However, he can hardly have been the only one.

As to war games' continuing popularity, at this point suffice it to say that in all my thirty-something years as a university teacher, the only time I had my students literally jumping on tables in excitement was during a seminar on war games. All but one of the students enrolled in the class were male; as the course ended, the lone woman made her contribution by presenting a cake baked in the form of a game of chess complete with all the pieces. Even the most cursory examination of such games suggests that serious preparation for war and mere entertainment, training and fun, make-believe and reality, are as closely entwined today as they have always been. As long as this remains the case, the culture of war will remain alive and well.

II

In War and Battle

In theory, war is a means to an end, a no-nonsense activity intended to serve the interests of one group of people who use whatever force they can muster in order to kill, wound, or otherwise incapacitate those who oppose that group. In reality, nothing could be further from the truth. First, far from being a simple act of naked force, war is riddled with ritual. Second, not only is it riddled with ritual but it has a powerful (one would like to say fatal) attraction, even to the point where fighting can lead to ecstasy very similar to that induced by various other kinds of stimulants. Third, not only does it have a powerful attraction that can culminate in ecstasy but it is surrounded by rules that determine what may and may not be done in it. In this part of the present volume, I shall discuss each of these subjects in turn, finishing my account with a chapter about the way wars are brought to an end.

.   .   .

5

Opening Gambits

Man, a culture-creating animal, surrounds himself with rituals—as, some would argue, many other animals also do.[1] The rituals start with those that surround even the most ordinary family meal, welcome, or parting; they extend all the way to the elaborate ceremonial in which the people of "advanced" countries dress on Christmas Day, Bastille Day, the Fourth of July, and similar occasions. Ritual, such as baptism and being given a name, is among the first things that greet us when we enter this world. Except under the most unusual, stressful, or hostile circumstances, ritual is also what surrounds us at the time when we leave it and marks our departure after we have done so.

The occasions on which men engage in ritual are almost infinitely numerous and infinitely varied. Here we are concerned with two kinds of ritual: those expressing fear and those that display power. Both are meant to reinforce one's self-confidence, and both do so by putting on an act. In the case of the former, acting out one's fears helps sublimate them, especially, as is usually the case, when it is accompanied by a supplication to or invocation of some higher power. In the case of the latter, the act consists of a show of strength, one that will both get one's adrenaline going and impress onlookers. War presents ample cause to engage in both kinds of ritual. On one hand, it is the most dangerous of all human activities, a thing to be approached with fear and trembling. For that very reason, nowhere else are displays of strength as important; as Tacitus says, it is always the eye that is defeated first.[2] Scant wonder that, in addition to making all sorts of practical preparations for war and battle, men have always surrounded those preparations with, indeed immersed them in, every sort of ritual, from prayers to reviews, flag-raising ceremonies, and taunting and challenging their enemies.

To begin with, let's consider the transition from peace to war. It is true that in many tribal societies in particular, the two are not as clearly separated in time as is the case in more sophisticated ones. Still, insofar as anybody who ventures into enemy territory turns him- or herself into fair game, it always exists. Peace, whether defined in terms of time or in terms of conditions that prevail in certain areas but not in others, is relatively safe. Conversely, war is so dangerous that, in some tribal societies, between 20 and 60 percent of all adult males (and between 13 and 32 percent of all adult females) die as a result of it.[3]

Another essential difference between the two, to be discussed in greater detail later in this volume, is that whereas in peacetime killing other people is prohibited, in the latter it is permitted, indeed required. In this way the transition is not simply a matter of the highest practical significance. It is that, but it also marks the abolition, the inversion even, of a taboo—the very taboo that makes civilized life possible in the first place. Given how important it is, one is hardly surprised to learn that, from ancient times to the present day, few if any societies did *not* mark it by some kind of ritual.

Many of the rituals in question are two-sided, which means that they involve some kind of interaction between the belligerents. In principle, and often in practice as well, such an interaction simply does not fit into the strategic framework most analysts use. War, after all, has always rested on taking the enemy by surprise. On the other hand, where surprise is absent victory is much harder to attain, and sometimes impossible. By communicating with the enemy, at least some of the element of surprise is inevitably lost.

The interaction may take countless forms, only a few of which can be discussed here. For example, in ancient Greece declaring war was a highly ritualistic act.[4] In the absence of permanent embassies, envoys were exchanged, demands made, the gods invoked, existing treaties abrogated, and the like. Certainly no self-respecting city-state would dream of starting hostilities without going through the rituals first, allowing us to question whether Thucydides's distinction between the excuse (*afourme*) and real cause (*aitia*) of the Peloponnesian War was really as clear-cut as he tries to make out.[5] The Romans, of whom nobody will say that they were either softheaded or ignorant of how to wage war, also used a two-sided procedure to make the transition, but in a different way. There was in Rome a college of priests known as *fetiales,* roughly translated as "poultry minders," since their main job was to look after the birds by which omens were read. When these priests had decided that a neighbor had committed such great offenses against Rome as to justify a war, four of them would be sent into enemy territory to present a list of grievances. The grievances had to be addressed within thirty days. If not, then in the presence of witnesses a member of the college would hurl a spear into enemy territory, thus formally declaring war.[6]

The Spanish conquistadors in what was to become Latin America followed a somewhat similar procedure. First they would produce a priest and have him read a declaration in which they demanded that the natives submit and accept the Catholic faith; once the Indians had refused, they started making war on them. British representatives in Africa in the last years of the nineteenth century also made use of ceremony. Local rulers were presented with blank surrender forms to sign. If they did not comply, then the redcoats would come and show them who had the power.[7] None of this is to say that the so-called primitive peoples of the continents in question did not have their own ways of informing the enemy that war was about to be declared or had been declared—far from it. For example, the Patagonians and Araucanians used to make an image of a man with long red teeth and a halter of hide, set it up so the enemy could see it, and surrounded it with spears, arrows, and clubs stuck into the earth.[8] Other tribes in other places had their own methods.

One of the most interesting rituals is the modern declaration of war. In its present form (or, at any rate, the form that was in fairly general use until 1945), it goes back to the Middle Ages. At that time ecclesiastics, who possessed immunity, were often used to convey messages between belligerents. During the Renaissance, this became the job of resident ambassadors.[9] The "civilized" procedure for declaring war is supposed to look roughly as follows: The foreign secretary or minister of the side that is about to start the war summons the other's ambassador for a meeting. The ambassador is presented with a paper in which the decision is announced and the reasons for it are explained. Having accepted the paper with better or worse grace (or, in some cases, demonstratively refused to do so) he is provided with a safe-conduct or passport and allowed to leave the country along with his staff; sometimes a skeleton staff is allowed to stay behind, or else the country on which war has been declared will ask the ambassador of some third country to look after its interests. Meanwhile, in the enemy capital, the same ritual is enacted. In this case it is the ambassador of the country that does the declaring who is supposed to take the initiative. Having obtained a hearing, he is expected to hand over the declaration, ask for his passport, and leave.

Quaint as some of these rituals are, they formed part and parcel of the culture of war at specific times and places, and as that culture changed, so did the rituals. One may argue that many rituals, perhaps most, were a mere sham, and often enough the charge was true. The conquistadors knew well enough that the Indians would not be able to understand what was wanted of them, but went to war nevertheless. In Rome, those who really decided on peace and war were not the fifteen or twenty *fetiales* but the Senate and the popular assembly (which passed the necessary legislation), so that anything the poultry minders did was purely ceremonial. To preserve surprise, many modern states have formally declared war only after launching their attack, and some have even dispensed with any declaration whatsoever. Yet none of this necessarily means that such things were not considered important. In fact, the opposite may be the case. On June 22, 1941, Adolf Hitler launched the largest surprise attack of all time. Even as the guns opened fire, he had his foreign minister, Joachim von Ribbentrop, and his ambassador in Moscow, Friedrich von der Schulenburg, follow the prescribed procedure and declare war.[10] Hitler was one of the most powerful and most cynical dictators of all time, and surely at that moment he had other things to think of. If he acted as he did, he must have had his reasons.

In general, one reason why going through the appropriate ritual is important is precisely because it forms part of the culture; meaning that, by not performing them, one ipso facto puts oneself at a disadvantage. However, in the case of the communications that precede a war, the rituals that mark the transition from peace to war, and declarations of war it may be possible to be more specific than this. In war, many people put their lives at risk and some die. The stakes are awesome, the highest that exist. Therefore, nothing is more important than that the combatants feel, and proclaim to the entire world, that their case is just; anybody who, going to war, lacks this conviction must be either criminal or simply foolish. As any lawyer knows, obtaining justice is largely a question of following the appropriate ritual and uttering the correct formulae. This explains why, when states go to war without declaring it, they almost always end up by explaining—read apologizing for—their failure. Conversely, only when a war is purely defensive are such declarations altogether superfluous.

The transition from peace to war having been made, preparation for battle could begin, and again we see that this often involved some kind of mutual communication, display, or ritual. Some of the most interesting used to be practiced by the Maring of New Guinea. Like many other tribal societies, the Maring recognized different kinds of war waged against different enemies under different circumstances in pursuit of different objectives. One of these involved a previous agreement as to the time and place where the armed encounter was to take place (and also concerning the weapons with which it was to be fought).[11] Australian Aboriginal tribes had similar customs, as did the Natchez of North America and many tribes in what is now Nigeria.[12] The effect was to turn not only preparation for battle but even battle itself into something very close to ritual or, if one wishes, a tournament. Yet to anybody who has followed the argument thus far, this hardly comes as a great surprise.

There were good reasons for such practices. Modern states are separated by borders, imaginary lines that run across the terrain and leave not a single inch between them uncovered. Not so tribal ones, which, lacking maps as well as a clear temporal distinction between peace and war, often sought safety by creating buffer zones many miles wide.[13] This in turn meant that if a battle (as distinct from a raid) was to take place at all, they had to agree on a place and a date. Nor were "primitive" tribes the only ones to behave in this way. In his *Histories*, Herodotus presents the Persian commander Mardonius explaining to his master—the "great king" Xerxes, son of Darius—the Greek way of making war.[14] So "foolish" are the Greeks, he says, that, forgoing any attempt at stratagem or maneuver, their method is to meet on a certain plain. There they confront and slaughter each other; clearly, this was possible only with the aid of a previous agreement, even a tacit one, as to the time and place.

In this particular case, we can only guess that there *must* have been a previous exchange of messages. The situation during early medieval history was entirely different. Nithard, a chronicler who described the struggles between Charlemagne's heirs, describes many occasions when commanders held parleys in an attempt to agree on the time and place a battle might be fought.[15] So do numerous other chroniclers such as Jordanes, Gregory of Tours, Dietmar, and more. Judging by their accounts, between about 850 and 1100, hardly an important battle took place without the commanders on both sides first exchanging emissaries and holding talks.

Nineteenth-century students took these episodes very seriously. Wrote Charles Oman,

> Strategy was absolutely inexistent. Nothing could show the primitive state of the military art better than the fact that generals solemnly set out and accepted challenges to meet in battle at a given place and on a given day . . . Even when the two forces were actually in presence, it sometimes required more skill than the commanders owned to bring on a battle.[16]

Twentieth-century scholars, especially those who came after 1945, took the other tack. They saw the commanders in question as followers of Machiavelli. The exchanges were neither necessary for battle to take place nor sincerely meant; instead, they were merely a thin veneer for all kinds of realistic strategic considerations. While the monkish chroniclers who had written the sources could not perceive those considerations, they themselves, being sharp-eyed, could and did. The hidden aim was the desire of one side to bring on a battle before the balance of forces could be redressed, move it to a more favorable location, and so on.[17]

While both lines of thought make some sense, neither provides a complete explanation. On one hand, the fact that some medieval battles started by accident (as, indeed, continues to happen today) proves that knowledge of strategy and geography, as well as command and control, were far from perfect. On the other, clearly men such as those who in 1066 organized the invasion of England, as well as those who to counter that invasion marched all the way from Stamford Bridge to Hastings, did not have to parley—certainly not on a regular basis—in order to locate their enemy and bring him to battle. It is probably true that commanders who exchanged proposals for fixing the time and place and manner of a coming encounter had all kinds of realistic considerations in mind, but this does not explain why such methods were limited mainly to the early Middle Ages. Were the Byzantine authors of the sixth-century *Strategicon,* which does not have a word to say about arranged encounters, and Edward I of England, toward 1300, less tricky and more knowledgeable about geography than commanders who lived in between those two dates? Or is it safer to assume that cultural attitudes surrounding war during the centuries in question dictate when and where such exchanges should or should not take place?

Another kind of ritual by which men prepare themselves for the awesome ordeal of combat is the challenge by champions. Challenges of this kind are known from many civilizations, including ancient Israel,[18] the Aryans of India, and early Rome.[19] Others are recorded by Homer. In the poems, almost any first-class warrior who meets an opponent he considers worthy of him pauses to deliver a speech—as, in fact, is expected of champions—before proceeding to the business at hand, either killing or being killed.[20] All are formulated in strikingly similar terms. Here is Aelfwine, son of Aelfric, delivering a challenge in preparation for the Battle of Maledon:

> I will make known my lineage to all, how I was born in Mercia of a great race. Ealhelm was my grandfather called, a wise ealdorman, happy in the world's goods. Thengs shall have no cause to reproach me among my people that I was ready to forsake this action and seek my home, now that my lord lies low, cut down in battle.[21]

Or, by way of a second example, a speech allegedly made by a Japanese samurai in 1156:

> I am not such a great man as men go, but I am an inhabitant of Iga province, a follower of the Lord of Aki, and 28 years old. My name is Yamada Kosaburo Koreyuki. I am the grandson of Yamada no Shoji Yukisue, who was well known among the aristocracy for being the first to go into battle under the Lord of Bizen at the attack on Yoshihito, Lord of Tsushima. My grandfather also captured innumerable mountain robbers and highwaymen. I too have been many times in battle and have made a name for myself.[22]

Taking Homer as our starting point, these examples cover a period of more than two millennia. Though the three cultures can hardly be said to have influenced one another, little changes.

Assuming it was a question of culture, under what circumstances could such a culture grow and flourish? First, the two sides had to stand in full view of one another. In other words, challenges were mounted before battles, not in the case of raids and ambushes; societies that did not have battles did not have challenges, either. Second, they had to be close enough to hear each other, which meant that the spread of firearms put a definite end to them. Third and most important, for a challenge of champions to take place, war had to be a personal matter. It was not merely a question of one group, one people, one country, or one army against another. It was that, but it was also a contest between individuals, those who occupied high rank and those who sought to distinguish themselves both in the eyes of their own side and in those of the enemy. All this explains why, by and large, challenges formed part of the martial culture of chiefdoms and feudal societies and not, for example, of those of Hellenistic Greece or post-Renaissance Europe. Limiting ourselves to the European Middle Ages, so numerous were challenges to single combat that one hardly knows where to start.

According to Procopius, the battles of Faenza (542) and Busta Gallorum (552) both opened with single combats between carefully chosen Ostrogothic and Byzantine champions.[23] The Battle of Pavia (889) opened with an encounter between Lombard and Byzantine champions.[24] Richter in his *Histoire de France,* Henry Huntington in his *History of England,* Wolfram von Eschenbach in *Willehalm,* the *Histoire de Guillaume le Marechal,* William of Malmesbury in the *Historia Novella,* and Joinville in his *Life of Saint Louis* all have similar stories to tell; somewhat later, Froissart's *Chronicles* are full of them.[25] The fact that a Muslim writer, Saladin's son Boha Ed Din, also mentions the practice provides independent confirmation of sorts.[26] It also proves that such things were not simply limited to a single military culture but, provided contact existed, were sometimes able to leap from one to the next.

Even kings and other great lords regularly challenged each other to combat, albeit with less success. William the Conqueror challenged Harald but was refused. Richard the Lionhearted challenged Philip Augustus; various proposals were exchanged, but nothing came of it. Edward III and Philip de Valois repeatedly challenged one another to single combat for the crown of France. In 1402, Louis d'Orléans, the brother of Charles VI of France, defied Henry IV of England to meet him, declaring that he wanted to revive chivalric glory by such means; Henry, of course, refused. Philip the Good of Burgundy appears to have had a passion for such contests, challenging many other lords in turn. Even as late as 1525, Emperor Charles V challenged King Francis I of France. Often we are told that the rulers in question wanted to accept and even that they started preparations, only to be dissuaded by their advisers.

Many modern historians have been unkind to challenges of this kind. If they did lead to combat, as very often happened among tribal peoples and in the *Iliad,* they were the product of "childish exhibitionism," "a total lack of military discipline," and "stupidity"; if they did not, then surely they proved the "decline" of chivalry from some lofty standard set in some past period when people were more "innocent" and less "realistic."[27] This, however, is nonsense. Whether or not they led to actual fighting, challenges, like two-sided declarations of war, had their uses. People used them, or at any rate could try to use them, to bring on battle, postpone it, justify their own cause, blacken that of the enemy, gain the moral high ground, and achieve a psychological advantage. Frequently it was hard to say where practical considerations ended and "childish exhibitionism"—read the culture of war—began. This is all the more so because the most effective exhibitions are often precisely those that seem as if they do not pay attention to practical considerations of any kind. Conversely, once an exhibition has been unmasked, then of course it loses any power to impress and persuade.

Even when two-sided declarations of war and challenges are dispensed with, so portentous is the entry into war and battle that it is rarely, if ever, made without ceremonies of some kind. I shall illustrate this by proceeding from some of the simplest known societies to more complex ones, although the fact that the technology at the former's disposal is indeed primitive hardly means that their culture and rituals also are. Among the Meru people of the Mount Kenya area, to go to war it was necessary to consult the appropriate priest (or, strictly speaking, ritualist, since a personal god is unknown) first. A delegation was sent to meet with him; a goat was sacrificed, its blood gathered in a vessel, and an omen taken. The same ritualist, or perhaps another one, also acted as a "curse remover," cleansing the warriors of whatever impurity they might incur that could impede success. Special powders, intended to provide magic protection, were prepared and blown into the wind, and magic incantations were chanted. Last but not least, the leaders were told which objects (such as a python or a hyena) spelled bad luck for them and should be avoided if possible or, in case they were met with, should cause the expedition to be aborted.[28]

Similar rites can be found among hundreds of different peoples all over the world—including, of course, those described in the Old Testament.[29] What is more, readers familiar with ancient history will easily recognize the similarity between them and the ones practiced in Greece and Rome. In the former, every war was preceded by consultation with the oracle at Delphi or some other, less famous shrine; what hap-

pened, or at any rate was supposed to have happened, to those who mis-
understood its commands or refused to follow them is sufficiently illustrated by the story of Croesus of Lydia, who lost his kingdom in this way.[30]
Animals would also be sacrificed and their entrails studied for omens.
Any commander who did not call on the appropriate personnel to perform the rites or who disregarded their advice would be certain to be accused of gross dereliction of duty if fortune went against him.

According to Xenophon, who spent the last years of his life among
them, of all the Greeks none were more careful in observing the rites than
the Spartans; it is even possible that, in calling them "craftsmen of warfare," it was this aspect more than any other he had in mind.[31] Certainly the
Spartans used omens to make, or at any rate justify, all kinds of military-
political decisions, such as when to send a force to the Athenians' aid at
Marathon (which resulted in their arriving too late to take part in the battle) and to have no more than three hundred men die at Thermopylae. On
the other hand, the fact that the Spartans took their religion seriously is
shown, among other things, by the fact that on the eve of the second
Persian War, they felt the need to formally atone for killing Darius's envoys
sent to them to state their demands on the eve of the first Persian War. So
determined was one Spartan commander to make sure that the gods were
on his side and the enterprise, on which he embarked, auspicious that he
took omens no fewer than four times;[32] Xenophon himself on one occasion
took omens no fewer than nine times.[33]

The Romans were even more famous for their military prowess and
devotion to omens of every kind. Here I shall follow their behavior as interpreted by Machiavelli (who in turn used Livy as his source), the reason being that in the whole of history, no man was less inclined to
"childish exhibitionism," let alone "stupidity."

> The Romans were more afraid of breaking an oath than of breaking
> the law, since they held in higher esteem the power of God than the
> power of man.

> It will be seen by those who pay attention to Roman history, how
> much religion helped in the control of armies . . . For, where there is
> religion, it is easy to teach men to use arms, but where there are
> arms but no religion, it is with difficulty that it can be introduced.

> Auguries were not only in large part the basis of the ancient religion
> of the gentiles . . . but they also contributed to the well-being of the

Roman republic. Hence the Romans took greater care in regard to them than in regard to any other institution . . . They made use of them in . . . entering upon military enterprises, in leading forth their armies, on engaging in battles . . . Never would they set forth on an expedition until they had convinced the troops that the gods had promised them victory.

Nevertheless, when reason told them that a thing had to be done, they did it anyhow, even should the auspices be adverse. But, so adroit were they in words and actions at giving things a twist that they did not appear to have done anything disparaging to religion.[34]

As the last two sentences show, Machiavelli was quite clear in his own mind that his admired Romans were not above manipulating religion in order to produce the desired outcome. This was true before the battle, when it could be used to raise morale or avoid a course of action that appeared undesirable without losing face, but it was also true after the battle when it could be used to pin the blame on certain people and actions and, by implication, absolve the rest. Moreover, as he says, religious acts "unless accompanied by true *virtu* [were] of no avail." All this is self-evident, and has since been repeated by hundreds if not thousands of commentators who congratulated themselves on their own cleverness in being able to see through the "tricks" that commanders and augurs practiced. Yet what Machiavelli, let alone most of his followers, does not say is that what makes such manipulation possible is not merely the adroitness with which the people in charge go to work. Rather, it is the fact that men, especially men who are facing momentous decisions on which their very lives depend, *need* reassurance in the form of ceremony and ritual. One side wants to be deceived, the other to deceive. Between them they create the culture of war.

Lifting our gaze to include other civilizations such as India, China, and Japan, we find that the list of methods various societies employed in order to obtain a lock on the future—especially, though of course not exclusively, the future that is linked to war—is almost infinite. Some sorted and tossed yarrow sticks. Others flipped special sets of coins on specially designed boards, read tea leaves, or placed shells near their ears and tried to interpret the sounds they thought they could hear. The heavens were searched for portents, especially unusual phenomena such as shooting stars and comets. So were the swirls created by streaming water or by clouds blown in the wind, and the movements of animals and birds.

A multitude of amulets, charms, and similar devices was produced, provided with some kind of blessing, and carried into battle.

People's dreams, especially those of rulers, commanders, and individuals with a reputation for holiness, were also studied; in this context, suffice it to mention Emperor Constantine's vision of a heavenly cross on which were written the words *in hoc signo vinces*. All these rites met a profound psychological need of men about to stake everything on a single throw, hoping for victory but expecting possible death. They must have been taken very seriously, or else they would hardly have been transmitted from one generation to the next and practiced over millennia on end. Yet, paradoxically, the fact that they were taken seriously did not exclude manipulation by, and on behalf of, the powers that be, for reasons very much like those Machiavelli mentions.

Monotheists, too, resorted to religion in making decisions pertaining to war and battle. The Pentateuch speaks of the *urim vetumim*, a form of divination carried out by the high priest with the aid of various precious stones that were attached to his breastplate.[35] Prophets stood up, proclaimed themselves to be speaking in the name of the one and only God, and either recommended some military course of action or advised against it. By way of providing proof of God's will, miracles were sometimes used. According to whether Moses did or did not hold up his arms during the Israelites' fight with the Amalekites, things went better or worse for the former.[36] At a later time, to make sure the Lord was serious about delivering the people, Gideon had Him soak a piece of wool that had been left outside overnight with dew while the ground around it remained dry. This, however, was still not enough. Next, a much greater miracle, he asked for things to be arranged the other way around and got his wish.[37]

By way of nonbiblical illustrations of such methods, let's focus on the European Middle Ages. At the Battle of the Standard in 1138, Archbishop Thurstan ordered the collection of saints' banners from the most important religious houses in the north of England, including those of Saint Cuthbert from Durham, Wilfrid from Ripon, and John from Beverley, to be hoisted from a ship's mast, at the top of which was secured a pyx containing the consecrated host, thereby forming the standard that gave the battle its name. At that time and in the following centuries, every Italian city-state had its war cart or *carrocio*. As long as peace prevailed the carts were reverently treated and flanked by two candles that had to stay lit at all times. In wartime they were taken out and used to carry religious insignia and pictures of saints into battle; such insignia acted as both rallying points and as spiritual powerhouses. The best-known standard of all was the French oriflamme. Originally it consisted of two separate flags that were fused together during the second half of the twelfth century. Most of the time it was kept at the monastery of Saint Denis, north of Paris, but in time of war it was brought out amid various ceremonies including masses, relicts, and benedictions.[38] Henry III of England imitated the French. He kept the royal war banner, a dragon worked on red cloth with eyes of sapphires and a fiery tongue, at Westminster Abbey, taking it out against the Welsh in 1257 and against the forces of Simon de Monfort in 1264.

The most potent means of securing divine aid was to bear relics into battle. According to William de Potiers, at Hastings, Duke William wore around his neck the relics on which Harald had sworn allegiance to him.[39] In Capetian France, during times of danger, the relics of Saint Denis were displayed on the altar and masses offered and prayers said for victory. Even more concretely, the lance of Saint Maurice, containing a nail believed to be from the True Cross, was carried by Otto I at his great victory over the Magyars at the Lech.[40] The invention at Antioch during the First Crusade of a still more potent lance, the one that had pierced Christ's side at the crucifixion, was a crucial boost to the morale of the Christian army.[41] Conversely, the capture of the True Cross by Saladin at Hattin in 1187 was comparable, in its demoralizing effect, to the capture by the Philistines of the Holy Arc three thousand years before.

To make light of one's sins in day-to-day life is easy. To do so when looking death in the face is a different matter; indeed, it is something that, if it is possible at all, marks people who are either absolute heroes or absolute fools. Most of them being neither the one nor the other, normally in preparing for the ordeal to come they feel the need to purify themselves. They may act either under orders, as King Saul's men did, or else on their own initiative.[42] Most likely they will abstain from food (or certain kinds of food), alcohol, and sex. They may undergo special rituals, such as vigils, designed to cleanse their bodies and their souls. Having done so, they put on clothes of a special color designed to show that they had taken their leave of this world, so to speak. All this is true regardless of whether they are animists or pagans or Shintoists or monotheists, Jews or Christians or Muslims. It applies to the most modern armed forces just as it did to those described in the Bible and, presumably, those of the Stone Age as well.

Other kinds of ritual that will almost certainly take place before battle is joined are designed to strengthen morale and reinforce group solidarity, the all-important factors on which victory often depends. Conditions permitting, first the troops, fully equipped and armed, will be drawn up for a review; insofar as most battles until about the middle of the nineteenth century involved fighting almost shoulder to shoulder in formation, positioning those formations itself was identical with preparing the review in question. Practically speaking, reviews permit commanders to take one last look to see whether everything is ready. Perhaps even more important, under most circumstances the very fact that they can see their comrades in array will raise men's confidence; under some circumstances a list of the units about to enter battle may be read.

Next, the commander will show himself. In doing so, their styles have differed very much. Though there were exceptions, before the French Revolution most commanders tried to look as splendid as they could. The purpose, as already explained, was to demonstrate their own confidence in the outcome, a need reflected by many of the more expensive, heavily decorated pieces of armor, dress, and equipment. After that, things began to change. A few commanders started wearing relatively simple uniforms when it suited them, one of them being Napoleon, who did so in order to set himself apart from the gilded royal commanders on the other side. A century and a half later Hitler, styling himself as a man of the people, did the same; as war broke out, he swore never to doff his field-gray uniform jacket until "final victory" was won. This, however, was but one element in a carefully calculated show. Rather than giving up sartorial splendor altogether, both Hitler and Napoleon transferred it to the members of their immediate entourage, who continued to wear splendid uniforms, gold braid, and so on. Thus they made themselves stand out even more, a process closely paralleled in parts of the civilian world.

In modern discussions of what commanders actually do in battle, the emphasis is always on command, control, and communications (sometimes, to make things as complicated as possible, with computers, sensors, and intelligence thrown in). All this is no doubt very important, but perhaps no more important than some other things that too often go unmentioned. At Lodi in 1796, Bonaparte, then a general, seized a flag and personally led the charge across a bridge with the Austrians firing at him from the other side. At Koeniggraetz in 1866, when it looked as if the Prussians were about to lose the battle, Moltke, offered a cigar by

Bismarck, who was standing nearby, carefully picked out the best of the lot—thus wordlessly persuading the chancellor, as the latter subsequently wrote, that everything was going to turn out well.[43] At Saint Omer in July 1944, Patton personally directed American military traffic breaking out of Normandy, inspiring his men and contributing as much to his army's victory as any commander ever has. Throughout the heavy fighting on the Suez Canal in October 1973, Ariel Sharon always kept a vase of flowers on his desk.

In questions of dress, the advent of modern firepower in the 1860s affected commanders much as it did other soldiers. On pain of becoming too conspicuous and too vulnerable, it forced them to rid themselves of their more splendid attire. Another factor was the spread of democracy. More and more, soldiers expected not to be commanded by their social superiors but to be led by their nominal equals, which meant that sartorial splendor had to be ended or at least assume different forms. We begin to come across commanders, such as Ulysses S. Grant, who were famous for the simplicity, even sloppiness, with which they dressed.[44] As time went on the trend toward simplicity spread until, from 1945 on, wearing fatigues became almost obligatory. This, of course, did not mean that commanders suddenly lost their age-old desire, and need, to set themselves apart from their subordinates. As the media began to make their presence felt on the battlefield from the middle of the nineteenth century on, moreover, their demands (and those of the public they served) also had to be considered.

Very often, the outcome was an attempt to combine simplicity with some kind of unique item. An excellent case in point was Douglas MacArthur. In a concession to the climate in the South Pacific he did away with the regulation tie, always appearing in an open-necked shirt. At the same time he used his famous pipe as a prop so as to make sure no soldier and no journalist would fail to make him out from the bevy of officers who surrounded him. Bernhard Montgomery, by wearing two grommets on his hat instead of one, did the same. So did Moshe Dayan. Visiting Saigon in 1966, Dayan had brought back a cap of the kind worn by the Army of the Republic of Vietnam troops; no other Israeli had one like it. Acting as minister of defense from 1967 on, he wore it when inspecting border fortifications, visiting troops (even during the October 1973 war), and the like. In that war, Sharon acquired a distinct look by putting on a dressing, covering what some said was a nonexistent wound to the head.

Other commanders still acted as if nothing had changed and dressed as flamboyantly as they could. J.E.B. Stuart, the Confederate cavalry commander famous for his extravagance, wore a red-lined gray cape, yellow sash, hat cocked to the side and decorated with a peacock feather, and a red flower in his lapel; not content with this, often he carried cologne as well. Making use of a little-known regulation that permitted general officers to design their own uniforms, George Patton wore what came to be known as an Eisenhower jacket. It came complete with gilt buttons, lacquered helmet lining, and the famous ivory-handled pistols. The latter were meant solely for display; for self-defense he carried a third one, loaded, under his shirt. As with many of his colleagues, all this was the result not of accident but of deliberation. Early in his career he had written: "Officers must assert themselves by example and by voice. They must be pre-eminent in courage, deportment and dress." Later he told a subordinate that "as an officer, you are always on parade"; this applied as much, if not more, during battle as at any other time.[45]

However they dress, commanders' way of presenting themselves to the troops was, and remains, crucial to preparing them for battle. Circumstances permitting, a formal review will be held. The commander will appear, perhaps after some deliberate delay whose purpose is to increase tension. Exuding self-confidence, he will pass along the lines, look deeply into the men's eyes, shake hands, ask a question or two, and do what he can to inspire them with determination and courage. If at all possible, there will be a speech. Certainly the exact content will differ according to circumstances and the eloquence of the commander or his staff. Still, in principle he who has read a single such harangue—a word closely related to the arrangement of units on the battlefield—has read them all.[46] In addressing the troops as equals, telling them that "the day" has come, appealing to their bravery, referring to the shame of those who refuse to fight, reminding them of their families, and looking back to the glorious past, the Spartan king Archidamus provides a model of the genre:

> Fellow citizens, the day has come which calls upon us to prove ourselves brave men and look the world in the face with level eyes. Now are we to deliver to those who come after us our fatherland intact as we received it from our fathers; now will we cease hanging our heads in shame before our children and wives, our old men and our foreign friends, in sight of whom in days of old we shone forth conspicuous beyond all other Hellenes.[47]

Since then, the only thing which changed is that, owing to the enormous growth in armies that has taken place, commanders can no longer make such proclamations face-to-face, as Archidamus, passing from regiment to regiment, did. Instead they are much more likely to be published as orders of the day or read over the radio and, more recently still, television. More than eighteen hundred years after Archidamus made his speech, another commander told his troops:

> Soldiers, Sailors, and Airmen of the Allied Expeditionary Force! You are about to embark upon the Great Crusade, toward which we have striven these many months. The eyes of the world are upon you. The hopes and prayers of liberty-loving people everywhere march with you. In company with your brave allies and brothers-in-arms on other Fronts, you will bring about the destruction of the German war machine, the elimination of Nazi tyranny over the oppressed peoples of Europe, and security for ourselves in a free world.
>
> Your task will not be an easy one. Your enemy is well trained, well equipped, and battle-hardened. He will fight savagely.
>
> But this is the year 1944! Much has happened since the Nazi triumphs of 1940–41. The United Nations have inflicted upon the Germans great defeats, in open battle, man-to-man. Our air offensive has seriously reduced their strength in the air and their capacity to wage war on the ground. Our Home Fronts have given us an overwhelming superiority in weapons and munitions of war, and places at our disposal great reserves of trained fighting men. The tide has turned! The free men of the world are marching together to Victory!
>
> I have full confidence in your courage, devotion to duty and skill in battle. We will accept nothing less than full Victory!
>
> Good luck! And let us beseech the blessing of Almighty God upon this great and noble undertaking![48]

The exhortation to battle having been delivered, very likely there will take place one final ritual aimed at reinforcing group solidarity, get the men's adrenaline running, and make them "forget themselves," as the saying goes. A war dance may be held, during which the men brandish their weapons and yell defiance at the enemy. Musicians may strike up and play, as in Sparta, Rome, among the Dervishes of the Sudan, and many modern armies down to World War I inclusive. A paean may be raised, as in most ancient Greek armies.[49] A war cry, such as "For Saint

George" (England), "*Vive l'empereur*" (France), and "Geronimo" (U.S. paratroopers in World War II) may be shouted out in a suitably stentorian voice and taken up by countless more or less dry throats—proving, once again, that war is as much a continuation of sports as of politics.

Over the last six decades formal declarations of war, which used to be seen as signs of "civilization," have become almost an endangered species. One reason for this is because modern weapon systems, missiles and aircraft in particular, are capable of covering extraordinary distances in extraordinarily short times. This fact makes surprise, especially strategic surprise at the outset of hostilities, even more critical, and in some ways easier to achieve, than it used to be, reinforcing the temptation to attack first and make speeches later. Had the Japanese declared war before striking at Pearl Harbor, surely they would have failed in that attack. Even as it was, the second wave of attackers met with stronger resistance, and suffered more losses, than the first one did.

Perhaps even more important, in the post-1945 world the great majority of wars have been waged not by one state against another but by states against other groups, such as insurgents, guerrillas, terrorists, or freedom fighters. Out of all the countless organizations that exist and jostle each other on this planet, only two hundred or so are called states and have the sovereign right to wage war. Understandably, what those two hundred fear is the possibility that by formally declaring war on others of a different kind, they will recognize the latter's right to do likewise; even as they do so, they may also lay themselves under all kinds of obligations spelled out in international law.[50] They much prefer to dress what they are doing in other procedures and use all kinds of other terms, such as a "state of emergency," "troubles," "pacification," and whatnot. But whereas states and the jurists who play such a large part in running them may be calculating animals, this does not change the psychology of fighting men. For them, the role of ritual in marking the march toward death and endowing it with meaning remains as great as it has always been.

Most modern scholars in such fields as political science, international relations, and strategy tend to look down on the kind of rituals that have been the subject of this chapter, either characterizing them as "primitive" or barely bothering to mention them. Some historians have done even worse. They have projected such attitudes back upon previous societies as well, explaining how the various gambits employed as preludes to hostilities were nothing but pure humbug. One of them, going back all the way to ancient Greece, tells us that "declarations of war should not deceive; they are for public consumption. Nothing objectively changes at the moment when war is declared, or officially halted; war may effectively have begun before it is declared, or may not begin until months later . . . The act of declaring war is primarily a legal, ceremonial and ideological statement."[51] That applies to war, but it applies equally well to very large parts of political, religious, and even intellectual life. Which is precisely why declarations of war, as well as countless other opening gambits whether one- or two-sided, have always mattered, still matter, and, as long as men remain what they are, will continue to matter.

6

The Joy of Combat

At all times and places, most men have probably hated war for the discomfort and the hardship it involves, the violence, the havoc, and the bloodshed it causes, and the grief and desolation it leaves in its wake. At all times and places, very often this hatred did not prevent men—even the same men—from enjoying it. They eagerly looked forward to it, reveled in it, and looked back on it with pride and satisfaction when it was over.

To begin at the beginning, at least one modern commentator has argued that Homer "deconstructs" and "subverts" the values of war even while he appears to celebrate them.[1] It is certainly true that he often calls war "awful" and terrible"; in particular, the last of the twenty-four books of the *Iliad* is entirely devoted to the pity and the sorrow. All the more remarkable, therefore, to find in it the following description of King Agamemnon, a hot-tempered character but not a particularly bloodthirsty one, in the full fury of action:

> [First] he struck Pisander with his spear, in the chest;
> off his chariot he fell, on his back, face up.
> Hippolochus leaped off; on the ground, the king slew him,
> lopped off his arms with his sword, cut off his head,
> and rolled him forward like a log in the throng.

He left them there, and hurried to the place
where the fighting was fiercest, sweeping the Achaeans along.
Foot soldiers killed foot soldiers, mounted men, their fleeing foes,
and the dust rose from under the thundering steeds' hooves.
With copper arms they fought, while King Agamemnon
felled men all around him, and led the way.
Just as a fire consumes a thicket that has never been pruned
raging all around, bringing down the tallest trees—
so did Agamemnon, the mighty man, make Trojan heads roll.
Horses galloped about, without a hand to guide them.
Men's bodies, once their wives' joy, were torn by the kites.
While Zeus plucked Hector from the darts and the dust—
keeping him from battle, blood, and the horrors of war—
Agamemnon pursued them, cheering on the Danaans.
The Trojans fled headlong. They ran through the field
past the ancient grave of Ilus, past the fig-crowned hill—
crowding to escape; but Agamemnon still pressed them.
He pursued, he roared, his hands all dripping with gore.
At the great oak, near to the Scaean gate,
they paused, waiting for the others to catch up.
And they too were in headlong flight, stampeding in terror
like cows caught by a lion as the time for milking comes.
He seizes one of them; with his mighty teeth
He breaks her neck, laps her blood, devours her guts.
Thus did mighty Agamemnon, son of Atreus, pursue the foe
killing the laggards, even as they fled.[2]

Two millennia later, Jean de Bueil in the *Jouvencel* had the following
to say about the matter:

War is a joyous thing: one hears and sees many good things and
learns much of value in war. One loves one's comrade so in war. One
thinks to oneself: Shall I let this tyrant by his cruelty take the property of one who has nothing? When one sees that one's cause is good
and one's blood is hot, tears come to one's eyes. There comes in the
heart a sweet feeling of loyalty and tenderness to see one's friend,
who so valiantly exposes his body to accomplish the commands of
our Creator. And then one determines to live or die with him, and
because of affection not to abandon him. From that resolve come
such a joy that he who has not experienced it cannot rightly say

what it is like. Do you think that a man who does that fears death? Not at all; for he is so strengthened, he is so joyful, that he does not know where he is. Truly, he is afraid of nothing. I believe that he is happy in this world and in the next, he who serves the profession of arms in this way, and that he is a true servant of God.[3]

Back in 1992, I asked a class of U.S. Marine Corps officers how many of them had been in the Gulf and how many of them would have missed it "for their lives." After the first question, some two hundred hands went up. After the second, every single one went down.

Quotes from Robert E. Lee ("It is good war is so terrible, or else we would love it too much"), Winston Churchill (for whom war had a "hideous fascination"), Adolf Hitler ("I passionately loved soldiering"), George S. Patton ("how I love war"), Moshe Dayan ("I know of nothing more exciting than war"), Ariel Sharon (telling a group of students about the October 1973 war, "We had a *great* time, didn't we?"), and countless others confirm how enjoyable war can be, and often is. Some such statements originate in the most unexpected quarters. Take Wilfred Owen, the British World War I officer best remembered as the author of violently antiwar poems such as "Dulce et Decorum Est." This is the very same man who, on another occasion, wrote that "there was extraordinary exultation in the act of slowly [going over the top and] walking forward, showing ourselves openly." The same is true of Guy Sajer, a Wehrmacht soldier whose memoirs evoke the terror of war as few other works have. Yet at one point he speaks of the "almost drunken exhilaration" that follows fear (and which can make "the most innocent youths on whatever side to commit inconceivable atrocities").[4]

Michael Herr was a Vietnam-era war correspondent who wrote a scathing account of the conflict. However, he also confessed that fighting and killing Vietcong left him with the "feeling you'd had when you were much, much younger and undressing a girl for the first time."[5] Expressions such as "gorgeously satisfying," "exultant satisfaction," "beautiful work" (all three referring to the act of bayonetting other people), and "the happiest moment of my life" abound. Some even come from the mouths of Christian priests whose lives are dedicated to serving the Lord.[6] Briefly, for every man who has ever said he loathed war, there was another one who felt that it was great "fun" and who "loved it" with all his heart.[7] At least for a time—and at least as long as things did not go

so badly that everything ran short, discomfort and suffering reached levels unimaginable in peace, the forces fell apart, defeat stared people in
the face, and they felt powerless to help their nearest and dearest.

Much more remarkable still, the same person will sometimes mix hatred for war and exultation in it in a single breath—proving, if proof were
needed, that the two are not separate but two sides of the same coin.
What follows is an exchange I had with a retired Israeli Air Force colonel
and squadron commander who, during the half-forgotten "War of
Attrition" of 1969–70, had flown a Phantom fighter jet against the
Egyptians over the Suez Canal. It emerged accidentally, as a result of him
expressing his disgust over the way Israel's government and general staff
had conducted the war. To my comment "As usual, it is the foot soldiers,
in your case pilots, who pay the price," he replied, "Let me tell you. Only
few have paid the price. We enjoyed the fighting, as fighter pilots who
seek fighting but hate wars. So young and hot we were, like children playing with wood-made guns."[8]

Just what is it that makes fighting as enjoyable an activity as it undoubtedly can be? In part, the answer is to be sought in the field of phys-
iology. The combination of violent movement and imminent danger
causes the brain and body to be flooded with dopamine and adrenaline;
this is a phenomenon that humans have in common with other animals.[9]
Here, however, what interests us is the psychological side of the question.

Building on our discussion of games, let us start by noting that, when
war and fighting begin in earnest, people take leave of the ordinary world,
entering a different one where normal rules of conduct cease to apply. As
tension rises, one's horizons shrink. Past and present, "because of" and
"in order to," are left behind, discarded the way a snake sheds its skin. So
are concerns, worries, obligations, relationships, and the many things
other people want of us and expect of us. In short, whatever was previously most important is forgotten and whatever was most oppressive is
lifted. This explains why some Australian veterans pointed to the
trenches as the happiest time in their lives, and they were certainly not
the only ones.[10]

Next comes the joy of grappling with and overcoming resistance.
Unlike many other dangerous kinds of game or sport, such as mountain
climbing or whitewater rafting, war pits us against the most powerful,
most intelligent, and most fearsome opponent of all, another man; compared to him and what he can do, every other challenge simply does not

count. Also, war is unique in that, alone among all games of strategy in which humans face each other, it does not have any rules that dictate what the enemy may do to us and we to him. It is the only one that permits, even requires, the mobilization not just of some human qualities but of all. Most of the time those qualities are like hounds on a chain—let them go and see where they fly.

As mortal danger stares people in the face, they seem to undergo a twofold process. On one hand, they bring the entire personality into play, no holds barred. At the same time there is an extraordinary focusing of the senses as everything superfluous is forgotten. The outcome is best described as a combination of concentration with lightheartedness and freedom—to speak, with Ernst Jünger, of a "pleasant kind of intoxication, the sort that one experiences, maybe, on a roller-coaster."[11] This is the kind of freedom most of us, but men perhaps more than women, keep seeking during most of our lives but experience only at rare moments, if at all—and which, since it is in a certain sense self-generated and can be neither granted nor imposed from outside, is perhaps the most absolute freedom a human being can experience.

If, for all these reasons, coping with death can be a source of joy, indeed the greatest possible joy, how about the other side of fighting, that is, killing? Some researchers have argued that killing does not come naturally to man. To make it possible, they say, it is first necessary to brutalize one's own side and dehumanize the enemy.[12] This seems to fly straight into the face of everything we know about war as it has been waged from the Stone Age on. From my terrier up, many animals seem to enjoy killing, seizing their prey, playing with it (as cats do), and never letting go until it is dead, when they proceed to carry and display the corpse as a trophy. So do many hunters, perhaps most. In this context it is by no means irrelevant that during perhaps 90 percent of our existence as a species, men hunted whereas women gathered. Whereas the former had the fun of the hunt bred into their genes, so to speak, the latter did not.

One reason why killing is, or at any rate can be, fun is because it involves overcoming resistance. Tearing up a living creature, drilling holes in it, breaking it to pieces, smashing it, doing away with it once and for all—speaking as a scholar whose self-imposed task in life is to try to understand people and society, if a greater manifestation of power exists, I would dearly like to know where to find it. There may be even more to the matter, however. Just as many weapons have a symbolic significance, so, as quite a number of direct quotes show, for men killing is often comparable to having sex.[13] Certainly doing so can easily lead to sexual excitement. As anybody who has taken part in war knows, no other activity will leave men feeling as ready, as driven, to discharge their seed into almost anything that moves.

Thus it comes as no surprise that the same terms are used for both activities. Ancient Greek, French, English, and modern Hebrew all provide examples of this; in these languages, one can "screw" an enemy just as one does a woman.[14] Furthermore, insofar as many cultures demand that warriors abstain from sex as long as hostilities last, doing the first may act as, and be deliberately used as, a substitute for the second. Things also work the other way around. The warrior who, having killed and seen his comrades being killed beside him, returns to find solace in a woman's embrace is a stock figure in the literature of all times and ages as well as in numerous works of art.[15]

Furthermore, for every person who kills, there are usually several who watch, whether in reality or, in modern life, by way of television and the movies. Quite a number of people even go to motor races specifically in the not-so-secret hope of seeing an accident take place; as long ago as ancient Rome, the same applied to chariot races. The more people that die and the more violent the way they do so, the louder the roar of the crowd and the more fun onlookers have both at the time and later, when telling those who were absent about what they saw (or claim to have seen). This is not necessarily because they are more bloodthirsty than average. Rather it is because, like the rest of us, they are simultaneously curious and afraid: afraid that something similar might happen to them, curious to know what it would feel like. Probably one reason why people so often enjoy killing is because it enables those who commit the act and watch it to come face-to-face with their fears. Since we must all face death in the end, inflicting it and seeing it inflicted could almost be called a form of psychotherapy.

Along with bloodshed comes destruction. To build is to cope and to overcome, but so is to destroy. Anyone who has ever watched children playing with wooden blocks or a Lego set knows that they enjoy destroying things just as much as, if not more than, putting them together; prevent them from doing the one and very likely they will cease doing the other. Without question the same is true of adults as well. Of course circumstances are almost infinitely varied, and various "rational" considerations, such as strategy and greed, will also help decide what is and is not destroyed in war. Still, at least as far back as the time when Alexander and his troops wrecked the royal Persian palace, the annals of war have always been full of acts of wanton destruction, including many that, as in this case, were committed for no better reason than that a drunken courtesan led an equally drunken band of warriors.[16]

Most destruction, like most of life itself, is merely banal. On occasion, however, it can be turned into artistry and carried to the point where it compels a sort of reluctant admiration, if not for the wisdom behind it, then for the imagination that was put into designing it and the fury it took to execute—as, for example, when King Sennacherib of Assyria boasted of having massacred the population of Babylon, demolished its buildings, and torn up the soil so it would wash into the sea; or when the Romans razed Carthage and seeded the soil on which it had stood with salt so it would never bear fruit again; or when Timur the Lame had pyramids built out of the skulls of his defeated enemies. Centuries after these acts were committed, they are still the subject of tales that make people shudder—in fact, the reason why they keep being told is precisely *because* they make people shudder. In the face of the evidence, it is useless to pretend that most people do not, or at any rate cannot, delight in destruction independently of any practical benefits that it may bring.

Both killing and destruction, of course, can also be the outcome of hatred and revenge. For reasons that are hard to understand, the role hatred plays in war has only rarely been made the subject of scholarly investigation.[17] Yet it can hardly be overestimated; even if it is absent at the beginning, escalation—the inherent tendency of war to go to extremes, as Clausewitz[18] puts it—will almost certainly cause it to raise its ugly head. Since war often involves very large numbers of people, the hatred that is part of its causation and to which it gives rise is seldom personal. On the other hand, even in the largest modern wars, there are cases when it is—as when several hundred million people came to see in Adolf Hitler the source of all evil. However that may be, once hatred has been aroused the resulting wanton killing and destruction will cause the desire for revenge to appear. Not only is revenge one of the commonest causes of war,[19] but it is also one of the most powerful and least controllable emotions. Taking revenge, we feel that we "get our own back," as the saying goes, compensating for power we have lost and gaining what we did not previously have.

Whatever its precise sources, quite often the joy of destruction and killing is carried to extremes. It is entirely capable of making an otherwise reasonable and well-balanced person to take leave of his senses. Either it causes him to break down or else it drives him to the point where, to

quote Jünger again, it lends wings to his stride. With supple body, determined face, and bloodthirsty eyes, he is no longer capable of feeling fatigue, pity, remorse, or even the pain that is caused by wounds. Elated, he
is struck by "blind fury" and becomes "ecstatically happy." He is overcome by a "daemonic lightness," which is sometimes attended by irre-
pressible laughter, and he understands, "as in a flash of lightning, the true
inner purpose and form of [his] life."[20] He fights much harder than he ever
knew he could fight or that it was possible to fight. To fight this hard,
cause and consequence must be left behind and absolute concentration
achieved. In this way, however paradoxical it may sound, going through
war, the most serious activity of all, as if it were some lighthearted game
may actually make a crucial contribution to survival and victory.[21]

All this is summed up in what the ancient Greeks called "the dance of
Ares" and what the Scandinavians meant by a "berserker." In both cases,
the terminology is taken from the realm of the supernatural. Ares, of
course, was one of the Olympic gods and the one who, by adulterously
sleeping with the love goddess Aphrodite, begot both Harmonia and
Eros. Berserkers were supposedly possessed by the spirit of animals, especially bears and wolves, in whose skins they dressed and whose grunts
and howls they imitated. Both tales suggest that one very important way
to leave the natural world for the supernatural one is to fight. Doing so,
one may forget oneself in the same way as believers sometimes do while
praying, singing, leaping, dancing, fainting, speaking in tongues, contort-
ing and convulsing their bodies, and perhaps flagellating themselves.[22]

In the case of both saints and warriors (or at least saints and warriors
of a certain kind), it is possible, indeed appropriate, to speak of madness.
In the case of both saints and warriors, the saving grace is that madness
grows out of and is acted out in the name of a cause. A cause, I hasten to
add, is not the same as an interest. *Interest* is the name that, speaking of
important things such as war and politics, we give to the practical benefits we hope to derive from our actions. It is the pillar on which modern—
and, as Polybios shows, not only modern—strategic thought rests; it is
the column of fire that, marching in front of the host, points to the way
ahead. Reading the literature, one is tempted to misquote Alexander
Pope's rhyme about Isaac Newton: "Strategy's world was shrouded in
dark and night / God said let interest be, and all was light."

Of course it is true that interest plays a very large role in war, particularly at the top, where the weightiest decisions are made. Now as in
Polybios's day, those whose task is to lead their people to war must follow

what they see as that people's interest; failing to do so, they are criminals if the failure is advertent and madmen if it is not. Yet it is also true that only rarely does such an interest percolate down the ranks and take hold of most, let alone all, of those who fight. Menelaus and Agamemnon had an interest in getting Helen back (both for her own sake, as the most beautiful woman in the world, and to deter other attacks in the future), but the overwhelming majority of the quarter of a million men they allegedly led did not. President George W. Bush may have had some kind of interest in attacking Iraq, but the overwhelming majority of the American people—least of all the soldiers who had to take leave of their comfortable lives and travel halfway around the world—did not.

As is also shown by the fact that few of us reserve any particular admiration for those who die serving their interest during, let us say, a robbery, the closer to the fighting line and death one gets, the less relevant interest becomes. Men may be willing to fight for God, king, country, people, family, their unit, their mates, or whatever. But to say that they do so because they have some kind of continuing interest in what may happen to others—even to their nearest and dearest—once they have left this earth is a travesty of reality and an insult to the intelligence.

By definition, a cause must be more important, greater, nobler than oneself, or else it cannot be worth dying for. Almost by definition, to be worth dying for it must be more than simply grasped or understood with the aid of the intellect. It must be so understood, but it must also enter a man, as it were, take him over, consume him, and possess him; it is not so much the brain that we are talking about as the heart. Without question, a cause as powerful as this is itself a form of madness. And yet, at the same time, the fact that the warrior (and the saint) has a cause is precisely what separates him from the madman, tying him back to the real world even as, "fighting mad," he takes his leave of it. This applies even to a berserker and even if, at the time he is possessed, he commits such terrible deeds as would cause nature itself to rise and vomit, so to speak.

As usual, it is Homer who provides the perfect illustration of this. Enraged by the death of his friend Patroclos and reconciled with King Agamemnon, Achilles stops sulking and resumes the fight. He kills so many Trojans, some of them as they kneel in front of him begging for mercy, as to make the river Scamander run with blood; the river god becomes angry at this and tries to drown him.[23] Having barely escaped with his life, he goes on to kill Hector and mutilate his body, the latter being a crime that really puts him beyond the pale of civilization as the Greeks, as well as most people coming after them, understood that term. And yet, throughout this tale of horror, there is not the slightest hint of "interest" on his part. Which is why, having repented, he is forgiven in the end.

So far, we have spoken of the individual. For good or evil, though, war is a collective enterprise and not an individual one. The very fact that people are under pressure (as long as the pressure is not so great as to push them beyond the breaking point) will cause them to come together, ending their existence as isolated atoms and forging them into a group. Things also work the other way around: if a cause had been lacking, then the mere creation of a group that is more than a gathering of atoms accidentally thrown together will quickly, almost miraculously, provide it. The combination of cause and outside pressure is, of course, much more intensive in war than in ordinary social life. Between them they can easily bring people to the point where they cease looking after their own interest. They cease to be themselves while at the same time becoming part of something much larger and more powerful. Feeling oneself part of something much larger and more powerful brings, yes, joy.

In the modern strategic literature, a favorite term is "force multiplier." By it is meant some factor—usually some kind of sensor, computer, data link, or precision-guided missile—that can greatly increase the ability of an army of a given size to carry out its mission and defeat its enemy. Too often, what is overlooked, or perhaps merely taken for granted, is that no other force multiplier is nearly as powerful as the sense of belonging or cohesion just described. Cohesion is what turns a unit, formation, or army from a gathering of people accidentally thrown together into a machine capable of setting goals for itself, fighting to reach them, and overcoming obstacles and taking losses as it does so; it is cohesion that enables a handful of guards to control thousands of prisoners. Conversely, without cohesion one cannot conduct war. I have set forth the organizational factors that make for cohesion in another volume.[24] Here I want to look at the cultural side of the question.

Cohesion both generates the ability to do things in a coordinated way—including the hardest thing of all, marching into battle and fighting—and is the result of doing those things. Training and education apart, as far back as we can look armies have employed a whole series of devices to help create it. Some appealed to the eye, others to the ear. Others still involved rhythmical movement or cadence. Among the oldest and best known of these devices are flags, banners, and standards. As developed in Rome, for example, originally standards acted as markers and rallying points as well as helping to command the legions and their subordinate units. In the last-named task, so important were they that many evolutions were themselves called after the signals in question, such as *signa tollere* (attention), *signa movere* (dismiss), *signa ferre* (forward march), *signa constituere* (halt), *signa inferre* (attack), *signa convertere* (about-face), *signa refere* (retire), *signa ad laevam ferre* (left turn), *signa obicere* (counterattack), and others.[25]

Standards were normally made in the form of animals or else provided with a cross piece or flag; in imperial times, the image of the emperor was added.[26] Most of the time they were kept in a kind of shrine and carefully guarded. They accompanied the forces on the march, and when a new camp was pitched they were the first to be ceremoniously pitched into the ground. Their importance may be judged from the many references to them in both literature and art. Here and there standards were even used tactically; by deliberately putting them at risk, a commander could force the troops to come to the rescue. To lose a standard to the enemy was considered the ultimate disgrace. Augustus arranged great celebrations when he obtained the return of the military standards lost by Crassus in Parthia over thirty years before, and he even had that fact recorded in his official *Res Gestae Divi Augusti,* or list of deeds. After Varus lost his three legions in Germany in A.D. 9 no effort was spared to find their standards.[27]

Another very important factor in cohesion is music. From an evolutionary point of view, music probably had its origins in the desire to display and attract a mate, as among songbirds.[28] From very early on, it was also deliberately used to create and maintain bonds among people, specifically including the very powerful bonds that war and fighting require. Many tribal warriors all over the world enter battle to the sound of musical instruments of every kind, be they horns or conches or instruments made out of elephants' tusks, as well as singing. From ancient Greece we have at least one painting of two phalanxes about to clash head-on, accompanied by a young flute player who looks as if he is trying to pierce the very heavens with his tunes. Roman legions came with their *tubicen* (trumpets) and *cornicen* (horns), apparently using them to draw the troops' attention to the orders the standards conveyed.

Historically many armies have deliberately sought to produce outlandish sounds, from yells to blasts of the trumpet, to intimidate and demoralize the enemy. In close combat, this is by no means rare even today. The interesting point is that doing so inevitably tasks the lungs and consumes oxygen, indicating the role culture may be allowed to play even if, considered realistically, it means an unnecessary expenditure of physical energy. Cultural differences are also important, since what some people experience as a cacophony sounds like music in the ears of others. Still, there is good reason to think that underneath the cultural differences that separate peoples, there is some psychological or even biological basis for all this. This is proved by the fact that in martial music around the world, strings are rarely used. Wherever we look, the main (usually the only) instruments are various kinds of wind instruments and percussion. The drum, a Chinese invention, seems to have been imported into Europe sometime during the fifteenth century. So hypnotic is its sound that, as at the Union monument at Gettysburg, it was often used as one of the symbols of armed force.

From the time the first regiments were established in the sixteenth century, every one of them had musicians as a matter of course. Toward 1700, possibly imitating a model originally provided by the Ottoman janissaries, those musicians started to be formed into real bands. The bands would play not only on the march, when they were very useful in countering fatigue, but strike up immediately before and even during battle.[29] In addition to popular tunes known throughout the army, each regiment had its own tune, thus strengthening cohesion still further; in the British army to this day, every officer from colonel on up has his so-called personal tune. The importance of music in creating a fighting spirit is brought out by the fact that following his victory over the Scots at Culloden in 1745, the Duke of Cumberland ordered captured bagpipes to be treated as "weapons of war" and smashed.

As armies grew during the nineteenth century the number of bands continued to increase. Certainly the military tunes were not to everybody's taste. On the other hand, the idea that everything military was necessarily inferior had not yet been born. Even in Britain, a nation of shopkeepers, military bands were considered inspiring enough to be invited to play at private social functions, such as parties and weddings, as well as public ones, such as dedications of buildings, bridges, and even churches. In 1819, after the public had been excluded from the Sunday performances of the Coldstream Guards' band at the Tower of London, the outcome was a flood of angry letters to the editor of the *United Services Journal*.[30] In 1914, the German army alone had no fewer than 560 bands.[31] In both world wars we hear of British troops leaving their trenches and attacking to the sound of bagpipes. Preparing for a last, desperate charge on the river Oder in 1945, German troops tuned their tank radios so that Wagner's "March of the Valkyries" would blare out of each and every one of them.

At all times and places, music has been capable of stirring people, rousing them, inspiring them with courage, even driving them out of their minds until they are no longer themselves. In martial music of the type familiar to modern Western people, rhythm, simple repetition of the same sounds, and the building of tension by playing the same tune at a higher and higher pitch are all deliberately used in order to achieve this. Whenever a martial band strikes up, there are few people in the audience who are not stirred to all kinds of semi-voluntary movement, such as tapping their feet, stamping with their legs, swinging their arms, and emphatically nodding their heads. Psychologists would no doubt explain that the people in question are being reduced from fully conscious humans into some kind of more primitive state of being, whereas snobs would say that they become machines. No matter; even if the charges are true, music still remains an essential part of the culture of war.

If music seems to appeal to some deeply rooted human need for rhythm, so does drill, to an even greater extent.[32] According to legend, Albert Einstein once said that in providing a brain to men who march in step, God has wasted His time, because to do that a spinal cord was

The drummer boy as the symbol of war: Thomas Nashe's *Reveille,* 1863
HARPER'S WEEKLY, 1863

enough. One understands what he meant, but this does not change the fact that, as every army under the sun knows, drill and marching are powerful instruments in building up cohesion and esprit de corps. What is less often noted, but in fact is self-evident, is how very enjoyable they can be. The following verse originated at the height of World War I. The author was not some Prussian militarist but a famous antiwar poet and conscientious objector (the reader will learn more about him in chapter 10). Nevertheless, he put his finger on the feeling in question:

> The barrack-square, washed clean with rain,
> Shines wet and wintry-grey and cold.
> Young Fusiliers, strong-legged and bold,
> March and wheel and march again.
> The sun looks over the barrack gate,
> Warm and white with glaring shine,
> To watch the soldiers of the Line
> That life has hired to fight with fate.
>
> Fall out: the long parades are done.
> Up comes the dark; down goes the sun.
> The square is walled with windowed light.
> Sleep well, you lusty Fusiliers;
> Shut your brave eyes on sense and sight,
> And banish from your dreamless ears
> The bugle's dying notes that say,
> "Another night; another day."[33]

Almost half a century after leaving the army, a famous American historian also recorded, not without surprise, how much he had liked "strutting around" on the parade ground.[34] "Words," he wrote, "are inadequate to describe the emotion aroused by the prolonged movement in unison that drilling involved. A sense of pervasive well-being is what I recall; more specifically, a strange sense of personal enlargement; a sort of swelling out, becoming bigger than life, thanks to participation in a collective ritual."

In today's world, troops exercising and marching in cadence, with or without the accompaniment of music, may be seen almost exclusively during drill and on parade. During much of history the situation was very different. Battles themselves constituted the greatest parades of all, which, as we saw, is one reason why warriors' bodies, armor, dress, and weapons were often as heavily decorated as they were. Every pitched battle (French, *bataille rangée*) would start with commanders arraying or marshaling their troops (which explains how field marshals got batons). Usually, though not invariably, they did so in full view of the enemy, and often they and their subordinates used ropes and similar means to mark the location of units. So important was the order of battle that in many Greek and Roman accounts it is given as much or more space than the actual combat. One can only guess that the historians who wrote the accounts derived a certain intellectual satisfaction from explaining how commanders did these things and why. By comparison, the fighting itself was a rough, confused, primitive business very difficult to describe in any kind of coherent way.

Obviously societies whose normal tactics consisted of sudden raids and ambushes did not need drill as much as those that gave battle, which explains why so many tribal societies did not have it but contented themselves with war dances instead. Even among armies of more complex societies, considerable differences existed. Drill was most suitable for the training and employment of heavy (later so-called line) infantry. By contrast, light troops and skirmishers relied on it much less; for them, war was much more a question of ambushes, raids, and skirmishes. Horsemen occupy much more space, and are more mobile, than infantrymen. This made it hard for signals to be seen and heard, with the result that cavalry could only be drilled in relatively small units. Still, even after taking all these factors into account, from the time the Greek phalanx beat the Persians at Marathon on, the most highly developed and, over the long run, most effective armies were those that not only used drill but drilled a lot.[35]

From ancient Egypt and Babylon come models and reliefs of soldiers in phalanx so vivid that one can almost hear them tramp. Detailed information about the complex evolutions of Greek and Macedonian phalanxes is provided by the first-century B.C. writer Asclepiodotus, albeit by his time such tactics had been rendered hopelessly out of date. Coming to the end of his work, he leaves no doubt that they were intended not just for the barracks but for the battlefield, too.[36] Here is one modern historian's description of how the Roman army marched into battle:

> The manipular legion was designed for fighting pitched battles . . . When a Roman army was close to the enemy, the legions marched in three parallel columns, the *hastati* on the left, the *principes* in the

center and the *triarii* on the right. To deploy into battle formation
these columns wheeled to the right to form the triplex *acies*. Each
maniple had to be positioned carefully in relation to its neighbors in
its own and the other two lines to ensure that the legion's front was
properly and uniformly supported. Even when the army had
camped only a few kilometers from the enemy it still formed itself
into three columns and marched to within one and a half kilometers
or less of the enemy position, and then, at the point which would
form the left of the army's position, wheeled to the right and
marched along the army's intended front to form the *triplex acies*.
It was a time-consuming process, even in an experienced and well-
drilled army, the whole column having to stop and wait as each maniple reached its appointed position and closed up from marching
formation into battle formation, before it could move forward again.
Deploying a Roman army took hours, and required constant supervision from the tribunes.[37]

Since the range at which armies engaged one another seldom exceeded a hundred yards, which is when bows and arrows would come
into play, all this could be done in relative safety.

In Roman times and later, armies entering battle did so in tight formation. In the Greek phalanx, according to Thucydides, soldiers were packed
so closely together that each man could shelter behind the shield of his
neighbor to the right, causing the entire formation to veer in that direction.[38] Even later, when spaces became a little larger, armies that operated
in this way faced two main problems. First, since marching was carried out
in column, whereas to fight an army had to spread out—some more so,
some less—the process of deployment tended to be slow and laborious.
Second, once an army had deployed and was facing the enemy, changing
the direction in which it moved was hard (sometimes, in the case of the
Macedonian phalanx, all but impossible) and might, if not carefully handled, lead to chaos and even disintegration. All this meant that formations
and cadence had to be maintained, as far as possible, even during battle,
with all the psychological consequences that this entails.

To what extent drill was used during the Middle Ages is hard to say.
Not only did feudal armies tend to be undisciplined, but the fact that the
most important forces consisted of mounted men made reliance on drill
problematic. Written sources refer to it rarely, if at all; on the other hand,
from about 1350 on we do have pictures that show hosts of armored soldiers, presumably dismounted knights (since few others can have owned

complete armor) marching or confronting one another in tight formation. Be this as it may, there is no question that the Swiss phalanxes, which started making their impact felt during the fourteenth century, did march in step and did carry out evolutions, skills they could only have acquired and kept up by engaging in close-order drill. The same applies to the 3,000-man-strong Spanish *tercios* that dominated European battlefields from the early sixteenth century. What is more, the *tercios* combined two weapons with very different characteristics, pikes and arquebuses. If anything, this made maintaining formation even more important and more complicated.

By the late sixteenth century, drill as practiced by these units had developed to the point that it was being imitated even as far away as China. Nevertheless, the commander usually credited with the introduction of drill into modern European armies is Maurice of Nassau, who led the Dutch in the revolt against Spain from 1584 on.[39] A highly educated man with knowledge of mathematics and the classics, Maurice looked to the Roman past for models. First, units were reduced in size and a new one, the battalion (corresponding to the Roman cohort), was created. Using drums—so much did they impress his countrymen that they declaimed ditties to imitate the sound they made—he taught the troops to march in step and perform evolutions, the most important of which, the countermarch, was taken straight from the ancient sources. Each movement necessary for loading and firing a musket or for using a pike was carefully analyzed and portrayed in drill books, the best known of which was produced by Jacob de Gheyn directly on Maurice's orders.[40] With officers and NCOs marching along and holding demi-pikes to instantly correct any soldier who moved out of line, all this was drilled into the troops until they could do it in their sleep.

The outcome was units capable of marching and firing volleys with machine-like precision, even as cannon thundered, muskets crackled, and clouds of white smoke billowed, and even as wounded men screamed and comrades went down right and left. From our point of view, more important even than military efficiency were the social and psychological consequences. The rank and file of seventeenth-century armies, like those of many others before and since, were usually made up of the flotsam and jetsam of society—"the scum of the earth, enlisted for drink," as the Duke of Wellington would say of his own troops two hundred years later. Drill, increasingly combined with uniforms, played a large part in turning these men into cohesive communities, membership in which made them proud of themselves. And of course, the fact that all this was done not merely by way of play, on the parade ground, but in real combat against real enemies added to the effect.

First the Swedish army, then the French and English ones, then the Russian one took over where Maurice left off. In particular, the Prussians, whose introduction to drill came at the hands (and the feet, since he was not above kicking his subordinates) of the "soldier-king" Frederick William I, were widely admired. Of them a contemporary, moving from one court to the next, wrote, "I never saw troops march with more order and state; it seemed as if they were all moved by one spring."[41] As flint-locks replaced muskets, bayonets were invented, and pikes were discarded, formations changed, growing longer and thinner. Nevertheless, soldiers remained fairly closely packed together; in 1800 each one took up perhaps twenty yards square, as opposed to two hundred times as much today.[42] Though reliance on lines increased, other formations, such as the column and the square, also remained in use. So did the need to deploy them, change their direction of march, and combine them with each other. Battles such as Rossbach and Leuthen (both in 1757) were decided partly by the unmatched precision with which the Prussian battalions maneuvered on the battlefield, marching, turning, holding their fire until they had come to close quarters with the enemy, halting, and letting loose two or three volleys per minute.

As a result, throughout the eighteenth century military writers continued to debate which formations were the best under what circumstances.[43] Even as late as the first decades of the nineteenth century writers such as Antoine-Henri de Jomini, who in some ways has the right to be called the founder of modern strategy, still took the trouble of discussing them in detail.[44] Reading the works in question and studying the relevant diagrams, one gets the impression that formations and tactics were considered to be almost identical. Most of the discussion was serious, or at any rate seriously meant. On occasion, though, some of those who designed the evolutions probably did so as much because they found the activity intellectually challenging, read fun, as for any other reason.

Even during the wars of the French Revolution and Napoleon, things remained much as they had always been. Battles were still parades, the greatest and most splendid parades of all. Tactical control continued to be exercised primarily by acoustic and visual means. This meant that music, especially trumpets and drums, and standards remained as important as they had ever been; for those in command, it was considered "ab-

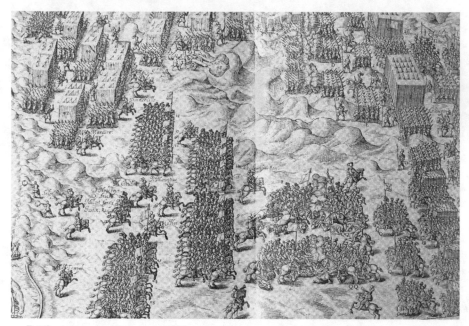

Battle as parade: Niewport, 1600   FROM *DE NASSAUSCHEN LAURENCRANS*

solutely necessary that they should at all times know what space a company, or any other division of the battalion, will occupy."[45] Under such circumstances, it is scant wonder that soldiers were passionately attached
to their colors, as they were now called. In each regiment, the colors were
carried by the most stalwart, most trustworthy men, known as
Fahnenjunker in German and as ensigns in English. Since the colors attracted the enemy, theirs was a dangerous job; hence, often they received
some special badge as well as special pay. Men kissed their colors, risked
their lives for them, and very often fought over them.

    In every army, losing the colors in battle was considered the ultimate
disgrace. For example, Napoleon after the Battle of Austerlitz awarded
one of his regiments a new eagle. However, he did so only after being informed about how the old one had been lost; as it turned out, the ensign
who carried it was killed, but his death went unnoticed among the confusion and the smoke. He then used the occasion to strengthen the men's
motivation, making them swear they would defend their eagle to the
death. Ten years later, a British unit that lost its standard at Waterloo had
another made in secret so as to avoid the stigma.[46] Conversely, the capture of an enemy flag was regarded as a great feat, and the soldiers who
accomplished it could expect a special reward.

Whereas the presentation of new colors was an important ritual, abusing them was subject to severe sanctions. As one British officer wrote: "The colours are always to be treated with the highest respect, any non-commissioned officers or soldier ever found to fail in this particular, either in conduct or language, shall be instantly brought to a court martial, and punished, in a most exemplary and severe manner."[47] Colors that had been damaged by enemy fire were considered special proof of valor, a fact that sometimes caused soldiers to deliberately place them, and thus themselves, in harm's way. Going on the parades that constituted battle, units competed to take up the place of honor, normally on the right, which traditionally led the attack and was thus often the most dangerous one of all. As a result, other things being equal, the higher a regiment's serial number the more likely it was to find itself near the left end of the array.

It was only during the 1860s that all this started to disappear—but not because commanders considered that the psychology of the troops had suddenly changed or wanted it to. Shortly after winning the Battle of Koeniggraetz in 1866, Moltke drew the lessons from it, writing that too many commanders had lost control of their units and that some way would have to be found to correct this problem,[48] to no avail. For millennia on end, the soldiers of some of the most powerful armies that ever existed had entered battle as well attired, armored, and decorated as their financial means, or those of their employers, permitted. They had stood up in parade-like formations, marched to the sound of some kind of music, and proudly held their standards aloft. Now, at last, firepower caught up with them, relegating much of this to the scrap heap.

Modern technology in the form of rifled breech-loaders and the weapons that followed them altered the skills demanded of the soldier. However, it did not do one thing to change the qualities of the warrior or the essential character of war itself. Realizing this, military organizations did not suddenly abandon standards, parades, music, and decorative attire of every kind. The former two had to be limited either to training or to ceremonial occasions (in 1945, during the victory parade held by the Red Army in Moscow, captured German standards were carried upside down and then thrown in a heap at Stalin's feet). The same applied to music, even though, as noted, it could still sometimes be broadcast on the radio, used to stir up feelings, and inspire heroic, even desperate deeds. Uniforms shed most of their former magnificence and became simpler. Nevertheless, men's urge to distinguish themselves from their comrades did not disappear. All it did was express itself in all kinds of other ways.

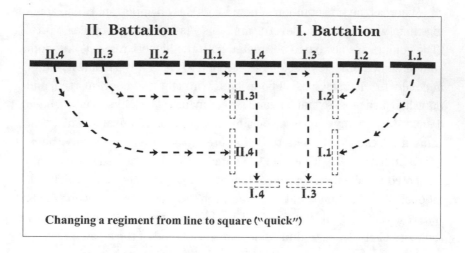

Changing a regiment from line to square ("quick")

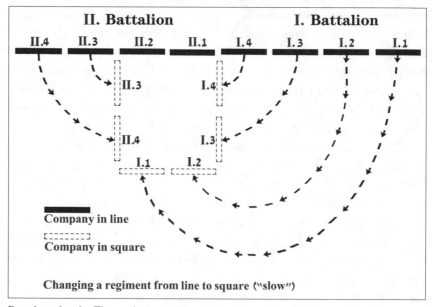

Company in line

Company in square

Changing a regiment from line to square ("slow")

Parade as battle: The evolutions of an eighteenth-century infantry regiment

In other respects, things changed little if at all. Now that military movement was increasingly carried out by vehicle and not on foot, soldiers driving into combat, even fighting, still derived immense satisfaction from seeing themselves part of a large, well-coordinated force that engulfed them and caused them to lose themselves inside itself. Partly because they saw themselves as part of a large force, partly because of the extreme pressure they came under, men continued to form cohesive groups. Once they had formed such a group they continued to experience, and often relish, a kind of comradeship rarely found elsewhere. They also continued to embrace causes of every sort and, in doing so, discarded their own interests even as, in another sense, they were fighting to realize them.

As had always been the case, war itself still consisted of long periods of discomfort and tedium, occasionally relieved by the arrival of a letter from home, a hot cup of tea to drink, the sound of music coming from the neighboring trench, and the presence of some animal such as an adopted stray dog. These periods were also punctuated at irregular intervals by moments of sheer terror and the most violent, most brutal, action imaginable. Certainly the violent action, and perhaps on occasion the terror as well, continued to have their own attraction; whatever proponents of political correctness may say, the same applied to destroying and killing. War also still involved grappling with the most powerful, most intelligent, most dangerous opponent of all. To quote Nietzsche, victory in it still remained the best cure for the soul; and, since testosterone levels are said to rise after a victory and fall after a defeat, not just the soul but the hormones as well.[49] Those who engaged in it still took leave of the world, with all the psychological consequences that this entails, and they still found themselves in a sphere where, since "because of" and "in order to" do not apply, there is a kind of freedom perhaps not found anywhere else. Finally, men still found it quite possible to hate war and love fighting at one and the same time.

Now as before, war was still capable of producing aesthetic effects *sans pareil*. As one historian of ancient Greece notes, a fully armed phalanx on the move, like a trireme with its oars in motion, was a "terrifyingly beautiful" object.[50] The same can still apply to a tank battalion charging, a warship breaking through the waves, the lines of tracer and flashes of guns being fired at night, searchlights looking for enemy aircraft in order to shoot them down, the trails fighter aircraft leave as they circle each other in combat, and the like. There simply is no question but that war can create color, movement, variety, and panoramic sweep. Here and there it even creates proportion and harmony.

From the time when medieval warriors stopped fighting, leaned on their swords, and watched as champions fought it out to the time when Israelis in 1991 mounted the roofs so as to see the Patriot missiles rising to intercept the Iraqi Scuds, all of this has always bewitched people, intoxicated them, and made them forget themselves.[51] Eager to see what is going on, they may jostle one another and ignore danger; at the same time, very often they are aware of how unusual, how out of the ordinary, what they witness is. They may seek to capture it by taking photographs, only to be disappointed when, as almost always happens, the results fall far short of expressing what they saw and felt. Many forms of modern art also use destruction (destructivism, brutalism), movement (kinetic art), and distorted forms (cubism, surrealism), but none of them can even remotely compete with real-life war. In the film *Jarhead,* the sergeant watches spellbound as the burning Kuwaiti oilfields create darkness at noon. So much does the spectacle move him that he exclaims, "I *love* this job."

A decade or so after the end of World War I, Freud published *Civilization and Its Discontents* with the objective of understanding the appalling death and destruction of war. In this work, he argued that the restraints that men, trying to lead a civilized life in common with other men, impose on minds and bodies—both their own and those of others—run counter to the basic drives underpinning the very minds that created those restraints.[52] If this is indeed true, then it comes as scant surprise that people are always looking for ways to break free, if only by pretending that the world, and they themselves, have ceased to be what they are; if only to a limited extent; and if only for a short period, after which they return to their senses, as the saying goes.

At all times and places, people have used a vast number of methods to reach this goal. They include alcohol ("the fastest way out of Liverpool"), drugs, games, sport, music, dancing, and every other sort of rhythmic movement, colorful display, ceremonial, religious worship, love, sex, aggression, and, yes, violent conflict up to and including war. Very often several of these methods are used at the same time. As a result, it would be hard to say whether it is these methods that lead to ecstasy or, to the contrary, ecstasy that leads to the methods being used; in which case, of course, they cease to be methods. Since even animals seem to experience at least some of this, he or she who does not do so must surely be a god. But if the meaning of being a god is never to be able to escape the bonds of rationality and interest, who wants to be a god?

7

The Rules of War

I f, comparing war with games, I said that war is a game without rules, here I am going to argue that, in another sense, war without rules is impossible. The reason why it is impossible is because war is an *organized* activity; whereas an organization without rules is a contradiction in terms.[1] One could go a step further still. Many scholars believe that one thing war does, or can do, is to provide an outlet for social tensions that may lead to chaos if they are not relieved.[2] What is seldom noticed, however, is that the way it achieves this goal is by channeling the tensions in question, pointing them in this or that direction, and surrounding them with all kinds of rules.

In all societies and at all times and places, some kinds of behavior, under some kinds of circumstances, for some kinds of reasons, with some kinds of goals, toward some kinds of people are considered part of war, whereas others are not. The former are required, cultivated, praised, rewarded, whereas the latter are rejected, excoriated, condemned, sometimes even punished. True, the bulk of the warriors may merely be provided with a few simple rules; after all, not everybody who attends church is an expert on theology either. Yet the existence of a vast scholarly debate, which in Western culture goes back as far as Greece and Rome, proves that the rules are anything but easy to formulate or master.

A very good way to understand how complex the rules can be is to project ourselves into some past civilization, study the way it went about

waging war, and compile a list of behaviors that were or were not considered acceptable. This, after all, is just what the group of people known as
reenactors do. Trying to create an authentic impression of the U.S. Army
in World War II, for example, they regularly end up with handbooks comprising hundreds of rules spread over dozens of pages. Even so, it is impossible to cover every point. Many remain in dispute, confirming the idea
that no organized activity can take place without a body of agreed-on
rules; often the outcome is that different groups of reenactors split up
and go their separate ways. How much harder it would be to reconstruct
the wars of some Stone Age society where patterns of behavior, the ties
that held men and groups together, and ideas concerning what did and did
not comprise of culture were so different from our own as to be almost incomprehensible. Perhaps that is why, the further back in time any reenacted event, the less authentic—more "farby," as reenactors say—it tends
to be.[3]

The origins of the rules vary greatly. Some are based on more or less
explicit cost/benefit considerations; in other words, they reflect what
might be called "best practice." Often the objective is to avoid alienating
the local population. Good examples are Mao Zedong's prohibition on
plundering the civilian population during the Chinese Civil War and the
"rules of engagement" issued to every U.S. soldier in Vietnam. Other rules
are the result of cultural factors. They comprise the things that, in any
given society and very often for reasons that are really no reasons at all,
are "done" or "not done." Such things may be spelled out in Holy
Scripture or else orally transmitted, as, for example, is done in the Koran
and other early Islamic traditions.[4] A third kind originates in agreement,
tacit or explicit, written or unwritten, between the belligerents.

Here one must note that war, however cruel and fearful it may be, is
not necessarily a zero-sum game in which one side can gain something
only at the direct expense of the other. Instead, as we shall presently see,
there may be, indeed often are, situations in which they share certain interests even as they tear each other to pieces over others. Both common
sense and the equations of game theorists tell us that in such situations
those who over time consistently stick to the rules (while always on their
guard against those who do not) will end up by gaining an advantage.[5]
The reason why they gain an advantage is because they build up a reputation for fair dealing; such a reputation is not without its uses in finding
allies, in obtaining reciprocity, and even in bringing the conflict to an acceptable end. Conversely, there are always some people who, putting

their own immediate interests first, disregard the laws of gods and men and thereby endanger everybody else. When the time comes, they can expect to be dealt with by the other side, and perhaps their own, too.

As to the categories themselves, far from being separate, they are interrelated. While culture, custom, and the like are very important, obviously no set of norms that has its origins in them but which clearly obstructs the practical demands of war can survive for very long. Two-sided rules that originate in common interests but are regularly violated by one side will not survive either; as the goose disregards them, so will the gander. To these problems should be added difficulties of communication as well as the usual ability of humans to make words and concepts mean what they want them to mean. For all these reasons, deciding what does and does not fall within the rules, let alone why, is extraordinarily complicated; why else have entire legal departments staffed by highly trained lawyers? Here all I can do is to provide a few examples of the rules, how they work, and what an important part they form both of the culture of war and war itself.

For any kind of society to wage any kind of war, the first question that must be answered is who may be treated as an "enemy." Clearly people who form part of the society itself cannot be so treated, or else it would very soon fall apart. This, however, is only the beginning. The vast majority of societies do not draw a simple line between friends and enemies. Instead, enemies are divided into different kinds, each of which is supposed to be fought by different means and treated in different ways. A very good example of this is provided by the book of Deuteronomy, which distinguishes between no fewer than three different kinds of enemies.[6] First there are the Amalekites, a hereditary enemy specifically condemned by the Lord, who must be exterminated whenever and wherever encountered. Next there are the pre-Israelite inhabitants of the Land of Israel. They, too, must be exterminated, but in their case this is not because of any special hatred but because of what, in a modern context, might be called a *raison d'état.* Finally there are "ordinary" enemies. Any wars the Israelites may wage against them are seen as purely instrumental, and accordingly the treatment they are to receive is quite different. And even this threefold classification still does not take into account civil war against other Israelites, a possibility that Deuteronomy does not discuss but which was actually realized on at least two later occasions.[7]

Nor are tribal societies, ancient or modern, the only ones to see things in such a way. In classical Greece, a clear distinction was drawn between two main kinds of enemies, Greeks and barbarians. As to what this could mean, suffice it to recall Aristotle: "barbarians," he says, are, "by nature, slaves."[8] The Romans distinguished between *inimicus* and *hostis.*[9] The Koran distinguishes between war waged by Muslims against other Muslims, war waged against other "peoples of the book" such as Jews and Christians, war waged against heathens, war waged against apostates, and war waged against brigands.[10] Enemies of each category were supposed to be treated differently; for example, whereas unbelievers could be enslaved, Muslims could not. Naturally these differences were mirrored by the Christians who waged war on the Muslims themselves. Thus war against the Saracens was not waged on the same principles as war against fellow Christians, albeit as the Crusades went on and the two sides got to know each other better, the differences between them tended to diminish.

On more than one occasion, such distinctions also governed warfare within the medieval *res publica christiana.* Fighting one another, French, English, Flemish, and German soldiers behaved in one way. Fighting others, such as the Irish, the Welsh, the Scots, or the Slavs in the east, they often behaved in an entirely different way, casting off most restraints and laying about them in a truly horrible fashion. Contemporary writers such as Gerald of Wales (1146–1223) were, of course, well aware of this. To explain the difference, they adduced all kinds of geographical, social, cultural, and military reasons.[11] No matter. Here, all we are trying to do is show that differences between different kinds of enemies did exist and were recognized. Which means that, in waging war against them, different sets of rules were applied.

Far from waning away along with the Middle Ages, such ethnic and religious distinctions continue to apply even today. From the time of Vasco da Gama on, European nations usually applied one set of rules when fighting each other. They used a second when fighting the Ottomans, and a third in their encounters with people outside Europe and the Mediterranean world; these differences persisted for hundreds of years. In World War II the Germans applied one set of rules when fighting Western countries such as France and Britain. A different set was used when confronting the Soviets in the east, and a third when fighting "bandits" in the occupied countries; regarding the latter, distinctions were also made between the west and the east, including the southeast.

To stay with this example, even in a country as disrespectful of international norms as Nazi Germany was, the shift from one set of rules to another was anything but self-evident or automatic. In order to make sure his generals understood what he required of them and carried it out, Hitler at one point summoned them for a highly unusual meeting at his Berchtesgaden mountain retreat.[12] Later in the war, although there may have been no orders from the top, the American military saw things in a similar light and behaved in a similar way. For the GIs, fighting Germans in Italy or France was one thing, doing the same against the Japanese in the Pacific Theater another. In the latter, racist stereotypes were superimposed on the already harsh realities of an all-out war between states, leading to, as one author puts it, a "war without mercy."[13]

When enemies are not classified by their religious beliefs or ethnic origins, they may be classified by their status or the class to which they belong. Particularly in the Middle Ages, war between members of the chivalrous classes was completely different from war between them and the lower classes.[14] In the former, opponents would often, though of course not always, be spared; in the latter, seldom if ever. In part it was a question of simple expediency, given that knights often had property and could be put to ransom whereas many others did not and could not. In part it was a question of class solidarity that sometimes transcended momentary conflict, and in part perhaps the hope that the way one treated one's opponents, and the kind of reputation that one gained thereby, could come in handy in case the fortunes of war reversed themselves. Again, no matter. The essential point is that there existed different kinds of war attended by different kinds of rules, even if they were fairly vague, even if they were never clearly written down, and even if they were sometimes violated.

Yet another method is to divide opponents into those who have the right to wage war and those who do not. Legitimate belligerents are usually classified as enemies, illegitimate ones as rebels, conspirators, guerrillas, terrorists, robbers, bandits, or criminals. If only because reciprocity is expected, legitimate belligerents are often treated with a degree of consideration. Not seldom, as in the Netherlands since 1621 or so[15] and in the rest of Europe from the second half of the seventeenth century on, this is done on the basis of explicit treaties, which themselves may be either bilateral or multilateral.[16] On the other hand, showing mercy to illegitimate belligerents might cast doubt on one's own legitimacy. As a result, normally they can expect no quarter. To the contrary, very often they are treated in ways consciously and explicitly designed to serve as a warning to others—for example, by being crucified as were Spartacus's

men, and a century and a half after them the Jewish survivors of the
Great Revolt.

Needless to say, there were occasions when the distinction between
legitimate and illegitimate belligerents could lead to remarkable results.
Take the case of medieval Japan. Japan being an island, for centuries on
end it did not wage war against external enemies, with the result that all
wars were civil wars by definition. There was, however, a curious twist. In
war, Japanese-style, all parties always claimed to be fighting on behalf of
the emperor and against the evil men who had captured him or misled
him; much the same reasoning also applied in Confucian China. In both
countries, it followed that the losers were ipso facto rebels and treated
accordingly. The leaders were executed in all kinds of interesting ways.
The followers were perhaps more likely to be pardoned or incorporated
into the victor's army, but in principle there was nothing to prevent them
from being executed as well.[17]

Yet another way the rules may operate is to distinguish between
what, for lack of a better term, I shall call "active" opponents and the rest.
The former are those on the enemy side who participate in combat and,
doing so, either kill the members of one's own side or at any rate do their
best to achieve that result. Not so the latter; depending on the society in
question, they may watch from the sidelines, provide medical and logistic
support, form part of the social and economic infrastructure without
which no war can be fought, or simply stay at home while waiting for the
outcome. Since different societies had different forms of military organization, the precise way in which the lines were drawn, as well as the technical means used to keep the various categories apart, were not fixed but
varied very much from one to the next.

Tribal societies usually distinguished between adult men, on one
hand, and women and children, on the other.[18] So did societies of the ancient Middle East. Take the reliefs that used to decorate the royal palace
at Nineveh and which show the Assyrian siege of Lachish, Judea, in 705
B.C. In them, the men are shown impaled, whereas women and children
are led away, apparently unharmed. Although there were exceptions, by
and large Greek, especially Hellenistic Greek, and Roman armies observed
similar distinctions. Medieval jurists tried to distinguish between combatants and innocent people, the latter comprising not only women and children but those whom today we would call noncombatants.[19] In Europe
since the second half of the seventeenth century, the basic distinction was
between those who, wearing the king's coat (as uniforms were often

called), were authorized to fight and those who were not. The former had it coming to them while the fighting lasted but were supposed to be protected once, for one reason or another, they were hors de combat; with the latter, the opposite was the case.[20] Reflecting the problem of the *franc-tireurs* that had arisen in the Franco-Prussian War of 1870–71, the international conventions signed during the early years of the twentieth century added the idea that even irregulars were entitled to certain forms of treatment. Provided, that is, they wore a distinguishing mark or dress, carried their arms "openly," and obeyed a clear chain of command.[21]

Whatever the precise categories adopted, very often the objective of the rules is to prevent escalation. To the side that is gaining the upper hand, pouring oil on the waters may be desirable in order to persuade the other to relax his efforts, refrain from going berserk, and perhaps surrender. On the side that is about to lose, doing the same may very well be the only way to avoid reprisals, even to make survival possible. Quite often, too, neither side is able to achieve a decisive victory. There may even be situations in which they do not want to—for example, with an eye to preserving the balance of power and turning an enemy into an ally in the not too remote future. In 1815, such considerations prevented the Congress of Vienna from depriving France of territory conquered before 1792 or even dismembering it. In 1866, similar ones led Bismarck to conclude peace with Austria without any attempt at annexation. On top of all this, both sides may have a common interest in preserving the infrastructure so as to ensure that once the war is over, a more or less civilized life can resume.

At all times and places, perhaps the factors most likely to lead to escalation are perfidy and gratuitous injury. Concerning the former, something has already been said when we discussed declarations of war. Not all societies have the custom, and even those that do, sometimes violate it in order to gain advantages, such as surprise. Yet surely such declarations are issued (and expected) by enough societies, and sufficiently often, to make an unprejudiced observer conclude that there must be some real advantages to doing so. Certainly those who do not do so are considered worthy of condemnation and punishment. Of course the annals of warfare are full of sudden raids, ambushes, and the like. Yet probably at no time and at no place was launching a totally unprovoked attack on a totally unprepared enemy considered a great feat.

Declarations of war apart, perfidy may also be committed during the hostilities themselves. Good examples are the assassination of enemy leaders (a practice that under the name of "targeted killings," remains as controversial today as it has always been), breaking truces, wearing false uniforms and other distinguishing marks (a practice specifically prohibited under modern international law), resuming the fight after being granted quarter, and the like. In both medieval Europe and Japan, military codes served explicit warning against engaging in it. The same is true of the list of rules issued by Muhammad's immediate successor, Abu Bakr.[22] The reason why they did so was not simply because perfidy is not "nice." Rather, it was because it was incompatible with the warrior's highest quality, his honor—precisely the factor that, when things got tough, could still bind knights, samurai, tribesmen, and other kinds of warriors to their lords and cause them to do their duty even unto death. This did not rule out the use of ruses. Was not Frontinus's *Strategemata* one of the most popular military textbooks of the Middle Ages, and had not Sun Tzu roundly declared that all warfare is based on deceit?[23] The difference was that ruses were permitted, even expected; however, violating one's freely given word was not.

To illustrate what was meant by perfidy, consider the following two incidents. In 1173, Louis VII of France, investing the Norman border town of Verneuil, was on the point of victory when, to save himself a final effort, he offered the inhabitants a three-day truce after which, if help did not arrive, they were to surrender. Probably he had hoped his opponent, Henry I of England, would be unable to come to the town's assistance in so short a time; when the Normans appeared nevertheless, instead of keeping his word he set fire to the town and tried to escape (only to be pursued by Henry). Again in the next year, Louis invested Rouen. Making little headway, first he granted a one-day truce in honor of St. Lawrence, he said—and then, pressed by his advisers—or so others said on his behalf—violated it. Contemporaries found his conduct heinous and roundly condemned it. Had the opportunity presented itself, they would have treated him as he deserved. Then as now, perfidy is considered perhaps the worst offense of all, and enemies who committed it, or who are accused of committing it, are likely to be executed out of hand.

Gratuitous injury is most often committed against those who are unable to resist, that is, the various kinds of people who are not active combatants, however defined, and those who have ceased to resist, a group encompassing the wounded and prisoners. The wounded do not have to be discussed at length, as during most of history they were not considered a separate category at all. Naturally those who had been wounded in the fighting might ask for quarter, as other warriors also did. However, it was only in the last three centuries or so, and then only in the West, that people started looking at them as a special group with rights similar to those of prisoners. First hospitals were turned into sanctuaries. Next neutral representatives such as those of the Red Cross were permitted access to them, and finally conventions prohibiting the capture of medical personnel and arranging for enemy wounded to receive treatment similar to the one meted out to one's own troops were signed.[24] From the West the idea spread to many other parts of the world. Today, violating the rights of the wounded, let alone butchering them, is considered a serious offense indeed. It is also one that invites retaliation and, in this way, escalation.

Some societies, when engaging in some kinds of war, do not take any kind of prisoners at all. Either those who do not fight or have retired from the fight enjoy immunity or else, going to the opposite extreme, they are simply killed whenever possible. Still, by and large these are exceptions. One reason for taking prisoners is because they often can be valuable, whether by way of their labor (both men and women), as sexual partners and breeders (women), or as a future source of manpower (children). In addition, prisoners can be used for gloating as well as for ceremonial purposes, subjects that will be treated in the next chapter. However it is done, every society has its rules as to whether prisoners should be taken in which kinds of war; which categories of people should be taken prisoners and which not, and how they should be treated once they have been taken.

In Europe, for several hundred years past, it is only members of the opposing armed forces (or, in case of guerrilla warfare and terrorism, their supporters) who may be taken prisoner. This proposition also works the other way around. Regardless of what their actual function is, anybody in uniform is considered an enemy and may be captured; this applies to rear-area troops just as much as to combatants at the front. During much of history, things were different. Very often, not only warriors or soldiers but also noncombatant men, women, and children—in fact, all members of the enemy society—constituted fair game. To illustrate, among the Meru of Kenya, life revolved around herds of cattle. So important was the role of cattle rustling in warfare that a warrior who wanted to surrender would call out, "Take cattle." Then he would place all weapons in both hands, point them upward, and push them toward his opponent. The victor would take the weapons and use his own cape to cover his captive, thus symbolically taking possession. Since the objective was to make a captive's family pay ransom, and since a future reversal of fortune was not unlikely, captives were rarely maltreated.

This, however, was just the beginning. Not just men but uncircumcised girls and those who had already been "cut" but were still waiting to be married could be captured (the scholars who gathered the material seem to have forgotten to ask about the fate of married women). Rarely, however, were they maltreated. Custom dictated that they could not be claimed as concubines or wives by their captors; instead, they would be exchanged for cattle in the same way as males were. Another method was for the captor to adopt the girl as his daughter. Eventually he would marry her off to a man of another clan, in return for which he and his family would, once again, receive cattle.[25]

Enslaving women and children is one thing, treating grown men in the same way, another. Most tribal (and, later, feudal as well) societies did not have the organization needed for the purpose, with the result that male captives had to be either killed or let go for a ransom. The situation in the ancient Middle East, Greece, and Rome was different. First, government was stronger and more articulated. This by no means meant that male prisoners were always spared—Egyptian, Assyrian, and Roman monuments often show us their fate in grisly detail. It did, however, mean that large numbers of adult men could be kept in permanent bondage and their labor exploited both on behalf of individuals and that of society at large. Second, the armies of these peoples, being much larger but not faster, probably found it harder to achieve surprise. Going on campaign, they were likely to find the country they passed empty. Usually the population would escape and take refuge in fortified cities. As happened, to cite but one instance, when the Spartans invaded Attica during the Peloponnesian War.[26]

Once a city had fallen, and unless surrender terms had been negotiated first, it would be sacked. A sack could be spontaneous, the result of soldiers' lust for revenge and plunder. As often, though, it was deliberately ordered by the victorious commander with an eye to revenge—sieges tended to be expensive in terms of losses suffered—profit, and the intimidation of future enemies. In the latter case it could be organized very carefully indeed; and, being organized, made subject to rules just as war itself was.[27] Men, women, and children were all seen as fair game to be treated as, using Roman terminology, the *ius gentium* or *ius belli* dictated. Men would be either killed, perhaps after being subject to torture to force them to reveal their belongings, or enslaved. Women and children were also enslaved, the former after being raped first (although exceptionally beautiful women, or such who formed part of the aristocracy, might be spared either to be presented to commanders or in order to increase their value when the time for ransom came). The city itself either was razed, as Carthage was in 146 B.C., or rebuilt and provided with a new population, as Jerusalem was in A.D. 137. Going from victory to victory as they did, Roman armies in particular were accompanied by professional slave dealers, chains at the ready. They would buy the captives from the troops and take them to the market.[28] The list of cities that at one time or another suffered this fate is almost endless, including, besides the above two, Troy, Babylon, Syracuse, and Rome itself (at the hands of the Vandals).

In modern Europe, the last time a real sack took place was at Magdeburg in 1635 (although Bajadoz in 1811 came pretty close). In both cases the commanders, Tilly and Wellington respectively, blamed the troops for getting out of hand. Even so, these were not Roman times. It is true that, in both cases, large numbers of men, women, and children perished. It is also true that many women were raped and the cities themselves ransacked in search of valuables. Still, there could be no question of systematically destroying the cities, let alone of carrying off their populations and putting in new ones. Children, women, and even men who had survived the initial fury were not taken prisoner or enslaved but allowed to resume their lives as best they could. Perhaps most important of all, whereas Xenophon had once written that "the losers' lives and property belong to the victors," by this time sacking a city was considered very much *hors du loi*. This explains why commanders, by claiming that the soldiers had acted on their own, took the trouble to apologize for what they had wrought.

By contrast, even Berlin, captured in the aftermath of the bloodiest war in modern history, was not sacked. Certainly there was plenty of robbery and rape. However, they were not carried out in an organized way. At no time did the Soviet high command issue orders, or even allow its troops to kill and destroy indiscriminately. As a result, paradoxically, such German men as were present, most of them either quite old or very young, had less to fear than German women did.[29] Yet this and many similar episodes do not mean that man is finally turning into a kinder, gentler animal. At most, one may say that those who break the rules are likely to be condemned, sometimes even punished; but that has always been the case. The real reason why enemy civilians, as opposed to enemy soldiers, are no longer captured is because from about 1700 on armies with their firearms became so powerful that mere civilians could not resist them anyhow.[30] As long as they did not resist, by and large conquerors found it more useful to treat them as part of the infrastructure on which they themselves relied. This situation, though, may not last forever. During the years since 1945 new forms of war, such as terrorism and guerrilla, have grown to the point where they are now almost the only ones left. The more important they are, the harder it becomes to maintain the distinction between combatants and noncombatants.[31]

In a modern economy based on free enterprise, slavery is generally regarded as inefficient. This probably explains why, although prisoners are often put to work, there can be no question of enslaving them. In this context, it is probably no accident that during and after World War II the only societies that deliberately captured and used large numbers of slave laborers were the totalitarian ones, Nazi Germany and the Soviet Union. Another factor has been the shift from polygamy (historically, most societies have been polygamous) toward monogamy. Along with modern contraceptives, this led to a highly peculiar idea: namely, that for a man to cheat on his wife is just as bad as for her to cheat on him. Alas for many men, the time when they could capture an enemy woman, take her home, sleep with her, and breed her is gone. But this does not mean that rape has less appeal for modern soldiers than it did in the past.

As already indicated, one possible objective of the rules of war may be the preservation of the economic infrastructure. Once again the Meru provide a good example of how it was done, or at any rate of how, in the glowing memories of old men speaking of long-dead traditions, it was supposed to be done: On one hand, the overriding objective of warfare was livestock rustling. On the other, engaging in it was considered not merely a serious business but also a game in which young warriors could discharge their energies and gain their spurs. Some care was taken to allow warriors to play the game without undue damage to the rest of society. Passing through their opponents' banana groves, raiders were permitted to take what they needed but forbidden to cut down or otherwise harm the trees. The same applied to fields of grain, yams, and arrowroot. Raiding parties could seize whatever they found within the enemy's huts but not destroy the huts proper. Weapons were seen as legitimate spoils of war, but agricultural tools were not. Warriors were forbidden to interfere with trade routes, both local ones and those linking the Meru with others. Such routes were solemnly marked in peacetime and were expected to remain open in wartime, too.

Rules broadly similar to those developed by the Meru may be observed in countless other societies as well. The Greeks had rules against poisoning wells and cutting down olive trees, which are notoriously slow to grow. The Koran has similar ones, as did medieval chivalrous custom.[32] Modern societies normally draw a line between military and civilian. The former may legitimately be attacked, bombed, demolished, and smashed to smithereens, while the latter may not. When William T. Sherman in 1864–65 made Georgia howl, this was precisely because, instead of observing the rules, he deliberately set out to violate them.[33] As might be expected, often there are problems of definition. Where does "civilian" end and "military" begin? Do the workers in an industrial district where munitions are produced form a legitimate target? Often the more complex a society, the harder it is to answer the question, the reason being that many kinds of equipment, communication and transportation arteries, and productive plants have dual uses. Still, most people would agree that *some* rules do exist and ought to be observed. Conversely, those who do not agree and target people and things indiscriminately are usually known as terrorists.

In this context it is necessary to say a word about the rules as they pertain to holy places and buildings. Under the modern law of war as it has existed for the last few centuries, such places are supposed to receive special attention and enjoy immunity. This is not because they are considered important; in a way, the contrary is true. In a secular society, the real reason why armies engaged in invading or bombing their enemies are supposed to spare churches and the like is precisely because most of us no longer believe that divine intervention may be, to speak with Machiavelli, "effective." Another reason may be the desire to avoid antagonizing the enemy population, as, for example, when Moshe Dayan ordered the Israeli army to take good care of the mosques on the Temple Mount after it occupied Jerusalem back in 1967.[34] Even so, the law says that holy sites, like the rest of the civilian infrastructure, must only be protected as far as "military necessity" permits.[35] In this way it provides a loophole wide enough to take not just a truck but a tank transporter, too.

Needless to say, previous societies had their own rules as to how these things should be done. To begin at the beginning, most tribal societies are closely identified with their gods. In fact, the belief in certain gods and not in others is precisely what distinguishes them from the rest and empowers them; consequently, when fighting other tribes, not only do they target the enemy's shrines, holy implements, and so on, but those implements and those shrines are often among the most important targets of all. Very good examples of this are provided by the Pentateuch, where the Lord explicitly commands the Israelites to smite not just their enemies but those enemies' gods as well.[36] Also included in the Bible is the story of the Ark of the Covenant. Ordinarily it was kept in the shrine, but at one point it was carried into battle as a miraculous rallying point and ended up being captured by the Philistines. So shaken was the prophet Eli when he heard the news that he fell off his chair, broke his neck, and died.[37]

Some readers may think that since tribal societies were small by definition, not too much should be made of them. This overlooks the fact that some of the mightiest empires ever—those of the ancient Middle East, the Arab ones, those of the Aztecs and the Inca—were in many ways little, but tribes writ large.[38] In these societies, rulers held their position by divine right. As a result, fighting those rulers also meant opposing the gods from whom they were descended or by whom they claimed to have been appointed. No wonder that when such empires waged war on each other or when other peoples tried to bring them down, religious objectives, far from being subject to special rules which protected them, were among the very first targets.

Here and there one may find really tolerant conquerors. Probably the best-known example is Rome. Of course, the Romans were by no means averse to robbing temples. Still, normally they would incorporate the gods of conquered peoples into their own pantheon.[39] Military and economic motives, not religious fury, determined what happened to the temples in question. Rome apart, most of the time the rules of war will only protect religious sites in two kinds of situations. One is when two or more belligerents profess the same faith. This was the case in ancient Greece and also in Europe before the Reformation. While in both societies there were cases when the rules were violated, each time an invasion threatened, people would take their belongings and pack them into the temples and churches; sometimes they succeeded in saving them in this way, sometimes not.[40] In Europe, this situation lasted until the Reformation and Counter-Reformation, when churches became targets par excellence. Next, after the Peace of Westphalia in 1648 caused religious passions to cool down, it more or less reasserted itself.

As already indicated, the other situation when religious assets are likely to be spared is when people no longer believe in God. Hence, "military necessity" permitting, they are content to treat such assets in the same way as they do others that have no special sort of holiness attached to them. It should, however, be noted that, in many cases, even self-styled "advanced" and "civilized" peoples are prepared to respect the rules concerning religious objects only as long as doing so does not carry negative consequences for themselves. For example, the British in 1900 relentlessly pursued the Golden Stool of the rebellious Ashanti tribe in the Gold Coast, present-day Ghana. Until, in the end, they succeeded in capturing it and planting their behinds on it.

Perhaps the most important set of rules of all, both in themselves and because they act as the necessary basis for all the rest, are those concerning communications between the belligerents. We have already seen how declarations of war are used to inform the enemy that one condition—that is, peace—has ended and been replaced by another in which different rules apply. Certainly not all war-making organizations issue such declarations. Some skip them altogether, and some publish them only as a kind of afterthought; still, there is no real proof that their use is in decline. For every modern state that breaks the rules in an effort to take the enemy by surprise and destroy its air force before it can even take off, one can find a terrorist organization that, seeking to draw supporters and perhaps gain some kind of legitimacy, publishes "manifestos" and declares "war" before starting to blow up things and kill people. In 1998 and again in 2000, the best-known terrorist organization of all, al-Qaeda, did just that.[42] In this case, as in many similar ones, the real problem was not that fair warning was not served but that nobody listened to what Osama bin Laden had to say.

Once hostilities have started, at least one side usually still considers it very important that some channels of communication remain open. One reason for this is to enable individual warriors and even entire units to surrender; though occasions when groups of people fight to the death do exist, they are perhaps less frequent than one might think. Another is to arrange truces and cease-fires, start peace negotiations, and the like. Truces in particular are very important. Were it not for them, waging war would be like traveling down a motorway that does not have places to stop, which is why, starting in the *Iliad,* the annals of warfare are full of them.[43] The most important reason for concluding a truce is to allow negotiations to take place, exchange prisoners, and the like. It may, however, also be used in setting up a kind of bet—as when a garrison,

hard-pressed, promises to surrender in so-and-so many days unless rein-
forcements arrive first. There are even occasions when truces are concluded simply to give both sides a break, as, for example, repeatedly
happened during the Vietnam War; and also when Israeli troops and
Hezbollah guerrillas in southern Lebanon arranged a cease-fire so both
could watch the world soccer championship on TV.

Since most war-making societies take prisoners, at least in some
kinds of war and under some circumstances, it is imperative that they
have more or less agreed-on methods to make surrender possible.
Probably the most common signals are visual ones, such as dropping
one's weapons, raising one's hands, going down on one's knees or even on
one's stomach, or, in the case of Rome, raising one's shield over one's
head. These forms of behavior are accompanied by appropriate verbal
formulae or other utterances whose purpose is to signify supplication.
Not only people but many kinds of animals are capable of giving such signals, recognizing them, and responding to them; as, for example, by turning tail, rolling over, or, in the case of females of many mammalian
species, crouching and presenting their behinds so the male may mount
them.[44] Backed as they are by a long evolutionary development, it is scant
surprise that the signals are still used even in the most recent conflicts
between the most advanced countries.

In case it is not individual soldiers but entire groups or units that
want to surrender or merely to parley, other methods are needed. One is
to employ a special class of envoys whose persons are sacrosanct and
who may therefore act as go-betweens. In both ancient Greece and medieval Europe, this was the task of heralds.[45] Europe also had a class of
people who belonged to a supranational organization, that is, the Church.
This, as well as the fact that the whole continent professed a single
religion, made it possible for ecclesiastics to be pressed into service as
intermediaries; churchmen, moreover, were prohibited from touching
weapons or shedding blood. Depending on conditions, other societies
have their own ways of doing these things and used other objects to make
their wishes known.[46] One of the most remarkable examples comes from
New Guinea. There making peace was regarded as women's work, the
reason being that women neither took part in war nor were considered
capable of doing so. As a result, delegations passing the "lines" regularly
included women.[47]

Returning to Europe, such methods only started to be abandoned
during the fifteenth and sixteenth centuries. First Italian city-states and

then other rulers started appointing permanent representatives in each other's courts, rendering the services of the Church and other go-betweens unnecessary.[48] At the same time, the advent of disciplined, semipermanent armed forces facilitated the development of rules that enabled armies to contact each other directly. To make sure that the envoys' identity and intent were not mistaken, often they carried flags of truce. The first time a white flag is mentioned is in China during the Eastern Han dynasty (A.D. 25–220). In Europe during the Middle Ages envoys sometimes wore a white tunic over their armor; just how this developed into the modern system is not clear.

Though signals indicating an individual's desire to surrender are as old as humanity or older, during most of history there was no obligation to take note of them; in other words, whether or not quarter was granted was entirely up to the warrior to whom the signals were addressed. Even as late as the first half of the seventeenth century, Hugo Grotius, discussing the problem, still did not cite any form of international law. Instead, he suggested that ordinary charity be brought to bear.[49] The situation of envoys was different. Regardless of who they were, it is hard to think of a time and place where they did not have a right to be heard, or at least allowed to depart unharmed. To disobey this rule has always been considered one of the worst "war crimes" of all. If, in the passage we have quoted and which describes Agamemnon's joy in battle, the king did not heed the pleas of Pisander and Hippolochus but mercilessly butchered them, then this was not because he was cruel; rather, it was because their father, Antimachus, had once suggested not only that the Achaean envoys' request for Helen should be turned down but that the envoys should be killed.[50]

By contrast, modern international law as it has developed since Grotius has tended to put matters upside down. Individuals who surrender in due form have a right to have their lives spared as well as to be decently treated during the captivity that follows.[51] Yet nothing obliges a belligerent to receive the envoys of the other side, let alone grant them a hearing. Sometimes such delegations, gingerly making their way across no-man's-land, are met by shots fired over their heads. If they do not take the hint and withdraw, then of course the next rounds may be aimed straight at them.

Not only do most societies have rules concerning the methods by which the desire to surrender may be signaled, but the concept itself implies certain forms of behavior concerning what the victor may do to the loser. Once again, let's use the *Iliad* as our example. For all the un-doubted savagery of Homeric warfare, Agamemnon, Odysseus, and the remaining heroes do seem to have recognized a standard formula under which cities might surrender. Under its terms, the defenders' depen-dents' lives and liberty would be spared, as would their own. This was done on condition that the losers swore not to conceal any of their be-longings and the victors would be allowed to take away half of them. At one point during the siege, Hector considered the possibility of making peace on such terms, only to reject the idea in the end.[52]

Almost without exception, the same applies to subsequent civiliza-tions. In particular, the history of siege warfare bristles with occasions when fortresses surrendered on terms that were considered acceptable by the contemporary culture of war.[53] Such occasions were often sur-rounded by pomp and circumstance; one need only think of Diego Velázquez's celebrated painting, *The Surrender of Breda* (also known as *Las Lanzas*). Often, the victors formed a kind of guard of honor as the defeated marched out with bands playing and banners flying. Normally their officers were permitted to retain their sidearms. That such cere-monies are by no means a matter of historical record only was shown, among other occasions, by the departure from Beirut of Yasser Arafat and his PLO fighters in 1982.

In fact, so incapable are men of escaping the culture they themselves have created that rules often exist even when their existence is denied. One example of this comes from World War II. To the Germans, the Allied demand for unconditional surrender came as an innovation, and many feared that they might be shot.[54] To the Americans, though, it was merely the formula Grant had used in all his victories and, in particular, at Appomattox Court House in 1865. The phraseology notwithstanding, there was no question of the Confederate troops being shot, their houses and property taken over, and their wives and children sold into slavery. Instead, having been supplied with food out of Union stocks (they were lit-erally starving), they were immediately allowed to return home and even take their horses with them. None of this is to deny that conventions con-cerning surrender are just as likely to be violated as any others. That, how-ever, simply takes us back to the question of perfidy already discussed.

As of the early twenty-first century, war remains the most fearsome of all human activities and one that, unless both sides exercise very strict control, is very likely to escalate out of hand. As of the early twenty-first century, too, it not only remains as rule-bound as it has ever been but cannot take place without rules to define what it is, and is not, about. Some of the rules are explicit, others tacit. Far from standing on their own, they are closely related to the culture of the society that created them, which explains why they vary widely between one society and the next. As society changes, so do the rules. As a result, probably there has never been even one war-making society that did not create and apply rules of this kind. Accustomed as we are to our own rules, we sometimes think that they are so simple as to be almost self-evident. That, however, is not the case. Otherwise the Japanese government, desperately trying to catch up with the West during the final years of the nineteenth century, would scarcely have sent out delegations to study them and submit recommendations as to how they might be applied.[55]

That even the most "civilized" societies often violate the rules of war is undeniable. It is also true that some societies at some times and places waged war with less restraint than others—and that the same societies have behaved with greater or lesser restraint at different times and when fighting different opponents. What cannot be proved, however, is the existence of a historical trend. One scholar, speaking of the years after 1789 and especially after 1914, claims that the advent of mass armies put an end to the "limited" cabinet wars of the eighteenth century. A second, speaking of Japan, claims that sixteenth-century samurai were less chivalrous than their medieval predecessors. A third, speaking of Europe, claims that late medieval warfare was conducted less chivalrously than that of the twelfth century, whereas a fourth, after a thorough examination, concludes that the warriors of the high Middle Ages were less chivalrous than the earlier Germans had been. We are even asked to believe that classical Greek warfare was less restrained than its archaic predecessor.[56] Accepting this logic, the inescapable conclusion is that human civilization peaked when our ancestors were still living in caves.

Nor is it true, as one author has written, that the rules are simply "the etiquette of atrocity," mere intellectual exercises designed to find reasons for committing crimes and to justify them after they have been committed.[57] Of course they are that—and so, in their own way, are all other types of rules as well. Nevertheless, over the millennia the rules of war have helped save the lives of millions of people as well as prevent the destruction of uncounted economic assets and cultural treasures of every kind. Had it not been for them, surely the destruction, the bloodshed, and the number of casualties would have been much greater than they already were. To mention but one example, what would have happened if, in World

War II, the Western Allies had treated German prisoners as the Germans themselves treated Soviet ones? In that case, surely in 1945 there would have been a few million fewer Germans than was actually the case.

Vice versa, perhaps the best way to understand what a conflict without rules, without even the possibility of communication of any kind, might be like is to turn to H. G. Wells's *The War of the Worlds* (1898). In this science fiction fantasy, Martians intent on exterminating the human race invade the earth. While provided with huge brains, they hardly have any bodies as we understand the term, with the result, as Wells explicitly says, that they are incapable of any kind of human emotion and perhaps of any emotion at all. Using heat rays and poison gas (which is then cleared away by jets of steam) they set out to methodically cleanse the earth of its inhabitants, treating humans "as men might smoke out a wasps' nest."[58] Surely in comparison with this, war as we know it, even war in its very worst and most atrocious forms, as waged by the Romans against Carthage or on the Eastern Front in 1941–45 or in the Pacific during the same years, can only come as a welcome relief.

8

Ending War

At a minimum, to end a war four things must be done, though not necessarily in this order. First, it is necessary to take care of casualties, both friendly and, especially in cases when territory has been occupied but there is no formal agreement, enemy ones, too. Second, it is necessary to distribute the spoils, be they prisoners, land, various other forms of property, or whatever. Third, it is necessary to celebrate one's triumph, reenact the ceremonies that marked the transition from peace to war in reverse order, and the like. Fourth, under most circumstances—unless the enemy has been more or less exterminated—it is necessary to reach some kind of understanding with the opponent so as to formally end the hostilities. All these measures may be taken either consecutively or simultaneously, carried out in cooperation with the former enemy or not. Perhaps the most remarkable thing about them is that in the whole of Clausewitz they are not even mentioned. And, as usual, as Clausewitz goes, so do his followers.

Depending on how large the war has been and how bloody, physically speaking, the problem of dealing with those who died in it may be either great or small. On the other hand, culturally speaking, its importance cannot be overestimated. In part, this is because man himself might be defined as the animal that, rather than leaving his dead as they are, takes care of them and looks after them; to paraphrase Aristotle, leaving this world and entering the next one is a social activity. In part, it is because few if any men are foolish enough to risk themselves in the future if the sacrifice their comrades have made in the past is not given the kind of recognition and respect they expect. Hence the society that does not honor those who died fighting for it has yet to be born. Had it been born, one would not expect it to survive for any length of time.

At all times and places, one of the first things victorious armies have done, when the campaigns in which they engaged came to a temporary or final halt, was to look after their own dead. In doing this, a very important role was played by social considerations. The more hierarchical it was, the greater the disparity between the treatment meted out to those at the top and to those at the bottom. One man might go to his eternal resting place amid great pomp and circumstance; meanwhile, thousands were disposed of rather less ceremoniously. A very good example of this is provided by the *Iliad.* At one extreme we have Patroclus. After he was killed his body was fiercely fought over, and only after several men had died doing so could it be secured and brought back to Achilles, who spent time mourning his friend and then proceeded to organize the funeral. The body was cleaned and made presentable as far as possible. A huge pyre was built and the dead man, along with his equipment, placed on it. To appease Patroclus's spirit Achilles personally took twelve captive Trojan youths and slaughtered them. After the body had been burned a series of athletic competitions was held, with prizes for the winners.[1]

This, of course, was exceptional. Even relatively egalitarian societies, such as the Vikings, only put their most important chiefs in longships and burned them, or else they would soon have run out of wood. A fortiori, in a highly inegalitarian one, such as the European Middle Ages, only lords and knights were taken to a church, formally interred, and had an effigy placed over their tombs and masses said in their memory. Ordinary soldiers were much more likely to be cremated en masse with little ceremony, as Greek ones in front of Troy were, or, if they were lucky, receive a simple burial accompanied by a blessing hastily imparted or a prayer quickly said. Occasionally an attempt was made to preserve the physical remains. One story has it that when a barrel containing the pickled body of a colonel of Napoleon's army was opened years after his death, it was found to have grown feet-long hair and inches-long nails.

In a world where many war-making organizations were small, many armies were disbanded as soon as the war itself had ended, and where most people could neither read nor write, it is not even clear whether a specific effort was made to record the names of the dead and notify the next of kin. Most campaigns were conducted relatively close to home and the size of the battles in which they engaged was not great; hence perhaps these things could be left to the survivors. European city-states as early as the Middle Ages, and larger polities from the seventeenth century on, started setting up mechanisms to look after dead soldiers' kin, which implied an orderly procedure for identifying bodies and informing relatives.[2] But there must also have been many armies, such as the imperial Russian one as late as the final decades of the nineteenth century, that never bothered to inform families at all. Either this was because the existing means of transportation and communication were inadequate for the purpose or else it reflected the contempt in which ordinary soldiers were held.

As might be expected, the armies of democratic societies did things very differently. Of particular interest in this respect were the ancient Greek city-states, given that in Greek religion those who had not received a proper burial could not enter the underworld but were instead condemned to an everlasting stay in limbo. To save their own men from this terrible fate, the defeated would send heralds to the victor—who, of course, remained in possession of the battlefield—asking for a truce and permission to gather their dead.[3] Custom, and the desire for reciprocity, obliged the victor to agree (though the Spartans on one occasion collected the enemy dead in order to extract payment for their bodies). As time passed, sending over heralds came to be seen as the normal way to concede defeat.

In Athens, about which far more is known than about any other city-state, bodies were gathered and cremated. Only once, after Marathon, were the remains buried on the spot; Thucydides, who is our authority on this matter, says this was done as a special tribute to the men's courage.[4] The normal procedure was to take the bones or ashes back to the city itself. There they were divided among the various tribes—Spartan soldiers even carried dog tags for the purpose—and displayed in a public tent so that friends and relatives could visit and pay their respects.[5] Three days later the caskets, plus an empty one to mark the Greek version of the Unknown Soldier, made their way to the cemetery in a procession attended by male and female family members as well as professional mourners. An appropriate speech was given, after which, Thucydides dryly informs us, the participants went home.

Partly perhaps because it was a republic for centuries on end, partly because of the far-flung campaigns in which its armies engaged, and partly because those armies tended to become more and more professional, Rome seems to have taken better care of these matters than any other country until modern times. Like the Greeks, the Romans believed that those who had not received a proper burial would be left in limbo, and indeed Queen Dido in the *Aeneid* calls this the worst fate than can befall a soldier.[6] That these duties were taken seriously is proved by Tacitus's description of Germanicus's troops coming across the remains of the three legions that had been lost to the Germans in A.D. 9, and at once setting out to provide them with a proper burial.[7]

Not content with this, many societies devised elaborate mythologies to explain what happens to their heroes in the afterlife. North American Plains Indian warriors—meaning the majority of adult males—famously went to the eternal hunting fields. Viking warriors who died in battle were picked up by the Valkyries and taken to the Hall of the Slain, or Valhalla. The place itself was an exhibition of the culture of war: its walls were made of spears, its roof consisted of shields, and its benches were covered with breastplates. It was there that the fallen heroes gathered, going out in thousands each day to practice for Ragnarok, the final battle between the gods and the giants, and returning each evening to feast on roast boar and drink intoxicating mead.[8]

Muslims who lost their lives fighting for the faith are known as *shahids,* or martyrs, and earmarked for the kind of heaven one would expect desert dwellers to construct—one in which they find running water, green meadows, and—given that, as polygamous nomads, they must have suffered from a shortage of women—any number of beautiful dark-eyed girls. Other traditions promise *shahid*s a seat at the table of Muhammad and Abraham and even a glimpse of Allah Himself.[9] Whatever the details, undoubtedly battlefield martyrdom has long been part of the Islamic culture of war. As many Westerners have recently learned to their sorrow, its role in inspiring the faithful to fight and die has been, and still remains, very considerable.

Whereas the Greeks normally permitted the defeated to gather their dead and bury them, most societies were less civilized. At best, the enemy's remains were hastily gathered and thrown into a pit, perhaps after being covered with lime to prevent disease from breaking out. At worst, they were left where they had fallen, prey first to human scavengers—in preindustrial societies, almost anything a soldier wore or carried had value—and then to animals and birds of prey. Among the Vikings, so self-evident was such treatment that, in the sagas, it became almost synonymous with defeat.[10] Bodies might also be mutilated. Sometimes this was done to express the hatred of one individual for another, as when Achilles tied Hector's stripped body to his chariot and dragged it around the walls of Troy. Perhaps more often, though, the victims were selected more or less at random. Ancient Egyptian tablets present us with severed heads, genitals that have been cut off and stuffed into their former owners' mouths, and the like. Such practices are not uncommon even today, the main difference being that instead of being officially condoned and proudly displayed, most of the time they must be concealed.

In 1905, excavations near the Swedish town of Visby brought to light several mass graves into which the remains of a battle that had taken place there in 1361 had been thrown.[11] Similarly, when Sir Walter Scott visited the battlefield of Waterloo not long after the event, he found the air filled with the stench of thousands of hastily buried bodies of men and horses.[12] This, however, was soon to change. Reminding us of ancient Greece, a growing move toward democratization caused practices originally devised for a few outstanding heroes to spread and be diluted, so to speak, until they embraced every dead soldier. During the French Revolution several proposals were made to gather the remains of the fallen and give them a proper burial. At the time, there was no question of setting up special cemeteries for them. Instead soldiers were to be interred in ordinary ones, where their ashes would be mixed with those of great men; thus enabling the "Braves" (as Napoleon called them) to enter the Pantheon.[13] Little came of it, however. The Grande Armée carefully registered its dead. It did not, and probably could not, alter the practice of disposing of most of them more or less on the spot.

Democracy aside, the other factor that led to change was the spread of mechanized means of transport, first railways and then motor vehicles. For the first time, they provided a practical method for moving the remains of dead soldiers to the places selected by the powers that be for disposing of them. During the nineteenth century the country in which both transport and democracy were the most advanced was the United States; perhaps this explains why, in 1862, it became the first one to establish (by an act of Congress, no less) dedicated military cemeteries. Partly because of their more pronounced class character, partly because many of them had remote colonies that made sending soldiers' remains home prohibitively expensive, European countries followed only much later. Even then many of them did not construct special military graveyards but contented themselves by reserving special plots for soldiers inside existing ones, as, for example, at the huge German cemetery at Stahnsdorf, outside Berlin.[14]

By the end of World War I every major country had established a special organization in charge of looking after the remains of those who had given their lives for it. As had always been the case, extraordinary heroes continued to be buried amid great pomp and circumstance. As was newly the case, ordinary ones were either disposed of en masse amid similar ceremonies or else received pale imitations of the treatment meted out to their betters. Reflecting ancient Greek practices, those whose remains could not be identified or even found started receiving special attention in the form of eternal flames, tombs of the Unknown Soldier, and the like. Previously bodies had been stripped of their belongings as a matter of course. Now, in theory at any rate, those belongings were supposed to be returned to the next of kin. Still, even in the age of railways and steamships, most of the time the dead soldiers were not transported home but buried not far from the spot where they had fallen. When the Germans withdrew from the countries they occupied they left numerous military cemeteries behind; British and American ones are scattered all over the world.

Most countries also extended the way they treated their own soldiers to include enemy dead as well. They may not expect any great ceremony; still, the 1929 Geneva Convention requires that they be respectfully treated, that is, not defaced or mutilated or subjected to procedures contrary to their own religion. It also requires that they be identified if possible. Their graves must be marked for future reference, and their names and personal effects handed over to the representatives of the Red Cross. The latter is supposed to send them to the enemy government, which in turn will inform the families. Not mere charity but the hope for reciprocity underlies these arrangements. With the sensitivities of its own population in mind, no country wants to stand accused of being the first to violate them. This probably explains why they are often kept, more or less. It also explains why countries that did not adhere to them, such as the Soviet Union during and after World War II, sometimes woke up years, even decades, after the event and decided that something needed to be done.

Disposing of the dead is one thing, putting them or parts of them to use another. Warriors of many times and places used to collect heads, scalps, ears, noses, and limbs. At times, the objective was simply to provide proof that the enemy was indeed dead. Reigning around 1200 B.C.,

King Saul asked David to bring him the foreskins of dead Philistines.[15] In
Japan before 1603, samurai who hoped to be rewarded by their lords had
to present the latter with severed enemy heads.[16] Nor, in spite of official
disapproval, are such practices unknown even today. Operating under
cover and thus unable to enforce formal discipline, insurgent organizations in particular may require that their members bring along body parts
of those whom they have killed. In doing so, the organizations' objective
is a double one. First, as in the past, parts of enemy bodies can act as
proof that those members' missions have in fact been carried out.
Second, by committing such acts, the perpetrators' links with the rest of
society will be cut, thus reinforcing their dependence on the organizations that sent them.

Whereas limbs or other body parts taken with this purpose in mind
were presumably disposed of after the event, in many societies the body
parts of enemies, having been suitably treated, were either carried on the
victor's person or put on display as trophies, as decoration, or to intimidate future enemies. Thus we hear of skulls being used as drinking vessels and paperweights, bones serving to embellish various kinds of
implements and furniture, and the like. Many of those who engaged in
these practices saw them as self-evident, very much part of the way
things had always been done and, by right, should be done. Even today,

Burying the dead; the entrance to the Polish soldiers' cemetery at Monte Cassino, Italy
DVORA LEWY

when they are officially frowned upon, they are far from unknown. Soldiers sometimes use the enemy's bodies as trophies, either collecting parts of them or propping them up and putting helmets on their heads and cigarettes in their mouths.[17]

As the discussion of prisoners has shown, not just body parts but intact human beings may be treated as booty. True, modern societies no longer take noncombatants prisoner and do not recognize the right of some individuals to reduce other individuals to slavery. However, there certainly have been occasions when they used war in order to subject entire peoples with the objective, among other things, of exploiting their labor for their own benefit. Some colonialists, notably the Belgians, made no bones about the matter, sending the natives of the Congo into the bush to gather rubber and cutting off their arms if they did not bring back enough of it.[18] Others used less interesting methods, but the objective was the same. To the extent that such things were done by "civilized" countries in Asia and Africa, they were seen as not only permissible but desirable, part of the famous "civilizing mission";[19] later Hitler had visions, never really carried out, of treating the occupied countries in Eastern Europe in the same way.[20] It was only his defeat, followed by the revolt of the colonial peoples, that finally ended this particular form of booty.

Depending on the society in question, treating people as booty could give rise to all kinds of organizational, social, political, and even ethical problems. Hardly ever, though, did such considerations apply to material objects, given that such objects neither need to be fed, nor put under guard, nor confined. Hence as far back into history as we may look, one of the very first things victorious warriors and armies did was to appropriate such objects for themselves. In tribal societies around the world, in China, in the ancient Middle East, in classical antiquity, and during the Middle Ages, the idea that the loser's property was forfeited was so self-evident that it was questioned rarely, if at all. As he so often does, Thucydides provides an excellent example of the way it was done. In the winter of 429–30 B.C., the Potideans, having withstood a siege of two and a half years, finally surrendered to the Athenians. The entire population was allowed to depart, but only on condition that they leave their property behind. All they could take along was a fixed amount of money for traveling expenses—presumably they went to seek shelter with relatives in other cities—plus one cloak per man and two per woman.[21]

While the material value of booty could be very considerable, that was not its only value. To inherit or buy or rent property is one thing;

using force to take it away from one's enemies in war, as distinct from robbery and the like, is another. Very often it is regarded as more honorable, the reason being that it provides tangible proof of what Machiavelli would have called *virtu* (prowess). Hybrias, a poet who lived in Crete around 700 B.C., expressed the idea as well as anyone can:

> My wealth is here, the sword and spear,
> the breast-defending shield.
> With this I plough, with this I sow,
> with this I reap the field.
> With this I tread the luscious grape,
> and drink the red-blood wine;
> and slaves around in order wait,
> and all are counted mine.
> But he, who will not rear the lance
> upon the battle field,
> nor sway the sword, nor stand behind
> the breast-defending shield,
> on lowly knee must worship me,
> with servile kiss adored.
> And peal the cry of homage high,
> and hail me mighty lord.[22]

At first sight, this is a straightforward admission that war is nothing but a quest for acquisition. However, another and, to my mind, better reading would be that the poem is really about (manly) pride. Not merely is war used in order to acquire dominion and possessions; rather, the speaker is proud of his possessions and his dominion *because* they were acquired in war. Nor is this the only place in Greek literature where such pride is expressed.[23] In fact, to say of something that it had been gained "by right of the spear," *doru*, was often considered the greatest praise of all.[24]

From then on, the only real change has been the distinction, which started to be made around 1700, between property that is public and that which is private. Reflecting the emerging trinitarian division of labor between a government that directs the war, armed forces that fight and die, and a civilian population that pays and suffers, it meant that public property could be legitimately taken, whereas private property could not.[25] Public property, once it had been taken, would be proudly displayed, whereas private property might be concealed and surreptitiously sold.

These, of course, are ideal cases and not too much should be made of them. The loophole called "military necessity" applied to material goods just as much as it did to people. In practice, often the difference was not as great as jurists required and international law ruled.

The last form of booty that must be discussed here is immovable property—land and the resources it contains. Most tribal societies do not really look at themselves as "owning" land. If anything, it is the land that owns them, given that it contains a variety of sacred objects that endow the life of the community with meaning. In addition, they often maintain wide stretches of no-man's-land among themselves. Hence, though they do fight one another over access to specific resources such as water, rarely do they aim at "conquest" in our sense of the term. This, of course, is not true of more developed, more structured, more hierarchical societies such as chiefdoms, empires (either centralized or feudal ones), city-states, and states. As far back as our sources allow us to look, organizations of this kind, large or small, strong or weak, have always understood the importance of owning land. Since they also had the organization needed to hold it and exploit it, very often they went to war specifically either to acquire more of it or to defend what they already possessed. This is what the ancient Egyptians under Ramses II did when they invaded Palestine. Three thousand years later, this was what the Germans under Hitler did when they invaded Russia.

In this respect, an important change overtook the culture of war in 1945, though its origins may already be seen several decades earlier.[26] The events of World War II, and specifically the attempt by Germany, Italy, and Japan to gain "living space" for themselves, caused the idea that war could and should lead to conquest, which as late as 1914 had still been almost self-evident, to be discredited. The charter of the United Nations, which was signed in 1946, specifically prohibited "aggressive" war and the use of force in order to annex territory. Gradually over the next few decades, this led to the idea that no war should be undertaken to bring about conquest or end before whatever territory was conquered in it had been returned to its rightful owner.

This, indeed, was a revolutionary idea. A Woodrow Wilson might have understood it; not so a Louis XIV, a Napoleon, or even a Wilhelm II or a Clemenceau. Perhaps, by right, it should have been rejected—after all, it ran directly counter to what most societies had aimed at and practiced for thousands of years. Instead, it took a remarkably short time to assert itself. Looking back, in all the years since 1945 it is hardly possible to find

even one case when a country succeeded in using war to move an international frontier, let alone have the change recognized by the international community. Instead, officially at any rate, all war suddenly became
defensive, though of course this did not mean that, under cover of the
phraseology, the forms it took and the activities it involved were
markedly different from their predecessors.

Closely linked to the question of what is considered booty is the question of who gets it. Starting once again with the simplest tribal societies,
the answer is that each warrior seizes what booty he can and takes it for
himself, a system that is sometimes known as coup counting. Other, more
strongly governed societies have devised their own systems. Very often
movable booty, or at least the part of it that individual warriors, acting with
or without permission, did not take for themselves and conceal, was gathered, stored, and put under guard. Next it would be distributed among the
victors in proportion to their supposed merit. First, the gods that be would
demand their share in the form of sacrifices, dedications, and so on.
Second, the commander in chief would probably take a considerable
share—usually between one-fifth and one-third of the total—for himself,
this on top of being presented with choice morsels such as valuable plate,
horses, animals, and women. Next his senior subordinates would receive
their share, and the rest was divided among the remaining troops. In addition there might be special awards, normally paid out of the commander in
chief's share, for those who had distinguished themselves in battle.[27]

The fate of immovable property was different. Regardless of what it
consisted of—land, natural resources such as forests, rivers, mines, or
buildings of every sort—it was seen as belonging to the victorious commander (or else to the ruler in whose service he worked). Almost the only
exception to this rule was formed by the ancient Greek city-states and the
Roman Republic. In them, rule and ownership were separate; hence conquered land, instead of going to the rulers, was turned into public territory
(Latin, *ager publicus*). Either it was kept in the hands of the polity or else
it was distributed to individuals whom the Romans called *coloni* and the
Greeks *kleruchoi*. By contrast, chiefs, barons, kings, emperors, and similar rulers took the conquered assets for themselves, after which they
might or might not divide them among their followers.

From about 1700 on, in Europe at any rate, there was a growing tendency to separate ruler and state so that the two were no longer the
same. As a result, movable property captured in war less often went to
the ruler but instead was taken over by the "artificial person" that, speak-

ing with Hobbes, he "carried" on his shoulders.[28] Subsequent developments strengthened the separation until for a ruler to personally receive any part of the booty came to be seen as treason or at the very least corruption. From Europe the idea of a strict separation between the rulers and the administrative structure at whose head they stood and whom they were supposed to serve spread to other continents. Often, of course, the distinction was more theoretical than real. Still, not even Saddam Hussein, occupying Kuwait in 1991, dared follow the example of Augustus who, more than two thousand years earlier, had invaded Egypt, driven its queen (Cleopatra) and her husband to commit suicide, and taken it as his private property. At present, this is where things rest. How long they will last is anybody's guess.

Man, a culture-creating animal, does not live by bread alone. Questions such as what constitutes booty and who is entitled to receive it in either ownership or usufruct are very important ones, but making the transition back from war to peace is equally so. The winner needs it to celebrate his victory and, having done so, readjust to the "normal" state of things. The loser, provided he still survives in an organized form, needs it for the second of these reasons, if not for the first. All this explains why the role of ritual in the immediate aftermath of war is no less important than at its beginning.

One very important way by which victory is celebrated is by symbolically taking possession of the battlefield and setting up a trophy. The word itself is Greek. *Trope* means the moment when the push of shields came to an end, the enemy gave way, and the rout began; it was to mark this moment that a trophy was erected. The earliest trophies may have consisted of trees whose branches were used to hang some enemy armor and clothing. For centuries they continued to be made of perishable materials such as wood, a fact that later writers tried to rationalize by saying that hostility between Greeks should not be allowed to become permanent.[29] The first to set up a permanent bronze trophy are said to have been the Thebans after the Battle of Mantinea in 362 B.C.; other Greeks first took them to task for doing so and then imitated them.[30] The most detailed description of a trophy is found in Virgil:

At earliest dawn, the victor first fulfilled his vows to the gods.
He sets up a great oak on a mound with its branches all lopped off,
and clothes it with shining arms,
the spoils of Mezentius, the enemy leader, as a trophy.

Oh great in war, he fastens to it the helmet crests dripping with blood
and the man's broken javelins.
The corselet twelve times struck and pierced,
he binds the bronze shield to its left hand
and hangs the sword with ivory hilt.[31]

As if to prove that nothing has changed, visitors to Gettysburg will
note a stone monument that marks "the high tide of the rebellion"—the
precise spot where on July 3, 1863, Pickett's charging troops broke, hesitated for a moment, and were pushed back. Even when we limit ourselves to the West, the list of peoples who, starting long before Mantinea
and ending long after Gettysburg, set up trophies to commemorate their
victories is all but endless: Romans, Vikings, Italians, Spaniards, French,
British, Germans . . .

Closely related to the erection of trophies are various other ceremonies. That different societies at different times and places have differed enormously in this respect goes without saying; one would scarcely
expect a nation such as the United States, with its three hundred million
mostly Christian people, to adopt the same rituals as a tribe numbering
perhaps five thousand whose most important god is himself, a warrior.
Still, in most societies it may be possible to find three basic components:
those linked to the celebration of victory per se, those that consist of
gloating, and those needed to purify the warriors or soldiers so as to help
their transition back from a situation in which almost anything was permitted to one in which a great many things are not.

To start with "pure" victory celebrations, almost certainly they will
comprise some kind of solemn procession, communal prayer, sacrifice to
the gods, music, the ringing of church bells, and the like. They will also include ceremonies such as hailing the victorious commander, presenting
awards to soldiers who have distinguished themselves, and speeches
praising the courage of the living and the even greater courage of the
dead; from the time it was delivered in 429 B.C., Pericles's funeral speech
has never been improved upon. A poet may be commissioned to write
verse in honor of the occasion, a sculptor or painter to commemorate it.
Most likely the proceedings will combine three elements: joy at the victorious conclusion of the war, gratitude to the gods that made that victory
possible (as in the Christian hymn "Te Deum"), and humility to prevent
those gods from turning their backs on the people the next time they are
needed, as in that other hymn, "Non Nobis."

In today's advanced societies, usually gloating over the enemy's defeat is not considered good manners. That, of course, does not mean that it does not take place; officially and in public, however, it is usually limited to more or less decorous forms. This includes symbolic acts, such as pulling down the enemy's flag (perhaps trampling on it and burning it, too) and hoisting one's own. It also means putting captured weapons on display, as European monarchs did for centuries on end and as Israelis and Arabs often did to each other from the first Arab-Israeli war of 1948 to the invasion of Lebanon in 1982. Many previous societies, not having undergone the so-called civilizing process, saw the matter differently. Far from being merely tolerated, gloating was encouraged. Indeed, it was considered more or less obligatory and treated as an essential component of that part of the culture of war that followed victory.

Many tribal societies in North America, Africa, and Polynesia took prisoners specifically in order to gloat over them. Often it was not lust alone but the desire to humiliate that caused female prisoners to be subjected to every form of sexual assault. Nor was this motive limited to "primitive" peoples. While it is mentioned in the *Iliad,* it is said to have played a large role in the Yugoslav civil war as well.[32] Male prisoners might also suffer sexual indignities. For example, a painting on a fifth-century B.C. Greek vase shows a barbarian, presumably a defeated one, presenting his naked behind to a Greek man who is holding his penis and about to penetrate him.[33] American guards at Abu Ghraib did not actually rape Iraqi male prisoners, but they did engage in sexual abuse. In this case, things were made even worse by the fact that some of the personnel involved were women.

While such things did happen, on the whole male prisoners were perhaps more likely to be mocked, physically and mentally humiliated, tied to stakes, and subjected to unspeakable tortures. Often the stronger and more renowned the prisoner, the more his captor had to gain by treating him in that way. Some societies took prisoners specifically in order to sacrifice them to the deities, the best-known (but by no means only) example being the Aztecs of Mexico. Even if none of these things was practiced, probably the least captives might expect was to be paraded through the streets so that the population could see them and inflict all kinds of indignities on them.

To focus on what may be the most extreme example of all, some societies—notably in the Pacific, New Zealand, Africa, the Caribbean, Brazil, and perhaps North America as well—killed their prisoners, cooked them, and ate them. On the whole, the existence of cannibalism seems sufficiently well established, even though a few anthropologists continue to deny it. Though its motives are by no means always clear, there must have been many cases when the practice had nothing to do with a shortage of protein. Instead, and as is also proved by the fact that enemy chieftains were sometimes considered a special delicacy, it reflected a desire to acquire the qualities of the defeated—and, at the same time, inflict the greatest humiliation of all: to be literally carved up, ingested, absorbed into another person's body, and excreted. Here and there all these things were done quite explicitly as the victor addressed his prospective meal and described what would happen to him.[34]

Celebrating victory and gloating is one thing, purifying oneself another. Many societies developed post-war rituals that returning warriors were obliged to undergo, such as discarding their bloodstained clothing and equipment, washing, spending time in isolation, abstaining from sexual activity for a certain period, praying, and the like; in many cases, they resembled those used after hunting.[35] Among the Meru, for example, it was done by sacrificing a ram and smearing its fat on one's spear. Now, this was a society where livestock was the most precious possession; to this extent, it is even possible that the obligation to do so had an inhibiting effect on the decision to go to war in the first place.[36] Seen from a sociological point of view, it is a question of readjusting one's behavior to the norms of peace. Seen from a psychological and perhaps biological one, it may also be understood as an attempt to stop the flow of adrenaline, calm down, and "find oneself" after having engaged in what is by far the most exciting human activity. Doing so is by no means always easy and may require a fairly protracted period.

By and large, the more prolonged the hostilities, the more casualties they claim, and the more horrific the forms they assume, the harder the transition from war to peace, and the more important therefore the rituals in question. In this context it should be added that, whatever the literature may say, there is no proof whatsoever that modern war is harder to bear than its predecessors; no reason, in other words, to think that seeing and hearing one's relative scream as he is being scalped alive is any worse than cowering in a trench and being subjected to an artillery bombardment. Given the high incidence of PTSD (post-traumatic stress disorder), and the like, are we to conclude that modern men are softer, less resistant, than their predecessors? Some people think so. Perhaps, however, the real explanation is different. A supposedly enlightened, supposedly rational, secular society no longer allows warriors to go through certain kinds of post-conflict ritual, let alone require that they do so before returning home and resuming day-to-day life. For these rituals, the treatments psychiatrists and psychologists have devised are, at best, but poor substitutes.[37]

The most famous of all victory rituals, in which many of the above elements were combined, was the Roman triumph.[38] Granted by the Senate to commanders whose troops had killed at least five thousand enemies, originally the triumph was a religious ceremony. The returning army underwent purification (*lustratio*) and thanked the gods for giving it victory. Only then could it enter the sacred limits of the city precinct, or *pomerium*. Starting in the second century B.C., the procession made its way along a fixed route. It departed from the Campus Martius, the place where troops were levied before the war and where exercises were held. It entered the city by way of the Porta Triumphalis, and made its way past various landmarks to the Capitol. At its head walked senators—presumably all those not too decrepit or too sick to do so—and other representatives of the government. Then, marching either on foot or on horseback, came the victorious troops. They brought along the spoils—including the most famous of all, the tabernacle from the Temple in Jerusalem, which is depicted on the Arch of Titus—tablets painted with scenes from the war, and, of course, prisoners in chains.

Near the end there appeared the victorious commander, riding a four-horse chariot and surrounded by his mounted staff. Originally he seems to have had his face painted red, indicating a link with Jupiter in his role as a war god. Later he wore a purple mantle and a crown of laurel, carried an ivory scepter, and had a slave hold a golden crown taken from the Temple of Jupiter above his head. All this, plus the acclamations of the crowd, was enough to turn the head of the best-balanced man; to avert the danger, the slave was also supposed to whisper the words "Remember you are mortal" in the victor's ear. The rest of the troops, often singing ribald songs in which they derided the enemy and made fun of their own commander, followed. The final goal was the temple of Jupiter. Here the enemy leader was solemnly executed. The commander consigned the insignia of victory for safekeeping, and the procession disbanded.

So far, the victors. But how about the losers? On the whole, the sources have little to say about the matter. One reason for this is because, as the saying goes, history tends to be written by the victors. In turn, one reason for *that* is because they are in a position to do so; another, because few, perhaps too few, people care to share the losers' pain and sorrow. Besides, quite often there are no losers. As Voltaire once slyly put it, both sides may find themselves praising god, each in his own camp.[39] For example, this was what happened after the 1973 Arab-Israeli War. During the months that followed, Egyptian president Anwar Sadat, Syrian president Hafez Assad, and then Israeli general Ariel Sharon all produced learned explanations as to why their respective countries had won the war and what the conclusions from this "fact" might be.

There are also cases when the losers are almost literally wiped out— killed, captured, enslaved, exiled, "ethnically cleansed." The process may be carried to the point where they are no longer capable of holding ceremonies of any kind, as in the case of Troy, Carthage, and countless other ancient cities. More often, though, at least some of them survive. Not only do they survive but, avoiding captivity, they continue to live in their own country, more or less in the same places as before, and retain some form of political organization, even if it is one that, as happened in France in 1940 and in Germany in 1945, has been created by the victors and was meant to transmit their orders.

Under such circumstances it is to be expected that the losers, too, will set up, and subject themselves to, various kinds of ritual. At a minimum, they will have to dispose of their dead. It speaks volumes in favor of the ancient Greeks that doing so was a right which the losers possessed and the victors were not supposed to deny them.[40] Other peoples were not always as civilized in this respect. Sometimes the losers were not granted permission at all as the victor avenged himself on the dead, or else tried to use the occasion to extract all kinds of concessions. For example, aware of how sensitive Israel is in this regard, Hezbollah terrorists in Lebanon have often turned negotiations for long-dead, half-rotten bodies and body parts into a grisly ritual.

Even in the unlikely case that the victors got rid of all the physical remains of the dead so there are none left for the losers to dispose of, probably the latter will still want to set up a memorial. This, for example, was what the Egyptians were allowed to do as part of their peace agreement with Israel. Nor is there any reason why, the victors permitting, the losers, too, will not hold all kinds of ceremonies, if not to celebrate and gloat, then at any rate to mourn and perhaps draw some conclusions for the future. Whether because their religion requires it or as a preliminary step on a process that may eventually lead to revenge, they may also want to cleanse themselves of their sins, real or imagined.

Even disregarding their human, material, and psychological loss, there will be enough for the losers to do to keep their hands full. One very interesting ceremony in which they, but of course not the victors, are likely to engage in is finding a culprit. In ancient Greece, generals who were perceived as having failed to perform as well as had been expected of them could expect to be investigated and put on trial in front of the popular assembly. If convicted, they might suffer the confiscation of their property, exile, or execution. One of those who were forced to leave their homeland in this way was the historian Thucydides.

From his time to our own little has changed. In 1967, Egypt's president, Gamal Abdel Nasser, was heavily defeated in his war against Israel. Thereupon he arranged a trial for his former deputy, Field Marshal Hakim El Amar, who was convicted and sentenced to death, and later committed suicide in his cell. Six years later it was the Israelis who, having been taken by surprise by the October 1973 war, set up a committee of inquiry to investigate minister of defense Moshe Dayan, chief of staff David Elazar, and several others.[41] In theory, trials of this kind are supposed to "get at the truth" and teach people how to avoid similar mistakes in the future. In practice, very often they act as rituals in which the defeated vent their anger on some poor devil of their own number so as to regain at least some of the feeling of power they have lost.

Finally, assuming the losers have neither been wiped out nor completely "subjugated" (as international law, recalling the days when defeated troops were made to pass under the yoke, calls it),[42] it will be necessary to end the war by concluding some kind of peace treaty. Such treaties are of many different kinds. Some are written, others not. Some are spelled out in enormous detail, taking up dozens and even hundreds of pages, whereas others do not need to because things are done more or less according to custom. Some are supposedly eternal, whereas others are only supposed to apply for a certain length of time. Some are designed to mark the final end of a conflict, others merely a cease-fire, a truce, or an armistice.[43] Here, what interests us most is not so much what the treaties say as the way in which they are made.

At a minimum, putting an end to war requires that one party—perhaps both—should launch signals indicating willingness to parley and that the other should register them and agree to hear what it has to say. Often this is the most delicate part of the proceedings; the one in which treachery or a simple misunderstanding is most likely to occur and reignite hostilities. For example, at the Battle of Cynoscephalae in

198 B.C. the Macedonian soldiers tried to surrender by holding their pikes upright; the Romans, however, went on slaughtering them until somebody explained the meaning of the gesture.[44] Communications having been established, either a neutral negotiator is appointed or emissaries, who in many cases also act as hostages, are exchanged. Probably there will be some kind of truce to suspend hostilities as long as negotiations last. That said, it is necessary to add that in many tribal societies the concept of peace itself is unknown and a truce is all that may be achieved.

The place where the meetings are held will be governed by the relative power of the peacemaking parties. Ancient Greek city-states used to send emissaries to address each other's *ecclesiae,* or popular assemblies. However, the final swearing ceremonies—there were no signatures— took place in some temple located in neutral territory. At Tilist in 1809, Tsar Alexander I of Russia and Napoleon agreed to meet on a raft anchored in the middle of the Neman River, which marked the border between their respective empires. By the rules of protocol both monarchs should have left their respective shores and reached the raft at exactly the same time. However, Napoleon's rowers, fortified by a round of brandy, were faster; this enabled him to get there ahead of his interlocutor and gain a slight psychological advantage by welcoming Alexander to the splendidly decorated pavilion.[45] A hundred and thirty-six years later, Field Marshal Chuikov in Berlin did not bother with such niceties. The Germans having used their radio to ask for somebody to come over and talk, he picked an officer of his staff and sent him to the German lines. When the major duly returned with a German delegation, the Soviets demanded that they, or their superiors, sign on the dotted line.[46]

Once talks get under way, both sides will try to impress each other with their power, determination, level-headedness, and generosity, but also with the constraints under which they operate and which, unfortunately, prevent them from making concessions.[47] At first they will proceed gingerly, even hesitantly. Later, as what modern political scientists like to call "confidence-building measures" take effect, things may loosen up. As in war itself, there will be patrols in the form of trial balloons, intelligence and counterintelligence, advances, retreats, ambushes mounted and sprung, and such. Nowadays much of this will probably be done with United Nations assistance, a fact that probably creates as many problems as it was designed to solve.[48]

The maneuvers may cause the talks to be broken off and hostilities resumed. On the other hand, the more advanced the talks, the greater the chance that the leaders on both sides will step forward and make a personal appearance. Either they will do so in order to take charge and avoid an unfavorable outcome; or else to claim the credit for themselves. Often this stage, even more than during the war itself, is the time for pomp and circumstance. Very likely this will include splendid clothes, highly decorated equipment, and magnificent horses (or, nowadays, limousines surrounded by outriders and screaming sirens). It will also include large and glittering retinues, an exchange of expensive presents to show one's own riches and display goodwill, and so on.[49]

The moment when the talks are finally crowned with success is also likely to be one of great solemnity. Weapons may be ceremoniously hung on trees, or broken, or buried.[50] Generous gestures, whether calculated or spontaneous, may be made. To produce a relaxed atmosphere, the pipe of peace may be taken out and smoked, as among the Sioux of North America. The two sides may share a festive meal and raise toasts to each other and to peace itself. They may draw some blood from their bodies, mix it, and drink the mixture, as in pre-classical Greece. They also may exchange women or share them. The former permanently, to cement the peace by forming new family alliances as with many tribal societies; the latter temporarily, as part of the fun, as when the Congress of Vienna attracted prostitutes far and wide.

The final step is usually to swear a solemn oath and invoke the gods to smite the side that violates it (in the final scene of Aristophanes's *Lysistrata,* Athenian and Spartan representatives trace the border between them on the naked body of a young woman standing for Irene, the goddess of peace). A treaty will be signed and sealed and copies of it exchanged. Hands will be shaken and the pens used for the signature solemnly noted. A ceremonial peacemaking fight may be staged—as among the Yolngu of north Australia—or a commemorative medal struck.[51] Often the proceedings are rehearsed in great detail, as when President Clinton practiced moves that would prevent Palestinian chairman Yasser Arafat from kissing him on the cheek, as is the Arab custom.[52] Nowadays all this is done in front of the TV cameras, and in fact anything that is not done in front of them hardly counts. Which, however, is not to say that the essence of things has changed, is about to change, or perhaps even can change.

III

COMMEMORATING WAR

Without question, war is the most terrible human activity by far; it is also one which very often traumatizes both those who participated in it and those who suffered from it. Logically, therefore, one would expect the men and women who have gone through it—and, perhaps even more so, those who have not gone through it—to do what they can to put it aside, turn their backs on it, and try to forget about it as best they can. Here and there, in fact, this is what happens. For example, Germany emerged from World War II almost totally destroyed. Much worse still, millions of people who had thought they had given their all for Führer, *Volk,* and fatherland suddenly discovered that, in reality, they had been little better than criminals serving a criminal government for criminal ends. No wonder the slogans "*Lieber tot als soldat*" (better dead than a soldier) and "*Nie wieder Krieg*" (never again war) gained in popularity until among wide circles they were almost turned into a dogma.[1] Something similar happened in Japan, a country with a long and very strong military tradition whose people have stubbornly resisted any attempt to have the national defense budget exceed 1 percent of GDP. In these and many other countries "militarism" has become the worst of all bad things, to be denounced, preached against, and avoided at almost any cost—even by violence, if need be.

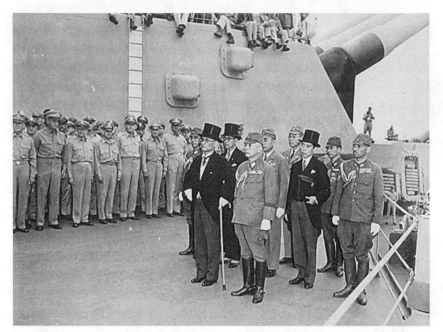

The shift from war to peace, and from peace to war, is usually attended by great ceremony. Japan surrendering, 1945   NATIONAL ARCHIVES

On the whole, however, such an aftermath is fairly unusual. In victory or defeat, officially or unofficially, publicly or privately, people are much more likely to look back at war as the decisive event of their individual or collective lives. After all, on its outcome depends their own fate; as well as that of the communities in which they live. Furthermore, they must think of the future as well. History is full of the corpses of those who would not or could not defend themselves. No wonder that people, groups, and nations in question study war, commemorate it by all available artistic means at their disposal, and often spend fortunes to build monuments to it. So it has been throughout recorded history. And so, unless human nature undergoes some radical changes, indeed, it is very likely to remain in the future.

. . .

9

History and War

When the first history—here understood in the sense of an attempt to record the past in prose, and in a more or less factual way—was written is unknown. What *is* known, though, is that, from the moment the first historical works were written, war has always occupied a large, often central place in it. Herodotus, in his capacity as "the father of history," set the tone for all his followers. His objective, he says, was to investigate and record the great deeds committed by both Greeks and Persians during the war between them so that future generations would not forget them.[1] Though this is not the only reason for writing military history, it remains as important as it has always been.

Among the ancient historians who followed in Herodotus's footsteps were Thucydides, Xenophon, Polybios, Sallust, Caesar, Livy, Josephus, Appian, Arrian, and Plutarch, to mention the most important ones only. Almost all of them possessed military experience of one kind or another. Several had commanded troops on campaign, usually with success. One is regarded as perhaps the greatest commander who ever lived; a grand master both of war and politics and of a clear, brief, style of writing that has never been surpassed.[2] None, not even Sallust, was a military historian as we understand the term, that is, a person who, working either for some organization or on his own, spends most of his life trying to investigate, record, and understand the wars of the past. Yet all of these historians made war into a central part of their various works—something that was warranted, indeed required, by the role armed force had played in the rise and fall of the rulers, peoples, and countries in whose fate they were interested.

This, of course, does not mean they approached history, specifically including the history of armed conflict, in a uniform way. For Thucydides, as he says, it was a question of writing the history of the largest and most important war ever fought until his day.[3] More critical and less inclined to mythologize than Herodotus had been, he accomplished his mission in a masterly way. His is a remarkably well-researched, well-rounded account. Not only does it shed light on every level on which war is waged—from the way shields were held to grand strategic planning—but it also illuminates the thoughts, emotions, and beliefs of the people and the societies who engage in it. Almost none of his successors, ancient or modern, are able to equal him in this regard.

By contrast, Xenophon was the kind of commander-historian who today might have used his retirement to write his memoirs as well as serious articles for serious newspapers. Polybios wrote military history as part of a grandiose project aiming to describe and understand what he saw as the greatest political development of his day: the rise of Rome to dominate the Mediterranean. He was deeply involved in and very familiar with political and military matters; still, he has neither Thucydides's rhetorical skill nor that historian's ability to describe the characters of his heroes or bring out the emotions that governed them. Livy at his best probably did have that ability, but his patriotic tone sometimes interferes with his objectivity to the point where one feels that what one is reading is not history but a fairy tale. One could go on and on explaining the approach each historian took, the sources he used, his strengths, and his weaknesses. The point to make, though, is that had it not been for war and warfare, many of them would have been left without much to write about at all.

While medieval people did not have military history either, they, too, were highly interested in accounts of past wars. Many of those they produced do not display the same close concern with finding out and recording what happened to whom, when, where, and why; hence they are perhaps best discussed under the heading of literature. There were, however, important exceptions. This was a period when, almost by definition, any important personages had to be either warriors or priests, explaining why authors such as Einhardt in his biography of Charlemagne and Joinville in his life of Louis IX devoted much space to narrating their respective heroes' military exploits. Another group of writers were the chroniclers. The chroniclers' task was to record the most important events of each year more or less as they took place. This naturally caused them to take a special interest in any unusual happenings that impacted on the societies in which they lived. And among such happenings, war occupied a central place.

Particularly during the early Middle Ages, almost all chroniclers were ecclesiastics and thus prohibited from participating in war. Given their status, they tended to see God's finger in almost anything. For them, the fact that a war had taken place in a certain year stood on a par with, say, the miraculous reappearance of John the Baptist.[4] Too often they explained victory and defeat in terms of divine intervention. On the other hand, their interest in military matters, such as campaign planning, tactics, logistics, and technology, was often less than it should have been. Whether this was due to lack of understanding or to their taking many things for granted is hard to say. What we get is not so much military history as the raw material for writing it, except that since the chronicles themselves usually represent the only available source concerning the events they describe, such a reconstruction is impossible.

Later, things changed. Increasingly, the chroniclers themselves came from the chivalrous classes. This fact caused them to take a deep interest in war, and helped them in their attempts to understand it and explain what had happened in it to posterity. A very good example is Jean Froissart (ca. 1333–ca. 1400). Froissart, who evidently felt at home both in French courtly circles and English ones, wrote during the last decades of the fourteenth century, taking as his subject the middle period of the Hundred Years' War. In many ways his work is more like an adventure story than history, bristling with challenges delivered and answered, battles fought, and brave deeds of arms performed by noble men on both sides. All these are described from the point of view of one who admired them and thought posterity should have a record of them.

In other parts of the world, other pre-modern civilizations had their own traditions of writing history. One of the most interesting came from China. Chinese society did not have a personal God or gods who could speak out, intervene in human affairs, reward, or punish. As a result, it assigned an enormous role to history as the most important source of knowledge of all. To this was added the dominant Confucian ideology; by emphasizing age and seniority, it had a built-in tendency to see the past as greater, more sagacious, and more worthy of emulation than the pres-

ent. The outcome was a tradition of historical writing, specifically including military historical writing, which sought to understand the present in
terms of the past.

In China, the dominant class has always consisted of governors/
scholars. Scholars professed to hold war in contempt, and to the extent
that they wrote of it they mostly limited themselves to generalities. The
task of looking at war in greater detail was left to soldiers; however, the
latter's place on the pecking order was below that of scholars. In
whichever way they approached the problem, both kinds of writers used
history as their starting point. So-and-so had emulated an ancient commander and had won the day. So-and-so had acted contrary to the ancients' advice and, getting his just deserts, was destroyed. For example,
when Ming dynasty generals during the second half of the sixteenth century had difficulty coping with the Mongols to the north, their instinctive
reaction was to turn their thoughts toward the period when their ancestors had used chariots.[5] All this made the job of the historian, specifically
including the historian whose concern was war, extraordinarily important
and extraordinarily dangerous as well. Historians who, from the point of
view of the powers that be, misrepresented history or drew the wrong
conclusions from it might very well pay with their offices or even with
their lives.

Returning to Europe, knights who wished to put their deeds on
record and who had the means to do so sometimes commissioned a specialist, as men such as William Marshal (1144–1219) and the Maréchal de
Boucicault (1366–1421) did. As one might expect, often the outcome,
however good as literature, was bad history, as men's motives and actions
were twisted to present them in the most favorable possible light. With
the waning of the Middle Ages from about 1420 on, things changed. The
rising new class of international mercenaries included a fair number of
well-educated men, both senior officers and not so senior ones, who were
quite capable of writing down their own memoirs. The result was a large
literature containing what, to modern eyes, often appears as a strange
hodgepodge of anecdotes, more or less credible adventures, noble deeds
performed, and moral homilies. Numerous useful strategic, tactical, and
technological tidbits may also be found. However, often they seem to be
arranged in no particular order; and the space they occupy is much less
than one might expect.

As we decipher the text, an explanation emerges. We learn that the
objective was not to provide a systematic or comprehensive account of

events, not even those that had befallen the author. Rather, it was to record the remarkable and the unusual while at the same time glorifying the author in the eyes of posterity.[6] As with Froissart, in some ways the material has more in common with adventure stories than with military history, or perhaps one should say that history existed to serve as the background to the deeds of prominent individuals, not the other way around, as became the case later on. Works such as those by Olivier de la Marche (French, 1426–1502), Jörg von Ehingen (German, 1428–1502), Diego García de Pareses (Spanish, 1461–1530), and George Gascoigne (English, 1501–1577) also aim at providing lessons concerning manhood and honor for readers who had no personal knowledge of armed conflict.[7]

Once the spigots had been opened, the memoirs of commanders and soldiers of all ranks soon turned into a mighty flood. The English Civil War alone produced some two dozen of them; such was their popularity that some were written by men with no military experience who were merely trying to exploit the market. It continues unstoppable to the present day. Some of the best representatives of the genre, such as the memoirs of Ulysses S. Grant and Churchill's massive histories of World War I (of which one contemporary said that "Winston has written a book about himself and called it *The World Crisis*") and World War II are real works of art. Carefully arranged to assist comprehension, provide perspective, and maintain suspense, they confront the reader with panoramic scope, enormous richness of detail at many different levels, considerable emotional depth, and, most important, clear expositions of what, in the author's view, happened and why it happened. They are also masterpieces of style, consciously or unconsciously using every possible device to enhance their prose; as such, they make for fascinating reading. Unfortunately, many more were produced by men who, whatever their virtues as commanders and soldiers, were without any serious training in either history or literature. They were intent only on glorifying themselves in case they had succeeded, or avenging themselves on their enemies—very often their own former superiors—if they had not.

The methods by which commanders compose their memoirs have also changed. During the three hundred years between 1600 and 1900, those who did not feel confident in their own literary abilities would often leave their papers to their descendants to pore over and publish. Today, spurred by promises of generous contracts and fat advances, they are more likely to hire research assistants and/or ghost writers, as General Norman Schwarzkopf did. Whether or not they published their memoirs,

many commanders also became the subject of biographies written with
or without their own consent—as happened to practically every one of
Frederick the Great's generals and Napoleon's marshals at one time or
another. Given an increasingly literate public, every war since 1600 has
brought a crop of works of this kind. Many achieved considerable popularity when first published, only to crowd the used-book shelves not
long thereafter; good examples are works by Field Marshal Bernard
Montgomery, General Dwight D. Eisenhower, and others.

Memoirs and biographies apart, the Renaissance also brought a new
appreciation of military history and the things it could do for commanders.[8] It was, however, military history of a new and different kind. It
showed less interest in divine intervention and the daring deeds of individuals, however chivalrous, and more in the impact of purposeful, organized human action. Take the writings of Machiavelli. Politician, diplomat,
defense official, thinker, historian, and writer of drama, Machiavelli's primary interest was politics rather than military affairs. Still, he did play a
role in organizing the defense of his native Florence, and he was almost
as familiar with war and armies as many classical writers had been. Like
the Chinese, he regarded the past as an example and a source of inspiration for the present. Unlike the Chinese, he did not automatically accord
priority to anything old. Instead he focused his admiration mainly on one
particular time and place, Republican Rome, almost entirely ignoring
anything that had happened between that period and his own. Indeed,
the strongest criticism that may be directed against his writings is precisely that they refused to recognize change. If the wise and virtuous
Romans had done something and succeeded, then who were we, their
less illustrious successors, to question it?[9]

What one might, for lack of a better term, call modern military history originated during the first half of the eighteenth century. By this
time all the essential pillars of modern war were in place: the idea that
war takes place (or at any rate should take place) between entities
known as states, the idea that internal and external wars are different
things and should if at all possible be waged by different organizations,
and the idea that it should be run on trinitarian lines with a clear division
of labor between government, armed forces, and people. Working within
this framework were civilian writers such as Voltaire. In the best tradition
of the Enlightenment they fulminated against war, its brutality, its barbarity, its lack of reason, and its tendency, as they saw it, to interfere with
the orderly progress of civilization.

In the spirit of the times, many philosophes saw war as not so much the ultimate reason of kings as the sport they practiced—the way in which they and the aristocrats by whom they were surrounded amused themselves at the expense of the troops as well as the general population. This idea, which permeates the works of the French physiocrats in particular,[10] may also be found in Adam Smith.[11] Logically it led to, and culminated in, Immanuel Kant's 1795 treatise *Perpetual Peace,* in which he suggested that such peace might be within reach if only all existing states were turned from monarchies into republics. Other authors, including Voltaire himself, were less optimistic. Though not primarily military experts, they recognized the role wars play in human affairs and did their best to provide readers with accounts of them.

The other contribution of the Enlightenment was, if anything, even more important. By the second half of the seventeenth century, the day of amateur warriors, feudal or mercenary, was largely past. France, Britain, Austria, Spain, and other European countries were busily constructing military academies where officers were to be produced seriatim. Though officers' lives remained dangerous, increasingly they were not supposed to fight but to plan, train, conduct, and lead; the day when even commanders in chief sometimes hacked around them, sword or lance in hand, were finally over. Those who staffed the academies were themselves professionals, field-grade officers presumably selected for their intellectual and didactic abilities. As time went on professionalism spread from the bottom of the officer corps upward, leading to the establishment of the first staff academies from about 1763 on. All this created an unprecedented demand for military literature. Much of the literature was historical in nature, its aim being to find out what happened and draw practical conclusions from it,[12] until not long after 1800 no less a soldier than Napoleon was ready to proclaim that the only way to become a great commander was to study and restudy the great campaigns of the past.[13]

Many of the authors in question, such as Jean-Charles de Folard and Charles Guischardt, followed Machiavelli. Like him, they took the wars of classical antiquity as their subject and sought to apply its lessons to their own time.[14] Others focused on those of the modern age, by which was meant approximately the period from the last decade of the fifteenth century on and which now became the subject of a growing literature. Whereas those two periods were considered to be relevant to the present, what was now coming to be known as the Middle Ages tended to be seen as a period of feudal darkness. As such there was little, if anything, that might be learned from it; all there was to see were small bands of often illiterate knights endlessly chasing each other while butchering (and, very occasionally, being butchered by) such urban militias and peasant levies as crossed their way.[15] Both Clausewitz and Jomini took this image for granted and, as a result, ignored the Middle Ages in their works. As late as 1929, the year in which the British pundit Basil Liddell Hart published the first version of what, after many permutations, was to become his celebrated work *Strategy,* it still persisted; indeed, traces of it may still be found in some very recent works.[16]

While the professionals who wrote and read military history might admire past commanders, especially, but by no means exclusively ancient ones, they had long done away with God as a serious actor in human affairs. Nor, except perhaps by way of an occasional embellishment to draw the reader's interest, did they care for the heroics of individual warriors. Instead, their primary concern was with the geographical-physical background, the plans of commanders, the movements of armies, and the evolutions and clashes of troop formations that ended in victory for one side and defeat for the other. As might be expected from a literature mainly written by professionals for the benefit of other professionals—some of it was actually sold by subscription, as Clausewitz's *On War* was—much of this was done in a highly technical manner. As a result, modern readers will often find the works in question tedious and hard to follow.

Another way to express the same idea would be to say that history and literature had finally gone their separate ways. Previously many, perhaps most, writers had written in order both to instruct and to inspire. To the extent that the latter and not the former was the main objective, they were often prepared to sacrifice historical accuracy for literary effect; also, to focus on individual people and feats to the detriment of the overall picture. By contrast, much of the military history written from the eighteenth century on aimed at providing instruction. The more systematic it became, the more it tended to leave the task of inspiring to other components of the culture of war, such as popular history, literature, poetry, and every kind of art. To the extent that individual people and feats continued to be mentioned at all, this was either because of their supposedly "critical" importance as commanders whose will made the military engine tick or simply by way of enlivening the text and making it more attractive to read. Works that violated this rule stood in danger of being classified as popular or juvenile, or at any rate as beneath the attention of serious professionals whose task was to think about wars, plan them, prepare them, run them, and then repeat the cycle until they themselves were either dead or on pension. Again, the attitudes thus created have tended to persist, in many cases down to the present day.

The wars of the American Revolution, the French Revolution, and Napoleon and the wars of liberation fought against the last-named led to a far-reaching, if temporary, democratization of armies. For a short time, everybody and his fellow soldier were given an opportunity to become heroes, or at least present themselves as such. Heroes wanted to put their deeds in the service of this or that great cause on record. The outcome was that the long-standing genre of more or less authentic, more or less truthful commanders' diaries, memoirs, and autobiographies were joined by vast numbers of similar works written and published by lesser men. All were accompanied by masses of popular military history, which, partly because of the spread of literacy and partly because this was the age of nationalism, was aimed at a much wider reading public.

That, however, was only part of the matter, and perhaps not the most long-lived one. To some, the French emperor was a revolutionary and a hero, the greatest commander history had ever seen. To others, he was an ogre, an evil genius who had shaken Europe to its foundations and come very close to destroying it. Either way, as even Clausewitz (who hated Bonaparte, as he called him) admitted, there was much to be learned from his campaigns: the ways in which they differed from previous ones, the organization, strategy, tactics, and logistics that had been employed, the things that had gone right and the things that had gone wrong. The same applied to the operations of those who, in the end, had defeated him. Given the exceptionally long period of peace that followed, such questions continued to preoccupy people, professionals and amateurs, at least until the wars of the middle of the nineteenth century; even then the French, seeking to understand how Moltke had succeeded in defeating them, continued to turn to Napoleon for inspiration. As the popular success of such works as David Chandler's *The Campaigns of Napoleon* (1966) and John Elting's *Swords Around a Throne* (1997) shows, interest in the wars in question has not faded.

From the time of Herodotus to that of Voltaire, writing history, military history included, had been mostly the province of amateurs, however knowledgeable and however gifted. Few if any had received any kind of historical training. From Xenophon down, many combined their work in this field with other kinds of literature, such as philosophy and drama; quite a number even sought to dress their histories in the form of verse.

By contrast, the first half of the nineteenth century saw the birth of academic history as we understand it today. The new academic historians worked in the universities and used the methods of scholarship they themselves had invented.

Writing ancient, even medieval, military history, these people had few scruples. As a result, their works on these periods bristle with accounts of wars waged, campaigns conducted, and battles fought; in time, they also became more scientific and more accurate. The academic writers in question did, however, usually draw the line when it came to modern military history. This, after all, was the period in which many governments did what they could to keep the bourgeoisie out of the military. Not having practical experience, many of our authors felt unqualified to write about strategy and were content to leave doing so to the "professionals."[17] Only a few had the courage to confront the professionals head-on, as, for example, Karl Marx's friend Friedrich Engels did. And Engels, of course, was not an academic but an amateur who, in his own words, had engaged in a serious study of the subject in order to master it as best he could.[18]

There were, it is true, a few exceptions to the rule. The most famous one was Hans Delbrück (1848–1929). At one point Delbrück, who taught in Berlin, had the temerity to suggest that the professionals had misinterpreted the strategy of Prussia's legendary commander Frederick the Great. Worse, by arguing that the strategy in question had been based on attrition rather than on annihilation, he called into question the plans of the great German general staff (which later became known as the Schlieffen Plan) for waging a future war against France. Scant wonder he came under attack on the part of officers on the staff. They told him, in no uncertain terms, that civilians did not and could not understand anything about military affairs;[19] several of his foreign counterparts, such as the British naval writer Julian Corbett, suffered a similar fate.[20] Though it may have been an accident, as late as 1969, the year in which I finished my studies at the Hebrew University in Jerusalem, there was not one course on the history of war in the entire curriculum. To this day, out of several thousand American universities, the number of those that offer programs in military history can be counted on the fingers of one hand.

The emerging split between military professionals, on one hand, and academics, on the other, also gave a new importance to the question as to whether military experience is or is not essential in writing about war and its history. As we saw, most of the famous Greek and Roman military historians had known war at first hand. As citizens, they had fought in the ranks.[21] Quite a number of them had even occupied high command posts. In this they have a noted advantage over modern academic historians; whereas many universities hire retired generals to teach students about the history of war, few if any defense ministers hire professors and put them at the head of armies. The exceptional quality of the authors in question strongly suggests the advantages of combining the tasks of commander and writer in a single person.

Even disregarding such problems as objectivity and perspective, however, there is another side to the question. Here I shall not list the renowned military historians, such as Sir John Keegan, who rose to the very top of their profession without ever having been in battle.[22] Instead there is a story told by Professor Martin Gilbert, himself a military historian of note and author of works on the Arab-Israeli conflict and on World War I. At a meeting, Admiral John "Sandy" Woodward, the man who had exercised command during the Falklands War, said that nobody who had not gone through war could really understand it. "If so, please explain it to me" was Gilbert's reply.[23]

Public interest in military history has never flagged. As the German professor Heinrich von Treitschke (1834–1896) once claimed, "the periods of peace form the empty pages of the history books." Every war waged not only in Europe but all over the world—after all, the nineteenth century, and its second half in particular, was the heyday of colonialism—brought a spate of more or less factual accounts written by participants, newspaper correspondents, and casual observers. Some of the last were well-known writers. One very good example was Theodor Fontane (1819–1898). A native of Prussia, Fontane was a successful author of travel diaries who later turned his talents to writing equally successful novels. Yet at one point he took off from his usual labors to produce a very readable history of the 1866 Prussian-Austrian War; aiming it not at the professional but at the interested, fairly well-educated, patriotic layman.

Some of these works were more reliable, others less so. Most probably glorified past wars, particularly those that had been won by their own countrymen but sometimes those that, allegedly fighting against great odds, they had lost as well. In particular, the American South, defeated in the Civil War, gave birth to any number of tales of this kind. As southern writers—many of them, to the present day—saw it, the war was forced on their country by an unjust North under that most unjust of presidents, Abraham Lincoln. Rising to the occasion, the South mobilized its forces.

Outnumbered and outproduced, it fought the good fight, struck and received many lusty blows, and finally succumbed to the overwhelming numerical and material superiority brought to bear against it by the other side. Works of this kind, as well as many others, often described the sufferings inflicted by a cruel and vindictive enemy in vivid detail. Nevertheless, during the second half of the nineteenth century, rare was the history focusing on the horrors of war and its miseries per se. Instead, since many writers were influenced by the prevalent nationalist and social Darwinistic ideas, there was a tendency to look at war as a necessary, even positive, part of human experience.

A new breed of military history, which made its debut during those years, was official military history produced by specially appointed personnel (either military or civilian) in specially created departments of the various general staffs. From ancient times on, commanders who were not at the same time rulers had often been required by their political masters to submit written after-action reports on their operations. At least from Alexander the Great on, many commanders who *were* rulers employed special officers responsible for collecting records and recording events;[24] there is some reason to believe that the authors of some works that have survived from the classical age, such as Josephus and Arrian, had access to records of this kind.[25] In 1779, Emperor Joseph II of Austria broke new ground by ordering his Hofskriegsrat, or Council for War, to compile documentary histories of every campaign the empire had waged from 1740 on. Regardless of just how it originated, ruler- or government-instigated history has often been reworked for use as propaganda, glorifying the victor, vilifying the loser, gloating over triumphs gained, concealing defeat or explaining it away, and the like. Under Napoleon, official accounts of military events were falsified to the point where the expression "to lie like a bulletin" became proverbial.[26]

That, however, is still not the same as having a specially appointed department, staffed by specialist personnel, charged with producing an official version of events. This sort of organization had to wait until the first half of the nineteenth century, when the first of its kind was set up by the Prussian army general staff.[27] The idea was to use campaign history as a tool in educating professional officers. As is proved, among other things, by the decision to divide the department into two sections, one responsible for gathering material and the other for writing, in a sense it was an attempt to show that, operating in their own field, they could do as well or better in researching the past, mastering it, and perhaps making use of what "lessons" it had to offer. The armed forces of other countries followed suit in due course. From the 1890s on, there was a tendency toward specialization, as each service, insisting it alone had the qualified personnel, started maintaining its own. The products were used not just for professional education, as originally intended, but also in the services' efforts to "enlighten" (read influence in the direction they considered desirable) the public and as data bases in their turf battles against each other.

Compared to their non-official colleagues, official military historians both enjoy some advantages and suffer from some disadvantages.[28] By far the greatest advantage they enjoy is ample means. Take, for example, the Bundeswehr's Militärgeschichtliches Forschungsamt in Potsdam. Backed by an annual budget of seven million euros per year, the historians working for it can afford a few things others cannot, such as administrative assistance and travel money for touring the terrain and conducting interviews.[29] Last but not least, they also receive guaranteed funding for publishing products that might otherwise be unpublishable and unsellable.

Probably even more important is access to documentation.[30] Traditionally this meant written records of every sort; more recently audiotapes and incredible amounts of photographic material have been added. On occasion, the material in question is highly classified. For example, some of the men, fine historians all of them, who produced the official U.S. history of World War II are now known to have been aware of MAGIC, the secret organization in charge of intercepting and decoding Japanese wireless transmissions, years before its existence was made public.[31] In any field of study, being the first and often the only one to peruse original material is a huge advantage. In one as surrounded by secrecy as war ordinarily is, it is even larger than usual.

On the other hand, historians whose task is to write official history while working for the powers that be must also labor under some difficulties. Even in democratic countries, knowledge of the side on which their bread is buttered will probably compel them to take some points of view and reject others.[32] As some of them admit, at the very least, scholars known to be especially controversial (which, in too many cases, means especially knowledgeable and especially original) are unlikely to be given the job in the first place.[33] In countries that are not democratic, supervision is much more stringent and can easily be carried to the point where they are reduced to acting as the government's mouthpieces. Following instructions, they write what they are told, regardless of any concern for historical truth and sometimes even as to whether the final product does or does not make sense. Worse still, policy may be altered at any moment. When this happens, historians who find themselves sitting at the wrong end of the table may well be penalized for their failure to change tack on time.

Even this, however, does not end the problems official historians face. Setting forth the history of their countries' armed forces at war, inevitably they must aim at being as comprehensive and as balanced as possible; failing to do so, they can be certain to bring all kinds of accusations down on their heads. Seeking to emphasize the general course of events rather than the exploits of any particular warriors, they also tend to be impersonal. On occasion, this is carried to extremes. Wending his way among multiple posts and offices that received such-and-such instructions or issued such-and-such commands, the reader may be forgiven for overlooking the fact that the occupants of those offices and posts are flesh and blood and even that they keep changing.

Almost invariably, the final outcome is a whole series of bulky tomes. Seeking to achieve a magisterial sort of overview, hardly ever do they appeal to the imagination, inflame the blood, or cause the adrenaline to flow. The following, taken from the Bavarian official history's description of the Battle of Fromelles in Flanders in May 1915, represents as good, or as bad, an example of the genre as may be found:

> In the fulfillment of a promise that General French, the English supreme commander, had given to the French military leadership, on 9 May the IV English Corps attacked to the northwest of this village. The assault met, in the center of the 6th BRD [Bavarian Reserve Division], the 16th RIR [Reserve Infantry Regiment]. At 7 A.M, two heavy mine explosions, which buried alive six groups of trench garrison troops, enabled the enemy to break into the position of the 16th RIR to a depth of some 200 meters. The flood was damned thanks to the bitter opposition of the remaining troops . . . as well as the help of neighboring troops from the 21st and 17th RIRs, while the well-placed fire of the artillery made it impossible for the English to reinforce their troops. In hard fighting, the front-line trenches were retaken during the day. Then the enemy, who had been drawn deep into the position and then cut off, were wiped out or hunted down. The desire for further attack was taken from the English.[34]

At their best, the official histories of war set a standard of comprehensiveness, thoroughness, and objectivity against which all others are measured. Seldom if ever, however, are they read from beginning to end—which, given that the official history of the United States Forces in World War II runs into no fewer than ninety-seven volumes (seven covering the navy, fifteen the air force, and seventy-five the army) would have been all but impossible in many cases. Hence they are perhaps most often used as reference books, and also, of course, as background in pictures of ministers, generals, and other dignitaries who wish to appear more learned than they actually are.

One thing official military history has in common with the history that is produced in academia is the quest for "scientific" status. The idea that studying the humanities is, or at any rate can be, a science was a product of nineteenth-century Germany. There, the term *Wissenschaft* was used, as it still is, to cover not merely the natural sciences but all fields of study from medicine to music. To earn the epithet "scientific" (*wissenschaftlich*), a work dealing with history, military history included, must meet at least four essential conditions. First, though the power of people's belief in God and the supernatural is readily acknowledged, the idea that such factors can effectively influence developments is taboo. In other words, human history must be explained in terms of human action, as Machiavelli had done, or else, following Hegel, in terms of "objectively operating," impersonal, all-powerful political, economic, social, cultural, religious, technological, and, of course, military factors. Second, the history in question must be "objective" in the sense of distinguishing between truth and fiction and sticking as close as possible to "what actually took place" (Otto von Ranke's celebrated phrase). Third, it must take a critical approach to sources and be documented closely enough to enable the reader to check on the way that the author has used them. Last but not least, it must be impartial in the sense of not favoring any particular actor—*sine studio et ira* (without flattery or ire), as Tacitus once put it.

Meeting these requirements can be very difficult. More to the point, the attempt to do so can easily result in volumes that are long-winded, pedestrian, boring, and even incomprehensible; on occasion, it almost looks as if academic historians, seeking "scientific" status for their work, deliberately try to make them so.[35] Hence it is not surprising that, side by side with "scientific" military history produced by either armed forces or

academia, the presses continued to pour out vast amounts of popular accounts of war and warfare. Prominent in the genre were more or less authentic diaries. Then there were collections (in reality, selections) of
official and unofficial letters, personal memoirs, biographies, and newspaper and magazine articles. Picture books filled with weapons, equipment, uniforms, and accounts of battles and campaigns catered to the
taste of men—women seldom read military history—of every age, class,
and degree of education. Often far from objective and deliberately written to include as much color as possible, these works may not always
have met strict academic standards. As the story about the angels who
appeared at Mons in 1914 illustrates, some even reintroduced divine intervention to explain how friendly forces were assisted or saved and the
wicked enemy smitten. Yet the lack of a "scientific" character did not prevent people from buying them and reading them.

Asked why they read military history as often, and with as much interest, as they obviously do, different men coming from different back-
grounds would have provided different answers. The greater majority
would probably have said that they considered accounts of past wars entertaining, even fascinating, finding in many a "rattling good story."[36] It
enabled them to hate or despise villains, identify with heroes, feel part of
something greater and nobler than themselves, go through many an adventure, and experience a gamut of feelings from danger to triumph, all
without any discomfort or risk to life and limb—especially if the story
could be told in personal terms (a quality not often found in serious, let
alone official, military history) and especially if it came with tales of love
and sex (which in these kinds of history is much less common still).
Others would have said that war is an essential part of human history
and, as such, deserves to be studied for the same reasons and as closely
as the rest.[37] To a fairly small minority, both in and out of the military, the
purpose in doing so was to understand war, learn from past war, provide
for the conduct of future war, discover the so-called principles of war,
and, in case one was philosophically minded or ambitious, come up with
some novel "system" or "theory" of war.

Without question, each of these reasons is a perfectly good one in itself and remains as important today as at least since the time Herodotus
decided to put his protagonists' deeds on record. Still, while they may
represent the truth, perhaps rarely do they represent only the truth, let
alone the whole truth. Among "serious" people, few are sufficiently honest to admit, as Liddell Hart at one point did, that what had really drawn

them to the field, at least originally, was the similarity between war and games; in other words, that the fascination with it has as much or more to do with the heart and the hormones than with the brain and its reasoning.[38] Yet unless that truth is fully understood, our understanding of war, let alone our ability to plan it and launch it and deal with it and profit from it, will always remain deficient.

10

Literature and War

Though one or two historians have received the Nobel Prize for literature—including the first prize of all, which went to an expert on ancient Rome, Theodor Mommsen—we today tend to draw a sharp line between literature, however accurate the descriptions it provides, and history, however well-written it may be. This was not the case during many past ages, especially when most people were illiterate, what was known of the past had to be orally transmitted; and especially when the two were often seen as one and the same thing. In those times, history, fiction, drama, poetry, especially epic poetry, and myth fell into the same rubric. Often the same persons wrote all three of them. Here I shall not enter into a discussion of the differences between these various genres except to say that history that invents things instead of trying to reach factual truth is not history at all.[1] If the writing of history often seems obsessed with war, the same applies to other forms of literature. In the words of Ernest Hemingway, a man who knew his way around both war and literature as few other modern men did, war is "just something irreplaceable."[2]

Though the term "war literature" only appeared in the 1920s, literary works whose subject is war, or which are filled with war, are at least as old as history itself. Even a short list would have to include many of the greatest compositions ever produced by human minds. A good starting point is the *Epic of Gilgamesh*. It was written down in Babylon about

2000 B.C. Its eponymous hero, whose battles and other adventures it nar-
rates, is a king who appears to have been historical and who lived some
seven centuries before that date. The list of heroic compositions would
pass through the *Iliad* (and parts of the *Odyssey* as well) and go straight
on to Virgil's *Aeneid*. All four of these, as well as similar epics originating
in other civilizations, have in common that they are literature and not history as we understand that term; in them, the desire to produce a work of
art is at least as important as any concern with historical fact. All four also
contain what we would regard as important mythological elements.

Some of these compositions vastly exaggerate the powers and deeds
of heroes, as the *Epic of Gilgamesh* does. Others describe free communication and even sexual intercourse between men and supernatural beings (the Greek and Roman epics as well as the *Epic of Gilgamesh*), or
else they introduce the reader to various imaginary monsters, such as the
Cyclops, Scylla and Charybdis, and the Sirens (the *Odyssey*). With the
exception of Virgil, who in many ways followed the example provided by
Homer, we know little or nothing about the way in which those who wrote
down the epics, apparently drawing on masses of preexisting oral material, saw the products of their minds. What we do know, though, is that to
those who listened to them or read them, those products did not represent fiction but events that had taken place in historical reality.

Realizing this fact is critical to understanding what followed. As they
composed their various histories, men such as Herodotus and Thucydides
did not deliberately set out to create a new kind of literary genre. Instead,
although writing prose rather than verse, in many ways they saw themselves as following in Homer's footsteps, more or less doing for the Persian
Wars and the Peloponnesian War what he had done for the war seven or
eight centuries earlier that had taken place near Troy. It is, of course, true
that both men took a critical approach to their sources, seeking to weed
out unreliable ones and resolve contradictions. However, an explicit demand for historical truth—requiring, before anything else, a sharp differ-
entiation between fact and fiction—only emerged with Polybios who
wrote in the first half of the second century B.C. Which, of course, is not to
say that, from this point on, all classical literature treated war, or other
kinds of past events, in a strictly historical way.

Referring to Greece, one modern historian has remarked that war
was even more prevalent in literature than it was in real life—which,
given the background of a world made up of hundreds of bickering city-
states, is saying a lot indeed.[3] Both dramatists and poets often took it as

their theme, producing masterpieces never surpassed to the present day. Some, such as Tyrtaeus and Archilochus, calling their fellow citizens to arms and instigating them to heroic deeds; some, like Aeschylus, celebrating the victories it produced; some, like Euripides, describing the sufferings it inflicted; and some, like Xenophon (in addition to his historical writings), philosophizing about it and even producing descriptions of entire imaginary battles meant to illustrate and to instruct. Of Xenophon, we have already said that before taking up residence as a sort of pensioner in Sparta, he had acted as a military commander and a very successful one at that. Of the rest, we know that they, or else their close relatives, had served in war and were sometimes injured or killed in the course of duty.[4]

Part myth, part law, part wisdom, part poetry, part history, the Old Testament is also full of war, particularly the Pentateuch, the books of Joshua, Judges, 1 and 2 Samuel, 1 and 2 Kings, and 1 and 2 Chronicles. Wars, especially those waged by Moses against the Amalekites, by Joshua against the Canaanites, and by the kings Saul and David against their various enemies, were an essential part of the process by which the people of Israel were shaped; war, this time against the Babylonians, also led to the fall of Jerusalem, and with it King Solomon's Temple, in 587 B.C. Clearly the biblical descriptions of these and other wars contain many historical elements, and indeed by and large the later the date the more realistic the account. Clearly, on the other hand, they also contain much material that most modern people would regard as ahistorical. The latter include one episode in which the battle's fortunes were decided by Moses's prayers and another in which Jehovah, at Joshua's request, gave special orders for the sun and the moon to stand in place so as to enable the Israelites to gain the upper hand.[5] Still, even in the less fanciful accounts, the real objective is not to satisfy anybody's historical curiosity, let alone teach strategy, tactics, technology, and similar military subjects. Rather, it is to demonstrate that wars are won when the Israelites remain faithful to the Lord's commands and lost when they are not.

Whereas, in classical antiquity, the point was finally reached where history was no longer confused with literature, during the Middle Ages the distance between the two narrowed once again. Chronicles apart, secular history as it had been understood in the ancient world all but ceased to exist. But even the chronicles were sometimes meant more to show the hand of God at work than simply to record human history as it unfolded. As works of art, medieval compositions such as *Beowulf,* the

Chanson de Roland, The Battle of Maledon, the *Nibelungenlied,* and many of the *chansons de geste* that followed them will stand comparison with the *Epic of Gilgamesh* and the classical epics. Like their predecessors, though, they cannot be regarded simply as historical truth describing the deeds and misdeeds of historical figures, even if their authors believed that they were historical truth, and even if many of them do contain some factual core whose exact nature and importance scholars are still trying to assess. Nor, apparently, did the quest for historical truth figure high among the objectives for which these works were composed. Some were mainly intended to glorify the ancestors of those who commissioned them and listened to them and, by extension, elevate their own status in the eyes of their contemporaries. Many others must have used the themes of war and battle in order to educate, inspire, and, yes, entertain.[6]

Both at the time of Homer and during the Middle Ages, the societies that gave rise to these compositions were proto-feudal or feudal. In other words, they were fairly decentralized in terms of the distribution of political power and almost completely dominated by a warrior class that imposed its values on most of the rest. The West was by no means the only region to give rise to societies of this kind; hence it is not surprising to find that more or less similar ones in other parts of the world came up with more or less similar literary works. In particular, Japanese literature generated during the Muromachi period—lasting roughly from 1336 to 1603—included vast numbers of historical, semihistorical, and pseudohistorical accounts of this kind.

As in medieval Europe, the authors were specialists hired or maintained for the purpose. Their task was to record and narrate the wars, deeds, triumphs, defeats, honor, and loyalty (or treachery) of the samurai. In much of this, truth can no longer be separated from fiction if, indeed, doing so was ever possible in the first place. Nor, in a sense, does it matter if a given samurai really existed and whether he really performed the military feats attributed to him or the motives attributed to him. Rather, as is also the case with the Homeric epics and the *chansons de geste,* the literature in question provides a faithful mirror of a society made up of warriors, their leaders, and their retainers. This includes its likes, its dislikes, its values, the way it understood itself, and how it sought to educate its members.

We have already noted that soldiers and commanders of the Renaissance produced much military history, and also that much of what they did produce was anything but scientific. At the same time, the Renaissance saw attempts by Italian writers in particular to model themselves on classical antiquity and revive the great tradition of epic poetry. Inevitably they focused much of their attention on war as one of the few fields capable of furnishing the desirable, and often highly profitable, combination of suspense, color, emotional depth, and sheer grandeur. These qualities may explain, for example, why Ariosto and so many other authors chose to write about armed conflict and not, say, in praise of raising livestock or mending clothes. Reading his famous *Orlando Furioso* (1516–32), one may be hard put to say whether it is love that forms the background to war or war the background to love. Both, it seems, are of equal importance, and both are cleverly contrasted with each other and used to enhance each other.

As with the classical epics, much of the material, particularly that referring to various Greek and Roman deities and fearsome (but at the same time delicate and loving) warrior women, is entirely fanciful.[7] The difference, of course, is that these were almost completely artificial creations that did not have deep roots in tradition and myth. True, the authors did their—often quite mediocre—best to set the tale they were telling in a more or less historical background; for example, Ariosto's heroes live in the time of Charles the Great. However, neither they nor their readers believed that the events narrated, or anything like them, had actually taken place or, perhaps, could have taken place. In this respect they are somewhat similar to the tales of J. R. R. Tolkien. The latter, of course, also include their fair share of war and battle. Still, however much people may admire them, few believe the characters they contain ever existed, let alone that by visiting Middle Earth one may find hobbits, magicians, orcs, and similar creatures and trace the adventures in which they engaged. All this amounts to saying that by the time of the Renaissance, the distinction between literature and history had been firmly established or, if we look back to Polybios, restored.

Other Renaissance authors also had much to say about war. The most famous one was undoubtedly William Shakespeare. From *Coriolanus* through *Julius Caesar, Richard II, Richard III,* and the various *Henry*s to *Hamlet,* many of Shakespeare's plays either take war as their main subject or are set against the background of war. Shakespeare, of course, was no historian and certainly not a modern "scientific" one. Even at the time they were written and produced, his historical plays did not claim to be absolutely faithful representations of past reality. What he did was to adapt the events he wrote about and the central outline of the plots from a variety of sources generally available at his time. Very often he subtracted and added and even invented characters, detail, and dialogue as it suited his dramatic purposes.

Shakespeare lived and worked at a time when England was at war with Spain and fear of invasion was always in the air. From the little that is known about him, it would seem he had rather less military experience than some of his fellow dramatists such as Christopher Marlowe and George Chapman.[8] Yet a unique combination of research—that he carried out such research is proved by his frequent use of technical terminology—and imaginative powers enabled him to breathe life into his plays and convey a sense of authenticity even when dealing with wars in faraway countries at faraway times. His descriptions of war and battle per se tend to be brief. If only because scenes involving large numbers of people are hard to stage, most of what took place is implied rather than enacted. For example, in the whole of *King Henry V* the battle of Agincourt proper only takes up two scenes in Act IV, and even these only present the doings of a handful of men.

In any case it is not strategy, tactics, or technology that engages Shakespeare's interest. Rather, it is the people who plan war, command in war, fight in war, celebrate war, enjoy war, and suffer from war. In presenting them to us, he goes all the way from the idea that "we go to war to gain a little patch of ground that hath in it no profit but the name"[9] to Henry V's harangue before the battle, perhaps the greatest of its kind ever written.[10] Does all this mean that we should now denounce Shakespeare as a "militarist"? Of course not. All it means is that, like countless others before and after him, he saw war as the greatest of all dramas. One which, besides bringing out every human quality to its fullest extent and offering unparalleled scope to his own talents, would also appeal to the audience he was addressing.

During the seventeenth and eighteenth centuries more or less fanciful literary works whose subject was war, or which at any rate used war as their background, continued to be produced in large numbers. Among the most interesting is Hans Jacob Christof von Grimmelshausen's *Simplicissimus* (1667). Grimmelshausen, who was born in 1622, enlisted in the Swedish army when he was just sixteen years old. He thus experienced war at first hand, even though most of the time he served not as an ordinary soldier but as a military clerk. His work is satirical, focusing not on the heroics of war but on its sufferings and the absurdities it involves. Time after time, the narrator, after whom the novel is named, takes the trouble to emphasize that the stories he is telling are "veracious." This does *not* mean that they actually took place or that Grimmelshausen believed they did. It does not even mean that he wanted his readers to believe that they did, or could have; in this respect there is a strong similarity with Joseph Heller's 1961 novel of World War II, *Catch-22*. The two also have in common that although almost every detail is pure imagination, overall the outcome rings true, despite Heller's telling the late historian Stephen Ambrose that his book was pure fiction and that, in reality, everything American troops stationed at the time and place he describes did was great and marvelous.[11]

To the many kinds of literature revolving around war, the nineteenth century added the historical novel. This was the time when, in the eyes of a growing number of people, history (and, from Darwin on, biology) began to take the place of religion in tracing the origins of humanity, its growth, and its development. It was also, as the previous chapter has explained, the time when academic history was invented and, having shaken free from religion on the one hand and from fiction on the other, sought to reconstruct the past as nearly as possible as it "really" had been. Yet writers of novels were seldom academics and academics seldom wrote novels. Rather, what novelists, or at any rate the better ones among them, really did was to study the precise knowledge academic historians had generated and use it in order to project their various characters, settings, and plots into the more or less remote past, in which war and warfare occupied an extremely prominent place.

Among the representatives of the genre were some of the greatest nineteenth-century writers, such as Walter Scott, Leo Tolstoy, Emile Zola, and Stephen Crane. Unlike the authors of the *chansons de geste* and also unlike Ariosto, they did whatever they could to make the background against which their characters enact their plots as realistic as possible. Seeking to make the background as realistic as possible, they ruled out divine intervention and magic of every kind. Furthermore, often they engaged in very considerable historical research aimed at reconstructing the wars of the twelfth century, Napoleon's invasion of Russia, the Franco-Prussian War of 1870–71, and the American Civil War, respectively. When Tolstoy in *War and Peace* describes the Battle of Austerlitz, or Zola in *The Debacle* describes the Battle of Sedan, there is no question but that these encounters actually took place. Equally there is no question but that the authors in question had studied them in depth and that many of the details, as well as the characters, are perfectly authentic. For example, Tolstoy's description of the Russian commander Mikhail Kutusov and other figures corresponds closely to the truth; that Tolstoy was a Russian nationalist who only liked Russian personalities is true but besides the point. Often, though, the story's real heroes are not authentic, nor is the reader asked to believe that they are. Neither Ivanhoe, his father Cedric, the mad Ulrike, nor the beautiful Rebecca are historical, and at no time did their inventor, Scott, pretend that they were.

Otherwise put, in essence the novelists invented characters and events that *could* have existed or taken place. Having done so, they fitted them into an accurate historical setting just as diamonds are fitted onto a ring. In this they differed from Renaissance writers, to whom such accuracy did not matter; too, with many countries moving slowly toward democracy, for the first time a great deal of attention was paid to the experiences of ordinary soldiers, which previous writers had tended to neglect.[12] Since producing historical novels requires both the historian's knowledge and understanding *and* the novelist's talent for creating a plot full of suspense, vivid writing, and emotional depth, doing so is anything but easy. The novels' popularity, which in many cases lasts to the present day, speaks volumes about both the authors' technical virtuosity in doing all of this and also about their capacity for empathy. One of the works in question, Stephen Crane's *The Red Badge of Courage* (1895), has been described as providing perhaps the best idea of what battle is like for those who fight in it.[13] What makes this achievement all the more remarkable is that Crane had never seen military service or been under fire. Once again, this raises the question of how important hands-on experience is when it comes to understanding war and battle and writing about them.

By the late nineteenth century, all these different kinds of literature began to be joined by yet another one. Discounting tales of Armageddon, which tended to be not only entirely imaginary but lacking in detail, hitherto most military fiction had been located in the past. From now on, increasingly, it began to colonize the future as well. One factor responsible for the emergence of this new kind of what today would be called science fiction may have been accelerated technological progress. Generated by the industrial revolution and unfolding almost daily under people's very eyes, it made the future into the subject of curiosity—the sort of curiosity that made possible the novels of Jules Verne. Another was the wellnigh universal feeling that the intense rivalry among the great powers of the time would sooner or later resolve itself in an outbreak of armed conflict. Thus writers both fed on people's fears and stimulated them.

Consider George Tomkyns Chesney's 1871 book *The Battle of Dorking; The Reminiscences of a Volunteer.* Born in 1830, Chesney joined the British army as an officer and had risen to the rank of lieutenant colonel by the time the book was published. He ended up as a general; next, having retired, he took a seat in parliament as a Conservative member for Oxford. It is written from the point of view of a veteran. Now an old man—the book is set in the year 1920—he describes to his grandchildren how England had neglected to keep up its defenses. As a result, it was taken by surprise by the Germans. Having defeated France, the latter succeeded in concentrating in secret, crossing the Canal, and landing in Sussex. In an encounter fought in the hills of Surrey, they inflicted such a decisive defeat on the English that Britain still had not recovered its position fifty years later.

An immense popular success, *The Battle of Dorking* found countless imitators in English (on both sides of the Atlantic), French, and German.[14] From its appearance until the beginning of World War I, hardly a year passed in which some tale of future war did not see the light of print. First they were serialized chapter by chapter in the magazines; later many of them appeared in book form. Very often their authors used them to drive home a political message of some sort, be it the need to arm (or disarm), the evils of plutocracy, the dangers of democracy or socialism, or whatever. Thus tales of imaginary wars, like histories of real ones, were adapted to every point of view and taste. As long as the tale was good, very often it did not matter much who won and who lost.

Most authors followed Chesney's example and placed their wars in the immediate future, but a few, such as the American Samuel W. Odell in *The Last War* (1898), projected their tales as many as seven hundred years ahead. Most imaginary wars took place in Europe, the great political, economic, and technological powerhouse of the time, and reflected contemporary international rivalries between France, Germany, Britain (each of which produced many tales in which their respective armies defeated each other), and Russia. Others were directed by "civilized" Europeans and/or Americans against "uncivilized" but rapidly breeding Africans and Chinese, ending in the latter's total defeat and even extermination.[15] A great many used the opportunity to describe all kinds of imaginary weapons, starting with bacteria (whose use, apparently, was not yet considered uncivilized) and culminating in nuclear energy. In 1895 a British novelist, Robert Cromie in *The Crack of Doom,* became the first to suggest that "one grain of matter" might contain sufficient energy "to raise a hundred thousand tons nearly two miles";[16] such awful powers, a few others thought, might even put an end to war as we know it.[17] Focusing on politics, war, and technology, as works of art few if any of these volumes could compare with the best historical novels in terms of scope, the depiction of character, and emotional depth. However, as good adventure yarns, they held their own, and as evidence about the way contemporaries saw war, they are indispensable.

The epics and the *chansons de geste* apart, our survey so far has been limited mainly to the prose literature surrounding war. From time immemorial, though, war has also given rise to a body of poetry so vast as to almost defy the imagination. Corresponding to every taste, from the truly sublime to the most vulgar drivel, most could probably be divided into three basic types. First there are works that call for war and encourage those who engage in it. In the words of poet laureate William Ernest Henley in the preface to his edited volume of *Lyra Heroica,* their task is "to set forth . . . the beauty and joy of living, the beauty and blessedness of death, the glory of battle and adventure, the nobility of devotion—to a cause, an ideal, a passion even."[18] While going back at least as far as ancient Greece during the sixth century B.C., this kind of martial poetry was never more popular than during the nineteenth century, when it joined forces with nationalism.[19] It reached one of its high points in 1862 when Julia Ward Howe wrote and published *The Battle Hymn of the Republic:*

Mine eyes have seen the glory of the coming of the Lord
He is trampling out the vintage where the grapes of wrath are stored
He has loosed the fateful lightening of His terrible swift sword
His truth is marching on.

Glory! Glory! Hallelujah! . . .

I have seen Him in the watch-fires of a hundred circling camps
They have builded Him an altar in the evening dews and damps
I can read His righteous sentence by the dim and flaring lamps
His day is marching on.

I have read a fiery gospel writ in burnished rows of steel,
"As ye deal with my contemners, So with you My grace shall deal;"

Let the Hero, born of woman, crush the serpent with his heel
Since God is marching on.

He has sounded forth the trumpet that shall never call retreat
He is sifting out the hearts of men before His judgment-seat:
Oh, be swift, my soul, to answer Him! be jubilant my feet!
Our God is marching on.

In the beauty of the lilies Christ was born across the sea,
With a glory in His bosom that transfigures you and me:
As He died to make men holy, let us die to make men free,
While God is marching on.[20]

There were works that celebrated victory and gloated over the
enemy's defeat. One such, attributed to the biblical prophet Deborah, is
worth citing in full:

Praise ye the Lord for the avenging of Israel, when the people willingly offered themselves. Hear, O ye kings; give ear, O ye princes; I,
even I, will sing unto the Lord; I will sing praise to the Lord God of
Israel.

Lord, when thou wentest out of Seir, when thou marchedst out
of the field of Edom, the earth trembled, and the heavens dropped,
the clouds also dropped water.

The mountains melted from before the Lord, even that Sinai
from before the Lord God of Israel.

In the days of Shamgar the son of Anath, in the days of Jael, the
highways were unoccupied, and the travelers walked through by-
ways. The inhabitants of the villages ceased, they ceased in Israel,
until that I Deborah arose, that I arose a mother in Israel.

They chose new gods; then was war in the gates; was there a
shield or spear seen among forty thousand in Israel?

My heart is toward the governors of Israel, that offered themselves willingly among the people. Bless ye the Lord.

Speak, ye that ride on white asses, ye that sit in judgment, and
walk by the way.

They that are delivered from the noise of archers in the places
of drawing water, there shall they rehearse the righteous acts of the
Lord, even the righteous acts toward the inhabitants of his villages
in Israel; then shall the people of the Lord go down to the gates.

Awake, awake, Deborah: awake, awake, utter a song; arise,
Barak, and lead thy captivity captive, thou son of Abinoam.

Then he made him that remaineth have dominion over the nobles among the people: the Lord made me have dominion over the mighty.

Out of Ephraim was there a root of them against Amalek; after thee, Benjamin, among thy people; out of Machir came down governors, and out of Zebulun they that handle the pen of the writer.

And the princes of Issachar were with Deborah; even Issachar, and also Barak; he was sent on foot into the valley. For the divisions of Reuben there were great thoughts of heart.

Why abodest thou among the sheepfolds, to hear the bleatings of the flocks? For the divisions of Reuben there were great searchings of heart.

Gilead abode beyond Jordan; and why did Dan remain in ships? Asher continued on the sea shore, and abode in his breaches.

Zebulun and Naphtali were a people that jeoparded their lives unto the death in the high places in the field.

The kings came and fought; then fought the kings of Canaan in Taanach by the waters of Megiddo; they took no gain of money.

They fought from heaven; the stars in their courses fought against Sisera.

The river of Kishon swept them away, that ancient river, the river of Kishon, O my soul, thou has trodden down strength.

Then were the horsehoofs broken by the means of the prancings, the prancings of their mighty ones.

Curse ye Meroz, said the angel of the Lord, curse ye bitterly the inhabitants thereof; because they came not to the help of the Lord, to the help of the Lord against the mighty.

Blessed above women shall Jael the wife of Heber the Kenite be; blessed shall she be above women in the tent.

He asked water, and she gave him milk; she brought forth butter in a lordly dish.

She put her hand to the nail, and her right hand to the workmen's hammer; and with the hammer she smote Sisera, she smote off his head, when she had pierced and stricken through his temples.

At her feet he bowed, he fell, he lay down; at her feet he bowed, he fell; where he bowed, there he fell down dead.

The mother of Sisera looked out at a window, and cried through the lattice, Why is his chariot so long in coming? Why tarry the wheels of his chariot?

Her wise ladies answered her, yea, she returned answer to herself,

Have they not sped? Have they not divided the prey; to every man a damsel or two; to Sisera a prey of divers colors, a prey of divers colors of needlework, of divers colors of needlework on both sides, meet for the necks of them that take the spoil?

So let all thine enemies perish, O Lord: but let them that love him be as the sun when he goeth forth in his might.[21]

Here, as in some other compositions of the same genre, the praise showered on the victor becomes even more pronounced by being contrasted with the misery of the loser.

There were also works that deplored the waste, pain, suffering, and sorrow of it all. There probably is not a place or time in history that did not produce poems devoted to these subjects. They tell of dead and mutilated bodies, raped women, starving children, flourishing towns and villages that have been turned into ruins, and entire districts that have been laid waste, often in violation of every rule of human conduct and often for no purpose at all. As might be expected, World War I, the greatest and most destructive war in history until then, was a particularly fruitful source of poetry of this kind. Siegfried Sassoon, the author whose poem in praise of the parade ground has been quoted in chapter 6, provides as good a sample of its kind as may be found:

To the Warmongers

(Spring 1917)

I'm back again from hell
With loathsome thoughts to sell;
Secrets of death to tell;
And horrors from the abyss.

Young faces bleared with blood,
Sucked down into the mud,
You shall hear things like this,
Till the tormented slain
Crawl round and once again,
With limbs that twist awry
Moan out their brutish pain,
As the fighters pass them by,

For you our battles shine
With triumph half-divine;
And the glory of the dead
Kindles in each proud eye.

But a cure is on my head,
That shall not be unsaid,
And the wounds in my heart are red,
For I have watched them die.[22]

There is no doubt that the poem is intense. But before we draw the wrong conclusions from it, let's take a closer look at the career of this famous antiwar poet. Sassoon was born in 1886, the scion of an immensely wealthy family. He led a privileged life and, like some other young men with too much money in the bank and too little real work to do, started writing verse with a vague idea of perhaps one day becoming a poet. Instead he became one of the first to volunteer for military service even before war had been officially declared. As he later wrote, doing so freed him from "any sense of personal responsibility."

Commissioned as a lieutenant, Sassoon quickly developed into a redoubtable killer, engaging in such daring escapades as to be nicknamed "Mad Jack" by his men. It was *after* he got his first taste of service in the trenches that he wrote:

I never thought to find such peace. If it were not for Mother and friends I would pray for a speedy death. I want a genuine taste of the horrors, and then—peace. I don't want to go back to the old inane life which always seemed like a prison. I want freedom, not comfort . . . The last fifteen months have unsealed my eyes. I have lived well and truly since the war began, and have made my sacrifices; now I ask that the price be required of me.[23]

As late as the beginning of July 1916, Sassoon was describing his experiences during the opening days of the Somme—remembered as the time when the British Army suffered the worst defeat in its entire history—as "great fun." It was only during a spell in the hospital, where he was recuperating from an illness, that he began to change his mind.

In his own words, what triggered the change was not so much what he had experienced in the trenches. Rather, it was "heavy lunches in London clubs" and his disgust with the "blighters" and "harlots" who, staying at home, were having the time of their lives; they made him long for the "freedom" and "greatness" of the front. Further disappointed by his failure to get a medal he thought he had deserved, Sassoon launched into several years of intensive antiwar writing.[24] Yet as late as the second half of 1918 he felt that war had been "an improvement on a lot of the aimless things one did in peace-time." Having said what he had to say about war, his creative impulse was exhausted; it took him three decades and a religious revelation to find another subject to write about. Thus his poetry, and that of a great many others as well, does not prove that war had no fascination for him. In fact, the opposite is the case.

As had been noted, Sassoon was not alone.[25] Poets such as Wilfred Owen (whose posthumous work Sassoon edited) and prose writers such as Erich Maria Remarque and Ludwig Renn also filled page after page showing their fascination with war even as they denounced its barbarity in the strongest terms they could think of.[26] But their influence, like that of many others of the self-styled "lost generation," should not be exaggerated. Both Remarque and Renn's novels were best-sellers, and deservedly so. However, Owen's poetry was a commercial failure.[27] At first Sassoon's did not do much better. While its aesthetic qualities were appreciated, even admired, it tended to be dismissed as the understandable outpourings of a young man who, having seen more action than was good for him, had gone slightly out of his mind.[28] It was only in the early 1930s that he and Owen began to have any real impact. By that time, some would argue, Adolf Hitler was already threatening to unleash an even more monstrous conflict. Thus the two of them, to the extent that they encouraged appeasement, may have done their country more harm than good.

Throughout the 1920s and 1930s, for every volume that presented the recent war as a vale of tears, suffering, pain, death, and sorrow, another one was published that exulted in it and glorified it. Among these works, the best-known example is Ernst Jünger's *Im Stahlgewitter* (*In the Storm of Steel*). No armchair soldier, Jünger had seen quite as much action as any other fighter. In the end, having been wounded no fewer than seven times, he even won the Pour le Mérite. Yet he shared neither Remarque's all-pervasive sense of idiotic futility nor Renn's feeling of incredible horrors endured and personalities forever wasted. For him, to the contrary, the war had come as liberation from the weight of the bourgeois civilization in which he had grown up, a civilization he experienced as so oppressive that, as a youth, he had run away from home to join the French Foreign Legion. However unpalatable the fact may be to some, aesthetically speaking *Im Stahlgewitter* will stand comparison with anything published about war between 1919 and 1939. Nor did Jünger change his mind later on. Insisting that he had described war as it was, not as it could or should have been,[29] he brought out several more volumes in which he evoked the world of the trenches.[30] Strange it certainly was, surreal, dangerous, and deadly, but also positively pulsating with life. As early as 1931 he began to look forward to the next war, a subject that led to yet another series of books culminating in *Auf die Marmorklippen* (*On the Marble Cliffs*, 1939). Eventually his fame brought him an offer to head the chamber of writers in the Third Reich—which he rejected.

For reasons that are not easy to explain, the country that during these years saw the publication of the greatest number of antiwar novels, plays, and poems was France. The country's losses, it is true, had been heavier than those of either Germany or Britain. In addition, some parts of the country that had been occupied by the Germans were so devastated that they took decades to recover. Still, in neither human nor material terms did France's loss compare with that of Russia, which went through two wars instead of one. Unlike Russia, moreover, France had come out of the conflict as one of the victors. Its empire remained intact and was, in fact, enlarged by the important addition of Syria; its position in Europe was stronger than it had been at any time since at least 1870. Certainly French writers were just as obsessed with war as Hemingway was and, given what their country had endured, perhaps more justified in being so. Unlike him, however, most of them spent almost all their energies deploring war, mourning the dead, encouraging youth to pacifism, and hoping against hope that there would be no repetition; this semi-official policy even had a title, "moral disarmament."[31]

The first and most famous French antiwar novel, Henri Barbusse's *Le Feu*, was published during the conflict itself, drawing a harrowing picture of the pointless sufferings of the *poilus* (the nickname given to French World War I infantrymen). Of those who followed him, perhaps the most successful were those who, like Sassoon in some of his poems, made their point by using black comedy. A good example is Pierre Drieu La Rochelle in *La Comédie de Charleroi* (1934); here, a mother uses her son's death in battle in order to increase her own prestige in the society in which she lives.[32] Those and a few others apart, much of the result amounted to sentimental trash and has rightly been forgotten. Here and there it is even possible to find an antiwar author, such as Jean Giraudoux, who ruefully admitted that, compared to war, peace was a wan, uninteresting, and simply boring subject to write about.[33]

By 1938, thirty-three-year-old Jean-Paul Sartre was describing the petty, empty selfishness of contemporary French society under the telling title *Nausea*. He need not have worried. War, and with it the "strange defeat" of 1940—strange in the sense that never in history was a great power overthrown with greater ease—did come.[34] After the inevitable early confusion and attempts at collaboration, the German occupation gave writers such as Elsa Triole, Louis Aragon, Maurice Merleau-Ponty, and of course Sartre himself something not only to write about but also, perhaps, to live for.[35] It also gave them readers, what with circulation figures of underground papers going up from zero in June 1940 to tens of thousands and even hundreds of thousands four years later.[36] Perhaps at few other times could so many people read about war and, simply by doing so, feel heroically involved in a great and noble enterprise of liberation.

Outside France's borders, the picture was much more mixed. In Mussolini's Italy and Hitler's Germany, writers who presented war as other than glorious were prohibited from publishing, if they were lucky, and landed in a concentration camp, if they were not. Conversely, in both countries writers who met the regime's expectations and stirred up martial feelings could expect substantial honorary and financial rewards. The result was vast amounts of trash, albeit of a very different kind from that produced by so many French writers. Focusing on Germany under National Socialism, war literature, instead of being sentimental, was shrill, full of "sacred" storms, "blossoming" youth, and "self-sacrificing" comrades who rushed into death loudly singing their country's anthem; having died, their light continued to shine through all eternity.[37]

Instead of endlessly diving into the various heroes' (and heroines') delicate and contradictory feelings, the literature in question was lacking in nuance, one-sided, and completely unrealistic. Yet this did not prevent writers such as Karl Broeger, Ernst Johannsen, Werner Beumelburg, and Fritz von Unruh from enjoying great popularity.[38] It is said that for every volume dealing with peace, there were twenty whose subject was war;[39] several of Unruh's works (e.g., *Way of Sacrifice*, 1928) were even translated into English. Little of the literature in question survived into the post-1945 period. In part, this was because it was just not good enough. In part, however, its disappearance was due to the fact that it was systematically execrated and boycotted.

In Stalin's Soviet Union, things were a little more complicated. Unlike Fascism and National Socialism, in principle, Communism was always "peace-loving." On the other hand, there was a growing "duty" to acknowledge the historical tradition of the struggle that had brought the Communist regime to power and, by implication, all other wars that could somehow be construed as being waged by the oppressed against their class oppressors.[40] As a result of this "duty," in the Soviet Union even more than in the other totalitarian states, literature often dealt not with flesh-and-blood men and women but with caricatures moved by the invisible cords of history and the relationships of production. Always and everywhere, they assaulted their enemies waving red flags and fell down yelling Communist slogans; after 1945, similar techniques were applied to "the Great Patriotic War" of 1941–45. In Stalin's hand even the term *realist,* which normally has positive connotations, was besmirched, coming to mean the opposite of "true." As far as it is possible to check, none of this did much to instill the fighting spirit the leadership sought. During much of the period between the world wars, Soviet military morale was low indeed, reaching a nadir in 1939–40.[41] In the end, it took the German invasion to shake the country out of its apathy.

Somewhere between France and the totalitarian states stood the United States and Britain. Both, it is true, produced large amounts of antiwar literature. The American equivalents of Remarque, Renn, Owen, Sassoon, were writers such as John Dos Passos, e. e. cummings, and Ezra Pound. The first two had volunteered for war before, shocked by its bestiality, they turned to describing its dehumanizing effects. The third, though he never came close to a battlefield (he spent the war living in London), was somehow able to find within himself even more effective words to denounce it, a fact that his subsequent turn toward fascism can by no means obscure.[42] For a time, even the pre-1914 tradition of aggressive science fiction seemed to have made a complete turnaround. Previously in such fiction the awesome weapons American scientists put into the hands of their wise and beneficial leaders had invariably led to the triumph of the equally wise and beneficial Anglo-Saxon civilization and with it a world government and the end of war. Now the possibility had to be considered that some very bad people across the Atlantic and Pacific oceans would be the first to lay their hands on the new devices, causing things to develop the other way around. As a result, many writers, instead of describing the glories and triumphs of future war, began to speculate about the need to prevent it from taking place.[43]

Yet this was but one side of the picture. As volumes such as Frederic W. Ziv's *The Valiant Muse* (1936) prove, even in Britain, and even at a time when the pacifist movement was at the peak of is strength, much published material remained as unshakably high-minded and patriotic as it had long been. Book for book, the public seems to have preferred patriotism to disillusionment;[44] here and there, an editor of anthologies even went so far as to exclude the works of Owen and Sassoon because they had too much to say about war's "passive sufferings" and not enough about the joy of those who entered it expecting to play with their lives.[45] As George Orwell once complained, authors of juvenile literature in particular seemed to have learned nothing and forgotten nothing.[46] Instead, they went on cranking out the same old war stories. All of them were set in the good old days around 1910, all of them were heroic, and all of them ended in the triumph of pleasant-faced, public-school-educated, courageous, fair-dealing British youths over their various nefarious adversaries.

Returning to the United States, tales about the horrors of war and the need to do something to prevent it from recurring only enjoyed a relatively short life during the early to mid-1930s. Next, the wind changed. Many American writers went back to their usual ebullient (some would say aggressive) selves. The larger the German and Japanese threats seemed to loom toward the end of the decade, the stronger the tendency to throw caution to the wind. By 1940, a time when many Europeans had already experienced what the bomber could do and the rest were tremulously anticipating its coming, fictional American scientists were once again building imaginary weapons more powerful than any in history and preparing to use them.[47]

Finally, one country that did experience war during the period in question, and which therefore may present a more fruitful field for inquiry than either "the west" or the totalitarian states, was Spain. Right from the beginning, the Spanish Civil War was regarded not merely as an internal affair but as a clash between opposing worldviews. As a result, it saw the participation of foreigners on both sides and was passionately followed even by people far removed from the scene. It produced a momentous amount of literature, including works by such well-known authors as Ilya Ehrenburg, Antoine de Saint-Exupéry, André Malraux, and Arthur Koestler.[48] Many others, such as the correspondent for the Nazi paper *Völkischer Beobachter,* Roland Strunk, have since been forgotten, but at the time they scribbled with the best.[49] Some of them were intent on little more than praising the heroic deeds and self-sacrifice they claimed to have witnessed—each one, needless to say, on his own side of the front.[50]

Others, particularly those whose work was only published after Franco had finally left the scene and democracy was restored, were more interested in the horror of it all.[51]

Perhaps the most famous books to come out of the war were George Orwell's *Homage to Catalonia* (1938) and Ernest Hemingway's *For Whom the Bell Tolls* (1940). Hemingway was an apolitical self-styled he-man who had known war at first hand in 1917–18 and rushed to Spain to report on the conflict, hoping it would provide him with material for his greatest novel of all.[52] Orwell was an extremely political left-wing socialist who had not yet known war directly and went to Spain to take part in it *and* report on it, doing "my best to be honest."[53] Both Hemingway and Orwell (who at one point had been a policeman in Burma) apparently acted as weapon instructors to untrained republican troops. Neither glorified war, and both were well aware of the misery, the squalor, and the atrocities. That apart, Orwell has much to say about the Communist betrayal of the democratic values for which men such as himself fought and sacrificed themselves; in the end, his objections to their methods almost cost him his life. By contrast, Hemingway seems preoccupied with death to the point of suicide (which he eventually committed in 1961). Yet to say their books were concerned exclusively with those aspects would be untrue. Orwell speaks of the rats in the trenches, but also of how much he enjoyed turning a group of volunteers into a cohesive unit and the fun he and his men had skinny-dipping during a lull in the fighting. With Hemingway, war, camaraderie, love of country, and love of women are always closely related. Had it been otherwise, neither could have produced the works of art he did.

At all times and places war has formed a subject for literature par excellence. Some authors feared it, some eagerly anticipated it. Some hated it, some exulted in it. Certainly its horrors caused many to experience a rude awakening, leaving them scarred for life and generating a sense of the futility of it all. However, this did not apply to everybody and perhaps not even to the majority. Quite a number looked back upon it as a great, perhaps the greatest, experience in their lives, one they never tired of describing in as many ways as they could think of. Furthermore, very often even the authors who were loudest in their professions of hatred for war could not resist the temptation to deal with it; in other words, neither horror nor futility translates into lack of interest. In the very greatest productions, including the *Iliad* and *War and Peace,* all the various emotions that war excites are mixed in different people at the same time and often in the same person at different times. To this should be added the ever-present gap between the narrator and his characters. As a result, often it is all but impossible to say which voices truly represent that of the author.

On one hand, people's lives certainly helped dictate what they did and did not write. On the other, and as is also the case among historians, perhaps the most surprising fact of all is the lack of any direct link between an author's experience of war and his ability to make his readers understand what it was like. No doubt the fact that Tolstoy, Owen, Sassoon, Jünger, Remarque, Renn, Cummings, Dos Passos, Orwell, and Hemingway did see war at first hand helped them both in selecting their subjects and in writing as they did. Yet the fact that Shakespeare, Crane, and Pound did not go through war neither prevented them from writing about it nor does it mean that their works are in any way inferior to the rest. As has already been mentioned, Crane was able to conjure up the experience of battle as perhaps no one before or after him had done. Pound in "Hugh Selwyn Mauberley" launched what is surely one of the most effective antiwar tirades ever, concluding that, having "walked eye-deep in hell," "a myriad / and of the best," had died "for an old bitch gone in the teeth / For a botched civilization."[54] In all these different ways, the relationship between life on the one hand and literature on the other is far from simple.

11

Art and War

Whereas writing is only a few millennia old (throughout the *Iliad* there is not a single reference to it), the plastic arts are much older. The oldest of all known paintings date to the upper Stone Age. Created 20,000 to 30,000 years ago, they were found in caves at Cougnac, Gabillou, Lascaux, Le Placard, Pech Merle, and Sous-Grand-Lac, all in modern France. In the past, whether or not they show men at war has been much debated; nowadays the prevailing consensus is that they do not. No such doubts surround more recent Stone Age paintings dating to perhaps 12,000 to 18,000 B.C. Some were discovered in caves located in the Iberian Peninsula. Others come from Çatal Hüyük in modern Turkey. What they show is armed men marching in column, deploying into line, shooting at each other with bows and arrows, and, in one case, using a sling.[1]

What made the ancient cavemen engage in war, or why they chose to commemorate their fights as they did, we do not know; trying to use the paintings to reconstruct their lives would be like trying to reconstruct Shakespeare's *Hamlet* from half-charred, centuries-old stage trappings left behind when the Globe Theater burned down. Concerning the people who produced a number of cave paintings in what is now South Africa, we can only assume that they may have been more or less like the San at the time before their "discovery" by the Europeans. Proceeding on this scanty basis, we may speculate that our remote ancestors depicted war much as they did other more or less important aspects of their lives, such as hunting, religious worship, the rites of birth, sex, death, and the like. Another possibility is that they were trying to achieve magical-religious objectives, such as inflicting injury on the enemy, appeasing the spirits, looking after their own souls and those of the dead, and so on.[2]

In this connection it is essential to point out that the distinction between "military" and "nonmilitary" art is a recent one. It dates back no more than a few centuries at most, and has everything to do with the fact that modern soldiers form a separate corporate body and are dressed in uniform. In earlier times, when secular society did not exist, almost all art—indeed, almost all culture—was either religious or military. Sometimes the two came together, as when warriors assumed the garb of saints and saints that of warriors; the Knights Templar, the Teutonic Knights, the Knights of St. John, and certain militant Muslim organizations all provide examples of this. To say nothing of the fact that, from Zeus down, many deities were themselves represented as warriors who made a specialty of smiting their enemies with mighty blows. One way or another, much of the time war and culture went together very well, reinforcing each other and drawing inspiration from each other—as it has been one of the goals of this book to explain.

What we might call "civilian" and "secular" art only appeared in relatively few societies that were not completely dominated by the military, or the priesthood, or both. One such society was China. Here organized religion was fairly weak. A class of priests responsible to the authorities for supervising society did not exist, and scholarly culture, as developed by the mandarins, was extremely important. Others were Greece and Rome, which in many ways invented what is commonly called civil society. But even in such societies, military art, far from occupying some special niche, was considered an integral part of art as a whole. Nor was there any question of treating it with contempt as, in the West, it often has been from World War I on.

As with historians and writers, artists were drawn to war for a variety of reasons. One was probably because of the role war had played in the history of the peoples and communities to whom they belonged; after all, when a city was sacked, the artist's workshop would be plundered, his wife and daughter raped, and he himself killed along with everybody else. That, however, was but one reason, and perhaps not the most important. Very often war allowed artists to engage their taste for display, splendor, and sheer pomp—to depict serried ranks of men, magnificently decorated horses prancing about, shining armor, polished weapons, colorful uniforms, banners fluttering in the wind, and the like. Artists originating in societies such as ancient Greece, which was infatuated with the beauty of the human body, could also use scenes of war and combat as an opportunity to present that body in all its various motions and in all its glory. Finally, and also as in the case of writers, war generated every sort of extreme emotion that artists might do their best to capture, from the fear of death to the ecstasy of fighting, from the glory of victory to the anguish of the defeated.

Ancient Greek vases, especially those originating in Athens, are universally admired as carrying some of the greatest figurative art ever created. Much as pacifists may deplore the fact, such vases are as likely to carry scenes of warriors and soldiers fighting as to show mythological scenes (many of which themselves revolve around war) or the day-to-day activities of peace. As far as we know, very large numbers of such vases were produced in relatively small, privately owned workshops comprising a master, his male family members, and perhaps a few slaves. Hence there could be no question of any political pressure being brought to bear. Most likely, the artists made the decision as to which paintings to cover their wares with in the hope of meeting expected demand. Going to work, they must have been assisted by the fact that in the world of Greek (and Etruscan) city-states, almost every soldier was a citizen and almost every citizen was a soldier, so that close personal acquaintance with war was very widespread. All the more reason why art and war, rather than going their separate ways, went together as a matter of course.

Though the number of large-scale paintings that have survived from the ancient world is small, we do know that some of those which did exist took war as their subject matter. Thus, a man by the name of Euphranor is known to have painted the Theban victory over Sparta at Mantinea in 362 B.C., a defeat from which the latter never recovered.[3] The Roman writer Pliny the Elder says that a late-fourth-century-B.C. painter, Philoxenus of Eretria, produced a panorama of the Battle of Issus in which Alexander defeated Darius in 333 B.C. Starting around the middle of the third century B.C., every time a victorious Roman commander returned home he would commission paintings of the campaign to display in his triumph, and these would later be deposited in temples and other public places. While almost all these paintings have disappeared, a mosaic that may have been based on Philoxenus's rendition of Issus was found in Pompeii and can now be seen in the National Museum of

Naples.[4] Many other Greek and Roman mosaics also show scenes of combat, even though, given the enormous effort involved (the number of stones in the Alexander mosaic is estimated at four million), they are more likely to focus on encounters between individuals than on full-scale battle.

What is true of painting is equally true of reliefs and sculpture. Greek sarcophagi, and later Roman ones as well, very often have their sides positively bristling with scenes of combat. Legions of statutes of every size and description also show warriors in action, resting on their arms, or, as in the case of the "dying Gaul" genre developed at Pergamon, expiring after having been wounded.[5] At times the artist added signs that refer back to mythology and permit the identity of the combatants to be established, but in a great many cases this is not possible. On both the sarcophagi and the vases, scenes of combat are often mixed with all kinds of other scenes, such as daily life, hunts, and religious processions. Even the heroes of the Trojan War, who are often identified by name, are not necessarily shown fighting. We also see them engaged in a variety of other activities: Peleus marrying Thetis, Achilles being discovered among the daughters of Lycomedes, Briseis being taken from Achilles, Achilles playing a game with Ajax, and the like.[6] Presumably this is another proof that creating a separate "military art" was the last thing the artists had in mind. Rather, they were out to portray the whole of life, of which war was very much a part.

Another peculiarity of the ancient vase paintings, the reliefs, and the sculptures is that, from Heracles down, a great many combatants, especially but not exclusively mythological ones, are represented nude or semi-nude. In fact, most Greek and all Roman soldiers wore metal armor in battle. Even the poorest among them covered themselves with dresses made of leather as, of course, did their barbarian opponents. Hence one can only guess that the artists in question had in mind some ulterior objective, such as presenting the human body in action and their own ability to capture it. This motive is even more in evidence when it comes to depicting female warriors, such as the Amazons.[7] Some Renaissance artists who specialized in martial scenes, such as Antonio Pollaiolo and Domenico Campagnola, were equally fascinated by the human body in action and equally prolific in producing images of it even if those images did not correspond to anything they could have seen in the real world.[8] Another reason why warriors are presented naked may have been to show how brave they were.[9]

From then to the present day, it would be hard, perhaps impossible, to find a society whose members did not find war fascinating and who did not try to present it as the best available technical means, and their own talents, allowed. Ancient Mesopotamia and Egypt, China, Japan, India, Byzantium, the Aztecs, and the Inca all had their share of military art in the form of paintings, reliefs, and sculptures of every size and description. Several of them had much more than their share; using the art in question to commemorate, intimidate, and in some cases serve a variety of magical and religious purposes. As to quality, think of the ranks of Chinese soldiers found in a Han-era tomb or of ancient Persian ones at Persepolis; the art in question will stand comparison with any other produced by any other civilization at any other time. To the extent that the prevailing interpretation of religion permitted figurative art, as was at some times the case in Iran and Turkey, the same even applies to Islamic countries. After all, Muhammad's importance as a commander is second only to his role as a prophet. Directly or indirectly, he is supposed to have participated in no fewer than thirty-seven battles; this fact is reflected in some Koranic manuscripts, and also in other artistic productions.[10]

Some of the vast body of material in question is fairly straightforward: it is clear that we are seeing a warrior. In other cases the paintings or sculptures themselves provide clues to what they are about, whereas in others still they come accompanied by written texts containing information about what the artists were trying to accomplish. There are, however, many cases when what we see is not so straightforward. Do the Lascaux paintings show men at war, or do they not? What are the strange watch-like devices worn by the Assyrian officers portrayed on the reliefs found in the royal palace at Nineveh and now in the British Museum? Were the wheeled contraptions shown on the same reliefs really battering rams? If so, why do they have sharp points, and why are those points aimed at the top of the walls of the besieged city and not at the bottom, as one would expect? Did the strange shields with narrow waists shown in early Greek art, looking somewhat like violins or cellos, really exist? These and similar questions have created an enormous scholarly literature aimed at figuring out whether or not the artists who produced the works were familiar with war, how objective or subjective they were, to what extent their products may be relied upon in our attempts to reconstruct reality, and so on. From our particular point of view, it does not really matter.

Medieval European artists, too, were much interested in war and often depicted it. In their case some of the interest was religious. Christianity, after all, predicts that the world will end in the battle of Armageddon, a subject that has long acted as a magnet to artists. It also has quite a number of heroes, such as Saint Martin, Saint George, Saint Joan of Arc, and several Saint Demetrioses of the Greek Orthodox Church who owed their fame to their martial exploits.[11] Consequently, one could often find war and warfare represented even in church; as the history of the Crusades and the wars of religion proves, Christianity was by no means always as pacifist-minded as some of its modern adherents claim. Other medieval artists worked for the chivalrous classes, whose demand for war-related scenes was all but insatiable. Some designed and created tapestries (though only one of these, the Bayeux Tapestry, survives, others are known to have existed), while others illustrated manuscripts of sacred and secular texts.

One peculiarity much in evidence is that medieval people, artists included, did not see history as a process of linear change.[12] As a result, very often when trying to re-create military episodes taken from periods long predating their own they tended toward anachronism, for example, by showing Macedonian and Roman soldiers as if they were knights on horseback and adding weapons and tactics that the ancients would not have recognized. Their presentations of contemporary war and warriors tended to be much more true to life, though inaccuracies did creep in. In terms of style, they range all the way from brutal realism—decapitated heads, limbs chopped off, blood squirting out—to idealization, symbolism, and allegory. As with other civilizations, their work forms a very important historical source, helping answer such questions as to just when the technique of couching the lance came into use.[13] As was also true of other civilizations, there are times when it raises more questions than answers.

The Renaissance is generally recognized as a time when artistic activity exploded, a fact that could not fail to leave its mark on the field in which we are interested. From Paolo Ucello, Giorgio Vasari, Leonardo da Vinci, Albrecht Dürer, Albert Altdorfer, Urs Graf, Daniel Hopfer, Niklaus Manuel, and Hans Sebald Beham down, many of the best-known Renaissance artists endlessly depicted skirmishes, battles, fortresses under siege, and soldiers. The latter are shown engaged in every conceivable activity: being recruited, leaving their families, in camp, marching, foraging, fighting, returning home, and carousing, as well as in death and with wounds. Some of the images are more or less realistic and may be used as historical sources.[14] Some are allegorical, whereas others still are perhaps best understood as caricatures.

In the opinion of some seventeenth-century art critics, battle paintings represented not just art but the highest type of art.[15] On one hand, the professional knowledge and artistic competence needed to integrate a very large number of people and details into a single composition were appreciated. On the other, military formations, by imposing order on irrationality and chaos, appealed to the Baroque taste for geometric forms. Many paintings referred to more or less contemporary battles such as Lepanto (1571) and the defeat of the Spanish Armada (1588). Others, such as Luca Giordano's *The Battle of Constantine,* had history as their subject—which does not mean that Renaissance artists were necessarily less guilty of engaging in anachronisms than their medieval predecessors had been. Some were much less true to reality than others, with the result that their reliability as historical sources has been debated.[16] Once again, from our point of view it does not matter.

Depending partly on those who purchased the paintings and partly on the artists' own talents, by the seventeenth century most such works could be divided into three basic types.[17] First, perhaps most numerous but least impressive artistically speaking, there were those which were meant for the professional use of officers and commanders. They filled their purpose by going into considerable technological and tactical detail. Such productions also included elaborate engravings showing the fortifications of various cities, the road that led to them, and the like. Many remain popular to the present day and can easily be purchased in the form of reproductions.

Second, there were those that sought to glorify the encounters, battles, and sieges they depicted. In them, inevitably, it was the victorious commander who took center place—even if, as was sometimes the case, he had not really been present or only arrived at the last moment to claim the credit for himself. Almost always he was shown mounted, reconnoitering the terrain, pointing his sword or scepter while issuing orders, or galloping at the head of his troops, either surrounded by a glittering staff or alone.

During the eighteenth and nineteenth centuries things changed. It is true that most governments remained firmly monarchical. Nevertheless, on the whole, rulers became somewhat less important, the states they ruled or the armies they commanded more so. As Frederick the Great succinctly put it: "I am the first servant of the state." This way of thinking may explain why, whereas nobody had thought to paint Gustavus meeting his fate at Luetzen, some artists began to produce a variation on the age-old theme of the victorious commander by showing him dying even as his forces were about to triumph. Those portrayed in this way included General James Wolfe, General Joseph Warren, General Richard Montgomery, General Hugh Mercer, and Admiral Horatio Nelson.

Third, there were decorative works that focused on artistic effects, such as the glint of bayonets, the flash of cannon, the smoke of gunpowder, and the like. One very good example of an artist who worked in this genre was a French painter, Jacques Courtois.[18] Works with titles such as *The Battle of Mongiovino* and *Joshua Stopping the Sun* enabled him to both gain commissions and give free rein to his fascination with light, shadow, and movement—a taste, of course, that he shared with many contemporary artists from Rembrandt down.

Whatever the category they belong to, the works in question came in every variety and were adapted to every pocket. The largest and most elaborate ones could be found adorning the walls of the palaces and castles of the mighty. The smallest, in the form of cheap woodcuts often made by unknown artists, illustrated the countless books and pamphlets that dealt with contemporary and historical affairs.

A fourth kind, which cannot be included in any of these categories, are artistic works that show the horrors of war. Images of this kind seem to have been especially popular in the Netherlands during the eighty-year struggle against Spain (1568–1648); however, Germany during the wars of religion (1555–1648) and France during the Thirty Years' War (1618–1648) also produced their share.[19] Sometimes the renditions took allegorical form, as when an anonymous follower of Rubens painted *The Consequences of War* (ca. 1638), which showed Mars tearing himself loose from Venus's arms in order to perform his bloody work.[20] It is certainly possible to find drawings of dead or mutilated soldiers, or even soldiers being eaten by dogs. Still, works that focus mainly, let alone exclusively, on such topics represent a small minority.

Some artists, such as Pieter Breughel the Elder, displayed an intriguing tendency to place such scenes not in the present but in the past. Thus they might paint sixteenth-century soldiers (easily recognizable by their equipment) maltreating the inhabitants of a very contemporary-looking Dutch village and call their work *The Murder of the Innocents*. Why they did so we don't know; members of Breughel's generation certainly had enough information at their disposal to know exactly what Roman sol-

diers had looked like. Perhaps he and the others were worried that plac-
ing such horrible scenes in a more contemporary context would reduce
the chance of their work selling.

With Velázquez in the lead, most artists probably produced military
art as part of their normal work in an attempt to satisfy their patrons'
tastes. Some, however, turned it into their specialty; by the end of the
seventeenth century, battle painting was recognized as a separate genre.
Thus Charles Le Brun both designed the Galerie des Batailles for Louis
XIV and produced some of the paintings it contains. At one point he was
also commissioned to decorate French warships; but such was the bill he
presented that he was paid his fee on condition he never set foot in the
shipyards again. The two Vanderveldes, father and son, specialized in
naval paintings and could be found in little boats bobbing around many a
battle, recording their impressions.[21]

From at least the time of Emperor Charles V on, some rulers and
commanders started paying artists to come along on campaign and produce sketches that could later be worked into paintings or tapestries,
such as those that decorate the Viennese Hofburg as well as Blenheim
Palace. Under Louvois, minister of war to Louis XIV, the French Army
created a corps of engineers, one of whose functions was to document
campaigns, battles, and sieges by producing sketches of them. They did
their work competently enough, but great art did not result.

As with historians and writers of literature, no direct link existed between a person's participation in battle and his ability to give artistic expression to what he had witnessed. The most experienced personnel
were probably those who, like Louvois's engineers, followed commanders
and armies on campaign, but this does not mean that their work enjoyed
the highest esteem. Many other artists probably witnessed war, for example when the cities in which they lived came under siege, even if they did
not take an active part in it. Things gradually changed, however. As modern territorial states were consolidated from about 1660 on, probably
many artists had fewer opportunities to see war at first hand than had
been the case a century or two previously.

One mid-seventeenth-century painter, Nicolas Poussin, wrote about
becoming less inclined to produce martial scenes after having experienced the original at first hand.[22] His, however, was by no means a normal
or even very frequent reaction. Most of his colleagues were happy to accept commissions; having done so, they did not trouble to leave their stu-
dios. Instead they worked on the basis of sketches provided by others,

complementing their knowledge by studying uniforms and weapons, con-
ducting interviews, and so on. Among those who worked in this way were
Philippe-Jacques de Loutherbourg (*Battle Scene,* 1765) and John
Singleton Copley (*The Death of Major Pierson,* 1783); the most famous
of all was undoubtedly Jacques-Louis David (*Napoleon Crossing the
Alps,* 1800). None of these men ever smelled powder.

As had been the case during the previous two centuries, artists who
depicted the glories of war far outnumbered those who focused on its
more shocking aspects. Even among the latter, some may have wanted to
warn against it, whereas others were trying to appeal to people's more
prurient instincts. Certainly there was no necessary link between the
artist's intentions and the way people reacted to his work. A good illustration of this particular problem is provided by Francisco Goya's *Los
Desastres de la Guerra,* a series of prints that are probably the most famous of their kind ever created. The fact that Goya was living in Spain
during the uprising against Napoleon is not in dispute, nor is the fact that
the uprising produced countless horrors of the kind he painted. However,
it is unknown whether he himself witnessed any of them; while he did
visit places where there had been fighting, he is not known to have participated even in a single skirmish. A scene such as the one in plate 5,
which shows a woman, baby at the hip, spearing a French soldier, could
hardly have taken place in reality.

Nor do we really know what motivated Goya.[23] At the time, he was
sixty-something years old. He had once been painter to the Spanish
court, producing many a brilliant canvas of royal personalities, proud
aristocrats, and ladies at play. At some point, however, doubts as to the
fairness of what today we would call the "system" seem to have crept in.
From 1800 on he gradually sank into a morass of despair. While motivated
partly by social and political conditions as he now understood them, a
combination of advancing deafness and a constant buzzing in his ears
could not have done much to improve his mood. The outcome was a
whole series of works, some preceding the *Desastres* and some following
them, known as the *Caprichos.* Many were almost as dark and forbidding
as the *Desastres,* yet they had little or nothing to do with war. Some related to real events, others to ones that, however poignant the titles he
gave them, had almost certainly taken place solely in his imagination. The
Desastres themselves were published only in 1863, decades after Goya's
death. Ever since, many critics have interpreted them as a warning
against war. Even on the assumption, which cannot be proved, that such

was indeed his purpose, it does not mean that his pictures did not prove capable of satisfying some sorts of ghoulish curiosity, too.

Just as the nineteenth century invented the historical novel, so it put great emphasis on historical paintings, including, of course, paintings of war and battle. Except in a few places such as Florence, where Vasari's paintings grace the Palazzo della Signoria, previously most images of this sort had probably disappeared into the residences of the powerful, the rich, or at least the well to do. Now, increasingly, they began to be displayed in public museums and exhibitions; the first half of the nineteenth century in particular was when many great museums were founded. This in turn was part cause, part outcome, of a growing tendency to use them as a vehicle for influencing public opinion; meaning the opinion of those who, as one country after another made the transition from professional armies to such as were based on conscription, had to provide the necessary cannon-fodder.[24] From the time of Marengo (1800) on, not a war and not a campaign was allowed to pass that did not result in panoramic images that celebrated them and glorified them for the edification of the folks at home.

As with the novelists, some of the paintings involved painstaking historical research of uniforms, weapons, formations, topography, and so on. As with the novelists, seldom did they present war as it really was. This was not for lack of technical ability on the artists' part; quite on the contrary. Rather, it was because capturing large formations of armed men on canvas's limited space is anything but easy. Very often doing so required the use of various devices involving composition and changes in perspective so as to make the objects depicted look "real" on canvas; a good example is Antoine-Jean Gros's 1808 masterpiece, *La Bataille d'Eylau*.[25] Capturing a long line of men-of-war sailing along creates even greater problems. One late-eighteenth-century critic even claimed that, technically, it was the most difficult feat of all.[26]

A few pictures were vast in size, not merely confronting the spectator but literally wrapping themselves around him. Producing them took years, required the erection of special buildings, and involved dozens if not hundreds of men. Some assisted the master by doing research, taking measurements, filling in details, and the like, while others painted or served as models; had the artists not received the willing cooperation of armies and governments, it could never have been done. Some of the resulting works, such as the Innsbruck "cyclorama" that depicts Andreas Hofer's 1809 rising against Napoleon, still exist and are open to the public.[27] Like others of the same kind, such as Anton von Werner's 7,000-square-foot panorama of the Battle of Sedan, it uses every trick of light and perspective to give visitors the illusion that they are standing in the midst of the events depicted. Without question, one reason behind the panoramas' enormous popularity was the fact that a great many of them had war and battle as their subjects. Conversely, if today they are seen as curiosities, it is not because the subject matter has become outdated. Rather, it is because the movies are now able to satisfy the same kind of interest much more effectively.

During the entire nineteenth century, no master of the battlefield genre attained greater popularity than an Englishwoman, Elizabeth Thompson.[28] Thompson, who was born in Lausanne in 1846, received painting lessons, as practically every good middle-class Victorian girl did. Apparently she got her inspiration during a visit to France, where she was exposed to paintings of the Franco-Prussian War. Not long after, she started producing a steady stream of large martial paintings. Their titles speak for themselves: *Roll Call* (the first in the series), *The Dawn of Waterloo, Scotland Forever, Steady the Drum and Fifes,* and others. Most famous of all was *Balaclava,* showing the heroic but utterly foolish charge of the Light Brigade in the Crimea in 1856. First exhibited in London in 1876, the picture created a sensation. Later, traveling the country, it attracted hundreds of thousands.

Thompson's subsequent fate provides an interesting example of how changing public attitudes can affect an artist independently of anything he or she does. *Roll Call* was purchased by Queen Victoria, who insisted on having it. To express her pleasure, the queen also gave Thompson a title so that she could call herself Lady Butler, after her husband's name. Even greater was Thompson's feat in causing the nineteenth century's most famous art critic, John Ruskin, to take back his statement that women could not paint.[29] But then things started going downhill for Thompson. By the standards of *Les Desastres de la Guerra,* Thomson's works had always been reasonably decorous. They did, it is true, include ragged soldiers, freezing soldiers, wounded soldiers, and even some dead soldiers. Yet there was no question of showing the real horrors of war. Whether because she did not want to include them or because, as a Victorian gentlewoman, she could not imagine them, the mutilated, bloated corpses, the hatred, and the cruelty, not to mention the stench, were left out. In the end, however great the sacrifice, the effect she created was always patriotic and even heroic. But not enough so, apparently, for the tastes of a public which, as the century neared its end, became progressively more jingoistic and less inclined to buy her pictures.

Later during the twentieth century, tastes changed again. While Thompson's works remained in limbo, this was now for the opposite reason: heroic and patriotic to the core, they did not show the horrors of war clearly enough. Her fate was shared by many other nineteenth-century artists who had specialized in painting historical battles. In their time, two of the most famous ones were Adolph von Menzel and Wilhelm Camphausen. Menzel did many paintings that showed Frederick the Great during the Seven Years' War, the one in which, overcoming every obstacle, he pulled up Prussia by its bootstraps and made it into a great power. Camphausen also did paintings of Frederick the Great at war, but to these he added others dealing with various other campaigns, from those of Cromwell to those waged by Prussia against Denmark and Austria in 1864–66. Both Menzel and Camphausen were enormously popular and enormously successful, receiving honors heaped on them by grateful rulers and commanders (whose portraits they also painted) and having their works universally admired. Both, needless to say, were appointed professors, and Menzel was awarded a high Prussian decoration. Yet today any museum that would dare to show their work would be accused of militarism or worse; apparently art that is not antiwar is not art at all.

In 1900–14, though, much of this turn away from war was still in the future. Like Ernst Jünger—indeed, like countless ordinary people in every European country—many artists were eagerly anticipating war. German expressionists such as Ludwig Meidner sought to express what it would be like in paintings with names such as *An Apocalyptic Landscape* and *Vision of a Marksmen's Trench.* So, on the other side of the border, did French cubists such as Roger de La Fresnaye and Jacques Villon. Several declared war even before it broke out. The best known was the Italian Futurist Filippo Marinetti. From 1909 on he fired off one manifesto after another, expressing his longing for war which he called "the only hygiene of the world"; later he was to become a fascist and a friend of Mussolini. He was, however, by no means the only one.[30] In Britain, we are told, "virility and aggression, amounting to a cult of violence, were the hallmark of the most radical *avant gardes,* including [Wyndham] Lewis and [Charles] Nevinson."[31] Others, such as David Bomberg, viewed it as an opportunity.

When war did break out, artists' reactions to it, like those of other people, varied. Some, such as Max Ernst (who managed to spend the en-

tire war in the rear area) and Ernst Ludwig Kirchner (who suffered a
nervous breakdown before he ever reached the front) were terrified by it.
Others reacted differently. Some went out of their way to admire "the
splendor of colors" (Oskar Schlemmer) and the "overwhelming sight[s]"
(Paul Klee) war produced.[32] The English painter John Nash told his wife
that he had been happiest in the trenches, where he discovered a zest for
life and a new appreciation for beauty. His compatriot Andrew Rothstein
spoke of "livid beauty"; he even went so far as to add that, had he been
asked whether war did not demand too high a price for seeing it, he
"should have been at a loss for an answer."[33] One very famous artist,
Fernand Léger, later wrote that he had been "dazzled by the open breach
of a 75-millimetre gun in the sunlight . . . that open breach of a 75 in the
full sunlight has taught me more for my plastic development than all the
museums of the world."[34] It was one of Léger's main artistic endeavors, as
reflected in such works as *Eléments Méchaniques* (1920), to capture
the movements of polished metal parts as the essence of modernity.
Apparently this purpose could be served at least as well by the *made-
moiselle soixante-quinze* as by any other machine of the time.

To have artists play with war as they thought fit was one thing, but to
harness them to their respective countries' effort was another. With
Germany in the lead, most of the belligerents in 1914–18 created bodies
of official war artists. Some were older men no longer subject to being
called up, whereas others were serving soldiers who were approached to
see whether they would join. Most were delighted to be invited—the wife
of one American artist, Harvey Dunn, recalls that her husband, asked
how long he would need to get ready to leave for France, shouted, "Two
hours!"[35] Some produced their work even as they served, using whatever
opportunities they could. At least one spent the war being chauffeured
around France in a Rolls-Royce. The armed forces gave them what they
needed—papers, administrative support, and in some cases transportation. Depending on the conditions of their employment, they might or
might not be given a commission, a salary, an expense account for buying
materials, and a guarantee that their works would be purchased. Yet on
the whole they were not a greedy lot; many worked for much less than
what their works had fetched in peacetime.[36]

In return, the official artists set out to document the war, producing
works that would stimulate the citizens of the belligerent countries to re-
double their efforts and perhaps persuade viewers in neutral countries to
take a more favorable attitude. From time to time there was friction with

the authorities. Either they insisted that artists produce monthly reports on their output, as American officials at one point did, or else they judged this or that painting unsuitable, read too ghastly, for official display and tried to prevent it from being shown in private exhibitions, too. Still, on the whole the various programs must have been considered successful, as proved by the fact that, when World War II was seen approaching in the late 1930s, many governments did not even wait for it to break out before turning to artists for help in preparing people for it.

In both wars, the result was thousands of paintings of greatly varying quality (in the United States in 1917–18 alone, 1,438 pieces were produced for fifty-eight agencies).[37] They covered every conceivable subject, as shown by titles that ranged from *Going over the Top* to *Soldiers Returning from Captivity,* and from *Battle of Britain* (probably the most famous work of all) to *Green Beach, Normandy.*[38] By this time armies had come to number millions of men and battlefields took up miles and miles of front. As a result, few artists tried to record major historical events in their entirety as so many of their predecessors had done; instead, in an effort to capture the character of the struggle, they would show universal scenes that had taken place nowhere but could be witnessed almost anywhere.[39] If only because few of the artists had specialized in painting war during peacetime, in many ways their works are typical representatives of the times and places at which they were produced. Some consist of simple drawings made by pencil or charcoal, while others are huge, colorful canvases. Some are extremely accomplished, others less so. In point of style they range from the realist through expressionist, cubist, or naive. Given that no hard-and-fast line separated those designated "official war artists" from the rest, this is not surprising.

Still, if the extensive published collections of the works in question are any guide, two facts stand out. First, the most abstract, entirely nonfigurative styles being developed during the period in question are almost entirely absent. Strangely enough, this seems to be even more true of paintings created in World War II than of those originating in World War I; to paraphrase Clemenceau, it is as if those who painted the events of 1939–45 felt war was too serious a business to be experimented with. Second, although there is often a good deal of pathos in the form of men in a variety of uncomfortable situations—huddled, wounded, captured, and even dead—only a very few works so much as try to capture the real horrors of war.

Those that do make the attempt do not all necessarily breathe a pacifist spirit. Rather, as in the case of Nevinson's *We Are Making a New World* and Charles Sims's *Sacrifice* (both 1918), the objective may be to point out that through fighting and suffering leads the road to redemption and resurrection.[40] In part, this choice of subject may have been the result of self-censorship, artists being as patriotic as everybody else. It must, however, also be remembered that the officials who selected the artists and commissioned the works did not have in mind a small crowd of avant-garde highbrows interested in discussing art so as to show each other how clever they were. Instead they aimed at a much wider public whose members cared about the war and whom they sought to nudge, however gently, in a certain well-defined direction.

The interwar division of much of the world into "democratic" and "totalitarian" countries, whose impact on literature has been briefly discussed in the previous chapter, could not fail to have its impact on the plastic arts, too. As with so many things, Nazi Germany represents a particularly interesting case. From Hitler on down, the Nazis were nothing if not militarists, intent on presenting war as if it were some kind of Boy Scout game. Worse still, the Führer understood himself as an artist and as a patron of the arts. Hence he deliberately set out to reform not only Germany's political, economic, and social system but its artistic life as well.[41] The Weimar Republic having fallen, art for art's sake was out, art in the service of life—including, not least, that very important part of Nazi life, war—was in. Artists unwilling or unable to understand what the regime wanted might one day receive a letter from the Gestapo. In it, they would find a *Malverbot* (prohibition on painting), as, for example, the "degenerate" Bauhaus painter Fritz Winter did. Conversely, those who pleased might be exempted from military service at the hands of Hitler personally.

Obeying this system of unnatural selection, artists resolutely closed their eyes to anything modern or abstract. Paradoxically, the outcome was a style of painting not too different from socialist realism, the one that was being produced, on the other side of the front, by National Socialism's mortal enemy, Communism. Take an exhibition called "War and Art." It was held in Vienna in 1942, just before the start of the great series of battles that ultimately led to Germany's defeat. Visitors opened their tour by filing past a bust of the Führer as well as two allegorical figures representing war whose details have not been preserved. There were some historical and foreign pieces, presumably meant to prove that the Nazis were not the world's first or only militarists.

The core of the exhibition consisted of well over two hundred contemporary paintings and drawings originating in every front where the swastika had so recently been planted. The works had titles such as *Flamethrower, German Destroyers in Battle, Tanks in Africa, Prisoners* [Allied ones, needless to say] *in the Harbor of Piraeus,* and, the closest any of the artists got to admitting that it was not all fun and games, *Leavetaking.* One Walther Tröge, a major in the Staff of the Deputy Commander, XVIIth Army Corps, wrote the introduction to the catalogue. Quoting Rudolf Binding, an author much favored by the Nazis, to the effect that "art seeks truth," he tells us that "real art is always looking for the great, the heroic"—as exemplified, one can only suppose, by a work titled *German Heroes' Cemetery in Parkina* (a village on the Karelian front).[42]

While artists living in Germany and other totalitarian countries were compelled to produce, or else willingly produced, realistic works that glorified war, others produced images that, though far from realistic, were able to repel and shock. Looking back, perhaps the best known are those of Otto Dix and Pablo Picasso. Like Sassoon (and also like another, wholly unknown young painter named Adolf Hitler), Dix enthusiastically welcomed the war, volunteering for military service when it came. Like Sassoon (and also like Hitler), he fought, was wounded several times, and was decorated. His first wartime works were crayons with titles such as *Going Over the Top, Dying Warrior, Hand to Hand Fighting,* and *Direct Hit.* In his biographies, they are often ignored; yet some of them might have satisfied even Tröge. What made him change his mind later on is not entirely clear, but it may have had something to do with his country's defeat. As with Goya, the mind-boggling, revolting awfulness of works such as *The Trench* (1923), *War Triptych* (1932), and *Flanders* (1934–36) went hand in hand with a sudden urge to create scenes of murder, rape, and dismemberment that had little if anything to do with his wartime experiences. As with Goya, apparently the decision to focus on such scenes reflected his own bleak state of mind as much as anything else.

The story of Picasso, and especially that of *Guernica,* is even more interesting. A Spaniard living in self-imposed Parisian exile, of a war he knew no more about than most civilians and rather less than his fellow artists, many of whom had served in World War I, in the Russian Civil War, or in Spain. In 1937 he was fifty-six years old and in a funk, vainly looking for inspiration for a painting he had undertaken to do for an exhibition on twentieth-century technological progress. Like most people, he learned the details of the attack by German bombers, in support of Franco, on the town of Guernica from the media. It shook him awake. There followed a demonic period of work. The result is not something actually seen by anyone from any angle at any moment; in fact, and presumably in an effort to remind the viewer that Guernica is not just any town but a Spanish town, the painting even contains elements taken from bullfighting. Yet Picasso did succeed in capturing the surprise, the horror, the helplessness, and, perhaps, most of all, the blind confusion war can inflict on people and animals as perhaps no one before or after him has. Caught in the bombardment and feeling their world burst into pieces around their heads, his mutilated figures dash around in screaming panic, not knowing where to hide or what to do first.

Like Thompson, Dix and Picasso provide object lessons concerning the way in which the perception of art, in this case art whose subject happens to be war, depends as much on changing public attitudes as on its own qualities (which, of course, remain the same). Dix's work came under attack even before the Nazi seizure of power. Early on, one of the participants in the chorus was the young mayor of the German city of Cologne. In 1925 he forced the municipal museum to get rid of it; his name, incidentally, was Konrad Adenauer. As for Picasso, though *Guernica* was praised in France, Britain, and the United States, it was hated in Nazi Germany, where it was dismissed as the work of a madman. Soviet critics also disliked it, even though the two totalitarian countries were each other's worst enemies, and even though, as long as the Spanish Civil War lasted, they fought one another by proxy.

After 1945 the cards were shuffled. In the Soviet Union, socialist realism continued to reign with a heavy hand and did so right down to the disintegration of the "evil empire" in 1989–91. Meanwhile, in the West, many now considered Picasso's *Guernica* to be "the major artwork of the 20th century."[43] Having narrowly escaped heavy punishment at the hands of the Nazis, Dix was rehabilitated. Conversely, in the former Axis countries—and, to a lesser extent, outside—anyone who still dared present war in realistic, let alone romantic, terms was in danger of being treated almost as badly as Dix and his fellow "degenerates" had been before 1945.

In Germany, as in Italy and Japan, thousands of "militarist" works were taken off the walls of museums and other public buildings. Yet the authorities were unsure what to do with them. On one hand, the paintings in question were no longer fit to be exhibited, considering the demands of the new democratic ideology. Nor, for the same reason, could they be sold off to the highest bidder, as other works sometimes are. On the other hand they were undeniably art, if only of the kind that, to use the German term, was now considered "despicable" (*verachtet*).[44] By way of a compromise, they were stored safely out of sight. Normally they may be viewed only by select persons, and then only for "scientific" purposes— which, presumably, do not include praising whatever artistic qualities they may have.

As if to sum up the entire subject of twentieth-century war art, in 1994 an international exhibition was held under UNESCO auspices to commemorate the eightieth anniversary of the outbreak of World War I. From the catalogue, we learn that there had been two kinds of artists. On the one hand there were "older ones, those most set in their old ways," who used "the tools of pictorial realism handed down from the previous century." "They observed biplanes, artillery guns, and soldiers in close detail, and equally methodically reproduced what they saw." Technically speaking many of their works were competent enough. Still, eighty years later they were considered interesting only for their "documentary value," if at all. In sharp contrast to them were "younger painters trained during the last twenty-five years of the nineteenth century," including impressionists and, a little later, post-impressionists, expressionists, cubists, futurists, and vorticists. For them, visitors were told, "the time for heroic realism and patriotic allegory was up." Rather, rejecting "once and for all the rules which had previously governed the painting of battle scenes," they invented whole new techniques to depict "the savagery of destruction."[45]

Alas, as we saw, reality is much more complex than this simple scheme of young versus old, "modern" antiwar art versus "traditional" pro-war works, suggests. The relationship between art and war goes back almost as far as art itself does. Over the millennia it has undergone countless changes, many of them curious and complex, yet most of the time the two went together well enough. Possibly because those who paid for it were also those who called the shots, often art was made to serve war. There were also cases when war was made to serve art; this applies not just to Courtois but to Dürer and, in at least some of his works, Goya, too. Starting with the scenes of combat on the Parthenon's friezes and ending with Picasso's etching *Combat pour Andromede Entre Persée et Phinée,* many artists have always found war fascinating, which of course helps account for the fact that works on the subject have always been among the greatest of all. Switching muses for a moment, we find even Wilfred Owen once admitted that compared with war, all other subjects seem "vapid."[46]

As the case of Elizabeth Thompson proves, often creations whose subject was war were able to rouse enthusiasm both among the public and professional critics even though, artistically speaking, they may not have been among the greatest. Many works, at one time admired, have sunk almost without a trace. That, however, was by no means always simply the result of artistic deficiencies, as is sufficiently proved by the fact that other works dating to the same periods and often employing much the same style and technique continued to be admired. Some works suffered the opposite fate. At the time they were produced they were execrated and even boycotted, only to become celebrated later on. In view of all this, it would take a brave man to claim, as the author of the UNESCO catalogue seems to do, that the last word has been spoken and that works that praise war have been relegated to oblivion once and for all—the more so because, as *Time* magazine ruefully admitted in 1945, the artistic tastes of the American public were quite similar to the Führer's own.[47]

At present, over most of the world, works that somehow smack of "militarism" may be found either in all sorts of military installations from the Pentagon on down (where they hardly count as art at all) or else in the attics and the cellars of other museums. Like Emperor Barbarossa under his mountain, there they lie, asleep but almost certainly not dead—waiting to emerge if and when, as has so often happened in the past, public attitudes change once again and they are called upon to do so.

12

Monuments to War

From the time they were first created, monuments to war can probably be divided into three basic types. First, there are those that record victory, whether real, exaggerated, or in some cases entirely imaginary; their purpose may be either to glorify the victor or to warn future enemies of what is in store for them should they get on the wrong side of him. Second, there are tributes to fallen heroes. Third, there are monuments whose purpose is to warn against war. Chronologically speaking, monuments belonging to the first type seem to be much older than the rest and, until at least 1918, the most numerous by far. Monuments to the dead came second, whereas those that warn against war came only after 1918 and remain limited to a few countries.

While nomadic peoples can and do set up trophies, permanent monuments of any size presume a settled society and, in most cases, an urban one that has at its disposal a considerable number of specialized craftsmen. This may explain why the first monuments known to have been made specifically in order to commemorate war are Egyptian by origin. Taking the form of stone palettes, the earliest ones go back to the predynastic era. Many others, dating to later periods, have been found at cities that, at the time the monuments were made, served as capitals or centers of royal power.

Originally the palettes served a practical purpose as well as a commemorative one. They consisted of hard stone surfaces on which various substances, such as cosmetics, could be ground into a powder and on whose reverse sides images were carved. At a later age they came to be carved on both sides, were used for ceremonial purposes, and thus acquired their value as monuments. Probably the best known is the so-called Narmer palette. Made around 3200 B.C., it received its (modern) name from a king called Narmer whose titles are listed at the top. Historically, he was the first king of the First Dynasty, who for the first time united Upper and Lower Egypt under a single government—a very great achievement whose consequences are with us to the present day.[1]

As monuments go, the Narmer palette is rather small, measuring about twenty-five inches from top to bottom. The front shows the king standing over a kneeling enemy whose hair he is grasping in one hand and whose head he is about to smash with the aid of a mace he holds in the other. Farther down are two naked enemies, presumably dead. The reverse side shows the king wearing the Red Crown of Lower Egypt (his original base was in Upper Egypt, whose symbol was the White Crown). Huge in stature, he is both preceded and followed by a number of standard-bearing soldiers on parade. The iconography is completed by two rows of decapitated bodies of enemies, their heads positioned between their legs, as well as an enemy being trampled by a bull (a bull was one of the symbols of Egyptian royalty). This particular palette apart, dozens of others have been found. Though not all record wars and victories, many do; just where they were originally positioned and how they were used is not known.

Another form of victory monument first developed in Egypt was the obelisk. The earliest ones were probably simple stones erected to represent divine power. From there, it was but a short step to using them to proclaim the king's military prowess and record his victories, the more so because in Egypt, as in so many subsequent empires, the pharaohs themselves enjoyed divine status and appropriated divine symbols, such as the sun, the bull, and others. Herodotus credits the invention of the obelisk to Pharaoh Sesostris I (1971–26 B.C.), who erected many obelisks on his various battlefields and had them inscribed with his name and the nature of his victories.[2] Of those obelisks, one still exists and, moved from its original place, is currently at Heliopolis near Cairo. It is hard, however, to make sense of Herodotus's account given that he also credits Sesostris with making conquests in remote regions, such as Thrace, that neither he nor any other Egyptian ruler ever reached.

Several pharaohs—including a female one, Hatshepsut—coming after Sesostris also erected obelisks. A few of those do not carry inscriptions, but most record the name of the pharaoh, the gods from whom he was descended or with whom he was identified, and the victories he claimed to have won. Some pharaohs wanted to save money or else to obliterate their predecessors' memory for a variety of political reasons, such as a change of dynasty. Accordingly, they had those predecessors' names erased from the monuments, substituting their own but usually leaving the rest of the text more or less intact. The smallest known Egyptian obelisk measures seven feet; the tallest one, which for the last four centuries has been standing in the square in front of the Vatican, is eighty-four feet. Proving that these monuments did indeed fascinate subsequent generations, out of the twenty-six surviving ones, only eight are still in Egypt, though not necessarily in their original positions.

Some of the remaining obelisks were taken away and re-erected by the Romans and Byzantines in Caesarea (present-day Israel), Rome, or Constantinople; taking over other people's property to display one's own power has always been one of the ways war was commemorated. After a long hiatus in which they went out of fashion, obelisks, with their simple geometrical form, returned to favor during the sixteenth century, when one of their number, originally brought to Rome by Emperor Caligula, was re-erected in front of the Vatican. They became even more popular toward the end of the eighteenth century when British and French expeditions started using them to decorate London and Paris. Focusing on those built to commemorate victory rather than for other purposes, obelisks from this period include the Battle of Bunker Hill Monument (1825–26) and the Moscow Victory Monument. The latter, completed as recently as 1993, is no fewer than 141.8 meters (432 feet) tall, the idea being to match the 1,418 days that the "Great Patriotic War," according to Russian reckoning, lasted.

A third form of victory monument is the column. At first sight it closely resembles the obelisk, and indeed it does not take a Freudian psychologist to see what they have in common. At another level, though, the similarity is misleading. An examination of the details reveals that the column continues a completely different tradition from the one that is behind the obelisk, namely, that of grave monuments set up by friends and relatives to commemorate individual soldiers from ancient Greece on. The first victory column, and one of the most famous, was erected by Trajan (reigned A.D. 98–117).[3] Standing a hundred feet tall in the forum named after the emperor, it was meant to commemorate his two Dacian wars, which brought what is now Romania into the empire. In many ways it is an astonishingly original creation, made all the more so by the unprecedented decision to have a chamber for the emperor's ashes carved into its bottom and to crown it with a gilded statue of him; to say nothing of the hidden spiral staircase that enables visitors to mount it from the inside.

Trajan's column served as a model for his third-in-line successor, Emperor Marcus Aurelius (reigned A.D. 161–80), who followed it fairly closely. Perhaps strangely, an interval of more than fifteen hundred years had to pass before the next one materialized. In 1722, a column went up in honor of the Duke of Marlborough at his residence at Blenheim Palace, near Oxford. Like the two earlier ones, it carries a statue of the victor, standing erect and imperiously gazing at his surroundings; unlike them, it is fluted and does not carry images of the war in which Marlborough commanded. Since then, imitation has caused such monuments to become somewhat more common. Among the best known is the column erected by Napoleon to commemorate his victory at Austerlitz (1806–10) and specifically designed to rival that of Trajan. Then there are Nelson's Column in Trafalgar Square (1840–43), Wellington's Column in Liverpool (1874–75), and the Siegessäule, built by the Germans in 1864–73 in order to remind the world of their triumphs over Denmark, Austria, and France.

The last of these differs from the rest in that it is not, nor ever was, topped by a statue of the victor. Probably the reason for this is that things had changed. Although Prussia's sovereign, William I, had been physically present at the battles of Koniggraetz and Sedan, he was a military commander in name only; on the other hand, it would not do to put the man who was actually in command, Helmut von Moltke, above his sovereign. The problem was solved by crowning the column with a symbolic image of winged Victory carrying wreath and scepter—a representation derived from a Greek original copied countless times thereafter.

Proving how long-lived the culture of war often is, these and other columns from before 1900 or so resemble each other not only in their general appearance but in several other respects as well. Many make use of equipment which was, or was said to have been, taken from the enemy in battle. Thus Napoleon's column was cast out of the bronze of Austrian and Russian cannon. Other monuments, such as Trajan's Column, Nelson's Column, Wellington's Column, and the Siegessäule, either depicted captured equipment or used actual items for decorative purposes.

All explain the events they commemorate through inscriptions, carved images, mosaics, and so on. All are placed in the middle of open space, some of it created especially for the purpose, in order that they may be admired from all sides.

While some commanders had their statues mounted on top of tall columns from where they could observe the world, most were not so lucky and had to make do with a simple base or pedestal. The first free-standing statues of victorious commanders intended to be displayed in public spaces, whether temple complexes or secular ones, seem to have been erected in ancient Greece. They and their pedestals were known as *propylaea;* over the centuries there must have been large numbers of them. In Rome, where similar structures started to be built during the third century B.C., they were known as *fornices.*[4] While few if any of these seem to have survived, we have plenty of statues of emperors. Many are dressed in military garb, and many pose as *imperatores,* or victorious commanders. Most stand on their own two feet, as Augustus in the famous statue of him does, but a few are mounted. Particularly important in this respect were an equestrian statue of Augustus, which stood in the Forum; a colossal one of Domitian, which was never completed; and an even larger one of Trajan, said to have stood forty feet tall.[5] Of all such statues that may have existed, the sole surviving example is the one of Marcus Aurelius on Capitoline Hill. One may dislike the "militarist" ideology it represented—after all, it would have been possible to represent the emperor writing his book, *The Meditations,* for which he is equally famous. But there can be no doubt concerning its nature as a magnificent work of art, never exceeded by anything created before or after.

Whereas the Middle Ages saw the creation of countless statues of knights, with few exceptions they were not freestanding and were not meant to commemorate specific victories. The vast majority served to cover tombs and are accordingly found inside churches; here the men in question were buried in the military garb that symbolized their status. Very often they lie in tandem with their wives, who of course had little to do with any wars in which their husbands may have commanded and triumphed. As in so many other things, it was the people of the Renaissance who picked up where the Romans had left off. The second half of the fifteenth century saw the erection of several equestrian statues of victorious commanders intended for display in public spaces. At least one, designed by Leonardo da Vinci to honor Francesco Sforza (1401–66), was never completed. Two others, representing Erasmo da Narni (1370–1443) and Bartolomeo Colleoni (1400–75) were. The last named is particularly fine; it may be the best image of an arrogantly victorious commander ever done.

During the early modern age, so much did the equestrian statue of the triumphant commander appeal to the imagination of generations of European monarchs that they reserved the right to have them erected for themselves. Every city of any importance got at least one, and they were still being put up as late as the early twentieth century. Some stood in the midst of city squares; others decorated thoroughfares. Mounted on top of massive pedestals taller than the tallest spectators, they deliberately forced people to look up at them. All were considerably larger than life, and all showed the monarch in military dress. Usually he carries a baton and points out the way ahead to his troops, even though fewer and fewer of the men thus portrayed ever exercised effective command in the field.

From about 1800 on, the tradition of erecting equestrian statues was carried to the United States, where it was applied to the generals who commanded the armies of the republic. Thus George Washington, Andrew Jackson, and John Pershing were all immortalized in stone or bronze. However, the largest number of statues commemorate the Civil War, a fact that reflects the importance of that conflict in U.S. history. The most important commanders represented are George McClellan, Joseph Hooker, Philip Sheridan, William T. Sherman, and, of course, the massive likeness of Ulysses S. Grant that is positioned in front of the Capitol and which, along with such treasures as the Washington Monument and the Lincoln Monument, forms one of the chief tourist attractions of Washington, D.C.

As one might expect, all of these follow their European models fairly closely. However, the United States is unique in that very often the initiative came not from officialdom but from ordinary citizens who formed associations and raised money for the purpose. As a result, it is possible to find statues erected not just for victorious commanders but also for those who, though the side they served lost the war, are perceived as having fought the good fight. They include famous Confederate generals such as Nathanael Greene, Nathan Bedford Forrest, and above all Robert E. Lee; in terms of sheer size, the statues along Monument Avenue in Richmond, Virginia, exceed anything to be found in the nation's capital.

The final form of victory monument that must be discussed in this context is the triumphal arch. As we saw, at all times and places it was customary to mark the end of hostilities by some kind of ritual, and parades took a prominent part. It was to provide the parades with suitable settings that triumphal arches were erected, first perhaps as temporary structures and then, from the second century B.C. on, as permanent ones. As time went by Rome was filled with them; by the imperial period, having lost their original function as gates under which the victorious army had to pass, they were being built in almost every part of the city without distinction. The most famous surviving ones are the Arch of Titus, the Arch of Septimus Severus, and the Arch of Constantine, though we do know of others. One was erected in honor of Augustus's victories in Dalmatia, in Egypt, and at Actium; in its final form, it was apparently surmounted by a four-horse chariot.[6] Other arches have been identified in every province, those discovered in Africa alone numbering over a hundred.

In Europe, victory arches reappeared during the Renaissance and have remained with us ever since. Among the many artists who drew up designs for them were Michelangelo and Leonardo, albeit their plans were never carried out.[7] A few monuments, such as the Porte de Peyrou in Montpellier and the arch near the Porte Saint-Denis in Paris, date to the second half of the seventeenth century, but most were built between 1700 and 1900. Among the earliest was Moscow's Red Gate (1735, demolished in 1935 on Stalin's orders). Others, which draw millions of visitors each year, are Madrid's Puerta de Alcalá (1768) and Arco de la Victoria (1956), Berlin's Brandenburger Tor (1788–93), Paris's Arc de Triomphe (1806–11), London's Marble Arch (1828, covered with marble stolen from the Arch of Constantine in Rome), and the arch on Moscow's Kutuzovskiy Prospekt that commemorates Russia's victory over Napoleon (1827–34).[8] Other arches, or gates, of victory can be found in New York State; Newport, Rhode Island; Mumbai, India; Pyongyang, North Korea; and Banjul, Gambia, even though some commemorate wars that most people would rather like to forget, and even though in some cases it is not clear what victory, if any, they were meant to celebrate.

Some monuments do no more than use the commander's statue or else some symbolic figure—a winged Victory, perhaps, or a chariot, or a star, or some national emblem—to achieve their purpose. Most, however, are decorated with pictures or reliefs representing the campaigns they were meant to celebrate. One of the earliest is the Stele of Eannatum, also known as the Stele of the Vultures. Made around 2450 B.C. in Mesopotamia, it is now in the Louvre.[9] Though only fragments survive, they suffice to reconstruct the main themes. It appears that one of the stone's two faces was narrative, the other symbolic, yet both refer to the same event.

A long inscription on the stele explains what happened. Following a boundary dispute between two cities, Lagash and Umma, the former defeated the latter and erected the stele on the newly drawn border. The side that carries the narrative has several different images carved into it. One shows the king of Lagash, Eannatum, standing in his chariot leading phalanxes of shield-carrying men; others present him sacrificing to the gods. Another shows men carrying baskets on their heads to make a mound, whereas still others show heaps of bodies (slain enemies, no doubt) and vultures feeding on them. The reverse side of the stele has a large seated Eannatum holding a net, which is full not of fish but of men. Modern archaeologists interpret this as the net he cast over the men of Umma, and, having caught them, he dispatched them with ease.

Victory monuments have usually paralleled battle paintings in presenting war as a grand spectacle. Scenes painted or carved on pedestals or on the monuments themselves show rulers, commanders, and soldiers as they assemble in camp. They prepare to go on campaign, gathering equipment and perhaps sacrificing to the gods or listening to the gods' instructions. Next they may be seen marching and crossing rivers; either swimming across them, as in some Assyrian reliefs, or else after having built bridges over them, as on Trajan's Column. They construct roads and fortifications. They deploy for battle, engage in combat, lay siege to

Commemorating victory; the Berlin Schlossbrücke   DVORA LEWY

fortresses, storm into the breach they made, and capture cities. Very often they also take the surrender of defeated enemies, who are shown kneeling and begging for mercy. Finally, they torture and execute prisoners—not seldom in gruesome ways such as impalement—gather and mutilate the bodies of dead enemies, divide the spoils, and the like. All of this accords with their function as demonstrations of power and as deterrents.

With the partial exception of ancient Greek city-states, which, being more or less democratically governed, were more inclined than most to honor common soldiers, almost all these monuments focus on the commander.[10] It was he who struck a heroic pose and received the lion's share of the glory; compared with him, everybody and everything else was put in the shade. Only during the nineteenth century did this convention begin to change. Two developments assisted the shift. First, in almost all European countries there was a growing movement toward democracy, on one hand, and general conscription, on the other. War was turned from the sport of kings into a national enterprise; as it did so, the way it was commemorated could not but be affected. Second, as the shift from Napoleon to Moltke illustrates very well, the sight of the heroic leader issuing orders from between his horse's ears gave way to that of the staff officer working at his desk.[11] Taken together, these processes explain why, almost for the first time in history, more and more often it was ordinary soldiers rather than commanders who, on the monuments, took center place.

In the West, one of the last colossal statues of commanders was the wooden one set up by the Germans late in World War I to honor Field Marshal Paul von Hindenburg.[12] Instead of merely gazing reverently at it, visitors used to drive nails into its legs. Whatever the precise meaning of this bizarre ceremony, it seems to show that, even in the authoritarian Second Reich, attitudes had changed; previously anything of the kind would have been considered sacrilegious. After 1950 or so, the only countries that still built colossal images of their always victorious rulers/commanders were those that, like the Soviet Union and North Korea, insisted on being "democratic" and totalitarian at the same time. Elsewhere, the place of such statues was taken by much smaller ones. Monuments to such men as Dwight D. Eisenhower, Bernard Montgomery, and many others, though often well done by excellent artists, are hardly spectacular. Almost all present their subjects as more or less faceless bureaucrats. Gone are the splendid uniforms, weapons, batons, and striking heroic poses. Instead, they are shown as ordinary, if brave and determined,

men—which, since they had lost their former independence and been reduced to paid state employees whose specialty happened to be the organization of violence, was just what they were.

As commanders went down, ordinary soldiers went up. Countless
monuments erected in France, Britain, the Soviet Union, and the United
States show them marching off to the Crimean War, the American Civil
War, World War I, World War II, and the Russian Civil War in particular;
even in Fascist Italy, besides the obligatory busts of Il Duce, the victory
over Ethiopia was commemorated by means of statues of ordinary, rather
dejected-looking Italian legionaries. Instead of being idealized, many of
the men are presented more or less realistically. Some brave obstacles, or
else they stand like a wall to block the enemy, as in a French monument
to the Battle of Verdun. Others storm forward with fixed bayonets. They
throw grenades, take their objectives, or plant their countries' flags in the
ground, as in the famous Marine Corps Memorial at Arlington National
Cemetery in Virginia. A few even lie dead or wounded. There is, however,
no question of showing the true horrors of war.

In almost all such memorials, commanders, if they are present at all,
are represented solely by junior officers. Often they differ from the rest
only by the kind of headgear they wear, the pair of field glasses they carry,
and similar minor pieces of dress and equipment; clearly the time when
they had been seen as belonging almost to a different species was past.
Taking democracy a step further still, perhaps for the first time in history
the contribution of those who had stayed at home also began to be considered worthy of commemoration. Thus, at least one French monument dating to the post–World War I period shows a woman at the plow.[13]

From monuments that showed one's own soldiers in more or less
heroic action it was but a short step to those specifically devoted to soldiers who had died. Once again, to find a precedent it is necessary to go
back all the way to ancient Greece. In Athens and elsewhere, the names
of those who had been killed while fighting for their country were gathered, arranged according to the year in which they had fallen, and put on
public display. This, however, remained an exception. As the city-states
were swallowed by the Roman Empire, the custom came to an end.
Friends and relatives of dead legionaries might set up graves for them;
sometimes they were paid for out of the savings of the deceased and carried an inscription chosen while he was still alive. However, public monuments neither carried their names nor were designed to honor them.

Proceeding to modern times, the first proposals to record the names of all those killed on behalf of *la patrie* by inscribing them on some kind of public monument were made by writers, such as Jacques Cambry, who were committed to the glories of the French Revolution. Though much discussed at the time, the idea did not take hold. When the Arc de Triomphe went up, the only names it carried were those of dead generals. Napoleon at one point wanted the structure known as the Madeleine, which he had re-designated as a temple to the glory of the Grande Armée, to carry the names of all those who had been killed in the wars from 1792 on. However, by the time he left the scene these plans had still not been realized, and the Bourbons, who followed him, had different ideas. In the event, the first modern community to publicly draw up and display a list of all its dead troops was not France but the German city of Frankfurt am Main. Ironically, they had lost their lives fighting *against* the message of democracy carried by the French Revolutionary armies, not for it.[14]

The nineteenth century saw the construction of a very large number of war monuments of all sizes and descriptions. Almost all were erected in honor of some king, ruler, or general, and many of them marked the place where these august personalities had watched the battle or commanded it. Almost all celebrated victory, though here and there it is also possible to find some dedicated to generals who had been killed while commanding their troops. Other monuments broke new ground by carrying inscriptions honoring the dead as a group; yet even as military cemeteries multiplied it was still not considered necessary to put the names of fallen soldiers on display. Instead, a few select ones might be chosen more or less arbitrarily to represent the rest—thus providing a foretaste of the cult of the Unknown Soldier to come.

For example, in the Husarentempel that went up near Vienna in 1810 to commemorate the great battles fought against Napoleon in the previous year, an inscription refers to "the noble bones of the brave warriors of Austria," five of whom are in fact buried on the spot. Yet this was by no means a universal practice. In 1815, when a British parliamentarian proposed that a monument to the Battle of Waterloo be set up carrying the names of every dead soldier, the foreign secretary, Lord Castlereagh, acting on behalf of the cabinet, turned down the idea.[15] Around the middle of the century some British monuments did begin to list the names of the fallen rank and file. Most, however, were located in the colonies and were erected and paid for by the units themselves, not by the government or other civilian authorities.

In this as in so much else, the real turning point was presented by

World War I. Originally it was considered a war like all others. Soldiers would march, fight, and die, whereas civilians, isolated from the clash of arms, would continue their lives as best they could while casting no more than an occasional look at military events. But things soon changed. This, after all, was the first "total war" in modern history.[16] Not only was the percentage of citizens who served much higher than in previous wars, but their social composition changed; both the rank and file and, even more so, the officer corps now included numerous well-educated members of the middle classes perfectly capable of expressing their feelings and opinions about the conflict in letters, pamphlets, and even entire books.[17] Furthermore, no previous war had reached back as far from the battlefield into what now became known as the "home front." No previous war had been covered by nearly as many instruments of mass communication, most of which saw it as their sacred task to refrain from criticism while helping cement the bond between those who took the field and those who had stayed behind. Certainly there were tensions between front and rear, and political, social, and economic conflict did not disappear. Still, perhaps more than in any previous war, the outcome was the creation of fighting communities comprising entire nations.

In the field of commemoration, apparently the first to realize that this war differed from all its predecessors was the British Imperial Permanent Memorials Committee, which was called into life in 1915 and later renamed the War Memorials Committee. By this time, the idea that fallen soldiers should not be interred in mass graves but deserved to be buried in individual ones bearing their names had become well established. Complicating things, however, was the fact that the War Office, seeking to save shipping space and also to protect civilian morale, prohibited the corpses of those who had been killed in the various theaters from being transported back to Britain for burial. Once the war was over, the cost of exhuming and reinterring them was considered too great. Instead, to enable friends and relatives to visit the graves, subsidized tours were organized, and these quickly became very popular.

That did not solve the problem, however. As in most wars, the conflict had given rise to a large number of men who went missing and were never found. But there was a difference; for the first time in history, it was felt that such men deserved to be publicly commemorated. Though some of the commemoration ceremonies could be conducted abroad, logistically it was far simpler to hold the main ones at home. One way or another, it became urgently necessary to find new ways to commemorate the nation's heroes, both those whose fate was known and those who had simply disappeared, the more so because the conflict was seen in messianic terms as the war to end all wars, and because in a world where troops that had been conscripted were fighting not for any kind of personal gain but simply in answer to their country's call were widely considered to deserve the "gratitude of generations."[18]

Staying in Britain, the earliest products of the new approach were the Cenotaph and the Tomb of the Unknown Soldier. The Cenotaph comprised an empty tomb built in Whitehall, central London, in 1920, where it took the place of a similar plaster structure set up in the previous year, in time to provide background for the victory parade.[19] Except for a carved wreath on each end and the words "To the Glorious Dead," the monument was left undecorated; instead it was flanked on each side by flags representing the Royal Navy, Army, and Air Force as well as the Merchant Navy. By contrast, the Tomb of the Unknown Soldier at Westminster Abbey does contain a soldier's corpse. The French having given permission, the corpse was selected in an elaborate ritual at Saint Pol, near Arras, and returned to England for reburial, the idea being that it should act as a symbol for the average, ordinary citizen who died in the war as well as for the nation's grief and its determination not to forget him.

From biblical times on, victory had almost always been seen as proof that God, or the gods, were on one's own side.[20] On the monuments, vic-

Democratizing sacrifice; names of fallen Israeli soldiers inscribed on a wall at the Armored Corps Museum, Latrun   MARTIN VAN CREVELD

torious rulers were often presented as gods, in the company of gods, or attended by religious symbols; so in Egypt, so in Mesopotamia, so in Greece, and so in Rome, too.[21] Conversely, the fact that the losers considered themselves as having been deserted by the deities was one more reason why they hardly ever built monuments even if, physically and economically and politically, they were in a position to do so. Now, for the first time in history, the idea was reversed. Cenotaphs and tombs containing the remains of anonymous soldiers suggested that bloodletting, as long as it was suffered in the name of the nation, *creates* holiness; and also that it was now the nation itself, rather than some other deity, that represented the highest value of all.

As if to show how much this idea corresponded to the spirit of the times, both London's Cenotaph and its Tomb of the Unknown Soldier were widely copied. Examples went up in New Delhi, India; Melbourne, Australia; Auckland, New Zealand; Vancouver, Canada; and Hong Kong. All these cities were ruled from London and some of their inhabitants had participated in the war more or less voluntarily. All set up relatively simple monuments that owed something to what were fast becoming the dominant artistic fashions of the time, cubism and art deco. Similarly in France, Germany, Austria, and Italy—in fact, throughout Europe—thousands of monuments were dedicated to the men who had been killed in the war. More surprisingly, cenotaphs also spread to non-European countries; as far away as Hiroshima, Japan, a cenotaph now commemorates the two hundred thousand people who died as a result of the atomic bomb. Here one can see reflected both the anonymous slaughter so characteristic of modern warfare and the way in which the effort at commemoration spread from soldiers to include civilians as well.

Tombs containing the remains of anonymous soldiers also spread like wildfire. As of the early twenty-first century, they could be found in at least thirty different countries, starting with Australia and ending with the United States. Crossing cultural boundaries, they even made their appearance in countries that at one point or another had been colonized by Europeans, including Iraq, which got its own version of the monument at the hands of dictator Saddam Hussein in 1982. Many tombs are provided with eternal flames symbolizing life, an idea variously said to have originated either in the Bible or in ancient Greece and which was first put into effect in Paris in 1921. Representing a sharp departure from previous practice, all these tombs and cenotaphs have little to do with victorious commanders. They also differ in that they do not present war as a triumphal act, let alone a spectacle. Instead, it is seen as an occasion for the most intense suffering men can undergo—a suffering that, hallowed by the need to ensure the nation's survival, is at times compared to that of Christ himself.

Another advantage of cenotaphs and tombs of anonymous soldiers was that they could be constructed not only by countries that had won their wars but also by those that had lost them, on occasion, as in South Tyrol, which was fought over by the Italians and the Austrians during World War I, the two kinds can still be seen standing right next to each other.[22] Most monuments of this kind pointed both to the past and to the future. On one hand, they expressed the survivors' grief over the dead and the determination not to forget them. On the other, they suggested that the sacrifice had not been in vain; indeed, a conscious effort was made to make death look like a beginning, not an end. One way to express the idea was by means of a symbol, such as a star or a cross, that is linked to eventual resurrection. Another was to make it explicit by means of an inscription such as the one on a monument in Hamburg that reads, "Germany will live even if we must die."

While some monuments expressed victory and others sorrow, in most of them there was a growing tendency to ignore the enemy. As we saw, ancient monuments erected by the Egyptians, Assyrians, and Romans, among others, very often carried graphic representations of the enemy's commanders and men, invariably being killed, captured, or abused in a variety of interesting ways. Looking back to tribal societies, it is quite possible that the earliest of all "monuments" consisted of captured enemy body parts set up to decorate and to deter. This was much less the case in medieval and early modern ones. In them, the enemy was much more likely to be represented as some monster lying or reclining on the ground; a model for this was available in the form of the dragon being slain by Saint George. Yet things did not stop at this point. One reason for this may be that the spread of modern firearms caused hand-to-hand fighting to cease and battlefields to grow much larger than they had been. This, in turn, made it possible, often even necessary, to represent warfare while relegating the enemy so far into the margins as to make him barely visible.

Another reason behind the change may have been the rising tide of bourgeois sensibilities directed against aristocratic license at one extreme and rural vulgarity at the other.[23] Starting in the late eighteenth century, those sensibilities caused public rituals, such as hangings, decapitations, and mutilations, to be gradually abolished.[24] This, of course, did not mean that society was now able to do without judicial punishments, some of them very cruel. All it meant was that those punishments were being carried out not in public, in the city square, but behind prison walls (from which, incidentally, they are now beginning to reemerge as the relatives of some slain Americans demand, and obtain, the right to watch the murderers die on closed-circuit television). The same phenomenon also explains why cemeteries, both the old civilian ones and the new military ones, started to be placed in out-of-the-way, fenced-off locations. There, they could be seen only by those who deliberately sought them.

Yet another reason for the change may have been that those who designed the monuments were unwilling to admit that the enemy's soldiers had suffered as much as their own and might, following the same logic, also share in the redemption to come. Certainly there was no way the enemy could be permitted to partake in the nation's sufferings, which, even more than its glory, were considered to be entirely its own. This was sometimes carried to the point where only native artists could be commissioned to design monuments and only native materials used in constructing them, one incidental outcome being that the use of captured enemy weapons either as decoration or as raw material all but ceased.[25] Whatever the reason, the enemy disappeared until, by the second half of the twentieth century, he could be found only in a very few places. Even when he was allowed to be present, he usually took on a symbolic form. Thus, in Berlin's Treptower Park, a gigantic Soviet soldier crushes a swastika with his foot; but monuments, such as the one in the former Yugoslavia that shows a German soldier lying on the ground and being bayoneted by a partisan, have become exceedingly rare. On the opposite side from this isolated sample there are thousands upon thousands of others that commemorate twentieth-century wars, including some of the most bloody, as if they had been fought against ghosts, not men.

Finally, at around the same time as wars and soldiers started to be commemorated in these novel ways, we find the first monuments whose purpose is to protest against war as such. As might be expected, such monuments grew out of those set up for the heroic dead and bear a superficial resemblance to them. In their more developed state, however, they differ in that the elements of redemption and resurrection are absent; they are directed entirely toward the past. In them, death is neither presented as a triumph and a promise of better times to come nor limited to those who took the field and fought. Instead, it is seen as a final tragedy inflicted on the innocent through no fault on their part and to no possible purpose that might justify it—even if those innocents were, in fact, soldiers who had fought as hard as they knew how to, and sometimes even if the cause for which they fought was as evil as can be.

An outstanding early example of the genre was produced by the German sculptor Käthe Kollwitz soon after World War I. Kollwitz's son, Peter, was killed early in the conflict, not long after she had escorted him to the mobilization center. That apart, she was a socialist and, following the left-wing wisdom of the day, was predisposed to see the conflict less as a great national struggle than as a disaster that had been brought on Germany (and other countries) by the ruling classes who were looking after their own profit. Thus it comes as no surprise that in 1932 she completed a statue—intended for a German war cemetery in Flanders—of a dead youth stretched out on the ground with his father and mother kneeling near him in sorrow.[26] In this celebrated sculpture, unlike many others, no doubt is left that he who has died will emphatically not rise again. Nor is he presented as an example for others to follow; if anything, it is the parents who are asking their dead offspring to forgive them for misleading and then forsaking him. Apparently these emotions were shared by any number of monuments showing grieving mothers, some with their dead sons, some without, which were built in France in particular. As one former British war correspondent, Philip Gibbs, put it, the purpose of the new monuments being set up all over the country was to serve as "warnings of what war now means in slaughter and ruin."[27]

Taking up where these monuments left off, there is the statue that commemorates the destruction by German bombardment of the Dutch city of Rotterdam in May 1940. As had by now become standard practice, the enemy is not in sight, and anyone not familiar with the history of World War II will find it hard to guess what the monument is all about. All there is is a statue of a shaken, eviscerated human figure as it spreads its arms to heaven in a gesture combining supplication, protest, and sheer terror. No question here either of sacrifice committed for some noble cause or of eventual redemption, let alone of fighting and heroism—only of slaughter, stupidly committed, to quote the sculptor, by the "human monster who contrived the atrocities which made his brothers pay for a crime they did not commit."[28]

More controversial than the one in Rotterdam are the monuments that some German cities, having been heavily bombed in World War II, set up to their dead. Given the fact that Germany was blamed for the war, and also in view of the unprecedented atrocities committed by the Nazi regime as long as it lasted, whether those casualties deserved to be commemorated at all has long been moot. The problem was solved, to the extent that it was solved, by setting up antiwar monuments known as *Mahndenkmale.* Some consist of specially erected structures, others of half-ruined buildings deliberately left in a state of disrepair, as in the Gedächtniskirche (Memorial Church) in the center of Berlin. To put it in a different way, public consensus to commemorate the disasters that overtook Germany could only be achieved on condition that the monuments also warn against war as such. Whether this will spread to other countries or remain an isolated phenomenon remains to be seen.

At all times and places, rulers, commanders, groups, peoples, and nations have felt the need to build monuments to the wars they waged. Doing so, very often they devoted vast resources and the best available artistic expertise to the enterprise. Quite often, too, they deliberately set out to put down the monuments set up by others; examples of this range from ancient Greece[29] to 1940, when the Germans demolished the monument to the World War I British raid on the town of Zeebrugge (in 1945, it was restored by the Belgians). In other cases they freely stole each other's monuments, rededicating them to causes for which they had never been designed; better proof of the importance attributed to the question could hardly be found. The earliest known monuments were erected in ancient Egypt and were designed to honor the victories, real or imaginary, of the pharaoh of the day. Countless others, taking a variety of forms, many of which are still in use, followed. Obelisks and pillars and arches and statues of commanders served to celebrate victory over past enemies and warn away future ones. For thousands of years on end, they came very close to monopolizing the scene.

Only at the very end of the eighteenth century, and then at first only in Europe and the U.S., is it possible to speak of real change. First, the sudden spread of democracy caused the attention allotted to commanders to diminish, that given to common soldiers to increase. Second, with absolute rulers in decline and common soldiers beginning to take center place, an entirely different kind of monument, dedicated to honoring the dead regardless of whether their country had won a victory or gone down in defeat, made its debut. As the emphasis shifted from the celebration of victory to the heroic suffering and sacrifice that war involves, commemorative monuments attempted to present nations as big families grieving for their sons; at the same time, the enemy, who for millennia had been shown in the act of being defeated and perhaps abused, all but disappeared from sight. Finally, the years since 1920 have seen the rise of a third kind of monument. Growing out of the second, and often hard to distinguish from it, its purpose is not so much to commemorate a specific war but to protest or warn against war as such. It is, however, important to note that such monuments are limited almost entirely to a relative handful of European or European-derived countries as well as Japan. Elsewhere, even today, they remain fairly rare and far between.

IV

A WORLD WITHOUT WAR?

The fact that, as far back into the past as we can look, war has always fascinated men above and beyond any political purpose it may have served is indisputable; but may we not be entering an entirely new epoch in which this fascination is about to lose its hold? Some authors, citing the decline in large-scale interstate war that has taken place since 1945 on, believe that such is indeed the case.[1] The way they describe it, serious opposition to the idea that war is a useful, let alone positive, thing first emerged in the West during the eighteenth century as a by-product of the anti-feudal, anti-hierarchical tendencies of the Enlightenment. Throughout the nineteenth century it continued to gather strength. One need only think of famous names such as Herbert Spencer, who thought that reason and consent were slowly taking the place of force in human affairs, or else of Norman Angell, who just five years before 1914 published a bestseller in which he argued that people would soon agree with him that war did not pay.[2]

The earliest organized movements explicitly aimed at abolishing war appeared during the second half of the nineteenth century. Their best-known leader was the Austrian-born Baroness Bertha von Suttner, agitator, lecturer, and author of a famous novel, *Die Waffen Nieder* (Lay Down Your Arms); at one time she had worked as a secretary for Alfred Nobel. Others were linked to the contemporary suffragette movement, or else to the socialist parties that were even then attracting growing numbers of voters in many European countries. From then to our own day innumerable peace movements have risen and blossomed.[3] Quite often they made use of the most modern communication techniques to conduct propaganda and spread their message.

During the interwar period the retreat from war continued, finding its greatest expression in the League of Nations. Only a few years after the organization had been established and had begun to function, most member states were ready to pay at least lip service to the idea that war should no longer serve as a method for settling international disputes. The Kellogg-Briand Pact of 1928, which aimed at abolishing war as an instrument of politics and was signed by most of the then-existing states, as well as the Geneva Disarmament Conferences of 1931–32, came and went. As the future was to prove, they did not succeed in putting an end to war; yet arguably the very fact that they came about indicated a significant change. Furthermore, their failure was due almost exclusively to the actions of just three self-declared "revisionist" states, Germany, Italy, and Japan. Yet even in those states, war had lost much of its popular appeal, with the result that, however hard Hitler, Mussolini, and Tojo tried to inspire their followers with the martial spirit, the outbreak of World War II witnessed hardly a trace of the enthusiasm that had accompanied its predecessor.[4]

After 1945 the process became even more pronounced. Operating under the aegis of the

Bertha von Suttner (on a 2-Euro Austrian coin) was probably the most famous pacifist ever; she died a month before the outbreak of World War I.
JONATHAN LEWY

United Nations, an organization specifically founded to preserve and promote peace, most countries found it necessary as well as useful to proclaim their opposition to war. In the United Nations charter, "aggressive" war was prohibited, but since there was no agreement on the definition of aggression, in practice the outcome was merely that attempts by one nation to use force in order to annex territory could no longer obtain recognition by the rest. The more time went on, the clearer it became that large parts of the world had become immune to war, especially the kind of war that is waged by major states against one another. What wars still took place were waged almost exclusively in the "developing" parts of the globe. Even these, so the argument runs, could not compare with their predecessors in points of size and organization. They were, in reality, little more than the handiwork of criminals and thugs.

On this view, war is a social institution, not a biological or psychological necessity.[5] Following the route taken by other age-old institutions, such as slavery, it is finally on its way out. The change in attitudes is neither short-lived nor accidental. Its origins may be discerned as long as a quarter of a millennium ago; its development reflects a mixture of advancing democracy, improving economic conditions, and international cooperation, all made possible as well as necessary by modern technology and communications. As war goes, so of course will the fascination it exercises and the culture it has given rise to—or perhaps one would be more correct to say that it is a growing disillusionment with, not to say revulsion for, war that is leading to the latter's demise. It is an optimistic vision, perhaps even a noble one, but is it true? In this part of the present volume, an attempt will be made to answer that question.

. . .

13

A Short History of Peace

Did the Enlightenment really bring about a fundamental change in attitudes, or are some of the antiwar ideas that it raised as old as history? For an answer, recall that both of the most important Chinese philosophies, Confucianism and Taoism, strongly opposed violence in all its forms. In the case of Confucianism, this was because it valued order and its prerequisites, such as seniority, submission, good faith, and decorum, above all else; take these pillars away, it taught, and the outcome would be chaos and the war of all against all. Taoism's main concern was less with society than with the individual and the rational life, which it saw as identical with "the path," or virtue. It therefore understood war as a manifestation of stupidity. Albeit one that, according to one of the greatest Taoist texts, Sun Tzu's *The Art of War,* was sometimes necessary and, in case it did break out, should be fought in the most rational manner possible.[1]

Turning from China to ancient Greece, nothing is easier than to find a longing for peace and a condemnation of war. This even applies to the *Iliad.* In many ways the epic represents the greatest cultural product of war ever. As the opening lines and many other passages testify, its very purpose is to record the deeds of heroes. Hence it delights in describing the splendid appearance of arms and armor, praises courage above all other virtues, and expresses the joy of fighting and bloodshed as few, if any, other literary creations have; not for nothing did Aristotle have the young Alexander study it.[2] Yet it is also suffused with a deep yearning for peace and the good life. Had it not been for that yearning, which balances the gory references to smashed skulls and spurting blood, then *qua* literature it would not be half as great as it is.

Throughout the poem, almost every time war is mentioned, it is joined to epithets such as "bloody," "full of tears," "deadly," "wild," "disastrous," "brazen," "bad," "sad," "full of suffering," "terrible," and "destructive."[3] The denunciations reach their peak in book V. There we find no less a person than Zeus telling his son, the war god Ares:

> Stop whining into my ear, you coward!
> Of all the gods, who live on blessed Olympus
> you are the most hateful. For you love
> war, fighting, and strife above all other things. »

Philosophers such as Xenophanes (ca. 570–ca. 478 B.C.), Pythagoras (ca. 580–ca. 500 B.C.), and Gorgias (ca. 483–ca. 375 B.C.), to mention but a few, went out of their way to praise peace and condemn war (especially, it must be conceded, war waged among Greeks as opposed to war waged by Greeks against barbarians).[4] At least two of the most important tragedies, Euripides's *Persians* and *Trojan Women,* can be interpreted in this sense; this is even more true of four of the best-known comedies, Aristophanes's *Acharnenses, Equites, Peace,* and *Lysistrata.* Indeed it has been argued that Aristophanes in particular was a lifelong fighter for peace, both because he feared for the fate of Athens during the Peloponnesian War and as a matter of principle.[5]

What is true of ancient China and Greece is equally true of other peoples at other times and places. If Polybios is to be believed, the Romans, among whom he lived for twenty years and whom he knew as well as they knew themselves, were uniquely inclined to solve every problem by using force. Yet, by the time of Emperor Augustus Horace, the Romans were celebrating the *pax romana* as the source of all blessings.[6] Augustus himself built the Ara Pacis, the altar to peace, a monument that in its own way is as original a creation as Trajan's column was later to be. A little less than two centuries later they brought forth Emperor Marcus Aurelius. His celebrated work, *The Meditations,* does not explicitly deal with questions of peace and war. Still, it is one of the strongest works in favor of the fellowship of men ever written.

Having its origins in the semi-monastic sects then forming in the Judean desert and intimately linked with the history of the Roman Empire, Christianity, too, started life at least in part as a protest against war and violence. Among the most celebrated words the Divine Savior ever uttered was his suggestion that the best way to resist aggression was to turn the other cheek.[7] Not much later, the Apostle Paul amplified his message, emphasizing man's duty to live peaceably with all.[8] Tertullian, Origen, and Lactantius were all firm opponents of military service; the first-named even composed a special treatise attacking it.[9] During the first few centuries after Jesus, Christians did in fact refuse to serve in the imperial army, an attitude that was both suitable for the practical needs of a small, esoteric sect and one of the reasons why that sect was so often persecuted. Many subsequent Christian movements were also strongly committed to peace. They included the Franciscans, the early Anabaptists, the Mennonites, the Amish, the Hutterites, the Jehovah's Witnesses, and especially the Quakers; all these retained their opposition to war through thick and thin.[10]

The above shows that it is simply not true to say that love of peace and hatred for war only made their appearance during the Enlightenment. Rather, all the Enlightenment did was to recast ideas that had been common currency for centuries if not millennia into its own peculiar mold. That mold was secular, nondenominational, and universal; from Rousseau and Diderot down, many philosophes believed that when it came to maintaining peace, Europeans had something to learn from the *bon sauvage*.[11] From then on, instead of following in Christ's footsteps, pacifism was supposed to be based on the "benevolence" and "philanthropy" that the Supreme Being had allegedly implanted in His creatures.

Finally, it is true that the second half of the nineteenth century witnessed the rise of the first organized movements dedicated specifically to supporting peace, but what does this fact prove? This was the great period when time and distance were cut. Railways, steamships, and telegraphs began girdling the earth, to say nothing of that most important invention, the postage stamp. Making use of the new technologies, hundreds of international organizations, both official and unofficial, sprang out of the ground as if by magic.[12] Delegates were elected (then as now, very often "delegates" represented nobody but themselves), meetings set up, congresses organized, speeches made, votes taken, and manifestos published. The organizations in question had all kinds of objectives, from charity through promoting world revolution to collecting antiques. No wonder that, among them, a few worked in support of peace.

Whatever their origins and precise nature, it would be hard to show that pacifist ideas had a strong impact on practical politics or that they reduced the frequency and intensity of war. Even in India, where Hindu religion emphasized *ahisma* or nonviolence, ruler-warriors waged war as often and as ferociously as anybody else; throughout precolonial Indian history, warriors (known as *ksatriya*) were considered the highest caste of all. For them, fighting was not just a means to an earthly end but one way, in fact *the* way, to gain merit that might come in handy when the time came for their souls to go through their next incarnation.[13]

All this explains why, in India, an organized antiwar movement emerged only during the middle decades of the twentieth century. Even then it was mainly an instrument for getting rid of the British; whenever Mahatma Gandhi proclaimed his intention to adhere to *ahisma,* the implication that violence could also be used was clear. Following independence, the movement floundered for some time as officials and defense intellectuals asked themselves how Gandhi's ideal might be reconciled with the new reality. However, in the newly resurgent, self-confident India of the late 1990s it has lost any influence. It was a government formed by a party professing traditional Hindu values, the Bharatiya Janata, that carried out India's nuclear tests in 1998.

For all its focus on the detached, virtuously rational or rationally virtuous individual, Taoism also brought forth what is probably the greatest text on war ever. In the whole of Chinese history there was no

Some pacifists could be quite belligerent; a Korean delegation brings Buddhism to Japan, A.D. 538.   DVORA LEWY

period when it was not studied; fifty commentaries and interpretations appeared between 1368 and 1628 alone. Today at least four different English translations are in circulation. As it was applied to other two-sided activities such as commerce, it ended up by introducing the principles of war into peace as well. Moreover, Taoism is closely related to some forms of martial arts, as one would expect from a way of thought (and life) concerned with using minimum or no force to overcome one that is much greater.[14]

Finally, some forms of Confucianism went along quite well with military action and war as long as it was directed against "evildoers" and "bandits"[15]—as, in theory, it almost always was. The most that all these religions may have done was help create occasional islands of peace in a dangerous world. During some periods of Chinese history they may also have somewhat diminished the status of warriors as opposed to scholars. That, however, was by no means always the case; as is proved by repeated intermediary periods when imperial power and peace broke down, giving warlords a free hand. On the whole, China's culture of war is quite as ancient and as highly developed as that of any other country. To realize this, all one has to do is look at the thousands upon thousands of terra-cotta warriors found in the tomb of Shih Huang-ti, the emperor who used fire and sword to unite China for the first time. Seldom if ever has there been such a powerful statement of unadulterated militarism.

For every ancient Greek poet or philosopher who denounced war, there was another who enthusiastically celebrated it, gaining fame and making his living by doing so. If it is true that Aristophanes spent much of his life calling for peace, surely he did so in vain; after all, the period when he wrote was precisely the one that, according to Thucydides, witnessed the greatest war the world had ever seen. As Augustus himself says in his *Res Gestae,* the Ara Pacis was only built after a period of seven centuries during which the gates to the Temple of Mars were hardly ever closed. Even so, one should not get a false idea. The altar carries, besides Augustus's own image, those of his adoptive father, Julius Caesar; his friend Marcus Agrippa; and his stepson, Tiberius. To a man, they had made their names as great commanders before turning, to the extent that they did, to works of peace. Marcus Aurelius's meditations did not prevent him from spending much of his life hunting Sarmatians, as he somewhat melancholically put it, nor from erecting the previously mentioned victory column with carved scenes of war much more violent than those on Trajan's column.[16]

The inability of the Church to put an end to war between Christians, as well as its frequent support for wars by Christians against other peoples, is notorious. The *pax dei* and the *tregua dei,* the former meant to regulate the times during which war could be waged and the latter to restrict the persons against whom it could be undertaken, were proclaimed and then forgotten.[17] A century or so later, the same fate overtook ecclesiastical efforts to ban certain weapons, such as crossbows. Often the Church did not even succeed in the less ambitious objective of creating islands of peace in the midst of war. This is not surprising: even the great scholar Saint Thomas Aquinas acknowledged that war could be waged on sacred days if necessary.[18] Throughout the Middle Ages (and before and after) there were countless cases when sacred buildings were looted, monks killed, nuns raped, and sanctuaries violated by force of arms.

One cardinal reason why its efforts failed was because, during long periods of its history, the Church itself either instigated war or waged it as intensely as anybody else. Even in the New Testament, which is one of the most pacific texts ever written, it is possible to find some extremely bellicose passages. As he set about cleansing the Temple, the Lord Himself proclaimed that his mission was to bring not peace but the sword; how many warriors found their inspiration in Saint John, imagining themselves as the hosts of the Lord fighting the Battle of Armageddon, is impossible to say.[19] Three hundred years after Christ's death, the process of "bellicization" started in earnest when Emperor Constantine, having dreamed that *in hoc signo vinces* and defeated his rival Maxentius, made Christianity into the empire's official religion. From that point on, Christians served in the army almost as a matter of course. Soon Saint Augustine was to write that "love of enemies does not exclude wars of mercy waged by the good"; in other words, it was possible to love one's enemy and kill him, too.[20]

It was in the name of the cross that Charlemagne used sword and fire to subdue the Saxons. Later in the Middle Ages, it was in the name of the cross that the nobility of Europe went on one crusade after another both in the Middle East and in their native lands, killing infidels and exterminating heretics. It was in the name of the cross that the Spaniards fought the Muslims in Spain, waged war on the Ottomans throughout the Mediterranean, and committed genocide in the New World. The Schmalkaldic War of 1543–44 was followed by the French Huguenot Wars (including the Saint Bartholomew's Day Massacre) of 1566–98 and the Thirty Years' War of 1618–48, to name only the most important ones. All these witnessed Christians of different denominations cutting each other's throats with an energy rarely surpassed before or since. It is true that after 1700, Europeans for the most part no longer fought each other in the name of their respective creeds. Still, most ecclesiastics continued to bless armies going on campaign as a matter of course, each one on his own side of the front.

As already noted, there were always some Christian denominations that insisted on opposing any war regardless of cause and consequence. On occasion their opposition was heroic. It was for their principled refusal to serve, among other things, that early Christians were routinely burned at the stake, thrown to the beasts in the arena, or beheaded as Saint Maximilian was. Early-sixteenth-century Anabaptists were tortured and executed. In the twentieth century, the likes of Hitler and Stalin sometimes locked up conscientious objectors in concentration camps. Sad to say, though, the numbers of those who resisted were never nearly large enough to make a difference. Concerning what would have happened if they *did* have the numbers—imagine, for example, an entire nation made up of Friends—one can do no more than guess. Perhaps such a nation would have stuck to its pacifist ideals. Its members could have refused to set up armed forces, relied on prayer to maintain their defense, and willingly paid the resulting price in the form of loss of property, liberty, and perhaps life.

More likely, though, the practical demands of life would have caused them to follow many other Christians and shed those ideals as a snake sheds its skin. To some extent, this is what happened in North America from about 1670 on. In particular, King Philip's War marked the time when conflict between whites and natives peaked and the outcome looked as if it were by no means predetermined. The recently established colonies scattered along the Atlantic coast did not have professional armed forces of the European type. Hence, normally the task of raising and commanding armies fell to magistrates at the town, county, and state level. By refusing to fill these functions, Quaker magistrates who helped run colonies such as Pennsylvania and Rhode Island avoided acting directly against their faith. Yet they certainly cooperated in the collection of military taxes, fully knowing what the money was intended for.

Some Quaker magistrates compromised. They would not wage offensive war, but they would build strongholds; once they had been built, it goes almost without saying that they offered refuge to white men—not just Quakers—but not to Indians. Others assuaged their consciences by commissioning other men to oversee military activities in their stead; as contemporary documents show, in doing so, they did not really succeed in satisfying anybody, not even themselves. Whatever the precise stance they took, once the wars had ended in the near extermination of the enemy, Quakers were not slow to vie with other colonists over conquered land.[21] The inescapable conclusion is that had the sect's members been left to fend for themselves for any length of time, inevitably they would have overcome their scruples, taken up the sword, and engaged first in defensive operations and then in offensive ones; equally inevitable, they would have developed their own culture of war just like anybody else.

Nor did pacifist feelings do much to limit warfare during the eighteenth century, and only too often did their authors (as many of them said) find themselves crying in the wilderness. To add to the irony, many contemporary commanders and officers were themselves children of the Enlightenment. They discoursed with the philosophers and prided themselves on their familiarity with the most advanced ideas of the time; the fact that they were on leave for months on end each year helped. The French logistician Jacques François de Chastenet de Puységur, the Austrian commanders Prince Eugen of Savoy and Marshal Leopold Josef Graf Daun, the French and Spanish commanders Antoine de Pas de Feuquières, Victor François de Broglie, and Álvaro José de Navia Osorio y Vigil, and others belonged to this type. All were highly cultivated men who felt almost as much at home in the study as they did in the field. Many of them collected books as well as other works of art. Some officers even made a name for themselves authoring literary best-sellers. Thus, having (as he says) done so much to help diminish the human race, the French expert on fortifications, Sébastien le Prêtre de Vauban, at the end of his life felt impelled to write a treatise on how it could be increased again.

The most famous specimen of the kind was King Frederick II of Prussia, aka the Philosopher of Sans Souci, aka Frederick the Great. While still a mere crown prince he penned a sharp rebuttal to Machiavelli. In it he did not rule out war, including preventive war. He did, however, express his astonishment at the lightheartedness with which many contemporary rulers approached the problem, and suggested that they should do what they could to spare their subjects from undergoing its horrors.[22] Throughout his life he continued to seek the company of Europe's best-known savants including, to mention but two, François-Marie Arouet de Voltaire and Moses Mendelssohn. This, however, neither prevented him from launching one war after another nor from keeping at it for as long as his treasury and his canon fodder lasted.

Several of Frederick's opposite numbers, notably Catherine the Great of Russia and Josef II of Austria, were almost as enamored of philosophical discourse and almost as "enlightened" as he was. Considering herself a "philosopher on the throne," Catherine founded the Hermitage Museum. She even wrote a treatise, inspired by Rousseau, on the education of young children. Josef took an interest in literature and played the harpsichord. Yet the wars that these and other crowned heads of the period waged were ferocious indeed.[23] Two of them, the Seven Years' War and the War of the American Revolution, spread over greater parts of the globe than any of their predecessors, clearly foreshadowing the twentieth-century world wars to come. Together, they caused the deaths of hundreds of thousands if not millions of people.

Whether they are bourgeois, socialist, communist, or anarchist, many modern ideas that see war as the product of a man-made social order that may one day be done away with can be traced back to Immanuel Kant and his 1795 treatise *Perpetual Peace.* In many ways, Kant was a typical son of the Enlightenment. Along with some of his predecessors and contemporaries, notably William Penn and Thomas Paine, Kant believed that war was simply a game played by monarchs and other aristocrats for their own benefit.[24] As long as hostilities lasted, many of these people remained safely ensconced in their palaces. Even if they took the field, for them the horrors of war were mitigated—for example, by being set free on parole when captured and having their property respected when on campaign; often they exchanged elaborate compliments. As they maneuvered this way and that, attacking, fighting, withdrawing; ordinary folk paid, suffered, and died. If that was true, then the next step was obvious. All that was necessary was to abolish monarchies, put an end to aristocratic privilege, and rearrange humanity in the form of republics so that power would be in the hands of ordinary people. Once this was done, war itself might be eradicated.

Though the Revolution certainly turned France into a republic, it was very far from meeting the hopes Kant put in it. Technically, in 1792–93, France may have been the victim of aggression, as the sovereigns of Europe, fearing for their thrones and even their heads, formed the First Coalition, declared war on it, and invaded its territory. Soon, however, the armies of the Republic found themselves using their bayonets in order to export *liberté, egalité,* and *fraternité* in all possible directions. First, using fire and sword and committing some of the worst atrocities on record, they set out to root out the pro-monarchist peasant uprising in the Vendé. The number of dead in that campaign is estimated at about a quarter of a million; in European history from 1648 to 1941, no other operation came closer to genocide.[25] That having been accomplished, they overran parts or all of the Low Countries, Germany, Switzerland, and Italy, reaching out as far as Egypt. Almost everywhere they went they were welcomed at first. Later, however, they met with resistance, and the more they tried to suppress it the stronger it became. Over the next few years, they set the continent ablaze.

As Napoleon took charge in 1799, the scale of warfare and the intensity with which it was waged increased still further. Whole libraries have been written to show how war assumed new and monstrous dimensions[26]—to the point where, according to no less an observer than Clausewitz, it came very close to assuming its "absolute" form.[27] From first to last, the wars took up an entire generation. Thus to argue that republicanism did much to limit war is not in the cards. If anything, it was a staunch supporter of absolute monarchy, Clement von Metternich, who organized the Congress of Vienna and restored peace. He even succeeded in maintaining it, more or less, for a period of thirty-three years after Waterloo.[28]

Over the next two centuries, Kant's followers often changed the villains' names. In his eyes they had been monarchs and aristocrats, useless leftovers from an earlier, pre-modern era. Depending on the ideology they embraced, some of his followers preferred to speak of "bourgeois" (the very people Kant, himself the most typical bourgeois of all, had thought were most strongly opposed to war). Others referred to "capitalists," "militarists," and "imperialists," as, for instance, in the works of the early-twentieth-century British economist J. A. Hobson and those of Vladimir Ilyich Lenin; others still blamed politicians in general.[29] No matter who they blamed, they remained wedded to Kant's idea that war originated in the selfish machinations of the elite, and not in the common people who were cheated or coerced into fighting it. Branching out into historical scholarship, some of them went on to apply this idea to remote periods long past.[30] The conclusion from this was obvious: to put an end to war all one had to do was make the government accountable to the people, as Kant and republicans coming after him suggested, or else do away with it altogether, as anarchists demanded.

In fact, neither before nor after 1795 did history provide much evidence to support Kant. Thucydides's description of Athenian democracy, its instability, and the way it was swayed by demagogues bent on fighting one war or another are among the most celebrated passages in his entire work.[31] A little later Plato described that democracy as "feverish," not a condition likely to promote peace.[32] The case of Sparta was exactly the opposite. Not only did Sparta have kings, but its character was always much more aristocratic than that of Athens. Partly for this reason, partly for others, it was famous for its reluctance to go to war. This was true in 480 B.C., when only an overwhelming threat finally convinced the Spartans to join the Athenians in repelling the Persian invasion. It was also true in Thucydides's own day and remained equally true a century after him. Alone among all Greek cities, Sparta refused to join Alexander the Great in his campaign against Persia. If the opprobrium that he heaped on it as a result made any difference, we have no record of that fact.

While it would not be true to describe Republican Rome as a democracy, neither was it a monarchy; there could be no question of a crowned person sitting in his palace saying, as Louis XIV once did, that whether or not a certain city would be lost he himself would still remain in power. The last thing one could say of the Roman aristocracy was that it was sheltered from war. In fact, serving in a certain number of campaigns was a prerequisite for entering politics and to getting oneself elected. Nor did any ancient civilization develop the niceties that, under the name of chivalry, sometimes did something to protect subsequent aristocrats from the worst that war could do. From the commander in chief on down, usually all that captives could expect was to be jailed, enslaved, mutilated, and perhaps executed in a variety of interesting ways. If our sources may be believed, after Carrhae in 53 B.C., the victorious Parthians poured molten gold into the captured Roman commander's mouth.

However important the consuls and the Senate might be, from the earliest days of the Republic the right to vote on peace and war always remained firmly in the hands of the various assemblies. It is true that some of these assemblies were deliberately structured to give the aristocracy a commanding voice, but from the end of the third century B.C. things began to change. The popular assembly, or *comitia plebis,* gained influence at the expense of the rest, and a hundred years later few magistrates even bothered to summon the other committees any longer. Yet, if anything, this move toward democracy, limited as it was, made Rome more ready to go to war, not less.

By the standards of the Middle Ages, and also by some of those that came later, the Swiss and, a few centuries before them, the Vikings were democratically governed. There were no kings. By the time the Nordic monarchies were formed, the great days of expansion were over; the Swiss, of course, always remained republican. Equally, there were very few aristocrats, and even those who did exist were expected to fight in the front line and risk their lives much as everybody else did. Even more than had been the case in Greece and Rome, the most important decisions on war and peace were made by popular assemblies. All free adult men attended, weapon in hand. Yet democracy did not prevent either the Vikings or the Swiss from counting themselves among the most belligerent people of all times; they assiduously prepared for war, defended themselves, and attacked others. The former also celebrated their exploits in sagas whose outstanding quality is their stark acceptance of war, bloodshed, and death.

Motivated by a mixture of belligerence and poverty, the Vikings and the Swiss acquired a reputation as fearsome warriors. At a later point in their history, they started renting themselves out to whoever was willing to pay for their military services. Whether on their own account or while in the service of others, the Vikings fought in places as far apart as North America, the northern shores of the Black Sea, and the Jordan Valley. The Swiss did the same, gaining fame for their willingness to change sides; as long as they were paid, they did not care why or for whom they fought. When Rousseau imagined his democratic society made up of warlike farmers, it was the Swiss, among whom he himself had been born and raised, that he had in mind.[33]

In 1812, the two great democracies of the period, Britain and the United States, again went to war against each other and kept it up for three years. Throughout the nineteenth century, often backed by a vociferous chorus of popular support, not a single year passed during which British troops did not engage in military operations in some part of the world. And while Lincoln's famous words at Gettysburg may sound impressive, the American Civil War was not a question of democracy fighting its opposite. Rather, what happened was that the most democratic country the world had ever seen broke up into two parts over an issue on which its citizens just could not reach agreement, and those parts, each under its democratically elected president, waged a truly ferocious war. Ere they were done, they left no fewer than six hundred thousand dead.

As Herbert Spencer's own triumphal tour of the United States proved, his philosophy, with its belief in the obsolescence of force and the inevitable spread of peaceful progress, was enormously popular in that country. The powerful, the well-connected, and the rich felt especially attracted by it; after all, by emphasizing success as the reward of "fitness," it vindicated their success. In 1896, the year when Spencer's influence reached its peak, no fewer than three Supreme Court justices declared themselves his followers.[34] Yet just two years later the United States launched what was by some accounts a totally unnecessary and totally unprovoked war against Spain. The irony did not escape some contemporaries.[35] In terms of bellicosity, and even more so in terms of statements that saw positive aspects in war, there was little to choose between Helmut von Moltke the Elder, chief of staff of a "reactionary," "authoritarian," and "militarist" country such as Germany, and Theodore Roosevelt, the popularly elected (and hugely popular) president of the most liberal, democratic, and progressive country of all.

Nor were those avowed opponents of war, the pacifists, the suffragettes, the socialists, and the anarchists, much better than anybody else. Throughout the period from 1871 to 1914, French pacifists had been prepared to abolish war—but only on condition that Alsace-Lorraine was returned to them first. Their German opposite numbers replied in kind. They said that the provinces were not on the agenda, that their French comrades had no right to discuss them, that the inhabitants of the two provinces were happy under German rule, and—by way of an *ultima ratio*—that German military strength would make it impossible for France to recover them by force.

It was, however, the Italian pacifists who raised the greatest number of eyebrows. Like the rest, they were prepared to renounce war, but only after South Tyrol, which had never belonged to Italy but which they insisted was really the Alto Adige, were taken away from Austria-Hungary. In 1911, when Italy unexpectedly attacked Turkey, the pacifists supported the war, thereby dealing their movement a mortal blow from which it never recovered. Throughout the period, perhaps the only pacifists who, for a time at any rate, did *not* put their country above their principles were the British ones. Their opposition to the Boer War was courageous, but it was also ineffective. So much did they antagonize the public that they needed police protection.[36]

Similarly, no sooner did World War I break out than the women's suffrage movement was divided. In all belligerent countries, the majority gave up their supposed pacifism and turned to support their respective countries instead.[37] One of the best known, Emmeline Pankhurst, immediately changed the title of her journal from *Suffragette* to *Britannia.* Another, Vera Brittain, envied her brothers for being able to go out and play "the great game of death."[38] This, however, was but part of the story. In all the belligerent countries, countless women were seized by a phenomenon known in Britain as "khaki fever." They put pressure on their menfolk to join the forces, and threw themselves into the arms of the first soldier they could find.[39] Later in the war, the time was to come when French, Italian, and German soldiers accused their womenfolk of having a ball while they themselves fought in the trenches and died by the millions.[40]

Probably for every socialist who rejected war there were two who had some good things to say about it. To Jean-Pierre Proudhon, one of socialism's founding fathers, war was a "divine thing," the origin of "religion's most brilliant mysteries" as well as "the entire system of justice."[41] Both Karl Marx and Friedrich Engels took a great interest in it. The former called the American Civil War "a spectacle without parallel," the pangs whereby an old world was giving birth to a new one.[42] The latter made it into his specialty, studying it with commendable thoroughness until his anonymous writings on that subject were sometimes believed to be those of a Prussian general. Among socialist leaders who came after them, most limited their opposition to offensive war between their respective countries, as the Frenchman Jean Jaurès did.[43] They did not object to defensive war, let alone to war as such. In this they strongly resembled many ancient Greeks, some Christians, and some Muslims.

Thus not only were socialists no pacifists, but many of them hoped to gain their objectives by resorting to arms. In theory, at any rate, that was how Engels, writing to Marx, justified the interest he took in the question.[44] When one leading socialist, Engels's former secretary and appointed heir, Eduard Bernstein, suggested that an armed struggle might be neither necessary nor desirable, so enraged were many of his fellow party members that the movement almost fell apart—proving, perhaps, that for them the vision of class war was something more than simply a means to an end.[45] When war did break out in 1914 practically all socialist leaders, afraid lest they be left without voters, supported it. Of the few who did not at least one, Ramsay MacDonald, paid the price by being forced to step down as his party's leader.

Finally, some anarchists were indeed pacifists. The best-known figure was Leo Tolstoy. As a young man he joined the tsar's army and saw action against the tribes of the Caucasus and also during the siege of Sebastopol. Many years later, he came to share Kant's idea that war was a mere swindle perpetrated on "the stupid laboring masses" by their self-appointed betters.[46] Having more or less withdrawn from the world, he could afford the luxury of living in accordance with his ideal, occasionally loosening a broadside that denounced war and preparation for it. Over time his warnings became mixed with Christianity so that it became hard to say what was more important, the writer's anarchist beliefs or his desire to follow in the footsteps of the Lord.

There did, however, also exist an important wing of the anarchist movement, known as syndicalism, which took the opposite tack. Far from embracing pacifism, it came very close to worshipping violence for its own sake—close enough to attract an unknown Italian laborer by the name of Benito Mussolini.[47] In a way, none of it mattered. When the bugles sounded and armies mobilized, almost all pacifist leaders, whatever the precise direction from which they approached the subject, changed their position. Some volunteered for military service. Others went on speaking tours to denounce their countries' enemies.[48] To most people, it was not so much a cause looking for a war as a war that was looking for a cause in whose name it could be fought.

Having been formed in a ferocious civil war, the Soviet Union started life as the first socialist country in a very belligerent mood. To Leon Trotsky, as to Marx before him, war was the "locomotive of history." Lenin himself had always had a violent streak in him, and it was his insistence on the inevitability of a bloody revolution that caused him to separate from the Mensheviks. He proved as good as his word, conducting a civil war that cost the lives of millions. Once in power he promised to spread the workers' revolution wherever he could. At the Eighth Bolshevik Party Congress in 1919 he predicted "a series of frightful collisions between the Soviet Republic and the bourgeois states."[49] He even set up a special organization, the Comintern, to prepare for the coming conflict. This phase lasted until 1927, the year when Stalin, as part of his struggle with Trotsky, brought it to an end. Having proclaimed "socialism in one country" as the official doctrine, from this point on he and his successors always took care to describe Communism as "peace-loving."

There was a certain logic to this claim. Like many before them and some after them, Soviet leaders believed, or claimed to believe, that war owed its existence to the selfish intrigues of the upper classes intent on maintaining their own rule and if possible making a profit for themselves. Now that those classes had been eliminated—this was called "resolving the contradictions"—the Soviet Union could no longer have any interest in waging war but would do so, if at all, only for self-defense. After 1945 the need to assist the working classes in other countries received a renewed emphasis, but until 1979 even that kind of military enterprise remained strictly limited. Let others dispute whether the men in the Kremlin were more hypocritical than the rest—whether, for example, Leonid Brezhnev had a greater personal interest in invading Afghanistan than George W. Bush did in trying to take over Iraq and its oil. In terms of theory, the Communist reasoning was probably as good, or as bad, as any that came before or after it. In any case, as realpolitik took hold, it made precious little difference.

The fact—to the extent that it is a fact—that war has declined from 1945 on is often attributed to the idea that democracies do not fight one another.[50] However, this argument does not hold water, either. That is not because there are exceptions—in fact, it is very hard to find any. Rather, it is because the same often holds true of countries that are anything but democratic. For example, after 1945 a newly democratic Germany no longer went to war against France as, in one guise or another, it had often done since 1187, when Emperor Otto IV was defeated by King Philip Augustus of France at Bouvines. However, neither did the democratic United States fight a war against nondemocratic countries such as the Soviet Union or, after 1953, China.

Though one may think of several reasons why there are fewer large-scale wars between Israel and its neighbors than there used to be before 1973, it is not because Arab states have suddenly ceased being brutal dictatorships. Whatever the reason Pakistan and India no longer wage large-scale war against each other, as they regularly did from 1947 to 1971, it is not because the former has changed its spots and turned into a model democracy; in fact it could be argued that a nondemocratic ruler, General Pervez Musharraf, has done more to normalize relations between Pakistan and its great neighbor than all his predecessors combined. Nor can democracy explain why, in spite of the very considerable border-disputes that divide them, India and China have not fought one another for over forty years.

To continue the list, Taiwan is more or less democratic, whereas China is not. The latter's rulers have often threatened the former with war in case it dares take such-and-such action. In practice, though, not a shot has been fired across the Straits for the last half century. Elsewhere in East Asia, half of Korea is more or less democratic, whereas the other has no such pretensions. As a continuous barrage of propaganda and occasional border incidents prove, the two sides have an outstanding capacity for hating each other, yet they have not gone to war against each other for over fifty years. Nor is there much reason to think that they will do so in the future. As of 2007, the most likely factor that could spark off war in the peninsula is precisely the collapse of North Korean's totalitarian regime, which is why other countries are trying to prop it up by means of subsidies. These facts, and many others like them, give those who attribute what peace the world is enjoying to the spread of democracy have some explaining to do. It is a task that few, if any, of them have attempted so far.

Throughout history there have been many people, including some highly influential ones, who courageously campaigned against war in the name of order, propriety, religion, compassion, humanity, civilization, economic expediency, and whatnot. The results were, to say the least, disappointing. Focusing as they do on the alleged machinations of elites, Kant and his many followers seem to underestimate the extent to which ordinary people are fascinated by war and, too often, desire war, clamor for it, and rejoice in it. This is not because they hope it will be directly useful to them in any material sense; except in cases of desperate self-defense, it hardly ever is. Rather, it is because they find it exciting as nothing else can be, and because once it breaks out, each man is ashamed not to be part of it as others are—a fact that also explains why some of war's most ardent supporters are found not at the front but in the rear. None of this is to say that there are no cases when the interests of the elite differ from those of the common people and when the former manipulate or coerce the latter; of course there are. Equally often, though, those interests, if that is indeed the proper term, may coincide, merge, and become inseparable. Never more so, it should be added, than precisely when the banners unfurl and the faith, or the fatherland, or national honor, or whatever, are in danger.

14

The Waning of Major War

If neither changing attitudes nor the spread of democracy can explain why major war among major powers seems to be on the wane, what can?[1] Taking a realistic view, rather than engaging in wishful thinking, one is tempted to answer the question as follows. First, God (or Robert Oppenheimer, or General Leslie Groves) created nuclear weapons and, by suffering them to be dropped on Hiroshima and Nagasaki, made sure those poor, deluded humans would understand the awesome things they could do.[2] After that, for a long, long time, He rested. Only then came any other reasons one might adduce, such as changing attitudes, spreading democracy, the (allegedly) growing cost of war, economic integration, the rise of international institutions, and so on and so on.

From the beginning of history, political organizations going to war against each other could expect to preserve themselves by defeating the enemy and gaining a victory. It is, of course, true that some victories had always been Pyrrhic, not worth the cost. Still, the eponymous King Pyrrhus got away with his life, as did most of the men he commanded. Now, assuming only that the vanquished side retains a handful of nuclear weapons ready for use, the link between victory and self-preservation has been cut.[3] The possibility must be taken into account that, the worse the disaster that the defeated party is facing, the greater also the danger to the survival of the victor. The leader of a nuclear belligerent whose country is threatened by the imminent prospect of total destruction—as, for example, happened first to France and Russia and then to Italy, Germany, and Japan during World War II—is all the more likely to react by pressing the button.[4] Some commentators even invented names for this scenario, speaking of a "ragged nuclear strike" and "broken-back warfare."

Hitherto, as we saw, pressures aimed at abolishing war, however well intended, had ended in failure. Now, with the ruins of Hiroshima and Nagasaki serving an awesome warning of what the most powerful war-making weapons could do, they had to succeed at all cost. In essence, two roads could lead toward that goal. One was to continue the time-honored method of refusing to serve in war, invoking God against it, speaking out or writing or rallying against it (from the 1960s on), and, in general, calling war a bad, bad thing. In democratic countries where elections were free, people were even allowed to vote in favor of parties that promised to act against war. Many of the parties in question were the direct successors of those that had campaigned for peace since before 1914. To this extent, there was nothing new in their activities.

From the British philosopher Bertrand Russell to the Soviet nuclear physicist Andrei Sakharov, those who raised their voices in favor of peace included prominent scientists, artists, and movie stars. Here and there, they were able to organize impressive mass rallies. Newsletters were dispatched, leaflets distributed, speeches given, and manifestos read. Arms were linked, candles lit, peaceful songs sung, and petitions signed by participants and sent to politicians. To provide intellectual ammunition in support of peace, an entirely new academic field, known as conflict resolution, was developed and has now existed for over half a century. Here and there antiwar candidates got themselves elected to parliaments. Yet no party that promised to go very far in this direction—for example, by unilaterally dismantling its country's armed forces—ever seems to have succeeded in attracting a mass following, let alone keep that following for long enough to make a difference.

To start with the most important country of all, in the United States pacifism never made any headway; it even could be argued that the American people became much more militaristic after 1945 than they previously had been.[5] One reason behind this obsession with the armed forces resulted from the change in the country's international position that took place after 1945; its very power meant that it came to be challenged in a way few, if any, others were. A second was the forces' own propaganda, a third one the often very considerable economic benefits that voters associated with having bases and arms-manufacturing corporations situated in their states and counties. The United States was also exceptionally prepared to use its forces.[6] Perhaps this had something to do with the fact that, until September 2001, it was always U.S. troops beating down on somebody else's country, never the other way around. Be the reasons as they may, throughout the Cold War both major American political parties catered to public paranoia, outdoing each other in promising that they alone would look after defense. Following the collapse of America's principal rival, they still do.

Conversely, any presidential candidate who looked as if he could not deliver on this count lost the election before he even started. If Harry Truman did not run again in 1952, it had everything to do with the way he handled Korea. If Jimmy Carter was defeated in 1980, it was in large part a result of the administration's manifest failure to cope with defense and foreign policy problems, such as the fall of the shah of Iran, the Soviet invasion of Afghanistan, and the Iran hostage crisis.[7] Conversely, once a candidate did get into the White House, normally one of the first things he did was take a "New Look" (as Eisenhower called it) at national defense and devise ways to reinforce it. The bottom line is that each time the United States has gone to war since 1945—in Korea, in Vietnam, in the Gulf, in Bosnia, in Afghanistan, and in the Gulf again—public opinion was, initially at least, very supportive.[8]

The situation in Europe was somewhat different.[9] Here pacifist sentiment developed out of the enormous losses suffered during World War II. In part, too, it was a logical response to the continent's feeling of impotence vis-à-vis the superpowers that now divided it among themselves. At any rate it was quite strong, providing a basis not merely for occasional protests but for organized political action on a national scale. Outside Scandinavia and Benelux, small countries with no conceivable enemy to fight (and no ability to do so), of all the parties that tried their hand at this game, it was the German Greens who were the most successful. Yet they never attracted more than 10 percent of voters; but this achievement was due at least as much to their other policies, such as protecting the environment. No more than any other left-wing, pro-peace European party did they succeed in taking their country out of NATO, as some of them had hoped to do. While forming part of the ruling coalition with Gerhard Schröder's Social Democrats from 1998 to 2006, the Greens could not prevent German forces from being sent first to bomb Serbia and then to fight in Afghanistan. On both occasions, their call to Bundeswehr soldiers to desert fell on deaf ears.

The impact on the nondemocratic countries of the former Eastern Bloc was probably even smaller, and no wonder. Seeing their country as the victim of Fascist aggression, Soviet leaders did what they could to keep the martial spirit alive. Besides, over there any attempt to present the government's policies as less than perfectly peaceful was quite often punished. The few antiwar activists who dared show themselves openly, as well as those who worked undercover but were discovered by the authorities, invariably lost their jobs. They also suffered from police harassment—some had their homes searched, others were beaten up—and were incarcerated either in prison or in psychiatric institutions. Since they were forced to operate underground, it is all but impossible to estimate how many of them there were.

In both East and West, to quote one author sympathetic to their cause, members of peace movements were well aware that their goals were "utopian." Indeed, it could be argued that, as with the Quakers, the only reason why they could exist at all was because there were relatively few of them; being few, they did not carry responsibility. In any case they hardly impacted on major decision making. The most they may have been able to do was to act as "peace witnesses," whatever that may mean.[10] Perhaps they also helped end a few wars—such as the French one in Algeria, the American one in Vietnam, and the 1982 Israeli one in Lebanon, all of which were already widely regarded as lost—somewhat sooner than might otherwise have been the case.[11]

The irony is reinforced by the fact that in trying to promote peace, some of the people involved could be very violent indeed. In the United States during the late 1960s, peace demonstrations led to massive unrest at party conventions and universities. Self-styled antiwar activists battled with the police, making it necessary to bring in heavily armed paramilitary forces in the form of the National Guard, culminating in a number of deaths. The climax came at the end of 1972, the time when the so-called Christmas Bombing of North Vietnam led to a quarter of a million people trying to storm the Pentagon. In Britain, Germany, and several other European countries, protesters demanding nuclear disarmament or the exclusion from their national territories of certain types of delivery vehicles, such as cruise missiles and Pershing ballistic missiles, often came to blows with their opponents. They blocked roads and railroads, laid siege to military bases, battled with the police, and sometimes went so far as to throw Molotov cocktails. In that, too, they resembled quite a number of their socialist predecessors; the road to hell is paved with good intentions.

As the Roman saying *Si vis pacem, bellum para* shows, the other road toward avoiding war—namely, deterrence—was not exactly new, either.[12] Rulers and countries have always sought to deter their enemies by building up their armed forces and putting them on display. From time to time they also issued threats concerning what would happen to their enemies if they dared do this or that. The difference was that, with the stakes as high as they were after Hiroshima, deterrence became vital as never before, to the point where it was turned into a central pillar of that most sacred cow, strategic theory. To achieve deterrence one had to be as powerful as possible—as former German chancellor Helmut Schmidt, once put it, "To be able to fight a war so as not to be compelled to." Technologies had to be developed, forces deployed, and doctrines adopted, that would make the threat of nuclear war "credible," as the phase went.

Let us start with technologies. The bombs that demolished Hiroshima and Nagasaki proved to be no more than the beginning. Bombs that were more powerful, more deliverable, and easier to store started being built almost immediately. By 1952–53, the development of hydrogen bombs opened the road to unlimited explosive power. By the time President John Kennedy assumed office in 1961, so many bombs were available that each Hiroshima-sized target could be "serviced" by no fewer than three weapons, each one sixty times as powerful as the one that had reduced that city to ashes. In the same year, the Soviet Union tested the largest of all nuclear devices. It turned out to have the power of fifty-eight megatons of TNT, equivalent to about four thousand Hiroshima bombs. By way of comparison, all the bombs dropped by the Allies during World War II on both Germany and Japan only amounted to a little over two million tons.[13] As Winston Churchill once put it, dropping larger bombs would only make the rubble bounce.

Such powerful weapons could only be used against an enemy who was many, many miles away (at the time of Hiroshima and Nagasaki, the American bases closest to Japan were 1,500 miles away). Partly to overcome that limitation and partly because threats to use such weapons (and thus invite retaliation) could hardly be made credible, before the 1950s were out, defense officials and scientists were turning their attention to developing much smaller warheads. In this way they opened the way to so-called tactical nukes, the least powerful of which may have developed rather less than the equivalent of one thousand tons of TNT. Technically speaking, developing small warheads is more difficult than building large ones; hence, doing so, and letting the fact be known, in some ways came to be considered a sign of nuclear maturity. Some nuclear weapons that have been developed, or could be developed, do not even create much heat or blast. Instead they create radiation, killing people but leaving the physical infrastructure intact.

Closely linked to the warheads themselves were their delivery vehicles. The first two atomic bombs had to be delivered by the largest, most powerful aircraft ever built until that time, the B-29 bomber. Still, the B-29 was not perfect for the purpose. First, it did not have intercontinental range; with an enemy as large as the Soviet Union, that meant many targets remained out of reach. Second, it was relatively slow and vulnerable. The first problem was solved by the construction of even larger aircraft. The second was dealt with by replacing reciprocating engines with jets, which led to a considerable increase in speed as well as range. Focusing on the United States, which built a larger arsenal and made known more details about it than anybody else, the B-36, B-52, B-58, B-1, and B-2, each one faster, larger, more powerful, and/or less vulnerable than its predecessor, came and went. Still not content with this, designers built "stand-off" missiles that could be launched from the bombers themselves, further extending the latter's range and making it harder to shoot them down.

The construction of smaller and smaller warheads opened the way to two further developments. First, it became possible to deliver them to target not only by heavy bombers but also by means of medium bombers, fighter-bombers, fighters, artillery systems, and even two-man bazookas mounted on a jeep. Second, they could be mounted on top of ballistic missiles. The first missiles were derived from the German World War II V-2 and only had a range of a couple of hundred miles. However, this figure was quickly increased until, by the early 1960s, practically any point on earth could be reached from any other and wiped off the map. At first missiles were liquid-fueled, but later they became solid-fueled, which meant that they could be kept in readiness at all times and launched much more quickly than before. At first each missile could carry only one warhead, but later this number was increased. By the late 1970s, some Soviet models (such as the formidable SS-18) could carry as many as ten.

During the 1970s, cruise missiles, small robotic jet aircraft capable of flying very low and delivering their warheads with great accuracy, joined the arsenal. Many of these different kinds of missiles could be based on land, either in fixed silos, on board special railway trains, or, in the case of the smaller missiles, specially developed vehicles. But it was also possible to base them in the air, where they were slung under the wings of bombers, or at sea, where they could be launched either from all kinds of surface vessels or from specially built submarines operating while submerged.

As was proved by the awesome arsenal that ultimately came into being, devising ways and means for turning much of the enemy country into a radioactive desert was relatively easy; compared to the cost of raising and maintaining strong conventional forces with their much larger demands on manpower, it was not even very expensive. The flip side of the coin was the extreme difficulty of defending one's own country against nuclear attack. This question has often been divided into two parts, protecting one's armed forces and protecting one's civilian assets. Force protection has also been divided into two parts: finding ways to defend one's nuclear delivery vehicles and waging conventional war under nuclear conditions.

Most, though not all, calculations pointed to the conclusion that enough aircraft and missiles could be built, and modes for basing them devised, to enable many of them to ride out a nuclear attack and launch a second strike. The situation in regard to waging conventional war under

The real source of Cold War peace; a B-52 bomber dropping ordnance during an exercise   DEPARTMENT OF DEFENSE

nuclear conditions was very different. Some military physicians insisted that troops should be indoctrinated so as to overcome the "bugaboo" of radiation. Some military administrators wanted soldiers to be divided into different categories according to the amount of radiation they had already received, so that they could be sent into battle accordingly. Then there were visionaries who envisaged the use of widely dispersed forces. They were to be equipped with the kind of vehicles and supply lines that would enable them to leap around nuclear mushrooms; others still came up with what was perhaps the most useful suggestion of all, proposing that the grave registration service should be greatly extended.[14]

All this might have been funny if it had not been accompanied by exercises in which troops, suspecting nothing, were taken to nuclear test sites and ordered to drive by ground zero soon after a weapon had been exploded. Given the close link between radiation and cancer, the best one can say of those who organized the exercises is, God forgive them because they did not know what they were doing.[15]

Meanwhile, attempts were also made to defend civilian assets against attack. Throughout the 1950s, schoolchildren were made to carry out air-raid drills by diving under their desks, putting their hands over their ears, and closing their eyes. Supposedly bombproof shelters, looking like the typical American living room magically transported underground, were designed and advertised, though how many of them were actually sold is not known. Some cities constructed a few radiation-proof public shelters, provided them with stores of food, water, and medicine, and settled down for an indefinite waiting period, during which the stores deteriorated and often lost whatever purpose they originally had. Except in a handful of countries such as Switzerland, where the government made money by taxing people who had *not* built shelters under their homes; after 1960 or so these efforts, too, were abandoned. In part, this was because an effective defense simply could not be provided; in part, because of the growing realization that, as John Kennedy once put it, in case a nuclear war broke out, the survivors would probably envy the dead.[16]

Attempts to devise an active defense looked more promising at first. As early as 1946 a Canadian general supposedly told the *New York Herald Tribune* that the answer to the atomic bomb was "clearly in sight," though just what that answer was has never been divulged.[17] Some of the plans were too crazy to merit serious attention even from the world's most committed Dr. Strangeloves. For example, at one point it was proposed that each potential target should have a hydrogen bomb buried not too far away.[18] As the incoming missiles appeared on the radar screens, the bomb would be set off, obscuring the atmosphere with a huge cloud of dust and debris that no warhead, coming in at hypersonic speed, could pass unscathed. The problem of radioactive fallout apart, one of the difficulties was that the cloud would clear away after thirty minutes or so, making it necessary to repeat the process at regular intervals. It sounds like the proverbial Vietnamese village that had to be destroyed in order for it to be saved, not to mention the even more interesting possibility of a false alarm.

From the 1950s on, there were many attempts to design and construct anti-ballistic-missile missiles—bullets that would hit other bullets in flight, as the saying went. Among the earliest to make their appearance were the Nike series, reaching from the Nike Ajax to the Nike Hercules and culminating in the Nike Zeus. Since the Zeus did not show sufficient promise, plans were drawn up to replace it by a more advanced Nike X (for "experimental"), which later received the nicer-sounding name of Sentinel. Next in line came the Spartan, then the Sprint. All these missiles were developed by the U.S. Army and Air Force, which saw them very much as instruments for extracting money out of Congress.[19] Meanwhile, the Navy, equally determined to obtain funding, went its own separate way, ending up with a completely different missile known as the Bomarc.

Starting in the mid-1960s, the Soviet response was to girdle Moscow with a similar system known in the West as the Galosh.[20] Like its American counterparts, this system, the only one to reach operational status, could easily be jammed. It could also be misled by various penetration aids as well as saturated by the multiple reentry vehicles (MRVs) that were just then being developed; such were its vulnerabilities that some experts wondered why it had been deployed at all. Like the rest, it suffered from the trivial disadvantage that it was not accurate enough to hit an incoming ballistic missile in midflight, so again like them, it relied on a nuclear explosion in the hope of pushing the target missile off course. Western observers estimated the force needed to do this at two or three megatons; even this was an improvement on the five megatons the American missiles were supposed to carry.

Since nobody knew exactly what would happen when a nuclear warhead exploded not too far from another, the possibility had to be taken into account that the incoming one might still cause immense damage by wiping out not Moscow but some other nearby town. Even if this did not happen, the consequences, in the form of radiation and electromagnetic

pulse (EMP), for the "protected" asset, might be too awful to bear thinking about. This last consideration explains why the Soviets later relented,
replacing (or claiming to replace) the defensive nuclear warheads with
conventional ones. Returning to the other side of the Iron Curtain, similar considerations applied to Washington, D.C., and New York. This also
explains why some of America's planned missiles, such as the Safeguard,
were meant to cover not cities but ballistic missiles in their silos, leaving
the civilian population as exposed as it had been.

Nor was the problem of defending against nuclear bombardment the
same as defending against a conventional one. In the latter case, the de-
fender might hope to intercept a sufficiently large number of incoming
delivery vehicles to repel an offensive and cause it to fail. This, for example, happened in 1940–41 when the Royal Air Force compelled the
Luftwaffe to stop its offensive against Britain's towns. It is also what almost happened to the Allied air offensive against Germany in late 1943,
when only the introduction of long-range fighters saved the fleets of
B-17s. Not so in the nuclear age, when even one surviving warhead may
cause enormous, perhaps almost inconceivable damage. The outcome is
to give the attackers such an overwhelming advantage over the defenders
as to turn the whole of military history on its head.

These considerations, plus financial constraints, helped turn the
1970s into a period of relative sanity. For a time, both superpowers, instead of sinking ever-growing resources into what looked more and more
like a black hole, preferred to negotiate. By means of mutual agreements
known as SALT (for Strategic Arms Limitation Talks) I and II, they froze
the number of delivery vehicles and put limits on the development of
anti-missile defenses. Fortunately for the defense industry, perhaps less
so for everybody else, the hiatus did not last. In 1983, President Ronald
Reagan breathed new life into the efforts to devise an anti-ballistic-
missile defense. His program, which was quickly dubbed "Star Wars," envisaged deploying a large number of space-based lasers to shoot down
incoming missiles. To provide the tremendous amount of energy required, one variant of the plan envisaged putting small hydrogen bombs
aboard earth-circling satellites and exploding them; enough said.[21]

When these plans proved too impractical and too expensive, efforts
to develop a ground-based interceptor were resumed. An early version,
consisting of Patriot missiles and their attendant radar, underwent its
first and only baptism of fire during the 1991 Gulf War. It turned out to be
a miserable failure, as *none* of the eighty or so Scud missiles aimed at

Countless failures in the attempt to develop anti-missile defenses; during the first Gulf War, Patriot missiles hit nothing　U.S. ARMY/JEFFREY HALL

Saudi Arabia and Israel were intercepted.[22] The Scuds were extremely primitive missiles: launched in small salvos of no more than three or four, they were without any kind of preparatory jamming or penetration aids, and they were so badly engineered and built that many of them fell apart in midflight. Extremely inaccurate and armed with conventional explosives, the damage they caused was negligible. Yet none of this should be the occasion for illusions. Had only a few missiles carried nuclear warheads, then neither their primitive construction nor their extreme inaccuracy would have mattered much. In that case, Israel, much of Saudi Arabia, and perhaps other parts of the Middle East as well would have ceased to exist—and so, most probably, would have the country from which the weapons had been launched.

A decade and a half later, another hundred billion dollars spent have yielded nothing better than twelve operational launchers (out of a hundred that were being planned in 1999) stationed in Alaska. However, they are operational in a very limited sense. The most recent test had originally been scheduled for August 31, 2006, but the air force announced that the weather forced it to be postponed by twenty-four hours.[23] Just what one is to make of this is by no means clear. The given reason may have been the true one, in which case all the story does is prove how utterly useless the system is. Or else it may have been an excuse to avoid an encounter with a North Korean missile test that was being scheduled for the same day. If no attempt to shoot down the Korean missile had been made, then the air force would have been embarrassed. If an attempt had been made and ended in failure, then it would have been more embarrassed. If the attempt had been made and succeeded, then the United States would have committed an act of war in the midst of peace, with incalculable consequences. Better, therefore, to play it safe—and all the more so because in two earlier tests held in 2004 and 2005, the antiballistic missiles did not even leave their launching pads. Part of the difficulty is technical, since the tests require computer programs consisting of millions of lines as well as split-second coordination among systems located thousands of miles apart. Part of it is economic, since each test costs about a hundred million dollars. Hence there is no way enough of them can be held—even assuming, which is by no means certain, that, given what the consequences of failure may be, the term "enough" has any meaning at all.

As these failures prove, so far the system cannot even guarantee the safety of America's northwestern Pacific region against a small-scale North Korean attack. This says nothing of the fact that the awesome arsenal that used to deter Moscow should be enough to deter Pyongyang as well. As a famous British commander put it long ago, the dog that takes care of the cat should scare off the kittens, too. Instead, all it has achieved is to help create a solid base for a strategic cooperation program between former bitter rivals Russia and China. Both countries are worried, or pretend to be worried, about the U.S. plans. Both have augmented their offensive ballistic missile programs. The objective is to make absolutely sure the United States will not have them at its mercy; President Vladimir Putin has even gone on record as saying that his country now has a new system capable of beating anything the United States may build.[24] Quite possibly the conclusion from all this is that the best defense is one that is never built.

Perhaps in order to assuage the conscience of its editors and readers, for decades on end the *Bulletin of the Atomic Scientists* used to publish its famous "nuclear clock" with the hands always pointing to some time very close to twelve. The idea that we were figurative seconds away from nuclear disaster may perhaps have been realistic in the early years after

1945, when few people had any idea as to what nuclear weapons really meant. The more time that went on, however, the clearer it became that the clock was nonsense, no more than a gimmick designed to draw attention to a periodical that would otherwise be almost completely unknown. Instead, the absence of a credible defense, combined with the vast damage nuclear weapons can inflict, meant that the doctrines for using them have always been surrounded by a certain air of unreality.

To again focus on the United States, the policies of "massive retaliation," "mutual assured destruction," "graduated response," "flexible options," and "decapitation" (to name but the five most important ones out of several dozen that were developed and, to one extent or another, adopted) came and went.[25] Some doctrines envisaged the possible use of all-out nuclear force even against small attacks in remote places, the consequences be damned. Others, particularly those devised from about 1970 on, were meant to make the world safe from nuclear war by advocating certain limits on the weapons' use so as to avoid the kind of retaliation that could very well leave the world in ruins. None ever even came close to carrying conviction, the more so because the Soviets always insisted that no such limitations would apply, and that any attack on them would lead to a full nuclear exchange right from the start.

In comparison with the United States, little is known about the nuclear arsenals and doctrines of other countries. One reason for this is the unparalleled openness in which these things are discussed in America, where inventing new and previously unheard-of kinds of war and devising doctrines for fighting them is part industry, part national hobby— more proof, if any were needed, that the culture of war is alive and well. Mainly, though, it is because not nearly as many people around the world care about the nuclear doctrines of countries such as Britain and France, or even those of Russia, China, and India.

For good or ill, no other member of the nuclear club impacts global politics nearly as much the United States does. At the same time, all of them enjoy all the advantages of latecomers. In other words, they are able to study the evolution of their predecessors' forces and doctrines, using them either as models to follow or simply to trigger their own thinking as to what ought to be done and how. Here I shall pass over the differences between the U.S. experience and that of the rest, focusing on the similarities instead.

First, all the members of the nuclear club (as far as we know) made their debut with a very small number of devices, which (with the exception of Israel) they proceeded to test either immediately or after an interval of some years.

Second, they followed up by building many more, expanding their nuclear arsenals until at some point considerations of cost-effectiveness caused them to say, "Enough."

Third, with the possible exception of North Korea (whose first test remains a mystery), they all started with relatively low-yield fission bombs, whether based on uranium, as in the case of Pakistan, or on plutonium, which require that a reactor be constructed first.[26] If they progressed, the next step was more powerful fusion bombs, on one hand, and small "tactical" warheads, on the other.

Fourth, depending on their size, strategic position, and technological and industrial possibilities, they either developed or purchased various kinds of delivery vehicles. The vehicles included heavy bombers (the Soviet Union, Britain), more or less advanced fighter-bombers (all nuclear countries), and ballistic missiles of various ranges (ditto). Some countries acquired cruise missiles (the Soviet Union, Israel, perhaps some others, too), artillery systems (the Soviet Union, perhaps Britain, France, China, Israel, and India as well), and missile submarines (the Soviet Union, Britain, France, Israel, and perhaps China). One country, Israel, was rumored to have constructed nuclear mines and buried them, ready for instant use, in the Golan Heights, though whether the stories have a basis in reality is impossible to say.[27]

Fifth, all these countries devoted much thought and effort to protecting their nuclear forces. To do so they concealed those forces (in the days of earth-circling satellites, not an easy task), based them in steep valleys where they could not easily be reached by ballistic missiles, or buried them deep in the ground. Some missiles were made rail- or road-mobile, whereas others were stationed aboard launchers placed in the air, at sea, or under the sea. In theory, every one of these defensive methods is capable of being overcome by a determined first strike based on really good intelligence and perfect coordination achieved by an equally perfect system of command and control. In practice, such is the difficulty and the risk that none of them was ever put to the test.

Sixth, though these things are not often discussed in public, all nuclear countries seem to have devised doctrines for using their forces if need be. For example, the Soviet Union's response to American hopes to limit nuclear war (so as to enable the United States to make "first use" against the enemy) was always "instant use of all weapons in case of attack"; since there was less emphasis on deterrence, this could be construed as an even more threatening version of the American "massive retaliation."[28] The Chinese, regarding themselves as a poor nation that cannot afford many missiles and having staked everything on rapid economic growth, seem committed to a low-key no-threat no-first-use doctrine (although, in reality, one can never know).[29] The French during the Cold War used to speak of "defending the national territory" against invasion and of "tearing off a [Soviet] arm." Since then they have altered their doctrine to warn off other, unspecified opponents. In 2006 they also tested a new surface-to-surface ballistic missile with a range of several thousand miles.[30]

Britain may have a nuclear doctrine, but few people care what it is or understand why it is needed at all.[31] To some extent, apparently, it is a question of keeping up with the Joneses. Take the provision that British forces may resort to nuclear weapons while waging conventional war against a conventional enemy. Britain is an island with no conceivable enemy within a thousand miles; hence, it is very hard to see how such a war could become so vital to the country's survival as to make such a move necessary. India and Pakistan have probably developed their own doctrines. The former's is based on minimum deterrence, which is not hard to achieve when your one serious enemy, Pakistan, is much smaller and weaker than yourself.[32] The latter's appears to center on first use in case India once again launches a large-scale attack that looks as if it might endanger the national existence, as happened in 1971.

Finally, the case of Israel. Since at least the late 1950s, Israel's greatest fear has been that some Arab country or another would acquire nuclear weapons. To avoid a nuclear arms race, it has steadfastly refused to admit that it possesses them; in December 2006, when the incoming American secretary of defense, Robert Gates, said that Israel was a nuclear power, Israeli commentators saw this as an embarrassment.[33] Consequently, it does not allow information concerning its doctrine to leak out, so that attempts to discuss the question in any detail are very likely to lead to arrest, trial, and imprisonment. Nevertheless, the semiofficial appellation "doomsday weapons" provides a fairly clear idea of what those weapons are meant for as well as the circumstances under which they might be used. So does talk about "the Samson option."

Whatever their doctrines may say, there is no reason to think that any of these countries got closer than the United States did to solving the problem of how to defend their industries, their economies, and their populations against nuclear attack. A few are so small that, should they use nuclear weapons against the enemy, the consequences could redound on their own populations—for example, how much fallout would Israel receive if, to stop a Syrian attack, it set off a warhead on the Golan Heights just as the wind blew in the wrong direction? All seem to have built extensive bunker systems in which their leaders may take shelter and from which they may direct whatever there may be left to direct. One or two may have engaged in desultory civil defense exercises. However, such exercises, if they are to be at all commensurate with the anticipated scale of death and destruction, must be enormously expensive and disruptive; their real value is indicated by a Cold War–vintage Moscow joke that had it that in case of a nuclear attack, the most important thing would be to prevent a panic. Hence they have remained few in number and far apart.

Outside the United States, only one country, Israel, has anything like an operational anti-ballistic-missile system, known as the Arrow. The product of over fifteen years of research and development, the system is like its U.S. equivalent in that it remains far too new and untested to deserve that title. As of early 2007, out of fourteen tests held, twelve had ended in some kind of failure. Yet critics charge that not one of them was held under conditions that could be regarded as completely realistic; in some ways, simply holding an exercise that *would* be completely realistic is extraordinarily difficult. One reason for this is geographical. Israel's Cape Canaveral is located on the coast south of Tel Aviv. If the test target missile was heading west, it would be moving away from the test site instead of toward it, which wouldn't reflect reality. If it was headed east, it would have to be fired from somewhere in the Mediterranean, and even if doing so were feasible, the possibility exists that it might get through the defenses and hit Israeli territory. Thus, whatever tricks those in charge might come up with, they cannot conduct a test in situ. No wonder that, even as the missile was tested, those responsible conceded that a watertight defense was not feasible—while overlooking the question whether anything less is of any value at all.[34]

No other member of the nuclear club has anything even remotely resembling America's financial, scientific, and technological resources. Several of them could be virtually wiped out by just a single bomb exploding over their largest city. Most could not survive more than a handful of bombs. Even if some reliable system for intercepting ballistic missiles could be devised, warheads could still be delivered to target by means of cruise missiles flying so low—a few hundred feet—as to put them beneath the reach of radar; this in an age where a crude cruise missile, propelled by a small, commercially available jet engine and capable of being guided to its target with a fair degree of accuracy, could perhaps be built in someone's garage.[35] Other weapons still might be put aboard a container ship and shipped into some port or simply loaded on a pickup truck and concealed at ground zero. Against this background, the unwillingness of virtually all countries to spend heavily in a futile attempt to develop, test and deploy either passive or active defenses can hardly be called surprising.

Both in the case of the great powers and in others, from time to time a crisis developed, meaning that some country threatened to use its nuclear arsenal but desisted in the end. There were scary moments in 1948, 1954–55, 1958, 1962, 1970, 1973, and 1989–90. Still, in the end, the balance of terror always prevailed. Much as the United States hated the Soviet Union and the other way around, they did not go to war against each other. The same applied, successively, to NATO and the Warsaw Pact countries, the Soviet Union and China, China and India (from 1962 on), and India and Pakistan. It also applied to the Korean Peninsula (where war might have led to a nuclear duel between the United States and China, and where North Korea now has its own nuclear force) and to the Straits of Taiwan (where there always existed the danger that a Chinese invasion might lead to U.S. intervention and escalation). It even applied to what in the eyes of many was the most difficult region of all, the Middle East; compared to the Arab-Israeli wars that used to be waged until 1973 inclusive, those that came later were mere skirmishes. To turn the idea around, even countries as poor and undeveloped as China in 1964, Israel in 1967, India in 1974, Pakistan in the late 1970s or early 1980s, and North Korea in the years immediately after 2000 proved able to build nuclear devices. No wonder major war between major states has declined.

Countless academic nuclear strategists like nothing better than to write lengthy treatises on whether this or that technological development, way of deploying nuclear weapons, or doctrine will make nuclear war more or less likely. In practice their speculations have proved almost entirely irrelevant, because they were never put to the test. All the strategists can do is play with words, sometimes supplemented with mathematical equations few people can understand and which may be even less relevant to any kind of reality than words are. As the most important historian of nuclear doctrine wrote many years ago: "*C'est magnifique, mais ce n'est pas la stratégie.*"[36]

It did not matter whether the "system" (whatever that may mean) of

nuclear states was made up of two states or of several. It did not matter
whether the nuclear arsenals those states deployed were large or small,
or whether the available delivery vehicles were sophisticated or primitive, multiple or single, accurate or inaccurate. It did not matter whether
the nuclear doctrine in force (if any) was coercion, deterrence (and
whether deterrence was to be practiced by denial or by punishment),
minimum deterrence, launch on warning, launch on impact, first strike,
second strike, massive retaliation, mutual assured destruction (which
alone came in four different versions), flexible response, countervalue,
counterforce, countervailance (a Reagan-era neologism not even its author could understand), or any of the dozens of others that one nuclear
power or another may have developed.[37]

Nor did it matter whether the balance of nuclear power was symmet-
ric or asymmetric. At the time of the 1962 Cuban missile crisis, the number of U.S. deliverable warheads exceeded that of the Soviets by perhaps
twenty to one.[38] The same was even more true in 1969–70 when the
Soviet Union was apparently contemplating a preemptive nuclear strike
against China. Another case of notable asymmetry was the 1989–90 confrontation between India and Pakistan; at that time, too, the balance of
nuclear forces was around twenty to one.[39] In a non-nuclear world such
discrepancies, combined with a fear of what the future might bring, could
very well have led to a preemptive strike against the weaker opponent.
Not so in a nuclear one, given that those who may have contemplated
such a nuclear strike were unable to guarantee that a nuclear bomb (or
perhaps several) would not explode on their own soil. Probably as a result, on none of these occasions did war break out. If some participants'
accounts may be believed, even in October 1962, which most commentators consider the most acute crisis of all, war was not even close to breaking out,[40] as is also proved by the fact that the Kremlin did not put its
nuclear forces on alert.[41]

It did not matter whether those who owned the bombs belonged to
similar civilizations, making it relatively easy for them to communicate, or
to different ones, which presumably rendered such communication more
difficult. It did not matter whether they were status quo societies seeking
to preserve the existing order, revolutionaries seeking to overthrow it, or
millenarians trying to bring about the end of history.[42] It did not matter
whether they were good, God-fearing Americans committed to free enterprise or wicked, godless Soviet Communists supposedly laboring
under a mixture of arrogance and inferiority complex. It did not matter

whether they were forgiving Christians, Hindus professing nonviolence, Muslims whose one desire was to go to heaven so as to enjoy the virgins there, or Jews allegedly afflicted by a Holocaust complex or Masada complex or whatever.

The famous, or rather infamous, transfer of nuclear technology from one country to another did not matter, either. This seems sufficiently demonstrated by the fact that in the past, Soviet nuclear technology has been transferred to China, U.S. nuclear technology has been transferred to Britain and France, Canadian nuclear technology has been transferred to India, Chinese and Dutch nuclear technology went to Pakistan, French nuclear technology went to Israel, Israeli nuclear technology went to South Africa, and Pakistani nuclear technology went to North Korea. In 1998, when India tested its bombs, the United States made its vigorous protest heard. Just eight years later, though, it signed an agreement to transfer nuclear technology to that country.[43]

It did not matter whether the person with his finger on the trigger was called Winston Churchill, who throughout his life enjoyed war and fighting as much as any man did; Stalin, who at the time he was handed his first weapon in 1949 was seventy years old and becoming even more paranoid and more murderous than he had always been; Dwight Eisenhower, who had long been confident that Detroit would enable the United States to win any future war; or Mao Zedong, who when asked about the prospect of nuclear war said he was ready to sacrifice three hundred million people to put an end to imperialism.

All these men started by assuming that nuclear weapons were merely more powerful versions of older ones and that if worse came to worst, they would be used to achieve political ends. Later all were convinced that a fundamental line separates nuclear weapons from the rest and that crossing that line could only lead to disaster.[44] In the words of Lyndon Johnson, "There is no such thing as a conventional nuclear weapon"; in those of Charles de Gaulle, "[After a nuclear war] the two sides will have neither powers, nor laws, nor cities, nor cultures, nor cradles, nor tombs"; in those of Leonid Brezhnev, "Only he who has decided to commit suicide can start a nuclear war in the hope of emerging victorious from it." All this gives us very good reason to think that others will arrive at the same conclusion. In the case of some of those others, such as Kim Jong-il, it seems to be happening already.

Returning from rulers to the people whom they claim to represent, to the extent that the latter were allowed to make their voices heard, they seem to have reacted to nuclear proliferation in two contradictory ways. First, as many polls held at different times in different countries showed, the possibility of a nuclear holocaust was very much on their minds. Some resigned themselves to it, others protested against it; as the adherents of the British movement for nuclear disarmament used to chant in the early 1960s, "Better Red than dead."[45] Second, as time went on, the manifest effectiveness of nuclear deterrence plus the obvious decline of major war among major states made most people feel more secure against outside attack than ever. The more secure they felt, the less willing they were to sacrifice either their offspring or their money to Moloch, a change that can be clearly documented in the decline of the percentage of national budgets allocated to defense. In this way, to the extent that antiwar attitudes did gain in strength from 1945 on, their rise was the outcome of the "long peace," not its cause.

For good or ill, none of this means that humanity has any absolute guarantee that nuclear weapons will never be used in anger, or that they will be used only under certain circumstances for certain purposes against certain targets. To the contrary; had any such guarantees been given, and supposing they could have been made credible, then nuclear weapons never could have deterred anybody at all. To this extent, any attempt to place limits on them is actually counterproductive. The point is precisely that such guarantees do not exist and, by the nature of things, cannot exist. As long as the capabilities are there, any promises not to use them or to use them only in certain designated ways will hardly be worth the e-mails by which they are transmitted. This has been called "the stability-instability paradox."[46]

Even in case the capabilities are dismantled, as actually did happen in South Africa and may perhaps happen in some other countries, they could still be rebuilt rather quickly. At a meeting in Johannesburg in 1996, I personally asked former president F. W. de Klerk (at that time executive deputy president) what had happened to the bomb's components; in response, all he could do was laugh. The price of peace, probably the only thing that can make humanity abandon its long-standing desire to try its hand at the game of war, is, unfortunately, fear.

15

Beyond the Pale

Sixty years after Hiroshima, any major state can acquire nuclear weapons (which, of course, is not to say that any major state will necessarily do so). Sixty years after Hiroshima, any state that is not yet able to acquire those weapons can be anything but major. As the previous chapter has shown, there can be no question but that the proliferation of nuclear weapons is one reason, probably almost the only reason, why major wars between major states have almost disappeared. But what about those regions where states are too weak or too undeveloped to build them, or else where wars are waged not by states among themselves but by and among other organizations? The answer is simple. *Pace* the optimists, in many of those regions war is not waning away. If anything, it is increasing.

By one list, between 1946 and 2002 there have been 226 armed struggles. Of those, 111 were large enough to qualify as wars, an average of two per year.[1] Though this might appear to be a very low figure, it is misleading on two counts. First, many of the wars in question were very long; some, such as the struggles in Vietnam, East Timor, the Philippines, Chechnya, the territories occupied by Israel, Angola, Mozambique, the Spanish Sahara, and the border area between Somalia and Ethiopia went on for decades on end. The same is also true of the one in Sudan. No sooner did one conflict end in the southern part of that unfortunate country than another broke out in the west; when it will end, if it ever does, is anybody's guess. Accordingly, at any one moment, there were quite a few of them going on in different parts of the world (one author has estimated the number at between ten and thirty).[2] Second, the number of casualties caused by any one struggle in any one year may not have been large enough to merit the term *war* being applied to it. However, given sufficient time, the number of people killed and the damage caused might be enormous.

The wars in question could be divided into several different, if to some extent overlapping, types. First, there are wars waged between nuclear states and non-nuclear states. Second, come wars waged between non-nuclear states on both sides. Third, it is necessary to consider wars that are waged by states against guerrillas and terrorists who operate outside their own borders. Fourth, civil wars that take place inside those borders. Sometimes by definition, sometimes for other reasons to be explained presently, what all four kinds have in common is that nuclear weapons are irrelevant to them. Conversely, the fact that nuclear weapons are irrelevant to them is the most important reason why they could be fought and most probably will continue to be fought.

Let us begin with wars between major (i.e., nuclear) powers and minor (i.e., non-nuclear) ones. The list opens with the Korean War, in which China, at that time a non-nuclear power, was also involved. It also includes the 1956 Soviet "intervention" in Hungary; the Suez War of the same year, which was waged by a nuclear-armed Britain, assisted by non-nuclear France and Israel, against Egypt; the 1973 Arab-Israeli War, waged at a time when Israel already possessed some nuclear weapons as well as the means to deliver them; the 1979 Chinese invasion of Vietnam; the 1979 Soviet invasion of Afghanistan; the 1982 Falklands War between Britain and Argentina; and the American campaigns in Iraq, the former Yugoslavia, Afghanistan, and, most recently, Iraq again. Depending on how one defines war, it may also include the 1968 Soviet invasion of Czechoslovakia and the United States use of armed forces in or against several Caribbean, Central American, and South American countries.

Some of these wars were very small, others very large. The number of dead in the Korean War alone is estimated at about a million and a half. The 1973 Arab-Israeli War did not lead to anything like that number of casualties, but it did see tank battles larger than any waged since 1945 or, indeed, in the foreseeable future. The first Gulf War involved eighteen hundred Allied aircraft and half a million American troops, to which must be added another quarter of a million sent to the theater by various members of the coalition. What made these wars and some others more or less like them possible is the fact that, throughout the period, states that either already had nuclear weapons or else were capable of building them so quickly that it hardly mattered remained a minority. Even as late as 2007, after more than sixty years during which the necessary technology had been steadily spreading, the figure still did not exceed twenty or so. The rest will require months or years to do the same.

Though their cases differ in detail, the fate of Imre Nagy, Alexander Dubcek, Hafizullah Amin, Manuel Noriega, Saddam Hussein, and Slobodan Milosevic speaks a clear language. In Thucydides's words, of men we know, and of the gods we believe, that the strong do what they can and the weak suffer what they must. Any state that cannot build or chooses not to build nuclear weapons must reckon with the possibility that someday, some other state that does possess them may use armed force in or against it for some reason—or for no reason at all. Neither distance, its small size, nor the weakness of its armed forces will necessarily protect it; who would have thought the United States would one day attack Serbia? All this is particularly true if it has the bad fortune of irritating the state with the largest number of nuclear weapons of all. The opposite, of course, is also true. Had the above six gentlemen possessed nuclear weapons, or had they even been strongly suspected of possessing them, then most likely the wars that brought about their downfall never would have taken place.

Whether hostilities are conducted under the rubric of war, intervention, humanitarian action, or peacekeeping is in many cases immaterial. In 1956, Nikita Khruschev's suppression of the Hungarians killed thousands, drove tens of thousands into exile, and left Budapest in ruins. In 1979 all Leonid Brezhnev may have planned was a swift coup de main with the intention of reestablishing an ousted Communist government in Afghanistan.[3] Instead, he plunged that country into a series of wars that have now lasted for almost three decades and which show no sign of ending. In 1982, officially at any rate, all Ariel Sharon planned was a brief "operation." Its purpose was to occupy parts of southern Lebanon so as to stop the Katyusha rockets from being fired at Israel from that region, as well as perhaps teach Syria a lesson; instead, he unleashed a war that killed tens of thousands, lasted eighteen years, flared up again in 2006, and may yet flare up for a third time. President Bill Clinton's decision to bomb Serbia in 1999 may well have had peacekeeping as his objective. Yet in the process he wrecked the country to a point from which it may take a long time to recover, if it ever does.

The six decades since 1945 have also witnessed a fair number of wars between non-nuclear, ergo minor, states. This list includes the first three Arab-Israeli wars fought in 1948, 1956, and 1967. It also includes the three Indian-Pakistani wars of 1947, 1965, and 1971 (although it is just possible that at the time the last of these took place, India already had a bomb in the basement, which would place this conflict in the previous category). In addition, there were the 1962 war between China and India, the 1970 Syrian invasion of Jordan, the 1974 Turkish invasion of Cyprus, the 1977 war between Ethiopia and Somalia, the 1978 war between Tanzania and Uganda, the 1980–88 Iran-Iraq War (by far the largest of the lot), and a handful of others too small to call.

Several of the states that were involved in these wars later went on to acquire nuclear weapons. The outcome was unsurprising. In 1973 the Arabs, making use of the fact that Israel had not tested its bomb (which at the time was an innovation) and limiting themselves to a narrow strip of occupied territory, fought one more large-scale war. After that, things settled down to a near absolute calm; along the Israeli-Egyptian frontier, along the Jordan, and on the Golan Heights, that calm persists to the present day. This is not necessarily because the rulers in Cairo and Damascus have grown fond of those in Jerusalem. Rather, it is because they are afraid lest a serious offensive on their part might lead to escalation.[4] Given this situation, they very much prefer to confront Israel by proxy in Lebanon and, to some extent, the Gaza Strip. Something similar happened in South Asia. Once China, India, and Pakistan had all acquired nuclear weapons they no longer dared go to war against each other, so even the latter two limited themselves to skirmishes over a remote Himalayan glacier.[5] While surprises cannot be ruled out, there is an excellent chance that this will remain true in the future, too.

One non-nuclear country, Iraq, would have acquired nuclear weapons at some time during the 1980s had not the Israeli raid on the Osiraq reactor demolished the necessary infrastructure and prevented it from doing so. What a nuclear-armed Saddam Hussein might have done is anybody's guess. Almost certainly he would have forced Iran to end the war against him earlier than was in fact the case, and perhaps on even better terms than he actually got; beyond that, who knows? He might have confronted Israel or, fearing nuclear annihilation, he might not have done so. He might have invaded Kuwait or, having enough money, he might not have. Even if he had invaded Kuwait and held on to it, he might have caused trouble in the region, he might even have caused the price of oil to rise, but he hardly would have put the world at risk. The man was a gambler and a very wicked one at that, but he was not mad.

As these lines are being written in 2007, Saddam's old enemy, Iran, may itself be in the process of developing nuclear weapons. Once again, what will happen if and when it succeeds in its quest is anybody's guess. Having been invaded by Iraq, Ayatollah Ruhollah Khomeini, a millenarian leader if ever one there was, was able to galvanize his countrymen through eight years of truly extraordinary feats of sacrifice. He went so far as to provide some of the youths who volunteered to fight with fake golden keys (made in Taiwan) promising them entry into heaven; however, in 1988 even he was forced to give way. In the two decades since then, little if anything has taken place to suggest that Iranians are more willing to commit suicide than anybody else.[6]

Khomeini's latest successor, President Mahmoud Ahmadinejad, is known as a hard-liner (though the exact link between his refusal to allow women to walk the streets without head covering and his foreign policy is by no means clear). He has gone on record as saying that the Holocaust is a myth and that Israel does not have the right to exist.[7] Some of his anti-Israeli statements are probably meant to reassure Iran's neighbors and prevent them, as far as possible, from starting their nuclear programs in response to Iran's own; after all, having the United States as one's enemy is enough without adding the Arab world as well. Of course, it is necessary to take the threats seriously, and Israel is even now initiating steps to deter the Iranians from trying to implement them. On the other hand, the prevalence of sanity is suggested by the fact that no leading Iranian has ever suggested that their country would be the one to put an end to Israel's existence. Ahmadinejad himself has said that this goal, desirable as it might be, would come about only as a result of Palestinian resistance and internal decay.[8]

Turning the problem around, much, perhaps most, of Ahmadinejad's blustering is clearly due to his fear that Israel and the United States may attack him as they did his former neighbor to the west. Both countries have made at least some preparations for such a strike. In both of them, leading statesmen have refused to rule it out.[9] Ahmadinejad's own military does not have and may never obtain what it takes to reach the U.S. homeland; indeed, not the least surprising thing about this may be that, Israel apart, the most vocal opposition to the Iranian program comes not from Russia, which is almost next door, but from seven thousand miles away. Aware of geographical realities, Ahmadinejad's real objective in speaking out against Israel may well be to deter an American attack on him. As also happened when India was facing Pakistan's nuclear program and the United States the one of North Korea, the most dangerous time is the so-called risk period *before* a country acquires nuclear weapons. Supposing Ahmadinejad succeeds in navigating through that period, there is at least an even chance that he will become less adventurous, not more so.

In all this, the really decisive fact remains that only a minority of states either have nuclear weapons or, like Japan, Taiwan, South Korea, and perhaps a few others, are in a position to assemble them so quickly that, according to their calculations, they can afford to wait. As to the remaining ones, it is of course absurd to say that all of them will go to war against their neighbors. In some cases, especially in North America, Latin America, and Europe, this is because they are on such good terms with those neighbors that war has become unthinkable; in others, especially in Latin America and Africa, it is because they simply do not have the armed forces needed in order to launch a serious attack on anybody outside their own borders. On the other hand, judging by past experience, some of them, especially in Asia, almost certainly will.

It is not impossible that one reason some states refrain from building nuclear weapons is that they believe they may find themselves at war against a nuclear enemy. A good case in point is Argentina. Without any question, Argentina has what it takes to go nuclear and could have done so several decades ago had it wanted to.[10] Passing over the country's relations with its South American neighbors, which are friendly on the whole, there is no secret about its desire to "recover" the Falklands (Malvinas), allegedly taken from it early in the nineteenth century. During the decades since the 1982 war, the issue may have been put to sleep, more or less. However, no government in Buenos Aires is likely to give up its claim to them.[11]

The islands' present owner, Britain, is a nuclear power with several hundred deliverable nuclear warheads routinely carried aboard its aircraft, ships, and submarines. Should another war break out and escalate, as wars tend to do, those weapons could be used to wipe much of Argentina off the map. Of this fact the Argentineans are fully aware; in response, they have been trying to press Britain into some kind of guarantee that nuclear weapons will not be introduced into their part of the world.[12] But does all this mean that, as a prerequisite for one day perhaps launching another bid to occupy the islands, Argentina should acquire nuclear weapons? To the contrary. Should it do so, then all it could achieve would be to increase the fear of escalation, thus perpetuating the present, highly unsatisfactory situation.

The case of Egypt is even more interesting. Egypt used to have a nuclear energy program that was cut short in 1986, ostensibly in connection with the Chernobyl disaster. However, as one of its former representatives to the International Atomic Energy Agency, Dr. Mustafa al-Fiqi, wrote in the semi-official *Al-Ahram*, it still retains the necessary funding and know-how; it also has two 22-megawatt reactors useful for research and training.[13] Had it wanted to, it could have acquired the weapons years ago. So why did not its leaders take that road? A possible answer is that they are worried lest circumstances may again force them to confront Israel, their only conceivable enemy, in the future. To quote one Egyptian academic, acquiring nuclear weapons would make a war between the two countries "unthinkable."[14]

Apparently the Egyptians' real aim is to create a nuclear-free zone in the Middle East by persuading Israel to dismantle its arsenal. Since the pressure they have exercised in this direction has been unavailing, though, they prefer the status quo to the alternative. After all, the one thing crazier than fighting Israel before acquiring nuclear weapons would be to go to war with it after doing so. A swifter, more certain way of terminating the existence of a six-thousand-year-old civilization could hardly be imagined.

With these examples in front of our eyes, it is very likely that North Korea's nuclear weapon test indicates not any preparation for an offensive against the South, but, to the contrary, a final decision on the part of Pyongyang to give up any thought of such an offensive. After all, it is not inconceivable that a conventional attack across the thirty-eighth parallel may succeed in breaking through the South Korean and U.S. forces, as actually happened in 1950. What *is* inconceivable is that North Korea will use nuclear weapons against the U.S. troops in the South, which also possess nuclear weapons, since doing so will certainly lead to its utter destruction. Thus, though we do not really know, the test may very well indicate that Kim Jong-il, well aware of his country's inferiority in every way, no longer has any plans to wage war—unless, of course, he himself comes under attack (which can come only from the United States, as Serbia and Iraq did).

The argument so far might make the reader think that the only measure needed to prevent war is to present every state, however small, with nuclear weapons, their delivery vehicles, and a command and control system sufficiently robust to ride out an attack.[15] As one long-serving Pentagon official with experience in such things once told me half seriously, it would be nice if all the world's leaders could be gathered together once every few years to see with their own eyes what a nuclear explosion can do.

The idea that unlimited, instantly usable, and irresistible force put into the hands of every person would lead to a much more peaceful and courteous world is not new. As far back as 1870, something similar was suggested by Edward Bulwer (Lord Lytton) in his novel *The Power of the Coming Race*. Living deep under the surface of the earth, the Ana, as they were called, had mastered a force known as *vril*. In one of its forms, *vril* could be focused into an easy-to-carry rod. As a result, "so completely [was man] at the mercy of man, each whom he encountered being able, if so willing, to slay him on the instant, that all notions of . . . force gradually vanished from political systems."[16]

Assuming no more new states are created, and using the pace at which proliferation has proceeded over the last sixty-something years as our basis, several centuries will have to pass before Bulwer's idea is put to the test. Even then there will probably remain other kinds of war that nuclear weapons cannot and will not prevent. The most important is the kind waged not by states against one another but by guerrillas, terrorists, and similar organizations against states, or the other way around. As has often been pointed out, the organizations in question form a very heterogeneous lot, though whether they are more diverse than states is moot. Politically and strategically all have one thing in common: the fact that the usual trinitarian distinction between a government that directs the war, armed forces that fight and die, and a civilian population that pays and suffers does not apply.

Taking a close look, we find that instead of a government, most of the organizations in question have a political wing.[17] Its task is to raise revenue, conduct propaganda, organize the people, and perhaps negotiate with the opponent. As they carry out these functions, the politicians are able to exercise some influence over the fighters, setting goals and recommending strategies to reach them. However, often they are in no position to command those fighters and tell them what to do; seen from the point of view of the guerrillas or the terrorists, this may also have the advantage that it provides them with a kind of flexibility that their opponents, whose chain of command is more centralized, do not possess. The outcome is the typical stop-go process whereby agreements with the guerrillas and terrorists are frequently made and cease-fires concluded, only to be violated within a matter of hours or days as one faction or another fails to receive its orders or disobeys them. Think of the Yugoslav civil war, think of Northern Ireland, think of Sri Lanka, think of Israel and the Palestinians.

Instead of commanding a civilian population, guerrillas and terrorists have more or less committed supporters. Either out of conviction or because they have been terrorized into cooperation, those supporters provide all kinds of goods and services: food, money, transportation (vital if the fighters are to reach their targets and make good their escape), intelligence (ditto), a technical infrastructure (repairing and manufacturing weapons and equipment), medical care, refuge, and so on. Some supporters also act as part-time fighters. Most of the time they lead normal lives, going about their business as usual. On occasion, though, they engage in active hostilities and then disengage as the enemy's movements and other circumstances may dictate.

Unlike the fighters, most supporters are more or less tied to the places where they live. Some are likely to be located across the border, where the other side cannot reach them or can do so only by paying a higher political-military price. Support may be provided not only by the citizens of a neighboring state but by their governments, too, in which case one may speak of "state-sponsored terrorism." In fact, whether or not terrorists and guerrillas can garner support from across the border is a significant factor in their success. For example, had not the "Terrs" (as they were called) in Rhodesia been assisted by Zambia and Mozambique, then today's Zimbabwe might not have come about. Had the government of the Irish Republic permitted the IRA to operate on its territory, then the "troubles" in Ulster might very well have ended differently.

Tactically speaking, the fighters do not operate in the open. While some guerrillas may put on uniforms when it suits them, terrorists never do. People belonging to both kinds of groups put great emphasis on concealing themselves by dispersing and blending with the civilian population—like fish in the sea, as Mao described it. Blending with the civilian population, they are much harder to control than regular forces are. Instead of being commanded from a single center, normally they form a network of loosely connected nodes. Compartmentalization, needed to guarantee secrecy, does the rest; many members of terrorists organizations would not know each other if they met on the street.

All this means that the organizations in question rarely have a clear center of gravity—a single group of people, installation, or location around which everything revolves and whose elimination or occupation would lead to their collapse. If an area is cleared, then it will remain clear only so long as the counterinsurgents stay in it. If they do stay in it, then the action will almost certainly shift to another. As to neutralizing the leadership, suffice it to say that the French at one point were able to capture all the top leaders of the Front de Libération Nationale (FLN). This, however, did not prevent the war in Algeria from taking its course.

Representing the weapon of the weak against the strong, both guerrilla war and terrorism are as old as history.[18] Both, however, seem to have acquired a new importance in the years immediately following World War II. In this period, nuclear weapons were steadily making their impact felt. At the same time the victors were anxious to exonerate the resistance movements that, often acting in contravention to international law as it then stood, had taken on the German and Japanese invaders. In 1949, this led them to draw up a new set of Geneva Conventions. Abandoning long-established practice, those conventions recognized the right of occupied populations to rise against their oppressors and enjoy combatant status.[19]

To put the idea in a different way, an attempt was made to draw a clear line between these forms of war and criminal activity—a radical departure indeed, since before this occupied people had no right to resist. Very often the conventions may not have meant much in practice, as guerrillas, terrorists, and those who fought against them committed acts defined as criminal and in response treated each other accordingly. Yet the conventions did define some situations in which the state's monopoly over the use of armed force might legitimately be broken as well as the way in which those involved should comport themselves; to this extent, they both reflected public opinion and pushed it along. Thus they encouraged many armed conflicts that might otherwise not have found the support they did.

Like other forms of war, guerrilla action and terrorism have a hideous fascination of their own.[20] Fighters see themselves as engaged with a much stronger force that they must outwit and outlast. They are prepared to undergo every kind of persecution, hardship, deprivation, and danger, including torture and a lonely death. In spite of this, *because* of this, guerrilla war and terrorism are capable of providing a way of life as well as moments of elation, up to and including what the Palestinians call the *bassamat al-farah,* the "smile of joy" flashed by some suicide bombers just before they activate the explosives that will kill them. That joy is probably one reason why, in an age where major wars are becoming increasingly rare, guerrilla and terrorist actions have proliferated to the point where, in terms of numbers, they have become the most important kind of war of all.

One of the first such campaigns to follow World War II was the Jewish revolt against British rule in Palestine. Involving no more than a few hundred active fighters, it started in the winter of 1944–45, lasted for some three years, and ended only when the imperial power with its one hundred thousand troops was forced to throw in the towel and leave the country.[21] The signal having been given, countless other uprisings followed. The Dutch were driven out of their East Indian colonies. The French were driven out of Indochina, Tunisia, Algeria, Morocco, and the rest of their colonial empire. Having given up India at about the same time as they lost Palestine, the British followed up by also losing control over Malaysia, Kenya, Cyprus, and Aden, to mention only those places where they tried to make a more or less determined stand. The Belgians failed to hold on to the Congo, the Spaniards to Spanish Morocco, and the Portuguese to either Angola or Mozambique.

As this list shows, during the early decades after 1945, most guerrilla and terrorist campaigns were directed against the old European colonial states. This was much less the case later on, when other countries also began to feel their power. Trying to take over from the French, the Americans found themselves embroiled in an unwinnable war in Vietnam and later Cambodia as well. The Soviets were defeated in Afghanistan, the South Africans in Namibia. The Indians tried to intervene in Sri Lanka and failed (even though the intervention force was larger than the entire Sri Lankan army). The Vietnamese tried to put down the Cambodian Khmer Rouge and also failed. The Israelis were forced to leave southern Lebanon and the Gaza Strip—although the outcome in the West Bank is still moot. After fighting for over two decades the Indonesians were forced to give up East Timor, which they had invaded and occupied.

Whether or not they were European, at the time they engaged in these campaigns several of the countries just listed already possessed nuclear weapons. Others gained access to such weapons even as they were doing their best to beat their elusive enemies, as, for example, Britain did

Beyond the pale; 9/11 as the largest terrorist act of all time   BETTMANN / CORBIS

in 1952, France eight years later, and South Africa at some point around 1980. Each time this happened, the rising mushroom cloud turned out to make no difference whatsoever. As Vietnam, Afghanistan (twice: in 1979–88 and from 2001 on), the second Iraq War, and Israel's 2006 war in

Lebanon were to show most clearly, guerrilla warfare and terrorism provided the method par excellence whereby even the most powerful nuclear states on earth might be confronted and, given enough time, defeated. Since the method was available, no wonder it was used.

Yet guerrilla actions and terrorism directed against foreign occupying powers only formed part of the story. A great many post-1945 wars were fought neither between states nor by states against guerrilla movements outside their national territories but by one part of their native populations against another. One factor that often causes wars of this kind is weak governments of questionable legitimacy whose one desire is to steal as much of the country's resources as they can; shot through and through with nepotism and corruption, they reach the point where it is no longer possible to say what constitutes legitimate activity and what does not. An excellent example was the Congo during the thirty-year rule of General Mobutu Sese Seko. Others are Liberia and Sierra Leone.[22] Equally important factors are overpopulation, environmental degradation that leads to a progressive diminution of resources, failing economies, and a tradition of ethnic and religious conflict. Which of these problems is the most important is extraordinarily difficult to establish and may also vary from one case to another. Only too often they lock into each other, creating a downward spiral that is very hard to stop.[23]

In fact, to the extent that the term *cause* presupposes a clear-cut distinction between peace and war, in many cases it may be misleading. This is because, as also used to be the case in many of the more "advanced" societies before the establishment of strong states at some time during the sixteenth and seventeenth centuries, armed conflicts are closely linked to a vast host of other factors—so vast that, taken together, they come very close to constituting the fabric of the societies in question.[24] Proceeding from the public sphere to the most intimate of all, this includes the cohesion of ethnic groups, tribes, villages, and clans and their ability to define themselves in relation to others of the same kind. It also includes adherence to a variety of religious, customary, and symbolic values, as well as the ever-present, never-ending competition between societies and individuals for power, riches, and status.

As important as anything else are relations between the sexes. Members of advanced societies are used to a situation where the streets are more or less safe so that women can walk them as well as men. This, however, is by no means universally the case. Many societies, especially nomadic ones, never had or could have a police force. In others, such as

Afghanistan, Somalia, or even parts of South Africa, what police forces did exist have broken down. Hence unprotected women are considered legitimate prey. Conversely, it is every man's first task in life to protect his female dependents, using physical force if necessary. Men who behave in this way, which of course also includes making sure that those dependents do not expose themselves beyond what is customary, will command their neighbors' admiration. Those who cannot or will not do so are not men at all. They will be despised by the men and deserted by the women—assuming, that is, that they can find any women to start with.[25] A stronger incentive for resorting to violence—which, ascending through family alliances ("we'll leave your women alone provided you do the same with ours") to clan and tribe, may escalate until it develops into full-blown armed conflict—could hardly be imagined.[26]

In fact, in much of the Third World, the real reason why armed conflict is widespread is that, far from representing an aberration created by decolonization, it actually serves to re-create traditions and values that colonial rule did its best to suppress. After all, usually the very first thing imperialists did was to prohibit their subjects from rising against their occupiers as well as fighting among themselves. They eliminated leaders, disbanded fighting organizations, and confiscated weapons; by so doing, they took away an important, some would say critical, part of those subjects' culture.

The inevitable result was the breakdown of other aspects of that culture as well. In the seventeenth century, that was what happened to the extremely warlike tribes of North America. Later the same fate overtook the mountain tribes of northwestern India and the Caucasus, the Maasai and Kikuyu of Kenya, the Baganda of Uganda, the Zulu of South Africa, the Maoris of New Zealand, the inhabitants of Papua New Guinea, and so many others as to make one lose count. In all of them, every male member of society had been a warrior by definition. In all of them, they lost that status. Having lost it, they found it very hard to discover a different role in life.

Conversely, if Somalia since the early 1990s has been in a state of more or less chronic warfare by all against all, then in many ways this simply represents a return to an age-old way of life that remained in force until the arrival of the Italian administration a hundred or so years previously.[27] Then, as now, government was extremely splintered and often extremely weak. Then, as now, gangs of youths seeking gain, recognition, and excitement went on the rampage. It was not so much a question of politics as of doing what youths do to prove themselves in their own eyes as well as those of others—the hooligan age without the normal constraints. Since the indigenous culture of war no longer exists, such gangs tend to be even less well organized and more prone to atrocities than their predecessors. That apart, the main difference is that instead of walking about with ancient blunderbusses, they carry machine guns and drive Toyota trucks.

The same applies to many other places. What we witness is not the establishment of a new disorder; instead, it represents a reversion to the old one. For example, Jean-Bédel Bokassa, the self-styled Napoleon of the Central African Republic, is said to have practiced cannibalism as a way of dealing with his enemies. If a figure such as Uganda's Idi Amin became famous for his brutality, including the use of opponents as crocodile feed, then to some extent at any rate this reflected his role as a "traditionalizer" acting in tune with the values of Ugandan society.[28] This is also proven by the fact that Amin's predecessor and successor, Milton Obote, behaved as badly, and probably killed as many people as Amin did. The fact that he carried the title of "doctor" made no difference. After all, how else does one make sure the members of the rival tribe will remain in their place and those of one's own will stay in control?

Under such circumstances, leaders, followers, and victims—all of whom may change places from time to time—come to see violence, including large-scale group violence, as a normal part of life. This even includes the women. In much of Africa, in particular, ties between husbands and wives are weak. The strongest ones link women and their offspring; looking for partners, women are accustomed to accepting the stronger one.[29] Abstract yearning for peace, even yearning as eloquently expressed as that of Rousseau, may exist. However, pacifist movements, even the weak and ineffective ones that exist in some "advanced" countries, do not find the soil fruitful for their development in the Third World. For example, both Kenya and South Africa at one time had followers of Gandhi. South Africa even had the saintly Gandhi himself; it was in that country that he first experimented with nonviolent ideas. Their voices, and those of others like them, were drowned by those clamoring for war to end colonialism, the domination of one race by another, and apartheid.[30]

In much of Africa and Latin America as well as parts of Asia, religion is on the march. Rivers of ink have been spilled concerning the rise of militant Islam, which, centered around the concept of Jihad or holy war, has produced outbreaks of violence in many countries across the world.[31]

Equally important, though less frequently noticed, is the emergence of militant forms of Christianity. Having been subordinated to the state and subjected to secularizing influences for over three hundred years, Christianity in Europe, and to a lesser extent in the United States, has long since lost its teeth. The former in particular seems to be dying; in the absence of an enemy to fight, most people find Christianity anemic and uninteresting, and vote with their feet.[32]

Very different is the case of many of Christianity's Third World variants. While showing sharp differences from one country to another, they can be very bellicose indeed. At the head of the sects stand priests and bishops of both sexes. Many of them are self-appointed, and some are so unconventional that Christians in developed countries would hardly recognize them as co-religionists. Incorporating all sorts of native traditions, their belief systems are shot through with magic. To many of their members, the main message of Christianity is not so much brotherly love as the ability to bring about supernatural cures and even raise people from the dead.[33]

Muslim or Christian, the sects are attracting a growing number of believers. Sometimes they direct their hostility against the ruling classes, accusing them of economic exploitation and discrimination. In other cases, they target their fellow citizens who belong to a different faith; very often, the two kinds of motives are mixed. Sometimes they attack, in other cases, they are attacked. Repeated outbreaks of violence in the Philippines, Indonesia, Sri Lanka, Uganda, Kenya, Nigeria, and Ghana (until 1981), and the Côte d'Ivoire, among other places, often leave thousands of dead in their wake; clearly, the last thing the adherents of either religion will do is renounce violence or turn the other cheek. Many Christians as well as Muslims believe that their religion obliges them to fight and that it will render them bulletproof. Those who live will bask in glory; those who die are assured of heavenly rewards. While Islam has always been a militant religion, in many ways these new Christians remind one of fifteenth- and sixteenth-century Hussites, Calvinists, Huguenots, and Lutherans. All carried crosses and chanted hymns as they joined battle in the name of the Lord.

These problems may be further exacerbated by political and military intervention from the outside. This was what happened in numerous Asian and African countries such as Laos, Cambodia, Lebanon, Afghanistan, Iraq (from 2003 on), the Spanish Sahara, the Congo (where the ongoing war of all against all has resulted in perhaps four million dead so far), Liberia, Sierra Leone, and so many others as to make one lose count. However, it also happened in the former Yugoslavia and may happen in any other country engulfed in civil war. The goal of the intervention may be to prevent disorder from spreading. In other cases, it is politically motivated as neighboring countries try to prevent each other from upsetting the regional balance of power or else use the ongoing conflict to fight each other by proxy. In other cases, it is a question of getting hold of resources, real or imaginary, whereas in others still it is a straightforward business proposition as one warring faction or another asks for outsiders to lend them a hand and promises to pay for doing so.

To focus on just one example, take the civil war in Chad. Punctuated by repeated coups, revolts, and revolutions, it has been going on with short intervals ever since the mid-1960s. At one time or another it involved contingents of Libyan, French, Congolese, Togolese, and Senegalese troops. Other forms of support, such as money, weapons, and training, came from Algeria, Sudan, Egypt, and Cameroon; even a country as far away as Lebanon provided mercenaries. Thanks to its reported reserves of uranium, Chad attracted foreigners as a garbage can attracts flies. All this helps explain how a thinly populated desert country with a pastoral economy and an income of less than a dollar per person per day can sustain a civil war for as long as it has without reverting to the use of spears, bows, and arrows. By the mid-1990s the number of dead was estimated at fifty thousand. How many have been killed since then is impossible to say.[34]

Some civil wars expanded until they took a more or less conventional form. That was what happened during the last phases of the Chinese Civil War (1946–49) and in Nigeria (1966–69), Vietnam (1963–75), Cambodia (1970–76), and the former Yugoslavia (1991–95). In the great majority of cases, however, it was a question of rulers using their armed forces in an attempt to combat insurgents. Pakistan's vain attempt to put down rebels in what is now Bangladesh (which developed into the Indian-Pakistani war of 1971), the Egyptian and Algerian struggles against Islamic militias, Syria's fight against Muslim extremists, Turkey's fight against the Kurdish Democratic Party and the attempts by Iraq and Iran to subdue the Kurds, the Omani and Yemeni fights against rebels, and the Russian effort in Chechnya all conformed to this type. So did the attempts of the government of Burma (Myanmar) to put down a whole series of ethnic revolts; the Pakistani Army's operations against al-Qaeda in the northwestern part of the country; the Indian fight in Kashmir, that of the government of

Sri Lanka against the Tamil Tigers; the struggles in Thailand, Indonesia, and the Philippines; and the civil wars that at one time or another have ravaged many Latin American and African countries.

Reflecting the situation where war and society are sometimes almost inseparable, many, probably most, of the insurgent organizations that wage these wars do not constitute armies as the citizens of advanced countries might understand that term. To use Weberian terminology, their leadership instead of being rational, goal-oriented, and bureaucratic tends to be charismatic. It was not so much UNITA that mattered as Jonas Savimbi, not so much the Christian Falange as Bashir Gemayel. At the height of the Lebanese civil war, no fewer than fifty different militias fought each other in that small country; anyone who could tell them apart (and not even their own members always could) deserved a medal. All this goes far to explain their tendency to divide, merge with others of the same kind, and divide again. Having divided, often they start fighting each other. Next, the leaders having resigned or fled or died, they disappear almost without a trace. Some troops wear standardized uniforms. Many others either put on what uniform-like bits and pieces they can find, devise their own, or simply make do with civilian clothes supplemented by some insignia or emblem. Some obey a central command structure, but many others do not and act more or less as they please.

As the breakup of the Serb-Yugoslav army in 1991–95 illustrates very well, some of the state-owned forces that try to fight these militias were initially cohesive, disciplined, and well organized, while many others can hardly be told apart from their enemies. By and large, the longer the conflict drags on, the more true this becomes. Like any other game where one player or team faces another, war is an imitative activity par excellence. Both sides are compelled to study one another and adapt; one cannot play basketball on one side of the court and tennis on the other. Regardless of whether they claim to be on the side of the government or its opponents, most militias consist of underage, undisciplined, untrained men with inflammable breath literally running about in search of loot. Many are supported by women who, voluntarily or not, provide rudimentary logistic services, do the laundry, and sleep with the fighters; sometimes they also provide intelligence. However, women rarely take up arms and fight. In Sri Lanka in the 1990s, only one out of thirty-three Tamil organizations included female combatants.[35]

Certainly the picture the militias presented was anything but pretty. Yet in East Timor, Sri Lanka, Afghanistan, Sudan, Nigeria, Angola,

Mozambique, Algeria, Somalia, Rwanda, Burundi, Congo, Liberia, Sierra Leone, and a great many other developing countries, these and other shortcomings did not prevent the fighters from committing murder on an enormous scale. They killed at least hundreds of thousands, drove millions more from their homes, and turned entire districts into deserts; it has been calculated that on a per-conflict basis, during the thirty-four years between 1968 and 1992 the number of refugees has increased fourfold.[36]

Against this background, to argue that humanity is losing its taste for war and that war itself is on its way to the dustbin of history is worse than misrepresenting the truth. Taking such an ostrich-like attitude almost amounts to a crime against that very humanity—the mostly poor, mostly undeveloped part of humanity that is beyond the pale. In fact, it is only some kinds of war waged among some kinds of political entities against each other on the basis of a certain type of military organization that are waning away. Even this limited shift is due less to any gradual change in attitudes, let alone human nature, than to the fears generated by the most powerful weapons of all. Had it not been for those weapons and those fears, then there is every reason to think that those organizations and the societies they claim to represent would have gone to war much to the same extent as they have from the time that Sparta took on and defeated Athens right down to the end of World War II.

The sudden (and entirely unexpected) waning of major war between major states constitutes a reversal of historical trends that go back to the early Middle Ages.[37] To this extent, its significance cannot be overestimated; to speak with Hegel; if ever there was a world-historical event, this is it. As far as it goes, it is also a very welcome development. Given the enormous "progress" made by the means of destruction since World War II, what could be worse than World War III? It cannot, however, change the fact that other forms of armed conflict, some of them enormously destructive and enormously bloody, are alive and well and may be spreading.

Too many Third World countries are even now sinking into the kind of hopeless poverty, confusion, and despair that formed the background to genocide in Rwanda. Many others, while more or less peaceful at the moment, harbor a potential for ethno-religious conflict that is waiting to explode and may well do so in the not too remote future. Those very factors are even now driving masses of immigrants into developed countries. Having arrived, they are torn between the need to build a new existence by assimilation and the wish to preserve their own traditions, and all this is complicated by discrimination. Wherever they arrive, their presence is creating social tensions that may one day not far off explode into large-scale violence. As of the beginning of the twenty-first century there are probably very few countries so homogeneous, so rich, and so wallowing in their contentment as to be, in principle, immune against the kind of outbreak that is already starting to affect several West European countries. Let those who have ears to listen, listen!

16

Quo Vadis, Homo?

Protected by their nuclear walls, immune against some of the worst things war can do—large-scale campaigning, bombardment from the air, and occupation—most inhabitants of major countries are no longer willing to pay for maintaining the military as they used to, let alone join the armed forces and get themselves killed on peacekeeping missions in some faraway country that presents absolutely no threat. But is it really true that war no longer fascinates them and that the culture of war is about to disappear? Judging by our television, radio, newspapers, movies, books, magazines, the military museums, the martial displays that are put forward from time to time, the countless games that boys of all ages like to play and on which fortunes are spent, the answer can only be a strong negative. Even in the most "advanced," most peaceful countries that have long done away with conscription, war retains a strong appeal to the popular imagination. Take that appeal away, and surely life would be very different from what it is; in that case, indeed, it is hard to say what people would watch, or read, or play with.

War has always made headlines; in almost any advanced country, it is nearly impossible to watch any news-oriented television program, listen to any radio program, or read any newspaper page (including pages displayed on the Internet) without coming across a reference to some war being fought somewhere in the world. Some of these countries have not fought a war for decades, even centuries; others are geographically far removed from the unfolding military events. Yet even in these places fresh outbreaks invariably lead to a surge of excitement—one that is perhaps best compared to a shot of adrenaline or an electric jolt.

For example, during the early stages of the Gulf War in January 1991, no fewer than sixteen hundred journalists were present, four times as many as had covered Vietnam during the peak days of the Tet offensive. The response they got was overwhelming. In Nairobi, people lined up six deep in front of electronics stores to watch the show, even though no Kenyan troops were involved or stationed anywhere near the Gulf.[1] It was largely thanks to the fortuitous presence of its man in Baghdad, Wolf Blitzer, that CNN, hitherto a small and unimportant station, was able to develop into one of the world's largest television news broadcasting services.

The size and importance of any specific war or violent act does not necessarily determine the amount of broadcasting time or newspaper space it occupies. Rather, however large or small a conflict may be, it tends to fill and even overcrowd that time or space. In the not so remote past, some of the most important armed forces waged their wars with the aid of hundreds of thousands or even millions of troops, overrunning entire countries and threatening to do the same with parts of continents. Now that both the number and the size of operations have been reduced to a small fraction of what they were, in many cases they are followed as closely as the larger events were before.

They may even be followed more closely, given that recent technological advances, such as satellite TV, cable TV, cellular phones, laptops, SMS, and much else, permit such coverage. It has even been argued that but for the attention the media pays them, certain forms of war would have played a much smaller role in world affairs than they do; even in 2001, about fifteen times as many Americans were killed in road accidents than in the events of 9/11. Without the presence of TV cameras to record what was going on, many terrorist events would have been non-events. Of this fact, of course, terrorists are well aware. Very often they alert the media after an event, explaining their action and issuing threats; here and there they do so before it has taken place. To this extent, it is not so much war that draws the media but the media that helps spread war.[2]

The coverage that war gets may be divided into many different kinds. There are words, either written or broadcast, and there are pictures. There are still pictures and moving pictures, real pictures and faked pictures, even staged pictures. An episode coming out of Bosnia in July 1992 illustrates the last-mentioned type: the local United Nations commander, a Canadian general, could not stop the warring sides from firing at their own positions so that CNN might film them.[3] There are serious stories, not so serious stories, and human-interest stories that tend to develop into either heroics or sob stories. There are true stories and false stories. There are even stories that can only be characterized as bullshit, meaning that those who invent them and spread them do not care whether they are true or false.[4]

Some wars are praised to the sky, whereas others are condemned in equally strong terms. However that may be, all tend to be followed, commented upon, and evaluated by journalists, military men (rarely, women), and academic experts (ditto).[5] As with any kind of game, usually, as time goes on, interest in any given war tends to diminish. When that happens, it is necessary to arrange some special effects, such as an extraordinary act of cruelty; or else to find another war that may step into the breach. Whenever a major military event takes place, it normally occupies the beginning of the show and is announced with the aid of the largest headlines. Had it not been for war, surely much of the news would have been even more boring than it already is.

So great is public interest in war, and so heavy the pressure to obtain and disseminate information about it, that there are many cases when coverage is much too close for comfort. After all, the publicity that forms the very lifeblood of the media has always been the enemy of military secrecy; besides, the military, like any other organization, prefers things to be told the way they see them and no other. This can lead to contradictory results. On one hand, journalists, in trying to satisfy the demand for their merchandise, are sometimes deliberately targeted by belligerents, who kill, injure, or kidnap them.[6] On the other, being human like the rest of us, they tend to be swept along by events. This is especially likely to happen when they cover wars waged by their own countrymen, with whom they can identify. Even in Vietnam, a war that attracted as much media opprobrium as did any other in history, some American journalists, while absolutely disgusted with the top brass, could not help but feel sympathy for the grunts who had to carry out orders and who paid the price for doing so.

Whether because they felt close to the troops or simply because they wanted to cut a figure, more than one journalist found himself trying to look like a soldier, walk like a soldier, and talk like a soldier.[7] Up to a point, this sort of thing is inevitable; to give the public some sense of what the men, whose activities he covers, were going through, a journalist has to be accepted by them. On occasion, this form of identification is taken to the point where the media become an embarrassment to the authorities. That was what happened, for example, when some British tabloids during the 1982 Falklands War engaged in what was known as "Argy-bashing," using coarse language.

Some journalists trivialize war, causing critics to accuse them of encouraging its outbreak by doing so.[8] The opposite, however, may also happen. Following the destruction of Hiroshima, the U.S. Army sent in photographers to shoot more than 100,000 feet of color film. The exposed film was then classified as "top secret" and stowed away, the objective being to ensure that the horror and the devastation should not become widely known, thus perhaps making Americans less willing to drop more nuclear bombs in the future.[9] Thirty years later, many people came to believe that Vietnam was lost not by the forces in the field but by TV in the living room.[10] Based on this American version of the German World War I *Dolchstoss* (stab-in-the-back) legend, some critics have credited the media with the power of presenting war in such a way as to make people turn their backs on it almost regardless of what really takes place in the field.

To cope with these and other problems, very often the military establishment does what it can to limit or deny access to reporters and to exercise censorship over their output. Depending on who is involved, where they take place, how intensive they are, and how well they are going, some wars are easier to control, others less so.[11] In both 1982 and 1991, geography helped the British and U.S. Forces keep the media under such tight control that they were barely able to present any kind of independent viewpoint. During the 2006 war in Lebanon, different circumstances and that most ubiquitous gadget, the cellular phone, made it almost impossible for Israeli censorship to do the same; even operational plans were sometimes made public before they could be carried out. Overall, such is the demand as to require entire departments whose sole job is to oversee the flow of news as far as possible while at the same time keeping away all sorts of curious people.[12] On occasion this has been carried to the point where there seem to be more public relations officers running around, many of them female, than there are soldiers fighting.

What is true of news is at least as true of the movies. From the earliest days of film, war has formed a critically important subject about which movies were made, and entire volumes have been written to document and explain this fact.[13] Some movies, such as the World War I British classic *The Battle of the Somme* (1916), were made by or at the behest of the authorities. Many movies were made to glorify war and excite public opinion in favor of its initiation or continuation, for example, the famous *Why We Fight* series of World War II. Some, such as *All Quiet on the Western Front* (1930), were meant to criticize war by focusing on its horrors and futility, but it has been claimed that even in interwar Britain such films formed a minority.[14] Probably the great majority were made simply in order to make money by catering to the seemingly inexhaustible public taste for blood and glory.

The ingredients of a good war story are age-old and well known. It must present some of its subject's terrors—for without terror there is no thrill. It must not, however, take this to the point where people close their eyes and start throwing up; movies that went too far in this direction usually did not enjoy either commercial success or critical acclaim.[15] Violence apart, the film must also involve love, betrayal, death, and triumph in various sequences and in various proportions. As Shakespeare knew very well, a little comic relief is usually welcome. However, one should not exaggerate to the point where the overall impression of deadly seriousness is undermined. Do that, and instead of a war movie what one gets is farce; entertaining, perhaps (as *Dad's Army* was), but in the end not really up to par. *Pace* those who believe in the gradual growth of peace, there is no indication whatsoever that public interest in this kind of show has diminished one bit.

Victorious wars, such as World War II, tend to be followed by waves of movies that show how heroic our boys were and, if only by implication, how just and noble was the cause for which they fought. Very good examples are *The Sands of Iwo Jima* (1949), *The Guns of Navarone* (1961), and *The Longest Day* (1964); as late as 1977, this was the recipe that made *A Bridge Too Far* into a smash hit. Seen in retrospect, many of these movies may be considered vapid at best, foolish at worst, but that was not how they were understood at the time. In 1961, by one survey, 50 percent of Marines at Camp Pendleton had joined the Corps after watching *The Sands of Iwo Jima*.[16] John Wayne, it turns out, was the best propagandist the U.S. Armed Forces ever had. He always had all the answers while blasting America's enemies left and right. Not for nothing did the Marine Corps award him its "Iron Mike" medal.

By contrast, wars that did not end in victory are likely to be ignored by the movies. Others, such as the one in Vietnam, are likely to be followed by almost equally big waves showing how cruel, unnecessary, and senseless they were. For example, a central theme in *All Quiet on the Western Front* was the tremendous gap that had opened between the civilians in the rear and the soldiers at the front as well as the civilians' complete inability to understand the sufferings of those doing the fighting. In *Apocalypse Now* (1979), the central theme is the mind of man and its seemingly unlimited capacity for cruelty. By contrast, *Platoon* (1986) revolves around the age-old theme of treachery. It ends with the words "We have seen the enemy, and he is us."

Normally the best way to end a war movie is by showing the triumph of the good guys. If circumstances make that impossible, a story may still be salvaged from the wreckage. One way to do this is by showing the badly wounded veteran triumph over himself, as in *The Deer Hunter* (1978) and *Born on the Fourth of July* (1989). Another, peculiarly American method is to use cinematic fiction in order to avenge a real-life defeat, as the *Rambo* movies did. Whether or not the war a movie portrays is good or bad, it may very well have an ending in which the wounds left behind are overcome and reconciliation is achieved. A good example is the German series *Dresden* (2006). The viewer having seen vast destruction, the series ends when the onetime British bomber pilot sets out to meet the German nurse who saved his life, but unfortunately he is killed in a plane crash while on his way to her. This sort of thing enables viewers to tell themselves that the horrors they have just watched, as well as their own interest in them, are somehow justified and forgivable.

As in the case of news, the link between movies and reality varies. Proceeding in supposed order of veracity, some movies claim to represent the raw truth and nothing but the truth. This sometimes gives rise to difficulties. In World War II, some German citizens had the impertinence to question the authenticity of newsreels that contained frontal shots of Wehrmacht troops charging. In response, Goebbels claimed that those scenes had indeed been filmed by members of his propaganda companies walking backward over the battlefield while turning their backs to the enemy; as he himself wrote on another occasion, the bigger a lie, the more people are inclined to believe in it. Other movies are said to be "based on real events," whatever that may mean. Some are documentaries; presumably this means that they stand in some kind of relation to the facts, even though the precise nature of that relation is not always clear. Finally, there are some that are admittedly fictional.

Seeking to create an impression of veracity, the first three types of movies do at least recognize some limits on the material they contain. This is not nearly as true of avowedly fictional ones. In them the locations where wars take place, the characters who fight in them, and the weapons with which they are fought are completely imaginary, often the more monstrous the better. As if the earth did not afford enough scope for bloody mayhem, some producers move their stories to intergalactic space millions of light-years away from earth and centuries in the future. Others make up, as their protagonists, strange creatures with outlandish-sounding names, improbable physiques, and the kind of mental capabilities that in ordinary life would land those who claim to have them in a lunatic asylum. Whoever the combatants may be, often they deploy weapons never likely to be seen outside the silver screen—such as the huge metal elephants marching through the snow that figured in the *Star Wars* series. All this shows that verisimilitude takes second place to excitement. Provided there is a good fight, almost anything goes, however foolish.

Illustrating the point, a very special kind of war movie is the one that shows warrior women in action. From the time of the ancient Amazons on, such women were almost entirely mythological. If they existed at all, they formed such a small minority of the forces as to be negligible. Some women were in fact awarded medals in recognition of their services; a few later wrote their memoirs. However, none is known to have performed any truly extraordinary feats. As the casualty figures from the most recent wars (2 percent females killed in action among the American forces in Iraq, less than 1 percent in the Israeli Defense Force during its 2006 campaign in Lebanon) prove, this continues to be very much the case today.[17] Briefly, women are infinitely more likely to be victimized by war than to take an active part in it. Yet these facts have not prevented movies that center around fighting females from attracting whole swarms of viewers.

In all this, the paradox is that the more like real-life soldiers the heroines look, the fewer people will want to watch them. Both male and female viewers are uninterested in female fighters who look or act like males— women perhaps because they cannot identify with them, men perhaps because they are frightened by them. Not by accident, the heroine of the TV series *Xena: Warrior Princess* had no male contacts, not even a father; once actress Demi Moore had shown some muscle in *G.I. Jane* (1997), her acting career went into a steep decline from which it did not recover.

To gain popularity, warrior women must have doll-like faces (Brigitte Bardot in *Viva Maria!* from 1965). They must also wear special clothing designed to emphasize their long legs, gigantic breasts, deep cleavages, and narrow waists (Jane Fonda in *Barbarella,* 1968; Pamela Anderson in *Barbed Wire,* 1998). The fact that these anatomic and sartorial characteristics would have made it hard for them to stand upright, let alone fight, is ignored. However one looks at it, such movies only have the most tenuous link with reality. Which, of course, makes even more interesting the question as to why they are as popular as they are.

What is true of movies is equally true of literature (quite often the two are linked, as books are made into movies and movies serve as the basis for novelizations). To be sure, there are some variations from one country to another; now it is the triumphal aspects of war that are emphasized, now its horrors. However, on the whole there is absolutely no indication that works whose subject is war are losing their popular appeal. This applies to highbrow literature, middlebrow literature, and especially lowbrow literature of the kind sold at countless newsstands; sometimes it seems that the more crude and simple-minded the material, the more copies it will sell. It applies to the kind of material where text is used almost exclusively; however, it also applies to the kind that consists almost entirely of pictures or else of drawings accompanied by lettering indicating grunts and the noise of explosions.

As with movies, modern war books can be categorized as military history at one extreme and fiction at the other, with quite a number of intermediate types, such as memoirs, reworked diaries, and the like. Using as our example, attempts to write the history of the greatest twentieth-century war of all may be divided into three main kinds. First, during the twenty-five years following the end of World War II, most authors tended to concentrate on theaters of war, great campaigns, and "decisive" battles (there were at least two books on the latter subject, each with a different list of battles). The overriding objective was to inform the reader how victories had been won and defeats suffered. The result was that, with the partial exception of the senior commanders who had been in charge, personalities did not matter very much; this also applies to the various official histories, whose outstanding quality is their blandness. By and large, this phase may be said to have come to an end in 1971, the year when Basil Liddell Hart's *History of the Second World War* was published posthumously.

Second, younger historians took up the challenge. Partly in order to

integrate military history with history in general, partly under the influence of the social sciences, they broadened the scope of their inquiries;
to the study of operations, large or small, they added logistics, intelligence, organization, politics, technology, economics, social affairs, and
even culture. To the result they gave the name "the new military history."
Much of this new military history was excellent, shedding light on hitherto neglected fields. However, at times it was taken to the point where
the real business of war—that is, killing and getting killed—almost disappeared from the printed page.[18] Much of it was dedicated to finding out
how things work and drawing lessons from them. However, more than a
few people found it too didactic; instead of dramatic moments and heroic
deeds, all it offered was tables and figures.

By and large, a reaction to that type of history had to wait until the
second half of the 1990s. That period saw the emergence of a third type,
probably best exemplified by the works of Antony Beevor about the battles of Stalingrad and Berlin. Like popular war literature of all times and
places, it all but ignores analysis, sometimes to the point where one wonders what it is that the author really wants to say. Perhaps more than
most popular war literature of all times and places—ours, after all, is the
age of the common man—it has shifted the focus from grand moves to
the ordinary, often all but forgotten soldier: his efforts, his sufferings, his
joys, and his sorrows. In so doing, historians made extensive use of diaries, letters, and personal interviews to tell a new generation of readers
with no hands-on experience of war what it had been like.

Not only is military history as much in demand as ever but, taking on
a new form, it has invaded the universities. This is an innovation. Until
1960 or so, few universities offered much by way of military history, modern military history in particular. To the extent that military personnel
engaged in higher study, they did so almost exclusively in their own institutions; such as officer schools, military academies, staff colleges, and
war colleges. Since then, things have changed. One reason behind the
change is that, sheltered by nuclear walls, soldiers in developed countries
in particular had much more time to study. Equally important was the
fact that the new military history was much closer to other forms of academic history as well as the social sciences. Previously war has often
been seen as standing apart from other fields. Now it came to be seen as
joining many of them together, given that there was hardly any part of life
that did not enter war and which, in turn, it did not enter.

As demand created supply and supply drove demand, almost any self-respecting university felt it had to set up a department of war studies, strategic studies, security studies, peace studies, or conflict resolution.[19] A few universities even have two or three of them side by side. In others, war is included under the rubric of political science or international relations; whatever their categorization, very often they could not be distinguished from each other. Normally those in charge of the departments are either civilian professors or retired military personnel who have taken academic degrees. Some of the students also consist of military personnel who, instead of attending their own schools, have been detailed to earn a degree. Others are intellectually minded civilians with an interest in war.

Can a person be both female and warlike? The sculpture of Athene at the Pergamon Museum is one attempt to solve the dilemma. DVORA LEWY

In Liddell Hart's words, to put an end to war it is necessary to understand it first. Whether many of those who study war in their capacity as faculty or as students really understand it is debatable; what is not in doubt is that their contribution to ending war is minuscule, if it exists at all. They flood the world with an avalanche of paper so great that in many cases ten words are printed for every bullet fired. All of which proves how fascinating war has become even among people and in institutions that for centuries did their best to ignore it or, if they couldn't, looked down their nose at it.

Among works of fiction, some fit events that *could* have taken place into a real setting, whereas others take real events and move them to an imaginary one. Others still are pure and acknowledged invention. On occasion the plot shows how war can improve the characters of those who engage in it—how the ordeal they undergo takes away their illusions and/or cynicism, turns them into better and more compassionate people, and even gets them to the point where they sacrifice themselves for others. Other works take the opposite tack. Their objective is to show how war can cause a character's lower nature to break through; as the story nears its end, that character is often conveniently disposed of as unfit to live in normal society. As with movies, many books tend to celebrate war, especially the kind of war waged by our own good boys against the wicked enemy. Add a lot of seemingly realistic technical details and stir well. The result is the unbeatable recipe that made Tom Clancy into a best-selling author.

Never mind that, with Clancy, all Americans are upright people who never let down their country, their friends, or their family. Never mind that, as events in Iraq showed all too plainly, his work has almost nothing to do with the often impersonal, highly bureaucratic world of the U.S. Armed Forces with its tendency to rely for canon fodder on the down and out.[20] Nor does it have much to do with the messy, dirty, stinking reality of armed conflict. With Clancy and those who imitated him, the pity and the sorrow are almost entirely absent. Above all, so is the pain—not only mental but physical as well. In this he is not alone. How does one put onto the printed page the pain felt by those who have their bodies perforated, their limbs broken or crushed or torn off? How does one make one's readers smell the burned flesh and hear the screams? Even Homer did not really find a way to do it; though there are numerous references to "black blood spurting" and "a rattling death cry," all his heroes without exception die a nearly instantaneous death. Conversely, had there been such a way, then perhaps war literature would have been a little less popular than it is—or perhaps not.

Among volumes that speak out against war, the most effective ones are probably not the maudlin ones but those that, like Joseph Heller's *Catch-22* (1961) and Kurt Vonnegut's *Slaughterhouse-Five* (1965), use black comedy as their instrument. As with Clancy, though, a great many simply seek to excite, entertain, and titillate; after all, to quote a U.S. fighter pilot with more than a hundred missions to his credit, combat is "the most fun you can have with your pants on."[21] If highbrow critics often look down on war, publishers most definitely do not. Indeed, one sometimes gains the impression that the main effect of the endless denunciations of lowbrow military literature issued by those critics, if they have any effect at all, is to encourage even more people (men, of course) to buy and read even more trash.

Almost none of this is new. Almost all of it represents a direct continuation of themes going back centuries, such as sin (if only the kind of sin that involves blindness and lack of preparation), struggle, heroism, suffering, and deliverance that may take place either before or after death.[22] From the *Iliad* through the Arthurian legends all the way to Tolstoy's *War and Peace,* some works are perennial favorites and keep being reissued in a variety of forms. Others, less well known, are sometimes reprinted, as Erskine Childers's *The Riddle of the Sands* was in 1999. Declining interest, let alone a break that could indicate a different mindset, is nowhere to be seen.

While some people watch war movies and others read war literature, many others express their obsession with war and armies by collecting militaria.[23] Presenting an even more sanitized way of dealing with war than any film or book does, originally militaria, whether native or captured, were located in the treasure rooms of kings and other commanders. Nowadays they are sold in every kind of establishment from specialist shops (including Internet shops) to traveling stands that are run off the back of a truck. They fall into many different types. Those who can afford to may collect real weapons ranging from antique samurai swords to machine guns and even larger systems such as halftracks, tanks, and combat aircraft. Such systems are bought from junkyards and carefully restored, a job that can be both prolonged and very costly. On special occasions they are put on display, driven, or flown; thus the line between tools and toys is difficult to draw. Other people make do with military uniforms, military hats (as at least one former U.S. chairman of the Joint Chiefs did), military gear, military insignia, and so on. Those who cannot even afford those will often collect models or pictures of the objects in question.

As with any other kind of collectible, the better the condition of any object and the closer it is to the real thing the harder it is to find and the higher the price it can command. For example, a copy of an SS dagger can be had for ten to twenty dollars. The original, provided it has been well preserved, may fetch ten times as much. As with every other kind of collectible, this fact has often led to all sorts of unsavory practices such as grave robbing. This is especially true in Eastern Europe.[24] That is where hundreds of thousands of more or less well marked, more or less well guarded graves of former Wehrmacht soldiers are located; for some inscrutable reason, militaria originating in the Third Reich have always commanded more than their share of public interest. It has also given rise to a minor industry that produces fakes. The need to avoid fakes, or "authentic replicas" as they are sometimes known, and make a profit if possible often means that collectors of militaria are as knowledgeable about their field of interest as, say, collectors of antique furniture are.

By far the largest collections of militaria are housed in our military museums. Unlike individual collectors, military museums often get their exhibits for free in the form of surplus war material handed over by the armed forces themselves (some armed forces, aware of the propaganda value that museums possess, run their own). Unlike most private collectors, they may have the means with which to restore the equipment and the space to put it on display. The result is some huge museums (for example, the Invalides in Paris, the Heeresmuseum in Dresden and Vienna, the Imperial War Museum in London, and others) and countless smaller ones. Quite a number of museums double as memorials to the fallen, as, for example, the Australian War Museum in Canberra, the Israeli Armored Corps Museum between Jerusalem and Tel Aviv, and the World War II Museum in Moscow's Victory Park. Others, such as the one at Anzio, Italy, are simply concerned with preserving as much history as possible.

Depending on circumstances, airfields, naval bases, and army camps all have been converted into museums. So have old warships, submarines, and the like. Berlin's Gatow Airfield now houses the Luftwaffe Museum. Columbus, Ohio, has the USAF Museum at Wright-Patterson Air Force Base. London has the World War II cruiser *Belfast.* New York and Charleston have the World War II aircraft carriers *Intrepid* and *Yorktown,* respectively (Charleston also has the only nuclear-powered freighter ever built, the *Savannah.* However, perhaps because it does not have any guns, its popularity cannot compare with that of the warships.) Boston is proud to present the USS *Constitution.* While several Scandinavian towns boast Viking ships, none of them can compete with Stockholm's seventeenth-century warship *Vasa* with its row upon row of gun ports. Such features, it seems, possess a strong appeal to the imagination.

At Peenemünde, on the Baltic, one can visit a former Soviet missile submarine. The astonishing thing about this particular exhibit is that it has absolutely no ties to the island. Besides being a well-known vacation spot, Peenemünde owes its fame to the fact that V-2 missiles were developed there during World War II; the submarine was bought and brought there with the sole purpose of attracting tourists. There is hardly a modern country that does not have such museums, and hardly one in which they do not attract large crowds. Every city can count itself fortunate if there happens to be a battlefield not too far away that may be sanitized and put on display. Had it not been for the events of July 1863, how many people would visit Gettysburg, Pennsylvania?

From collecting militaria to playing at war is but a short step. One type of wargame that, starting in the United States, has gained considerable popularity in recent years is the one played by the reenactors already mentioned in Part II.[25] Some reenactors have personal experience of war, while others do not. In terms of education, profession, and income, they come from all walks of life. As also happens in the real-life military, this fact often results in people who would normally have led entirely separate existences coming together and feeling much closer than would otherwise have been the case; doing so is considered part of the fun. They spend considerable sums of money and sacrifice considerable amounts of leisure time in order to engage in their hobby of researching and reenacting historical battles. Practically all of them are men; the few women who take part are usually sisters or girlfriends. Some groups of reenactors, seeking authenticity, do not allow women to join. Others, to the contrary, are constantly on the lookout for female recruits who could fill the ranks of their "medical corps."

Some reenactors choose to portray American Revolutionary soldiers serving with Washington and crossing the Delaware. Each year as Christmas comes there is likely to take place a reenactment of that campaign; sometimes they succeed in crossing the river, sometimes not.[26] Others pretend they are World War I French *poilus* or World War II Soviet Guards. Some may give evidence of being on the peculiar side by choosing to reenact the German Waffen SS. Surprisingly, even an army that had little to show but defeats, such as the World War II Italian one, has its reenactors, as some enthusiasts dress up and act like one of Mussolini's units in Russia.[27] All this requires vast amounts of preparation and study. Strange as their hobby may seem, few people take military history more seriously, or know more about it, than many reenactors do.

Though there are different approaches to reenacting and even different "schools" of reenactors who adhere to them, most participants do what they can to make sure that the encounters should be as authentic as possible. A rifle, a pocket knife, a watch even, that do not fit the time and the place about to be reenacted are considered enough to spoil the fun.

So does a piece of clothing that looks either too new or too old. In the former case this is because the item in question is probably a fake; in the latter, because it does not appear as it did at the time it was actually issued and worn. Such problems often lead to heated arguments, and groups of reenactors have been known to break up because of disagreements over what is and is not acceptable.

As with most collective activities, much of the time devoted to the hobby is spent on either technical preparations or socializing. However, some of it is spent digging trenches in the soil, dragging equipment into position, running up and down hills under the hot sun, wading through slush and snow, lying on the ground pretending to be dead, eating K-rations, and in general doing almost anything to experience (or reexperience) what war at the time and place selected was like. Here it should be said that, of all forms of war games, reenactments come closest to capturing at least some of the friction, deprivation, and physical effort that real-life war involves. To that extent, they also provide the most realistic training for it.

Most reenactments are performed by a relatively small number of enthusiasts at their own expense and for their own enjoyment in more or less secluded locations that are rented for the purpose. Some, however, are organized by or in cooperation with local authorities with the aim of reaching a much wider public and, if possible, making money. In the United States, Britain, and several other countries performances of this kind can involve hundreds if not thousands of participants. Even in Germany, where the memory of World War II has turned "militarism" into the dirtiest of all dirty words, things are changing; in October 2006 a reenactment was held to mark the two hundredth anniversary of Napoleon's triumph over Prussia at Jena. In Italy, the Battle of Custozza (1866) is now being commemorated annually.

Compared to the private events, most large-scale public reenactments are not nearly as thorough in their attempts to reproduce contemporary uniforms, weapons, and tactics. Some, such as the annual staging of a "Roman" battle held at Fiesole, near Florence, are better understood as burlesque, though even there the significant point is that it is mock fights, rather than something else, that people flock to laugh about. The shows, for that is what they are, are capable of attracting huge crowds made up of both sexes and all ages. Perhaps surprisingly, most of those who watched the one in honor of the Battle of Jena were not youths but middle-aged couples with an interest in history. A reenactment of the

Civil War Battle of Manassas that I attended many years ago caused such huge traffic jams that it took hours to reach the event and leave it. The occasions also provide opportunities for every kind of vendor of militaria to hawk their wares. In many ways, they are simply open bazaars where entertainment takes the form of mock warfare rather than, say, a magician or a circus.

An unkind soul would say that, based as they are on make-believe, all these forms of playing at war merely represent a trivial form of amusement for people who have never grown up.[28] Up to a point that is true, but it is also true that they reflect the close relationship that has always existed between war and games. Even some of those who criticize the hobby tend to be caught up in it. They flock to watch the reenactments and loudly express their approval or disapproval of what they see. Next they start recounting their own experiences, real or imaginary, and get involved in the reenactors' own debate. Often they end up having as much excitement trying to find out what is and what is not authentic, what can and cannot be reenacted, as well as the purpose of it all, as the reenactors themselves do.[29]

Other war games also continue to be played as they have always been. On one hand, there are "free" games suitable for the exploration of high strategy.[30] On the other, there are the old structured games, including also the kind that is played with the aid of toy soldiers, toy cannon, toy field toilets, and the like.[31] These structured games have been joined by two new devices that transformed the field, giving it an entirely new lease on life and reaching millions of people. First, at some point during the 1960s, the chess-like squares with which boards had been marked since the last decades of the eighteenth century were replaced by hexes.[32] This seemingly trivial change was a stroke of genius. It permitted the various pieces to move in six directions instead of four, thus greatly increasing flexibility and realism. It also permitted terrain features that influence strategy and operations, such as roads, rivers, borders, and the like, to be represented much more accurately than before. Soon war games based on hex maps, some of them commercially available and some custom-designed for certain purposes, were being played by professionals and amateurs alike.[33]

War games of this kind are capable of dealing with most levels of war from the grand-strategic to the purely tactical. To provide anything like a realistic picture of the campaigns and battles they seek to portray, they must be based on extremely detailed information concerning the capabil-

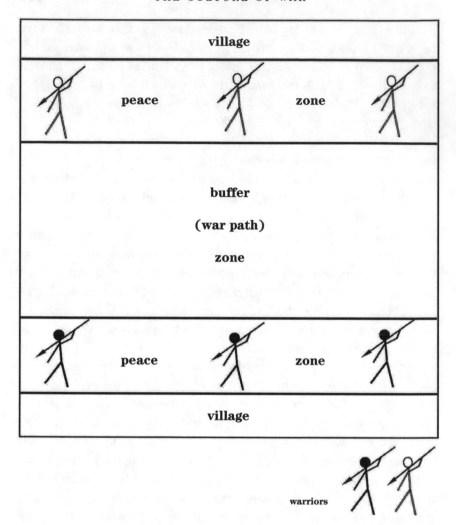

As this North American Indian example shows, board games representing war have a
long history.

ities of weapons and units, the impact that enemy action may have on
them, the effect of external factors such as terrain, day and night, the
weather, and so on. Some games even take morale into account, multiply-
ing or dividing units' capabilities as appropriate. The amount of study
many of them involve, as well as the ingenuity needed to combine the
various factors being modeled, can only be called prodigious; in some
ways they differ little from modern operations research. Nor is it rare for
experts in one of these fields to move to the other. If you can design a

true quantitative model of a battle of any size, then you can do almost anything.

The flip side of the coin is that the larger games in particular can be very difficult to play. Suitable surroundings, such as a large table reserved solely for the purpose, must be available. First, players must master the rules. Though common designers and a common background (for example, the Napoleonic wars or World War I) mean that some games have certain characteristics in common, the details tend to differ, and different companies may produce different versions of the same battle or campaign. Very often the rules take up several dozen closely printed pages that resemble nothing so much as a legal text with numbered paragraphs, sub-paragraphs, and sub-sub-paragraphs; within the artificial world of the game, of course, they *are* legal texts. Next it is necessary to set up the pieces on the board. Given that there may be several hundred of them, doing so is a time-consuming, often quite tedious task.

Since the players must take turns in moving their pieces and rolling dice to see the results of "combat," the game proceeds very slowly. Since different kinds of troops, represented by different kinds of pieces, have different capabilities and will impact enemy ones in different ways, a tremendous amount of calculation is needed. Usually it is carried out on specially provided forms as well as innumerable little pieces of paper; starting in the 1970s, calculators became an indispensable tool. All this means that games can last for weeks, months even, and that a considerable amount of organization is required if they are to be played at all. Nevertheless, between about 1960 and 1990 they were sufficiently popular for special shops to be set up to sell them and magazines to be published to review and advertise them; apparently playing at war was enough fun for enthusiasts to overcome all the difficulties.

In the end, hex board games were brought down not by any obvious boredom with the subject but by the diffusion of a different kind of game, namely, the kind that is played with the aid of computers.[34] Initially the number of people, most of them scientists and military planners, who were able to play war games by programming and running the enormously costly, and hence precious and far-between, computers of the 1950s was strictly limited. But the invention of microchips allowed almost anybody, professional or amateur, to access a computer and to play the games not just for serious training, modeling, and simulation but for amusement as well. Computers eliminated the most important disadvantage of chess and other games that are based on it, namely, the demand that players take turns instead of acting simultaneously, as would be the case in real life. They also enabled the huge amounts of information some games require to be processed quickly and efficiently.

Increasingly, as their power grew, computers permitted the creation of entire virtual worlds, thus adding realism to the games. Yet another advantage of computers was that once they had been programmed, they could go through even the most complex games at low cost and enormous speed. This made it possible to play the same game over and over again. Meanwhile, programming changes enabled the parameters to be altered as often as necessary so as to see the different outcomes that would result.

In many modern war games the opponent is not a human being but the computer itself, and computers that do this are often known as simulators.[35] Even some of the simplest simulators, which can be purchased for a few dollars at any computer shop, incorporate a vast amount of data about the physical world they claim to represent; whether that world is imaginary or real is, in the end, immaterial. The same is even more true of the simulators that armed forces use to train their troops. Some of the first simulators were developed during World War I and were intended for basic pilot training. In World War II a company by the name of Link built thousands of them for the U.S. Army Air Forces, which used them to train pilots. These were crude devices, made to look more or less like the inside of aircraft and provided with hydraulically or pneumatically operated controls so as to give trainees a feel for what flying that aircraft was like. In the 1950s, to add realism, instruments, recorded noises, and films that enabled trainees to see the "outside world" were added.

From about 1970 on, the growing power of the available computers permitted the machines to be made much more complex and much more realistic still. Seen from the outside, the devices currently in use look like huge, rather ungainly boxes. They are mounted in large, often specially constructed buildings and supported by all kinds of hydraulic contraptions designed to tilt them at various angles; control is exercised from a desk provided with numerous screens, switches, and buttons. From the inside they look and feel almost exactly like real aircraft complete with every instrument from seat harness through altimeter and artificial horizon to sights and firing button. In a sense they *are* real aircraft, but they also incorporate the enormously complex electronic, visual, mechanical, and acoustical devices needed to simulate not only the machine itself but also the environment in which it operates. Thanks to the computer, all these devices can be tied together and coordinated. This in turn allows the simulation of almost any kind of mission, performed under almost any kind of conditions.

Some of the performances and conditions in question are too dangerous to try in real life. That is precisely why algorithms for them are written, the objective being to enable pilots to practice them in a risk-free environment. On the other hand, where there is danger, even simulated danger, there will always be men, and perhaps a few women as well, who see it as a challenge, play with it, and have fun with it. Thus I am told that Israeli (and presumably not only Israeli) pilots training at Maxwell Air Force Base in Alabama asked their USAF instructors to program the simulator so as to represent their Hercules transport aircraft as "flying" under the bridges spanning the Mississippi at Saint Louis. First they practiced in the ordinary way. Next, having mastered the technique, they proceeded to do the same upside down.[36] The experience is absolutely hair-raising; yet that is just why men love it so much.

From aircraft the use of simulators spread to other weapon systems, such as tanks, armored cars, ships, submarines, and guided missiles of every sort. As with aircraft, the initial objective was to teach trainees to operate their machines safely and cheaply. It is true that simulators can be very expensive. On the other hand, they have the very great advantage that they do not require real-life ammunition. Operating and maintenance costs also form no more than a small fraction of what training with real equipment under real conditions involves. As in the case of aircraft, soon enough the opponent started to be simulated as well. Rapid technological advances in fields such as data processing, imaging, and communication followed. The most recent models enable not just individuals but entire groups to practice against each other.

Yet the simulators used by the military only represent the tip of the iceberg. For just a few dollars anybody can buy a box containing a disk, install the software on his or her personal computer, and start pretending he or she is a pilot, a tank gunner, a submarine commander, or whatever. Other games may be downloaded from the Net. Some, such as the most recent versions of *Warcraft,* permit as many as a hundred different players to participate simultaneously. These simulators cannot compete with their larger and more expensive counterparts in the amount of detail they provide. Still, the information on which they are based is sufficiently extensive to fill entire encyclopedias.

As the game opens, players are often offered a choice as to which war they want to play at—one disk may store several of them. Next they can decide which aircraft or other systems they want to fly or operate, how they want to arm them, what kind of missions they want to carry out in what kind of terrain, under what conditions, and against what kind of opposition. The games may also contain surprises, forcing players to cope with the unexpected; as in real life, practice makes perfect. Professional soldiers say that many of them provide a good feel for what operating the weapon system is like as well as reasonable approximations of real-life combat. Since some of those soldiers are themselves involved in the design process, this is not surprising.

For those who are not content with the computer games available to ordinary mortals and seek greater excitement still, it is now possible to take tours in real-life, if perhaps slightly outdated, combat aircraft. The first who hit on the idea of using such aircraft to generate revenue were the Russians during the 1990s. With the state broke and unable to pay its armed forces, many combat aircraft inherited from the Soviet Union were standing about in their hangars, rusting away. What better solution than to rent them out as if they were parts of some amusement park? For the paltry sum of fifteen thousand dollars per hour, tourists could put on a pressure suit, take the trainer's seat behind the pilot, and enjoy a spin in some MiG or Sukhoi fighter that would otherwise have to be put out of service; it is an experience, I am told, that no roller coaster can match. Later the idea spread to other countries. In the United States and elsewhere, there are now companies that enable their clients to fly combat aircraft, drive tanks, and the like, all simply so they can play at war and experience some of the thrill it can provide.[37]

Finally, even as countless kinds of games are deliberately designed to simulate war, some forms of war have become so much like certain kinds of games as to be virtually indistinguishable from them. This is because much modern combat, particularly air-to-air, ground-to-air, air-to-ground, and sea-to-sea, has long ceased to be fought against flesh-and-blood adversaries. In many cases, the "target" is too far away or moves too fast to be seen or heard. In others it may be hidden by darkness, cloud, or (as with submarines) water. Its presence is detected "over the horizon," as military men say, sometimes (as with anti-ballistic-missile defense) when it is thousands of miles away. This is done by radar, or else by some other device such as FLIR (forward-looking infrared) or sonar.

Once contact has been formed, the impulses bounced off or generated by the target are converted into electronic signals, fed into computers, processed, and projected onto a fluorescent screen. It then becomes the task of the commander, pilot, or weapons officer to use some blips, representing his sights, to aim other blips, representing his own missiles, at a third group of blips, representing the enemy. Even as he does all this he must also pay close attention to a fourth category of blips, ones that tell him where he is, in what direction he is flying, whether he is flying straight or upside down, where the other members of his force or unit (if any) are, and the like.

The blips are supposed to represent objects in the real world, but that is by no means necessarily the case. As anyone who has ever visited a video arcade knows, they might equally well be fed into the system by a computer program or, for that matter, some malevolent gnome who has hijacked the machine and is now playing games with the player. To those who watch the screens and operate the controls it does not make the slightest difference; they see what they see, and they do what they must do. In this way a situation is created where fighting, training, and play merge into one another to the point of becoming indistinguishable. Back in 1986, when *Newsweek,* describing the combat over Tripoli Bay when two Libyan aircraft were shot down by U.S. fighters, headlined it "The Ultimate Video Game," it hit the nail right on the head; since then, of course, the use of electronics in war has only expanded.[38]

To play a video game well, two qualities are needed: manual dexterity—although it is possible that in the not so remote future some games will be activated by thought alone—and absolute concentration on the task at hand.[39] For such concentration to be achieved, cause and consequence must be put aside. So must the entire outside world, with all its tensions and distractions. The player should enter the arcade as if he were entering a temple with his head bare, so to speak. In fact, for him *not* to know whether the signals that flash about on his screen represent anything in the real world can actually represent a critical element in his ability to perform. The less he worries about what may or may not be behind them, the better able he may be to manipulate them with the necessary assurance, flexibility, and speed. Thus insulation can help lead to mastery, whereas acquiring and exercising mastery is a source of joy at least equal to any other. Play merges into war, and war turns into play. Far from the culture of war being a more or less irrelevant appendage to the "real thing," in many cases it and the "real thing" have literally become one and the same.

V

CONTRASTS

In theory, war is simply a means to an end, a rational, if very brutal, activity intended to serve the interests of one group of people by killing, wounding, or otherwise incapacitating those who oppose it. In reality, nothing could be further from the truth. Facts beyond number prove that war exercises a powerful fascination in its own right—one that, while it affects participants, is by no means limited to them. Out of this fascination grew an entire culture. Like any other culture, the one associated with war consists largely of "useless" play, decoration, and affectations of every sort. On occasion, affectations, decoration, and play are even carried to counterproductive lengths.

But what if, for one reason or another, the culture of war fails to develop, or assumes a mechanical character, or is deliberately strangled? In that case, four different outcomes are possible. Outcome number one is the wild horde. Outcome number two is the soulless machine. Outcome number three is men without chests. Outcome number four is feminism. History knows many examples of the first three; the fourth, though not entirely un-precedented, has become particularly important during the last few decades. Each one in its different way is quite capable of wrecking a military organization and rendering a society inca-pable of defending itself.

.   .   .

17

The Wild Horde

Any cohesive and disciplined group of men working together for a considerable time will develop a culture of their own. Indeed, it has been argued that groups of bonded males, sometimes joined by a lone female who serves as glue and inspiration, are the originators not just of the culture of war but of all culture.[1] On the other hand, it is culture that holds the group together; without a set of norms so familiar that much of it is taken for granted, there can be no discipline and no cohesion. Finally, it is culture that distinguishes one group from another and of which the members are proud.

Not every group that finds itself at war does form a culture or is able to sustain it. Sometimes this is because the men simply have neither the time nor the conditions to develop the necessary cohesion and discipline—with the result that they remain strangers to each other, cannot trust each other, and can only cooperate with each other to a very limited extent. In others it is because they have been heavily defeated. As the cry *Chaque homme pour lui-même, sauve qui peut* is raised, culture may very well melt away like snow under the sun. Attempting to get away, men may overrun and turn on each other, which is one reason why casualties suffered in the aftermath of a battle often exceed those during the fighting itself. Later still there is likely to take place an identity crisis. What used to be most cherished turns out to be of no value, and what used to be most valuable turns out to be false. No longer knowing who and what they are, men allow the ties that bind them to lapse, turning them from a fighting organization into a mob. Time and very great effort will be needed to restore them, and there may be circumstances where they cannot be restored at all.

Yet another situation in which the culture of war will break down is when a force strong in numbers, organization, equipment, training, and tradition is made to face a much weaker one for too long. Almost inevitably, the outcome is demoralization. If they sit still and suffer repeated pinpricks, then they will become demoralized. If they lash out at the enemy without success—when fighting the weak, the fact that the conflict is not decided itself signifies the lack of success—then they will also become demoralized. As they become demoralized they will blame each other, accelerating the process still further. In Nietzsche's words, nothing is more boring than a victory endlessly repeated. In those of Lao Tzu, a sword thrust into saltwater will rust.

Historically speaking, the list of wild hordes is a long and dishonorable one. Among the earliest about whom we have more or less detailed information were the Roman *latrones,* best translated as "outlaws" or "bandits." *Latrones* were common in many Roman provinces and could be found during most of the centuries from the late Republic to about A.D. 200 (from that period on, so large was the number of rebellions and civil wars as to make it almost impossible to distinguish between *bellum,* war, and *latronicum,* the kind of large-scale police action that was directed against robbers). As ancient historians and jurists used the term, it referred to groups of armed men who were more than simple robbers; though every *latro* was necessarily a robber, not every robber was necessarily a *latro.* What set *latrones* apart was that instead of acting individually, they ganged together and, openly using armed force, set out to plunder the countryside. Thus their status stood midway between ordinary criminals and public enemies of the state. This also explains why, when dealing with them, the use of ruses (*doli*) such as treachery was considered not only permissible but even honorable.[2]

As might be expected, *latrones* were not evenly distributed. They tended to infest regions with difficult terrain, such as mountains, forests, and deserts from where they emerged to attack villages and highways. As the New Testament shows, they represented one of the main hazards of travel; it was the attack on a traveler, left half dead by robbers, that provided the Good Samaritan with the opportunity to perform his good deed.[3] Similar references come from the life of the Apostle Paulus,[4] the writings of the philosopher Seneca,[5] the poet Juvenal,[6] and many others. Few people, however elevated, could claim to be entirely safe against them. For example, the future emperor Hadrian, then on a mission to inform the candidate for the throne, Trajan, of his predecessor Nerva's death, fell victim to an attack by *latrones*. Having lost his transport, he had to continue his voyage from Mainz to Cologne on foot.[7]

Latrones came from all social classes.[8] Among them were escaped slaves and free men, citizens and foreigners, military and civilians, humble folks and high-ranking persons who for one reason or another had broken with civilization. Most of our sources having been produced by members of the aristocratic or at least well-to-do classes, they rarely describe the lives of *latrones* in detail. Accordingly, the best extended account of them is found in an early second-century-A.D. novel, Apuleius's *Golden Ass*.

The story, which we only need to follow in part, is set in Thessaly. A small band of outlaws has taken up residence in a wild mountain stronghold, far from civilization, where they have their housework done for them by an old woman. As individuals they are not without courage, but they are volatile, tricky, treacherous, and cruel. They go out on an almost daily basis, robbing, murdering, and taking back loot, part of which they sell to the inhabitants of a nearby village. One day the loot includes both the hero, Lucius, a man whom magic has changed into an ass, and a young woman of good family whom they snatch away just before her wedding party and hold for ransom. Since we lose sight of them at the point in the story where the ass, Lucius, succeeds in escaping from the stronghold while taking the woman with him, it is impossible to say how the robbers end up. Presumably, having gone too far in making a nuisance of themselves, sooner or later a company of soldiers was sent to deal with them and they were caught and punished, only to be replaced by others of the same kind.

Like terrorists and guerrillas at many times and places, small-time, garden-variety robbers of the kind described by Apuleius tended to be persistent. This was all the more the case because the members of some professions, notably shepherds, were regarded as naturally inclined to banditry. Though slaves in law, the kind of life they led gave them an unusual degree of freedom; at the same time, by permitting mobility and demanding frugality, it instilled them with warlike qualities. Some shepherd slaves even practiced robbery with the tacit consent of their owners, who were thus relieved of the need to take care of them.[9] On top of this some people, particularly the Lusitanians of modern Portugal, were seen as being naturally disposed toward the outlaw's life. All this explains why such emperors as Augustus and Tiberius, both of whom took energetic action against them, failed to get rid of them completely.[10] Still they hardly constituted a threat to the immense structure that was the Roman Empire.

There did, however, also exist other kinds of wild hordes that presented a much greater challenge, with the incidental result that we are much better informed about them. Some of the most notorious were made up of escaped slaves. The largest slave revolts in the ancient world were those that took place between about 134 B.C. and 70 B.C. Their *locus classicus* was Sicily; however, uprisings also took place in Asia Minor and Greece—both of which were heavily penetrated, if not conquered, by Rome during the second century B.C.—as well as Italy itself. Some of the slaves worked in mines, which were known as the worst places of all, whereas others, such as Spartacus and his early followers, were being trained as gladiators. Most, however, must have been among the thousands upon thousands of agricultural slaves who lived and worked on immense estates where there were few free citizens to keep them in check. If our sources may be believed, they were often subject to acts of almost unbelievable cruelty growing out of the owners' feeling of power over, or fear of, their slaves.

From escaped slaves and their leaders it was but a short step to guerrilla chieftains. Some set themselves up at the head of their peoples, started a rebellion, and fought the Romans for as long as they could. Others were pretenders or rivals to thrones, whereas others still aimed at avenging political assassinations by taking the law into their own hands. Here it is important to realize that, following well-established literary codes, our sources divide *latrones* into noble bandits and ordinary ones. The former are often presented as contrasts to, and examples for, corrupt Roman civilization; while the Romans had lost their edge, the *latrones,* living far from civilization and its amenities, retained it. Sometimes a contrast is also drawn between the noble leaders and their men. The latter were riffraff, yet look what the heroic leader was able to do with them! Strip the sources of their literary bias, and both types of *latrones* become much more similar to one another and to what most of them really were—that is successful, if sometimes righteous, brigands. Successful, that is, until defeated by the relentless might of Roman arms supported by what Caesar calls a superior military tradition and what we have dubbed a superior culture of war.[11]

The first great slave revolt took place in Sicily, starting in 136 B.C. and ending four years later. The first actors were shepherds. Their activities consisted of what we today would call a mixture of terrorism and criminal activities, making the highways unsafe at night; according to Diodorus, the first-century-A.D. writer who is our principal source, they lived under the open sky, carried clubs and spears and staves, and dressed in the skins of wolves and boars. Followed by ferocious dogs, they were terrible to look at. Feeding on plenty of milk and meat, physically and mentally they became savages.[12] As more slaves started escaping, the movement expanded and charismatic leaders made their appearance. The most important was Eunus, originally from Apamea in Syria. If Diodorus may be believed, he was neither brave nor an able commander. Instead he was a trickster. Pretending to read the future and using "magic" to spew out sparks and flames, he convinced his followers that he enjoyed divine support; the fact that his name happened to mean "good fortune" helped.[13]

From then on the revolt spread like wildfire. It involved first hundreds, then thousands, and finally, if our sources may be believed, tens of thousands; "their pressing needs and their poverty forced the slaves to regard everyone as acceptable, giving them no opportunity to pick and choose."[14] Without any real strategy, acting almost indiscriminately, the bands moved about the island, "[measuring] their authority only by the excessive suffering of the freeborn."[15] "They fell upon the city of Enna, with Eunus at their head and working his miracle of the flames of fire for their benefit. When they found their way into the houses they shed much blood, sparing not even sucking babies. Rather they tore them from the breast and dashed them to the ground, while as for the women—and under their husbands' very eyes—but words cannot tell the extent of their outrages and acts of lewdness."[16] According to Florus, so great was the destruction as to exceed that caused by the First Punic War.[17]

At one point in the uprising poor free people started joining the slaves, increasing their numbers and engaging in even worse depredations than the slaves themselves. Finally, having resisted several attempts to subdue them, the rebel bands were brought to heel by Roman forces under the command of a consul, Publius Rupilius. Besieged in the town of Tauromenium (modern Taormina), toward the end they were reduced to such straits that they started eating first children and women, then each other. Of their leaders one, Comanus, was captured but succeeded in killing himself by stopping his breathing. Not so Eunus. Along with a cook, a baker, a masseur, and another man whose duty it had been to amuse him at drinking parties, he was dragged out of a cave, imprisoned, and died as his body disintegrated, possibly owing to gangrene.[18]

The second Sicilian slave revolt lasted from 104 to 101 B.C. Even before it started, there took place a number of small slave uprisings in various places in Italy that were quickly suppressed. The Sicilian revolt itself opened with the murder of a Roman knight, Publius Clonius, by eighty of his slaves. Since the local governor was slow to act, the number grew quickly. Six thousand rebels elected a "king" by the name of Salvius; Diodorus claims that he had been "a flute player of frenetic music at performances for women" who, like Eunus before him, also claimed the ability to foresee the future.[19] A second leader was a Silician by the name of Athenion, an experienced estate manager with great knowledge of astrology. "He adopted an attitude just the opposite to that of all the other rebels. He did not admit all who revolted, but making the best ones soldiers, he required the rest to remain at their former labors."[20]

As the rebellion spread, "the whole of Sicily was sunk in chaos, a veritable *Iliad* of woe."[21] The free poor living in the countryside also rose, robbing, plundering, and murdering "indiscriminately so that nobody could report on their insane and illegal activity."[22] The outcome was "anarchy." Having anointed himself king and calling himself Triphon, Salvius was joined by Athenion, and the two of them ended up facing the Romans in the open. They were defeated, but the battle did not prove decisive and it took another year to put down the remaining slaves. Athenion, who from beginning to end is presented as the only rebel leader who was more than a mere bandit, died fighting bravely on the battlefield. What happened to Triphon is not clear.

In antiquity as well as today, the most famous ancient slave revolt was that led by Spartacus between 73 and 70 B.C. Spartacus himself is described as a noble barbarian, strong in body and mind. Later he proved himself a capable and wily commander; such were his virtues, says Plutarch, that he might almost have been taken for a Greek.[23] Committed to a school for gladiators, he escaped, carrying with him initially several dozen companions. Next he was joined by tens of thousands; including, to follow Plutarch again, "many of the herdsmen and shepherds of the region, sturdy men and swift of foot," who excelled as scouts and light infantry in particular.[24]

The men, however, proved unworthy of their commander. Having won several victories over the Roman detachments, they moved north, finally reaching ancient Galia Cisalpina (modern Lombardy). Well aware of their limitations, Spartacus suggested to them that they should leave Italy and return to their countries of origin, but they refused. Sallust, in one of his surviving fragments, explains why: "Shamefully, they forgot their homeland; many of them, following their slavish nature, did not seek anything but loot and cruelty."[25] Instead, he marched them all the way to Lucania, in southwestern Italy, intending to take them to Sicily, where he hoped to incite another slave revolt.[26] For that, however, he could not procure the necessary ships.

Retreating into the province of Rhegium, "immediately, and acting against their commander's orders, the escaped slaves started raping young and mature women . . . Others set houses on fire. Many rebellious slaves, fit by nature to be [Spartacus's] allies, went into hiding places and dragged out the masters' treasures or the masters themselves. To the barbarians and those of slavish nature, nothing was sacred. Spartacus, though he begged them to stop lest they make themselves hated, could not call them to order. They were busy committing cruel slaughter."[27] Whereas the slave hordes were too undisciplined to adopt a coherent strategy, their enemies rallied under the command of consul Marcus Licinius Crassus, the subsequent triumvir.[28] Crassus quickly built a wall right across the toe of the peninsula, an astonishing feat of engineering. To the slaves, all that remained was to fight with the courage of desperation. This they did, but to no avail. As the end approached Spartacus was deserted by his companions. He fought on until he was finally killed.

To trace every uprising that threatened the peace of ancient Rome would take us much too far. Even a short list would have to include the Lusitanian outlaw Viriatus (died 139 B.C.), the Spanish tribal leader Sertorius (defeated 72 B.C.), the Numidian deserter Tacfarinas (died A.D. 24), and the bandit Aniktos of Pontus (eliminated A.D. 69). Time after time, our sources insist that many rebel leaders were brave and strong, as were at least some of their followers. However, hastily thrown together, undisciplined, and sometimes without a common country of origin, they were lacking in everything that we have included under the rubric of the culture of war; how could it have been otherwise? Lacking a culture of war, they found it very hard to engage in any kind of organized, sustained action except atrocities. Time after time they ended up being defeated by the regular forces sent out against them.

Nor was the ancient world the only period to witness wild hordes in action. Skipping over fourteen hundred years, let us take a look at the great French peasant uprising known as the Jacquerie. The deep background to the revolt was formed by the intense hatred of the serfs, who were tied to the soil and subject to all kinds of exactions as well as contempt and ridicule, by their self-appointed betters.[29] Its immediate cause was the great French defeat at the hands of the English in the Battle of Poitiers (1356). In this battle, the king of France was taken prisoner. The ruling classes were decimated—the list of dead reads like an aristocratic who's who—leaving government in the hands of the eighteen-year-old dauphin, the future Charles VI.

While the Estates took over Paris, adding to the confusion, unpaid soldiers, commanded by disgruntled barons, roamed the countryside. One band, under a certain Regnault de Cervoles, infested Provence. Another, under a Welsh captain called Ruffin, blocked the roads between Paris and Orléans; a third, under Robert Knollys, a companion of England's Black Prince, operated in Normandy. The activities of these and many others are sufficiently well indicated by the French words used to describe them: *écorcheurs* (skinners) and *routiers* (highwaymen). They attacked towns and villages, robbed travelers, and kidnapped people and held them for ransom.

Against this background of growing anarchy, two courses were open to the peasantry.[30] One was to leave their habitations, seek refuge in forests and other desolate places, and take up guerrilla warfare. The other, perhaps less frequent but more dangerous, was open revolt. Representing the second form, the Jacquerie got under way on May 28, 1358. Its epicenter was at the village of Saint-Leu in the Oise valley, north of Paris, a region that previously had been left almost untouched by the war. Apparently a group of soldiers, commanded by one Raoul de Clermont, had orders to establish themselves there so as to guard a crossing of the Oise River, whereupon they took up quarters in the local abbey and demanded that the village bring them provisions.

That evening, after vespers, two hundred "Jacques"—the name seems to have been derived from the padded jacket that formed an essential item of peasant dress—held an impromptu meeting in the local cemetery. There they gave voice to their grievances, including the heavy taxation made necessary by the need to ransom noble prisoners in English hands and the inability of the king, who as just said was himself a prisoner, to hold it in check. Encouraging each other by shouting, they rushed to the nearest manor house, killed the knight, his wife, and their children, and set the place on fire.

As so often, the revolt spread quickly. It involved not only peasants but some members of the urban lower classes as well. Here and there towns opened their gates to the rebels, providing them with food, drink, and shelter. Later, of course, they claimed that they had been coerced into doing so. The claim may well have been true in some cases, which may explain why, when all was over, those involved were able to earn letters of pardon. Within two weeks, the entire region around Paris was up in arms; isolated uprisings took place as far away as Rheims and Rouen.

The Jacques' principal leader was a well-to-do peasant by the name of Guillaume Caillet. As so often, he is presented as personally charismatic, courageous, and strong, as indeed he would have to be to create something out of practically nothing. It is claimed that he tried to rein in his followers and impose some order on them. However, he and other leaders exercised only very limited control over the diverse bands of peasants. Scattered over the countryside, lacking in everything that constitutes the culture of war, most Jacques were little better than mobs— murderous, destructive, and according to some sources gorged with blood and often drunk; in the apt phrase of one modern historian, "with no aim and no morrow."[31]

From such bands, nothing but the worst could be expected. Their activities are best described by Jean Froissart, who admittedly was not an eyewitness and whose sympathies lay entirely with the upper classes.

> These evil men, who had come together without leaders or arms, pillaged and burned everything and violated and killed all the ladies and girls without mercy, like mad dogs. Their barbarous acts were worse than anything that ever took place between Christians and Saracens. Never did men commit such vile deeds. They were such that no living creature ought to see, or even imagine or think of . . . I could never bring myself to write down the horrible and shameful things they did to the ladies. But, among other brutal excesses, they killed a knight, put him on a spit, and turned him at the fire and roasted him before the lady and her children. After about a dozen of them had violated the lady, they tried to force her and the children to eat the knight's flesh before putting them cruelly to death. They had chosen a king from among them, and they elected the worst of the bad . . . Taken together, they easily numbered a hundred thousand men. When they were [captured and] asked why they did these

things, they replied that they did not know; it was because they saw others doing them and they copied them. They thought that by such means they could destroy all the nobles and gentry in the world so that there would be no more of them.[32]

Using other chroniclers as his source, Froissart puts the total number of manors and castles sacked by the Jacques at over a hundred.

On June 9, a band of Jacques—their number supposedly reached nine thousand—entered the town of Meaux, in the valley of the Marne. Taking shelter in the local citadel were the dauphin's wife, Jeanne de Bourbon; his sister; his infant daughter; and three hundred other ladies and their children. As it happened, the Jacques' arrival coincided with that of two barons, Jean de Grailly (the Captal de Buch) and Gaston Phoebus. Originally based in the south of France, they were on their way back from Prussia, where they had campaigned with the Teutonic Knights. Buch was an aristocrat praised by Froissart as a model of chivalry; later he was to throw in his lot with the English and die in prison for his pains. Gaston, whose nickname, Phoebus, had to do with his good looks, was the Comte de Foix and thus one of the greatest French noblemen.

On this occasion, all they had with them were forty "lances." Counting men at arms and pages, this works out to some two hundred troops; the number of knights is put at just twenty-five. Yet dressed in armor, "with pennants of argent and azure displaying stars and lilies and couchant lions,"[33] this small force was able to rout the crowd of undisciplined peasants, slaughtering, if our sources are to be believed, several thousand of them. It has been explained that, caught in the narrow streets of the town, the Jacques could not bring their numerical superiority to bear.[34] That is true. However, it is equally true that such streets hardly formed the best place for armored cavalry to fight, as was proved just a few days later when a party of nobles trying to enter the town of Senlis (which had cooperated with the Jacques) was repulsed with loss.

From this point on, things went downhill for the Jacques. At the head of the forces now arrayed against them was King Charles of Navarre, aka Charles the Bad, aka the Duke of Normandy (1323–73). On the day after the events at Meaux he caught up with the Jacques at Clermont, a little distance east of the place where it had all started. Like so many similar captains before and after him, Guillaume Caillet pleaded with his followers not to stand and fight against a better-organized, better-armed opponent but to take refuge in Paris, which was in the hands of a rebellious commune led by a wealthy draper, Etienne Marcel. Once again, he was disobeyed.

The Jacques, numbering perhaps three thousand to five thousand, gathered in a field at Mello. By now they were sufficiently well armed to form separate units of archers and crossbowmen; six hundred were mounted and constituted a rudimentary cavalry force. Opposing them, the noble army may have numbered perhaps fifteen hundred to twenty-five hundred men of whom, assuming that the customary division into "lances" was maintained, probably no more than one-fifth were knights on horseback. Caillet himself was invited to parley in the barons' camp, an offer he foolishly accepted. Arriving there, he was arrested, put in chains, and later tortured and executed. This was not an uncommon fate for men of his kind. Perceived as having broken the laws of gods and men, they could hardly complain if similar treatment was meted out to them. The ensuing battle was furious but short. The Jacques were beaten as easily in the open field as their comrades had been in the alleys of Meaux. Hundreds were killed, the rest scattered and later hunted down like rabbits. Many of the surrounding villages in which they tried to take shelter now betrayed them; others witnessed atrocities much like those that had been recently committed by the Jacques themselves. By the end of August, everything was over.

Considered as a peasant revolt, the Jacquerie was neither the first nor the last of its kind. As in the case of the ancient slave revolts, the motives that led to it are understandable, some would say praiseworthy. However, lacking strong leadership, proper organization, and a clear direction, it accomplished nothing and changed nothing. Like so many wild hordes before and after them, all the Jacques left behind was a reputation for terror of the worst kind, one that was answered by similar terror accompanied by better discipline and a more highly developed culture of war.

The last example of wild hordes I want to consider here is taken from the civil war that raged across the former Yugoslavia from 1991 to 1995. The state of Yugoslavia was created in 1919 by joining Serbia and Montenegro, themselves liberated from Ottoman rule in 1878 and extended by means of the Balkan Wars of 1911–12, with some provinces taken from the disintegrating Austro-Hungarian Empire. However, the marriage of Serbs and Montenegrins with Croats, Slovenes, and Muslims (primarily in Kosovo and in Bosnia-Herzegovina) proved unhappy from the beginning. Throughout the twenty years up to the outbreak of World

War II, a Croat separatist movement in particular was active. From time to time, it also received Italian support.[35] In April 1941, Yugoslavia's ethnic diversity and unresolved conflicts contributed materially to the country being overrun in a blitzkrieg campaign that lasted all of two weeks and cost the Wehrmacht fewer than 250 German dead.

The country's next ruler, the former guerrilla leader Jozef Broz, nicknamed Tito, was himself a Croat. He sought to override the ethnic problems by imposing a single ideology, Communism, and as long as he lived he was fairly successful in this task. However, the price he had to pay for maintaining control was growing decentralization; his death in 1980 started the processes that would ultimately lead to disintegration. Following the collapse of the Eastern Bloc, the first multiparty elections were held in November 1990. Croatia and Slovenia voted for independence; two years later they formally seceded from the federation, leaving the quarter million Serbs of Croatia high and dry. Even more ominously, separating Slovenia and Croatia from Serbia was the ethnically mixed province of Bosnia-Herzegovina.

The Yugoslav National Army (sometimes known as JNA), which was sent to put down the two rebellious provinces, was originally well trained, well organized, and well equipped with Soviet weapons, and could look back on a formidable military tradition going back for centuries on end. First, as already mentioned, the Serbs spent five hundred years fighting the Ottoman Empire, from which they were finally able to gain their independence in 1878. Next they withstood the Austrian Empire in World War I; after that, they formed the core of the forces that waged a successful guerrilla campaign against Hitler. Yugoslavia came out of World War II as the only country that expelled the German invaders without being overrun by foreign armies. This in turn is one reason why, in 1947–48, Tito was able to thumb his nose at Stalin when the latter tried to impose his own brand of Communism on him.

Had it been a question of dealing with Croatia and Slovenia alone, the JNA, still intact and ably commanded, might conceivably have succeeded in its mission. It could not, however, simultaneously put down unrest in those provinces and look after Bosnia-Herzegovina in its rear—to say nothing of growing discontent in Macedonia and Montenegro, both of which also ended up by proclaiming their independence. As a result, Slovenia, located in the northeastern corner of Yugoslavia, farthest away from Serbia, had to be let go, so the country gained its independence with hardly a shot being fired. No such good fortune for Croatia, where

Yugoslav—in reality, Serb—forces clashed with hastily established local militias and succeeded in occupying the district of Krajina. And no such good fortune, above all, for centrally located Bosnia-Herzegovina.

In Bosnia-Herzegovina, Croats, Serbs, and Muslims—the last supposedly the descendants of Turkish settlers—had been living together for centuries, now quarreling, now at peace. As Yugoslavia broke up, all three groups hastily set up militias to deal with one another. Taking up the cause of the Bosnian Serbs, the JNA started disintegrating. Most Croat soldiers deserted, preferring to join their brethren either in Bosnia-Herzegovina or in Croatia itself. Some Serb soldiers also deserted, either because they wanted to join the Serbs in Bosnia-Herzegovina (where many of them originated) or because, instead of risking their lives, they preferred to go home to Serbia. At the same time as it lost these troops the JNA also started taking in some Bosnian Serb volunteers. Within a matter of months the once proud regular force had virtually ceased to exist, becoming all but indistinguishable from the other militias.

The most important militias were the Bosnian Serb one, led by former JNA general Radko Mladić, and the Bosnian Muslim Green Berets. Most of their members, as well as those of the smaller Croat militias, possessed some military experience, having served either in the JNA or in the territorial forces maintained by each Yugoslav province. However, none had the time to get properly organized. They could, moreover, hardly be told apart. All fought with each other, negotiated with each other, kidnapped and executed each other's leaders. Now Croats and Muslims fought against Serbs, now Serbs and Croats united forces against Muslims.

However, not even those bitter enemies the Serbs and the "Turks" (as the Serbs called them) eschewed occasional cooperation. For example, the Muslims around Mostar tried to bribe the Serbs (who had the most firepower) to shell the Croats. In July 1993, Muslims charged with defending Sarajevo against the Serbs sold their positions to the latter.[36] Four months later a Muslim leader by the name of Fikret Abdić, onetime Communist Party strongman in Bihac and now a freebooter, signed a private ceasefire with the Serb militias opposing him. Next, he tried to set up an autonomous region in the Cazinska district. Attacked and defeated by Bosnian government forces, he and an estimated twenty thousand followers escaped into Krajina, the province of neighboring Croatia, which at that time was being held by the Serbs.[37]

Complicating things even further, Bosnia-Herzegovina is a mountainous country with deep valleys joined by narrow, winding roads. Movement from one town to another can be quite difficult, especially in winter, and communications are easily cut. The upshot was that each town, Serb or Muslim or Croat, set up its own militia to supplement, or oppose, that of the next. Some of the militiamen were conscripted—to the extent that the rival governments, the Serb one under Radovan Karadžić and the Muslim one under Alija Izetbegović, were able to have their orders obeyed—whereas others took up arms out of their own free will.

Some towns had more than one militia. Take the case of Sarajevo, soon to become world famous as its inhabitants were besieged and shelled by Bosnian Serb forces. Early in the war the Green Berets in the city were commanded by Jusuf Prazina, a soldier turned mafioso. The defense of the neighborhood of Dobrinje was organized by Ismet Bajramović-Ćelo, commander of the city's military police, who was also in charge of the local prison and used that position to let out criminals on condition they fight for him. The Croat suburb of Stup was controlled by a local Croat, Velimir Marić. A certain Musan Tolalović, aka Caco, ran the part of the city on the left bank of the Miljacka River. Some of them saw themselves as serving the Bosnian Muslim government, others not. By one count, the total number of militias that joined the struggle at one time or another, in one way or another, reached eighty-three.[38]

During the four years of confused fighting, the Serb militias, which had progressively swallowed up what remained of the JNA, acquired a particularly bad reputation.[39] In countless media reports as well as at least one (entirely fictional and fairly idiotic) movie they are often presented as adventurers, thugs, and even football hooligans. Provided with weapons from former JNA stores by Yugoslav (in reality, Serb) president Slobodan Milošević, they wore bits and pieces of uniforms as well as Yugoslav army insignia. They are portrayed as a canaille that blundered about from one Muslim town to another, killing, torturing, raping, driving tens of thousands from their homes, looting anything they could lay their hands on, and setting fire to what they could not carry. Often they were fortified by alcohol. For example, the Serb hordes that carried out the massacre at Srebrenica were roaring drunk.

In many cases, the description was apt. However, it does the Serbs an injustice in that it applied almost equally well to the remaining militias. In Sarajevo and other mixed towns, Croat and Muslim militiamen treated the Serb population almost as badly as the Serbs treated them.[40] Thus, when Croat forces took Krajina late in the war, two hundred thousand

Serbs lost their homes amid scenes of destruction very similar to those that had taken place in Bosnia-Herzegovina. In particular, cultural landmarks, such as Orthodox churches and graveyards, became targets. All that was left of them were blackened ruins; a community that could trace its origins four centuries back in history simply ceased to exist. The longer the war went on, the more alike the warring groups became. Within a matter of months, they could hardly be told apart.

Furthermore, not one of them represented a really cohesive force. Cut off from each other by mountain passes, recruiting their men wherever they could find them, subordinate leaders did more or less as they pleased; that was one reason why, of the countless cease-fires agreed on at one time or another, few held up for more than a handful of days or even hours. Under cover of war between ethnic groups, criminal activities multiplied and countless personal accounts were settled, gun in hand. The other face of the coin was that many members of the rival militias knew each other from before the war, a time when they had lived together more or less peacefully as neighbors. This made it easy for them to negotiate with each other, trade with each other, and occasionally carry out special missions, such as assassination, on behalf of each other.

As the wild hordes, for that is what they had become (or had been from the beginning), chased each other, an additional element of confusion was introduced by the presence of the international media and of foreign (United Nations) forces. For reasons that are difficult to fathom, almost from the beginning of the conflict most of the world media turned against the Serbs, accusing them of atrocities that their opponents committed equally. As the media went, so did much of public opinion from President Bill Clinton and his secretary of state, Madeleine Albright, on down. Yet the Serbs themselves never understood why they were being singled out.[41] All they were doing was trying to hold the country together as best they could; furthermore, had not their enemies, both Croats and Muslims, cooperated with Germany in World War II?

In an attempt to justify the role they played, some members of the media claimed that, by their presence, they helped document atrocities and perhaps prevent a few of them. This may be true, but it is also true that all the warring sides were quite prepared to harness the media by staging incidents for their own benefit. For example, Bosnian Muslim militias sometimes refused to allow the United Nations to evacuate their civilian co-religionists from battle zones, only to turn around and blame the Serbs for the plight of those very civilians.[42] By some accounts there

The wild horde has been here; refugees in Bosnia.   CORBIS

were even occasions when Muslim forces, with the same objective in
mind, opened fire on their own citizens.[43]

The first United Nations Protection Force (UNPROFOR) units were
introduced into the country in August 1992 and numbered fifteen hundred men. Later they were progressively reinforced until, two and a half
years later, their strength reached twenty-three thousand. Since the intention was merely to "ameliorate" the situation, however, at no time did
they operate as a single body. Instead, being scattered in small groups all
over Bosnia-Herzegovina, all they could do was help carve the country
into smaller and smaller, but less and less coherent, enclaves. Their commanders desperately tried to understand what was going on, designated
"safe zones," escorted convoys to beleaguered towns, and negotiated
cease-fires. However, the fact that those commanders had to be in constant touch both with UN headquarters in Zagreb and with the various
TCNs (troop-contributing nations) did nothing to help.

Among the TCNs, not a single one had any intention of committing
its troops to battle or indeed putting them at risk in any way; this attitude
was carried to the point where UNPROFOR commanders who did open
fire, even in self-defense, were reprimanded.[44] Deliberately or by accident, very often the peacekeepers found themselves interposed between

the warring militias. As a result, much of the time they were both vulnerable and ineffective: vulnerable to potshots taken at them, to kidnapping (some troops of the Dutch contingent were tied to Serb guns, acting as human shields), and to having their communications cut; ineffective in accomplishing their mission and putting an end to the hostilities or even considerably reducing their intensity.

Separated from each other, the various Yugoslav militias found that they could not conquer territory—between the end of 1994 and the middle of 1995 the front lines hardly moved.[45] But they were still able to fire at each other to their hearts' content, an opportunity they began to use as soon as spring arrived. As even one of its own commanders admitted, for much of the time UNPROFOR may have been part of the problem, not the solution. Arguably the force's main contribution was to increase the already tremendous chaos by making it even harder for the warring parties to adopt a cohesive strategy and focus their efforts. It prevented victory from going to one side or another, and probably prolonged hostilities beyond what might otherwise have been the case.[46]

As if to confirm all of this, following years of confusion and rivers of blood, the commander of UNPROFOR finally reached a decision (or rather, had one forced on him by his superiors in London, who intended to withdraw a battalion of troops without planning to replace them). Acting in secret, he evacuated the area around Sarajevo, thus making sure that the Serbs would not again take his men hostage as they had done on previous occasions. The outcome, which appears to have been entirely unexpected, was to give NATO freedom of action to use its airpower against the Serbs. A few days' bombardment, to which the Serbs were unable to respond, did the job.

Even so, the effects should not be exaggerated. First, in terms of equipment destroyed, and even more so personnel killed or injured, General Mladić's losses were moderate. For example, out of an estimated seven hundred artillery tubes, just seven were destroyed.[47] As so often happens, a number of precision-guided bombs missed their targets and hit civilians instead; though the Serbs cried foul, nobody listened. Second, the attack only hit the Serb forces deployed around Sarajevo. The rest, busy laying siege to various other Muslim-held enclaves, remained unaffected. By that time, though, the Serbs had become thoroughly demoralized by their own activities. These were made necessary in part by the fact that Belgrade, in an effort to end the UN-imposed sanctions, had ceased to support them or pay for their upkeep. As a result, a single hard kick sufficed to make the men melt away and the remaining leaders negotiate.

One of the commentaries on Sun Tzu's *The Art of War* speaks of "mad bandits," an apt expression.[48] Either because they lack a common culture or because they have discarded it, wild hordes respect neither heavenly commands nor human ones. They understand neither themselves nor the enemy. As a result, they are hardly able to take organized action on any scale. Though luck may favor them on this occasion or that, in the long run they cannot win; in one sense, indeed, the term *winning,* when applied to them, loses its meaning. Having gained a victory, they are rarely able to follow up. Having suffered a defeat, they tend to become demoralized and disintegrate. Perhaps the best they can hope for is the kind of confused stalemate that prevailed after Poitiers and in Bosnia, given that it extends their life and allows them freedom of action they otherwise would not have possessed. Working themselves into a blind fury, often they do not distinguish between friend and foe. This in turn may mean that they lash out so brutally and so indiscriminately as to create even more enemies than they already have. Wherever they turn, they spread first fear and then hatred.

Lawless, disorganized, and universally hated, wild hordes cannot trust anybody or make anybody trust them. The one way they can hold on to anything is by utterly destroying it. However, the destruction they wreak is in many cases counterproductive, given that the dead are useless to the living and that a ruined country cannot sustain human life. They tend to be extremely wasteful of resources, both their own and those they may have taken from the enemy. Either they neglect to husband those resources or they willfully destroy them; when some of the English commanders turned to banditry and ravaged the French countryside after Poitiers, what did their activities benefit their king? All this may explain Clausewitz's contemptuous dismissal of such troops when he recommends that they be stationed only "in prosperous areas where they can enjoy themselves."[49] In war, however, they tend to be more or less useless, as great a menace to their commanders and to themselves as to their enemy.

18

The Soulless Machine

A soulless machine may be the product of two opposed sets of circumstances. In most cases, it is a question of the culture of war developing to the point where it takes over from war itself. Applied mindlessly and mechanically, instead of helping make the forces disciplined, cohesive, and effective, it turns counterproductive and contributes to their defeat; this is especially likely to happen during the period that follows upon a great victory. It is, however, also possible to find some cases when, for one reason or another, an existing culture of war is deliberately set upon, pulled down, and so thoroughly demolished that, for good or ill, it may *never* rise again. While focusing on Germany, the present chapter will provide one example each of these two possibilities.

The Prussian army was established by the Great Elector, Frederick William (reigned 1640–88), who was the first to make it into a recognizable factor in European power politics. Next, it was almost literally kicked and beaten into shape by the Elector's grandson, Frederick William I (reigned 1713–40). However, the "soldier king" much preferred the culture of war to war itself. Throughout his life, he wore a uniform; as legend has it, when lying on his deathbed he vowed to keep it on even when he would go to meet his maker in heaven. Here on earth, the king's most famous creation was the regiment of *lange Kerle*, or tall grenadiers; in an age when people on the average were smaller than now, they had to be at least six-foot-four to join. He had painters produce portraits of his favorite soldiers, using them to decorate the rooms of his palaces. As the Austrian ambassador to his court noted, so much did he cherish them that there was something childish about it.[1]

Frederick William's heir, Frederick the Great, was a completely different character. He discarded some of his father's more flamboyant forms of martial display, including both the grenadiers and a troop of cuirassiers so proportioned as to deserve the appellation "giants riding elephants."[2] At the same time he built up the Prussian army until it became one of the most formidable military organizations of all time. Over a period of twenty-two years, from 1741 to 1763, he used it in a series of ferocious wars against all the European great powers in turn. The wars enabled him to double Prussia's territory as well as its population, but they left the country almost in ruins.

During Frederick's last twenty-three years—he died in 1786—the army he had commanded so successfully started going downhill. In Prussia, as in other eighteenth-century countries, the educated middle classes were not required to serve. Now, however, in an effort to get the economy back on its feet, a growing number of country dwellers—the famous *Kantonisten*, after the mobilization districts from which they were drawn—were also exempted from conscription so that they could continue to work in agriculture. To fill the ranks of a force that continued to expand, foreigners were enlisted until, by the time of Frederick's death, they outnumbered natives two to one.[3] Yet the Prussian state was notoriously parsimonious, with the result that the men were of low quality and deserted at the first opportunity. To compensate for their shortcomings, very great emphasis was put on the culture of war until it was driven to almost insane lengths, including, notoriously, the use of the whip.

In part, it was the king's own fault. He had always been a cynic; now, prematurely old and exhausted, increasingly he came to prefer form over substance. Under him, the man most responsible for the new trend was Lieutenant General Friedrich Christoph von Saldern. Born in 1719, originally he had been a capable commander who proved his strong nerves, as well as his excellence in moving troops quickly and precisely, in the murderous battles of Hochkirch, Liegnitz, and Torgau. His physical appearance was striking: "a picture of the God of War, tall [in his time he had been one of the *lange Kerle*], very well formed, fully of majesty and dignity" was the description one contemporary left of him.[4] He was also a man of some integrity, having at one time refused Frederick's order to destroy a hunting lodge that belonged to one of the king's Saxon enemies, and fallen into temporary disfavor as a result. In 1763 Frederick made him army inspector in Magdeburg, a post he retained until 1785. In this capacity he was able to convince his fellow generals, all of whom were veterans of the Seven Years' War like himself, that the essence of military training, indeed the whole of military life, consisted of regularity in carrying out tactical evolutions.

At this time, the king's reputation was already beginning to assume legendary proportions; to some extent, he seems to have fallen in love with his own system. Year after year he came to observe the maneuvers. Year after year he was intrigued as von Saldern, commanding from the tower that overlooked the town's market square and making full use of his stentorian voice, had the troops go through an ever more complicated series of evolutions. Many were especially devised for the king's benefit; the most spectacular, if not the most useful, movement of all was turning a battalion on its own axis, like a top. Georg von Berenhorst, a former Prussian staff officer who had turned into a well-known military writer, has left us a description of what it looked like: "A battalion of 200 or 250 files makes a fine impression as it advances on a broad front towards the dilettanti who are standing directly in front. The soldiers' legs, with their elegant gaiters and close-fitting breeches, work back and forth like the warp on a weaver's frame, while the sun is reflected blindingly back from the polished muskets and the whitened leatherwork. In a few minutes the moving wall is upon you."[5]

For this kind of perfection to be achieved, uniforms had been made so tight-fitting that simply putting them on required a great deal of work. More seriously, every cog in a machine made up of thousands upon thousands of human components had to function very precisely and without fail. A commander who succeeded in this task could win great acclaim, Prussia's highest medal, the Pour le mérite, included. A single error, though, and the king's wrath would put an end to an officer's career: generals were jailed, colonels cashiered in front of their troops, cavalry officers transferred to the less prestigious infantry. To prevent their menfolk from falling victim to such a catastrophe, wives, mothers, children, and other relatives would address their prayers to heaven. With the men drilled for weeks ahead of time, heavily punished if so much as a button was missing from its proper place, it is no wonder they turned out robot-like.[6]

The reviews may have helped cement the ties between the king and his army. Frederick himself is said to have remarked that the most surprising thing about them was not the regularity with which they were carried out but rather that in the face of tens of thousands of heavily armed men, he and his entourage were able to stand and watch in perfect safety. However, the extent to which the culture of war had taken over from war itself is nicely illustrated by two contemporary stories. One had von Saldern earnestly debating the pros and cons of increasing the regulation marching speed of seventy-five paces a minute to seventy-six; according to the other, when he went to heaven and explained his system of maneuvers to Gustavus Adolphus, the king answered that he was not aware that in the years since his death the earth had been made flat.[7] Briefly, a thousand details—"pedantries" as Field Marshal Gebhard von Blücher was to call them later on—that had originally served a useful purpose now became detached from reality, so to speak. They continued to float about solely as parts of a highly developed culture, one that no longer made sense in any terms except its own.

Following Frederick's death the situation deteriorated still further. The king's successor was his nephew, Frederick William II. Nicknamed the "fat giant," he neither had much personal experience of war nor any interest in it. An amiable man, his main concern was the endless string of mistresses he maintained. In 1788, his commanders attempted to modernize the army by issuing new regulations for the light infantry. Even then, however, most of the text continued to focus on close-order drill: dress ranks, forward march, so and so many steps a minute, right turn, left turn, and so on. As a result, the training of the light infantry differed little, if at all, from that of the rest.[8]

Attracted by the reputation left behind by Frederick the Great, foreigners flocked to watch the parades, hoping to glean from them something that might prove useful. One of the more knowledgeable was General Charles Cornwallis, the former commander of the British forces in North America who, unfortunately for him, had acquired firsthand experience of the most recent forms of warfare. He was not impressed by what he saw. Two long lines of soldiers, dressed in all their finery and precisely arrayed with the aid of stakes and ropes, were positioned on a field and marched toward one another. Coming within six yards, they halted and opened fire, keeping at it until the last training cartridge had been spent. So ridiculous were the maneuvers, Cornwallis later wrote, that the worst general in England would be hooted for practicing them; as we shall see in a moment, though, this was just how the Prussian troops fought in the Battle of Jena.[9]

Another visitor was Louis-Alexandre Berthier, Napoleon's chief of staff. In the early summer of 1806 he went to Magdeburg to observe the maneuvers held by the Duke of Brunswick. Like everybody else, he noted the perfect order with which the troops went through their evolutions. However, instead of firing their weapons they used wooden clappers to simulate the noise of shots; such troops could scarcely present a danger to the experienced French army. What Berthier could not know was that at exactly this time, the commander of the Potsdam regiment was telling Berlin that his muskets had become so worn with endless cleaning and polishing that they could no longer be used to fire live ammunition; yet other Prussian officers were claiming that the French evolutions did not match their own standards.[10] The state of the cavalry, which under Frederick had been regarded as Prussia's most formidable arm, was no better. When the time came, so accustomed had the troops become to operating in dense formation that it was impossible to make them go on patrol or conduct reconnaissance.

As the French Revolutionary and later the Napoleonic armies overran Europe, Prussia stayed on the margins. Its forces invaded France in 1792 but were repulsed by the famous cannonade at Valmy in September of that year. After that they took no further part in the wars. Instead, they turned into a military backwater where commanders, convinced of their own superiority, clung obstinately to tradition, including the obligation on all officers and men to follow the sovereign and wear ponytails. Particularly prominent was Ernst von Rüchel, von Saldern's disciple and a man of whom Clausewitz wrote that he looked and acted as the "concentrated essence" of Prussianism. On one occasion he claimed that the Prussian army had many Napoleons. On another he was present when the Berlin Military Society, whose founder was the future military reformer Gerhard von Scharnhorst, discussed the possibility that infantry officers, instead of merely riding with their units as the regulations required, should learn how to command them in battle. Whereupon this general, who was to play a critical role in the unfolding events, exclaimed: "A Prussian nobleman never walks!" What a change from the time when, at Torgau in 1760, Lieutenant General Johann von Hülsen, having had his horse shot out from under him and unable to mount another one owing to his injuries, had himself dragged to the front on top of a gun.[11]

By 1806, Prussia had signed an alliance with Russia and was preparing to fight Napoleonic France. The reigning monarch was Frederick William III. He had ascended the throne in 1797 and was to remain on it until 1840. As a boy, his tutor had been General von Scheelen, precisely one of those "demon drillmasters" who formed the backbone of the Prussian army. He himself was pious and well-intentioned but narrow-minded and shy, a man completely dominated by his beautiful young wife, Queen Louise. Napoleon, who spent quite some time dining with him in the summer of 1807, said of him that he was "good." However, he also found that the king would talk of little but "military headgear, buttons, and leather knapsacks"; other subjects, including military matters, were beyond his comprehension.[12] Out of 142 Prussian generals, 4 were over eighty years of age. Thirteen were over seventy-nine, and 62, Rüchel himself included, over sixty. Even among the regimental and battalion commanders 25 percent were over sixty.[13] Such men could be expected to safeguard old bottles but not to pour new wine into them.

The commander in chief was the abovementioned Duke of Brunswick. Forty years earlier Frederick II, one of whose principal lieutenants he had been in the Seven Years' War, had called him "my young hero." Tremendously brave, he ably commanded the Hanoverian army in northwestern Germany; his victory at the Battle of Krefeld (1758) made him famous throughout Europe. Now, however, he was seventy-one years old. A minor incident that took place on October 4, 1806, showed how attached to the culture of war, how hidebound, forty years of peace had left him. Frederick William had called a conference of his senior commanders at Erfurt. The palaver took longer than expected, and it was still not over at eleven o'clock, the appointed hour for changing the daily password. As officers started gathering outside, the king, noticing them through the window, gave Brunswick a new password to announce. The commander in chief emerged from the door and immediately noted a minor catastrophe: the NCO and four men who should have been present in order to prevent strangers from coming close and listening in were not standing at their appointed posts.

With the king watching, the old field marshal marched around, berating his subordinates but unsure what to do next. Somebody pointed out the possibility of using the two guards stationed at the entrance to the building, but this still left him two men and one NCO short of the required number. Luckily, help was at hand. A cart loaded with bread for a battalion of grenadiers rumbled by. The soldier riding in it provided the necessary NCO, but now a fresh disaster took place. The soldier did not carry a carbine as per the regulations; instead, he had tied it to the cart so as to keep his hands free! In the face of such a flagrant breach of discipline, what to do? If he employed the man to defend the password from prying ears, he would be flouting the regulations; if he punished the soldier as he deserved, the password could not be issued at all. Great consternation and helplessness reigned until the field marshal cut through the Gordian knot by issuing a special order. Only then could the new password be announced. "And that," commented a future general and minister of war, Hermann von Boyen, on whose eyewitness account these paragraphs are based, "was the man who was about to lead us against Napoleon."[14]

A few weeks later, at the double Battle of Jena-Auerstadt on October 14, 1806, Nemesis arrived. This is not the place to analyze the strategic plans of both sides or describe the divisions that existed inside the Prussian high command. Nor do I want to dwell on the immense gulf that separated officers, who were privileged to wear the king's coat, from the downtrodden rank and file, most of whom were still serfs, little more than human cattle without civic rights of any kind, brought to the battlefield by the lash and kept there by their NCOs' demi-pikes. This is the factor to which most historians, especially nonmilitary ones who want to show how "feudal" and "absolutist" Prussia still was, have attributed the defeat; why should such soldiers fight? Yet while it is true that armies reflect the civilian society of which they are a part, it is also true that any army is a separate organization held together by bonds, which we have called the culture of war, that civilian society shares, if at all, only to a limited extent.

A closer look at what actually happened on the field reveals a picture that is rather different from the accepted one. The Prussian army that went to war against Napoleon numbered little short of 200,000 men. It also numbered 7,000 officers, a proportion not at all unusual for the armies of the period. Of those officers, though, only 190—just over 2½ percent—were killed.[15] The total number of Prussians who lost their lives in the double battle is estimated at some 10,000; in other words, proportionally far fewer of Frederick William's officers died for their country than did those in the rank and file. Yet these were highly privileged, handpicked men, bred and raised for and in the service, sworn on their honor to defend their sovereign, and steeped in a culture that, as Rüchel's remark illustrates, was carried to the point where it had become counterproductive.

The behavior of the rank and file was entirely different. At Jena, the most important single Prussian body consisted of twenty thousand infantrymen under the Prince of Hohenlohe-Ingelfingen. For hours on end they stood in line, three deep, near the village of Vierzehnheiligen at the center of the front. Mechanically, they loaded, rammed the bullets down the barrels, primed, aimed, fired their muskets, and poured volley after volley into—what? Opposing the Prussians were French *tirailleurs,* or skirmishers, who had taken cover among the buildings of the village itself. Behind the Prussians, Rüchel, with fifteen thousand men, was coming to their aid, but for some reason he took four hours to cover six miles. Isolated from the rest of the army, coming under murderous fire directed at them by enemies they could not see, blanketed by the white smoke rising from their own weapons, gradually covered with soot, their bravery (or perhaps it was merely unthinking stolidity) was amazing; probably no other men in the world could have done half as much. Even as most of their comrades lay on the ground dead or dying, clumps of soldiers still went on with their routine.[16]

Had the outcome of the battle been determined by the resentment felt by the common man against the sociopolitical conditions of the Prussian state and his refusal to fight on its behalf, then the rank and file should have fled while the officers held their ground. What happened, however, was just the opposite. A culture of war developed from about 1700 on and was forged in the deadly struggles of the Prussian state against its enemies. Crowned with success, naturally it was turned into the country's outstanding symbol of power. As such, it was applied mechanically and relentlessly for another forty years until it became second nature. The effect on the officers was to make them conceited, timid, and unwilling and unable to think. Any attempt to tamper with existing forms was prohibited, any sort of enthusiasm discouraged.[17] The effect on the men was to make them do just what they had been drilled to do, even under the most difficult circumstances, even though what they were doing was entirely senseless, and even though, as the figures show, few of their commanders were there to hold them in line. When the casualties became intolerable, the army, and the culture that held it together, collapsed like a house of cards.

As everything they had cultivated for decades on end proved to be useless, the forces disintegrated very quickly. Having performed prodigies of valor but finally unable to hold on, the remnants of Hohenlohe's infantrymen fled. As they did so, they collided with Rüchel's troops, who, moving with the usual steadiness on the parade ground, were just then coming up from the rear. The result was the most indescribable chaos; the German term *versprengte,* meaning "leaderless troops who have been blown apart," is said to have originated in this episode.[18] Weeks, even months were to pass before order was restored. Meanwhile, in the words of one of Napoleon's marshals, Jean Lannes, "the Prussian Army is so terrified that it lays down its arms whenever even a single Frenchman makes his appearance."[19] The emperor was no less derogatory. In the twenty-second bulletin of the Grande Armée he rhapsodized: "The Prussian Army has vanished like autumn mist in front of the rising sun."[20]

Reality lived up to this description. Previously even the critical Scharnhorst had thought the bonds that held the army together would survive a defeat, perhaps even more than one defeat; "our honor," he wrote, "as well as mutual trust, will remain intact."[21] Nothing could have been further from the truth. Entire units, including many that had never fired a shot, fled as if they had been pursued by the devil, or else they fell over each other in their haste to give themselves up. Take Hohenlohe, who had commanded the Prussian center. Though defeated and obliged to retreat, he still commanded a strong force of over ten thousand men. He also had with him sixty-four guns, twenty more than the number with which the French marshal Louis-Nicolas Davout had defeated a Prussian force twice as large as his own at Auerstadt, and thirty-nine more than those Napoleon himself had concentrated in order to form his "Grand Battery" at Jena.[22] Nevertheless, on October 28, having credulously accepted Marshal Joachim Murat's bluff that he was surrounded by a hundred thousand French troops, he laid down his arms. Informing his officers of the decision, he found that not one of them demurred; yet with proper leadership they ought to have been able to get away to Stettin.[23] Later not even the future victor of Waterloo, Blücher, was able to avoid capture.

Untouched by the battles of October 14 were the great Prussian fortresses at Erfurt, Magdeburg, Spandau, Stettin, and others farther east in Silesia and along the Oder. Many of them were better-provisioned and better-armed than the field army had been. Erfurt alone contained more than ten thousand men, albeit they were demoralized and disorganized; Magdeburg took in twenty-five thousand. Yet their governors, often elderly veterans of the Seven Years' War who had been given their posts so as to save on pensions, did not even try to make a stand. One fortress, Küstrin, fell when its commander, Colonel von Ingersleben, accepted a bribe. At one point, so many places opened their doors more or less simultaneously that Murat was hard-pressed to report their fall to his imperial brother-in-law. The governor of Berlin, the same who had issued the famous proclamation that the king had lost a battle and that it was the citizens' "first duty" to remain calm, fled. In the armory he left fifty thousand muskets—brand new, and technically somewhat superior to those used by the French. Later, Napoleon used them to equip the troops he raised in Poland.

Too soon, the French had reached as far east as the river Vistula. Once again, history does not quite support the idea that it was the alienation of the middle classes from the Prussian state that was responsible for the defeat. As he retreated, not to say fled, in front of the French, Captain August von Gneisenau, the future field marshal, found the population well disposed toward him and the handful of troops he had been able to rally. Wherever he went, they were willing to help, providing him with shelter, food, warm clothing, transportation, and information; had it not been for the assistance he got, he never would have been able to get away.[24] As had already been the case at Jena, the Prussian collapse proceeded from the officer corps down, not the other way around.

One evening, as the French approached the fortified town of Kolberg in Pomerania, the burghers tried to rouse the colonel commanding the garrison, only to be told that he had already gone to bed and could not be disturbed. On the next day, when the first cannonballs were fired, they learned that he wanted nothing more than to hoist the white flag as soon as he could. In the end, they had to prevent him at the point of a bayonet from doing so.[25] Not long after this, Gneisenau arrived, now carrying his new rank of major. Taking charge, he was able to hold on until peace was finally signed at Tilsit in June 1807. He was, however, entirely exceptional. In the weeks following Jena-Auerstadt, so many of Frederick William's officers gave themselves up that Napoleon, not knowing what to do with them, set most of them free on parole.

Writing not long before the war, the aforementioned Gerhard von Scharnhorst voiced his opinion that when it came to carrying out evolutions, the Prussian army had achieved "an excellence perhaps never to be surpassed." For that very reason, though, as soon as its officers reached the field, they had no clue as to what they were to do. In putting the "art of war" above the military virtues, the state was putting its existence in jeopardy. Writing not long after the debacle, his protégé Carl von Clausewitz agreed: endlessly drilled on the parade ground, the "spirit of the army" had become "completely unwarlike."[26]

On the other side of the hill, Napoleon, whose ability to arrange a show was not the least of his qualities as a commander, was well aware of the role that the culture of war had played in all this. First he had the monument to the great Prussian victory over the French at Rossbach in 1757 dismantled and transported to Paris, where it was re-erected not far from the Palais Royal.[27] He also took the trouble of traveling to the Garnisonkirche in Potsdam, where he paid a solemn visit to Frederick's tomb and took away the king's three-pointed hat and dagger. A magnificent victory parade through Berlin's Brandenburg Gate sealed the victory.

Like the phoenix, the Prussian army did not die but rose out of its crushing defeat. Taking the "wars of liberation" of 1813–15 as their starting point, but increasingly looking back to the great days of Frederick II as well, Prussian (later German) commanders during the nineteenth and twentieth centuries continued to cultivate the culture of war.[28] No army on earth took greater pride in its uniforms, trappings, flags, music, and parades. None held its past in higher regard or devised more elaborate ways of celebrating it; there was scarcely a public ceremony in which the military, often supported by the numerous veterans' organizations, did not take a prominent part.

Still, in many ways this was now a progressive force, not a reactionary one.[29] However powerful the emphasis put on symbolic values inherited from the past, never again was there any question of allowing tradition to smother the present to the extent that had been the case between 1763 and 1806. Partly sustained by their culture, the army, later the armed forces as a whole, were able to develop a singular combination of cohesion, strict discipline, high initiative, and the command system known as mission-type orders (*Auftragstaktik*).[30] These qualities in turn helped the forces win a series of signal victories in the Wars of Unification of 1864–71. Later they put on an outstanding, if ultimately unsuccessful, military performance in both world wars.

Inside Germany during the century and a half in question, some groups did what they could to rein in their country's culture of war, which they took for an instrument of reaction, feudalism, capitalism, imperialism, and so many other bad things that one loses count. Some, especially on the left, denounced it. Others, especially among the educated middle classes, ridiculed it.[31] However, there can be little question that the majority always admired it and supported it. Throughout the century and a half after 1813, it was always the army that acted as the "school of the nation," not the other way around. Even during the days of the Weimar Republic, when the Reichswehr was restricted to a hundred thousand men, the veterans' organizations numbered millions, thus helping preserve and spread the military tradition. Had it not been for the strong and widespread public support that the army and its culture received, then of course none of the abovementioned wars would have been conceivable.

Outside Germany, attitudes were even more divided. Some foreigners admired the magnificence of it all and tried to adapt it for use in their

own armed forces. This even applied to former enemies. In the years between the end of the Seven Years' War and the outbreak of the French
Revolution, "à la Prusse" became the model in places as far apart as Paris
and St. Petersburg. If Russia's Peter II did not fight Frederick II to the
end, this was in part because of his admiration for the Prussian army; if
his wife, later known as Catherine the Great, may be believed, he tried to
emulate that army with the aid of toy soldiers that he even took to bed
with him.[32] Something similar took place in the Anglo-Saxon world during
the last few decades before 1914, a time when few people in either
Britain or the United States, officers least of all, had any doubt that the
German army was the world's best and most powerful.[33] Not everybody,
though, was enchanted with the unfolding spectacle. There were always
those who shook their heads at the manifest spirit of "militarism." Either
they saw it as a leftover from pre-modern times, as Herbert Spencer did,
or else they perceived it as a danger to their own countries, in France in
particular.

As a result of World War I, and even more so after World War II, many
historians started blaming militarism for everything that had gone wrong
with Germany. First, the armed forces were made to shoulder part of the
blame for the fact that the country had taken so long to turn itself into a
democracy. Next, they were accused of failing to resist Hitler and for
making possible, if they did not help commit, some of the worst war
crimes and atrocities of all times.[34] Without question, there was a great
deal of truth in all this; still, there is no denying that, however terrible the
consequences, militarism helped account for the country's unquestioned
military effectiveness.[35] In a way, it did not matter. Whatever their position, both sides, each in its own way and for its own purposes, freely acknowledged the role played by the culture of war in constructing one of
the most formidable armed forces in the whole of history. As a practically
endless stream of publications and legions of collectors of militaria all
over the world prove, to this day it exerts a powerful—some would say
hideous—fascination.

As the German Democratic Republic and the German Federal
Republic started rebuilding their armed forces in the early 1950s, the
question of culture—in other words, what traditions they would cultivate
and how they would relate to their predecessors—had to be confronted.
The solutions adopted by the two states could not have been more different.[36] East of the Iron Curtain, the leaders of the GDR claimed to have
carried out a complete social, economic, and political revolution.

Supposedly they cut all links with the previous state and society, putting in their place one representing the very workers and peasants whom the Nazis, capitalist toadies that they were, had brutally suppressed. This break meant that they felt free to build up a new culture of war without worrying too much about accusations of "militarism." The way they saw it, their state, having shed its old class character and led by the Communist Party, could do no wrong. Neither, of course, could that state's armed forces.

The outcome was a paradox. The Nationale Volksarmee (NVA), or National People's Army, as it was called, regarded itself as the very opposite of the old Prussian-German militarism, not entirely without reason. After all, the "Junker caste," which for two and a half centuries had formed the backbone of that militarism, had been eliminated; those of its members who did not cooperate were physically liquidated. Partly for inner political reasons, partly because they always had their Soviet "friends" looking over their shoulders, NVA commanders also went much further than their Western counterparts in getting rid of old, allegedly unreliable former Wehrmacht personnel—even if, as often happened, doing so involved a loss of military efficiency.[37]

On the other hand, precisely because the forces' commanders and their political bosses claimed that they had discarded that legacy, they felt no compunction about taking up many of the trappings of that very militarism. That included very strict discipline imposed from the top down; the goose step; field-gray uniforms; insignia surprisingly similar to those Hitler's soldiers had worn; and even the jackboot. As early as 1956, all of these were rehabilitated. As the official decree put it, the government of the German Democratic Republic had successfully accomplished its self-imposed mission of purging the country's culture of war of its "reactionary" and "militarist" elements. As a result, that culture was once again fit for use by the armed forces.[38]

Trappings alone, however, do not a culture of war produce. An armed force with no tradition is like a person without a face; it does not know what it is, let alone what it stands for and is supposed to fight and die for. Marxism-Leninism had always had a strong historical orientation. Accordingly, before long the GDR leaders, as well as the NVA's own commanders, started scouring history for traditions they could adopt as their own so as to provide "exemplary role models" and develop the troops' "sense of honor."[39]

First and foremost was the shining Soviet example as set in 1919–20 and during the great anti-Fascist struggle of 1941–45.[40] While it is true that Prussians and Russians had cooperated in the war against Napoleon, this emphasis on "socialist internationalism" sometimes led to strange results. For example, Seelow, on the river Oder, saw the construction of a vast monument, accompanied by a museum, to commemorate the victory of the Red Army in its battles *against* the German Wehrmacht in April 1945—surely the only time in history a monument was built in a country to celebrate the defeat of that very same country.

Second only to the heroic Soviet liberators came "German revolutionaries" of various periods. Prominent among them were the leaders of the Peasants' Revolt of 1525; some of the less wealthy, less bourgeois leaders of the abortive revolution of 1848; the Spartacists, especially Karl Liebknecht and Rosa Luxemburg, who had tried to launch an equally abortive Communist coup in 1919; and the troops of the Ernst Thaelmann Battalion who had fought for the republic in Spain during the civil war there. Some, but by no means all, of the members of the group that tried to assassinate Hitler on July 20, 1944, were rehabilitated and joined the pantheon. So were a few "progressive" elements of the old Prussian army. For example, Scharnhorst was metamorphosed from the son of a former NCO in the army of Frederick the Great into a peasant's son (*Baurensohn*). Having had his record cleaned in this manner, in 1966 he enjoyed the honor of having the NVA's highest medal named after him; at a later point, he even had a television film made about his life and career.

In 1979, other heroes of the "wars of liberation" also had medals minted in their honor. The more time that passed, the more pronounced the tendency of the GDR, whose territory did after all include the core provinces of the old Prussian state, to adopt at least some of the traditions of that state as its own. Gradually figures such as Frederick William I and Frederick William II came to be seen in a different light; from feudal monarchs who had conspired with the nobility to exploit the peasants and the workers they were transformed into men who had served their country well.[41] In 1979, even the statue of Frederick II, the greatest "militarist" of them all, was rescued from oblivion and restored to its place on the Unter der Linden in Berlin, where it still remains.

Looking back over the forty-five-year history of the GDR, we can see how at first the state tried to make a complete break with Germany's traditional culture of war. Later, however, the process went into reverse gear—the more so because the GDR, like its neighbor to the west, always claimed to represent the entirety of the German nation. Slowly and hesitantly, the NVA tried to harness additional elements of German history to its cart, even if they were not strictly "proletarian" and "revolutionary," and even if they were not quite "internationalist." All this preoccupation with tradition was deliberately designed to promote the ideological "steeling" of GDR troops in preparation for the "socialist class struggle" to come.[42] As official propaganda had it, by taking up and developing these traditions, the NVA had made itself into the most worthy, most progressive armed force in German history, a sharp contrast to the Bundeswehr, which had never purged itself of its predecessors' sins.

But did the culture thus called into being truly take root, or was it just so much claptrap forced on the troops by power-hungry leaders who themselves did not believe a single word they said? In post-unification Germany, where almost everything East German is denounced and denigrated (often with very good reason), it is hard to get a reliable answer to this question. During the last two decades or so of its existence, the NVA was widely regarded as perhaps the most efficient non-Soviet armed force in the Warsaw Pact nations.[43] Publishing their memoirs, some of its former troops expressed considerable pride in their service; its representatives, acting as advisers, spread all over the Third World from East Africa to Cuba.[44] On the other hand, it was never tested in battle. Furthermore, the GDR was a totalitarian state where dissent and criticism were not permitted; in it, merely to cast doubt on the effectiveness of tradition was a punishable act. Perhaps the fact that in 1989 this state collapsed with hardly a single officer or soldier lifting a finger to save it speaks for itself.

While similar in the sense that an old culture of war had to be discarded and a new one created, in other ways the situation in the Federal Republic was entirely different. To be sure, the Western Allies made an attempt at "de-Nazification," having every German citizen fill in forms concerning his or her involvement with the regime and imposing some penalties on a minority of them. That apart, however, no far-reaching purge, no redistribution of property, no revolution, not even the kind of revolution that the Soviet Union forced on the Democratic Republic, took place on West German soil. Instead, guided by Chancellor Konrad Adenauer, a Catholic conservative, the West Germans went on to build up a constitutional, democratic, law-abiding state provided with powerful guarantees for human rights. Doing so, they came under constant scrutiny by their allies in NATO and, later, the European Union; those allies were always looking for signs of regression, as they still do.

Thus both internal considerations and external pressures dictated that when the Bundeswehr was established, it went far to reject the legacy of the past. Two ideas in particular were critical to the process. First there was the "citizen in uniform," a notion that had few precedents in the history of a country where the very term *militia* had long been prohibited and where soldiers had always been an instrument, first of the sovereign and then of the state. It meant that the army lost its special position in society, including of course the special status and the special privileges that its members had long enjoyed. The second innovation, "inner leadership" (*Führung*), was even more revolutionary. Here the objective was to put an end to the strict old top-down discipline that, during World War II, had provided countless soldiers with an excuse for participating in countless atrocities—including, by way of a minor footnote, the execution of more than fifteen thousand of their own comrades.[45]

The task of putting these concepts into practice proved very difficult. As West Germans started rebuilding their country after 1945, millions of them retreated into private life. Opposition to everything military was both widespread and very vehement. For many years the most popular slogan was "*Nie wieder Krieg*" (never again war); if in the years since Germany's reunification and the end of the Cold War that slogan is no longer heard as often as before, in large part this is because it is taken for granted.[46] Yet West Germans were not necessarily ready to make a complete break with the state's previous armed forces. After all, millions of their friends or relatives, or they themselves, had served in those forces; they would resist being criminalized merely for having done so.[47] As early as the late 1940s public opinion was rejecting both Allied and German attempts to put former officers on trial, and by the mid-1950s it largely succeeded in bringing those attempts to an end.

Caught between these pressures, the highly select group of defense officials and former officers, which from 1953 on started planning for the establishment of the Bundeswehr, had to tread very carefully indeed. On one hand, the members of the Amt Blank, as it was known, had to avoid any appearance of "militarism," which became, and has remained, one of the dirtiest words in the language. At the same time, they could not go very far in denouncing Germany's military past, specifically including its recent past. Finally, unlike the GDR, the Bundesrepublik very soon turned itself into a functioning democracy. Failure to take voters' wishes into account would readily be reflected in the opinion polls and in the vote counts.

The situation inside the Bundeswehr was equally complicated. Those who founded the force and commanded it during its first three decades or so were, without exception, former Wehrmacht personnel, including some ten thousand officers and thirty thousand NCOs. To be sure, they had been handpicked to guarantee that they were "unblemished"—*unbelastet,* as the saying went.[48] Still asking that they apply their expertise while at the same time requiring that they discard, even actively condemn, the culture in which many of them had served for years was perhaps more than human nature could bear. For example, should they or should they not be allowed to wear their wartime decorations? In principle, Wehrmacht decorations were no different from those of other armies. However, some of them had been awarded by Adolf Hitler personally, and every one of them was stamped with the swastika. The eventual compromise, permitting the medals to be worn without the swastika, satisfied nobody.

As on the east side of the intra-German border, the results were paradoxical. As far as external trappings went, the Bundeswehr resembled the Federal Republic as a whole in that it was much less "German" and much less "militarist" than its eastern counterpart. Field-gray uniforms and goose-stepping parades were done away with, and hopefully never to return. American-type combat boots and helmets, as well as the uniforms worn by the troops, made them look very different from any previous German armed force—a little less martial, perhaps, and not quite as sharp. Nowhere was the change more evident than in the dress uniforms officers wear. Breeches have been replaced by trousers, boots by parlor shoes, tunics by shirts with civilian-type ties and dinner jackets. Much of this seems designed to make commanders look as much like lackeys as possible. Some people, indeed, would argue that they *are* lackeys.[49]

Yet the Bundeswehr differed from the NVA in that it was not an ideologically committed force serving a revolutionary regime, but a supposedly apolitical organization on the Western model. Hence originally it did not go nearly as far as the NVA in banishing other remnants of Germany's military tradition. Instead, a line was drawn between a supposed minority of "bad" soldiers who had been Nazis and participated in atrocities and the great majority of "good" ones who had merely served their country. The former should be, and allegedly had been or would be, isolated, denounced, and even punished. The latter should be left alone. They might even deserve an honorable niche as soldiers who, however wicked the leadership under which they had fought and the cause for which they had fought, had done their duty in an "honorable" way.

As time went on, there was a growing tendency to include even the troops of the Waffen SS, an organization that the international military tribunal at Nuremberg had designated as "criminal," in the second category. How problematic all this was, and remains, was perhaps illustrated most dramatically in May 1985. As U.S. president Ronald Reagan prepared to visit Germany, he was invited by Chancellor Helmut Kohl to inspect the military cemetery at Bitburg, where thousands of former Wehrmacht troops are buried side by side with a few fallen Waffen SS members. Following extensive diplomatic negotiations, Reagan complied, but only after he and Kohl had paid a joint visit to the memorial to the victims of the Bergen-Belsen concentration camp, and only after he had delivered an emotional speech in memory of those victims.

From time to time some Bundeswehr personnel would overstep the limits of what was considered permissible—often, it must be said, without any intention of doing so. Each time, the alarm announcing the presence of "right-wing extremist" tendencies was sounded and a public scandal would ensue. This in turn would cause successive ministers of defense to issue new, more restrictive decrees on what was considered tradition-worthy and what was not. A few things, such as putting on display swastikas of any size, in any form, and for any purpose, have always remained *hors de loi.* The same applies to German martial music originating in the Third Reich. Inside Germany, disseminating it and playing it are strictly prohibited—which, of course, has given rise to a black market in tapes and CDs as well as any number of Internet sites.

Concerning other traditions, a lively debate has raged. Now it was permitted to honor former Wehrmacht generals by celebrating their birthdays, inviting them to speak, and so on; now doing so was prohibited under severe penalties. Now units, bases, casernes, and streets could be named after World War II heroes; now all those names were proscribed and assigned to oblivion. What made the situation even more confusing was that some of the things German law did not allow were considered permissible, even desirable, in other countries. For example, if one wishes to see Wehrmacht flags, standards, uniforms, and insignia as they really were, it is necessary to visit a museum located outside Germany's borders. And throughout the years 1975–85, the Pentagon often invited former Wehrmacht commanders to participate in war games so as to learn from their experience and put it to use.

Whenever a change was made, a lively debate would ensue. Socialists were constantly claiming that what was taking place reflected a feeling of nostalgia for, or even a return to, the bad old days. Confronting them, conservatives always argued that not everything in the past had been absolutely bad and that an army, if it was to be a fighting force and not just a bureaucratic machine, could not dispense with that past.[50] Whenever a left-wing government held office, as was the case from 1969 to 1982 and again from 1998 to 2006, it would ratchet up the list of prohibitions—as, for instance, Helmut Schmidt's minister of defense, Hans Apel, did. Whenever a right-wing government took over, as from 1982 to 1998 and from 2006 on, it could do little to change the situation for fear of being called Nazis both by its own people and by others.

Under such circumstances it is scant wonder that the "tradition-worthy" sections of history from which the Bundeswehr was allowed to draw its inspiration have tended to become progressively narrower. The process worked in several directions. First, the distinction between "good" and "bad" Wehrmacht generals was put aside, so anyone who had been a senior commander under Hitler was ostracized. Next, the process started moving down the military hierarchy. In the end, even figures such as Hans-Joachim Marseille, an ace fighter pilot who gave his life for his country in 1942 after having shot down more Allied aircraft than anyone else (and who, as a devoted Catholic, was anything but a supporter of National Socialism), were banned.

At first, only the years 1933–45 were exorcised. From 1968 on, however, there was a growing tendency to extend the shadows until they covered previous periods of German military history as well. Not only the Panzer leader Heinz Guderian, not only the desert fox Erwin Rommel, but Hans von Seeckt, Paul von Hindenburg, Erich Ludendorff, Alfred von Schlieffen, and Helmut von Moltke disappeared. From heroes who had served their country, they were turned into "militarist," "reactionary," and "imperialist" villains; in today's casernes, it is in vain that one looks for their names or their portraits. Moreover, the Federal Republic during most of its history has been vehemently anti-Communist and still retains this character to some extent. Hence it could not follow the GDR by taking up left-wing revolutionary traditions; in this respect, its situation was even worse than that of its sister on the other side of the border.

As of 2007, the results are there for anyone to see. The total number of men who went through the German armed forces in 1939–45 is estimated at almost eighteen million; how many more did so in the two centuries before World War II is impossible to say. Of these, the only ones whose deeds are still considered worthy of official recognition are those who tried to assassinate Hitler on July 20, 1944—a group that numbered a few hundred officers at the very most, and whose members were anything but representative of the forces as a whole. The situation is made doubly ironic by the fact that most of the officers in question were not liberal democrats, let alone politically correct left-wing pacifists. Instead, almost to a man, they were old-fashioned, dyed-in-the-wool Prussian-German nationalists.[51] Their objective was to save Germany as they understood it—meaning, essentially, a return to a pre-1914, even pre-1871, regime that would incorporate many authoritarian elements. Had General Ludwig Beck, Colonels Schenk von Stauffenberg and Henning von Tresckow, and their fellow conspirators been able to witness some of the uses to which their names are put today, no doubt they would have wished that they had never been born.

Service personnel taking military education courses in other countries will spend some of their time mulling over the things those countries stand for and they themselves are supposed to risk their lives for; not so Bundeswehr personnel, who are made to spend at least as much time discussing warnings concerning the awful things Germans did when they were still Nazis and which should never, ever, be repeated. Throughout the Bundeswehr's numerous installations, one will look in vain for any attempt to celebrate the periods in military history before 1813 (when "patriarchal feudalism," "militarism," "authoritarianism," and other "preindustrial values" allegedly reigned) and after 1815 (when those bad things not only reigned supreme but became increasingly mixed up with nationalism and National Socialism as well).[52] In comparison with similar institutions in other countries, German military academies, staff colleges, and other educational institutions have an empty, bare, functional, and soulless appearance. The relics of the "wars of liberation" apart, almost the only items on display pertain to the Bundeswehr's own history. However, since the Bundeswehr has never gone to war, the ability of those items to excite and inspire is limited. It is not colored pieces of metal, wood, and cloth that count but the deeds they represent. The Bundeswehr in 2003 was able to earn some praise by helping build dikes along the Elbe; however, as a basis for military tradition, this is clearly insufficient.

Yet even as the list of those whom Bundeswehr personnel are allowed to remember is being progressively cut, more than a few Germans feel that the purge has still not been carried sufficiently far. Take the case of Ralph Giordano. The son of an Italian father and a German Jewish mother, Giordano spent World War II in Hamburg trying to prevent the Gestapo from catching up with him; later he became a well-known journalist. As he wrote in 2000, to him and his family the Wehrmacht was the enemy. Every victory it won was a disaster, every defeat it suffered a blessing that brought deliverance that much closer. In his view, an armed force whose operations permitted genocide to take place does not have, cannot have, anything that is worth preserving for the present; nor did any of its predecessors during at least the previous 130 years. Yet Giordano is but one prominent voice in a chorus made up of left-wingers. Had they had their way, the Bundeswehr would have called its bases exclusively after figures such as Otto Bruser, a seventeen-year-old Jehovah's witness who in the spring of 1944 refused to enlist and subsequently was put on trial, convicted, and executed.[53]

THE **Goose Step** IS **Verboten**

The German Army Today

Eric Waldman

Fp   *The Free Press of Glencoe*

The soulless machine; title page of a book about the German Bundeswehr
FROM *THE GOOSE STEP IS VERBOTEN*

Given the terrible historical background, all this is perfectly understandable. On the other hand, it is indisputable that an armed force, if its members are to fight and die for their country, must have a culture of war—and also that the examples on which that culture draws cannot be of the kind that Giordano and many others inside and outside Germany regard as the only suitable ones. Contrary to what one might expect, the fact that over sixty years have passed since 1945 does not make things any easier. Partly because practically all those involved are now dead, partly because the end of the Cold War has in some ways pulled the rug out from under the Bundeswehr's feet, in many ways the more time that passes, the more thorough the soul-searching that has been going on. Both inside and outside Germany, many would consider the constant confrontation—*Bewältigung*, "overcoming," as it is called—with the past to speak in the country's favor. For the Bundeswehr, however, it has made things very difficult indeed.

Though "inner leadership" has become the subject of a vast litera-

ture, nobody knows what it stands for. Merely to understand the code of
military justice, with its countless paragraphs, reservations, and qualifi-
cations, requires a legal genius. In too many cases the system, such as it
is, has led to lax discipline; in others it has degenerated into the so-called
eleventh commandment, "Be nice to each other." The idea of the "citizen
in uniform," too, has led to some remarkable results. Conscripts, most of
them originating in the lower social classes (the sons of the higher ones
are much more likely to opt for civilian service instead), look and behave
as if they had caught a bad number in a lottery. Professionals, officers
above all, regard themselves as little but uniformed state employees who
happen to wear a funny sort of clothes to work and whose specialty—
more in theory than in fact—is the use of violence on behalf of the state.[54]
One does not have to be a "militarist" or a right-wing extremist to note
the peculiar smell that prevails throughout the Bundeswehr. That smell is
made up of impersonal bureaucratic procedures, political correctness,
and the obsequiousness that results when people worry lest speaking up
will lead to bad consequences.

Representatives of the right lament the situation, claiming that this is
no way to build a fighting force and that if Germany ever again goes to war
the consequences could be dire. Many representatives of the left also
lament it, either because they feel that Germany's culture of war still carries too many relics of the past or because they object to any culture of the
kind and would like to see it abolished altogether—"an army without
pathos," as the forces' founding fathers put it. Meanwhile, the Bundeswehr,
though many of its personnel are as able and as willing as soldiers anywhere else, is caught in the middle. Much of what other armed forces, its
own allies included, take for granted is prohibited to it; it is damned if it
does and damned if it does not. As far as active soldiers are concerned,
merely to mention that the problem exists may lead to instant dismissal. A
former inspector-general, who after his retirement enjoys greater freedom
than the rest, put it very well: "We are a broken nation."[55] How much time
must pass until the situation changes, and what the consequences for
Germany and the world may be if it does change, remains to be seen.

19

Men Without Chests

"Men without chests" are men who, not having a culture of war and perhaps even looking down on the very idea, refuse to stand up and defend themselves almost regardless of the provocation to which they are subjected. As long as peace prevails, they do their best to look away. When war gets under way, instead of arming themselves and fighting, they either hide, run, or pray. For our purpose, the sequence of cause and consequence is immaterial. In other words, it does not matter whether the neglect of the culture of war leads to the failure of the will to fight or the other way around. Nor, since the readiness to fight and the culture in which it is partly rooted are mainly mental phenomena, does it matter whether it is perceived or real.

As one might expect, men without chests are not the product of a single society. They may be found at all times and places—but especially in societies that have enjoyed the blessings of peace for very long. Here is Priam, king of Troy, giving some of them a piece of his mind: "Worthless children, shameful creatures! If only all of you had been killed together, instead of Hector . . . I begat the best sons in Troy, and I tell you not one of them is left . . . But these shameful ones are still here, these boasters and dancers, the best men of the dance-floor, robbers of sheep and goats among their own people!"[1] Or take the Chinese idea of *wen,* best understood as "cultural attainment." It has no use for physical strength, speed, and endurance. Instead it makes scholars civilized, gentle, refined, humane, soft-spoken, bashful, and often possessed of a feminine body as well; lack of exercise and a sedentary lifestyle do not normally for a war-like nature make.[2] In all this it is the opposite of *wu,* or martial virtue.

Perhaps the best single example of a people without chests are the Diaspora Jews—though some would say that modern Europeans, refusing to confront the growing Muslim threat in their own countries and abroad, are moving in the same direction.[3] As many parts of the Old Testament bear witness, originally the Israelites who left Egypt, crossed the Sinai, conquered the land of Canaan, and went on to found the Kingdom of David were as warlike as any other contemporary people and developed a culture to match.[4] The tradition was continued through late Hellenistic times, when a Jewish state ruled by the Hasmoneans was able to maintain an independent existence over a century or so, and when Jews were apparently employed as mercenaries by the kings of Egypt. It had its last great revival in the vast rebellions against Rome that swept over Judea in A.D. 66–70 and 132–35. A few traces of it can still be found in the Talmud, which was written in the two and a half centuries after those events, and which expresses some pride in the second of these episodes in particular.[5]

As the armies of the emperors Vespasian, Titus, and Hadrian put down the rebellious Jews, the country was devastated. Hundreds of thousands lost their lives or were captured and enslaved; the rest, inspired by a famous rabbi named Yochanan Ben Zakai (ca. A.D. 1–80), went on to build up an entirely new kind of Jewish culture. In it, the national identity was based almost exclusively on religious worship and scholarship, and neither war nor its culture was allowed to play any part. The same was even more true of the growing majority of the Jewish people who were driven into exile or, seeking a better life, went there of their own free will. Widely dispersed, living on foreign soil, without a polity of their own, often barely tolerated, and always almost completely defenseless in the face of their more numerous neighbors, it is hardly surprising that they quickly lost touch with their warlike past.

As the centuries progressed, things went much further still. It appears that some Jews continued to serve in the Roman army, only to be expelled from it by the Christian emperor Theodosius II, who issued a series of laws against them in A.D. 410–39.[6] Later, Jews were entirely absent from the medieval heroic tradition, be it *Beowulf,* the *Chanson de Roland,* the Arthurian legends, the Scandinavian sagas, or the *Nibelungenlied.* As one mid-twentieth-century song jokingly put it, being a knight and slaying dragons was no job for a fellow called Gruenbaum. On rare occasions, individual Jews might join armies belonging to the rulers of the countries in which they lived and participate in war. In that case, however, the question always remained what they should do if they encountered each other in the field. Should they put the service allegiance that separated them ahead of their religious bonds, or the other way around?

Moreover, keeping up the Jewish way of life while on campaign could be very difficult, as it consisted of hundreds upon hundreds of commandments, such as gathering the ten men needed to pray to the Lord (*minyan*), observing the Sabbath, eating kosher food, consuming alcoholic drinks, finding a Jewish bride, and even obtaining the kind of burial that would lead to resurrection on the Day of Judgment. Hence, the few Jews who served—including, apparently, a few convicted Marranos in seventeenth-century Peru who, instead of being executed in an auto-da-fé, were sentenced to the galleys—always stood in danger of losing touch with their own people.[7] This was what often happened to the youngsters from the Pale of Settlement forcibly enlisted in the army of the Russian tsar during the first half of the nineteenth century.[8]

Some popular religious festivals, notably Hanukkah, which was celebrated in memory of the Hasmoneans and their uprising against King Antiochus of Syria in 168 B.C., still preserved some traces of martial pride, but most did not. Jewish leaders involved in foreign affairs focused on placating Gentile rulers, often with the aid of bribes. Meanwhile, the rabbis drew further and further away from any involvement with war and its culture. The process whereby the quill took the place of the sword was carried to the point where passages in the Old Testament were reinterpreted to remove any reference to military affairs. For example, the book of 2 Samuel presents King David as a conquering hero. Along with his army, he went on countless campaigns against every neighboring people in turn until his rule extended from Damascus all the way to the Red Sea. Yet medieval sources put an allegorical gloss on the story, turning him into a rabbi who taught his yeshiva students how to worship the Lord.[9]

None of this is to deny that surviving in the Diaspora often required enormous courage. However, it was the courage not of the warrior, with which we are concerned throughout this volume, but that of the victim and the refugee. The former centers on honor, pride, and the determination to sell one's life dearly if necessary, emotions that are inconceivable without a well-developed culture of war. The latter, by contrast, rests on evading, hiding, and turning the other cheek in a desperate attempt to survive at almost any cost save surrendering one's religious adherence. In time the belief that Jews, lacking a martial tradition, were cowards born and bred who could not, would not, stand up for themselves even when pressed became well-nigh universal. So much so, in fact, that it would be hard to say who was more strongly attached to the stereotype, anti-Semitic Gentiles or the Jews themselves.

To the Enlightenment, with its strong anti-religious bent and emphasis on toleration, Jews were no longer simply the devilish enemies of God they had been for centuries on end. Instead, though their basic humanity was granted, they became a blot on the landscape, a glaring eyesore whose very presence put in question the anticipated progress of man toward equality and perfection.[10] Hence the rise of the idea, during the last years before 1789, that they should be freed from discrimination and educated. Having once overcome their "clannish religious opinions," they would cease to be Jews and become citizens instead.[11] However, the relevance of this to our theme is limited. Many representatives of the Enlightenment set themselves up against existing states, specifically including the allegedly often foolish and often unnecessary wars that those states waged among themselves. The emphasis was on creating human beings, not soldiers. To most of those who wished to emancipate the Jews, doing so meant infusing them with culture in general, rather than instilling them with the culture of war.

This kind of reasoning did not survive the dawning of the nationalist age. Increasingly as the nineteenth century progressed, the equality and perfectibility of all men were replaced by the perfectibility of each nation separately and its claim to superiority over all the rest. Furthermore, the Enlightenment had put its faith in timeless, universal reason. By contrast, the nineteenth century, and its last two-thirds in particular, was the age of historically based ideologies. Wherever one looked, states and nations, attempting to establish their own unique origins and nature, were busily manufacturing histories for themselves. Wars, campaigns, battles, commanders, soldiers, and heroic deeds figured very prominently in those histories. Sometimes this was taken to the point where these elements of war almost supplanted everything else; decades of scholarship went into rediscovering and refurbishing them. At the same time they were pressed into the service of patriots bent on maintaining their countries' power and increasing it if possible.

Against this background, the Jews were like a flag on a windless day.

While others had fought and bled, they had been confined to the over-crowded, filthy ghettos. Hardly ever had they taken part in the armed struggles for independence and territorial expansion, real or imaginary, that were now being elevated to the essence of each nation's history; in Austria, for example, the prohibition on Jewish soldiers was lifted only in 1788. Even after the emancipation had begun, the legacy of centuries of seclusion, voluntary or other, prevented them from breathing free and spreading out. They remained an almost exclusively urban population, af-flicted with all the diseases that such a population suffered. Supposedly this gave them furtive movements—later, the Nazis were to compare them with rats. They also were alleged to have flat feet, huge noses, squinting eyes, crooked backs, and sunken (the Nazis said apelike) chests.

Jews were said to possess rounded, effeminate bodies. They could neither stand up straight, stride proudly, talk clearly, nor look people in the face, let alone endure the physical exertion and deprivation that wag-ing war requires. Unruly and unable to either obey or command, they could not even cooperate with one another to form an army, engage in training, and take unified action. To cap it all, Jews, although well known for trading in horses, were unable to ride those indispensable instru-ments and symbols of war; so unwarlike was their nature that they had to be saved from their enemies by their dangerously scheming, if darkly at-tractive, women.[12] On occasion these images were projected far back in time so as to cover not just contemporary Jews but their biblical ances-tors as well—as, for example, in *Judith,* a play by the famous Austrian author Johann Nestroy (1801–62).

Still, both during the Enlightenment and in the first half of the nine-teenth century the "Jewish problem" was thought to be religious, eco-nomic, and political. To be sure, the qualities attributed to Jews were unpleasant enough. However, it was supposed that they originated in their owners' false education and the difficult conditions under which they lived, not in what would nowadays be called "genes" and what people at that time used to call "blood." Drag them out of their backwardness—even by discriminating against them, if necessary—and those qualities and the Jews themselves would ultimately disappear. Throughout the hundred years from 1780 to 1880, the objective was to acculturate and assimilate (first into humanity, then into each nation separately), not to segregate and ultimately destroy. This was true even of famous anti-Semites such as the writer Paul de Lagarde and the historian Heinrich von Treitschke.[13]

As racist thought began to take hold during the second half of the nineteenth century, the situation changed. Perhaps the best-known representative of the new form of anti-Semitism was Houston Stewart Chamberlain (1855–1927). An Englishman born and bred, Chamberlain turned his back on his own country, which he accused of being sunk in materialism and commercialism. Instead he became an admirer of Germany and of Wagner, and ended up marrying the latter's only daughter. In 1899 he published *The Foundations of the Nineteenth Century,* a wide-ranging, pseudo-scholarly treatise that was to become the bible of at least two generations of anti-Semites.

The way Chamberlain reconstructed history, the best Israelites had not really been Israelites at all. For example, Moses was "probably a perfect Egyptian." King David, of whom the bible says that he had "red" (blond, Chamberlain claimed) hair and "beautiful eyes," was an "Amorite."[14] This, however, was by no means the whole of the picture. Originally the Israelites, miserable creatures though they were, comprised two separate if closely related peoples, the Josephites (whose principal tribes were those of Ephraim and Manasseh) and the sons of Judah. Of the two, the former were much more important and successful. The latter, by contrast, were a kind of sickly appendage made worse by an admixture of Hittite blood.[15] They were only able to keep alive thanks to their manlier, more heroic brethren to the north. With the destruction of the Kingdom of Israel at the hands of the Assyrians in 721 B.C., the Israelites disappeared from the stage of history, leaving the miserable sons of Judah alone in a world with which they were ill suited to cope. It was from these people that subsequent Jews inherited their racial soul.

The nature of that soul could be seen in every field from scholarship to music and from productive work (in which Jews did not engage) to politics. Still, perhaps the one in which it was most manifest was precisely the one in which we are interested in here. Chamberlain explains that there were Celtic, Germanic, and even Slavic and Indian heroes; he specifically speaks of Siegfried, Tristan, Perceval, Roland, Marco Kraljevich of Kosovo fame, and Rama.[16] All of them were characterized by their heroic courage, their clear preference for honor over earthly possessions, and their fealty unto death, qualities in which they were often inspired by their "tender, brave and chaste" women. Most important of all, they were endowed with the singular ability to transform the most crushing defeat into posthumous victory, thus turning them into the stuff of legend on which subsequent generations could and did build their culture of war. Contrast that, Chamberlain continues, with the biblical Samson, the only Jewish hero (most Jewish heroes, as we saw, were not Jews at all) he mentions by name. Samson's strength lay in his hair. In the end, as we know, he allowed himself to be shorn both of his hair and of his strength by a scheming, sluttish woman.

Strange as they may seem in retrospect, Chamberlain's ratiocinations concerning the Jews' nature in general and lack of a proper martial spirit in particular were entirely typical and were endlessly repeated both in scholarly literature and in more popular works sold in the streets. At best the Jews, having gone through so much, were graciously forgiven for what they had become. A very good example was the French writer Charles Péguy (1873–1914). Péguy was a fervent nationalist who nevertheless surrounded himself with Jewish friends and was reluctant to part with them. What he admired were the sufferings inflicted on their people by history, and the spiritual depth that was the result of those sufferings.[17] At worst the accusations were vulgarized, as in Hitler's *Mein Kampf,* where German Jews are accused—falsely, as it turns out—of failing to do their duty in the world war and of spreading syphilis as well.[18]

What makes all this really interesting is that it was not limited to Gentile anti-Semites but was often taken over by the Jews themselves. At times they even used the image for their own purposes. For example, the first Polish partition of 1772 brought large numbers of Jews under Prussian rule (previously only a relative handful had been permitted to settle). Their representatives traveled to Berlin in order to persuade their new sovereign, Frederick II, that they would not do as soldiers and should be exempted from military service. The king hesitated, asked around, and conducted some experiments. However, in the end he granted their request—after making them pay additional taxes. Consequently the enlistment of Jews into the Prussian army was delayed by forty years. It was only in 1812, during the period of military reform, that the laws concerning conscription were extended to Jews so that they could serve in the "wars of liberation" like anyone else.[19] Half a century after that, the spectacle of Jewish soldiers wearing uniforms, bearing arms, and going on campaign for the first time was still considered sufficiently interesting to inspire some works of art.

Once the ghetto had been left behind, a growing number of assimilated Jews tried to gain acceptance on the part of Gentile society by rendering faithful service in the armed forces of the countries in which they lived. This was especially true in countries that had introduced general conscription, and especially in Germany and France. Jewish soldiers participated in every one of Prussia's wars from 1813 on. Napoleon's summoning of a Sanhedrin (Jewish supreme council) in 1806 was specifically meant to ensure that Jews, as a condition for retaining the equal rights they had been granted in 1791, would serve in the army like anyone else. Dreyfus, after all, was a brilliant graduate of the École Polytechnique and a promising officer on the general staff.

That, however, was but part of the story. Though Jews did serve, very often they failed to obtain the kind of martial recognition they craved, causing some of them to descend into self-hatred. Here is what one extremely successful businessman, government official, politician, and author had to say about the matter just before the turn of the twentieth century:

> Your east Mediterranean appearance is not very well appreciated by the northern tribes. You should therefore be more careful . . . [not to become] the laughing stock of a race brought up in a strictly military fashion. As soon as you have recognized your un-athletic build, your narrow shoulders, your clumsy feet, your sloppy, rounded shape, you will resolve to dedicate a few generations on the renewal of your appearance.[20]

As if this were not provocative enough, the article carried the title "Hear, O Israel," after the most important Jewish prayer of all. Its author was Walter Rathenau, who one historian said "incarnated the spirit of the times in his own person."[21] For reasons that were part personal, part social, Rathenau's fondest wish was for his sovereign, Emperor Wilhelm II, to appoint him a lieutenant of the reserve. His failure to realize his dream may well have been the bitterest disappointment of his life, sending him into a mental crisis from which he took several years to recover. Perhaps it was fitting that in 1922 he was killed at the hands of anti-Semitic assassins.

Zionists, too, took up the image of the unmilitary Jew, and indeed as time went on its role in building up their movement's own ideology and culture grew. Among its propagators were many of the movement's most prominent leaders and writers, figures whose names are still carried by streets, squares, and neighborhoods in practically every Israeli city, town, and settlement. Consider the most important leader of all, Theodor Herzl.

Herzl was born in Budapest in 1860, the son of a well-to-do and assimi-lated family. Later he was given a typical liberal education that laid very little stress on Judaism but centered around the humanist values instead.

Throughout his eight-year period of Zionist activity, Herzl tended to underplay the role that armed force, as distinct from political, economic, and organizational activities, would have to play in the "colonization" of Palestine by the Jews. In part, he may well have been sincere in his atti-tude; one of his closest friends was Bertha von Suttner.[22] There may, how-ever, have been other considerations, too. First, the conversations he held with various European rulers gave him good reason to believe that the powers that be, above all the Ottoman Empire, would not take kindly to the establishment of a strong Jewish state in the Middle East.[23] Second, there was no need to draw the attention of his fellow Zionists to the violent resistance that their movement probably would meet on the part of the settled inhabitants of the Land of Israel.

Be this as it may, in his diary Herzl struck a different tone. Already during his student days in Vienna he was confronted by the fact that some of the dueling societies there would neither admit Jews nor give Jews satisfaction. The resulting humiliation continued to preoccupy him for decades thereafter. It may explain why, daydreaming about the fu-ture, he noted that the Jewish state would permit and even encourage dueling so as to restore the Jews' long-lost sense of honor.[24] Visiting the Land of Israel in 1898, he considered the Jews he met there shy and narrow-minded. What a surprise, then, to watch a demonstration by some early Zionist settlers who, imitating their Arab neighbors, galloped around on their horses and fired their weapons into the air to welcome him. This flew straight in the face of every anti-Semitic stereotype; so strong was the impression that it brought tears to his eyes. He considered the episode sufficiently important to work it into his programmatic novel, *Old-New Land*. There, a crusty old Prussian officer named Otto von Koenigshof is made to compare the Jewish horsemen with Frederick II's cavalry at Rossbach, no less.[25]

The most important early-twentieth-century Jewish poet was Chaim Nahman Bialik. Born in 1873, a native of the Ukraine, Bialik grew up in poverty and later made his living as a teacher and a masterly writer of Hebrew. Right from the beginning he was obsessed with the humiliation of being Jewish and with reviving ancient Jewish heroism, only to be dis-appointed by what followed. The disappointment in turn led to the com-position of his best-known work, a poem called "The City of Slaughter."

The city in question was Kishinev, in western Ukraine. In April 1903 it witnessed a pogrom, the same one that caused the family of future Israeli prime minister Golda Meir to leave for the United States. The poet minces no words in denouncing the rabble's deeds, including murder by means of spikes driven into people's heads, and shaking his fist at the God who had permitted those deeds to take place. However, his strongest censure is reserved for the Jews themselves. Physically degenerate (Herzl had claimed that "they have the bodies and souls of small tradesmen"), lacking courage, the only thing they cared about were their possessions; in his notes, taken on the spot, Bialik explains how they mourned each broken piece of crystal. Untrained in the use of weapons, when the mob came for them they could think of nothing better to do than to hide in "shitholes." Next, the men who had not been killed "like dogs" ran to the rabbis to ask whether the law still permitted them to sleep with their poor violated wives.[26]

Bialik's poem was translated into Russian by Ze'ev Jabotinsky

(1880–1940), the man who later founded the right-wing Zionist Revisionist movement, which in turn became the parent of the present-day Likud Party. Jabotinsky added a preface in which he called Bialik "my elder brother in spirit" and claimed that "The City of Slaughter" reflected the Jewish experience as no other did.[27] His own strictures on Jewish life might have come (and perhaps did come) straight out of some anti-Semitic handbook:

"The Jew . . . is always afraid, frightened of the sound of a driven leaf"; Ze'ev Jabotinsky in the uniform of a British lieutenant.

We live in the narrow confines of the ghetto and see at every step the contemptible pettiness which developed as a result of oppression over many generations, and is so unattractive . . . And what is truly exalted and glorious, our Hebrew culture, we do not see. The children of the masses see a bit of it in the *heder* [rabbinical elementary school], but there Judaism is presented in such a pathetic form and in such ugly surroundings that it cannot inspire love. It is different with the children of the middle class; these are denied even that; practically none of them know anything at all of the history of our people; they don't know about its historic function as a "light unto the nations" of the white race, its great spiritual power . . . they only know the Judaism which their eyes see and their ears hear. And what is it that they see? They see the Jew who is always afraid, frightened of the sound of a driven leaf; they see that he is chased from every place and insulted everywhere and he doesn't dare to open his mouth and answer back . . . Each time a Jewish boy leaves home for school, his mother tells him not to stand out, lest he be seen or heard.[28]

Lamenting or denouncing Jewish weakness, cowardice, and lack of a martial spirit was one thing, doing something about it another. At least one Zionist, Adolf Bruell (1846–1908), advocated the use of mixed marriages in order to infuse the Jews with soldierly blood.[29] As Turkey joined World War I at the end of 1915, Jabotinsky, now a well-known Zionist leader, sought to solve the problem in a different way. He devoted much of his efforts to the establishment of a Jewish Legion under British command.

The volunteers he had in mind would come from neutral countries such as Scandinavia and, before 1917, the United States as well. Others would be drawn from belligerent nations where, since they were living there as foreigners, they were not subject to conscription. First they would go to Egypt and receive military training. Next they would assist in the British war effort that was being mounted against the Ottoman Empire; after that, they would act as the nucleus of a Jewish army to come. As one of the soldiers who joined the scheme later put it, their goal was not so much "strategic" as to "shed their blood as an educational value for future generations."[30] In other words, they would set an example on which a new culture of war could be built.

On the whole, the movement was not a success. One reason for this was because the War Office was not interested in setting up a force whose minuscule military value would probably be much outweighed by the political trouble it would create among Britain's would-be Arab allies in the Middle East. Even after the wind changed and it reluctantly gave its assent, most of the men Jabotinsky had in mind, lacking both fighting spirit and a culture in which it might have been rooted, preferred to stay where they were. He personally went to Whitechapel, a poor district in east London, in a quest for volunteers among the Russian Jews who had settled there. The borough was just then going through a tremendous boom. Its residents lost no time in telling their would-be savior that they were tailors; the last thing they wanted was to play at war in the ranks of an imperial power to which they did not feel any strong bonds.[31] So vehement was the opposition that at one point the police had to rescue Jabotinsky from being mobbed. In the end only a few hundred men signed up and served against the Ottomans, first at Gallipoli and later in the Sinai Desert and Jordan Valley.

Though he was unwilling to speak up publicly about these matters, Herzl himself spent hours speculating about the methods necessary for the "maintenance of manly discipline" among his followers. At the same time, it would be necessary to inoculate the new Jewish army against various kinds of irregularities that afflicted other armed forces. There would be "national festivals with gigantic spectacles, colorful processions, etc.—e.g., on the foundation day of the State." Using yellow as its preferred color, the state would hand out decorations similar to the French Légion d'Honneur; above all else, it would adopt a flag. "A flag, what is that? A stick with a rag on it? No, Sir, a flag is more than that. With a flag one can lead men wherever one wants, even into the Promised Land. For a flag men will live and die; it is, indeed, the only thing for which they are ready to die in masses, if one trains them for it."[32]

Another way to transform the "little Jews"—the contemptuous expression, originating with the anti-Semites, is found repeatedly in Herzl's diary—was to provide them with a proper physical education. In his book, he proposed to do this by means of rifle clubs, ball games, and rowing. All of these had proved their value in Switzerland and England; why not use them to transform the Jews as well?[33] The most prominent exponent of sport as a vehicle for national regeneration was his close friend Max Nordau (1849–1923). Like Herzl, Nordau was born in Budapest. From there he made his way to Paris, where he worked as a physician and came into close contact with the city's downtrodden—but also with contemporary modern art, for which he had no appreciation whatsoever. In

1892 he published an international best-seller, *Degeneration,* which set forth the supposedly nefarious effects of modern civilization. Prominent among them were urban life, commerce, consumerism, and the speed of transport made possible by the rise of the railways. Another factor was the superabundance of news arriving from all quarters of the world; in the face of all those disasters, how could one expect to retain one's sanity? All this spelled ruin for people's minds and bodies, inducing uncertainty, effeminacy, neurasthenia, and in the end, madness.

As with so many of his fellow Jews, some of Nordau's ideas can be traced back to the anti-Semites. In his case the key figure was Friedrich Ludwig Jahn (1778–1852). The proclaimed ideal of the "father of German gymnastics" had been to create sound minds in sound bodies. Though Jahn had prohibited Jews from joining his movement, Nordau was quite prepared to acknowledge his influence. What could be more natural than to try to regenerate the Jews by applying his methods to them? In particular, the Jewish reaction, or lack of it, to the Dreyfus affair left Nordau disappointed. While the mob was yelling for Dreyfus's blood and theirs, French Jews hardly even dared to gather and raise their voices in protest. Instead, "slinking along the walls," they showed how "morbid" their nature had become.[34] Clearly they were in even more urgent need of salvation, both physical and mental, than everybody else.

At Herzl's invitation, Nordau attended the second Zionist Congress in 1898. There he put forward the importance of developing, side by side with a political program, one of physical training. It would lead to the creation of a new, proud, straight-backed type of "muscular Jews"; possibly he was also influenced by the "muscular Christianity" that during those very years was being propagated in the United States.[35] His speech was received with tumultuous applause. In the following years he went on to publish several essays on the subject, which were later included in his collected *Zionist Writings.* Furthermore, Nordau, like Herzl, was much concerned with the Jews' alleged lack of courage and the need to correct it. In 1907 he produced a play whose hero, Dr. Kohn, striving to save his people's honor, engages in a duel with a German officer—and, having lost his life, is posthumously turned into a symbol.

By that time, Jewish gymnastic clubs, formed partly in response to Nordau's call and partly because Gentile ones were steadily expelling their Jewish members, were no longer rare. Seeking to manufacture a tradition for themselves, most took on the names of ancient Jewish heroes. At least one, in Vienna, called itself simply "The Force." When the sixth

Turning Jews into heroes; a postcard in honor of the Jewish battalion of the British
Army, 1918   Y. BEN DOV

Zionist Congress held its opening ceremony in 1903 it invited several
dozen Jewish athletes. They gave a demonstration of their prowess, thus
proving that the situation was not hopeless and that the Jewish people
could still be saved.

In more ways than one, all these images of what Jews were and were
not, could and could not do, came together in the person of the abovementioned Jabotinsky. Jabotinsky was an excellent speaker and a brilliant linguist—he could write in eight different languages—as well as a
political organizer. In his own lifetime, as well as after his death, he was
considered the most prominent Zionist "militarist" of all (though still not
radical enough for some of his followers, including future prime minister
Menachem Begin). In a passing reference early in his career he rejected
the fashionable idea that war was an outgrowth of economic competition.
In reality, he suspected, it was akin to fashion, the result of men's unceas-
ing competition for honor and excellence; the clue to understanding
human behavior was Homer, not Marx.[36]

Though he was sometimes accused of Fascism, politically speaking,
Jabotinsky always remained a liberal. He insisted on democratic elec-
tions, human rights, and individual freedom ("every man a king").
Perhaps even more important, he never overlooked the role of private

property as a guarantee for that freedom.[37] At least until the outbreak of the so-called Great Arab Revolt in the Land of Israel in 1936, what set him apart was his readiness to admit, even advocate, the role that armed force (an "Iron Wall") would and should play in the Zionist attempt to re-settle the Land of Israel and establish a Jewish state there.[38] To bridge the gap between the need for an army and his liberal values, he proposed a version of "inner commitment" that was to prove much more attractive and much more successful than that of the Bundeswehr.

The way he saw it, ceremonies and ritual constituted "almost three-quarters" of human culture; yet Jews "do not know how to stand straight, how to greet each other, how to address a comrade and how to address a superior; we are, in short, formless."[39] This problem he and a few others set out to correct. In 1923 they founded Betar, a right-wing youth move-ment named after the last fortress held by the Jewish rebels who had fought against Hadrian in A.D. 135. With branches in several countries, no sooner had Betar been established than it immediately made its bellicose intentions clear by adopting the lines, "In blood and fire Judah fell / in blood and fire Judah will rise!" as the opening of its anthem. It also put great emphasis on paramilitary education. In a community noted for its slovenliness, lackadaisical attitudes, and lack of formal discipline, uni-forms (complete with ties) were obligatory. Members spent much of their energy making sure their shoes were properly polished. They also in-spected each other, saluted each other, hoisted flags, drilled, held pa-rades, and so on.

Partly because they were followers of Marx, partly because they saw Judaism as part of the set of circumstances that had deprived the Jews of their onetime martial prowess, many of the most important Zionist lead-ers had little patience with religion. Not so Jabotinsky and Betar, who, though fundamentally secular in outlook, took a more positive line. In their eyes the Old Testament was not simply a sacred book but contained a strong admixture of secular elements as well; accordingly, they tried to harness it by emphasizing its nationalist, instead of ethical and religious, contents. Overall, the intention was both to change Jewish attitudes and to impress non-Jews. This was true in Poland, the country where Betar had its largest membership; in Italy, where Mussolini personally, hoping to gain support against the British, provided the movement with an un-usually favorable climate and even allowed some serious paramilitary training to take place; and also in the Land of Israel itself. Setting the ex-ample, Jabotinsky never overcame his habit of handing out photographs that showed him in a World War I–vintage British officer's uniform, complete with cap and crossbelt.

In 1933, to counter those who accused him of "militarism" (and whom he in turn accused of having bouillon run in their veins instead of blood), Jabotinsky penned an article on the subject. He noted that both in the world at large and among the Jewish community in the Land of Israel, many left-wing, self-styled pacifist movements used military terminology and methods to inspire their members and provide them with cohesion and set a course. They, too, set up paramilitary organizations. They talked of "advances" and "retreats," wore insignia, adopted military ranks (as the Salvation Army did), wore uniforms, raised flags, held marches, and the like; obviously there was something to be said in favor of such things. War, he thought, was ugly and should be waged only in a just cause, but that was no problem—since the Jews were a small and persecuted minority, their cause was just by definition.

Military life, he continued, "in and of itself," was "distinguished by many fine aspects."[40] The parts of it he liked best were ceremony and discipline. "There is nothing in the world that will make as great an impression on us as the ability of the masses, at particular times, to feel and also to act as one unit, moved by one will, acting in uniform tempo; because that is the entire difference between a mob, a rabble, and a nation."[41] They were vital to raise "our race" (by this time Jews were embracing racial ideas almost as strongly as anti-Semites did) out of its ghetto existence and into the light.[42] Properly applied, they would result in a fighting spirit as well as *hadar. Hadar* was a quality that stood for everything that, in Jabotinsky's view, the Jews did not have. It is best translated as "forms of appearance and bearing that command respect"—as in keeping one's body clean and trim, walking straight, refraining from gesticulation, speaking in a firm but measured way, and the like.

Having originated among turn-of-the-century Zionists and later adopted by the Jewish community in the Land of Israel, the supposed contrast between Herzl's weak, effeminate "little Jews" and the masculine, muscular, martially minded "new Jews" became critically important in the State of Israel. After all, the latter's very raison d'être was, if not to bless Jews with absolute security, at any rate to provide them with the wherewithal, physical and mental, to defend themselves—make them stand straight, as the saying went. Hence the contrast continued to be propagated by every available means well into the 1950s and 1960s. One outcome was that during those years the term "Diaspora Jew" became one of the strongest expressions of contempt in the entire Israeli vocabulary. Even Holocaust survivors, instead of being treated sympathetically, often found themselves despised for allegedly allowing themselves to be led "like lambs to the slaughter."[43] I personally recall how, while still attending elementary school around 1960, my classmates and I were made to memorize and sing in unison a song that presented them and their dead relatives as "calves."

As so often with stereotypes, the image of "men without chests," which Zionism first adopted and then sought to alter, was part fiction, part real. Originating with some of the most vicious anti-Semites as long ago as the Middle Ages,[44] it was fiction insofar as it included elements that were entirely mythological, such as the idea that Jews, lacking virility, were more liable to the female disease of hysteria.[45] It was also insufficiently nuanced; just as not all non-Jews were heroes, so there were always some Jews who did not conform to the pattern. Finally, to the extent that it was adopted by the Jews themselves, it bordered on the pathological. Yet it was real insofar as most Jews, living through centuries and centuries of exile, did indeed lose touch with their own culture of war. As to adopting that of others, either doing so was prohibited or else they did so only with considerable reluctance. Given the circumstances, how could it have been otherwise? With rare exceptions, such as the great scholar Maimonides (1135–1204) who had much to say about the law of war in particular, they did not see any need for it.[46] To the extent that traces of it still existed, they did their best to reinterpret it or to push it aside. This attitude was taken to the point where, if the opening pages of Herzl's diary may be taken literally, one of his first concerns was to convince his would-be fellow Zionists that they needed a flag at all.

Once the Zionist movement got under way and it became clear that the Land of Israel would not be won without a fight, the construction of a new martial tradition became imperative and was carried out quite consciously. Parts of it were drawn from Jewish history, above all the Old Testament. Here also Jabotinsky tried to lead the way. Perhaps one reason for this was because he and his right-wing followers were a minority within the Zionist movement. This enabled him to say openly what others, from Herzl, Chaim Weizmann, and David Ben-Gurion on down, could only express in private; the last in particular was as much enamored of the "new Jew" as anybody else. As part of his efforts, Jabotinsky wrote a novel about Samson. In it, he sought to correct the hero's image as a muddleheaded, skirt-chasing muscleman who was always getting into trouble and had to fight in order to get out of it. Instead he presented him as a farsighted leader. As Samson confessed to his jailer, throughout his life he had been "in love" with the Philistines and tried to make his own people appreciate their enemies' "order and dignity in warfare," without success.[47]

Other ingredients of the newly forming military tradition were the Hasmonean revolt against the Seleucid Empire as well as the legacy of those who had risen against Rome and lost their lives fighting for their people's independence. Prominent in the latter was the story of Masada, a massive, hard-to-access rock in the Judean desert overlooking the Dead Sea. It was there, according to the ancient Jewish historian Josephus Flavius, that the last Jewish rebels had chosen to commit collective suicide rather than surrender to their enemies. Like so many other elements in the Jewish culture of war, over the centuries Masada was wiped from the national consciousness; even its location was forgotten. One reason for this was that Josephus had written in Greek, whereas a Hebrew translation of his work appeared only in 1923.

Starting around the middle of the nineteenth century, when the rock was rediscovered by German archaeologists, its fame gradually grew. At the time Jabotinsky wrote his article about the blessings of military life it was just beginning to be turned into a national symbol at the hands of the Zionist establishment.[48] The time was not far away when it became an object of pilgrimage. Its use as part of the culture of war culminated in the turbulent 1960s and 1970s. Recruits forming part of Israel's armored corps, carrying lit torches, were made to scale the rock in darkness so as to greet the rising sun. Next they would form up on the top and were then sworn in under the slogan "Masada will not fall again." Part disapprovingly, part admiringly, foreigners spoke of the national "Masada complex." So, in response, did some Israelis, including Prime Minister Golda Meir.[49]

Certain elements of the Israeli military culture, especially uniforms, drill, parades, and ceremonies, were borrowed in more or less modified form from various foreign armed forces around the world. Photographs of reviews held during the early 1950s speak volumes concerning the debt it owed to the British armed forces that had policed Palestine for thirty years and in which many of its members, including several chiefs of staff, had cut their teeth. In time, a lively debate arose as to which of these very different traditions should be given priority. Was a culture originating in an ancient, even tribal past suitable for the modern world? How to reconcile the religious elements in the Jewish culture of war, as expressed in the Old Testament above all, with the predominantly secular nature of modern Israeli society? Was the Jewish (later Israeli) Defense Force to adopt a spick-and-span attitude like so many others, or would it draw its moral strength from different sources?[50] Assuming a culture of war was indispensable, how to instill it while avoiding that worst of all bad things, "militarism"?

For some fifty years, from the anti-Jewish riots of 1929 until the conclusion of peace with Egypt in 1979, the issue was overshadowed by the concept of *en brera,* "no choice." *En brera* resulted from the fact that, in its own view and to a considerable extent in reality as well, the country was a David fighting a Goliath; to realize that, all one had to do was take a look at the map. However, by the turn of the twenty-first century Israel had developed into a regional giant. The Israeli Defense Force (IDF) was one of the world's most powerful. It had in its arsenal enough nuclear weapons and delivery vehicles to demolish all its enemies combined, causing the ethos that had sustained it since the beginnings of Zionism to lose much of its force. Other developments common to Israel and other advanced societies, such as the declining number of children per family and a consequent rise in the average age of the population, pushed the change along.[51] Last but not least, the need to fight the Palestinians in the occupied territories led to demoralization as well as the opening of a growing divide between Israeli society and its armed forces. Conversely, whenever the armed forces attempted to assert themselves and repair their lost prestige they were accused of "militarism."[52]

Nemesis came in the summer of 2006. Going to war against Hezbollah in Lebanon, an irregular Islamic guerrilla force consisting of just a few thousand fighters and armed with few heavy weapons to speak of, the IDF performed poorly. The political leadership and general staff were plagued by internal divisions, indecisiveness, and, above all, fear of fighting and taking casualties. The troops turned out to be willing but lackadaisical, insufficiently trained and motivated as well as badly led. Apparently the ethos that had long made commanders rally their men with the cry "Follow me" was forgotten. Plagued by these shortcomings, the Israeli forces took weeks to achieve their objectives, to the extent that they did so at all. Nor were things any better in the rear, which came under rocket fire, than they were at the front. The perceived failure led to turmoil in Israel, culminating in the resignation of the chief of staff. Still, it had the effect of rekindling the debate concerning the true sources of fighting power and the role of a martial tradition in sustaining it.

At present, it is impossible to foresee what answer may emerge. Clearly, however, in the absence of peace, Israel's ability to sustain what armed struggles the future may bring depends on such a tradition being found and as thoroughly assimilated into the consciousness of the troops as well as that of the nation at large as "no choice" used to be. Thus the Jewish-Zionist-Israeli experience provides an object lesson concerning what has happened, and may still happen, to a people who, for one reason or another, have lost touch with their culture of war.

20

Feminism

From the day when the first band of cavemen put on war paint and took up clubs to kill their neighbors (often with the objective, among other things, of capturing the latter's women),[1] the relationship between women and the culture of war has been complex and contradictory. This continues to be the case today, and in spite of efforts at reform by feminists and various other groups it is very likely to remain the case in the future.

As even a superficial glance at history will reveal, women are absolutely essential to war. In the main this is not because they have taken an active part in combat, although here and there it is possible to find a handful who did so either while wearing disguise (mainly in the eighteenth century) or, even less often, openly.[2] Nor is it because, whether dressed in uniform, as in the military of today's advanced countries, or without it, while acting as camp followers, they have often supported men, contributing to such fields as logistics, administration, transportation, medical work, intelligence, and the like.[3] In both of these capacities, all women have done was to imitate men and act as surrogate men. In the latter, they sometimes enabled more men to go out to the front and do the real work of war, fighting. This has been reflected in their low status, meager pay, and limited opportunities for promotion; indeed, one reason why armies employed any women at all was because, compared to men, they tended to be cheap.

By contrast, when women behave as women, their impact on men, fighting men above all, cannot be overestimated. "Come back with your shield or on it" was the parting shot a Spartan mother addressed to her son who was leaving for the battlefield. On one occasion, when Cyrus's men were running from battle, the Persian women called them "base cowards" and lifted their skirts to emphasize the point.[4] We are told similar stories about other civilizations, such as the Zulu of South Africa.[5] Throughout history, countless anxious women presented their menfolk who were going into battle with pictures, amulets, pieces of dress (including intimate ones), and other souvenirs. In 1914, British women distributed white feathers to "slackers" and told them, "We do not want to lose you, but we think that you should go." "Mount and enter," an obscene adaptation of a traditional Jewish blessing, uttered when worshippers are called on in synagogue to read from the Torah, was the greeting Israeli women allegedly addressed to their husbands as they returned from the 1973 war.

In both reality and fiction, it is women who loudly demand that their men protect them against the things that lecherous enemy males are planning to do to them. In both reality and fiction, very often one of the most important objectives for which war is waged is to save women from those things. Hence it is women who cheer on those men as they deck themselves in their martial finery, take up their weapons, dress ranks, and march away on campaign; pray for them while they are fighting; greet and embrace the victors as they come marching home; console the losers once they have ceased running away; dress the wounded (how much better to be looked after by a woman than by a man); and, as a last favor, mourn the dead and bury them. The victors in a war will surely target the women of the defeated. "To every man a damsel or two," as the mother of the biblical commander Sisra put it; no sense of female solidarity here, incidentally.[6] The losers' women may well be turned into booty as they are subjected to every kind of atrocity and indignity culminating in rape or murder (or both).

Women who do not conform, as by refusing to mourn their dead menfolk or by finding new partners too soon, can expect to be ostracized both by men and by other women. Those who cross the lines, as by voluntarily consorting with the enemy, can expect punishment, perhaps even very serious punishment. No sooner did Odysseus come back from his travels and avenge himself on Penelope's suitors than he hanged twelve of his maids, who had slept with those suitors, by the neck, "like thrushes or pigeons in a net."[7] In liberated Europe immediately after World War II, women who had associated with German soldiers were often paraded in the streets after having their hair shorn off. In Iraq, in Afghanistan, any woman who dares come too close to the foreign occupation troops may very well have signed her own death warrant.

Briefly, had it not been for the tension between the sexes war would have been almost inconceivable. Indeed, it might have been pointless. Men who are without a future—in other words, without women and their off-spring—would not have had much reason to fight each other over honor or possessions, either, and would have ceased to do so soon enough.[8]

What applies to war applies equally well to its culture. Everything else apart, one very important reason why men have created the culture of war was in order to impress women with their own martial glory. They would scarcely have done so if women had not been as capable of being swept along by that culture as men are; but for the admiration that they excite in women, what use are glittering weapons and suits of armor, painted faces and bodies, plumes, splendid tight-fitting uniforms, gladia-torial fights, knights' tournaments, reviews, parades, victory celebrations, monuments, and so much else? Many years ago I was present when U.S. Marines in San Diego, mounting a somewhat dangerous demonstration of their skills, were watched by their female relatives and friends, several of whom were nervously sucking their fingers. It would scarcely be too much to say that women are what war and its culture are all about—and this, as Horace says, since "long before Helen of Troy ever lived."[9]

Observing the magnificent appearance of Bernier, the hero of the twelfth-century poem *Raoul de Cambrai,* his admirer, Bernice, ex-claims: "How fortunate one would be, to be the lover and the engaged bride of such a knight! Anyone who was allowed to kiss and embrace him would find it better for her than meat and drink."[10] The person who in-vented Bernice and put the words into her mouth was a man. However, women concur. Writing soon after the largest war in history until then, the English feminist Virginia Woolf made the point as well as anybody could. "Women," she says, "have served all these centuries as magnifying mirrors possessing the magic and delicious power of reflecting the figure of men at twice its real size." Had it not been for that power, "probably the earth would still be swamp and jungle. The glories of all our wars would be unknown . . . mirrors are essential to all violent and heroic action."[11]

Quite a number of feminists have argued that war, and of course its culture, are typically wicked male products that (supposedly) do not appeal to the "real" nature of women.[12] Hence women who try to join in wars are traitors to their own sex; what they should do is stay away from them and resist them as much as they can. Reality, however, is much more complex. Consider the following passage, written by a member of the U.S. Women's Auxiliary Army Corps (WAAC) in the midst of World War II:

Without women, no war; Jewish women in festive dress bidding farewell to their departing menfolk, Palestine, 1918   ZIONIST ARCHIVE

All eight hundred of us marched out on the Parade Ground to be re-
viewed by Colonel Faith. We certainly put our hearts into column
left, and by the right flank, and when we went by the reviewing
stand, out heads snapped around so energetically that I'm surprised
a few didn't go bowling off down the field. Being out there, with all
those trim, eager women moving perfectly in ranks, and the band
playing, and the sun on the colors, was the most tremendous experience I've had yet. There is nothing that can equal the feeling of
being part of something infinitely larger than yourself.[13]

But do women enjoy war and combat as much as many men do?
Judging by the fact that, once they have left puberty behind, very few of
them participate in war games of any kind (including those that do not
demand physical strength, such as computer games) even when they are
invited, the answer is negative. My own attempts to search the few books
written by women who fought, as opposed to those who merely served or
watched from the sidelines, also failed to turn up phrases similar to those
often uttered by men. Instead, such women tend to emphasize the difficulty they have encountered in casting off a woman's role and assuming
that which is normally reserved for men.

For example, take Nadezhda Durova's *Cavalry Maiden*. The author
was a young Russian noblewoman. At the age of twenty-seven or so, she
ran away from home in order to join the tsar's forces and fight against
Napoleon—as a woman, she felt that the army offered her greater freedom than home life did. Writing long after the event, she often describes
how "dreadful" things were. War and combat certainly caused her excitement, even wild excitement, but normally her reaction seems to have
been one of anxiety and fear. Throughout the book, not once does she express her joy in them.[14]

Perhaps the real reason why women so seldom enjoy battle, or at any
rate seldom express their enjoyment of it, is because there is a catch. War
and masculinity reinforce each other, so that fighting men have always
been envied by men and attractive to women. Simone de Beauvoir describes the scene. No sooner had the Germans (who, she does not forget
to say, were "perfectly groomed") occupied Paris in 1940 than they were
surrounded by prostitutes, both professional and amateur.[15] In 1945, as
the Allies overran first Western Europe and then Germany itself, the
same happened in reverse. These are but two of countless examples that

could be cited. One Israeli woman, gazing at her weapon-carrying male compatriots, thought they were "gods."[16]

For women, things work exactly the opposite way. The more like hardened fighters they look and behave, the more difficult they will find it to maintain their femininity, and the less attractive to men they will become. Hence the efforts, noted in a previous chapter, to make fighting women who figure in the literature or appear on the screen look as feminine as possible so that men, mainly young men, will want to read about their adventures, watch them in action, or play computer games with them; the fact that in real life such creatures would be impossible is simply put aside. Rousseau, who himself was a great womanizer and who knew about such things, hit the nail on its head. "The more you try to be like us, *mesdames,*" he wrote, "the less we shall like you."

Nor does the blame for this rest on "male chauvinists" alone. Many men find a woman who plays at war cute—as, for example, when World War II artist Alberto Vargas, who specialized in illustrating men's magazines such as *Esquire,* painted some of them wearing high heels, short pants, a semi-buttoned blouse, and a rakishly tilted service cap. However, women, knowing the score at least as well as men do, are unimpressed. For every uniformed female who has ever graced the cover of magazines such as *Vogue, Cosmopolitan,* or *Marie Claire,* there are a thousand beautiful models and actresses who have done the same. The fact that these magazines and others like them are edited by women merely serves to emphasize the point. Such attitudes may very well deter at least some women who might otherwise have decked themselves in the apparel of war and expressed the joy of war as many men have done; therefore, the question concerning their innate qualities must remain open.

Men and women do, however, differ in other respects that are germane to the subject. First, physically speaking, women are considerably weaker and more vulnerable than men—a fact that, when it comes to an activity such as war in which bodily strength, robustness, and endurance have always played and continue to play a crucial role, cannot and should not be overlooked. The most important differences between the sexes may be summed up as follows:[17] On average, women are about five inches shorter than men. They have only 72 percent of the overall strength and 55 percent of the upper-body strength that men possess. Women's joints are constructed in a different way. This makes them less adept at activities such as climbing, leaping, running, and throwing. Thinner skeletons, especially skulls and shins, make them more susceptible to injuries that may result from either blows or stress.

Women's weaker anatomy means that they are less resistant to infection, hence dirt and life in the field, than men are. Their sensitive breasts, which tend to grow larger as they grow older, require special protection and present an obstacle to certain kinds of movement. When it is a question of reaching an enemy, women's shorter arms and legs handicap them. Smaller lungs mean that they cannot match men in every kind of aerobic activity; in fact, the aerobic capacity of a fifty-year-old man equals that of a twenty-year-old woman.[18] Furthermore, male muscles differ from female ones. As a result, a period of intensive training, instead of closing the gap between the sexes, will cause it to increase still further.[19] The fact that since 1970 or so the gap between men's and women's times in running and the like has narrowed somewhat merely proves how very low women's starting point used to be.[20] Finally, women, like men, are capable of driving themselves, or being driven to, very great physical effort far exceeding their ordinary capabilities. For women, however, the long-term results may include osteoporosis, amenorrhea, and barrenness.[21]

In view of the physical differences between the sexes, devising a training course that will prepare members of both for war on an equal footing while at the same time making sure they are, in fact, ready for it is almost impossible. Make women train as hard as men do, such as in climbing or running or marching with heavy packs (or merely doing without showers), and the result will be that a very high percentage will be injured, drop out, and/or fail to qualify.[22] Thus, in one Canadian experiment, only one out of a hundred women who entered infantry training survived the course; in Israel, so small is the number of women who do graduate that it cannot justify the resources invested.[23] Do the opposite, that is, hold male trainees to female standards, and the men will end up receiving hardly any training at all. Worse still, a training course that does not present a challenge, instead of making trainees more self-confident, is very likely to be regarded with indifference and will also lead to demoralization. There is, moreover, an additional disadvantage: the less strenuous the course, and therefore the less it makes trainees push themselves to their utmost limits, the less it can be used as a vehicle of selection to separate the goats from the kids.

It is, of course, possible to devise a system that will start by measuring the relative capabilities of men and women, then separate the trainees by sex and put each of them through the kind of regime their bodies can sustain. This method has the disadvantage that, instead of finding out what female trainees will have to do on campaign and designing the course in such a way as to provide the best possible preparation for it, it only takes into account their own capabilities. It ignores the fact that no training is hard enough for real-life war—and also that in war the cost of inadequate training is unnecessary losses. Hence it is not just an error; rather, it represents a crime both against the forces as a whole and against the women it contains.

This system also has another disadvantage, namely, that it will make men train much harder than women for the same reward. For example, they may have to run five miles instead of three or complete a course in forty-five minutes instead of an hour or scale a seven-foot wall instead of a five-foot one or throw a hand grenade to a distance of sixty yards instead of thirty-five or carry a pack that is half again as heavy. Being made to train much harder, the men may well ask what the point is, given that women, who are held to lesser standards, obtain the same credit and end up in the same units supposedly doing the same jobs and garnering the same pay and privileges.

Some military schools try to cope with the problem by concealing these discrepancies—for example, by issuing men and women training hand grenades that look similar but are made of different materials and have different weights, or else by making men and women run separate courses (longer for men, shorter for women) but with a common starting point and a common finish. All such measures rest on the belief that the men are stupid—and will therefore tend to make them even more cynical and bitter. As long as the number of women does not exceed token levels, somewhere between 10 and 15 percent, these and similar problems may be handled as men, acting with good grace or ill, help them cope so that things can go ahead.[24] Put in more, however, and once again the inevitable outcome will be demoralization.

What can cause the difficulty to increase still further is the very real possibility that available facilities will be insufficient, so compromises will have to be made. When that happens the men, besides being worked much harder, will invariably draw the short end of the stick in regard to housing, sanitary facilities, dining facilities, and so on.[25] The army that, given a choice, will prefer women over men has not yet been created; should it try to do so, then without question it will be met with howls of protest both by the female trainees themselves and by their civilian relatives and supporters. All these problems explain why, throughout history, men and women (even on the exceedingly rare occasions when the latter were present at all) undergoing military training have very seldom lived together or done their physical exercises together. Conversely, at times when training is conducted in common, as for the gigantic reviews sometimes put on by Communist countries such as North Korea, the objective is not to maximize the trainees' skills and capabilities but simply decorative.

When it is a question of training teams rather than individuals, things become much more difficult still. Any team is only as strong as its weakest member. Put in a woman, and unless she is a true Amazon (experiments show that only a very small percentage of women are able to keep up even with the weakest men),[26] she will become a liability, forcing her male comrades to work extra hard so as to compensate for her weakness and her vulnerability. Much of the time the liability will only be a minor irritant, as happened during the 1991 Gulf War, when male GIs always had to help female ones when it was a question of moving camp, packing and unpacking ammunition, and so on.[27] However, in some situations it may become life-threatening both to her and to the men who, instead of focusing on the mission, have to protect her and look after her.

Nor is the situation of the woman herself a comfortable one; always coming in last and always having to ask for special dispensation or else for help in carrying out various tasks.[28] If she is not properly grateful she'll be abandoned, perhaps deliberately sabotaged. The smaller the number of women around and the less contact soldiers can have with the females of the surrounding civilian population, the more intense the pressure to hand out sexual favors; among the U.S. troops in Iraq, this was sometimes carried to the point where, busy repelling the advances of her male comrades, the female soldier can no longer function at all.[29]

Finally, in every military around the world there are some types of training where physical contact between instructors and trainees, as well as among the trainees themselves, is indispensable. Examples are hand-to-hand combat; medical work, as in bandaging, heart massage, mouth-to-mouth resuscitation, and the like; evacuation, as in carrying the wounded; and resistance, as when trainees are put through mock torture to prepare them for what may be coming. Require men and women to touch each other, and assuredly the outcome will be complaints about what the present generation knows as sexual abuse and that previous ones used to call gross immorality. Demand that they keep their distance, and training will degenerate into an absurd ritual with no link to reality. Such ritual, resembling a carefully orchestrated ballet, may in fact be observed in many modern armed forces in the United States and elsewhere.[30]

As we saw, a very large part of the culture of war arises in, and from, the institutions and procedures whereby future warriors are put through their paces while being prepared to fight and perhaps sacrifice their lives. With the stakes as high as they are, under no circumstances should the system be unfair or be so perceived. If it is, then it is almost certainly going to break down. Instead of being admired and cherished, it will be hated and detested; instead of generating cohesion and fighting power, it will prevent them from being formed. To be sure, such fairness is hard to maintain under the best of circumstances. However, when men and women are mixed together as closely as many kinds of military training demand, doing so is almost impossible.

There is probably an even more important reason why fairness is so hard to maintain. In every known society since the world has been created, whatever is considered suitable for a man is perceived as too hard for a woman. At the same time, whatever is seen as suitable for a woman is perceived as being too easy for a man. Nor is it only a question of exerting physical strength, as is proven by the fact that when it comes to meting out punishments to men and women, the same situation prevails. Swear at a man and he is supposed to take it; not so a woman. This asymmetry explains why for a very strong woman such as former Israeli prime minister Golda Meir or former Indian prime minister Indira Gandhi to be called a man, as both often were, is a compliment (albeit one that, had they been looking for husbands, would have caused them problems). But for a man to be called a woman represents the maximum possible humiliation.

This asymmetry has important consequences both for men and for women. As noted by the most famous female anthropologist of all time, Margaret Mead, in all societies both men *and* women value men's achievements much more highly than those of women;[31] as the Dutch poet Chawwa Wijnberg, put it, if only men had periods even the sanitary napkins would look large and impressive.[32] Uneasy about being regarded as women, men are compelled to spend a considerable part of their energies making sure women do not outclass them. If, as happens when women start entering a male field in any significant number, men cannot do so, then it is only a question of time before they start to leave. Once that happens, the social status of the field in question will start declining. So will the economic rewards that it provides as well as its ability to attract good personnel.[33] Things also work the other way around, as is shown, for example, by the rise in the prestige since 1970 or so of activities such as cooking as men joined in, it emerged from the women's programs and magazines, where it had long been hidden from sight, into the mainstream media that now devote plenty of attention to it.

How to explain the above processes? Clearly they have something to do with the greater physical strength of men; however, since they apply equally well to fields in which such strength is irrelevant, such as playing chess (practically all great chess players are men) that is by no means the complete explanation. A better one might perhaps run as follows: Since men are capable of producing many more offspring than women, from an evolutionary point of view their lives are not nearly as precious. In any given human group, a large percentage of men may die, whether in war or for other reasons. Nevertheless, barring a real catastrophe, the remainder will almost always be able to fertilize as many women as there are around. Provided there is enough food and no external enemy, eventually the balance between the sexes will be restored and the existence of the group will not be put in jeopardy. In fact, and again taking an evolutionary point of view, it will not be put in jeopardy even if there *is* an external enemy, one who, having killed the men, will take over the women, either adopting their children and/or having additional ones with them.

Wherever we look, the much higher value that society puts on women's lives is evident. In every known society, criminal violence kills far fewer women than men—to the point where such violence itself is largely a male-on-male affair.[34] Society also tends to be far more forgiving of violent women than of violent men. In the United States, for every convicted female murderer who is sentenced to death, there are eight males; when it comes to the number of executions that are carried out, the discrepancy is much greater still.[35] Since far fewer women work in dangerous jobs, they suffer far fewer accidents.[36] The largest gap of all, however, may be seen in the movies. In them, for every woman who loses her life, roughly two hundred men share the same fate.[37] Even this figure underestimates the difference between the sexes. On the screen, unless a female character is very wicked indeed, her death is almost always presented as tragic. By contrast, the same fate overtaking a man is simply part of the fun.

Not only are the lives of men grossly undervalued in comparison to those of women, but male hormones, such as testosterone, also make them more inclined to aggressive, assertive, and competitive behavior.[38] These facts are crucial. They explain why men are considerably more inclined to take risks in almost every field, including many, such as investing money, gambling, and even taking multiple-choice exams, that have nothing to do either with war or with physical strength.[39] By definition, risk-taking behavior demands courage, and courage has always been admired as perhaps the greatest human quality of all—no less so by women than by men.

These considerations may finally solve the great riddle that Margaret Mead and many others have posed but few have tried to answer: why, in every known society, men garner such a disproportionate share of the honors that those societies have at their disposal. Many of the things men do (including, some would say, waging war) are entirely without sense: for example, extreme sports, such as the most dangerous kinds of mountaineering, rodeo riding, car and motorcycle racing, ski jumping, and whitewater canoeing. In these fields there are hardly any women participants. It is not the things themselves but the way, or perhaps merely the perceived way, in which men go about doing them that counts. As long as they do not miserably fail, the more recklessly they pursue their goals the louder the applause they draw.

In fact, provided the odds are bad enough and the cause good enough, even failure may acquire an aura. Courage itself is a very great virtue; even the perpetrators of the Great Train Robbery got a certain amount of public sympathy. When it is demonstrated not for one's own sake but for the benefit of others, one may speak of self-sacrifice, sometimes growing into true nobility. In civilian life, the classic example is the fireman (there are hardly any firewomen) who enters a burning house to save a child and dies as a result. The fact that men are much less important for society's survival than women means that they are expected to sacrifice their lives, and do so, much more often. Furthermore, a man who sacrifices his life to save a woman will be admired. By contrast, one who permits a woman to die so as to save *his* life can expect nothing but contempt. Male self-sacrifice in the face of predators may be observed even among some species of animals, such as zebras and baboons.

Of all human activities, war is practically the only one in which people, almost exclusively men, are deliberately ordered to do this and that even if it means their lives are going to be forfeited. If they hide or refuse, they may be tried, punished, and perhaps executed for cowardice. The

Roman practice of decimating units—killing every tenth soldier *pour encourager les autres*—is famous as one of the harshest examples of this practice. But it is certainly not the only one; in World War II, the Red Army alone executed tens of thousands of men (but few if any women) for these offenses. It is to prepare men for sacrifice, as well as reward them for the risks they have taken, that much of the culture of war was first invented and has continued to develop across the ages. To share it equally with women who, thanks to their biological function as childbearers and child minders, are rarely asked, let alone ordered, to sacrifice their lives, would represent the height of iniquity and lead directly to that culture's collapse.

In theory, if scarcely in practice, it is possible to imagine some mad dictator who would try to ride roughshod over these problems. Her or his starting point might be simply the desire to maximize the available forces, but it might also be some extreme version of "equity feminism" bent on proving that women can do anything as well as men can. In any case, she or he will start by drafting female subjects (including, one supposes, mothers; have not many feminists claimed that men are as capable of looking after children as women?) as well as the male ones. She or he will then proceed to train soldiers of both sexes, either separately or together, either to different standards or to the same ones. Putting aside any other considerations, men will be put in charge of women as often as women are put in charge of men. Members of both sexes will be assigned, promoted, and rewarded solely according to their proven abilities. In the process, no attention will be paid to the fact that, like it or not, society does not value the achievements of men and women equally, so that the outcome will be humiliating to men.

Next, having instilled men and women with the culture of war as part of their training, our dictator may order them into battle on an equal basis. Having sacrificed them equally, she or he will reward the survivors equally for heroic deeds committed and victories won. She or he will, however, also punish the survivors equally—for example, by assigning deserters to penal battalions where their chances of surviving will be slim, or else by putting them in front of a firing squad made up of both men and women. Of course, any army that tried to arrange things in such a way would either see so many women receiving so many injuries during training as to make the exercise counterproductive or be forced to deal with hordes of half-trained, thoroughly disgusted men and women. Socially it would fall apart long before it ever came within the guns' range.

Inevitably, such arrangements would lead to many more female casualties than is currently the case even in the most "advanced" Western armed forces. Probably this is why even the most radical feminist utopias of the 1970s did not suggest, let alone demand, anything of the kind: one does not gather supporters, least of all female supporters, by promising that as a reward for acting like men and being treated as harshly as men, they will get killed as often as men are. Behavior of the kind just described may be found, if at all, only in extremis, such as during the last, dying moments of beleaguered cities that, their gates having been stormed and walls breached, face being sacked and destroyed.[40] Even then, the women who mount the roofs and throw objects on the enemy below are almost certain to fight of their own accord, out of despair, and not because some organization has ordered them to do so.

In this day and age, certainly in "advanced" Western countries, it is much easier to imagine the opposite scenario—which, however, will lead to exactly the same result. Imagine a society whose female members

The best antidote to war is women's ridicule; Lysistrata   *THE YELLOW BOOK,* 1895

in particular have been wallowing in such a long period of peace that they no longer see any need either for war or for its culture. As the men preen and strut and bluster, the women, instead of cheering, turn their faces away. They spit on the uniforms and tear off the decorations. They laugh at the hats and tell the troops who are departing for war—this actually happened to one of my friends during the Vietnam era—that they hope the men will be killed.

Some of the more radical feminists go further still. Like Aristophanes's Lysistrata, they reject not only the culture of war but

also the men who, throughout history, have been its main creators, carriers, and beneficiaries. As this kind of feminism gains in force, the culture
of war—the flags, the insignia, the music, and the monuments—is
pushed away from the streets into the barracks. From the barracks it retreats into the halls of the museums and from there into the unvisited,
half-forgotten basements where, in the end, nothing but a few dusty remnants are left. As the culture of war retreats, this kind of feminism gains,
and so on in a cycle that keeps reinforcing itself.

Women have always been absolutely essential to the culture of war
and, through it, to war itself. For that very reason, there are two different
ways in which women, turning toward feminism, may make their destructive impact on the culture of war felt. One is by following Lysistrata's example by turning against the culture, deserting it, and, worst of all,
ridiculing it. The other, which is almost equally bad, is bringing pressure
to bear so as to make armed forces take in too many women and have
them occupy too many important positions—in short, by trying to imitate
men. In either case, the culture in question will have to do without
women's "delicious power" to reflect it and magnify it. As a result, it will
surely collapse like the house of cards any kind of culture is—and so, if
and when war comes, will the ability to fight it and to win it.

The Great Paradox

In theory, war is simply a means to an end, a rational, if very brutal, activity intended to serve the interests of one group of people by killing, wounding, or otherwise incapacitating those who oppose that group. In reality, nothing could be further from the truth. War, and combat in particular, is one of the most exciting, most stimulating activities that we humans can engage in, capable of putting all others in the shade; quite often, that excitement and that stimulation translate themselves into pure joy. This fact alone is, or should be, enough to lift it out of the realm of mere utility, as Clausewitz and many of his "realist" followers would have it, and into that of culture. Indeed, it could be argued, as my friend Edward Luttwak does, that if war is not enjoyable, then likely something is very wrong with the purpose for which it is waged.

The obvious reason why war is supremely exciting is because it is a life-and-death struggle. It is one of the very few activities in which humans, almost all of them men, deliberately court death, and the only one in which they do so while taking on an opponent who is as strong and as intelligent as themselves. They may even be ordered to risk their lives against their will and on pain of the most severe punishments. These facts are reflected in its culture. It was, indeed, very largely to counter the fear of death that the culture of war was created many, many millennia ago and has been maintained ever since.

Whether or not the culture of war belongs to war's "essence," as those who fight in it often seem to believe, or whether it is just a decorative appendage, as too many defense officials and academic strategists think, will not be discussed here. It may be true that the real essence of war is fighting, that fighting has neither rules nor any other sort of culture, and that, to quote Clausewitz, it stands to war as cash payment stands to commerce.[1] However, a treatise on commerce that focuses on cash payments alone while ignoring everything else (if such a thing were possible) would be not just senseless but incomprehensible. It is like saying that the essence of a closet consists of the space it provides for the various kinds of objects that are put into it. Though technically correct, such an argument ignores the fact that it is the sides, the rear, the doors and the shelves that create this space and define it.

While the ostensible function of the culture of war is to make men willing, even eager, to look death in the face, it can do so only if it is understood not as a means to an end but as an end in itself. Those who give their lives for the eagle know very well that it is just an image of a rather nasty bird, painted this or that color and put on top of a pole. A commander who before giving a speech, making the trumpet sound, holding a review, or arranging for a ceremony in which fallen comrades are honored informs listeners or participants that his goal is to "psych them up" for battle will earn nothing but ridicule and/or contempt. Thus reality and pretense mix; to be of any use, the culture of war *must* be useless. Such is the great paradox referred to in the title of this chapter.

In fact, the term *understood,* by putting the emphasis on the intellect, may itself be the wrong choice. Partly because of the sheer terror in which it unfolds, partly because it involves a clash with an enemy who has his own free will and whose actions are often unpredictable, war has an inherent tendency to degenerate into uncontrollable mayhem, the kind of thing that modern strategic parlance, with its penchant for euphemisms, calls "escalation," "inadequate information," and "friction." To prevent this from happening, or to minimize the impact when it does happen, it is not enough for the culture of war to be understood. Instead, it must be felt, experienced, incorporated into the fighters' souls to the point where it and those who are its bearers fuse into one and can no longer be told apart.

All this explains why, whereas weapons, organization, tactics, strategy, and everything else connected with war change, often rapidly and radically, its culture, rooted as it is in human psychology, is largely impervious to change. In one sense, the older it is the better, given that age provides it with a certain patina that cannot be artificially created and for which there is no easy substitute. Other things being equal, the more venerable any element of the culture is, the greater its impact. Which, of course, is one reason why those elements are often adhered to blindly and stupidly, even to the point where they become counterproductive.

We know the past, and we must live with it regardless of whether we want to or not. But how about the present and the future? Is humanity now reaching, will it ever reach, the point where it can heave a sigh of relief, do away with the culture of war (as well as war itself), and concentrate on leading the comfortable life?[2] Some people believe so, and hope to use the opportunity to rid society of "militarism," among other bad things.

Personally, I am more skeptical. It is true that, considering the increase in the earth's population and the growing resources at the disposal of the most powerful political entities, war has become steadily smaller from 1945 on. It is, however, not at all true that this decline has resulted from a change of heart, let alone a change in the nature of the human animal. Almost as far back into history as we can look, there have always been some people who preached the cause of peace. Yet their words and gestures seem to have had precious little impact on a bellicose world. Quite often the champions of peace, instead of sticking to their convictions through thick and thin, ended up advocating war for a cause that they considered right; others were pacifists only because they knew that in case of need their countrymen would do their dirty work for them. To the extent that change did take place, it was due almost exclusively to fear of a nuclear holocaust that would render meaningless the very objective of war, victory.

While this fear has prevented the world's most powerful political entities from going at each other's throats as they used to, it has been almost completely powerless to prevent war against or between lesser entities. Take Korea, take Biafra, take Vietnam. Take the Indo-Pakistan War of 1971; take the eight-year Iran-Iraq War, take the former Yugoslavia, take Angola, take Mozambique; take the Soviet invasion of Afghanistan; take Colombia, take Rwanda, take Sudan. The groups and armies responsible for these conflicts did not always have the best available organization or the best available weapons. But this fact did not prevent them from behaving as ferociously and committing as many atrocities as their larger and better-equipped predecessors.

Even in the developed world, and even in many of the countries where rulers and opinion makers like doing nothing better than denouncing other people's tendency toward "militarism," the warlike spirit is often alive and well. This is proved, if proof were really needed, by people's tendency to read books about war, watch movies whose topic is war, play games that imitate or are based on war, and experience a surge of interest every time some war breaks out in some other country, however remote and unimportant it may be. It is true that some of these manifestations of the old warlike spirit are trivial; not every armchair strategist is prepared to go out and risk his or her life. On the other hand, some deserve to be taken seriously. They suggest that Thor's hammer, though it has long been at rest, has not been forgotten. If and when the occasion demands, it may yet be taken up by a firm, determined hand.

As Sun Pin, a Chinese commander and military writer who lived some twenty-three centuries ago, said, "However mighty the state, whoever takes pleasure in war will perish."[3] It is, however, also true, as Sun Pin himself said, that "though war may take place only once in a hundred years, it must be prepared for as if it could break out the very next day." Almost any kind of human activity will be conducted more effectively and almost any kind of human product improved if those who engage in it or manufacture it do not just plod along but take pleasure in what they are doing. Why, then, should preparing for war and waging it be an exception?

If war is to be waged at all, let alone if it is to be waged successfully, then keeping up its culture is a sine qua non. Should circumstances make doing so impossible, or should things be taken too far, then, as we saw, four different outcomes are possible. The first is the wild horde, a force that, having no discipline and no cohesion, can wage war only as long as there is no enemy. The second is the soulless machine, made up of robots rather then men; the third, men without chests, who neither can nor will defend themselves when the need arises. The fourth is feminism. Like the other three, feminism both reflects a declining culture of war and acts as a factor that can cause such a decline. Unlike the other three, it is a two-edged sword. When it comes to maintaining the culture of war, too many women joining the military and trying to gain their share of that culture are just as dangerous as women who turn their backs on it.

Like so many books, this one ends where it began. I am neither a commander nor a defense official; in deciding to become an academic and choosing the *vita contemplativa,* my aim has always been not so much to offer guidance or change the world as simply to understand. It appears to me now, as it did when I started working on this project, that the culture of war does not deserve the contempt in which some people tend to hold it. Instead, it is at least as interesting, at least as important, and at least as worthy of being studied as any other subject I might have chosen. If, having got to this point, the reader shares this feeling, then I have achieved all I set out to do.

ACKNOWLEDGMENTS

The idea for this book came to me in October 2005, when the Musée d'Art et d'Industrie in Saint-Étienne, France, asked me to do an introductory essay for the catalog of an exhibition it was preparing under the title *Bang! Bang!*. I therefore wish to thank the director of the museum, Ms. Veronique Baton.

At the time, I was living in Postdam, Germany, and I was fortunate to have the gracious assistance of the staffs at the Staatsbibliothek, Berlin, and of the library of the Militärgeschichtliches Forschungsamt, Potsdam. Without them, this book would never have been completed, let alone seen print. Later, the staffs at the Library of the Hebrew University, Mount Scopus, and at the National Library, Givat Ram, were equally helpful in trying to meet my sometimes rather strange requests.

My good friends in Berlin and Potsdam were forced to listen to me endlessly discussing the project; I ask their forgiveness. I am especially grateful to Ms. Aiga Mueller, a splendid artist whose works always give me something to think about. Then there are Dr. Erich Vad, Dr. Anneke Vad, Mr. Mortiz Schwarz, and Prof. Konrad Jarausch. In addition to being a most gracious host, Mr. Jarausch also helped me get a position at the Institut fuer Zeitgeschichte.

I wish to thank the Axel and Margaret Axson Johnson Foundation, Stockholm, and especially its director, Mr. Kurt Almquist. The foundation generously provided me with a grant during my year in Potsdam. Originally it was supposed to support another book, *The American Riddle*, but as often happens, by the time I was able to get the grant, *that* volume was already more or less finished. I hope the foundation does not mind getting two books for the price of one.

My agents, Gabriele Pantucci and Leslie Gardner, of Artellus Ldt., London, have been their usual marvelous selves. Their only shortcoming is that they do not visit me in Israel, where I would be able to return the hospitality that they have so often extended to me. I hope they'll do so very soon.

My editor, Mr. Ryan Doherty, did all an author can expect and more. I am grateful for that.

My son, Uri van Creveld, my stepdaughter, Adi Lewy, and my step-son, Jonathan Lewy, all discussed things with me—often, whether they wanted to or not. Thanks for that—and for everything you do and are.

Finally, for you, Dvora. You, who are worth as much to me as all my books combined, and then some; you, who have given me nothing less than life itself. You are my butterfly, and what holds you is a net of words, whispers, and gestures that is known as love.

NOTES

INTRODUCTION

1. See on this, above all, C. von Clausewitz, *On War,* Princeton, NJ, Princeton University Press, 1976, pp. 75–99.
2. On the "uselessness" of culture and its affinity to play see, above all, J. Huizinga, *Homo Ludens,* New York, Beacon, 1971 [1939], especially chapter 1.
3. Deuteronomy: 20.10–20.
4. Chretien de Troyes, *Le roman de Perceval ou Le Conte du Grall,* S. Hannedouche, ed., Paris, Triade, 1969, lines 1632–35; P. de Bourdeille, Brantôme, *Oeuvres completes,* L. Lalanne, ed., Paris, Renouard, 1862–64, vol. 6, pp. 476–77.
5. A. Santosusosso, *Soldiers, Citizens, and the Symbols of War,* Boulder, CO, Westview, 1997.
6. See, for a good discussion of such lines, M. Lissak, "Boundaries and Institutional Linkages Between Elites: Some Illustrations from Civil-Military Relations in Israel," *Research in Politics and Society,* 1985, pp. 129–48.

CHAPTER 1: FROM WAR PAINT TO TIGER SUITS

1. See, for numerous examples of the use of war paint, L. H. Charles, "Drama in War," *Journal of American Folklore,* 68, 26, 1955, pp. 254–59.
2. *Bellum Gallicum,* v. 14. Here and in subsequent references the edition used, unless otherwise indicated, is that of Loeb Classical Library.
3. C. James, *Regimental Companion,* London, Egerton, 1813, vol. 3, pp. 468–69.
4. C. H. Enloe, *Does Khaki Become You?* New York, South End, 1983; A. J. Bacevich, *The New American Militarism,* New York, Oxford University Press, 2005; B. Goshen, *War Paint,* New York, Ballantine, 2001.

5. D. G. Chandler, *The Campaigns of Napoleon*, New York, Macmillan, 1966, p. 226.

6. S. Freud, "Medusa's Head" [1922], in S. Freud, *Standard Edition*, London, Hogarth Press, 1973, vol. 18, pp. 273–74.

7. *Iliad*, 11.14–46.

8. *Iliad*, 18.474–609, 20.268–72.

9. Xenophon, *Memorabilia*, 3.10.14.

10. *Constitution of the Lacedaemonians*, 11.3.

11. R. Justin, *Epitome of the Philippic History*, Atlanta, Scholars Press, 1997, ii.7.

12. *Iliad*, 4.466–75.

13. See on this, J. Garbsch, *Roemische Paraderuestungen*, Munich, Beck, 1978, p. 3.

14. See, for Xenophon, W. K. Pritchett, *The Greek State at War*, Berkeley, University of California Press, 1985, part IV, p. 242.

15. Livy ix. 40.21–6.

16. Caesar, *Bellum Civile*, 67; Plutarch, *Pompey*, 69.

17. Tacitus, *Agricola*, 32.

18. Ammianus Marcelinus, 18.2.17; Vegetius, *Roman Military* (*Epitoma rei militari*), Philadelphia, Pavillion, 2004, p. 88.

19. See on this, B. Bar Kochva, *The Seleucid Army*, Cambridge, Cambridge University Press, 1978, pp. 20–47.

20. See K. Gilliver, "Display in Roman Warfare: The Appearance of Armies and Individuals on the Battlefield," *War in History*, 14, 1, January 2007, especially pp. 15, 19–20.

21. See on these finds, H. Schutz, *Tools, Weapons and Ornaments: Germanic Material Culture in Pre-Carolingian Central Europe, 400–750*, Leiden, Brill, 2001, pp. 155, 157.

22. Periodization by C. H. Ashdown, *Armor and Weapons in the Middle Ages*, London, Harrap, 1925, p. 9.

23. D. Bashford, *Handbook of Arms and Armor, European and Oriental*, New York, Metropolitan Museum of Art, 1930, p. 91, figure 48.

24. On the links between armor and fashion see R. E. Oakshott, *European Arms and Armor: From the Renaissance to the Industrial Revolution*, Guildford, Lutterworth, 1978, pp. 78–88.

25. See the excellent illustrations in S. Bull, *A Historical Guide to Arms and Armor*, New York, Facts on File, 1991, pp. 38–39.

26. See, for some examples, Bashford, *Handbook of Arms and Armor*, p. 63, figure 27.

27. Ibid., pp. 70–71, figures 33 and 35.

28. See F. Lachand, "Armor and Military Dress in Thirteenth- and Early-Fourteenth-Century England," in M. Strickland, ed., *Armies, Chivalry and Warfare in Medieval England and France*, Stamford, Watkins, 1998, pp. 358–59.

29. J. Huizinga, *The Waning of the Middle Ages*, Harmondsworth, Penguin, 1965

[1924], passim. The same idea runs though R. L. Kilgour, *The Decline of Chivalry as Shown in the French Literature of the Late Middle Ages*, Gloucester, MA, Smith, 1966 [1937], pp. 3–57.

30. M. G. A. Vale, *War and Chivalry: Warfare and Aristocratic Culture in England, France, and Burgundy at the End of the Middle Ages*, Athens, University of Georgia Press, 1981.

31. Huizinga, *Homo Ludens*, pp. 195–213.

32. See C. Beaufort and M. Pfaffenbichler, *Meisterwerke der Hofjagd- und Ruestkammer*, Vienna, Kunsthistorische Museum, 2005, pp. 206–7.

33. *L'Apparicion de Maistre Jehan de Meun*, Strasbourg, University of Strasbourg, 1926, vol. v, 459ff; Ph. de Commynes, *Memoires*, J. Calmalte, ed., Paris, Libraire Ancienne, 1924, vol. II, p. 102.

34. See, for some examples, G. N. Pant, *Studies in Indian Weapons and Warfare*, New Delhi, Singh, 1970, pp. 122–25.

35. Taira Shigesuke, *Code of the Samurai*, T. Cleary, trans., Boston, Tuttle, 1999 [ca. 1700], p. 72.

36. See on this episode, S. Trumbull, *Samurai Warfare*, London, Arms and Armor, 1996, pp. 110–11.

37. *My Reveries on the Art of War*, Harrisburg, PA, Army War College, 1940, pp. 194–95.

38. R. Koser, "Aus den letzten Tagen Koenig Friedrich Wilhelms I," *Hohenzoller-nerJahrbuch*, 7, 1904, p. 25.

39. See on this, E. H. Gombrich, *The Sense of Order: A Study in the Psychology of Decorative Art*, London, Phaidon, 1984.

40. See on this subject, S. H. Myerly, *British Military Spectacle: From the Napoleonic Wars Through the Crimea*, Cambridge, Harvard University Press, 1996, pp. 18–19, 22–27, 78.

41. Major General John Mitchell, *Thoughts on Tactics and Military Organization*, London, Longman & Co., 1838, p. 225.

42. The illustrations are reprinted in K. P. Merta, *Uniformen der Armee Friedrich Wilhelms III*, Berlin, Brandenburgisches Verlagshaus, 1993, plates on pp. 45–47.

43. See, for example, Major John Patterson, *Camp and Quarters; Scenes and Impressions of Military Life*, London, 1840, vol. 1, p. 240.

44. See on this, Myerly, *British Military Spectacle*, pp. 111–12.

45. A. Zahavi, "Mate Selection—a Selection for a Handicap," *Journal of Theoretical Biology*, 53, 1975, pp. 205–14; A. Zahavi, "The Cost of Honesty," *Journal of Theoretical Biology*, 67, 1977, pp. 603–5.

46. Quoted in R. A. Janssen, *Growing Up in Ancient Egypt*, London, Rubicon, 1990, pp. 103–4.

47. A. Somerville, *The Autobiography of a Working Man*, London, MacGibbon, 1967 [1848], p. 125.

48. H. Dollinger, *Wenn die Soldaten . . .* Munich, Bruckmann, 1974, p. 32, reproducing a pre-1914 caricature by E. Heilemann.

49. Colin Powell, *My American Journey*, New York, Random House, 1995, p. 26.

50. H. Newman, *Auto-Biographie,* Munich, Goldmann, 2002, p. 303.

51. See, on some of these variations, P. Fussell, *Uniforms,* Boston, Houghton Mifflin, 2002, pp. 17, 27, 28–29, 56.

52. G. Sajer, *The Forgotten Soldier,* London, Cassell, 1971, p. 460.

53. See J. Thompson, *War Games: Inside the World of Twentieth-Century War Reenactors,* Washington, DC, Smithsonian, 2004, p. 68.

54. Quoted in Fussell, *Uniforms,* p. 27.

CHAPTER 2: FROM BOOMERANGS TO BASTIONS

1. These remarks on China are taken from M. Loehr, *Chinese Bronze Age Weapons,* Ann Arbor, University of Michigan Press, 1955, passim.

2. See, for the following, G. Philip, *Metal Weapons of the Early and Middle Bronze Ages in Syria-Palestine,* Oxford, B.A.R, 1989, pp. 115, 145–46, 151, 154–55, 175, 179, 184, 196–97, 205.

3. Quoted in R. E. Oakshott, *The Archaeology of Weapons: Arms and Armor from Prehistory to the Age of Chivalry,* London, Lutterworth, 1960, p. 17.

4. Shahrum Yub, *The Keris and Other Short Weapons,* Kuala Lumpur, Museum Association of Malaysia, 1991, passim.

5. See on this, H. R. Ellis Davidson, "The Ring on the Sword," *Journal of the Arms and Armor Society,* 11, 10, June 1958.

6. Taira Shigesuke, *Code of the Samurai,* T. Cleary, trans, Boston, Tuttle, 1999 [ca. 1700], p. 13.

7. Oakshott, *The Archaeology of Weapons,* pp. 224–28.

8. Ibid., pp. 214–23.

9. I. Bottomley and A. Hopson, *Arms and Armor of the Samurai: A History of Weaponry in Ancient Japan,* New York, Crescent Books, 1988, p. 8; G. N. Pant, *Studies in Indian Weapons and Warfare,* New Delhi, Singh, 1970, p. 80.

10. Pant, *Studies in Indian Weapons,* p. 89.

11. *Chanson de Roland,* S. C. Moncrief, trans. (1919, available online at http://omacl.org/Roland/), lines 2303–54.

12. Bottomley and Hopson, *Arms and Armor of the Samurai,* p. 36.

13. *Inscriptae Grecae* (2), 1614–28.

14. See D. H. Kennedy, *Ship Names: Origins and Usage During 45 Centuries,* Newport News, VA, Mariners' Museum, 1974.

15. E. Jüenger, *The Storm of Steel,* London, Penguin, 2004, p. 261.

16. H. Olsen, "Nose Art," 2005, available at www.nps.gov/wapa/indepth/PacThreatTopics/noseart.htm.

17. See the picture in S. Bull, *A Historical Guide to Arms and Armor,* New York, Facts on File, 1991, p. 24.

18. G. Smith, "The Saddamizers," *Village Voice,* April 9–15, 2003.

19. See, for a picture of the tank in question, www.perthmilitarymodelling.com/reviews/vehicles/echelon/ech_t35004_5.htm.

20. See the picture in M. van Creveld, *Technology and War,* New York, 1989, following p. 128.

21. See on this entire subject, F. T. Elsworthy, *The Evil Eye: The Classic Account of an Ancient Superstition,* New York, Dover, 2004.

22. S. Freud, *The Interpretation of Dreams,* New York, Macmillan, 1913, especially pp. 131–62.

23. See C. Cohn, " 'Clean Bombs' and Clean Language," in J. B. Ehlstain and S. Tobias, eds., *Women, Militarism, and War,* Boston, Rowman & Littlefield, 1990, pp. 33–42.

24. See the comments, some of them by personnel with combat experience, at www.gadgetopia.com/post/4258.

25. The History Channel, "Battle Stations: Attack Helicopter," shown on January 21, 2004. Details available at www.thehistorychannel.co.uk/text_only/tv_listings/full_details/Technology/programme_2522.ph.

26. A good introduction to this subject is G.-Michael Duerre, *Die Steinerne Garnison: Die Geschichte der Berliner Militaerbauten,* Berlin, Dürre, 2001. I wish to thank the author for presenting me with this work.

27. See E. Porada, "Battlements in the Military Architecture and Symbolism of the Ancient Near East," in D. Frazer et al., eds., *Essays in the History of Architecture Presented to Rudolf Wittkower,* London, Phaidon, 1967, pp. 1–12.

28. S. Trumbull, *Samurai Warfare,* London, Arms and Armor, 1996, pp. 83, 89.

29. Ibid., p. 83.

30. See S. Pepper, "Ottoman Military Architecture in the Early Gunpowder Era; A Reassessment," and S. S. Blair, "Decoration of City Walls in the Medieval Islamic World; The Epigraphic Message", both in J. D. Tracy, ed., *City Walls: The Urban Enceinte in Global Perspective,* Cambridge, Cambridge University Press, 2000, pp. 282–316 and 488–529, respectively.

31. S. Pepper, "Siege Law, Siege Ritual and Symbolism of City Walls," in Tracy, ed., *City Walls,* p. 584.

32. S. Pepper, "Artisans, Architects, and Aristocrats; Professionalism and Renaissance Military Engineering," in D.J.B. Trim, ed., *The Chivalric Ethos and the Development of Military Professionalism,* Leiden, Brill, 2003, pp. 142–43.

33. The following is based on R. K. Morris, "The Architecture of Arthurian Enthusiasm: Castle Symbolism in the Reigns of Edward I and His Successors," in M. Strickland, ed., *Armies, Chivalry and Warfare in Medieval England and France,* Stamford, Watkins, 1998, pp. 63–75.

34. See on this, T. A. Heslop, "Orford Castle, Nostalgia and Sophisticated Living," *Architectural History,* 34, 1991, pp. 36–58.

35. See on this, C. Coulson, "Structural Symbolism in Medieval Castle Architecture," *Journal of the British Archaeological Association,* 132, 1979, pp. 73–90.

36. Morris, "The Architecture of Arthurian Enthusiasm," p. 63.

37. See on this form of "Christianity," D. L. Bergen, *Twisted Cross; The German Christian Movement in the Third Reich*, Chapel Hill, University of North Carolina Press, 1996, pp. 192–205.

38. See, for a general account of the military cultures in question, M. J. Meggitt, *Blood Is Their Argument; Warfare Among the Mae Enga Tribesmen of the New Guinea Highlands*, Palo Alto, CA, Mayfield, 1977.

CHAPTER 3: EDUCATING WARRIORS

1. Von Salomon, *Die Kadetten*, Hamburg, Rowohlt, 1957 [1942], p. 29.

2. J. Fadiman, *An Oral History of Tribal Warfare: The Meru of Mt. Kenya;* Athens, Ohio University Press, 1982, pp. 71–73, 76–84.

3. For the little we know about the training of medieval knights see M. Keen, *Chivalry*, New Haven, Yale University Press, 1984, pp. 9, 26, 226, 227.

4. See on this period, for example, J. F. Leahy, *Honor, Courage, Commitment; Navy Boot Camp*, Annapolis, MD, Naval Institute Press, 2002, pp. 8–9.

5. See on this, M. Volkin, *The Ultimate Basic Training Guidebook*, New York, Savas Beatie, 2005, pp. 53–55; K. B. Galloway and R. B. Johnson, *West Point: America's Power Fraternity*, New York, Simon & Schuster, 1973, pp. 44–61.

6. Johannes Leeb, *Wir Waren Hitlers Eliteschueler*, Munich, Heyne, 1999, p. 62.

7. G. Sajer, *The Forgotten Soldier*, London, Cassell, 1971, p. 201.

8. Xenophon, *Constitution of the Lacedaemonians*, 2.3.

9. See, for the methods used by the U.S. Armed Forces to condition men to killing, D. Grossman, *On Killing: The Psychological Cost of Learning to Kill in War and Society*, Boston, Little, Brown, 1995, pp. 252–59.

10. Volkin, *The Ultimate Basic Training Guidebook*, p. xv.

11. This and the following pieces of information on Sparta are taken from N. M. Kennell, *The Gymnasium of Virtue: Education and Culture in Ancient Sparta*, Chapel Hill, University of North Carolina Press, 1995, p. 134.

12. See A. Fuks, "Agis, Cleomenes and Equality," *Classical Philology*, 57, 3, 1962, pp. 161–69.

13. See M. van Creveld, *The Training of Officers; From Professionalism to Irrelevance*, New York, Free Press, 1990, p. 29.

14. J. Moncure, *Forging the King's Sword: Between Tradition and Modernization: The Case of the Royal Prussian Cadet Corps, 1871–1914*, New York, Lang, 1993, p. 110.

15. See G. S. Pappas, *To the Point: The United States Military Academy, 1802–1902*, Westport, CT, Praeger, 1993, pp. 102–3.

16. See G. Horsmann, *Untersuchungen zur militaerischen Ausbildung im republikanischen und Kaiserzeitlichen Rom*, Boppard/Rhein, Boldt, 1991, pp. 6–8.

17. See, for Israel, D. Kaplan, *Brothers and Others in Arms; The Making of Love and War in Israeli Combat Units*, New York, Harrington Park, 2003; for the Philippines, A. W. McCoy, *Closer Than Brothers; Manhood at the*

Philippine Military Academy, New Haven, Yale University Press, 1999, especially pp. 35–73.

18. Xenophon, *Constitution of the Lacedaemonians,* 6.

19. Plutarch, *Lycurgus,* 16.8.

20. Pollux, *Onomasticon,* Stuttgart, Teubner, 1967, 9.104.

21. For a discussion of what military history can and cannot do for military education see T. E. Griess, "A Perspective on Military History," in J. E. Jessup and R. W. Coakley, eds., *A Guide to the Study of Military History,* Washington, DC, U.S. Government Printing Office, 1979, pp. 25–40.

22. Polybios, *The Histories,* ix.1–2; Niccolo Machiavelli, *The Discourses,* B. Crick, ed., London, Penguin, 1998, introduction, pp. 50–62.

23. Kennell, *The Gymnasium of Virtue,* pp. 121, 125–26, 132.

24. See on this Moncure, *Forging the King's Sword,* pp. 180, 183; also van Creveld, *The Training of Officers,* pp. 27–28.

25. See E. J. Krige, *The Social System of the Zulus,* London, Longmans, 1936, pp. 106ff.

26. Horsmann, *Untersuchungen zur militaerischen Ausbildung,* pp. 77–82.

27. Quoted in D. Ayalon, "The Mamluk Military Institution," in *The Mamluk Military Society; Collected Studies,* London, Variorum, 1979, pp. 54–55.

28. *Laws,* 830c–831a.

29. For a list of shortcomings in one such base see Leahy, *Honor, Courage, Commitment,* pp. 81–82.

30. See on the standards, A. Goldsworthy, *Roman Warfare,* London, Cassell, 2000, pp. 97, 128; also Garbsch, *Roemische Paraderuestungen,* pp. 14–15.

31. Pappas, *To the Point,* p. 139.

32. See, for Crete, Strabo, *Geographies,* 10.483–84, quoting Ephorus. The Spartan novitiate, known as *krypteia,* is described in Plato, *Laws,* 633b, and Plutarch, *Lycurgus,* 28.

33. See, for Athens, Thucydides, *The Peloponnesian War,* 2.13.7, 4.67.2, 8.92.2, as well as Aischines, 1.49, 2.167–68. For a somewhat fanciful reconstruction of the training period as it existed in Athens, see P. Vidal Naquet, "The Black Hunter and the Origins of the Athenian Ephebeia," in R. L. Gordon, ed., *Myth, Religion, and Society,* Cambridge, Cambridge University Press, 1981, pp. 147–62.

34. See F. Gies, *The Knight in History,* New York, Harper & Row, 1984, pp. 81–82, 92–93; also Keen, *Chivalry,* pp. 224–27.

35. See on this, M. van Creveld, *Fighting Power; German and U.S. Army Performance, 1939–1945,* Westport, CT, Greenwood Press, 1982, p. 72.

36. Kennell, *The Gymnasium of Virtue,* p. 109.

37. The best discussion of dubbing and the ceremonial by which it was surrounded is Keen, *Chivalry,* pp. 64–82.

38. Kaplan, *Brothers and Others in Arms,* pp. 84, 208.

39. See, for the details, www.combatreform.com/extremeexcrement.htm.

40. *Greek Historical Inscriptions,* M. N. Tod, ed., Oxford, Clarendon, 1948, vol. 2, no. 204.

41. See Kennel, *The Gymnasium of Virtue*, p. 43.
42. For example, J. D. Winkler and P. S. Steinberg, *Restructuring Military Education and Training; Lessons from RAND Research*, Santa Monica, CA, RAND, 1997, as well as the large bibliography on which it rests.

CHAPTER 4: GAMES OF WAR

1. E. Longford, *Wellington: The Years of the Sword*, New York, 1969, pp. 16, 17.
2. In this, as well as my understanding of games in general, I am following J. Huizinga, *Homo Ludens*, New York, Beacon, 1971 [1939], especially pp. 1–27.
3. *The Will to Power*, W. Kaufmann, ed., New York, 1967, fragment no. 649, p. 344; no. 656, p. 346; no. 658, p. 347; no. 649, p. 353.
4. "Über Strategie" [1871], in Generalstab, ed., *Moltkes Militaerischen Werken*, Berlin, Mittler, 1891, part 2, p. 291.
5. J. S. Henderson, *The World of the Ancient Maya*, Ithaca, Cornell University Press, 1997, p. 230.
6. 2 Samuel, 2.14–15.
7. See on this, J. Keegan, *The Face of Battle*, London, Cape, 1976, pp. 299–302, 308.
8. See on this M. Golden, *Sport and Society in Ancient Greece*, Cambridge, Cambridge University Press, 1998, p. 37.
9. See on the culture in question D. Ayalon, "Notes on the *Furusiyya*," chapter 2 in idem, *The Mamluk Military Society: Collected Studies:* London, Variorum, 1979.
10. Plato, *Laws*, 823b; also Isocrates, *Panathenaikos*, 163.
11. C. B. Stanford, *The Hunting Apes: Meat Eating and the Origins of Human Behavior*, Princeton, NJ, Princeton University Press, 1999, p. 5 and passim.
12. See, for the reasons why men hunt, F. Wood Jr., *The Delights and Dilemmas of Hunting*, Lanham, MD, University Press of America, 1997, pp. 10–39.
13. See D. M. Carroll, *An Interdisciplinary Study of Sport as a Symbolic Hunt*, Lewiston, NY, Mellen, 2000, especially pp. 29–69.
14. Stanford, *The Hunting Apes*, pp. 3–4; R. Wrangham and D. Peterson, *Demonic Males: Apes and the Origins of Human Violence*, Boston, Houghton Mifflin, 1996, pp. 5–6, 16–18.
15. See the interesting article by M. Pastoureau, "La Chasse au Sanglier: Histoire d'une Dévalorisation," in A. Paravicini Bagliani and B. van den Abeele, eds., *La Chasse au Moyen Age: Société, traités, symboles*, Turnhout, Brepols, 2000, pp. 7–32.
16. J. M. Barringer, *The Hunt in Ancient Greece*, Baltimore, Johns Hopkins University Press, 2001, pp. 2–3.
17. See, for example, D. Petersen, *A Hunter's Heart*, New York, Holt, 1996, p. 2; G. E. Dowd, *A Spirited Resistance; The North American Struggle for Indian Unity*, 1745–1815, Baltimore, Johns Hopkins University Press, 1992, pp. 9–22; H. S. Knight, *The Creed of Kinship*, New York, Dutton, 1935, p. 34.
18. Xenophon, *On Hunting*, R. D. Doty, ed., Lampeter, Mellen, 2001, 2.1, 12.1.

See, for similar views, Xenophon, *Cyropaedia,* 12.10–11; Plato, *Republic,* 549A; *Plato Laws,* 763b; *Plato, Soph.,* 219d–e, 222c.

19. N. Machiavelli, *The Discourses,* B. Crick, ed., London, Penguin, 1998, p. 511.
20. See on this, J. A. Mangan and C. McKenzie, " 'Pig-Sticking Is the Greatest Fun'; Martial Conditioning on the Hunting Fields of Empire," in J. A. Mangan, ed., *Militarism, Sport, Europe: War Without Weapons,* London, Cass, 2003, pp. 97–119.
21. See on this, Keegan, *The Face of Battle,* pp. 314–18.
22. G. S. Patton, *War as I Knew It,* New York, Bantam, 1981 [1947], pp. 317–18; Z. Dror, *The Life and Times of Yitzhak Sadeh* [Hebrew], Tel Aviv, Hakibbutz Hameuchad, 1996, p. 151.
23. See, for the ancient Greek case, Barringer, *The Hunt in Ancient Greece,* pp. 7, 21, 23, 27, 33, 34, 35, 43; for the Indians of North America, A. Starkey, *European and Native American Warfare, 1675–1815,* Norman, University of Oklahoma Press, 1998, pp. 27–28.
24. W. J. Baker, *Sports in the Western World,* Totowa, NJ, Rowman & Littlefield, 1982, p. 8.
25. Quoted in M. B. Poliakoff, *Combat Sports in the Ancient World,* New Haven, Yale University Press, 1987, p. 96.
26. *Iliad,* 23.820–25.
27. Plutarch, *Pyrrhus,* 23.6; *Plutarch,* Pelopides, 7.3.
28. Plutarch, *Cleomenes,* 27.2.
29. Valerius Maximus, *Memorable Doings and Sayings,* Cambridge, Harvard University Press, 2000, 2.4.7.
30. Karl Meuli, "Der Ursprung der Olympischen Spiele," *Die Antike Welt,* 17, 1941, pp. 189–208.
31. See on these developments, D. G. Kyle, "From the Battlefield to the Arena: Gladiators, Militarism and the Roman Republic," in V.A. Mangan, ed., *Militarism, Sport, Europe,* pp. 10–27.
32. Tertulian, *De Spectaculis,* Florence, Nuova Italia, 1961, 22.
33. Augustine, *The Confessions,* Cambridge, Cambridge University Press, 1993, 6.8.3.
34. Cicero, *Murena,* 39.
35. Suetonius, *Claudius,* 34.
36. *Iliad,* 23.664–75.
37. *Anabasis,* 5.8.23.
38. *The War Songs of Tyrtaeus,* J. Banks, trans., London, Bell, 1881, fragment 12W.
39. *Autolykos,* fragment 228N, quoted in Poliakoff, *Combat Sports,* p. 99.
40. *Republic,* 403e–404b.
41. See on them, Poliakoff, *Combat Sports,* pp. 99–100.
42. Lucian, *Anacharsis,* J. F. Kindstrand, ed., Uppsala, University of Uppsala, 1981, 15.30; Philostratus, *Concerning Gymnastics,* T. Wood, ed., Ann Arbor, University of Michigan, 1936, 9.11.43; Plutarch, *Moralia,* 639a–640a.
43. See on this, Poliakoff, *Combat Sports,* pp. 97–98.

44. Xenophon, *Memorabilia,* 1.2.4, 3.5.15.

45. Aristophanes, *The Clouds,* Harmondsworth, Penguin, 1973, line 1012.

46. Aristotle, *Politics,* 8.4.1338b.

47. Florus, *Epitome of Roman History,* 2.8.14.

48. Valerius Maximus, *Memorable Doings and Sayings,* 2.3.2; see also Vegetius, *Roman Military,* 1.11.

49. See, for what follows, M. Keen, *Chivalry,* New Haven, Yale University Press, 1984, pp. 85–101.

50. Quoted in F. H. Cripps-Day, *History of the Tournament in England and France,* London, Quaritch, 1918, p. xxv.

51. See on this subject, R. V. Barker, *The Tournament in England, 1100–1400,* London, Boydell, 1986, pp. 45–69.

52. See, for the knight's training and the role played by tournaments, J. F. Verbruggen, *The Art of Warfare in Western Europe During the Middle Ages,* Woodbridge, Boydell, 1997, pp. 27–36.

53. See, above all, the career of William the Marshal as set forth in G. Duby, ed., *Guillaume le Marechal,* Paris, Fayard, 1984.

54. J. Larner, "Chivalric Culture in the Age of Dante," *Renaissance Studies,* 2, 1988, p. 122ff.

55. See on this entire subject, Barker, *The Tournament in England,* pp. 101–11.

56. The episode is mentioned in J. Stowe, *Survey of London,* Oxford, Clarendon, 1908 [1603], vol. 1, p. 268.

57. J. K. Rühl, "Wesen und Bedeutung von Kampfsagen und Trefferzhalenskitzzen für die Geschichte des spaetmittelalterlichen Tourniers," in G. Spitzer and D. Schmidt, eds., *Sport zwischen Eigenstaendigkeit und Fremdbestimmung,* Bonn, Institut für Sportwissenschaft, 1986, pp. 82–112.

58. See, for a short discussion of this problem, K. Chase, *Firearms: A Global History to 1700,* Cambridge, Cambridge University Press, 2003, p. 59.

59. R. Eales, *Chess: The History of a Game,* New York, Facts on File, 1985, chapter 1.

60. See on this entire subject, P. P. Perla, *The Art of Wargaming,* Annapolis, MD, Naval Institute Press, 1990, pp. 15–60.

61. See on its various versions, "Winning at Stratego", n.d., available at www.drewcampbell.net/stratego/variations.html.

62. See Wilbur Gray, "Military Wargaming," 1995, available at www.nhmgs.org/articles/historyofwargaming.html.

63. See Perla, *The Art of Wargaming,* pp. 61–104; also J. Prados, *Pentagon Games: Wargames and the American Military,* New York, Harper & Row, 1987, p. 4.

64. For example, in preparation for submarine warfare in the Atlantic and the invasion of Russia in 1941. See K. Doenitz, *Ten Years and Twenty Days,* Westport, CT, Greenwood, 1976 [1959], pp. 32–33; and F. Halder, *Kriegstagebuch,* Stuttgart, Kohlhammer, 1962, vol. 2, pp. 201, 205, entries for November 29 and December 3, 1940. Incidentally, the man in charge of this particular game was General von Paulus, who later surrendered at Stalingrad.

65. H. G. Wells, *Little Wars: A Game for Boys from Twelve Years to One Hundred and Fifty and for That More Intelligent Sort of Girl Who Likes Games and Books*, London, Arms and Armor, 1970 [1913].

66. F. Jane, *How to Play the Jane Naval War Game*, London, Sampson Law, 1903.

67. See, for the possibilities such games offer, S. P. Glick and L. Ian Charteris, "War, Games, and Military History," *Journal of Contemporary History*, 18, 4, October 1983, pp. 567–82.

68. See V. Giginov, " 'Fitness 'Wars': Purpose and Politics in Communist State-Building," in Mangan, ed., *Militarism, Sport, Europe*, p. 277.

CHAPTER 5: OPENING GAMBITS

1. See K. Lorenz, *On Aggression*, London, Methuen, 1963, pp. 94–99.

2. *Germania*, 43.

3. L. Keeley, *War Before Civilization; The Myth of the Peaceful Savage*, New York, Oxford University Press, 1996, p. 196, appendix, table 6.2.

4. See V. D. Hanson, *The Wars of the Ancient Greeks*, London, Cassell, 1999, pp. 68–69.

5. Thucydides, *The Peloponnesian War*, I.23.5–6.

6. Livy, *The Histories*, 24.32.

7. T. Pakenham, *The Scramble for Africa, 1876–1912*, New York, Random House, 1991, pp. 452–69, describes how it was done.

8. J. M. Cooper, *Analytical and Critical Bibliography of the Tribes of Tierra del Fuego and Adjacent Territory*, Washington, DC, Bureau of American Ethnology, 1917, Bulletin No. 63, p. 154.

9. See M. van Creveld, *The Rise and Decline of the State*, Cambridge, Cambridge University Press, 1999, pp. 72–73, 133–34.

10. The Moscow ceremony is described in W. L. Shirer, *The Rise and Fall of the Third Reich*, New York, Simon & Schuster, 1960, pp. 1110–11.

11. See C. Lowman, *Displays of Power; Art and War Among the Marings of New Guinea*, New York, Museum of Primitive Art, 1973.

12. See H. H. Turney-High, *Primitive War: Its Practice and Concepts*, Columbia, University of South Carolina Press, 1971 [1949], pp. 167–68, 245–46.

13. S. Leblanc, *Constant Battle: The Myth of the Peaceful, Noble Savage*, New York, St. Martin's, 2003, pp. 144, 155.

14. Herodotus, *The Histories*, vii.9.

15. Nithard, *Historiarum Libri IV*, Hanover, Han, 1955, II.3., p. 33; II.9, pp. 23ff; IV.3, p. 44.

16. C.W.C. Oman, *The Art of War in the Middle Ages*, A.D. *378–1515*, Ithaca, NY, Cornell University Press, 1963 [1885], pp. 61–63.

17. K. G. Cram, *Iudicium Belli: Zum Rechtskarakter des Krieges im Deutschen Mittelalter*, Muenster, Boehlau, 1955, passim.

18. 1 Samuel 16:1–11.

19. See, for India, R. C. Dutt, trans., *The Mahabharata*, London, Macmillan, 1899, pp. i, vi–x; for Rome, Dio Cassius, "Fragment of Zonoras," *Roman History*, 2.6.7.

20. See, for this entire subject, T. R. Walsh, *Fighting Words and Feuding Words: Anger and the Homeric Poems,* Lanham, MD, Lexington, 2005, pp. 141–62.

21. *The Battle of Maledon,* E. V. Gordon, ed., London, Methuen, 1937, 11.216–23.

22. Quoted in S. Trumbull, *Samurai Warfare,* London, Arms and Armor, 1996, p. 25.

23. Procopius, *History of the Wars,* VIII.28.8–9.

24. *The Works of Liudprand of Cremona,* F. A. Wright, trans., London, Routledge, 1930, pp. 48–50.

25. See on them M. Strickland, "Provoking or Avoiding Battle," in D.J.B. Trim, ed., *The Chivalric Ethos and the Development of Military Professionalism,* Leiden, Brill, 2003, pp. 327–37.

26. Boha ad Din, *The Life of Saladin,* C. L. Conder, trans., Palestine Pilgrims' Texts Society, London, 1897, vol. 12, pp. 161–62.

27. J. J. Glück, "Reviling and Monomachy as Battle-Preludes in Ancient Warfare," *Acta Classica,* 7, 1964, pp. 26, 31; Turney-High, *Primitive Warfare,* p. 72; R. L. Kilgour, *The Decline of Chivalry,* Gloucester, MA, Smith, 1966 [1937], pp. 10–11, 375–76.

28. J. Fadiman, *An Oral History of Tribal Warfare: The Meru of Mt. Kenya,* Athens, Ohio University Press, 1982, pp. 99–100, 109, 122.

29. For example, 1 Samuel 30:7–8; 2 Samuel 2:19–20.

30. Herodotus, *The Histories,* I.53.

31. P. Cartledge, *The Spartans,* Woodstock, NY, Overview Press, 2003, p. 148.

32. Ibid., pp. 58, 116, 176–77.

33. *Anabasis* 6.4.13–6.5.2.

34. N. Machiavelli, *The Discourses,* B. Crick, ed., London, Penguin, 1998, pp. 139, 148–49, 494–95.

35. Leviticus 7:8.

36. Exodus 17:10–12.

37. Judges 6:36–40.

38. See on this, R. W. Kaeuper and E. Kennedy, eds., *The Book of Chivalry of Geoffroi de Charny,* Philadelphia, University of Pennsylvania Press, 1996, pp. 15–16.

39. William of Poitiers, *Histoire de Guillaume le Conquerant,* R. Foreville, ed., Paris, Belle Lettres, 1952, pp. 180–82.

40. K. Leyser, "The Battle of the Lech, 955," *History,* 50, 1965, pp. 1–25.

41. S. Runciman, "The Holy Lance Found at Antioch," *Analecta Bollandiana,* 68, 1950, pp. 179–209.

42. 1 Samuel 14:24–6.

43. See on this episode, M. van Creveld, *Command in War,* Cambridge, Harvard University Press, 1985, p. 138.

44. See, for Grant, J. Keegan, *The Mask of Command,* New York, Penguin, 1987, pp. 202, 206, 208.

45. Quoted in P. Fussell, *Uniforms,* Boston, Houghton Mifflin, 2002, p. 39.

46. See, for this entire subject, M. H. Hanson, "The Little Grey Horse—Henry V's Speech at Agincourt and the Battle Exhortation in Ancient Typology," 1998, available at www.dur.ac.uk/Classics/histos/1998/hansen.html#n3, particularly sections 2 and 3.

47. Speech delivered at Malea, quoted in Xenophon, *Hellenica*, 7.33–4.

48. Dwight D. Eisenhower, speech available at www.kansasheritage.org/abilene/ikespeech.html

49. See W. K. Pritchett, *The Greek State at War*, Berkeley, University of California Press, 1971, part I, pp. 105–8.

50. See on this K. Watkin, "Warriors Without Rights: Combatants, Privileged Belligerents, and the Struggle Over Legitimacy," Program on Humanitarian Policy and Conflict Research, Harvard University, Occasional Paper no. 2, winter 2005.

51. G. Shipley, "Introduction: The Limits of War," in G. Rich and G. Shipley, eds., *War and Society in the Greek World*, London, Routledge, 1993, p. 5.

CHAPTER 6: THE JOY OF COMBAT

1. S. Weil, "The Iliad or the Poem of Force," in S. Miles, ed., *Simone Weil: An Anthology*, London, Weidenfeld & Nicolson, 1986, pp. 162–95.

2. *Iliad*, 11.143–78.

3. J. de Bueil, *Le Jouvencel*, Paris, Laurens, 1887, 2.20–21.

4. G. Sajer, *The Forgotten Soldier*, London, Cassell, 1971, p. 286.

5. Quoted in P. Fussell, *The Great War and Modern Memory*, Oxford, Oxford University Press, 1975, p. 271; M. Herr, *Dispatches*, London, Picador, 1977, p. 24.

6. See, for these and many more quotes, complete with sources, J. Bourke, *An Intimate History of Killing*, New York, Basic Books, 1999, pp. 18–21, 272–74.

7. Quote from W. Broyles, "Why Men Love War," in W. Capps, ed., *The Vietnam Reader*, New York, Routledge, 1991, pp. 71–72.

8. E-mails exchanged on December 29–30, 2005. The identity of S.G. is available on request, provided he agrees.

9. See on these changes, U. Mayer and B. Baker, "Neuroendocrine Stress Responses to Aggression," in J. Haller and M. Kruk, eds., *Neurobiology of Aggression*, New York, Humana Press, 2003, pp. 93–118.

10. B. Gammage, *The Broken Years: Australian Soldiers in the Great War*, Harmondsworth, Penguin, 1975, p. 270.

11. E. Jünger, *The Storm of Steel*, London, Penguin, 2004, p. 171.

12. See, most recently, D. Grossman, *On Killing: The Psychological Cost of Learning to Kill in War and Society*, Boston, Little Brown, 1995, especially pp. 4, 29 (quoting S. L. A. Marshall) as well as pp. 249–61.

13. Ibid., pp. 137–41.

14. For a discussion of the Greek terminology see E. Vermeule, *Aspects of Death*

in Early Greek Art and Poetry, Berkeley, University of California Press, 1979, p. 101; of the Hebrew one, L. Sion, *Images of Manhood* [Hebrew], Shine Working Paper, no. 3, Jerusalem, 1997, pp. 90–92. For a general discussion of the terminology that war and sex have in common, see Denis de Rougemont, *Passion and Society,* London, Faber & Faber, n.d., pp. 248–50; as well as C. Cohen, "Sex and Death in the Rational World of Defense Intellectuals," *Signs,* 12, 1987, pp. 687–718.

15. See, for a good firsthand discussion of these issues, J. Glenn Gray, *The Warriors: Reflections on Men in Battle,* New York, Harper, 1959, pp. 59–96.

16. Plutarch, *Alexander,* XXXVIII; E. N. Borza, "Fire from Heaven: Alexander at Persepolis," *Classical Philology,* 67, 4, October 1972, pp. 233–45.

17. One of the few exceptions is J. A. Ballard and A. J. McDowell, "Hate and Combat Behavior," *Armed Forces and Society,* 17, 2, winter 1991, pp. 229–41. See also Bourke, *An Intimate History of Killing,* pp. 127–58.

18. *On War,* pp. 75–77. For some quotes showing that things do indeed work the way Clausewitz describes them, see Bourke, *An Intimate History of Killing,* pp. 215ff.

19. See, for example, J. B. Ross, "Effects of Contact on Revenge Hostilities Among the Achuara Jivaro," in R. B. Ferguson, ed., *Warfare, Culture, and the Environment,* Orlando, FL, Academic Press, 1984, pp. 101–5; and T. Boist, "Ecological and Cultural Factors in Plains Indian Warfare," in Ferguson, ed., *Warfare, Culture and the Environment,* pp. 152–53.

20. Jünger, *The Storm of Steel,* pp. 93, 216, 232, 281.

21. For an excellent analysis of this point, see C. O. Scott, *Ender's Game,* New York, Doherty, 1985, especially the last chapter.

22. For a good description of such practices as they appear in American evangelist churches see R. M. Anderson, *Vision of the Disinherited: The Making of American Pentecostalism,* Peabody, MA, Hendrickson, 1979, pp. 10–27.

23. *Iliad,* books 20 and 21.

24. M. van Creveld, *Fighting Power: German and U.S. Army Performance, 1939–1945,* Westport, CT, Greenwood, 1982.

25. See J. Garbsch, *Roemische Paraderuestungen,* Munich, Beck, 1978, pp. 14–15.

26. B. Campbell, *War and Society in Imperial Rome,* London, Routledge, 2002, pp. 37–38.

27. Tacitus, *Annales,* II.18–9. 25.

28. G. Miller, "Evolution of Human Music Through Sexual Selection," in M. L. Wallin et al., eds., *The Origins of Music,* Cambridge, MIT Press, 2000, pp. 320–60.

29. See Maurice de Saxe, *Reveries on the Art of War,* Carlisle Barracks, PA, Army War College, 1943, pp. 30–31.

30. S. H. Myerly, *British Military Spectacle: From the Napoleonic Wars Through the Crimea,* Cambridge, Harvard University Press, 1996, pp. 142–43.

31. According to B. Matthews, *Military Music and Bandsmen of Adolf Hitler's Third Reich*, Winchester, Tomahawk, 2002, p. 16.

32. B. Merker, "Synchronous Chorusing and Human Origins," in M. L. Wallin et al., eds., *The Origins of Music*, Cambridge, MIT Press, 2000, pp. 31–48.

33. S. Sassoon, *Collected Poems*, London, Faber & Faber, 1947, p. 95. A pre–World War I German paper came up with something similar: "Wenn so ein heissen Sommertag / Stramm lasse exerzieren / Un so ein Luftzug weht den Duft / Von Schweiss un Lederzeug rüber. / Na, bis jewiss sonst für reine Luft / Aber der Duft jeht über. / Hochrjefühl das! Man spürt den Jeist / Der Armee sichtbarlich wehen! / Kann ein Zivilmensch / Behaupte ich dries / Überhaupt nicht verstehen." Dollinger, *Wenn die Soldaten*, Munich, Bruckmann, 1974, p. 61.

34. W. M. McNeill, *Keeping Together in Time: Dance and Drill in Human History*, Cambridge, Harvard University Press, 1995, p. 2.

35. See V. D. Hanson, *The Western Way of War*, Berkeley, University of California Press, 2000, pp. 16–17.

36. Asclepiodotus, *Tactics*, 12.11.

37. A. Goldsworthy, *Roman Warfare*, London, Cassell, 2000, pp. 49–50.

38. Thucydides, *The Peloponnesian War*, 5.71.1.

39. See on him, W. H. McNeill, *The Pursuit of Power: Technology, Armed Force, and Society since* A.D. *1000*, Oxford, Blackwell, 1982, pp. 125–35.

40. J. de Gheyn, *Wapenhandligne van Roers, Musquetten ends Spiessen, Achtervolgende de Ordre van Syn Excellentie Maurits, Prince van Orangie*, The Hague, 1607.

41. K. L. von Poellnitz, *Memoires*, Liège, 1734, vol. 1, p. 21.

42. According to Dupuy, *Numbers, Theories, and War*, Indianapolis, Bobbs-Merrill, 1979, p. 32, figure 2-4.

43. See on this, R. Quimby, *The Background to Napoleonic Warfare*, New York, Columbia University Press, 1957.

44. *The Art of War*, New York, Dover, 2007 [1838], pp. 267–84.

45. Orders for the Assistance . . . of Non-Commissioned Officers . . . 79th Regiment, Colchester, n.d., p. 20.

46. T. Morris, *Recollections of Military Service in 1813, 1814 and 1815*, London, n.p, 1845, p. 251.

47. Quoted in Myerly, *British Military Spectacle*, p. 97.

48. See on this, G. F. Henderson, *The Science of War*, London, Longman, 1905, pp. 3–8.

49. See, out of a huge literature, O. C. Shultheiss and others, "Effects of Affiliation and Power Motivation on Salivary Progesterone and Testosterone," *Hormones and Behavior*, 46, 2004, pp. 592–99.

50. V. D. Hanson, *The Wars of the Ancient Greeks*, London, Cassell, 1999, p. 128.

51. For example, H. Froissart, *Chronicles*, Harmondsworth, Penguin, 1968, p. 179.

52. S. Freud, *Civilization and Its Discontents*, New York, Norton, 1961 [1930], pp. 25–38, 48–61, 68–71, 81–82.

CHAPTER 7: THE RULES OF WAR

1. See on this aspect of the problem, "Temperamenta Belli: Can War Be Controlled?" in M. Howard, ed., *Restraints on War: Studies in the Limitation of Armed Conflict,* Oxford, Oxford University Press, 1976, pp. 1–4.

2. For example, R. Cohen, "Warfare and State Formation: Wars Make States, and States Make Wars," in R. B. Ferguson, ed., *Warfare, Culture, and Environment,* Orlando, Academic Press, 1984, pp. 329–58.

3. J. Thompson, *War Games: Inside the World of Twentieth-Century War Reenactors,* Washington, DC, Smithsonian, 2004, p. 40.

4. R. Firestone, *The Origin of Holy War in Islam,* Oxford, Oxford University Press, pp. 73–77.

5. See R. Axelrod, *The Evolution of Cooperation,* New York, Basic Books, 1984, pp. 27–55, 162–91.

6. Deuteronomy 20:10–10.

7. Judges 11:1–6, 20:14–47.

8. *Politics,* I, ii.19–21.

9. *Cassell's New Latin Dictionary.*

10. Y. H. Aboul-Enein and S. Zuhur, *Islamic Rulings on Warfare,* Carlisle Barracks, PA, Army War College, 2004, available at www.strategicstudiesinstitute .army/mil/pdffiles/OUB588.odf#search-'Islamic%20rulings%20on%20warfare', pp. 4–5. See also S. Gieling, *Religion and War in Revolutionary Iran,* London, Tauris, 1999, pp. 41–42.

11. Gerald of Wales, *The Journey Through Wales / The Description of Wales,* L. Thorpe, ed., Harmondsworth, Penguin, 1978, p. 269.

12. Halder, *Kriegstagebuch,* vol. 2, pp. 335–37, entry for March 30, 1941.

13. J. W. Dower, *War Without Mercy: Race and Power in the Pacific War,* New York, Pantheon, 1986.

14. Much the best modern treatment of this entire question is M. Strickland, *War and Chivalry; The Conduct and Perception of War in England and Normandy, 1066–1217,* Cambridge, Cambridge University Press, 1996, pp. 153–82.

15. See on the rules as applied during the last phases of the Dutch struggle of independence against Spain, F. Gonzalez de Leon, "Soldados Platicos and Caballeros: The Social Dimension of Ethics in the Early Modern Spanish Army," in D. J. B. Trim, ed., *The Chivalric Ethos and the Development of Military Professionalism,* Leiden, Brill, 2003, pp. 259–65.

16. See G. Best, *Humanity in Warfare,* New York, Columbia University Press, 1980, pp. 59–67.

17. See K. F. Friday, *Samurai, Warfare and the State in Early Medieval Japan,* London, Routledge, 2004, pp. 149–51.

18. See, for Islamic doctrine on this question, Aboul-Enein and Zuhur, *Islamic Rulings on Warfare,* p. 18.

19. For example, H. Bonet, *The Tree of Battles,* Liverpool, Liverpool University Press, 1949 [1401], pp. 188–89.

20. See G. Best, "Restraints on War by Land Before 1945," in M. Howard, ed., *Restraints on War: Studies in the Limitation of Armed Conflict,* Oxford, Oxford University Press, 1976, pp. 27–31.

21. Hague Convention IV, 1899, "Rules and Customs of Warfare on Land," articles 1–3, available at http://www.lib.byu.edu/~rdh/wwi/hague.html.

22. See, for Europe, Strickland, *War and Chivalry,* pp. 126–28; for Japan, Friday, *Samurai, Warfare and the State,* pp. 140, 144–45; for Islam, Aboul-Enein and Zuhur, *Islamic Rulings on Warfare,* p. 29.

23. *The Art of War,* T. Cleary, trans., Boston, Shambhala, 1988, p. 49.

24. For the origins of this system see *International Review of the Red Cross,* 18, 206, September–October 1978, pp. 247–49.

25. The following is based on J. Fadiman, *An Oral History of Tribal Warfare: The Meru of Mt. Kenya,* Athens, Ohio University Press, 1982, pp. 41–42, 46–47.

26. Thucydides, *The Peloponnesian War,* II.18–23.

27. See, for Rome, Polybios, *The Histories,* 10.15.4–17; also A. Ziolkowski, "*Urbs direpta,* or How the Romans Sacked Cities," in J. Rich and G. Shipley, eds., *War and Society in the Roman World,* London, Routledge, 1993, pp. 69–72.

28. See K. Bradley, *Slavery and Society in Rome,* Cambridge, Cambridge University Press, 1994, pp. 39–43.

29. An excellent account of what life in Berlin was like during those days is Anonyma, *Eine Frau in Berlin,* Frankfurt/Main, Eichborn, 2002.

30. See on this development, van Creveld, *The Rise and Fall of the State,* p. 165.

31. See on this, G. Best, *War and Law Since 1945,* Oxford, Clarendon, 1994, pp. 141–47.

32. See Aboul-Enein and Zuhur, *Islamic Rulings on Warfare,* pp. 18–19, 22.

33. See on Sherman, E. Hagerman, *The American Civil War and the Origins of Modern Warfare,* Bloomington, Indiana University Press, 1988, pp. 284–93.

34. M. Dayan, *Story of My Life,* London, Sphere, 1976, pp. 387–89.

35. See on this subject, Best, *Humanity in Warfare,* pp. 18–19, 47–50, 145–47, 176–78, 226–27, 249–52, 259–60.

36. Deuteronomy 7:5.

37. 1 Samuel 4:18.

38. van Creveld, The *Rise and Fall of the State,* pp. 36–37.

39. A. Wardman, *Religion and Statecraft Among the Romans,* London, Granada, 1982, pp. 109–22; F. Altheim, *A History of Roman Religion,* London, Methuen, 1938, pp. 14–29.

40. See Strickland, *War and Chivalry,* pp. 79–80.

41. See on the stool's importance, F. Boateg, "African Traditional Education: A Method of Disseminating Cultural Values," *Journal of Black Studies,* 13, 1, March 1983, pp. 321–36.

42. "Fatwah Urging Jihad Against the Americans," *Al Quds al-Arabi,* February 23, 1998, available at www.ict.org.il/articles/fatwah.htm; and O. bin Laden, "Letter to America," *The Observer,* November 24, 2002, available at http://observer.guardian.co.uk/worldview/story/0%2C854725%2C00.html.

43. *Iliad,* 3.111–12, 7.55–6, 7.288–90.

44. K. Lorenz, *On Aggression*, London, Methuen, 1963, pp. 112–17, 150–53.

45. See, for ancient Greece, W. K. Pritchett, *The Greek State at War*, Berkeley, University of California Press, 1979, part IV, pp. 246–49; and, for the Middle Ages, M. Keen, *Chivalry*, New Haven, Yale University Press, 1984, pp. 137–38.

46. For example, the New Hebrideans used palm fronds; C. B. Humphreys, *The Southern New Hebrides*, Cambridge, Cambridge University Press, 1926, p. 59.

47. G. Landtman, *The Kiwai Papuans of British New Guinea*, London, Macmillan, 1927, p. 165.

48. M. Garret, *Renaissance Diplomacy*, Boston, Houghton Mifflin, 1955, pp. 17–54.

49. *The Rights of War and Peace*, New York, Dunne, 1901 [1625], p. 346.

50. *Iliad*, 11.137–42.

51. Best, *Humanity in Warfare*, pp. 125–27.

52. *Iliad*, 22.111–28.

53. See, on the way these things were handled during the Middle Ages for example, Strickland, *War and Chivalry*, pp. 204–21.

54. V. Subbotin, "How Wars End," in V. Sevruk, ed., *How Wars End: Eye-Witness Accounts of the Fall of Berlin*, Moscow, Progress, 1969, p. 153; V. Vishnevksy, "Berlin Surrenders," in Sevruk, ed., *How Wars End*, p. 165.

55. W. Gong, *The Standard of Civilization*, Oxford, Clarendon, 1988, pp. 74–76.

56. D. Bell, *The First Total War*, Boston, Houghton Mifflin, 2006; S. Trumbull, *Samurai Warfare*, London, Arms and Armor, 1996, p. 10; R. Vernier, *The Flower of Chivalry: Bertrand du Guesclin and the Hundred Years War*, Woodbridge, Boydell, 2003, p. 197; Cram, *Iudicium Belli*, p. 87.

57. G. Parker, "The Etiquette of Atrocity: The Laws of War in Early Modern Europe," in G. Parker, ed., *Empire, War and Faith in Early Modern Europe*, London, Allen Lane, 2002, pp. 143–68.

58. H. G. Wells, *War of the Worlds*, London, Penguin, 2005, p. 90.

CHAPTER 8: ENDING WAR

1. *Iliad*, 23.175ff.

2. See, on the way it was done in Prussia, e.g., G. L. Mosse, *Fallen Soldiers: Reshaping the Memory of the World Wars*, New York, Oxford University Press, 1990, pp. 45–46.

3. A brief description of the proceedings is found in Plutarch, *Nicias*, 6.5.

4. Thucydides, *The Peloponnesian War*, 2.34.1–7

5. Diodorus, *The Histories*, 8.27.2

6. Virgil, *Aeneid*, 4.858–63.

7. Tacitus, *Annales*, 7.

8. Price, *The Viking War*, pp. 331–32, 335.

9. S. Gieling, *Religion and War in Revolutionary Iran*, London, Tauris, 1999, pp. 55–56.

10. See sagas quoted in S. Strualson, *Heimskringla: The Lives of the Norse Kings,* New York, Dover, 1990, pp. 229, 236.

11. Anonymous, "The Battle of Visby Burials," n.d., available at http://homepage.ntlworld.com/peter.fairweather/docs/visby.htm.

12. *The Letters of Sir Walter Scott,* H.J.C. Grierson, ed., London, Constable, 1933, p. 79.

13. J. Cambry, *Rapports sur les sculptures, presentés a l'Administration Centrale du Départment de la Seine,* Paris, Quimper, 1799, p. 66.

14. See, for these developments, Mosse, *Fallen Soldiers,* pp. 44–46.

15. 1 Samuel 18:25–27.

16. Information kindly provided by Prof. Ben Ami Shillony, February 19, 2006.

17. See J. Bourke, *An Intimate History of Killing,* New York, Basic Books, 1999, pp. 25–29, for examples as well as sources.

18. See T. Pakenham, *The Scramble for Africa, 1876–1912,* New York, Random House, 1991, pp. 598–600.

19. See, above all, L. Pyenson, *Civilizing Mission: Exact Science and French Expansion, 1870–1940,* Baltimore, John Hopkins University Press, 1993.

20. *Hitler's Table Talk, 1941–1944,* H. R. Trevor Roper, ed., London, Weidenfeld & Nicolson, 1953, pp. 290, 588–89.

21. Thucydides, *The Peloponnesian War,* 2.70.14.

22. The translation here used, with some slight changes, is by D. Sandford, in D. Burges, ed., *The Greek Anthology,* London, Bell, 1876.

23. See, for example, *Iliad* 23.826–35.

24. See, for example, Diodorus, *The Histories,* 17.17; and, for the entire subject, M. Austin, "Alexander and the Macedonian Invasion of Asia: Aspects of the Historiography of War and Empire in Antiquity," in G. Rich and G. Shipley, eds., *War and Society in the Greek World,* London, Routledge, 1993, pp. 207–8.

25. See M. van Creveld, *The Transformation of War,* New York, Free Press, 1991, pp. 35–42.

26. See, for a short discussion, M. van Creveld, *The Rise and Decline of the State,* Cambridge, Cambridge University Press, 1999, pp. 349–52.

27. Two examples of the way it was done may be found in Plutarch, *Cimon,* 13 (the Greeks) and in M. Khadduri, *War and Peace in the Law of Islam,* Baltimore, Lawbook Exchange 1955, pp. 118–32 (the early Arabs).

28. T. Hobbes, *Leviathan,* Oxford, Blackwell, 1946, p. 105.

29. Diodorus, *The Histories,* 13.24.3–6.

30. According to Cicero, *On Invention,* 2.23.69–70.

31. *Aeneid,* 11.4–11.

32. *Iliad,* 2.235; M. Kaldor, *New and Old Wars,* Cambridge, Polity Press, 2006, pp. 54–55.

33. Reproduced in E. E. Keuls, *Reign Phallus: Sexual Politics in Ancient Athens,* Berkeley, University of California Press, 1985, p. 262.

34. See on ritual cannibalism, A. Vilaca, "Relations Between Funerary Cannibalism and Warfare Cannibalism: The Question of Predation," *Ethnos,* 66,

1 March 2000, pp. 88–92; T. S. Abler, "Iroquois Cannibalism; Fact, Not Fiction," *Ethnohistory,* 27, 4, 1980, pp. 309–16; and A. P. Vayda, "Maori Women and Maori Cannibalism," *Man,* 60, 1960; W. Balee, "The Ecology of Ancient Tupi Warfare," in R. B. Ferguson, ed., *Warfare, Culture, Environment,* Orlando, FL, Academic Press, 1984, pp. 247–48; R. Carneiro, "Chiefdom-Level Warfare as Exemplified in Fiji and the Cauca Valley," in J. Haas, ed., *The Anthropology of War,* Cambridge, Cambridge University Press, 1990, pp. 199–200, 205.

35. D. M. Carroll, *An Interdisciplinary Study of Sport as a Symbolic Hunt,* Lewiston, NY, Mellen, 2000, p. 47; F. Clark Howell, *Early Man,* New York, Time-Life, 1970, pp. 126–37.

36. J. Fadiman, *An Oral History of Tribal Warfare: The Meru of Mt. Kenya,* Athens, Ohio University Press, 1982, pp. 118–19.

37. See D. Grossman, *On Killing: The Psychological Cost of Learning to Kill in War and Society,* Boston, Little Brown, 1995, pp. 270–73; also, for the way psychologists act as priests, P. Martin, "Living with Pain," *Psychology Today,* November 15, 1981, p. 68.

38. The following is based on B. Campbell, *War and Society in Imperial Rome,* London, Routledge, 2002, pp. 143–44. See also W. Deiseroth, *Der Triumph-bogen als grosse form in der Renaissancebaukunst Italiens,* Ph.D. thesis, Munich, Ludwig-Maximillian Universität, 1970, pp. 1–2, and H. S. Versnell, *Triumphus: An Inquiry into the Origin, Development and Meaning of the Roman Triumph,* Leiden, Brill, 1970, pp. 1, 55, 166.

39. *Candide,* New York, Bantam, 1962 [1759], p. 13.

40. See on this, H. van Wees, *Greek Warfare: Myths and Realities,* London, Duckworth, 2004, pp. 136–37.

41. The Israeli proceedings even resulted in a fat volume known as the *Agranat Committee Report,* Tel Aviv, Am Oved, 1975.

42. Livy, *Roman History,* ix.6.1–3.

43. For the origins of these terms, and the differences between them, see S. D. Bailey, *How Wars End,* Oxford, Clarendon, 1982, vol. 1, pp. 29–41.

44. Polybios, *The Histories,* 18.26.10–2.

45. D. Chandler, *The Campaigns of Napoleon,* p. 586.

46. See, for a firsthand account of the way it was done, Vishnevsky, "Berlin Surrenders," in Sevruk, ed., *How Wars End,* pp. 159–94.

47. Much the best volume on all of this, easily eclipsing all the rest, is T. Schelling, *Arms and Influence,* New Haven, Yale University Press, 1966, especially pp. 1–34.

48. Bailey, *How Wars End,* vol. 1, passim.

49. See R. Cohen, *Theater of Power,* London, Longman, 1987, on how it is done.

50. For example, in Papua, G. Landtman, *The Kiwai Papuans of British New Guinea,* London, Macmillan, 1927, p. 165.

51. W. Lloyd Warner, *A Black Civilization: A Social Study of an Australian Tribe,* New York, Harper, 1958, pp. 155–56.

52. W. J. Clinton, *My Life,* New York, Knopf, 2004, pp. 543–44.

PART III: COMMEMORATING WAR

1. See on this, G. Latsch, "Lieber Tot als Soldat," *Spiegel Special*, 1 January 2006, pp. 135–37.

CHAPTER 9: HISTORY AND WAR

1. Diodorus, *The Histories*, 1.1.
2. See, on Caesar as a military historian, F. Adcock, *Caesar as a Man of Letters*, Cambridge, Cambridge University Press, 1956, pp. 19–76.
3. Thucydides, *The Peloponnesian War*, I.1.1.
4. *Anglo-Saxon Chronicle*, online edition, available at http://omacl.org/Anglo/part1.html, Anno 448.
5. See K. Chase, *Firearms: A Global History to 1700*, Cambridge, Cambridge University Press, 2003, pp. 162–63.
6. See on this kind of literature, Y. Harari, *Renaissance Military Memoirs*, Woodbridge, Boydell, 2004, pp. 25–66.
7. See, for short biographies of these men, ibid., pp. 196–203.
8. See, for example, T. Proctor, *On the Knowledge and Conduct of War*, Amsterdam, Da Capo, 1970 [1578], preface.
9. See on Machiavelli as a military theorist and historian, M. van Creveld, *The Art of War: War and Military Thought*, London, Cassell, 2000, pp. 68–73.
10. On the views held by the *philosophs* on these questions see E. Silberner, *La guerre dans la pensée économique du XVI au XVII siècle*, Paris, Librairie de Recueil Sirey, 1939, particularly part 2.
11. *An Inquiry into the Wealth of Nations*, Chicago, University of Chicago Press, 1976 [1776], pp. 455–56.
12. See on this J. Nowosadtko, *Krieg, Gewalt und Ordnung*, Tübingen, Diskord, 2002, pp. 4–56.
13. "*Extraits de recits de captivité*," in *Correspondence de Napoleon Ier*, Paris, Plon, 1870, p. 379.
14. J. C. De Folard, *Nouvelles découvertes sur la guerre, dans une dissertation sur Polybe*, Brussels, Feppons, 1724; C. Guischardt, *Mémoires Militaires sur les Grecs et les Romains*, Lyon, Bruyset, 1758.
15. See, for example, G. H. Von Berenhorst, *Betrachtungen über die Kriegskunst*, Leipzig, Fleischer, 1796.
16. For example, V. D. Hanson, *Carnage and Culture: Landmark Battles in the Rise of Western Power*, New York, Doubleday, 2001.
17. See on this, H. Von Treitschke, "Cavour," in *Historische und Politische Aufsaetze*, Neue Folge, 1, part 1, Leipzig, 1870, p. 474.
18. See on this, B. Semmel, *Marxism and the Science of War*, Oxford, Oxford University Press, 1981, pp. 3–12.
19. Nowosadtko, *Krieg, Gewalt und Ordnung*, pp. 84–87.
20. A. Gat, *The Development of Military Thought: The Nineteenth Century*, Oxford, Clarendon, 1992, p. 222.

21. For a list of those who did so, see V. D. Hanson, *The Wars of the Ancient Greeks,* London, Cassell, 1999, p. 56.

22. See, for Keegan's own reflections on the question, *A History of Warfare,* pp. xiii–xvi.

23. Told to this author in a private conversation.

24. See on them, D. W. Engels, *Alexander the Great and the Logistics of the Macedonian Army,* Berkeley, University of California Press, 1978, pp. 58, 68, 157–58; also W. W. Tarn, *Alexander the Great,* London, Milford, 1936, vol. I pp. 12–13, and vol. II p. 39.

25. See, for Josephus, E. M. Smallwood, introduction to *The Jewish War,* London, Penguin, 1988, pp. 18–26; for Arrian, J. R. Hamilton, introduction to *The Campaigns of Alexander,* Harmondsworth, Penguin, 1971, pp. 18–23.

26. See J. D. Markham, *Imperial Glory: The Bulletins of Napoleon's Grande Armée,* London, Greenhill, 2002.

27. See L. Morton, "The Writing of Official History," in R. Higham, ed., *Official Histories,* Manhattan, Kansas State University Press, 1970, p. 36; also, at greater length, H. Umbreit, "Von der Preussisch-deutschen Militärgeschichtsschreibung zur heutigen Militärgeschichte," in V. von Gersdorff, ed., *Geschichte und Militärgeschichte,* Frankfurt am Main, Bernard & Graefe, 1974, pp. 17–54.

28. See on this entire subject, R. Higham, ed., *The Writing of Official Military History,* Westport, CT, Greenwood, 1999; and J. Grey, ed., *The Last Word? Essays on Official History in the United States and the British Commonwealth,* Westport, CT, Greenwood, 2003.

29. Information provided by Prof. Beatrice Heuser, formerly chief historian at MGFA.

30. See on the importance of this, M. Blumenson, "Can Official History Be Honest History?" in Higham, ed., *Official History,* pp. 40–41.

31. See A. S. Cochran, " 'Magic,' 'Ultra,' and the Second World War: Literature, Sources, and Outlook," *Military Affairs,* 46, 2, 1982, p. 88.

32. See on the way it was done in Britain after World War I, S. W. Rosskill, "Some Reasons for Official History," in Higham, ed., *Official History,* pp. 11–12. For some very instructive examples of official history dealing with historical truth see J. F. Williams, *Corporal Hitler and the Great War, 1914–1918,* London, Cass, 2005, pp. 86–127.

33. J. Butler to B. H. Liddell Hart, August 29, 1947, Liddell Hart Papers, 4/28, quoted in J. Black, *Rethinking Military History,* London, Routledge, 2004, p. 208.

34. Bayerischen Kriegsarchiv, eds., *Die Bayern im Grossen Kriege 1914–1918; Auf Grund der Kriegsakten dargestellt,* Munich, Bayerischen Kriegsarchiv, 1922, pp. 221–23. The translation is from Williams, *Corporal Hitler and the Great War,* p. 99.

35. See on this, H. R. Trevor-Roper, *History, Professional and Lay,* Oxford, Oxford University Press, 1957, p. 15.

36. See on this aspect of the question, A. Beevor, "The New History," *Waterstone's Books Quarterly,* 4, 2002, p. 36.

37. See J. C. Allmayer-Beck, "Die Militärgeschichte in ihrem Verhaeltnis zur historischen Gesamtwissenschaft," in Gersdorff, ed., *Geschichte und Militärgeschichte,* pp. 177–200.

38. *Memoirs,* London, Cassell, 1965, vol. 1, p. 8.

CHAPTER 10: LITERATURE AND WAR

1. See on these problems, as far as they relate to military history, M. Taylor, *The Vietnam War in History, Literature and Film,* Tuscaloosa, University of Alabama Press, 2002, pp. 14–32.

2. Quoted in M. Hanrez, *Los Escritores y la Guerra de España,* Barcelona, Libros de Monte Avila, 1977, p. 13.

3. W. R. Connor, "Early Greek Land Warfare as Symbolic Expression," *Past and Present,* 118, February 1988, p. 6.

4. See, for a short list of Greek historians and poets who commanded in war or at least participated in it, V. D. Hanson, *The Wars of the Ancient Greeks,* London, Cassell, 1999, p. 19.

5. *Exodus* 17:11–2.

6. See, for example, the work of Rudolf von Ems, as explained in W. H. Jackson, "Warfare in the Works of Rudolf von Ems," in C. Saunders et al., eds., *Writing War: Medieval Literary Responses to Warfare,* Cambridge, Brewer, 2004, pp. 50–51.

7. See on these women, M. van Creveld, *Men, Women and War,* London, Cassell, 2001, pp. 58–61.

8. See on this, N. de Somogyi, *Shakespeare's Theater of War,* Aldershot, Ashgate, 1998, pp. 1–2.

9. *Hamlet,* 4.4.19–9.

10. *Henry V,* 4.3.40–70.

11. S. E. Ambrose, *The Wild Blue: The Men and Boys Who Flew the B-24s Over Germany,* New York, Simon & Schuster, 2001, pp. 143–44.

12. See on this neglect, A. Wagner, *Krieg und Literatur in einem Frankreich des Wandels,* Salzburg, Müller-Speiser, 1990, pp. 224–25.

13. P. Covici, introduction to *The Red Badge of Courage,* Harmondsworth, Penguin, 1983, pp. 7–8.

14. The European side of the story is summed up in I. F. Clark, *Voices Prophesizing War,* London, Oxford University Press, 1966; the American one, in H. Bruce Franklin, *War Stars: The Superweapon and the American Imagination,* New York, Oxford University Press, 1988, pp. 19–53.

15. W. D. Hay, *Three Hundred Years Hence,* London, Guilford, 1881; J. London, "The Unparalleled Invasion," reproduced in I. F. Clark, ed., *The Tale of the Next Great War, 1871–1914,* Liverpool, Liverpool University Press, 1995, p. 265.

16. R. Cromie, *The Crack of Doom*, London, Digby, 1895, p. 20.

17. J. Barnes, *The Unpardonable War*, New York, Macmillan, 1904, pp. 338, 340; A. C. Train and R. W. Wood, *The Man Who Rocked the Earth*, Garden City, NY, Doubleday, 1915, p. 142.

18. W. E. Henley, ed., *Lyra Heroica*, London, Macmillan, 1936 [1892], p. vii.

19. G. L. Mosse, *Fallen Soldiers: Reshaping the Memory of the World Wars*, New York, Oxford University Press, 1990, pp. 20–22.

20. Lyrics available at www.law.ou.edu/ushistory/bathymn.shtml.

21. Judges 5:2–31.

22. S. Sassoon, *War Poems*, London, Faber & Faber, 1983, p. 77.

23. See, for these and the following Sassoon quotes, J. M. Wilson, *Siegfried Sassoon: The Making of a War Poet*, London, Duckworth, 1998, pp. 179–80, 221, 268, 291, 317, 319, 510.

24. According to Wilson, *Siegfried Sassoon*, pp. 351, 356.

25. For example, R. Wohl, *The Generation of 1914*, London, Weidenfeld & Nicolson, 1989, p. 219.

26. S. Sassoon, *The War Poems of Siegfried Sassoon*, London, Heinemann, 1919; E. Remarque, *Im Westen nichts Neues*, Berlin, Propylaeen, 1929; L. Renn, *Krieg*, Frankfurt am Main, Frankfurter Societas, 1929.

27. G. Walter, ed., *Robert Brooke and Wilfred Owen*, London, Everyman, 1997, p. xxi.

28. P. Lyon, ed., *Twentieth-Century War Poetry*, London, Palgrave, 2005, pp. 49–51.

29. See A. D. Harvey, *A Muse of Fire: Literature, Art and War*, London, Hambledon, 1998, p. 131.

30. *Der Kampf als inneres Erlebnis*, Berlin, Mittler, 1922; *Feuer und Blut*, Magdeburg, Stahlhelm, 1925; *Das Abenteuerliche Herz*, Berlin, Frundsberg, 1929.

31. See M. L. Siegel, *The Moral Disarmament of France: Education, Pacifism, and Patriotism, 1914–1940*, Cambridge, Cambridge University Press, 2004.

32. D. la Rochelle, *La Comedie de Charleroi*, Paris, Gallimard, 1934.

33. See E. Golding, "Giraudoux le Pacifique," in D. Bevan, ed., *Literature and War*, Amsterdam, Rodopi, 1990, p. 49.

34. M. Bloch, *Strange Defeat*, New York, Norton, 1968 [1957].

35. See on this, E. Triolet and L. Aragon, *Oeuvres Romanesques Croisées*, Paris, Laffont, 1964, vol. 5, pp. 13 and 14.

36. See, for some figures, *Catalogue des Periodiques Clandestines diffuses en France, 1939–1945*, Paris, Bibliotheque Nationale, 1954, pp. 39 and 52.

37. See on this, U. Brunotte, *Zwischen Eros und Krieg: Maennerbund und Ritual in der Moderne*, Berlin, Wagenbach, 2004, pp. 122–24.

38. F. Von Unruh, *Opfergang* [Way of Sacrifice], Frankfurt am Main, Societas, 1931; K. Bröger, *Bunker 17*, Jena, Diederichs, 1937; E. Johannsen, *Vier von the Infanterie* [Four Infantrymen], Hamburg, Fackelreiter; 1929; and W. Beumelburg, *Die Gruppe Bösemueller* [Bosemueller's Squad], Oldenburg, Stalling, 1930.

39. W. Wette, "From Kellogg to Hitler," in W. Deist, ed., *The German Military in the Age of Total War,* New York, Dover, 1985, pp. 88–89.

40. See, for this period, N. Thun, *Krieg und Literatur: Studien zur sojewtischen Prosa von 1941 is zur Gegenwart,* [East] Berlin, Akademie Verlag, 1977, p. 8.

41. See R. R. Reese, *The Soviet Military Experience: A History of the Soviet Army, 1917–1991,* London, Routledge, 1991, pp. 52–70, 112–19.

42. See on them, J. Walsh, *American War Literature, 1914 to Vietnam,* London, Macmillan, 1982, pp. 9, 42–50, 69–78.

43. See on this, Franklin, *War Stars,* pp. 141–48.

44. See on this, R. M. Bracco, *Merchants of Hope: British Middlebrow Writers and the First World War, 1919–1939,* Oxford, Berg, 1993.

45. W. B. Yeats, ed., *The Oxford Book of Modern Verse, 1892–1935,* Oxford, Clarendon, 1936, pp. xxxiv–xxxv.

46. G. Orwell, "Boys' Weeklies," in *Collected Essays, Journalism and Letters,* Harmondsworth, Penguin, 1970, pp. 189–90.

47. See, for example, F. Althoff, "Lightning in the Night," *Liberty Magazine,* August 24, August 31, September 7, September 14, September 21, Octobcr 5, October 10, October 19, October 26, November 2, November 9, November 16, 1940.

48. See, for a list, P. Monteath, "The Spanish Civil War and the Aesthetics of Reportage," in Bevan, ed., *Literature and War,* pp. 69–70.

49. See on him, H. Volck, *Der Traum von Tode: Das Phantastische Leben des brühmten deutsche Weltreporters Roland Strunk,* Berlin, Holle, 1940.

50. For example, A. Berea, *Valor y miedo,* Madrid, Esteban, 1980.

51. For example, J. E. Zuniga, *Largo noviembe de Madrid,* Barcelona, Bruguera, 1980.

52. See on him, F. R. Benson, *Writers in Arms: The Literary Impact of the Spanish Civil War,* New York, New York University Press, 1967, pp. 60–63, 125.

53. G. Orwell, *Homage to Catalonia,* London, Secker & Warburg, 1938, p. 153.

54. E. Pound, *Collected Shorter Poems,* London, Faber & Faber, 1952, p. 208.

CHAPTER 11: ART AND WAR

1. This is the interpretation put on the paintings by A. Ferrill, *The Origins of War: From the Stone Age to Alexander the Great,* London, Thames & Hudson, 1985, pp. 17–22, 25.

2. This is the traditional interpretation as presented by, for example, F. Windells, *The Lascaux Cave Paintings,* London, Faber & Faber, 1949, pp. 47–68. For the opposite view see P. G. Bahn, "Where's the Beef? The Myth of Hunting Magic in Paleolithic Art," in A. Rosenfeld and P. Bahn, eds., *Rock Art and Prehistory,* Oxford, Oxbow, 1991, pp. 1–13.

3. See R. Vasic, "Some Observations on Euphranor's 'Cavalry Battle,'" *American Journal of Archaeology,* 83, 3 July 1979, pp. 345–49.

4. See on it, most recently, A. D. Lee, "The Alexander Mosaic," *Classical Review*, 48, 2, 1998, pp. 431–33.

5. See on it, S. Howard, "The Dying Gaul, Aegina Warriors, and Pergamenese Academism," *American Journal of Archaeology*, 87, 4, October 1983, pp. 483–87.

6. See S. Woodford, *The Trojan War in Ancient Art*, London, Duckworth, 1993, especially pp. 60–64.

7. See, on artistic representations of nude Amazons, T. H. Carpenter, *Art and Myth in Ancient Greece*, London, Thames & Hudson, 1991, pp. 125–26.

8. See J. Hale, *Artists and Warfare in the Renaissance*, New Haven, Yale University Press, 1990, pp. 159–62.

9. According to C. Alexander, "Unpublished Fragments of Roman Sarcophagi in the Metropolitan Museum of Art," *Metropolitan Museum Studies*, 3, 1, December 1930, pp. 38–46.

10. See one such picture, showing the Koran being revealed to Muhammad in the midst of a battle, at www.retecool.com/mirrordir/Mohammed%20Image%20Archive.htm.

11. See on them, C. Walter, *The Warrior Saints in Byzantine Art and Tradition*, Burlington, VT, Ashgate, 2003.

12. See, on the way they saw history, A. J. Gurjewitsch, *Das Welbilddes mittelatlerlichen Menschen*, Munich, Beck, 1982, pp. 98ff.

13. See on this, L. White, *Medieval Technology and Social Change*, Oxford, Oxford University Press, 1962, pp. 31ff.

14. See on the question of verisimilitude, R. and T. Wohlfeil, "Das Landskecht-Bild als Geschitchliche Quelle: Ueberlegungen zur Historischen Bildkunde," in M. Messerschmidt, ed., *Militärgeschichte: Probleme—Thesen—Wege*, Stuttgart, Deutsche Verlags-Anstalt, 1982, pp. 81–99.

15. T., Kirchner, "Paradigma der Gegenwärtigkeit: Schlachtmalerei als Gattung ohne Darstellungskonventionen," in S. Germer and M. F. Zimmermann, eds., *Bilder der Macht—Macht der Bilder*, Munich, Klinkhardt & Biermann, 1997, p. 108.

16. See R. and T. Wohlfeil, "Das Landsknecht-Bild as geschichtliche Quelle," pp. 81–99.

17. According to M. Marrinan, "Schauer der Eroberung: Strukturen des Zuschauens und der Simulation in den Nordafrika-Galerien von Versailles," in Germer and Zimmermann, eds., *Bilder der Macht*, p. 272.

18. See on him, L. Popelka, "Schlachtenbilder—Bemerkungen zu einer verachteten Bildgattung", in J. Huttier, ed., *Schlachten, Schlachten, Schlachten. Eine Ausstellung der Gemäldegalerie mit dem Institut für Bildnerische Erziehung*, Vienna, Akademie der Bildende Kuenste, 1985, p. 11.

19. See on this, Hale, *Artists and Warfare in the Renaissance*, pp. 255–56.

20. See on this genre, K. Bussmann and H. Schilling, *1648: Krieg und Frieden in Europa*, Muenster/Osnabrück, 1997, pp. 155–88; and, on the anonymous painting, ibid., p. 260.

21. See on them, G. S. Keyes, *Mirror of Empire: Dutch Marine Art,* Cambridge, Cambridge University Press, pp. 421ff.

22. See H. Keazor, " 'Je n'ai plus assez de jouy ni de sante pour m'engager dans ces sujects tristes': Gewaltdarstellingen bei Nicolas Poussin vor und nach 1638," in M. Meumann and D. Nitfanger, eds., *Ein Schauplatz herber Angst; Wahrnehmung und Darstellung von Gewalt im 17. Jahrhundert,* Goettingen, Wallstein, 1997.

23. See, about the origins of the Desastres and the problems that they raise, R. Hughes, *Goya,* New York, Random House, 2004, pp. 272–319.

24. See S. Germer, "Taken on the Spot: Zur Inszenierung des Zeitgenoessen in der Malerei des 19. Jahrhunderts," in Germer and Zimmermann, eds., *Bilder der Macht,* p. 28.

25. See C. Pendergast, *Napoleon and History Painting: Antoine-Jean Gros's La Bataille d'Eylau,* Oxford, Clarendon, 1997, p. 8.

26. According to W. Gilpin, *An Essay upon Prints: Containing Remarks upon the Principles of Picturesque Beauty,* London, 1768, 1, p. 65.

27. See, for details, www.panorama-innsbruck.at/e/thema/maler1.htm.

28. See on her, P. Usherwood and J. Spencer-Smith, *Lady Butler, Battle Artist, 1846–1933,* London, National Army Museum, 1987, especially pp. 166ff.

29. Quoted by Anon, "Elizabeth Thompson," n.d, available at www.spartacus .schoolnet.co.uk/Jbutler.htm.

30. Marinetti's Manifesto is available at http://cscs.umich.edu/~crshalizi/T4PM/ futurist-manifesto.html.

31. Quote from S. Malvern, *Modern Art, Britain and the Great War: Witnessing, Testimony and Remembrance,* New Haven, Yale University Press, 2004, p. 108.

32. Quotes from A. D. Harvey, *A Muse of Fire: Literature, Art and War,* London, Hambledon, 1998, p. 108.

33. Nash letter reprinted in P. Nash, *Outline; An Autobiography and Other Writings,* London, Faber & Faber, 1949, p. 189. Rothstein statement in W. Rothenstein, *Men and Memories: A History of the Arts, 1872–1922,* New York, Tudor, n.d, vol. 1, p. 333.

34. Quote from Harvey, *A Muse of Fire,* p. 110.

35. A. E. Cornebise, *Art from the Trenches: America's Uniformed Artists in World War I,* College Station, TX, A&M University Press, 1991, p. 25.

36. See on this Malvern, *Modern Art,* p. 82.

37. Cornebise, *Art from the Trenches,* p. 8.

38. See, for these and a great many other official paintings, M.R.D. Foot, *Art and War: Twentieth Century Warfare as Depicted by War Artists,* London, Headline, 1990. The American side of the story is covered by Cornebise, *Art from the Trenches.*

39. Harvey Dunn as quoted in E. M. Howell, "An Artist Goes to War: Harvey Dunn and the AEF," *Smithsonian Journal of History,* 2, 4, winter 1967–68, pp. 49, 51.

40. According to Malvern, *Modern Art,* pp. 34–35.
41. See, for some of Hitler's ideas on art, A. Speer, *Inside the Third Reich,* New York, Macmillan, 1970, pp. 28–31, 43–45, 55–56.
42. OKH, *Krieg und Kunst,* Vienna, Kuenstlerhaus, 1942, p. 5. In 1943, the book was re-issued under the title, *Feuer und Farbe* (Fire and Color).
43. P. Haim, "Echoes of Guernica," n.d, available at www.legacy-project.org/index.php?page=exhib_intro&exhibID=4.
44. See W. Schmidt, "Maler an der Front," in R. D. Mueller and H. Volkmann, eds., *Die Wehrmacht, Mythos und Realitaet,* Munich, Beck, 1999, pp. 644–46.
45. All quotes are from the show's Web site, www.art-ww1.comgb/present.html and www.art-ww1.com/gb/visite.html.
46. Wilfred Owen to Susan Owen, August 15, 1917, in Wilfred Owen, *Collected Letters,* H. Owen and J. Bell, eds., Oxford, Oxford University Press, 1967, p. 485.
47. Issue of October 8, 1945.

CHAPTER 12: MONUMENTS TO WAR

1. A good discussion of the Narmer palette is available at http://www.ancient egypt.org/index.html.
2. *The Histories,* II.102–11.
3. See, for the considerations that led to its creation, P.J.F. Davies, "The Politics of Perpetuation: Trajan's Column and the Art of Commemoration," *American Journal of Archaeology,* 101, 1, January 1997, pp. 41–46; also B. Campbell, *War and Society in Imperial Rome,* London, Routledge, 2002, pp. 135–37.
4. See L. Pietila-Castren, *Magnificentia publica: The Victory Monuments of the Roman Generals in the Era of the Punic Wars,* Helsinki, Finnish Society of Sciences and Letters, 1987, pp. 72–74.
5. See on these monuments, P. Zanker, *The Power of Images in the Age of Augustus,* Ann Arbor, University of Michigan Press, 1988, pp. 83–84.
6. Dio Cassius, *Roman History,* 49.15.1, 51.19.1, and 54.8.3.
7. See Deiseroth, *Der Triumphbogen,* pp. 3–4.
8. A brief treatment of these and other gates may be found at Wikipedia under the title "Triumphal Arch," available at http:/en.wikipedia.org/wiki/Triumphal_arch.
9. A good description of the stele is available at http://galileo.spaceports.com/~notabene/vultures.html.
10. V. D. Hanson, *The Wars of the Ancient Greeks,* London, Cassell, 1999, pp. 70–71.
11. See on this, M. van Creveld, *Command in War,* Cambridge, Harvard University Press, 1985, p. 57.
12. See J. W. Wheeler-Bennett, *Hindenburg: The Wooden Titan,* London, Macmillan, 1967, p. 270.
13. The French monument is at La Côte Saint André: see A. Becker, *Les Monuments aux Morts: Patrimoine et Mémoire de la Grande Guerre,*

Paris, Errance, 1998, p. 80. For the Port Sunlight monument see A. King, *Memorials of the Great War in Britain,* Oxford, Berg, 1998, p. ix.

14. See G. L. Mosse, *Fallen Soldiers: Reshaping the Memory of the World Wars,* New York, Oxford University Press, 1990, pp. 39–40.

15. *Parliamentary Debates,* first series, vol. xxi, pp. 1049–51, session of June 29, 1815.

16. See R. Chikering and S. Foerster, eds., *Great War, Total War,* Cambridge, Cambridge University Press, 2000, especially pp. 19–56.

17. See P. Fussell, *The Great War and Modern Memory,* Oxford, Oxford University Press, 1975, pp. 155–90.

18. See on all this, S. Malvern, *Modern Art, Britain and the Great War: Witnessing, Testimony and Remembrance,* New Haven, Yale University Press, 2004. pp. 75–76.

19. See, for the Cenotaph's history, King, *Memorials of the Great War in Britain,* pp. 141–49.

20. See, for example, 1 Samuel 4:8.

21. See, for Rome, R. Kousser, "Conquest and Desire: Roman Victoria in Public and Provincial Sculpture," in S. Dillon and K. E. Welch, eds., *Representations of War in Ancient Rome,* Cambridge, Cambridge University Press, 2006, pp. 222–24.

22. See, for war monuments in this province, G. Sola, ed., *La Memoria Pia: I Monumenti ai Caduti della I Guerra Mondiale nell'Area Trentino Tirolese,* Trento, Dipartimento di Science Filologiche e Storiche, 1997.

23. See on this, N. D. Garland, *Punishment and Modern Society: A Study in Social Theory,* Chicago, University of Chicago Press, 1990, pp. 213–48, 104ff.

24. See M. Foucault, *Discipline and Punish: The Birth of the Prison,* London, Penguin, 1977, pp. 104–34.

25. See on this, King, *Memorials of the Great War in Britain,* pp. 155–56.

26. See on this monument, J.R.M. Winter, *Sites of Memory, Sites of Mourning,* Cambridge, Cambridge University Press, 1995, pp. 108–10.

27. Quoted in King, *Memorials of the Great War in Britain,* p. 76.

28. Ossip Zadkine as quoted on the official site of the Netherlands Bureau of Tourism, http://www.holland.com/oorlogssporen/gb/index.html?page=http://www.holland.com/oorlogssporen/gb/operations/monument.html.

29. See T. Hoelscher, "The Transformation of Victory into Power," in Dillon and Welch, eds., *Representations of War in Ancient Rome,* p. 30.

PART IV: A WORLD WITHOUT WAR?

1. The most important writer in this vein was Francis Fukuyama in "The End of History?" originally published in *The National Interest,* 16, summer 1989, pp. 3–18. Since then the literature on the subject has grown to monstrous proportions; see, above all, J. Mueller, *The Remnants of War,* Ithaca, NY, Cornell University Press, 2004, and E. Luard, *The Blunted Sword: The Erosion of Military Power in Modern World Politics,* London, Tauris, 1989.

2. H. Spencer, *The Data of Ethics,* London, Williams & Novgate, 1907, pp. 3–15; N. Angell, *The Great Illusion,* New York, Garland, 1972 [1910].

3. See, for a short history of these movements, C. Chatfield and R. Ilukhina, *Peace/Mir, an Anthology of Historical Alternatives to War,* Syracuse, NY, Syracuse University Press, 1994.

4. See on this, Mueller, *The Remnants of War,* pp. 53–54, 57–59.

5. See, for a recent restatement of this view, D. P. Fry, *Beyond War: The Human Potential for Peace,* Oxford, Oxford University Press, 2007.

CHAPTER 13: A SHORT HISTORY OF PEACE

1. On *The Art of War* as a Taoist text see Tom Cleary's introduction to Sun Tzu's *The Art of War,* pp. 1–17; also M. van Creveld, *The Art of War: War and Military Thought,* pp. 24–25.

2. Plutarch, *Alexander,* VIII.2.

3. *Iliad,* 1.284, 2.165, 2.686, 2.833, 4.240, 4.281, 5.732, 6.254, 7.376, 9.440, 9.650, and many other places.

4. See on these three, N. Spiegel, *War and Peace in Ancient Greek Literature* [Hebrew], Jerusalem, Magnes, 1986, pp. 54–55, 59–62, 152–54.

5. Ibid., 94–109.

6. *The Complete Works of Horace,* London, Dent, 1945, Ode 4.5.17–24, The Saecular Hymn, 57–60, ibid.

7. Matthew 5:38–39.

8. Romans 8:6.

9. *De Corona,* Paris, Presses universitaires de France, 1966.

10. Franciscans; Franciscan Rule, 1223, available at http://www.fordham.edu/halsall/source/stfran-rule.html; Anabaptists: P. Brock, *Pacifism in Europe to 1914,* Princeton, NJ, Princeton University Press, 1972, pp. 69–71; for the others, F. Shlachbach and R. T. Hughes, eds., *Proclaim Peace: Pacifism from Unexpected Quarters,* Urbana, University of Illinois Press, 1997.

11. Perhaps the most powerful brief statement of the myth is D. Diderot, "Supplement to Bougainville's Voyage" [1772], reprinted in M. L. Berneri, *Journey Through Utopia,* New York, Schocken, 1950, pp. 202–6.

12. See on this, M. van Creveld, *The Rise and Fall of the State,* Cambridge, Cambridge University Press, 1999, pp. 382–83.

13. *Santi Parva,* Section 55, in Patrap Chandra Roy, ed., *The Mahabharata,* Calcutta, Oriental Publications, 1962, p. 118.

14. C. Hansen, *A Taoist Theory of Chinese Thought,* New York, Oxford University Press, 1992, p. 289.

15. H. Ooms, "Neo-Confucianism and the Formation of Early Tokugawa Ideology," in P. Nosco, ed., *Confucianism and Tokugawa Culture,* Princeton, NJ, Princeton University Press, 1984, pp. 46–47; W. Nakai, "Tokugawa Confucian Historiography: The Hayashi, Early Mito School, and Arai Hakuseki," in Nosco, ed., *Confucianism and Tokugawa Culture,* pp. 78–79.

16. *Meditations,* Harmondsworth, Penguin, 1964, X.10.

17. See H.E.J. Cowdrey, "The Peace and Truce of God in the Eleventh Century," *Past and Present,* 46, 1970, pp. 42–67.

18. *Summa Theologia,* Question 40, Article 4, Part II, Second Part, London, Washburne, 1912–41.

19. Matthew 10:34.

20. *Letters,* W. Parsons, trans., New York, Fathers of the Church, 1955, ii, 15, 138.

21. M. B. Weddle, *Walking in the Way of Peace: Quaker Pacifism in the Seventeenth Century,* Oxford, Oxford University Press, 2001, pp. 180, 228–29.

22. *The Anti-Machievel* [1739], available at http://www.geocities.com/daniel macryan/antimac.html, chapter xxv.

23. For a challenge to the conventional view of eighteenth-century war as "limited," see J. Childs, *Armies and Warfare in Europe, 1648–1789,* New York, Holmes and Meier, 1982.

24. W. Penn, "An Essay Towards the Present and Future Peace of Europe," in W. Penn, *The Fruits of Solitude and Other Writings,* London, Dent, 1915 [1690], p. 20; T. Paine, *Collected Writings,* New York, Library of America, 1955, vol. I, pp. 453, 454, 456.

25. Bell, *The First Total War,* p. 156.

26. The work with the greatest resonance was J.F.C. Fuller, *The Conduct of War, 1789–1961,* London, Eyre & Spottiswode, 1961, especially pp. 29–41. See also, more recently, Bell, *The First Total War,* pp. 120–85.

27. *On War,* pp. 75–77.

28. See on Metternich's achievement, H. A. Kissinger, *A World Restored,* London, Weidenfeld & Nicolson, 1957, especially pp. 312–24.

29. J. A. Hobson, *Imperialism: A Study,* New York, Gordon, 1975 [1902]; V. I. Lenin, "Imperialism, the Highest Stage of Capitalism," 1916, available at http://www.fordham.edu/halsall/mod/19161enin-imperialism.html.

30. See, for example, J. Rich, "Fear, Greed and Glory: The Causes of Roman War Making," in J. Rich and G. Shipley, eds., *War and Society in the Roman World,* London, Routledge, 1993, pp. 38–68.

31. *The Peloponnesian War,* II.65, III.36, IV.65 provide good examples of this.

32. *Republic,* 556 E.

33. See H. Rosenblatt, *Rousseau and Geneva,* Cambridge, Cambridge University Press, 2006.

34. W. Sweet, "Herbert Spencer," 2006, available at http://www.utm.edu/research/iep/s/spencer.htm.

35. For an explicit comparison between the ideas of Moltke and Roosevelt see N. Angell, *The Great Illusion,* New York, Garland, 1972 [1910], pp. 138–39.

36. See on all this, S. I. Cooper, *Patriotic Pacifism: Waging War on War in Europe, 1815–1914,* New York, Oxford University Press, 1991, pp. 67, 157, 165, 168–69, 173, 175–76.

37. See J. Berkman, "Feminism, War and Peace Politics: The Case of World War I," in J. B. Ehlstain and S. Tobias, eds., *Women, Militarism, and War,* Boston, Rowman & Littlefield, 1990, pp. 147–50.

38. Quoted in Lynne Layton, "Vera Brittain's Testament(s)," in Margaret R. Higonnet et al., eds., *Behind the Lines; Gender and the Two World Wars*, New Haven, Yale University Press, 1987, p. 72.

39. See on this, A. Woollacott, "Khaki Fever and Its Control: Gender, Class, Age and Sexual Morality on the British Homefront in the First World War," *Journal of Contemporary History*, 29, 2, 1994, pp. 325–47.

40. F. Thebaud, "The Great War and the Triumph of Sexual Division," in F. Thebaud, ed., *A History of Women in the West*, Cambridge, MA, Belknap, p. 37; S. M. Gilbert, "Soldier's Heart: Literary Men, Literary Women, and the Great War," in Higonnet et al., eds., *Behind the Lines*, pp. 204–12.

41. *La guerre et la paix*, in *Oeuvres Completes*, Paris, Libraire des sciences politiques et socials, 1863, vol. 7, pp. 29, 33, 41.

42. "The American Civil War" [1862], printed in Semmel, ed., *Marxism and the Science of War*, pp. 129–35. The quote is from p. 129.

43. See J. Joll, *The Second International*, London, Weidenfeld & Nicolson, 1955, p. 153.

44. See Semmel, ed., *Marxism and the Science of War*, pp. 6–7.

45. See his *Evolutionary Socialism*, New York, Schocken, 1961 [1899].

46. "Christianity and Patriotism" [1898], reprinted in S. Nearing, ed., *War, Patriotism, Peace, by Leo Tolstoy*, New York, Garland, 1973, p. 30.

47. See, above all, G. Sorell, *Reflections on Violence*, London, Collier, 1961 [1908], pp. 90–91.

48. For a list of those who did so, see Cooper, *Patriotic Pacifism*, pp. 189–90.

49. "Report of the Central Committee of the Russian Communist Party (Bolsheviks) at the Eighth Party Congress," *Selected Works*, Moscow, Foreign Languages Publishing House, 1946, vol. 2, p. 33.

50. See W. R. Thomson, "The Democratic Peace and Civil Society as Constraints on Major Power Warfare," in R. Vayrynen, ed., *The Waning of Major War: Theories and Debates*, London, Routledge, 2006, pp. 209–38.

CHAPTER 14: THE WANING OF MAJOR WAR

1. See J. Mueller, *Remnants of War*, Ithaca, NY, Cornell University Press, 2004, pp. 161–82.

2. See, for some of the resulting impressions, M. J. Hogan, ed., *Hiroshima in History and Memory*, Cambridge, Cambridge University Press, 1996.

3. See, above all, T. S. Schelling, *Arms and Influence*, New Haven, Yale University Press, 1966, chapter 1; also R. Jervis, *The Meaning of the Nuclear Revolution*, Ithaca, NY, Cornell University Press, 1989, pp. 6–8.

4. The best work about the breaking of the link between victory and survival, and indeed nuclear strategy in general, remains Schelling, *Arms and Influence*.

5. See on this, A. Yarmolinsky, *The Military Establishment: Its Impact on the American People*, New York, Harper & Row, 1971, pp. 25–37; and, more recently, A. J. Bacevich, *The New American Militarism*, especially pp. 9–33.

6. See on this, the Brookings Institution Report as reported in *Time*, January 17, 1977.

7. See L. Sigelman and P. J. Conover, "The Dynamics of Presidential Support During International Conflict Situations: The Iran Hostage Crisis," *Political Behavior*, 3, 4, 1981, pp. 303–18.

8. See F. V. Larsen, *Casualties and Consensus: The Historical Role of Casualties in Domestic Support for U.S. Military Operations*, Santa Monica, CA, RAND, 1996; and J. Mueller, "The Iraq Syndrome," *Foreign Affairs*, 84, 6, November/December 2005, pp. 44–54.

9. See on the differences between Europe and the United States, R. Kagan, *On Paradise and Power: America and Europe in the New World Order*, New York, Knopf, 2003.

10. A. Carter, *Peace Movements: International Protest and World Politics Since 1945*, London, Longman, 1992, p. 268.

11. See, on the case of Vietnam, M. Small, "Influencing the Decision Makers: The Vietnam Experience," *Journal of Peace Research*, 24, 2, 1987, pp. 185–98.

12. See G. Quester, *Deterrence Before Hiroshima*, New York, Wiley, 1966.

13. Figure from R. Overy, *The Air War, 1939–1945*, London, Europa, 1980, pp. 100 and 120.

14. A. J. Bacevich, *The Pentomic Era: The U.S. Army Between Korea and Vietnam*, Washington, DC, National Defense University Press, 1986; D. Lindsay, "No Time for Despair," *Armor*, 65, May-June 1956, pp. 38–39; R. W. Ernst, *Military Review*, 36, August 1956, pp. 55–62.

15. See on these tests, J. Miller, *Under the Cloud: The Decades of Nuclear Testing*, New York, Free Press, 1986, especially pp. 133–94.

16. JFK to Eleanor Roosevelt, July 28, 1961, quoted in H. Parmet, *JFK: The Presidency of John F. Kennedy*, Norwalk, CT, Easton, 1983, p. 198.

17. Quoted in B. Brodie, *The Absolute Weapon*, New York, Columbia University Press, 1946, p. 7.

18. A. B. Carter, "BMD Applications: Performance and Limitations," in A. B. Carter and D. N. Schwartz, eds., *Ballistic Missile Defense*, Washington, DC, Brookings, 1984, pp. 121–22.

19. D. N. Schwartz, "The Historical Legacy," in Carter and Schwartz, eds., *Ballistic Missile Defense*, pp. 340–42.

20. See, for some of the details, IWG (Independent Working Group) Report, "System A-135," 2007, available at http://www.missilethreat.com/systems/a-135.html.

21. See, for some of these plans, A. M. Cunningham and M. Fitzpatrick, *Future Fire: Weapons for the Apocalypse*, New York, Warner, 1983, especially pp. 59–103.

22. T. Postol, "Lessons of the Gulf War Experience with Patriot," *International Security*, 16, 3, 1991/92, pp. 119–70.

23. Reuters, "U.S. Plans Anti-Missile Test over Pacific," August 31, 2006, available at http://www.prisonplanet.com/articles/August2006/310806Anti-Missile.htm.

24. A. Nemets, "China Missile Threat Greater Than Believed," NewsMax.com, September 13, 2004, available at http://newsmax.com/archives/articles/2004/9/12/233044.shtml; AP, "Putin: Our Missiles Can Beat Your System," January 13, 2006, available at http://www.usatoday.com/news/world/2006-01-31-russiamissiles_x.htm.

25. By far the best work on this subject remains L. Freedman, *The Evolution of Nuclear Doctrine*, New York, St. Martin's, 1984.

26. AP, "France: North Korean Nuclear Test Was a Failure," November 11, 2006, available at http://www.msnbc.msn.com/id/15217370/.

27. Anon, "Israel's Nuclear Mines Program," 1997, available at http://nuclear weaponarchive.org/Israel/.

28. V. D. Sokolovsky, *Soviet Military Strategy*, 3rd ed., London, MacDonald, 1975.

29. See S. Pande, "Chinese Nuclear Doctrine," *Strategic Analysis*, 22, March 12, 2000.

30. A. Bernard, "France Broadens its Nuclear Doctrine," *International Herald Tribune*, January 20, 2006, available at http://www.iht.com/articles/2006/01/20/news/france.php.

31. See, for the latest developments, A. Oppenheimer, "Her Majesty's New Nukes," *Bulletin of the Atomic Scientists*, 59, 2, March–April 2003, pp. 16–18.

32. R. M. Basrur, *Minimum Deterrence and India's Nuclear Security*, Stanford, CA, Stanford University Press, 2006; also P. R. Chari, "India's Nuclear Doctrine: Confused Ambitions," *The Non Proliferation Review*, fall-winter 2000, p. 131.

33. Z. Schiff in *Haaretz* [Hebrew], December 10, 2006.

34. Yediot Ahronot [Hebrew], February 2, 2007.

35. See "Aardvark," "A Do It Yourself Cruise Missile," May 2006, available at http://www.interestingprojects.com/cruisemissile/.

36. Freedman, *The Evolution of Nuclear Doctrine*, p. 400.

37. MAD 1, 2, 3, and 4; according to Jervis, *The Meaning of the Nuclear Revolution*, p. 95.

38. See, for the figures, S. D. Sagan, "SIOP-62: The Nuclear War Plan Briefing to President Kennedy," *International Security*, 12, 1, 1987, p. 22.

39. See, for the last-named case, G. Perkovich, "A Nuclear Third Way in South Asia," *Foreign Policy*, 91, summer 1993, pp. 93–105.

40. McG. Bundy, *Danger and Survival: The Political History of the Nuclear Weapon*, New York, Random House, 1988, p. 616.

41. See M. Trachtenberg, "The Influence of Nuclear Weapons in the Cuban Missile Crisis," *International Security*, 10, summer 1985, p. 157.

42. See on these differences, W. C. Martel, "Deterrence and Alternative Images of Nuclear Possession," in V. Paul et al., eds., *The Absolute Weapon Revisited*, Ann Arbor, University of Michigan Press, 1998, pp. 213–34.

43. J. Vandehei and D. Linzer, "U.S., India Reach Deal on Nuclear Cooperation," Washingtonpost.com, March 3, 2006, available at http://www.washingtonpost.com/wp-dyn/content/article/2006/03/02/AR2006030200183.html.

44. See J. L. Gaddis et al., eds., *Cold War Statesmen Confront the Bomb: Nuclear Diplomacy Since 1945,* Oxford, Oxford University Press, 1999, pp. 171–93 (Churchill), 39–61 (Stalin), 87–119 (Eisenhower), and 194–215 (Mao).
45. See, for example, *Times* Education Magazine, "The Slogan Society," October 16, 1964, available at http://www.time.com/time/magazine/article/0,9171,876274,00.html.
46. See on this, K. Boulding, "Confession of Routes," *International Studies Notes,* 2, spring 1986, p. 32.

CHAPTER 15: BEYOND THE PALE

1. See M. Erickson et al., "Armed Conflict, 1989–2002," *Journal of Peace Research,* 40, 2003, pp. 593–607.
2. See A. Hironaka, *Never Ending Wars,* Cambridge, Harvard University Press, 2005, p. 39, figure 2.3.
3. See A. Bennet, *Condemned to Repetition? The Rise, Fall and Reprise of Soviet and Russian Military Intervention,* Cambridge, MIT Press, 1999, pp. 167ff.
4. See on this, M. van Creveld, *Nuclear Proliferation and the Future of Conflict,* New York, Free Press, 1993, pp. 107–18.
5. For the Siachen conflict, see A. S. Wirsing, "The Siachen Glacier Dispute," parts 1, 2, and 3, *Strategic Studies,* x, 1, autumn 1987, pp. 49–66; xi, 3, spring 1988, pp. 75–94; and xii, 1, autumn 1988, pp. 38–54.
6. For the way Iranians see their security problems, see F. Mokhtar, "No One Scratches My Back: Iranian Security Perceptions in Historical Context," *Middle East Journal,* 59, 2, 2005, pp. 209–29; for a point of view opposed to the one here presented, E. Inbar, *The Need to Block a Nuclear Iran,* Ramat Gan, BESA Center for Strategic Studies, 2006.
7. "Ahmadinejad: Israel Will Disappear," *Jerusalem Post,* December 2, 2006, available at http://www.jpost.com/servlet/Satellite?pagename=JPost%2FJPArticle%2FShowFull&cid=1164881801325.
8. Bloomberg.com, "Ahmadinejad Predicts Collapse of Israel," November 29, 2006, available at http://search.yahoo.com/search?p=Ahmadinejad+israel&fr=yfp-t-501&toggle=1&cop=mss&ei=UTF-8.
9. See, for example, "Iran Vows Deterrence After Bush Refuses to Rule Out Attack," *International Herald Tribune,* January 18, 2005.
10. See R. W. Jones and M. G. Mcdonough, "Argentina," *Non-Proliferation,* 1998, available at http://www.ceip.org/programs/npp/nppargn.htm.
11. VOA News, "Argentina Reasserts Claim to Falkland Islands," January 3, 2007, available at http://www.voanews.com/english/archive/2007-01/2007-01-03-voa29.cfm?CFID=47093395&CFTOKEN=93208398.
12. See BBC News, "Argentina Seeks Nuclear Apology," December 7, 2003, available at http://news.bbc.co.uk/2/hi/americas/3297805.stm.
13. Al Aharam, May 2002, quoted in E. B. Landau, "Egypt's Nuclear Dilemma," *Strategic Assessment,* 5, 3, 2002.

14. Adel Safty, "Egypt's Nuclear Challenge," *Gulf News,* September 10, 2006, available at http://archive.gulfnews.com/opinion/columns/region/10073217.html.

15. The first, as well as most prominent, advocate of this view was K. Waltz, *The Spread of Nuclear Weapons: More May Be Better,* London, IISS, 1981.

16. E. Lytton, *The Coming Race; or the New Utopia,* London, Routledge, 1870.

17. The best work on how terrorists operate is B. Hoffman, *Inside Terrorism,* New York, Columbia University Press, 1998.

18. The most detailed history is R. Asprey, *War in the Shadows: The Guerrilla in History,* New York, Doubleday, 1975.

19. See G. Best, *Law and War Since 1945,* Oxford, Clarendon, 1994, pp. 115–32.

20. See, for some quotes to this effect, Hoffman, *Inside Terrorism,* pp. 100, 175–76.

21. A very good firsthand account of this struggle is M. Begin, *The Revolt,* Jerusalem, Steimatzky, 1951.

22. See on this, J-F Bayart and others, *La Criminalisation de l'état en Afrique,* n.p., CERI, 1996, especially pp. 17–54.

23. See for a short analysis, Hironaka, *Never Ending Wars,* pp. 89–103.

24. See on all this, the seminal article by A. B. Bozeman, "War and the Clash of Ideas," *Orbis,* 20, 1, spring 1976, pp. 61–102.

25. See on the way these things worked in East Africa, for example, D. Ocaya-Lakidi, "Manhood, Warriorhood and Sex in East Africa," in A. A. Mazrui, ed., *The Warrior Tradition in Modern Africa,* Leiden, Brill, 1977, pp. 152–53.

26. For some reflections of the role of women in causing war see A. Gat, *War in Human Civilization,* Oxford, Oxford University Press, 2006, pp. 67–76; also M. van Creveld, *Men, Women and War,* London, Cassell, 2001, pp. 27–33.

27. According to H. H. Adam, "Somalia: A Terrible Beauty Being Born?" in L. W. Zartman, ed., *Collapsed States: The Disintegration and Restoration of Legitimate Authority,* Boulder, CO, Lynne Rienner, 1995, p. 78.

28. See A. A. Mazrui, "Soldiers as Traditionalizers: Military Rule and the Re-Africanization of Africa," in Mazrui, ed., *The Warrior Tradition in Modern Africa,* pp. 236–58.

29. See E. Todd, *The Explanation of Ideology: Family Structures and Social Systems,* Oxford, Blackwell, 1985.

30. See A. A. Mazrui, "Gandhi, Marx and the Warrior Tradition in African Resistance," in Mazrui, ed., *The Warrior Tradition in Modern Africa,* p. 187.

31. For example, D. Kapustyin and M. Nelson, *Soul of Terror: The Worldwide Conflict between Islamic Terrorism and the Modern World,* New York, International Press, 2007; B. Lewis, *The Crisis of Islam; Holy War and Unholy Terror,* New York, Random House, 2004; and J. L. Esposito, *Unholy War: Terror in the Name of Islam,* New York, Oxford University Press, 2002.

32. See, for a short account of these developments, Y. Lambert, "A Turning Point in Religious Evolution in Europe," *Journal of Contemporary Religion,* 19, 1, January 2004, pp. 29–46.

33. See P. Jenkins, "The Next Christianity," *Atlantic Monthly,* 290, 3, October 2002, pp. 53–68; also, at greater length, P. Jenkins, *The Next Christendom: The Coming of Global Christianity,* Oxford, Oxford University Press, 2002, especially pp. 108–39, 168–90.

34. See on this and other African conflicts, A. Hoeffeler, "On the Incidence of Civil War in Africa," *Journal of Conflict Resolution,* 46, 1, 2002, pp. 13–28.

35. C. Nordstrom, "Women and War: Observations from the Field," *Minerva: Quarterly Reports on Women and the Military,* ix, 1, spring 1991, p. 2.

36. M. Weiner, "Bad Neighbors, Bad Neighborhoods: An Inquiry into the Causes of Refugee Flows," *International Security,* 21, 1, 1996, pp. 5–9.

37. See M. van Creveld, "Through a Glass, Darkly: Reflections on the Future of War," *Naval War College Review,* 53, 4, autumn 2000, pp. 25–44.

CHAPTER 15: *QUO VADIS, HOMO?*

1. According to M. Alleyne, *International Power and International Communications,* London, Macmillan, 1995, pp. 10–11.

2. See, for a short discussion of the relationship between terrorism and the media, B. Hoffman, *Inside Terrorism,* New York, Columbia University Press, 1998, pp. 131–56.

3. See L. MacKenzie, *Peacekeeper: The Road to Sarajevo,* Toronto, Douglas & MacIntyre, 1993, p. 308.

4. See on this kind of story, H. Frankfurter, *On Bullshit,* Princeton, NJ, Princeton University Press, 2005, pp. 30–34.

5. See on this, C. Lemish and T. D. Tidhar, "Where Have All the Young Girls Gone? The Disappearance of Female Broadcasters in Wartime," *Women and Language,* 22, 1999, pp. 27–32.

6. See, for example, Committee to Protect Journalists (CPJ), "Iraq: Journalists in Danger," 2007, available at http://www.cpj.org/Briefings/Iraq/Iraq_danger .html.

7. L. Carruthers, *The Media at* War: *Communication and Conflict in the Twentieth Century,* New York, St. Martin's, 2000, pp. 158–59.

8. German playwright Karl Kraus as quoted in C. Coker, *War and the Twentieth Century,* London, Brassey's, 1994, p. 52.

9. See on this episode, P. Wyden, *Day One: Before Hiroshima and After,* New York, Simon & Schuster, 1984, p. 324.

10. Carruthers, *The Media at War,* pp. 146–53; also A. Trevor Hall, *War in the Media Age,* Cresskill, NY, Hampton, 2000, pp. 49–54.

11. P. Schlesinger and others, *Televising Terrorism: Political Violence in Popular Culture,* London, Comedia, 1983, p. 111.

12. See most recently UPI, "The Pentagon Reaches Out to Bloggers," *Post Chronicle,* March 7, 2006, available at http://www.postchronicle.com/news/ security/printer_2129382.shtml.

13. See, in particular, M. Paris, *Warrior Nation: Images of War in British Popular Culture, 1850–2000,* London, Reaktion, 2000, pp. 142–44, 151–53.

14. Ibid., pp. 53, 55, 60.

15. Carruthers, *The Media at War,* pp. 276–78.

16. Quoted in M. Taylor, *The Vietnam War in History, Literature and Film,* Tuscaloosa, University of Alabama Press, 2002, p. 100.

17. U.S. figure, 3.2.2007; CNN report available at http://edition.cnn.com/ SPECIALS/2003/iraq/forces/casualties. In Operation "Summer Rain," a single Israeli female nurse was killed when the helicopter in which she flew was shot down.

18. See on this, D. Showalter, "A Modest Plea for Drums and Trumpets," *Military Affairs,* February 1975, pp. 71–73.

19. See, for what these disciplines actually do or claim to do, C. Gray, *Strategic Studies: A Critical Assessment,* Westport, CT, Greenwood, 1982.

20. See, for some of the latest on this, D. M. Halbfinger and S. A. Holmes, "Military Mirrors Working Class America," *New York Times,* March 30, 2003.

21. Quoted in P. G. Jones, *War and the Novelist: Appraising the American War Novel,* Columbia, University of Missouri Press, 1976, p. 100.

22. See on the thematic continuity, J. L. Weston, *The Quest for the Holy Grail,* London, Cass, 1965, especially pp. 90–95.

23. The best source for this entire subject is the *Militaria International* magazine series.

24. See C. Martinkat, "Stoerung der Totenruhe," *Junge Freiheit,* November 17, 2006, p. 12.

25. The following is based on J. Thompson, *War Games: Inside the World of Twentieth-Century War Reenactors,* Washington, DC, Smithsonian, 2004, especially pp. 76–94, 201–36.

26. See, for the details, http://www.pacpubserver.com/new/enter/12-16-98/ crossing.html.

27. See, for some pictures of an event held in May 2006, http://www.militarypho tos.net/forums/showthread.php?t=80549.

28. See, above all, T. Horwitz, *Confederates in the Attic: Dispatches from the Unfinished Civil War,* New York, Vintage, 1999, especially pp. 6–9.

29. Thompson, *War Games,* pp. 284–85.

30. See on the way it is done at the Pentagon, T. B. Allen, *War Games,* New York, McGraw-Hill, 1987, pp. 148–50.

31. See D. Featherstone, *Featherstone's Complete Wargaming,* n.p, David & Charles, 1989.

32. See on this, N. Palmer, *The Comprehensive Guide to Board Wargaming,* New York, Hippocrene, 1977, pp. 23–26.

33. A very good review of this kind of war game, and the way it relates to real-life war, is Glick and Charteris, "War, Games, and Military History," pp. 567–82.

34. See, for a general account, J. Lundy and B. Sawyer, *Engines of War: Developing Computer Wargames,* Scottsdale, AZ, Paraglyph, 2004.

35. See on this entire subject, J. M. Rolf and others, eds., *Flight Simulation,* Cambridge, Cambridge University Press, 1988.

36. This author will provide the name of the pilot who told the story on request, provided he agrees.

37. For the details of one such company see flymig.com, available at http://www.flymig.com/forum/?161.

38. *Newsweek,* April 17, 1986, p. 7.

39. See Goudarzi, "Teenager Plays Video Game Just by Thinking," *Livescience,* December 10, 2006, available at http://www.livescience.com/technology/061012_teenage_videogame.html.

CHAPTER 17: THE WILD HORDE

1. For example, K. Weissmann, *Maenner Bund,* Schnellroda, Antaios, 2004.

2. See, for a general discussion of *latrones,* T. Grünewald, *Rauber, Rebellen, Rivalen, Raecher: Studien zu Latrones in Roemischen Reich,* Stuttgart, Steiner, 1999, pp. 21–48.

3. *Lukas,* 10.30–36.

4. 2 Corinthians 11:26.

5. Sen. *De Ira,* 3.43.3.

6. *Satire* 10.19–22.

7. *Historia Augusta* [German], Munich, Artemis, 1985, Hadrian, 2.6.

8. See Grünewald, *Rauber,* pp. 231–34.

9. Ibid., p. 82.

10. See, for example, Suetonius, *Augustus,* 32.2; Suetonius, *Tiberius* 37.1.

11. *Usum ac disciplina; The Gallic War,* 1.40.5.

12. Diodorus, *The Histories,* 34/35.2.29–30.

13. Ibid., 34/5.2.14.

14. Ibid., 34/5.2.44.

15. Ibid., 34/5.2.25.

16. Ibid., 34/5.2.11.

17. Florus, *Epitome of Roman History,* 2.8.1–7.

18. Diodorus, *The Histories,* 34/5.2.22.

19. Ibid., 36.4.4.

20. Ibid., 36.5.2.

21. Ibid., 36.4.6.

22. Ibid., 36.4.11.

23. *Crassus,* London, LCL, 1951, 8.3.

24. Ibid., 9.3.

25. Fragments of the *Histories,* London, Association of Classical Teachers, 1978, No. 98.

26. Plutarch, *Crassus,* 10.2.

27. Sallust, Fragment No. 98.

28. Plutarch, *Crassus,* 11.4–5.

29. See on this, J. Le Goff, *Medieval Civilization,* Oxford, Blackwell, 1988, pp. 299–304.

30. See on this, N. Wright, *Knights and Peasants: The Hundred Years War in the French Countryside,* London, Boydell, 1998, pp. 80–83.
31. E. Perroy, *The Hundred Years War,* New York, Capricorn, 1965, p. 135.
32. J. Froissart, *Chronicles,* pp. 151–53.
33. In the words of B. Tuchman, *A Distant Mirror,* New York, Ballantine, 1978, p. 180.
34. Ibid.
35. See A. Suppan, "Yugoslavism Versus Serbian, Croatian, and Slovene Nationalism," in N. M. Naimark and H. Case, eds., *Yugoslavia and Its Historians,* Stanford, CA, Stanford University Press, 2003, especially pp. 116–28.
36. M. Kaldor, *New and Old Wars: Organized Violence in a Global Era,* 2nd ed., Oxford, Polity, 2006, pp. 53–54.
37. See, for all these leaders and forces, S. L. Burg and P. S. Shoup, *The War in Bosnia Herzegovina: Ethnic Conflict and International Intervention,* Armonk, NY, Sharpe, 1999, pp. 128–39.
38. Kaldor, *New and Old Wars,* p. 49.
39. See, for example, the description in J. Mueller, *The Remnants of War,* Ithaca, NY, Cornell University Press, 2004, pp. 88–95.
40. See on this, G. Igric, "Not Just the Victim," *War Report,* 57, December 1997–January 1998, pp. 9–10.
41. See T. A. Emmert, "A Crisis of Identity: Serbia at the End of the Century," in Naimark and Case, eds., *Yugoslavia and Its Historians,* pp. 161–62.
42. R. Smith, *The Utility of Force: The Art of War in the Modern World,* London, A. Lane, 2005, p. 357.
43. See C. G. Boyd, "Making Peace with the Guilty: The Truth About Bosnia," *Foreign Affairs,* 74, 5, September–October 1995, pp. 22–38.
44. See Kaldor, *New and Old Wars,* p. 67.
45. Burg and Shoup, *The War in Bosnia Herzegovina,* p. 153.
46. See Smith, *The Utility of Force,* p. 153; also E. N. Luttwak, "Give War a Chance," *Foreign Affairs,* 78, 4, July/August 1999, pp. 36–44.
47. According to R. L. Sargent, "Deliberate Force Combat Air Assessments," in R. C. Owen, ed., *Deliberate Force: A Case Study in Effective Air Campaigning,* Maxwell Air Force Base, AL, 2000, p. 431. The figure of 700 comes from Kaldor, *New and Old Wars,* p. 49, table 3.1.
48. *The Art of War,* S. B. Griffith, trans., Oxford, Oxford University Press, 1963, p. 84.
49. *On War,* p. 632.

CHAPTER 18: THE SOULLESS MACHINE

1. Quoted in F. Ergang, *The Potsdam Fuehrer,* New York, Octagon, 1941, pp. 81–82.
2. J.D.E. Preuss, ed., *Oeuvres de Frédéric le Grand,* Berlin, Nauck, 1846–57, vol. 1, p. 221.

3. G. Rothenberg, *The Art of Warfare in the Age of Napoleon*, London, Batsford, 1977, p. 341.
4. J. W. Archenholtz, *Geschichte des Siebenjaehrigen Krieges in Deutschland*, Berlin, n.p, 1840 [1791], vol. 2, p. 82, quoted in C. Duffy, *The Army of Frederick the Great*, London, Purnell, 1974, pp. 202–3.
5. Berenhorst, *Betrachtungen ueber die Kriegskunst*, vol. 2, pp. 424–25, quoted in Duffy, *The Army of Frederick the Great*, p. 88.
6. See on all this, J. Burgoyne, "Observations upon the Present Military State of Prussia, Austria, and France" (1767), in E. B. Fonblanque, ed., *Political and Military Episodes . . . from the Life and Correspondence of the Right Honorable Burgoyne*, London, n.p., 1876, p. 66.
7. V. Marcu, *Das Grosse Kommando Scharnhorst*, Berlin, Deutsche Buch Gemeinschaft, 1928, p. 38; Berenhorst, *Betrachtungen*, vol. 2, 423.
8. According to E. von Hoepfner, *Der Krieg vom 1806 und 1807*, Berlin, Schropp, 1855, vol. 1, pp. 53, 56.
9. C. Ross, ed., *Correspondence of Charles, First Marquis Cornwallis*, London, Murray, 1859, vol. 1, p. 205.
10. According to P. Schrekenbach, *Der zusammenbruch Preussens im Jahre 1806*, Jena, Diederichs, 1906, p. 24.
11. Archenholtz, *Geschichte des Siebenjaehrigen Krieges in Deutschland*, vol. 2, p. 110; M. Lehman, Scharnhorst, Leipzig, Hirzel, 1886, vol. 1, p. 322.
12. Quoted in T. Stamm-Kuhlmann, *Koenig in Preussens grosser Zeit*, Berlin, Siedler, p. 255.
13. F. L. Petre, *Napoleon's Conquest of Prussia—1806*, London, Lane, 1906, p. 42.
14. Quoted in H. Otto, *Gneisenau: Prussens unbequemer Patriot*, Bonn, Keil, 1979, pp. 178–79.
15. Figure from S. Fiedler, *Grundriss der Militaer- und Kriegsgeschichte*, Munich, Schild, 1978, vol. 3, p. 255.
16. See on this episode, F. N. Maude, *The Jena Campaign*, London, Sonnenschein, 1909, p. 156.
17. See, for how the Prussian army treated "enthusiasm," R. Hoehn, *Scharnhorsts Vermaechtnis*, Bonn, Athenaeum, 1952, pp. 33–34.
18. Otto, *Gneisenau*, p. 196.
19. Quoted in Maude, *The Jena Campaign*, p. 159.
20. *Correspondance de Napoleon 1er*, Paris, Plon, 1863, vol. 13, p. 436.
21. Lehman, *Scharnhorst*, vol. 1, p. 365.
22. See, for the figures, Petre, *Napoleon's Conquest of Prussia*, pp. 23, 150, 176, 180.
23. Ibid., pp. 245–49, 251.
24. Otto, *Gneisenau*, p. 207.
25. See on this episode, F. Uhle-Wettler, *Hoehe- und Wendepunkte Deutscher Militärgeschichte*, Main, v. Hase, 1984, pp. 107–8.
26. Quotes from Hoehn, *Scharnhorsts Vermaechtnis*, pp. 112–13; G. Eckert,

Von Valmy bis Leipzig, Hanover, Norddeutsche Verlags Anstalt, 1955, pp. 102, 105.

27. See on this episode, C. Duffy, *Prussia's Glory: Rossbach and Leuthen, 1757,* Chicago, IL, Emperor's, 1990, pp. 188–89.

28. See, for a short description of how it was done, Duffy, *The Army of Frederick the Great,* pp. 208–12.

29. See D. Showalter, "Army and Society in Imperial Germany: The Pains of Modernization," *Journal of Contemporary History,* 18, 4, pp. 583–618.

30. T. N. Dupuy, *A Genius for War, the German Army and General Staff, 1807–1945,* London, MacDonald's, 1977, pp. 116, 268, 307.

31. The most famous anti-militarist tract was L. Quidde, *Caligula* (1894), reprinted in H. U. Wehler, *Caligula: Schfriften über Miltiarismus und Pazifismus,* Frankfurt am Main, Syndikat, 1977, pp. 61–80.

32. See on him, B. R. Berghahn, *Militarism: The History of an International Debate, 1861–1979,* Cambridge, Berg, 1981, pp. 11–14.

33. See, for Britain, S. Wilkinson, *The Brain of an Army,* Westminster, Constable, 1895; and, for the U.S., E. Upton, *Armies of Asia and Europe,* New York, Greenwood Press, 1968 [1878].

34. See, for example, T. Veblen, *Imperial Germany and the Industrial Revolution,* London, Macmillan, 1915, especially pp. 66, 70, 78, 80; R. J. Evans, *The Coming of the Third Reich,* New York, Penguin, 2004; and H. Mommsen, *The German Army and Genocide: Crimes Against War Prisoners, Jews and Other Civilians, 1939–1944,* New York, New Press, 1999.

35. G. Craig, introduction to H. Rosinski, *The German Army,* Washington, DC, Infantry Journal, 1944, p. 7.

36. See, for a short discussion on which the following is based, W. von Bredow, "Die Last der Tradition," in *Deutsche Studien,* 18, 72, December 1980, pp. 366–68.

37. See D. R. Herspring, *East-German Civil-Military Relations,* New York, Praeger, 1973, p. 186.

38. O. Bluth, *Uniform und Tradition,* Berlin (East), Ministerium für Nationale Verteitigung, 1956, p. 73.

39. H. Hoffman, *Traditionen und Taditionspflege der nationalen Volksarmee, in Sozlialistische Landesverteitigung. Aus Reden und Aufsätzen,* Berlin, DTSB, 1971, p. 463.

40. See on this, P. Heider, "Militärische Traditionen der DDR und ihrer Streitkräfte," *Militärgeschichte,* 1979, 4, p. 440ff.

41. See E. Foertsch, "Historische Traditionen in Systemswettsreit: Das Beispiel Preussen-Bild in der DDR," *Deutsche Studien,* 18, 72, December 1980, pp. 350–51.

42. W. Gerhardt, "Erfahrungen aus der Arbeit von Traditionszirklen in Truppenteilen der NVA und Grenztruppen der DDR," *Militärgeschichte,* 14, 1975, p. 233; "Tradition der NVA," *Militärlexicon,* Berlin, Militärverlag der DDR, 1973.

43. D. Holloway and J.M.D. Sharp, *The Warsaw Pact,* Ithaca, NY, Cornell University Press, 1984, p. 74; T. O. Cason, "The Warsaw Pact Today: The East European Military Forces," in R. W. Clawson and L. S. Kaplan, eds., *The Warsaw Pact,* Wilmington, DE, Scholarly Resources, 1982, pp. 150–51.
44. See, especially, T. Fischer, *Die Letzen Tage der DDR,* Aachen, Helios, 2006, chapter 1.
45. M. Messerschmidt and F. Wuellner, *Die Wehrmachtjustiz im Dienste des Nazionalsozialismus,* Baden-Baden, Nomos, 1987, p. 63ff.
46. See on this, W. Wette, "Die deutsche militärische Füehrungschicht in der Nachkriegszeiten," in G. Niedhart and D. Riesenberger, eds., *Lernen aus der Krieg? Deutsche Nachkriegszeiten 1918 und 1945,* Munich, Beck, 1992, pp. 39–66.
47. See, on West German resistance to the trials of former Wehrmacht officers, N. Frei, *Vergangenheitspolitik. Die Anfäenge der Bundesrepublik und die NS Vergangenheit,* Munich, Beck, 1996, pp. 133–306.
48. See, for a short discussion of their ideas, D. Abenheim, *Reforging the Iron Cross: The Search for Tradition in the West German Armed Forces,* Princeton, NJ, Princeton University Press, 1988, pp. 126–38.
49. See on this, R. Günzel, *Und Ploetzlich ist alles politisch,* Schnellroda, Antaios, 2005, pp. 71, 76–77.
50. See, for the origins of the debate, D. C. Large, *Germans to the Front: West German Re-Armament in the Adenauer Era,* Chapel Hill, University of North Carolina Press, 1996, p. 193; and, for its present state, D. Stein, "Eine Armee Ioscht ihre Gedaechtniss," *Junge Freiheit,* June 3, 2006, p. 1.
51. See on their political views, T. Hamerow, *On the Road to the Wolf's Lair: German Resistance to Hitler,* Cambridge, MA, Belknap, 1999, pp. 320–21, 334.
52. See, for one list of banned items, W. Graf von Baudissin, *Soldat für den Frieden,* Munich, Piper, 1970, p. 119.
53. See R. Giordano, *Die Traditionslüge; Vom Kriegerkult in der Bundeswehr,* Cologne, Kiepenheuer, 2000, pp. 19, 397.
54. See on this, Günzel, *Und ploetzlich ist alles politisch,* pp. 70–71, 77.
55. General Hans von Sandart, interview with Moritz Schwarz, *Junge Freiheit,* 24.6.2006, p. 3.

CHAPTER 19: MEN WITHOUT CHESTS

1. *Iliad,* 24.28–62.
2. Song Geng, *The Fragile Scholar: Power and Masculinity in Chinese Culture,* Hong Kong, Hong Kong University Press, 2004, pp. 13, 61, 79–80.
3. For example, H. Broder, *Hurra, wir Kapitulieren! Von der Lust am Einlenken,* Berlin, WJS, 2006.
4. See, above all, the books of Deuteronomy, Joshua, Judges, 1 and 2 Samuel, as well as 1 and 2 Kings.
5. Jerusalem Talmud, Ta'anit, chapter 74.

6. *Codex Theodosianus,* C. Pharr and T. S. Davidson, eds., Nashville, TN, Vanderbilt University, 1946, sections 8.16 and 16.

7. According to S. B. Liebman, "The Great Conspiracy in Peru," *The Americas,* 28, 2, October 1971, p. 176.

8. See on them, A. Ofek, "Cantonists: Jewish Children as Soldiers in Tsar Nicholas' Army," *Modern Judaism,* 13, 1993, pp. 277–308.

9. See on this, S. A. Cohen, "The Bible and Intra-Jewish Portraits of King David," *Jewish Political Studies Review,* 3, 1991, pp. 49–66.

10. See on this, R. Liberles, "The Historical Context of Dohm's Treatise on the Jews," in Friedrich Naumann-Stiftung, ed., *Das deutsche Judentum und der Liberalismus—German Jewry and Liberalism,* Königswinter, Comdok, 1986, pp. 44–69; also G. L. Mosse, *Germans and Jews,* New York, Grosset & Dunlap, 1970, pp. 39–42.

11. See C. W. Dohm, *Ueber die burgerliche Verbeserung der Juden,* Berlin, Nicolai, 1781, especially vol. 1, pp. 26–28, 39, 119, 130.

12. See C. A. Lea, *Emancipation, Assimilation, and Stereotype: The Image of the Jew in German and Austrian Drama, 1800–1850,* Bonn, Grundmann, 1978, pp. 96–101.

13. See on this, H. Bender, *Der Kampf um die Judenemanzipation in Deutschland in Spiegel der Flugschriften,* Jena, Frommann, 1939, p. 69; also P. Pulzer, *The Rise of Political Anti-Semitism in Germany and Austria,* London, Halban, 1988, pp. 221–22.

14. H. S. Chamberlain, *Die Grundlagen des Neunzehnten Jahrhunderts,* Munich, Bruckmann, 1909, vol. 1, p. 499.

15. Ibid., vol. 1, p. 429.

16. Chamberlain, *Die Grundlagen,* vol. 1, pp. 560–62.

17. N. Wilson, "Péguy, the Jews and the Jewish Question," in B. Cheyette and N. Valman, *The Image of the Jew in European Culture,* London, Mitchel, 2004, pp. 178–83.

18. A. Hitler, *Mein Kampf,* Mumbai, Jaico, 2001 [1925], pp. 168–69.

19. See M. Messerschmidt, "Juden in preussisch-deutschen Heer," in F. Naegler, ed., *Deutsche Jüdische Soldaten: Von der Epoche der Emanzipation bis zum Zeitalter der Weltkriege,* Hamburg, Mittler, 1996, p. 39.

20. Quoted in P. Mendes-Flohr and J. Reinharz, *Jew in the Modern World: A Documentary History,* Oxford, Oxford University Press, 1995, p. 232.

21. G. Heckler, "Walter Rathenau und sein Verhältnis zum Militaer," in Naegler, ed., *Deutsche Jüdische Soldaten,* p. 147.

22. See A. T. Levenson, *Between Philosemitsm and Antisemitism: Defenses of Jews and Judaism in Germany, 1871–1932,* Lincoln, University of Nebraska Press, 2004, pp. 107–8.

23. R. Patai, ed., *The Complete Diaries of Theodor Herzl,* New York, Herzl Press, 1960, vol. 2, pp. 760–61.

24. See R. Wistrich, "Herzl's Zionism Between Myth and Utopia" [Hebrew], in D. Ochana and R. Wistrich, eds., *Myth and Memory,* Tel Aviv, Hakibbutz Hameuhad, 1996, p. 111.

25. *Altneuland,* Haifa, Haifa Publishing Company, 1960, p. 37.

26. *Selected Poems of Hayim Nahman Bialik,* I. Efros, ed., New York, Bloch, 1965, p. 119.

27. D. Meron, ed., *Underneath the Bough: Ze'ev Jabotinsky's Poetry,* Tel Aviv, Hidekel, 2005, pp. 135–37.

28. "Exile and Assimilation," Tel Aviv, Salzman, 1946, pp. 100–1.

29. A. Bruell, *Die Mischehe im Judentum im Lichte der Geschichte,* Frankfurt am Main, Hofmann, 1905. pp. 201ff.

30. Quoted in U. Ben Eliezer, *The Making of Israeli Militarism,* Bloomington, Indiana University Press, 1998, p. 2.

31. "My Life," in *Writings,* Jerusalem, 1961, vol. 1, p. 154.

32. Patai, ed., *The Complete Diaries of Theodor Herzl,* vol. 1, pp. 27, 33, 43, 168.

33. *Altneuland,* p. 62.

34. M. Nordau, *Degeneration,* Lincoln, University of Nebraska Press, 1993, p. 16.

35. See T. S. Presner, " 'Clear Heads, Solid Stomachs, and Hard Muscles': Max Nordau and the Aesthetics of Jewish Regeneration," *Modernism,* 10, 2, 2003, pp. 269–96.

36. Z. Jabotinsky, "The Muse of Fashion" [1916], in *Writings,* vol. 13, p. 216.

37. "My Life," pp. 44–45.

38. See, above all, "The Iron Wall" (1923), available at http://www.marxists .de/middleast/ironwall/ironwall.htm.

39. M. Yizraeli, ed., *Jabotinsky on Hadar* [Hebrew], Tel Aviv, Betar, 1961, pp. 26, 28, 29.

40. Z. Jabotinsky, "On Militarism," in *Writings,* vol. 11, pp. 41–42, 47.

41. Ibid., 47.

42. See T. M. Endelman, "The Social and Political Context of Conversion in Germany and England, 1870–1914," in T. M. Endelman, ed., *Jewish Apostasy in the Modern World,* New York, Holmes & Meier, 1987, p. 102.

43. D. Bar-On, "The Others' Within Us: A Socio-Psychological Perspective on Changes in Israeli Identity," Beer Sheva, Ben Gurion University, 1998, available at http://www.bgu.ac.il_Danbaron/Docs_Dan/introduction.doc., pp. 13–14.

44. See E. R. Wolfson, "Eunuchs Who Keep the Sabbath; Becoming Male and the Ascetic Ideal," in J. J. Cohen and B. Wheeler, eds., *Becoming Male in the Middle Ages,* New York, Garland, 1997, p. 153.

45. See on this, S. L. Gilman, *Jewish Self-Hatred: Anti-Semitism and the Hidden Language of the Jews,* Baltimore, Johns Hopkins University Press, 1986, pp. 288–91.

46. See G. J. Bildstein, "Holy War in Maimonidean Law," in J. Kraemer, ed., *Perspectives on Maimonides,* Oxford, Oxford University Press, 1991, pp. 209–21.

47. Z. Jabotinsky, *Prelude to Delilah,* New York, Ackerman, 1940 [1926], p. 304.

48. See N. Ben-Yehuda, *The Masada Myth: Collective Memory and Myth-making in Israel,* Madison, University of Wisconsin Press, 1987, pp. 83ff.

49. See, for quotes and a discussion, "Iconoclast," August 1, 2006, available at http://www.solami.com/masada.htm.

50. See on this, M. van Creveld, *The Sword and the Olive: A Critical History of the Israel Defense Force,* New York, Public Affairs, 1998, pp. 50–51, 124–26.
51. See E. N. Luttwak, "Where Are the Great Powers? At Home with the Kids," *Foreign Affairs,* 73, 4, July/August 1994, pp. 23–28.
52. See, for example, Y. Levy, *The Other Army of Israel; Materialist Militarism in Israel* [Hebrew], Tel Aviv, Yediot, 2003; as well as H. Gor, ed., *The Militarization of Education* [Hebrew], Tel Aviv, Babel, 2005.

CHAPTER 20: FEMINISM

1. On women as the objective of war, see, most recently, A. Gat, *War in Human Civilization,* Oxford, Oxford University Press, 2006, pp. 67–76.
2. See on them, R. M. Dekker and L. C. van de Pol, *The Tradition of Female Transvestism in Early Modern Europe,* New York, St. Martin's, 1989.
3. For a short account of women's role as combatants (in or without disguise) and camp followers, see M. van Creveld, *Men, Women and War,* pp. 54–66, 88–98, 126–48.
4. Both of these stories are found in Plutarch, *Moralia,* 240ff.
5. For example, the Zulu: J. Krige, *The Social System of the Zulus,* London, Longmans, 1936, p. 279.
6. Judges 6:30.
7. *The Odyssey,* 2.468.
8. See on this, M. van Creveld, "A Woman's Place: Reflections on the Origins of Violence," *Social Research,* 67, 3, fall 2000, pp. 825–47.
9. *Satires,* 1.3.107–8.
10. *Raoul de Cambrai,* ed. and trans., S. Kay, New York, Oxford University Press, 1992, p. 333.
11. V. Woolf, *A Room of One's Own,* New York, Harcourt, Brace and Jovanovich, 1957, pp. 35–36.
12. See, above all, D. Gioseffi, ed., *Women on War: An International Collection of Writings from Antiquity to the Present,* New York, CUNY Press, 2003.
13. E. R. Pollock, *Yes Ma'am; The Personal Papers of a WAAC Private,* Philadelphia, Lippincott, 1943, p. 31.
14. N. Durova, *The Cavalry Maiden,* London, Paladin, 1988 [1836], passim.
15. S. de Beauvoir, *The Prime of Life,* Harmondsworth, Penguin, 1962, pp. 452, 454.
16. Quoted in U. Ben Eliezer and J. Robbins, "Gender Inequality and Cultural Militarism" [Hebrew], in Gor, ed., *The Militarization of Education,* p. 266.
17. The best short summary is B. Mitchell, *Women in the Military: Flirting with Disaster,* Washington, DC, Regnery, 1998, pp. 141–42.
18. See table, "Aerobic Capacity Norms," published by Health Drgily, 2007, available at http://health.drgily.com/walking-test-peak-aerobic-capacity.php.
19. See on this, G. Zorpette, "The Mystery of Muscle," *Scientific American,* 10, 2, summer 1999, p. 48.
20. See C. Dowling, *The Frailty Myth: Women Approaching Physical*

Equality, New York, Random House, 2000, pp. 192–96; A. Fausto-Sterling, *Myths of Gender,* New York, Basic Books, 1992, pp. 218–20.

21. See K. J. Colson, S. A. Eisenstadt, and T. Ziporyn, *The Harvard Guide to Women's Health,* Cambridge, Harvard University Press, 1996, pp. 238, 241, 322, 379, 388.

22. Mitchell, *Women in the Military,* pp. 141, 148.

23. Ben Eliezer and Robbins, "Gender Inequality and Cultural Militarism," p. 269.

24. Figure suggested by R. Kanter, *Men and Women of the Corporation,* New York, Wiley, 1991.

25. See, for example, G. J. DeGroot, "Whose Finger on the Trigger? Mixed Anti-Aircraft Batteries and the Female Combat Taboo," *War in History,* 4, 4, November 1997, p. 437; F. Pile, *Ack-Ack, Britain's Defence Against Air Attack During the Second World War,* London, Harrap, 1949, pp. 190–91.

26. D. Morris, *Manwatching: A Field Guide to Human Behavior,* New York, Abrams, 1977, pp. 239–40.

27. Cf. GAO Report to Sec/Def, U.S. GAO, Washington, DC, 1993, pp. 2–5; S. Gutmann, *The Kinder, Gentler Military: Can America's Gender-Neutral Fighting Force Still Win Wars?* New York, Scribner, 2000, pp. 15, 258.

28. See on this, H. Rogan, *Mixed Company: Women in the Modern Military,* Boston, Beacon, 1981, pp. 23–24.

29. See, for the experiences of one woman who found herself in this situation, K. Williams, *Love My Rifle More Than You: Young and Female in the U.S. Army,* London, Orion, 2005, especially pp. 18–23.

30. See Gutmann, *The Kinder, Gentler Military,* pp. 59–60 passim.

31. *Male and Female,* London, Gollancz, 1949, pp. 159–60.

32. C. Wijnberg, "If Men Were to Bleed," in E. de Waard, ed., *The New Savages in Passion* [Dutch], P. Newint, trans., Amsterdam, van Gennep, 1998, p. 2.

33. B. P. Reskin and P. A. Roos, *Job Queues, Gender Queues; Explaining Women's Inroads into Male Occupations,* Philadelphia, Temple University Press, 1996.

34. For some enlightening figures on this, see G. Greer, *The Whole Woman,* New York, Anchor Books, 2000, p. 285.

35. Nancy Levit, *The Gender Line: Men, Women and the Law,* Albany, State University of New York Press, 1998, p. 107.

36. See on this, for example, J. Waldron and S. Johnson, "Why Do Women Live Longer Than Men?" *Journal of Human Stress,* 2, 2, 1976, pp. 19–30.

37. According to W. Farell, *Why Men Are as They Are: The Male-Female Dynamic,* New York, McGraw-Hill, 1988, p. 362.

38. See, out of a huge literature, S. Creel, "Social Dominance and Stress Hormones," *Trends in Ecology and Evolution,* 6, 9, 2001, pp. 491–97; J. Archer, "The Influence of Testosterone on Human Aggression," *British Journal of Psychology,* 82, 1991, pp. 1–28; and D. Olweus et al., "Circulating Testosterone Levels and Aggression in Adolescent Males," *Psychosomatic Medicine,* 50, 3, 1988, pp. 261–72.

39. See, out of the huge literature, T. Bltiz-Miller et al., "Cognition Distortions in

Heavy Gambling," *Journal of Gambling Studies,* 13, 3, September 1997, pp. 253–60, available at http://www.springerlink.com/content/xr3285666034307h/; J. J. Mondak and M. R. Anderson, "The Knowledge Gap: A Reexamination of Gender-Based Differences in Political Knowledge," *Journal of Politics,* 6, 2, 2004, pp. 492–512, available at http://web.ebscohost.com/ehost/pdf?vid =3&hid=108&sid=75aecdb4-c901-49aa-bab7-931ecd6d8f0e%40sessionmgr107; V. Bajlets and A. Bernanski, "Why Do Women Invest Differently Than Men," *Financial Counseling and Planning,* 7, 1996, pp. 1010, available at http://www.afcep.org/doc/vol%2071.pdf.

40. See, for one such episode, Josephus, *The Jewish War,* iii.7.32.

CONCLUSIONS: THE GREAT PARADOX

1. *On War,* p. 97.
2. See, for what that life might be like, F. Fukuyama, *The End of History and the Last Man,* New York, Penguin, 1993, passim.
3. *Military Methods,* R. D. Sawyer, ed., Boulder, CO, Westview, 1995, p. 84.

INDEX

ABOUT THE AUTHOR

MARTIN VAN CREVELD, professor of history at Hebrew University, Jerusalem, is one of the best-known experts on military history and strategy. Born in the Netherlands, he was educated in Israel and England and began his academic career in 1971. He has written eighteen books, which have been translated into fourteen languages. Among the most notable are *The Changing Face of War, Supplying War, Command in War,* and *The Transformation of War,* widely regarded as the most important text on the future of armed conflict, as well as a critical history of the Israeli Defense Force.

Professor van Creveld has consulted to the defense establishments of numerous governments, including those of the United States, Canada, and Sweden. He was the second civilian expert ever to be invited to address the Israeli General Staff, and has lectured or taught at practically every institute of strategic military study. He has made many appearances on CNN, BBC, and other international networks, and has written for and been interviewed by hundreds of magazines and newspapers, including *Newsweek* and the *International Herald Tribune.*

ABOUT THE TYPE

This book was set in Century, a member of the Century family of type-faces. It was designed in the 1890s by Theodore Low DeVinne of the American Type Founders Company, in collaboration with Linn Boyd Benton. It was one of the earliest types designed for a specific purpose, the *Century* magazine, because it was able to maintain the economies of a narrower typeface while using stronger serifs and thickened verticals.